S0-CDI-630

Dakhleh Oasis Project: Monograph 3

GREEK PAPYRI FROM KELLIS: I

Dakhleh Oasis Project: Monograph No. 3

GREEK PAPYRI FROM KELLIS: I

(P.Kell.G.)

Nos. 1–90

Edited by K. A. Worp

in collaboration with

J. E. G. Whitehorne and R. W. Daniel

Oxbow Monograph 54
1995

The Monographs of the Dakhleh Oasis Project
are published by Oxbow Books
Park End Place, Oxford OX1 1HN

ISBN 0 946897 97 2

This book is available direct from
Oxbow Books, Park End Place, Oxford OX1 1HN
(Phone: 01865-241249; Fax: 01865 794449)

and

The David Brown Book Company
PO Box 511, Oakville, CT 06779
(Phone: 203-945-9329; Fax: 203-945-9468)

Printed in Great Britain at The Short Run Press, Exeter
from camera-ready artwork prepared by the author

PREFACE

A preface usually contains, *inter alia*, a list of people and institutions entitled to the gratitude of the author(s); this preface is no exception to that practice. Before, however, giving such a list I should like to present to the readers some background to what is, I think, a rather unusual volume of Greek documentary papyri.

In May 1992 I was invited by Dr. C.A. Hope (Monash University, Melbourne, Australia) to undertake the editing of the Greek documentary texts from the Dakhleh Oasis Project excavations at Ismant el-Kharab (ancient 'Kellis'). This work entailed making several trips to the excavation site (some 600 kilometers to the south-southwest of Cairo in the Western desert of Egypt) where the original documents are kept in a magazine near the excavation house at Ezbet el-Bashendi. First work on the Greek papyrus fragments was done during a stay of 7 weeks early 1993, subsequently during slightly shorter visits in early 1994 and 1995, in the working room in the excavation house. There an initial classification of Greek and Coptic papyri was made, as many matching fragments as possible were brought materially together and first transcripts were recorded (mention must be made here of preliminary work on the assembling of documents and on transcribing some texts done by Dr. R.G. Jenkins [University of Melbourne]) and there the results of joining these fragments were photographed. In this connection it must be stressed that working conditions in Egypt 'in the field' differ from those in an office somewhere in a Western country and that, e.g., it was not always possible to make photos which satisfy the highest quality demands, while a well-equipped papyrological library was not available on the spot for immediately exploring the consequences of any idea which came to mind while trying to read a difficult passage. This situation must be constantly kept in mind when making a judgement about the quality of the work in this volume.

In Amsterdam I was fortunate in obtaining the assistance of various colleagues for preparing a first publication of the texts from Kellis, notably that of Dr. J.E.G. Whitehorne (Brisbane) and Dr. R.W. Daniel (Cologne). Dr. Whitehorne undertook the preparation of 13 texts (Nos. **3**, **5**, **6**, **8**, **10**, **11**, **13**, **49**, **65**, **67**, **70**, **71** and **76**) for final publication, while Dr. Daniel studied the magical texts published in this volume, nos. **85** - **88**; both worked on the basis of photos of the papyri and of information communicated by me who had seen the original papyri and who subsequently checked various suggestions for alternative readings contributed by them. Furthermore, Dr. T. de Jong (Groningen/Amsterdam) helped me with studying the astronomical and astrological aspects of the horoscope **84**. Finally, Dr. Whitehorne helped me with reading the computer-produced manuscript of the texts I had prepared and with checking the word indices. Also to be recorded here must be the help of Prof. R.S. Bagnall (New York) whose remarks made on the basis of his reading through an early version of most of the documentary texts were extremely beneficial.

I am particularly grateful to Dr. Colin A. Hope, the director of the excavations at Ismant el-Kharab, who invited me to publish the texts in this volume, made various trips to Egypt financially possible and provided us with the indispensable photo material and all kinds of background information concerning the excavations. His generosity has facilitated our work in many more ways than can be expressed in these few lines. The various members of the excavation team working at the site, especially M. Berry, G. Bowen and O. Kaper, also deserve warm thanks for making every effort to make my visits to Egypt a unique and productive experience.

It is a real pleasure for me to enjoy the collaboration of Dr. A. Alcock (Witzenhausen, Germany) and Dr. I.E.G. Gardner (Edith Cowan University, Perth, Western Australia). They are working on the Coptic papyri coming from the same excavations and their unique experience with these texts and their wide learning gave us unparalleled benefit. They will recognize in our publication many of their own ideas and suggestions. Evidently, many problems in the Greek documentary papyri published here find their counterparts in the Coptic material they are working on.

I am deeply grateful to the Director of the Dakhleh Oasis Project A.J. Mills, his wife Lesley, and various other members of the Project's team 'κατ' ὄνομα' for their hospitality, stimulating encouragement and general help. It is also my great pleasure to record on the Egyptian side the wonderful cooperation offered by various inspectors of the Egyptian Organization for Antiquities, especially Mr. Ashraf es-Sayed Mohammed. My stay in Egypt was made a memorable and happy event in particular thanks to the excellent cooking of Mssrs. Mansour and Taha.

The Photographic Section of the Department of Geography and Environmental Science of Monash University, deserves thanks for their effort in processing the prints of the many photographs taken during various excavation seasons.

Work at the site during the 1991-1993 seasons was funded by the Australian Research Council (Co-investigators: Dr. C.A. Hope and Dr. R.G. Jenkins), while the 1994 season was funded by the Egyptology Society of Victoria (Australia); the 1995 season was funded by a new, three year grant from the Australian Research Council (Co-investigators: Dr. C.A. Hope and Dr. I.E.G. Gardner). We are very grateful for the exceptionally magnanimous support given by these organizations.

The Director of the Netherlands Institute for Archaeology and Arabic Studies at Cairo, Dr. F. Leemhuis, his wife, and the staff of the institute should be thanked for their hospitality always extended so generously.

Last, but not least, the Faculty of Arts and Letters of the University of Amsterdam, in particular Drs. A.J.H.A. Verhagen and Drs. H.A. Mulder, and the Board of the Institute for Mediterranean Studies deserve warm thanks for enabling me to visit and work in Egypt several times. My colleagues in the Departments of Classics and Ancient History should be thanked 'κατ' ὄνομα' for their interest and cooperation.

Amsterdam, May 1995

CONTENTS

NOTE ON EDITORIAL PROCEDURE

Texts in this volume are presented according to the usual papyrological practices. In all printed texts punctuation, accents and breathings are added; in the critical apparatus cases of dihaeresis, breathings, accents, punctuation and other lectional marks as actually occurring in the ancient texts have been indicated. The following signs have their usual senses:

( )	Resolution of abbreviation or symbol
[ ]	Lacuna in the papyrus (in the translations, however, these [ ] are not taken over; only unfilled lacunas in the texts have been indicated in the translations by horizontal dashes)
[ca. 7]	Approximate number of letters lost in a lacuna and not restored
⟦ ⟧	Letters written, then deleted by the scribe
< >	Letters omitted by the scribe
{ }	Letters erroneously written by the scribe
\`α β γ´	Letters later inserted by the scribe above the line and not intended to indicate an abbreviation
α̣ β̣ γ̣	Letters, the reading of which is uncertain or would be uncertain outside of the context
. . .	Letters which have not been read

Where scribal orthography differs from the standard forms of Greek, the latter is given in the critical apparatus or in the commentary to an individual text.

No consistent attempt has been made in this volume to accentuate all Egyptian personal and geographical names, especially in the case where one is dealing with a new name.

Papyri are cited according to the *Checklist of Editions of Greek and Latin Papyri, Ostraca and Tablets*^{4}, ed. by J.F. Oates, R.S. Bagnall, W.H. Willis and K.A. Worp (BASP Suppl. 7; Atlanta, Georgia 1992). It is hoped that the sigla for a few volumes not yet listed in there will be self-explaining.

Bold-face type is used to indicate the numbers of texts included in this volume.[1]

The articles ὁ, ἡ and τό and the copula καί have been omitted for compiling the word indices.

Unless stated otherwise, all dates in this volume are 'A.D. ...'.

[1]) In order to elucidate the inventory numbers given with the papyri in their palaeographical description: the numbering system 'A/(numeral between 1 and 5) /(numeral)' refers to the registration numbers given to all objects found during the excavations; 'A' = Area A; the first following numeral (between 1 and 5) refers to: '1' = House 1, '2' = House 2, '3' = Structure 4, '4' = the street between Areas A and B (north of Houses 1 and 2), and '5' = House 3. The second numeral refers to the number of the object itself. All wooden boards have object numbers, as do some of the papyri. Most of the latter, however, do not and this is because initially papyrus was found in small quantities. This method of registration rendered it difficult when papyrus fragments had to be moved from one glass frame to another. The system then adopted was to assign a P.+ number which related to the specific deposit (the archaeological context and location).

Rigorous consistency throughout the volume, e.g. with the transliteration of Greek and Latin names (endings of Greek names in -os vs. endings of Latin names in -us), has not been attempted.

Photographs of the Papyri appear in catalogue order at the end of the book

TABLE OF PAPYRI

AN INTRODUCTION TO THE GREEK PAPYRI FROM KELLIS

The publication of a first volume of Greek documents from ancient Kellis in the Dakhleh Oasis calls for some preliminary remarks. For general archaeological information about the site, see the excavation reports published by C.A. Hope (Monash University, Melbourne) in: Mediterranean Archaeology 1 (1988) 160-178; Journal of the Society for the Study of Egyptian Archaeology 15 (1985) 114-25; 16 (1986) 74-91; 17 (1987) 157-176; C.A. Hope et alii, 19 (1989) 1-26; Bulletin of the Australian Centre for Egyptology 1-5 (1990-1994), passim. A full archaeological discussion by Dr. Hope is scheduled to appear in a forthcoming publication of Coptic texts prepared by Dr. I.E.G. Gardner. The technicalities concerning the editorial procedures of the present publication are dealt with elsewhere in this volume, various other questions are dealt with here.

A. *Some background information on the preservation of the texts published in this volume*:

This first volume of Kellis papyri contains 90 texts (some in 2 copies [**38.a,b**; cf. also **34** and **34.appendix**] or with individual texts on recto and verso [**19.a,b**], some with two individual texts belonging originally to one sheet or roll [**85.a,b**); 83 have been written on papyrus, 7 on wood. These texts share the same provenance, Area A in the excavation site at Ismant el-Kharab, and they were found over several seasons of excavations starting in 1986. During these excavations several thousands of papyrus fragments, ostraka and wooden boards inscribed with Greek or Coptic, a few times with Syriac and Latin texts, were found. Only a small number of these were found in House 1, quite a few more in House 2, while House 3 turned out to contain a real treasure trove. Some texts were found in a fairly or even remarkably complete state; in most cases, however, one is dealing with more or less fragmentarily preserved texts written on papyrus. After first conservation the material (now kept in more than 150 glass frames of various sizes) needed to be sorted, first of all according to the language used for a text. For that purpose various fragments and scraps were taken out of various glass frames and as many combinations as possible or promising had to be (and were) tried in order to reconstruct an original text. In fact, one is dealing with a kind of giant jigsaw puzzle and, as usual with such puzzles, in some cases a seemingly attractive match had finally to be given up. Though it cannot be excluded that more matches are still possible, the 'Law of diminishing returns' is applicable, and it remains to be seen whether there are still many more possible.

As far as the state of preservation of the wooden boards inscribed with Greek texts is concerned, next to the completely preserved, multi-board codices of Isocrates and the Harvest Account Book, there is a large number of incomplete fragments of boards, and a substantial number of more or less complete single boards have been preserved (especially among the Coptic texts).

In this volume are edited most of the 'publishable' Greek papyri from Houses 1, 2 and 3 and Structure 4 *and* the 'publishable' texts on wood from House 3. Only a small number (10) of documents and private letters from House 3 came to our notice after the manuscript had been closed off (cf. **19.a.appendix**); though their 'information value' is limited, they will get a full publication in the future. Further unpublished material from Area A is found also among the wooden boards from Houses 1 and 2 and the unpublished ostraka from Structure 4.[1] The residue of inscribed material coming from these houses is a fairly substantial amount of abraded or very scrappily preserved (often enough only 'postage stamp size' or even smaller) papyrus fragments which are apparently unconnected with other texts. In general it may be taken for granted that this material will not yield much interesting new information.

The collection of the 90 texts published in this volume is, of course, not sufficient for writing the complete history of ancient Kellis. Even if the ongoing excavations were to stop yielding inscribed material and if the texts already excavated were the only sources to reckon with as far as written material is concerned, one would need for writing such a history at least a full publication of the Coptic texts and of the other Greek texts still awaiting full publication,[2] next to a full publication of the archaeological and artefactual material excavated. Still, the texts in this volume offer already now a broad range of glimpses into the daily life of people living in a village in the Dakhleh Oasis during the fourth century. These glimpses are the more fascinating as until quite recently hardly any documents from or about the Dakhleh Oasis had been published (G. Wagner, *Les Oasis d'Egypte à l'époque grecque, romaine et byzantine d'après les documents grecs* [Cairo 1987] 188-196 exploits the exiguous existing documentation as fully as possible; for Môthis [p. 189-90] add SB XVI 12754, for Kellis [p. 190] add PUG II Append. (p. 73f.) and P.Duke inv. G. 9 in BASP 25 [1988] 129f.).[3]

NB: Before all we should like to stress that in our publication we have tried to strike a balance between a speedy publication (probably containing a substantial number of errors or omissions) and an 'ideal' edition (satisfying much more severe demands). Of course, the latter would have taken much more time to produce.

B. *Some principles guiding the organisation of the contents of the volume*:
Rather than giving all documents in, e.g., a strictly chronological or thematical (or other) order we have adopted a mixed application of two principles, viz. the 'topographical' and the 'thematic'. The 'topographical' principle made us distinguish

[1]) For the wooden boards from Houses 1 and 2 cf. Mediterranean Archaeology 1 (1988) 168 (House 1), 171 (House 2); JSSEA 17 (1987) 163, 166 (House 2); for the ostraka cf. *ibidem* 160 n.6 (at p. 175). We are not aware of any progress with the publication referred to there.

[2]) Next to the already mentioned wooden boards and ostraka from Houses 1 and 2 and the remaining 10 texts from House 3 there are also the papyri, ostraka and wooden boards from House 4 in area A, from the Area B and from the Main temple complex and adjacent buildings [Area D].

[3]) To be sure, many of the documents listed by Wagner *loc.cit.* 3ff. refer to oases other than the Dakhleh Oasis.

between documents coming from the surface of Area A (**1**) and from the individual Houses 1 (**2** - **3**), 2 (**4** - **16**) , Structure 4 (**17** - **18**) and House 3 (**19** - **90**); within each cluster we have arranged documents thematically (e.g.: petitions, official documents, sales or letters are mostly given together). For various reasons, however, strict maintenance of rigid consistency throughout the volume has not always been achieved.

C. *The dispersal of fragments over various houses and rooms*:

One of the immediately striking phenomena in the papyri from Houses 1 - 3 is the fact that in quite a few cases various fragments originally belonging to a single document were actually found at often very diverse places. We notice the following cases and refer to the plans of Houses 1 - 3 and to the more detailed plan of House 3 (pp. 5-6).[4] From Houses 1 and 2 we have the following texts with such a 'complex' background:

3, P.Kellis inv. A/1/75+76 (from *House 1*, floor of room 9) + P. 92.12 (*House 3*, room 1, level 1). The combination of fragments apparently coming from two different houses but obviously belonging to one single document is quite remarkable; see the description of **3**. It is difficult to tell whether the document in its complete form was kept originally in House 1 or in House 3; as the largest part comes from House 1, the whole document has now been assigned to that place, but it is possible that vice versa the original document was kept first in House 3, then broke into various parts the largest of which was deposited by the wind in the entrance of House 1. It may even be that the original document was *not* kept in either House 1 or 3, but that parts were blown by the wind from elsewhere into Houses 1, resp. 3.[5]

6, P.Kellis inv. A/2/83 (House 2, *room 5*, level 3, at corner to room 6) + A/2/92 (*room 6*, level 3, near door). According to the plan of House 2 rooms '5' and '6' are adjacent and not separated by a wall.

8, P.Kellis inv. A/2/84+85+86+87 (House 2, *room 5*, floor deposit) + A/2/89+93 (*room 6*, level 3, near door). Again, according to the plan of House 2 rooms '5' and '6' are adjacent and not separated by a wall.

14, P.Kellis inv. A/2/96+97+106 (inv. A/2/96+97 from House 2, *room 7*, understairs cupboard, on base of bed; inv. A/2/106 from *room 3*, level 1, found in cupboard in NE corner). The plan of House 2 shows that rooms 3 and '7' are adjacent and not separated by a wall.

15, P.Kellis inv. A/2/79 (House 2, *room 3*, level 6, under the pots) + A/2/110 (*room 5*, level 3, Northeast corner of room). As the plan of House 2 shows, rooms 3 and '5' are at some distance of each other (separated by room '6'); however, the Northeast corner of room '5' is relatively close to room 3.

From House 3 come:

21.a, P.Kellis inv. P. 17.Q + 20 (both from *room 10*, level 3) + P. 18 (*room 10*, level 1) + P. 63.B (*room 8*, level 4). The text is a copy of **21** (room 8, levels 4 and 3).

4) Not discussed are fragments of one single text which were all found in the same room, though at different levels.

5) Note that all fragments were found in the entrances of Houses 1 and 3.

22, P.Kellis inv. P. 56.F (*room 9*, level 3, Western doorway) + P. 61.W (*room 8*, level 4).

24, P.Kellis inv. P. 59.B+E (*room 3*, level 3) + P. 60.A (*room 9*, level 4) + P. 81.B (*room 6*, level 4).

26, P.Kellis inv. P. 78.D (*room 6*, level 3)+ P. 90.A (*room 6*, level 4, West wall) + P. 92.35.G (*room 11*, level 4) + P. 93.B+D (*room 6*, level 4).

27, P.Kellis inv. P. 97 = P. 90.B (*room 6*, level 4, West wall) + P. 92.A+B (*room 6*, level 4, South wall) + P. 92.14 (*room 1.a*, level 1) + P. 92.18 (*room 1.a*, level 2).

28, P.Kellis inv. P. 31 (*room 3*, level 1) + P. 52.C (*room 9*, level 3).

29, P.Kellis inv. P. 92.B (*room 6*, level 4, South wall) + P. 92.7 (*room 2*, level 3).

30, P.Kellis inv. P. 71 (*room 6*, level 3) + P. 52.A+C (*room 9*, level 3) + P. 56.F (ibidem, Western Doorway) + 'Unnumbered # 2' (House 3, provenance not stated).

31, P.Kellis inv. P. 61.L (*room 8*, level 4) + P. 68.A+E (*room 6*, level 3).

33, P.Kellis inv. P. 17.L+W (*room 10*, level 3) + P. 50 (*room 6*, level 1).

34, P.Kellis inv. P. 52.B+C+D+H (*room 9*, level 3) + P. 56.A+C (ibidem, Western doorway) + P. 61.D (*room 8*, level 4).

36, P.Kellis inv. P. 17.BB (*room 10*, level 3) + P. 63.A (*room 8*, level 4).

38.b, P.Kellis inv. P. 52.H (*room 9*, level 3) + P. 65.L (*room 8*, level 3).

42, P.Kellis inv. P. 59.D (*room 3*, level 3) + P. 60.B (*room 9*, level 4).

43, P.Kellis inv. P. 1 (*room 6*, level 1) + P. 43 (*room 5*, level 3).

48, P.Kellis inv. P. 56.C (*room 9*, level 3, Western doorway) + P.61.F+G+U+V (*room 8*, level 4) + P. 65.F+J (*room 8*, level 3).

77, P.Kellis inv. P. 41 (*room 7.a*, level 2) + P. 78.D (*room 6*, level 3) + P. 92.A (*room 6*, level 4, South wall).

84, T.Kellis inv. A/5/198+263 (# 198 from *room 6*, level 3, # 263 from *room 1*).

In House 3, therefore, we find the following movements of 'wandering fragments' dispersed over the house (texts with a 'room 6' component have been clustered first, other rooms are listed in numerical order):

Room	+ *Room* +	*Room*	*Text*	*Room* +	*Room* +	*Room*	*Text*
6	1		**84**	6	9	?	**30**
6	1.a		**27**	6	10		**33**
6	2		**29**	6	11		**26**
6	3	9	**24**	3	9		**28**; **42**
6	7.a		**77**	8	9		**22**; **34**; **38.b**; **48**
6	8		**31**	8	10		**21.a**; **36**

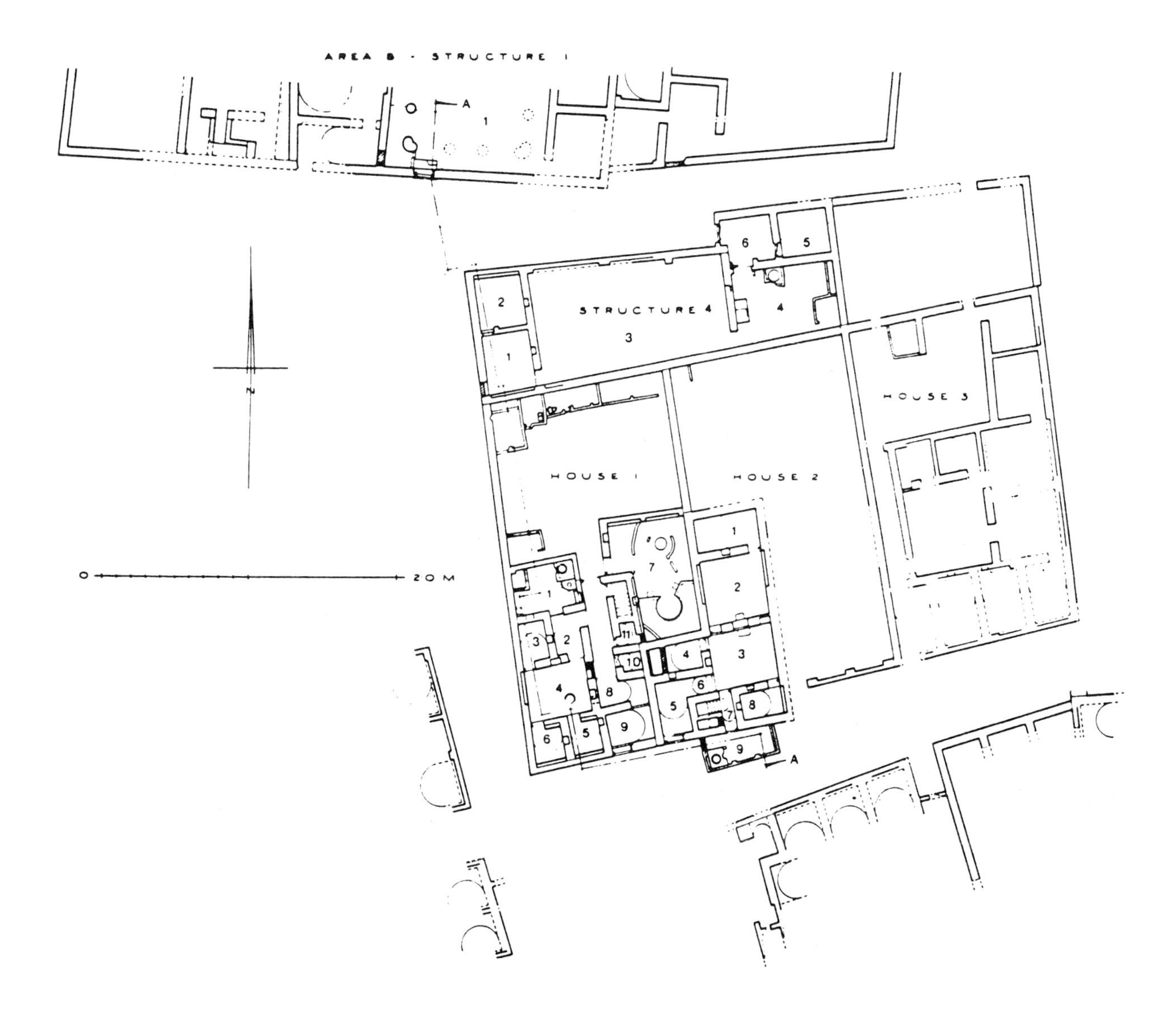

Plan of Areas A-B showing results of the 1986–88 excavations

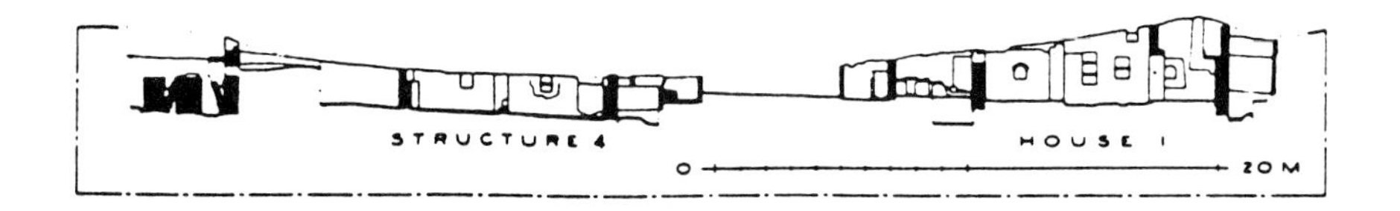

Section A–A through excavations

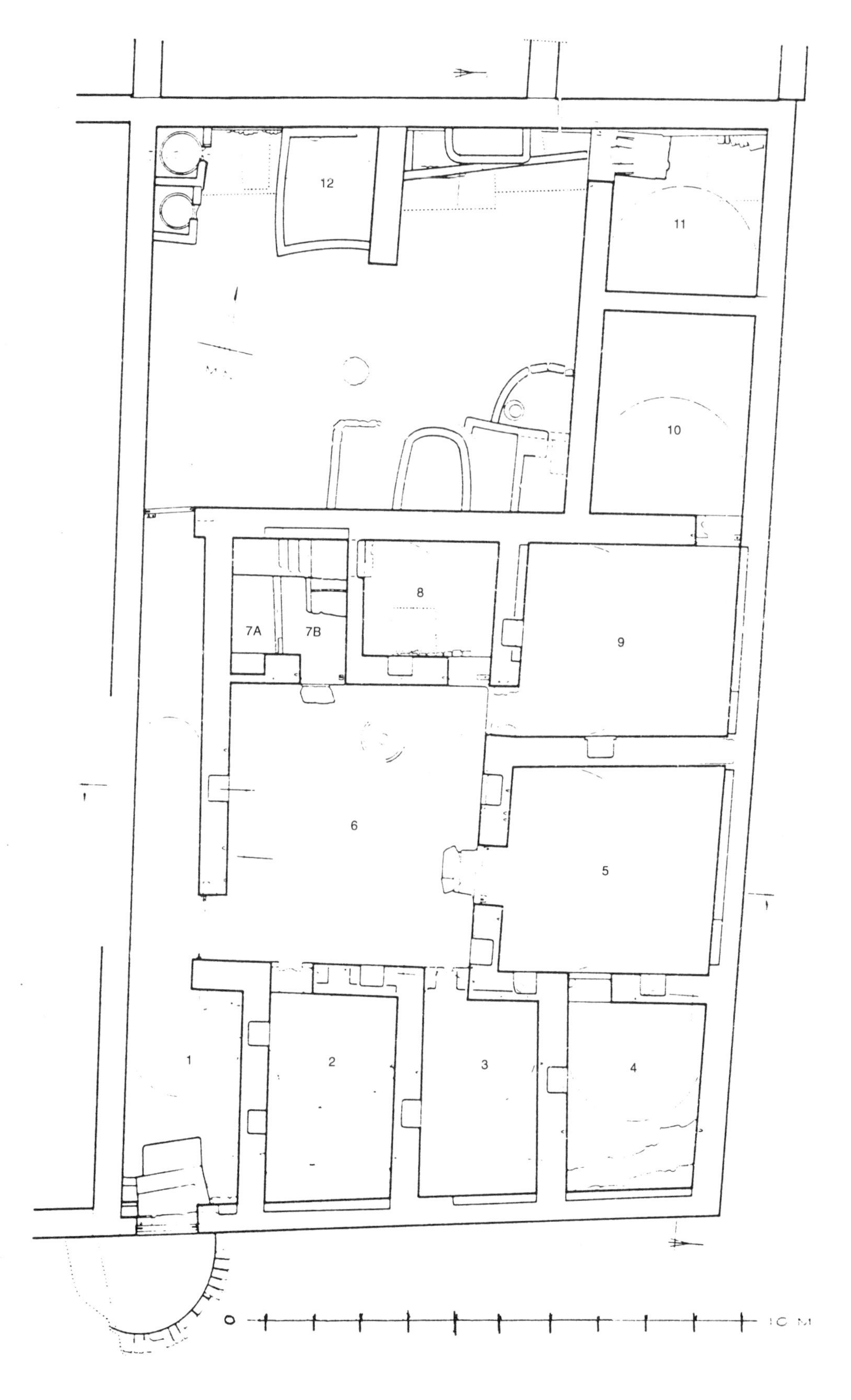

Plan of Area A House 3, with locations of sections

A glance on the plan of House 3 will easily show that room '6' (a very central room in that house) stood in virtually immediate connection with rooms '1' - '3', '8' and '9'; the connection of room '6' with room '7.a' goes through room '7.b' and the connection with room '10' only through (the rather large) room '9'; the connection, however, between rooms '6' and '11' is only very indirect and it is not easy to see how part of **26** (inv. P.92.35.G) came into room '11'. Rooms 3 and '9' were not directly adjacent; the doors of both rooms opened into room '6' and any traffic between rooms 3 and '9' must have gone via that room. Rooms '8' and '9' were adjacent and therefore the phenomenon of papyrus fragments wandering from one room to the other is easily acceptable. Traffic, however, between rooms '8' and '10' had to go through room '9'.

D. *New insights coming from the Greek Kellis papyri*:

Though there are obviously many parallels and resemblences between the contents of the 90 documents from a village in the Dakhleh Oasis published for the first time in this volume and the many thousands of documents from the Nile valley or the Fayum published over more than a century[6], one must reckon in general with the possibility, that the documentation from Kellis may show all kinds of divergences versus the documentation coming from the Nile Valley and that various aspects of life in the Oasis are different from life in the Nile valley.[7]

Some new items of interest found in the Kellis papyri deserve to be highlighed:

1. Next to a multitude of well-known personal names, a substantial number of new personal names are found throughout these documents, i.e. we are dealing with names not listed in the usual onomastica of F. Preisigke's *Namenbuch* or D. Foraboschi's *Onomasticon Alterum Papyrologicum*. As far as these names have an Egyptian background they deserve further study, especially by competent Egyptologists.
2. There are a number of interesting new prosopographical data about, e.g., terms of office of high officials like the *praesides Thebaidos* (cf., e.g., **15**, **19.a**, **20**, **23**, **26**, **27**.2n.) and about *ekdikoi*, *logistae* and *syndikoi* of the Mothite nome (**21**, **25**, **29**).
3. We get some further information about the topography of the Hibite Nome (**2**, **35**), the Panopolite Nome (**30**), and especially highly important first information about the Mothite Nome; one finds a number of village names and the name of a district 'Mesobe' within the nome (cf. Index VI), while **27** offers the first instance of a *pagus* in the Mothite nome.

[6]) We have not found a marked difference between the quality of the Greek language as used in the new texts from Kellis and that in documents from Arsinoe, Hermopolis, Oxyrhynchos, or any other place in the Nile valley). It is true, however, that in some cases the Kellis papyri feature phrasings not commonly found in the papyrological documentation from elsewhere; cf., e.g., the notes to **31**.19ff. and **37**.12ff.

[7]) There is, e.g., no flooding of the Nile to reckon with. It is a also worthwhile to record here that in the Kellis papyri one finds, e.g., reflections of dating practices having become obsolete elsewhere in the Nile valley (cf. D. Hagedorn - K.A. Worp, *Das Wandeljahr im römischen Ägypten*, ZPE 104 [1995] 243-255).

4. Various points of administrative and judicial procedure and the collection of taxes are illustrated; cf., e.g., **15** (selection of collectors of the *chrysargyron)*, **19** (petition to the governor of the Thebaid + *hypographe* (?) on the verso), **20** (petition because of theft), **21** (petition because of assault), **23** (selection of comarchs in a petition concerning assault), **24** (declaration to the bureau of the *dux*), **27** (notification to the *praepositus pagi*), **29** (collection of the costs of transportation of statues to Alexandria), **76** (letter concerning the collection of *chrysargyron*). Especially interesting are also the data concerning the administration of the Mothite nome separately from the Hibite nome (cf. **41**.4n.).
5. The many private letters in the volume (actually, circa 1/3 of all Greek papyri published in this volume are personal letters and short business notes; for unpublished Kellis material cf. above, sub 'A') offer much information about the personal life of inhabitants of the village, but sometimes also tell us something about people living in the Nile valley.[8] Exceptionally interesting is **63** with its Manichaean background. The considerable distance between the Kellis and the Nile Valley (a stretch of ca. 300 km of extremely desolate desert land) might be taken to be an unsurmountable obstacle against regular traffic, but in fact communications seem to have been rather regular. In this respect it should also be noted that the ceramics and various artefacts found at Kellis show many indisputable links with the Nile Valley.
6. Next to petitions to some government official, other official texts (**1**, **3**, **15**, **19** - **29**), and private letters, this volume contains also a number of various interesting juridical texts, e.g. leases (**31** - **33**), sales and gifts (**8**, **34** - **39**), loans of money and oil (**18**, **40** - **47**, **49**), a manumission of a slave (**48**), an exchange of property rights (**30**), and a *parachoresis* of land (**4**); in a number of cases the nature of a mutilated contract cannot be established more precisely.
7. The wealth of new economic data coming from these papyri deserves special attention: we get, e.g., interesting new data about interest paid on loans of money and this stimulated further research into that subject (cf. the introduction to **40** - **47**). The texts from Kellis also provide us with unique information about the manufacture of commodities and prices and about agricultural production and consumption in the Dakhleh Oasis in the 4th century A.D. Also interesting are the numismatical practices reflected by some documents (talents actually paid in *nummi*; cf. also **29**).
8. Finally, the astrological, magical and medical texts **82** - **89** highlight these facets of life in Kellis, while **90** is a school text which at the same time illustrates, again, a facet of the local economy.

[8]) The following communitities in the Nile Valley (ἡ Αἴγυπτος, cf. **76**, **81**) maintaining relations with Kellis in the Dakhleh Oasis are mentioned in the Greek documents: Aphrodite (cf. **30**, **32**, **42** - **44**), Antinoopolis **71**, **77**), Hermopolis (cf. **21**, **51**, **52**, **66**) and Panopolis (**30**).

FROM THE SURFACE OF AREA A

1: FRAGMENTS OF AN OFFICIAL DOCUMENT (A PREFECTURAL DECREE?)

(293 - 294)

P.Kellis inv. A/0/1 (Area A, Structure 4, surface of room 1). H. 12.6 x B. ca. 11.3 cm. The glass frame contains several papyrus fragments all featuring on the recto (not published here) an identical type of 'chancery writing' (for a palaeographical analysis of this cf. G. Cavallo in Aegyptus 45 [1965] 216-49); it cannot be established how these fragments fit together. The verso of one of the fragments is also inscribed (the writing runs across the fibers) and it is this text (written by a well-trained cursive hand) which is published below. The text was mentioned previously in JSSEA 17 (1987) 173-74).[9]
NB: A small fragment mounted in the same frame does not belong to this papyrus.

1 Ἔτους [*ἐνάτου τοῦ κυρίου ἡμῶν* Γαίου Αὐρηλίου]
2 Οὐαλερ[*ίου Διοκλητιανοῦ καὶ ἔτους η τοῦ κυρίου*]
3 *ἡμῶν* Μ[*άρκου* Αὐρηλίου Οὐαλερίου Μαξιμιανοῦ Αὐτοκρατόρων]
4 Καισάρῳ̣[*ν* Γερμανικῶν *μεγίστων* Σαρματικῶν *μεγίστων καὶ* (*ἔτους*) *α*]
5 *τῶν κυ*[*ρίων ἡμῶν* Φλαουίου Οὐαλερίου Κωνσταντίου]
6 *καὶ* Γαλε[*ρίου* Οὐαλερίου Μαξιμιανοῦ *ἐπιφανεστάτων*]
7 Καισάρῳ̣[*ν* Εὐσεβῶν Εὐτυχῶν Σεβαστῶν, *ὑπατείας* Διοκλητιανοῦ *τὸ ε*]
8 *καὶ* Μαξ[*ιμιανοῦ τὸ δ* Σεβαστῶν, *τῆ̣ πρὸ* --]
9 Καλανδ̇[*ῶν* Month name. Ῥουπίλιος (?)]
10 Φῆλιξ *ὁ δ̣*[*ιασημότατος ἔπαρχος* Αἰγύπτου
11 *καὶ προ*[
12 *οὕτως* [
13 *ν̣ον α* ̣[
14 *σαντος̣*[
15 *φειν κα̣*[
16 Ἀπολλ ̣[
17 *τὰ πλεῖσ*[*τα*
18 *ρακαιτο*[
19 *ἀ̣* ̣*ιοσ* ̣ ̣[
\- - - - - - - - - - - - -

"In the ninth year of our lord Gaius Aurelius Valerius Diocletianus and in the 8th year of our lord Marcus Aurelius Valerius Maximianus *Imperatores Caesares Germanici maximi Sarmatici maximi* and in the 1st year of our lords Flavius Valerius

[9]) The hand of the chancery writing features resemblances to that of the unpublished P.Kellis inv. A/2/90+91 (from House 2) and the verso of that papyrus also shows text written by a cursive hand. Though the handwriting on the verso of both papyri looks similar, the cursive writing of inv. A/2/90+91 cannot be matched with that of **1** (its size is different) and for that reason any thought of a combination of **1** with inv. A/2/90+91 must be rejected.

Constantius and Galerius Valerius Maximianus *nobilissimi Caesares, Pii, Felices, Augusti*, in the 5th consulate of Diocletianus and in the 4th consulate of Maximianus the *Augusti*, on the nth day before the Kalends of the month --. Rupilius Felix, *vir perfectissimus, praefectus Aegypti* --"

This tantalizing scrap contains in its present stage not much more than the remnants of an elaborate, largely restored dating formula after the emperors Diocletian and Maximian and the Caesars Constantius and Galerius (for their most elaborate regnal formula cf. R.S. Bagnall - K.A. Worp, *Regnal Formulas in Byzantine Egypt* 9f.; cf. also ZPE 61 [1985] 97-98 on P.Lond. III 958), probably followed immediately by a consular dating formula[10]. This direct combination of dating elements is rare in papyri from this period (cf. P.Laur. IV 176.18-20n.; for a parallel from a much earlier period cf., e.g., BGU I 140.3-5 + BL IV 3 and VIII 19). If the example of the BGU-text is followed, the dating formula may be related to a rather special, highly official type of dating of a document and within the context of such a dating one may be attracted to think that after the name Φῆλιξ in l. 10 an epithet and the office of governor of Egypt should be restored (see note ad loc.); if this is acceptable, it is a short step further to restore *τάδε λέγει* and regard this papyrus as the remnants of a prefectural decree (for such decrees preserved in papyri from Roman Egypt, see P. Bureth in RHD 46 (1968) 246-262 and his article 'Le préfet d'Egypte, 30 av. J.-C. - 297 ap. J.-C.' in ANRW X.1 [1988] 472-502 [with addenda by G. Bastianini, *ibid.*, 503-517]; cf. also G. Bastianini, "Ἔπαρχος Αἰγύπτου nel formulario dei documenti da Augusto a Diocleziano', ANRW X.1 581-597). It must be stressed, however, that all of this is very speculative; of course, the actual contents of the prefectural decree cannot be reconstructed with any confidence.

1ff. In view of the size of the lacuna it seems reasonable to suppose that at least some numerals of the regnal years were written out in full; regnal years 9, 8 and 1 (running from 1.iii - 28.viii.293) or 10, 9 and 2 (29.viii.293 - 28.viii.294) may be thought of; cf. below, l. 10n. Of these alternative sets of years it may be slightly more attractive to think of the earlier set, as it looks probable that the ordinal 'ninth' was written out in full (on this phenomenon cf. J.D. Thomas in ZPE 24 [1977] 241-43, H.C. Youtie in *Scriptiunculae Posteriores* I 455-56, and A. von Stylow & J.D. Thomas in Chiron 10 [1980] 537-551) and the lacunas are better filled if this goes with Diocletian in 293 rather than with Maximian in 294. It is, however, not absolutely excluded to restore the numerals as *δεκάτου* (Diocletian), *θ* (Maximian) and *β* (the Caesars), and if one prefers their restoration and a date of 294, the consulate in ll. 7-8 should be restored as

7 Καισάρω[ν Εὐσεβῶν Εὐτυχῶν Σεβαστῶν, ὑπατείας Κωνσταντίου]

8 *καὶ* Μαξ̣[ιμιανοῦ *τῶν ἐπιφανεστάτων* Καισάρων, *τῇ πρὸ* --]

Of course, a consulate of a Maximian in 2nd position also occurs in 297 (Maximianus Aug. V & Gal. Maximianus Caes. II), 299 (Augg. Diocletianus VII & Maximianus VI), 300 (Constantius Caes. III & Gal. Maximianus Caes. III), 303 (Augg. Diocletianus VIII & Maximianus VII) and 304 (Augg.

[10]) We should like to thank our colleague R.S. Bagnall who offered the correct solution for restoring this part of the dating formula.

Diocletianus VIIII & Maximianus VIII), but any of these years is problematic in view of l. 10 (cf. note ad loc.)

Under all circumstances, however, the restoration of the regnal formula implies some twisting; while the papyrus has broken off at the right rather straight, present restorations count 32 letters in l. 1, 33 letters in l. 2, 44 letters in l. 3, 42 letters in l. 4, and 36 letters in both ll. 5 and 6, while for Diocletian V as first consul in l. 7 a restoration of 46 letters is needed (42 letters, if only *Κωνσταντίου* is restored). If restorations within the 32-36 letters range are to be applied throughout, those now proposed in ll. 3-4 and 7 are too long, but it is always possible that some words in these lines were written with abbreviations, or that they were simply omitted.

3-4. One regularly finds in papyri from this period the words *Αὐτοκράτορες Καίσαρες* at the very start of the formula. That, however, is ruled out here by *ἡμῶν* at the start of l. 3, which suggests a restoration of *τοῦ κυρίου* at the end of l. 2 and the restoration of the same element *τοῦ κυρίου ἡμῶν* before Diocletian's name in l. 1.

4. For the (restored) victory titles for Diocletian and Maximian cf. Tyche 4 (1989) 229-32.

9. No doubt a name of a Roman month followed Καλανδ[; an indication of an 'n^{th} day before the Kalends of month N.N.' may have stood before it, unless reference is made to exactly the first day (Kalends) of the month in question. For the use of Roman months in datings in Greek papyri from Kellis cf. **22** and **41**.

10. The omicron before the very much damaged δ̣ on the right hand edge (of this letter only a speck of ink remains slightly above line level) could, of course, also be the initial vowel of a noun, but within the context of this papyrus (featuring chancery writing on its other side and an unusually long dating formula + extended imperial titulature in the opening lines on this side) it seems reasonable to assume that the Latin name Felix was followed by an article (ὁ) and that we are dealing with a high official whose name was followed by '*vir perfectissimus*' (*ὁ διασημότατος*). The only such Felix occupying a high position in Egypt who fits into the chronological time frame 293 - 294 (cf. the regnal formula in ll. 1-7) is Rupilius Felix, known to have been the *praefectus Aegypti* in 292/3 (cf. T. Barnes, *The New Empire of Diocletian and Constantine* [Cambridge, Mass. 1982] 149; as his first-known successor is Aristius Optatus (297), there is no obstacle against dating this papyrus to either 293 or 294.

FROM HOUSE 1

2: DECLARATION ON OATH

(301)

P.Kellis inv. A/1/74+76 (House 1, floor of room 9). H. 11.4 x B. ca. 16.5 cm. Written parallel with the fibers. Two vertical folds are still visible, while the left hand edge of the papyrus is probably another fold. The verso of the papyrus is blank. The text was mentioned JSSEA 17 (1987) 172-73.

1 [῾Υπατείας Ποστουμίο]υ Τιτιανοῦ̣ κ̣α̣ὶ̣ Ο̣ὐ̣ι̣ρ̣ί̣ο̣υ̣ Ν̣ε̣π̣ωτιανοῦ V a c a t
2 [Τῇ τάξει τοῦ ἡ]γουμένου Θ̣ηβα̣ίδος ἐπακολουθοῦντ̣[ος
3 [N.N. ὀφ]φικ̣ιαλίου [τ]ῆ[ς] αὐτῆ̣ς τ̣άξεως V a c a t
4 [Παρὰ Αὐρηλίου . . . . .] Πασαιτ̣ο̣[.] μ̣ητρὸς Τ̣σ̣ε̣νεντήριος ἀπὸ ᾿Ιβιτῶν πόλεως [
5 [. . . . . ῾Ο]μ̣ολογῶ [ὀμνὺς τ]ὴν̣ ο̣ὐ̣ρ̣ά̣ν̣ιον τύχην τῶν κυρίων ἡμῶν Διοκλητ̣[ια-]
6 [νοῦ καὶ Μαξιμιανοῦ <Σεβαστῶν> καὶ Κ]ωνστ[αντίου καὶ Μ]α̣ξιμιαν̣ο̣ῦ τῶν ἐπιφανεστάτων Καισ̣άρων καιτ[. .]
7 [. . . . .]η̅ε̅ιν̣[. . . . . τo]ὺς δύο ἐκ μητρὸς Τβήκιος ἔτι τὲ καὶ τῆς σ̣ε̣α̣υ-
8 [τοῦ τάξεως . . . .]ο̣υπ̅[. . . . .]ν̣οῦφιν ἀκολούθως τοῖς ὑπομνηματισθεῖσι
9 [. . . . .]ω̣νια̣[. . . . .]τ̣ο̣ῦ̣ ὄντος μηνὸ̣ς Μεσορὴ καὶ ἀξιῶ τὰ καρπιζό-
10 [μενά . . . . . . μοι ἀποδ]ο̣θῆναι, π̣[άρε]σχον δὲ ἐμαυτοῦ ἐγγυητὴν παρόντα καὶ συνευδο-
11 [κοῦντα Αὐρήλιον . . .]ν Πεκῦ̣σ̣ι̣[ο]ς̣ ἀπὸ κώμης Μα̣δ̣ιώφ̣ριος τοῦ ᾿Ιβίτου νομοῦ.
- -

2 θηβαΐδος Pap. 4 πασαϊτ̣[, ἴβιτων Pap. 7 δὲ 8 ϋπομνηματισθεισι Pap. 11 ἴβιτου Pap.

"In the consulate of Postumius Titianus and Virius Nepotianus. To the office of the *praefectus Thebaidos*, with the concurrence of N.N., *officialis* of the same office, from Aurelius N.N. son of Pasai- and Tsenenteris, from the city of Hibis ---. I acknowledge, swearing by the heavenly fortune of our lords Diocletian and Maximian *Augusti* and Constantius and Maximian *nobilissimi Caesares*, - - - the two sons of Tbekis and, moreover, of your office (?) - - - nouphis according to the recorded - - - of the current month Mesore, and I demand that the harvested produce be returned to me and I have put forward N.N. son of Pekysis from the village of Madiophris of the Hibite nome as my surety, who is present and consents - - -."

Though we have a sizable portion of this document dating from Mesore 301 (cf. the consular date in l. 1 and l. 9, τ̣ο̣ῦ̣ ὄντος μην̣ὸ̣ς̣ Μεσορή; probably one folding is missing at the left), its actual content is not clear. The document was sent by an inhabitant of the city of Hibis (l. 4) to the office of the praefect of the Thebaid, with the concurrence of an official of the same office (ll. 2-3, ἐπακολουθοῦντος N.N. ὀφφικιαλίου τῆς αὐτῆς τάξεως), and it appears to contain a declaration (confirmed by an oath by the emperors, ll. 5-6) that something had been done, or would be done, by/to two persons who were the sons of a woman Tbekis (cf. l. 7, το]ὺς δύο ἐκ μητρὸς Τβήκιος) and who perhaps belonged to the office of the praeses addressed (cf. ll. 7-8, ἔτι τε καὶ τῆς σ̣ε̣α̣υ- | [τοῦ τάξεως; the reading of σ̣ε̣α̣υ- and the supplement is all but secure); furthermore something has happened (or, [rather ?], should happen) in accordance with the officially recorded notes (cf. l. 8, ἀκολουθῶς τοῖς ὑπομνηματισθεῖσι). Finally, the petitioner apparently asks that the harvested crop will be returned to him (cf. ll. 9-10, ἀξιῶ τὰ καρπιζό- | [μενα μοι ἀποδ]ο̣θῆναι) and he provides a surety for himself in the person of a son of a certain Pekysis from a village in the Hibite nome (cf. ll. 10-11, π̣[άρε]σχον δὲ ἐμαυτοῦ ἐγγυητὴν κτλ.). It is conceivable that this document contains a complaint that the petitioner's crop had been stolen by the two sons of Tbekis and that the surety was intended to back up the petitioner's story.

1. These are the consuls of the year 301, cf. R.S. Bagnall a.o., *Consuls of the Later Roman Empire* (Atlanta 1987; hereafter: *CLRE*), s.a. The restoration of the lacuna at the left contains 17 letters against 11 letters now restored in ll. 2; was line 1 written with some ekthesis? Cf. also l. 5-6n.

2-3. [τ]ῆ[ς] αὐτῆς τ̣άξεως in l. 3 implies the restoration of at least the word τάξις in l. 2; the present restoration (11 letters) seems too short (cf. l. 1n.), but a restoration of, e.g., [Τῇ τάξει τοῦ πρίνγκιπος τ]οῦ κτλ. (i.e. 21 letters restored) may be just a bit too long (cf. also l. 5-6n.); the same objection may be raised against restoring, e.g., [Τῷ N.N., πρίγκιπι τάξεως τ]οῦ κτλ.

The opening of a document with the element ἐπακολουθοῦντ̣[ος [N.N. ὀφ]φικ̣αλίου in the address seems unparalleled.

4. As the name of the petitioner's mother is specifically mentioned (for the name's ending -νεντῆρις cf. CPR XVII.A 4.4-5n.), one may assume that the name preceding this must refer to the petitioner's father. Probably one should restore/read it as Πασάιτ̣ο̣[ς] or Πασαίτ̣ο̣[υ]; a name Πασάις/Πασάιτος, however, is not yet listed in the usual papyrological onomastica, but cf. names like Τασάις and Πισόις.

4-5. A restoration of τῆς Μεγάλης 'Οάσεως (16 letters) would fill the lacuna between πόλεως (l. 4) and 'Ο]μ̣ολογῶ (l. 5) satisfactorily, but an alternative restoration like τῆς ἄνω Θηβαίδος (14 letters) cannot be excluded.

5-6. In general an oath is intended either to confirm a statement that something has happened in the past, or to confirm a promise to do something in the future (for the distinction between these two kinds of oaths, see in general E. Seidl, *Der Eid im römisch-ägyptischen Provinzialrecht* [München 1933-1935]). In the present case it looks as if the oath was taken in order to confirm a past event, before a specific request for future action was made (l. 9 ff.). The formula of the imperial oath found here (referring to the emperors Diocletian and Maximian and to the Caesars Constantius and Maximianus Galerius) has not occurred before, cf. K.A. Worp's collection of imperial oath formulas for the period 284-641 in ZPE 45 (1982) 199-223; a rather similar oath formula for Diocletian and his colleague(s) omits the adjective οὐράνιον before τύχην and adds the words καὶ νίκην thereafter. The first known case of an imperial oath referring to the οὐράνιον τύχην of the emperors is found in SB XIV 11551.4 (Hermop., 324 - 337, much restored). It is certainly odd to see in the restoration of the lacuna at the start of l. 6 the word Σεβαστῶν between < >, but the lay-out of the papyrus seems to make it certain that l. 5 was sufficiently filled

already with Διοκλητ[ια- (one expects some blank margin after it, cf. the next lines); the following syllable -νοῦ and the copula καὶ cannot be squeezed also into that line. Under the present circumstances the restoration at the start of line 6 counts already 20 letters (for the length of the lacuna cf. notes to ll. 1, 2.) and after the name of Maximian there is no simply space for the expected element Σεβαστῶν; of course, one may also speculate about leaving καὶ Μαξιμιανοῦ out while restoring the title Σεβαστῶν, i.e. restore 15 letters. So much is certain that the oath formula ends with τῶν ἐπιφανεστάτων Καισάρων. After that one expects the letters καιτ- to belong to an infinitive going with ὁμολογῶ (l. 5), but we have not found a suitable infinitive. Reading καρπ̣[instead of καιτ[may seem attractive in view of l. 9-10, τὰ καρπιζό- | [μενα, but is palaeographically difficult.
7. One may also restore, of course, υἱο]ύς.
7-8. The reading and restoration of τῆς σ̣ε̣α̣υ-[τοῦ τάξεως is all but secure. In fact, readings like τῆς σ̣π̣ο̣υ-/[δῆς or even τῆς δ̣ε̣ο̣ύ-/[σης seem also possible.
8.]ν̣οῦφιν looks like the accusative of a personal name; restore, e.g., 'Ορσε]ν̣οῦφιν.
9.]ω̣νια̣[: one may also read]μ̣α̣νια̣[or even think about reading ἡγε]μ̣ο̣νία̣[ς. The declaration was written evidently in the period 25.vii - 23.viii.301 (cf. = τ̣ο̣ῦ̣ ὄντος μηνὸ̣ς̣ Μεσορῆ = 'the current month Mesore').
11. The ink trace before ἀπὸ can only be read as belonging to the horizontal stroke of a sigma. Pekysis must have been the father of the surety put forward by the sender of the document.

A village name Madiophris (or read λ instead of δ and/or β, or even ε, instead of ρ?) in the Hibite nome is not yet known. For the geography of the Hibite nome in general cf. G. Wagner, *Les Oasis d'Egypte* 155f.

3: DOCUMENT CONCERNING IRRIGATION

(Mid-4th century)

P.Kellis inv. A/1/75 + 76 (both from House 1, floor of room 9) + P. 92.12 (House 3 [!], room 1, level 1). The papyrus consists of several fragments now combined into two contiguous units, Frag. I = A/1/75+76 (H. 14 x B. 13.3 cm.) and Frag. II = P. 92.12 (H. 12 x B. 3.3 cm.). There is a top margin of 2 cm. and a blank space of ca. 2.5 cm. between ll. 16 and 17. The writing runs parallel with the fibers, the verso is blank. Frag. I has three vertical folds at ca. 3.5 cm. intervals and is broken along similar folds at left and right; Frag. II is similarly broken along the folds at the left and right. Since all the extant folds are at regular intervals of ca. 3.5 cm. it seems most likely that the papyrus was originally rolled up and, when it was flattened by pressure, it broke into a number of strips all of about the same width. The space needed to restore two or more names + patronymics at the start of l. 1 and a (post-) consular formula at the start of line 6 suggests that there are at least 2 strips (possibly more), each of that width, missing from the left hand edge plus a similar number from the right hand edge. The original sheet was therefore at least 9 x 3.5 cm. = 31.5 cm. wide (not counting margins) and at least 4/9ths of the written text is lost. For organizational purposes the papyrus fragment A/1/75 was referred to previously as 'P.Kellis 13' (mentioned JSSEA 17 [1987] 172; plate in Mediterranean Archaeology 1 [1988] 177, ill. 14 [with wrong caption, cf. *ibidem* 168, where 'ill. 15' is referred to]).
NB: It is quite remarkable that fragments belonging to the same document were found in two different, even not directly-adjacent houses (Houses 1 and 3); probably at least one of these was taken by the wind from one house and dropped at random into the other house ca. 20 meters away (cf. the plan of Houses 1 - 3, p. 5).

1 [Αὐρήλιοι NN. καὶ NN. ἀπ]ὸ κώμης Κέλλεως τοῦ Μωθίτου νομοῦ Ạ[ὐρηλίῳ] Τιβερίῳ [

2 [Βουλόμενοι ἐπίδοσιν λιβέλλ]ων ποιήσασθαι παρὰ τῇ ἀνδρείᾳ τοῦ κυρ[ίου διασημ]μ[ο]τάτ[ου ἡγεμόνος/δουκὸς

3 [ὅτι μηδὲν ἀδι]κοῦμεν μετριώτατοι ὄντες καὶ μηδὲν [. . . . με]νοι καὶ ὅτ[ι

4 [ἡ]μᾶς δυσκληρίαν τῆς κώμης. Ὕδατα γὰρ ο[ὐκέτι με]ταφέρομεν δια[

5 [ ]οῦντα ἡμῖν. Κυρία ἡ ἐντολὴ ἁπλῆ γραφε[ῖσα ἐφ' ὑπο]γραφῆς τῶν [ἑξῆς ὑπογραφόντων καὶ ἐπερωτηθέντες ὡμολογήσαμεν.

6 [το]ῦ λαμπροτάτου κόμιτος. Αὐρήλιος[ca. 8] Κόρακος καὶ [

7 [ ]ουτβαντς καὶ Ψεκῆς Πρεμενούριος κ[αὶ ca. 6] θης χαλκε[

8 [N.N. Τι]βερίου ἐθέμην τὴν ἐντολὴν ὡς πρόκε[ι]ται. [Αὐρήλι]ος Ψάις Πετε[-- ἔγραψεν ὑπὲρ αὐτῶν γραμμάτα μὴ εἰδότων.]

9 [ ]ων παραχύτος καὶ Πινούθης Γενᾶ κ[α]ὶ ο[. . .]σιος καὶ Σαρα[π-- ἐθέμεθα τὴν ἐντολὴν ὡς πρόκειται. Ἔγραψεν ὑπὲρ αὐτῶν γραμμάτα μὴ εἰδότων

10 [Αὐρήλιος N.N. ἀπὸ κώμης Κέλλε]ως. Αὐρήλιος Καλλικλῆς καὶ Παταιᾶς κ[αὶ . . . .]τωνος καὶ [ἐθέμεθα τὴν ἐντολὴν ὡς πρόκειται. Ἔγραψεν]

11 [ὑπὲρ αὐτῶν γραμμάτα μὴ εἰδότω]ν Αὐρήλιος Τιμόθεος Τιβερίου ἀπὸ τῆς[αὐτῆς κ]ώμης. Αὐρ[ήλιο

12 [ ]μοις καὶ συνηθείᾳ, φυγάδευσαι δὲ τοῦ πλ.[ca. 6]ρος τῆς κώμ[ης

13 [ ]διὰ τοῦτο καὶ πρότερον εἰς μεταφο[ρὰ]ν [τῶν ca. 3] χρήματων[

14 [ ]ς γὰρ οἱ βοηθούμενοι διὰ ταισσάρων σημ[αινομένων] πρὸς προσπο[

15 [κωμ]ογραμματέα ἀπαγάγων εἴς τινα ἐρη[μον τόπον π]λείστους τ[ύπους

16 [ ] τοὺς ἀθλίους τούτους καὶ πένητας κ[αὶ . . . . . φ]υγαδεύεσθ[αι

(Space of 2 or 3 lines)

17 (M.2)]. ἐκ δέλτου αὐτοῦ τὰ ὑπομνήματα ἐκλαβεῖν [. . .]ιανὸς ὁ διασ[ημότατος ἡγεμών/δούξ

8 ψαϊς Pap. 10 παταΐας Pap. 14 τεσσάρων (first σ written over ι) 15 ι of τινα written over α

So much of this document is missing that it is difficult to make any consecutive sense of what remains. An attempt at analysis produces the following result:
(1) l. 1: Opening, probably of the 'A (+ ?) to B *χαίρειν*'-type.
(2) At first sight the document is an *ἐντολή* = 'order, mandate, power of attorney' (cf. l. 5) closed off by a dating + subscriptions (ll. 6-11). In ll. 2ff. reference is made to a hearing or deposition of a petition before a *praeses* (or a *dux*, cf. l. 2n.); this would explain why the *ἐντολή* now follows. Line 3 would then contain a reference to the authors' modest status which they invoke in approaching a high official (cf. **20**.5n. for this rhetorical *topos*). At issue is the transport or transfer of water. The petitioners claim apparently that they have done no wrong and that they are not responsible for the *δυσκληρία* of the village since they no longer (?) transport the water (l. 4). Ll. 2-5 are, then, the body of the *ἐντολή*. (cf. also l. 8.).
(3) The start of l. 6 apparently preserves part of a dating formula (cf. note ad loc.).
(4) Starting with the second half of l. 6 a number of names are given of people subscribing to the *ἐντολή*; their number (a considerable number of people seem to have been involved) suggests that this was issued at the local, village level; cf. **24**.
(5) It is unclear, however, how the *ἐντολή* is connected with the present petition. Did it arise earlier as a result of a previous hearing and is it now included in this document as part of the petitioner's case[11]? In ll. 12-16 we find references to banishment and to 'these poor and wretched ones' (l. 16). No doubt therefore the claimants had not only been saddled with a responsibility which was not rightly their's, but they had also been wrongly punished, so they felt, for their failure to carry it out.
(6) The document ends with a note (l. 17) made by a second hand on what had been or needed to be done on the matter; reference is made to the records of an official whose honorific *διασημότατος* suggests a *praeses Thebaidos* or a *dux* (cf. l. 2 n.).

For problems concerning water-rights in another Egyptian village (Karanis, 439) cf. P.Haun. III 58 + ZPE 99 (1993) 89f.

The writing of the papyrus is the same as that of **15** from 357 (cf. below, l. 8n.), hence the date of this text to the mid-4th century; the consular dating [?; cf. l. 6 n.] is not incompatible with such a dating.

1. Ạ[*ὐρηλίῳ*] or Ạ[*ὐρηλίοις*: although only a corner of the letter remains and alpha is by no means certain, the size of the following lacuna more or less compels the reading.

For the Mothite nome cf. **41**.4n.

Though the beta of Τι*βερίῳ* is damaged, Τι*θ̣έριῳ* (cf. **50**.9 and note ad loc.) cannot be read.

2. This line seems to contain reference to a hearing or an enquiry or a deposition of a document; the supplement at the start is inspired by **23**.14. For the supplement at end cf. l. 17. Instead of *διασημ*]*μ*[*ο*]*τ̣ά̣τ*[*ου ἡγεμόνος* one could restore *διασημ*]*μ*[*ο*]*τ̣ά̣τ*[*ου δουκὸς*, cf. **24**.1 (352): *τάξε*]*ως τοῦ̣* [*κυ*]*ρίο̣υ̣ μου̣ διασημ̣ο̣τάτου δουκὸς*. Though the evidence shows that the honorific abstract *ἀνδρεία* refers predominantly to the provincial governor (cf. CPR V 7.9n.), there is in itself no reason to think that it could not apply to a *dux* and his 'virtus'.

[11]) It should be noted that all of ll. 1-16 was written by one hand, so one might argue that somewhere in ll. 3-11 a copy of an earlier document [a dated *ἐντολή* + subscriptions] was cited within the context of a new document.

3. The supplement at the start is 'exempli gratia'. Petitioners typically claim that they have done no wrong; *μετριώτατοι* is a self-characterization of their status.
4. *δυσκληρία* is an *addendum lexicis papyrologicis*; it occurs in patristic authors, cf. G.W.H. Lampe, *A Patristic Lexicon* s.v.

ọ[: the omikron is broken but secure; *ο[ὐκέτι με]ταφέρομεν* would fit the space adequately and make reasonable sense. For *με]ταφέρομεν* cf. l. 13, *μεταφο[ρὰ]ν*.
6. *το]ῦ λαμπροτάτου κόμιτος* may be part of a consular dating formula. If so, likely dates are the years 344 (Sallustius *comes*) or 347 (Fl. Eusebius *v.c.*, *comes*), cf. R.S. Bagnall a.o., *CLRE* under these years (cf. also *op.cit.* the note to 345 on Fl. Albinus). The years 372, 374, 392 are less likely, as from 368 onwards the governor of the Thebaid was usually a *vir clarissimus* (λαμπρότατος), not a *vir perfectissimus* (*διασημότατος*), cf. J.Lallemand, *L'administration civile* 61-2. The handwriting is also likely to be slightly earlier than this. The fact that no month + date have been given does not need to detain us (cf. in general **8**.13n.).

The occurrence of a Korax as the father of an Aurelius Kapiton in **24**.15 suggests a restoration [Καπίτων], which would fit the lacuna well.
7. *]ουτβαντς*: perhaps write *]ου Τβάντς*. Although not listed as a name by F. Preisigke, *Namenbuch*, or D. Foraboschi, *Onomasticon Alterum Papyrologicum*, there are several Egyptian names of the Τβ-type.

The name Πρεμενοῦρις is not listed by Preisigke or Foraboschi, *opp.citt.*, although an Egyptian name-type in Πρεμ- (derived from Demotic p3-rmt?) is well attested; cf. W. Spiegelberg, *Ägyptische und griechische Eigennamen aus Mumienetiketten der römischen Kaiserzeit* (Leipzig 1901 [repr. Chicago 1978]) 32* Nr. 224.

χαλκε[: not listed by Preisigke or Foraboschi *opp.citt.* as a personal name. It may well be that this is rather an occupation name, *χαλκε[ῦς*, cf. l. 9, *παραχύτος*.
8. Tiberius at the start of this line was perhaps the same man as the father of Aurelius Timotheos son of Tiberius in l. 11.

Depending upon how many names are lost in the lacuna at the start, the singular *ἐθέμην* should perhaps be changed into the plural *ἐθέμεθα*.

An Aurelius Psais son of Pete--- occurs also in **15**.2-3 (357).
9. *παραχύτος*: not known as a personal name; it may be a new variant of *παραχύτης*, 'bath attendant' (cf. P.Oxy. XII 1499.2-3: *παραχύτης δημοσίου βαλανείου*), or 'water carrier'; cf. M. Wisseman in Glotta 62 (1984) 80-89. Either meaning would fit the context of the document well; cf. above l. 7n. on *χαλκε[ῦς*. The variants *περιχύτης* and *πυριχύτης* are also attested; see P.Sorb. II 69, 102.D3n.

Πινούθης: cf. *Πινοῦθις*, *-θος*, *-τι* etc.; all can be taken as variants of the Egyptian name Πανοῦτε.

Γενᾶ: for the name cf. **76**.33-34n.
10. For the name Παταιᾶς cf. **16**.4n.
10-11. For the restoration of *ἔγραψεν ὑπὲρ αὐτῶν γραμμάτα μὴ εἰδότω]ν* Αὐρήλιος Τιμόθεος Τιβερίου, *κτλ.*, cf. the sequence of subscriptions in **13** and in **24**.
14. *οἱ βοηθούμενοι*: most usually said of an advocate's clients, but it is difficult at this stage to see the document as a report of judicial proceedings.

προσποϙ[: *προσπο[ίησιν*, 'acquisition of, claim to' seems unavoidable, although the word is apparently new in the papyri.
17. In itself it is conceivable that this line contains a prefectural (or ducal) *hypographe* given in response to a petition. For such *hypographae* cf. CPR XVII.A, Append. C. For *praesides* of the Thebaid cf. J. Lallemand, *L'administration civile*, 251-255 and the supplements to her list in TYXH 1 (1987) 192f; there are a number whose name ends ...ianus.

FROM HOUSE 2

From House 2 we have the following texts:

4) Parachoresis by Pausanias, 331
5) Letter to Pausanias, from Gena
6) Letter to Gena, from Pausanias
7) Letter to Gena son of Pataias, from Harpokration

---

8) Sale of a slave to Tithoes son of Petesis, 362
9) Agreement with Tithoes son of Petesis
10) Order for payment to Tithoes, from Ammonios
11) Order for payment to Samoun son of Tithoes, from Ammonios
12) Letter to Tithoes, from Samoun

---

13) Division of an inheritance, 333
14) Agreement by Horion, 356
15) Notification to the *Praeses Thebaidos* from Aurelius Psais, 357
16) Memorandum to Gelasius, from Aionianus

It is clear that among the papyri coming from this house certain clusters can be distinguished which may be related to occupants of this house, cf. esp. texts **4**-**7** (texts related to Pausanias and Gena) and **8**-**12** (texts related to Tithoes and his son Samoun). It should be noted that a letter written in Coptic, inv. A/2/76+77[12], also belongs to the latter cluster. Within each cluster the exactly dated texts have been given first. Texts **13**-**16** apparently do not belong directly to either of the previous clusters, nor are they clearly interrelated among themselves; their relationship, therefore, to any of the other known occupants of House 2 remains problematic. As regards **16** it should be noted that one may be dealing with persons who occur also in a papyrus (still unpublished) from House 4 in Kellis.

[12]) Cf. the description in JSSEA 17 (1987) 163 and 173.

4: CONTRACT OF *PARACHORESIS*

(331)

P.Kellis inv. A/2/63+69 (both from House 2, room 2, level 2 [A/2/63 low in level 2 in NE corner of room]). The papyrus consists of several fragments which can be combined into two larger units; these, however, cannot be combined further with each other with any certainty. Frag. I: H. 2.5 x B. 3.5 cm. Frag. II: H. 20 x B. 5 cm. At the bottom of Frag. II is a margin of 8 cm. The verso is blank.

Frag. I:
1 [Αὐρήλιος Πανσανίας Οὐαλερίου ἄρξας τῆς]
2 [Μωθιτῶν πόλεως] Αὐρηλίῳ Π[. . . . . ἀπὸ]
3 [κώμης Κέλλεως] τῆς αὐτῆς [πόλεως χαίρειν.]
4 [Ὁμολογῶ παρακεχω]ηκέναι σο[ι τὸ ὑπαρχόν μοι Object
5 [ἐκ μέρους ἀπη]λιωτικοῦ τ[ῆς κώμης
6 πήχεις] τεκτονικὸ̣[υς Numeral
7]πήχεις τ̣[εκτονικοὺς Numeral; γείτονες

\- -

Frag. II:
8]..[
9]ητος ἀδελφ[
10 ψ]ε̣ιλοῦ τόπου ἐ̣[
11 [ἢ οἳ ἐὰν ὦ]σ̣ι̣ [γε]ί̣τ̣[ω]νες πάντοθ[εν, τῆς βεβαιώσεως]
12 [ἐξακολο]υθούσης μοι διὰ παντὸς [ἀπὸ παντὸς τοῦ ἐπελευ-]
13 [σομένο]υ̣. Κυρία ἡ παραχώρη[σις ..... γραφεῖσα]
14 [ἐφ' ὑπογρ]αφῆς μου βέβαια ἔσ̣τ̣[ω καὶ ἔννομος]
15 [ὡς ἐν δημ]οσίῳ κατακειμένη [καὶ ἐπερωτηθεὶς]
16 [ὡμολόγησ]α̣.

17 [Ὑπατεία]ς Ἰουνίου Βάσσου [καὶ Φλ(αουίου) Ἀβλαβίου]
18 [τῶν λαμπρο]τάτων, Τῦβι β̅ [
19 (M.2) [Αὐρήλι]ος Πανσα̣ν̣ί̣ας Ο̣[ὐαλερίου ἄρξας]
20 π̣α̣ρ̣[εχώρ]ησα τὸ προκ[είμενον Object]
21 κ̣α̣ὶ̣ ἐ̣[περ]ωτηθεὶς ὡ[μολόγησα.

10 ψιλοῦ 11 ἄν, γείτονες

"Aurelius Pausanias son of Valerius, former magistrate of the city of the Mothites, sends greetings to Aurelius P--, from the village of Kellis belonging to the same city. I acknowledge that I have ceded to you the (parcel) belonging to me - in the eastern part of the village -, *n* x *n* carpenter's cubits in size -- (indication of neighbours), or whoever the neighbours may be at every side, while the right of eviction rests upon me under all circumstances against every person raising a claim. The document of cession must be authoritative, written in *n* copies with my signature, and guaranteed and legal as if deposited in a public archive and in answer to the formal question I have replied positively. In the consulate of Iunius Bassus and Fl. Ablabius, *viri clarissimi*, Tybi 2. (M. 2) I, Aurelius Pausanias son of Valerius, former magistrate, have ceded the aforementioned (parcel) and in answer to the formal question I have replied positively."

This papyrus contains a badly preserved *parachoresis* or 'contract of cession' (cf. ll. 4, 13); despite its fragmentary condition it is clear that at least a house or a plot of land was involved (cf. l. 10, *ψ*]*ειλοῦ τόπου*, and also l. 11, 'neighbours on all sides', which evidently refers to the ceded immovables). Originally such *parachoreseis* involved only catoecic land but later all kinds of private land could be ceded. For such contracts of cession cf. R. Taubenschlag, *The Law of Greco-Roman Egypt in the Light of the Papyri* (Warsaw 1955²) 228f., 238, and H.J. Wolff, *Das Recht der Griechischen Papyri Ägyptens* 166f.; cf. also the remarks by P.J. Sijpesteijn in ZPE 19 (1975) 96 n. 15 and H.A. Rupprecht in Gedenkschrift Kunkel (Frankfurt/Main) 365ff. and the full discusion by B. MacGing in P.Dub. 3. For recently published cessions from Oxyrhynchus cf. P.Oxy. XLIX 3482 (where there is also a list of relevant parallels) and LI 3638, LII 3690; cf. now also the full text of P.Oxy. III 663 published by B. Nielsen in BASP 29 (1992) 143-152, while two more such contracts from Oxyrhynchus will appear in a forthcoming volume of P.NYU II. Such documents are also known from the Arsinoite nome; cf., e.g., SB VI 9618, VIII 9906 and XVIII 13764. Apparently they are not yet known from the Great Oasis (the *parachoresis* in SB VIII 9873 [244] deals with the cession of a half part of the activities of an undertaker).

1, 19. The name Pausanias (restored in l. 1 on the basis of l. 19) is one of those 'classical' Greek personal names occurring remarkably frequently in papyri from the Dakleh Oasis cf. G. Wagner, *Les Oasis d'Egypte* 225ff. This name also occurs in other texts from Houses 2 and 3, cf. especially **38.a**.1 (where also Pausanias' office as ἄρξας Μωθιτῶν πόλεως is found), and the note ad loc.; there seems to be no obstacle against referring all of the attestations to one person.

2. It is just conceivable that one could restore here the name of the addressee and that of his father as: Αὐρηλίῳ Π[αμοῦρ Ψάιτος ἀπὸ]. After all, Pausanias had some at least some kind of relationship with Pamour, cf. **38.a**.1-2, 9-11. If we restore below in l. 13 *δισσὴ γραφεῖσα* it could be assumed that 1 copy went to Pamour (evidently living in House 3), while the other copy was kept by Pausanias; was Pausanias perhaps living in House 2?

2-3. *τῆς αὐτῆς* [*πόλεως*: the restoration of *πόλεως* is suggested by, e.g., **38.a**.2-3. For the relationship between the village of Kellis and the city of the Mothites cf. **20**.3-5n.

5-7. Probably these lines contain an indication of the situation of the plot of the land ceded and its size, cf. **38.a** and **38.b**.6ff. The Greek adjective *ἀπηλιωτικός* = 'Eastern' (NB: one cannot read here *ἰ*]*διωτικός*!) suggests that the land was situated in the eastern part of the village. For the *πῆχυς τεκτονικός* = 'the carpenter's cubit' (also used in **38.a** and in **38.b**.7ff.) as being the most common cubit (45 cm. long, as it consisted of 6 *παλαισταί* [palms] at 7.5 cm. each) cf. P.Oxy. IV 669.34-35n.; in general cf. K. Maresch, *Beobachtungen zu den Längen- und Flächenmassen Ägyptens in römischer und byzantinischer Zeit* in P.Köln VII p. 177-87 and S.P. Vleeming, *Demotic Measures of Length and Surface, chiefly of the Ptolemaic Period* in Pap.Lugd.Bat. XXIII 208ff., esp. 214 § 9.

11-12. For the restoration at the start of l. 11 cf. **38.a** and **38.b**.11. For the warranty formula used here cf. the references to various contracts of sale from Kellis given in the introd. to **36**. The lacuna in l. 11 between tau and nu in *γε]ί̣τ̣[ω]νες* is so wide that it must have contained an omega rather than an omikron.

13f. For the adjective to be restored before *γραφεῖσα* cf. above, l. 2n. For the formula used in ll. 13-15 cf. the note to **37**.12ff. and H.J. Wolff, *Das Recht* 162-63, for its juridical meaning cf. also M. Hässler, *Die Bedeutung der Kyria-Klausel in den Papyrusurkunden* (Berlin 1960) 77f.

17-18. The consulate is that of 331, cf. R.S. Bagnall a.o., *CLRE* s.a. As 331/2 happens to be a leap year, Tybi 2 = 29.xii.331. It is possible, of course, that the document was dated, like a number of other private contracts from this region, '*κατ' Αἰγυπτίους*', in which case Tybi 2 in 331 would fall 89 days earlier, i.e. on 1.x. On the question of the survival and use of the Egyptian '*annus vagus*' in Roman Egypt cf. D. Hagedorn - K.A. Worp in ZPE 104 (1994) 243-255.

5: PRIVATE LETTER

(Ca. 330)

P.Kellis inv. A/2/109 (House 2, room 7, understairs cupboard, on base of bed). H. 26.5 x B. 10 cm. Complete with margins (2.5 cm. at the top, 1.5 cm. at the left, and 3.5 cm. at the bottom) intact. The pattern of worming suggests that the sheet was folded at some stage across the middle from top to bottom. Written along the fibres. Mentioned in JSSEA 17 (1987) 173. For organizational purposes the papyrus was referred to previously as 'P.Kellis 22'.

1 Τῷ δεσπότῃ μου
2 Παυσανίᾳ
3 Γ̣ε̣νᾶ χαίρειν. Π̣ρ̣ο̣[ηγο]υ̣-
4 μέν[ως] πολ[λὰ τὴν] ε̣ὐ̣[γέ-]
5 [νειάν σ]ο̣υ προσαγορεύω
6 [μετὰ τῆς κυρ]ί̣α̣ς̣ μ̣ου Τ̣α̣μοῦ
7 [καὶ τ]ῶ̣ν υἱῶν εὐ̣χόμενος ὁλο-
8 κ̣λ̣ηρεῖν διὰ παντός· ὡς ἐκέ-
9 λ̣ε̣υ̣σ̣εν ἡ σὴ εὐγένεια, ἤθελον
10 ἐ̣ξαυτῆς ἐλθεῖν πρὸς τ̣ὴν σὴν
11 [χ]ρη[σ]τότ̣ητα, ἀλλ' ἐπειδὴ ἐν τῷ
12 [. . .]. . . . . . Π̣μ(οῦν) Βερι βορινοῦ
13 [. . . .] ἡμερῶν μετὰ πλησ̣ου
14 [το]ῦ καρποῦ, διὰ τοῦτο̣ τέως̣ ὑπερ-
15 [ε]θ̣έμην, ἵνα μὴ ἔλθω
16 [μηδ' ἀ̣]φανίσθῃ τὸ πρᾶγμα.
17 [Ὡ]ς̣ ἴστε̣, καιρ[ό]ς ἐστιν̣ τῆς
18 κατασπορᾶς. Εἰ ἔ̣δοξεν ο̣ὖν
19 τῇ εὐγενείᾳ, πέμψον το̣ν̣ ἀδελ-
20 φο̣ν̣ Τιμόθεον, ἵνα ποιήσῃ

21 τὸ πρᾶγμα ἀντ' ἐμοῦ, καὶ γράψον
22 μοι ὄνον πρὸς Γάιον
23 ἵνα ἐπ̣ειχθῶ, ἐπειδ[ὴ] οὐκ
24 ἔχω [̣]νι ̣ κτῆν̣ο̣ς̣. 'Ε̣ρρῶ-
25 σθαί σε εὔχομαι, δέσπο-
26 τά μου, πολλοῖς εὐτυχοῦν-
27 τα χρόνοις.
Verso:
28 Τῷ̣ δ̣ε̣υπότῃ μ̣[ου] Χ Π̣[αυ]σ̣α̣νί̣α̣
29 Γενᾶ τέκτονος

10 ἐλθεῖν: ἐ- ex corr. 11 αλλ´ Pap. 15 ϊνα Pap. 21 αντ— Pap. 23 οὐκ— Pap. 29 τέκτων

"To my master Pausanias, Gena sends greetings. First of all I send many greetings to your nobility together with my lady Tamou and your sons, praying for your well-being for all time. Since your nobility bade me to, I wanted to come to your goodness straightaway, but since ... in (the village of) Pmoun Beri ... days with ... for the crop, for this reason I delayed a while, lest I come and the business be lost. As you know, it is the time of the sowing. So if it seems good to your nobility, send brother Timotheos to transact the business instead of me. And please write to Gaius for me about a donkey, so that I may make haste, since I do not have a ... beast. I pray that you are well, master, and prosper for many years." (Verso) "To my lord Pausanias, Gena the carpenter."

A letter from the carpenter Gena to Pausanias. Both parties are found also in **6** written by Pausanias (for him, see **4**.1n.) to Gena. Although Gena is addressed there as 'my lord brother', the fact that here he calls Pausanias his 'master' (ll. 1, 25-26), 'your nobility' (ll. 4-5, 9, 19) and 'your goodness' (ll. 10-11) suggests that their relationship is one of master and servant rather than of equals. In fact in both texts Gena is found acting as an agent for Pausanias for in ll. 11-14 of this letter he seems to be involved in some business on Pausanias's behalf while ll. 18-21 concern some unspecified matter which Gena suggests might be undertaken by Pausanias's other agent Timotheos rather than by himself.

4-5. εὐγένειαν is supplemented from ll. 9 and 19. Although ἡ σὴ εὐγένεια may seem to rule out ἡ εὐγένειά σου, both forms are found; the latter is more usual in private letters, see P.Oxy. LIX 4004.10n. (also containing further literature for the use of the term εὐγένεια).
6. The initial letters of the personal name Τ̣α̣μοῦ are abraded but secure; either an indeclinable variant, or perhaps a gen. sing. Ταμοῦ of Ταμοῦς, cf. D. Foraboschi, *Onomasticon Alterum Papyrologicum*. Maybe she was Pausanias' wife.

11. Although *χρηστότης* as a honorific is often found in a Christian context (see P.Oxy. LVI 3863.6 n. with reff.), it also occurs from the 2nd century onwards of any patron; see F. Preisigke, *Wörterbuch* III, Abschn. 9, s.v.
12. Although there are some traces, *ἐποικίῳ* cannot be read before Πμ(οῦν). For names in Πμοῦν in the Oases, see G. Wagner, *Les Oasis d'Egypte* 29; for the element Βερ<ρ>ι- (= 'new, young' in Coptic) cf. *ibidem* 163.
13. The sense has to be something like 'since I was in north Pmoun Beri for some days on account of sowing the crop', but the precise wording is unclear. There is insufficient space for [πολλῶν] ἡμερῶν; perhaps a numeral before ἡμερῶν was preceded by ἦν. The meaning of μεταπλησου is equally unclear; separating μετὰ from πλησου does not solve the question how the latter should be interpreted.
19-20. The 'brother Timotheos' referred to here may be identical with the Timotheos who acts as Pausanias's agent in **6**.4, 27, 51.
24. Though the singular may be somewhat surprising (not listed by F. Preisigke, *Wörterbuch* I, but cf. LSJ s.v. κτῆνος, 2) the reading κτῆ̣ν̣ο̣ς is fairly reliable; it remains uncertain, however, whether it was preceded by [ὀ]νικ̣(ὸν). Why the author of the letter would have used here the ponderous wording ὀνικὸν κτῆνος rather than a simple word ὄνον (cf. l. 22), must remain an open question.
24-27. This more elaborate closing formula of a letter seems to be found more frequently in letters from the 2nd and 3rd century (cf. F. Preisigke, *Wörterbuch* s.v. εὐτυχέω) but there are some other 4th-century examples among the Kellis papyri cf. the closing formulas of **46**, **64**, **69**, **72**.
29. For τέκτονες in the papyri cf. Th. Reil, *Beiträge zur Kenntnis des Gewerbes im hellenistischen Ägypten*, Diss. Leipzig 1913, esp. 74ff. The trade is fairly well represented in the papyri from Kellis, cf. the attestations listed in Index IX.

6: PRIVATE LETTER

(Ca. 330)

P.Kellis inv. A/2/83 (House 2, room 5, level 3, corner room 6) + A/2/92 (room 6, level 3, near door to room 3). H. 30.5 x B. 7.3 cm. Written across the fibers and continued down the fibers in the lefthand margin. After writing, the papyrus was then turned over from the right to the left and the letter finished off on the lower half of the back. The address was written on the upper half and the papyrus was folded across the middle with the result that it was split into two pieces of roughly equal size which became separated at some time in the past. Mentioned in JSSEA 17 (1987) 173. For organizational purposes the two papyrus fragments were referred to previously as 'P.Kellis 20' and 'P.Kellis 21'.

1 Κ̣[υ]ρίῳ̣ μου ἀδελφῷ̣
2 Γ̣ε̣[ν]ᾷ̣ [Π]α̣υσανίας
3 χα[ίρει]ν. [Ἐ]νετειλάμην
4 τῷ̣ [ἀδελφ]ῷ̣ Τιμοθέῳ̣
5 ἀ̣π̣[οστεῖλαι] χοιρίδιον
6 απ̣[ca. 7]̣ νος εἰς τὰ
7 αν̣[ca. 7]ου ⟦επ⟧ καὶ ἐ̣παν-
8 ελ̣[θεῖν. Ἐπεὶ] ἐζήτησα περὶ
9 τῶ[ν χοιριδ]ίων, φήσει
10 ὁ ἀ[δελφὸς ὅ]τ̣ι Εὗρον δύο

11 παρ' Αὐρη[λίο]υ Βησᾶτος
12 τέκ[τονος ἀπ]ὸ Πμ(οῦν) Τεκαλε
13 ὑπὲρ [τοῦ ἑν]ὸς ἑκάστου
14 σίτ[ου καγ]κ(έλλων) δώδεκα ἀχιρ-
15 ⟦ισ⟧[. . . .]υ. Ἔσπευσα
16 οὖν [πέμ]ψαι πρὸς ὑμᾶς
17 τὸ[ν ἡμέτ]ερον Σινέα.
18 Δι[ὸ] οὖν [ἀ]ποστείλ[η]ς ὑπὲρ
19 \`τοῦ ἑνὸς´ σίτου καθαροῦ καγκ(έλλους)
20 [δ]ώδεκ[α], ὅπως ἀξιω-
21 θεὶς ἀνέλθῃς μετὰ τού-
22 [το]υ τοῦ Σινέως καὶ ποι-
23 [ήσῃς τὸ]ν αὐτὸν υἱὸν
24 .[ ].[ ]. . . . . .υνα. τὰ
25 χοιρίδια. Κ[αὶ εἰ] μὲν
26 εὑρήσεις τὸν ἀδελ-
27 φὸν Τιμόθεον, ποίη-
28 σον αὐτὸν ἀναδέξασθα[ι]
29 αὐτῷ τοὺς ἄλλους
30 δώδεκα καγκ(έλλους) σίτου
31 εἰς τὸν καιρὸν ὑπὲρ
32 τοῦ ἄλλου. Εἰ τὲ πάλιν
33 οὐκ εὑρήσεις, δῆλον
34 σὺ αὐτὸς ἀναδέξα[ι]
35 τὸ μέτρον τῶν γενη-
36 μάτων καὶ ἀπόστει-
37 λον τὰ δύο χοιρίδια
38 καὶ ἐὰν δηλώσῃς
39 μοι ὅτι εἴς τινα
40 γεωργὸν θέλεις
41 τὴν ἀποχὴν τῶν
42 δώδεκα καγκ(έλλων) σίτου, ἀπο-
43 στελῶ σοι χωρὶς ἀμε-
44 λείας διὰ τῶν ἐλθόν-
45 των ⟦.⟧ δύο καθαρτῶν
46 ἐπ' αὐτόν. Ἐρρῶσθαί
47 σε εὔχομαι, κύριέ ⟦μου⟧
48 ἄδελφε, πολλοῖς χρό-
49 νοις.

Left hand margin, downwards along the fibers:

50 Ὡς προεῖπον οὖν, ἔπεμψα διὰ Σινέ[ως εἰς τιμ]ὴν τοῦ ἑνὸς ἐν σίτῳ ⟦ου⟧ καγκ(έλλους) ὀκτώ, ὅπως τὰ δύο ἀποστεί-
51 λατε. Ἰδοὺ γὰρ ἔπεμψα

On the verso, lower half of the document upwards:
52 *τῷ ἀδελφῷ* Τ*ιμοθέῳ τὰ εἰκότα ἔτι μὴν καὶ*
53 *τῷ ἀδελφῷ* Σ*αρᾶπι.*
On the upper half of the papyrus:
54 Τῷ ἀδελ[φ]ῷ Γενᾷ Χ Π̣α̣υ̣σ̣ανίας.

9 *φήσι* 10 *ηὖρον* 31 *τὸν*: *τ* ex *κ* 32 *εἰ δὲ* 38 *καὶ*: *κ* ex corr. 39 *ὅτι* ex corr. 50-51 *ἀποστείλητε.*

"To my lord brother Gena, Pausanias sends greetings. I instructed brother Timotheos to send a pig ... for the ... and come back. When I made enquiries about the pigs, our brother said: 'I found two at Aurelius Besas's, the carpenter from Pmoun Tekale (?), at twelve *cancelli* of wheat for each one'. So I have made haste to send our (son) Sineus to you. Therefore you must send twelve *cancelli* of clean wheat for the (first) one, so that as requested you may return along with this Sineus and make the same son ... the pigs. And if you find brother Timotheos, get him to guarantee the other twelve cancelli of grain for him for the opportunity for the other one. And if in turn you don't find him, you must of course guarantee the measure of the produce yourself and send the two pigs. And if you let me know that you want the receipt for the twelve cancelli of grain made out to a particular farmer, I'll send it to you without any trouble via the two cleaners who are coming to him. I pray that you are well for many years, my lord brother."
(Left hand margin and back) "So as I said before, I have sent for the price of one of them in grain eight *cancelli* via Sineus, so that you may send the two. For look, I have sent to brother Timotheos what is reasonable and also to brother Sarapis. Pausanias, to brother Gena."

Pausanias writes to Gena with instructions about buying two pigs in exchange for grain. The exact details of the transaction are obscured by the broken state of the upper part of the papyrus. Nonetheless, what seems most likely is that Pausanias's original agent Timotheos, who had been instructed to buy one animal (ll. 3-8), had found two for sale (ll. 8-15) at 12 *cancelli* per pig. Timotheos had some funds (l. 51), but not enough to buy both. Pausanias now informs Gena that he has sent his agent Sineus and orders (l. 15ff.) Gena to come up with twelve *cancelli* (eight of which apparently had been sent in the meantime by Pausanias to Gena through Sineus, cf. ll. 15-17, 50) for the first pig and gives instructions for Gena to pass on to Timotheos in order to secure the other pig against a guarantee of twelve *cancelli* in the future (ll. 25-32). If Timotheos could not be found, Gena himself was to act as guarantor (ll. 32-37). The transaction may seem unnecessarily complex but it has obviously been complicated by Pausanias's inability to contact Timotheos directly as well as by the need to provide a guarantee in addition to more funds.

The ecology and economics of pig-raising in Egypt in the New Kingdom period have been discussed by R.L. Miller, JEA 76 (1990) 125-140; it is likely that many of his conclusions remain valid for this later period.

2f. Pausanias (cf. **4**.1n.) and Gena are also known from **5** in which Gena is the writer and Pausanias the addressee. A brother Timotheos (here ll. 4, 26-27, 51) also occurs in **5**.19-20.
5. For the supplement cf. ll. 36-37.
7-8. For the supplement cf. ll. 20-21.
12. For place names starting with an element Πμοῦν cf. **5**.12n.
14. For σῖτος replacing πυρός from the 4th century onwards, see H. Cadell, CdE 48 (1973) 329-38. For the *cancellus* measure, see **10**.5n.
14-15. ἀχιρ-⟦ισ⟧[. . . .]υ: Or perhaps ⟦ιε⟧? A term ἀχείριστος, 'unworked' is found in P.Charite 12.3 and P.Herm. 22.14 (BL VIII 149), used of flax. It is difficult to see how it might have been applied to grain. Although the word is unattested, a possibility is that this was an attempt at writing ἀχ(ε)ιριστικοῦ, a negative form of χειριστικός, 'entered in a list', which is used of πυρός in P.Oxy. XII 1444.4 and 1526.4. A meaning 'off the record' would accord with what seems to be an offer by Pausanias in ll. 38-44 to perform some creative accounting with the ἀποχή.
17. For unknown reasons the name Σινεύς is not listed by F. Preisigke, *Namenbuch* or D. Foraboschi *Onomasticon Alterum Papyrologicum*, though it occurs in P.Giss. 103 = M. Naldini, *Il Cristianesimo in Egitto* # 43, ll. 29 and 38. This papyrus also comes from the Great Oasis.
23. τὸ]ν αὐτὸν υἱὸν: the reading is certain, but the transaction is complicated enough without another party being involved. It may be assumed that 'son' is here used as a term of familiarity for Sineus (cf. l. 17, τὸ[ν ἡμέτ]ερον Σινέα) in the same way that Timotheos is called 'brother' in ll. 4 and 10.
24. Perhaps one can read δο]ῦ̣να̣[ι] τὰ at the line end.
25-26. εἰ] μὲν εὑρήσεις κτλ.: these lines correspond with ll. 32-33, Eἰ τὲ (l. εἰ δὲ) πάλιν οὐκ εὑρήσεις κτλ.. For the use of εἰ + ind.fut. in the protasis instead of the expected ἐάν + subj. cf. B.G. Mandilaras, *The Verb in the Greek Non-Literary Papyri* (Athens 1973) § 408.
30. While the standard translation of δῆλον is 'manifestly', a translation 'of course' seems to fit here better.
45. The word καθαρτής, 'cleaner', is new in the papyri. What they were to clean is unknown; it is just possible (but not likely) that they cleaned pig-sties. City cleaning is attested as a liturgy in late 2nd century Oxyrhynchus (P.Harr. II 193) and payments are made for city cleaning in 5th-6th century Hermopolis (SB XIV 12699). It is possible, of course, that in SPP III 694.1 one should resolve καθαρ( ) into καθαρ(τής) rather than into καθαρ(ουργός).
46. The epsilon of ἐπ' looks rather like an ypsilon.
50. For the eight *cancelli* sent via Sineus cf. above, ll. 18-20.

7: PRIVATE LETTER

(Ca. 350 ?)

P.Kellis inv. P. A/2/94 (House 2, room 6, level 3, near door) + A/2/95 (room 6, level 5, near door). H. ca. 25 x B. 7.5 cm. The bottom margin is 5 cm., the margin at the left 1 cm. wide. The writing on both sides of the sheet runs parallel with the fibers.

(A/2/94)
1 Κυρ[ίῳ μο]υ ἀδẹ[λφῷ]
2 [Γεν]ᾳ̣ Πατ̣[αιᾶτος]
3 [Ἁρποκρατί]ων χ̣α̣ί̣ρ̣ε̣ι̣[ν].
4 [Ἀσπά]ζ̣[ομαι] π̣ο̣λ̣λ̣ά̣ σ̣ε̣ μ̣ε̣τ̣ὰ̣
5 [τ]ῶν παρὰ̣ σ̣οὶ ἀδελφῶν κατ' ὄ̣νο-
6 [μ]α εὔχ[ο]μενός ὁ̣λ̣οκληρεῖν·
7 [ἀ]ξιωθεὶς μὴ ἀμελήσ̣ῃ̣ς
8 ὑ̣πὲρ ο̣ὗ̣ ἠξίωσ̣ά <σε> παρόντα
9 καὶ τάχειον ἀποστεῖλαί μοι
10 διά τινος πεπιστευμένου
11 [τ]ὸ δελματίκιόν μου·
12 ὑπόδειξον δέ μοι, ἢ χοι-
13 TRACES
14 TRACES
15 TRACES
16 TRACES

- -

(A/2/95)
17]ὑ̣π̣οδειξ[
18 TRACES π̣[ε]ρ̣ὶ̣ [ὧν] β̣ο̣ύ̣λ̣ε̣ι̣ γ̣ρ̣[άψον
19]μοι ἡδέως ἔχοντι .[
20]ἐ̣[ρρῶ]σθαί σε εὔχομαι π[ολλοῖς]
21]VACAT χρόνοι[ς.
22 Τὸν ἀδελφὸν Γελά̣σ̣ι̣ο̣ν̣ καὶ
23 Πανχάριον καὶ Ἀνου( ) πολλὰ
24 ἀπ' ἐμοῦ πρόσειπε.

Verso:

25 Κυρίῳ μου ἀδελφῷ \ / Ἁρπο̣[κρατίων
26 Γενᾳ̣ Παταιᾶτος / \

9 τάχιον (ο ex corr.) 23 παν'χαριον Pap.

"To my lord brother Gena son of Pataias, Harpokration sends greetings. I greet you many times and by name the brothers who are with you, while I pray for your well-being. As requested, please don't neglect as to what I asked you when you were here and send me as quickly as possible through a trusted person my 'Dalmatian' robe; and indicate to me whether --- (ll. 18ff.) Give me your orders about your wishes, as I am happy (to carry them out). I pray for your health in many years. Greet from me many times my brother Gelasius and Pancharios (?) and Anou( )." (Verso) "To my lord brother Gena son of Pataias, Harpokration."

The subject of this mutilated private letter is, like that of so many others, a request to the addressee to convey greetings to people staying with him and to send something (here a cloak) to the writer of the letter.

2. A Gena (with the nomen Aurelius) son of Pataias also occurs in **76**.33-34 (second half of the 4th century). For the name Pataias cf. also **16**.4n.
3. Is this the same Harpokration as mentioned in **23**.8, 10, 16 (353)? There he is a former magistrate of Mothis who was evidently an influential person in Kellis. If this identification is correct, one could assign this letter to the middle of the 4th century.
11. For 'Dalmatian' robes in the papyri, see S. Daris, *Il lessico Latino nel Greco d'Egitto*[2] (Barcelona 1991) 38-39 s.vv. *δαλματική*, *δελματική* and related words. See also the notes to P.Oxy. LI 3626.16ff.
12. *χοι-* looks like the opening of some form of *χοῖρος*/*χοιρίδιον*. For the subject of pigs in Kellis cf. **6** and **23**.16ff.
22. For Gelasius cf. **16**.1-2n. The reading of the name is here, too, not quite comfortable, but it seems preferable to Γε̣ν̣ᾶ υ̣ἱόν̣.
23. The name form Παγχάριος (or Παγχάριον for a woman?) is not well-attested in the papyri; cf. F. Preisigke, *Namenbuch* s.n. Παγχάρης. 'Ανου( ) may be expanded to, e.g., 'Ανου(βίων).

8-12: Texts related to Tithoes

Texts **8** - **12** are related to Tithoes son of Petesis, a carpenter in Kellis, who apparently lived in House 2. The name Tithoes reflects the popularity of the local god Tutu; cf. C.A. Hope in Mediterranean Archaeology 1 (1988) 163 and O. Kaper in Bulletin Australian Centre for Egyptology, 2 (1991) 59ff. The only precise date for this person is given by text **8** from 362. By using information kindly provided by I. Gardner about a still-unpublished Coptic letter (A/2/76+77) his family tree can be reconstructed as follows:

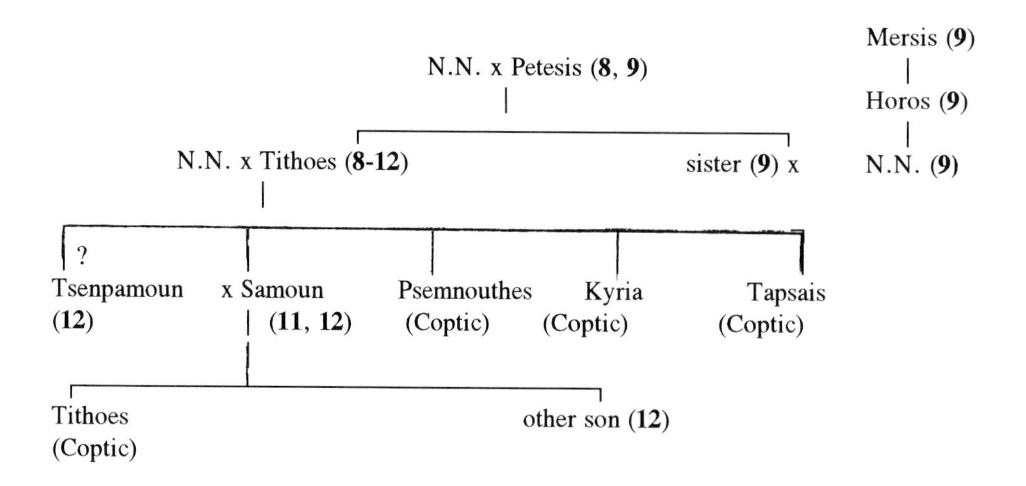

8: SALE OF A SLAVE

(29.viii - 27.ix.362)

P.Kellis inv. A/2/84+85+86+87 (House 2, room 5, floor deposit) + A/2/89+93 (room 6, level 3, near door). H. 24 x B. 30.7 cm. Written along the fibers on a large sheet with substantial margins left at the top (2.5 cm.), bottom (4 cm.) and left hand side (4 cm.). The back is blank. The text was mentioned in JSSEA 17 (1987) 173, where the largest fragment (A/2/84) is referred to as 'an official document'. For organizational purposes the papyrus was referred to previously as 'P.Kellis 35'.

1 Αὐρήλιοι Ψάις Πεκ̣[ύσιος] Παλιτοῦτος καὶ Τατ̣οῦπ ἡ [αὐτ]ο̣ῦ̣ γυνή, ἀμφότεροι ἀπὸ [κώ]μης Κε̣λλ[ε]ω̣ς

2 τοῦ Μωθίτου νομοῦ κ̣[ατα]μ̣ένοντες ἐν ἐποικίῳ Ε̣ ̣ ̣[.... Αὐρ]ηλίῳ Τιθοεῖ Πετήσιος τέ[κ]τονι ἀπὸ τῆς αὐ-

3 τῆς κώμης τοῦ αὐτοῦ [νο]μοῦ χαίρειν. Ὁμολογοῦ̣[με]ν πεπρακέναι σοι καὶ καταγεγραφέναι ἀπὸ τοῦ

4 νῦν ἐπὶ τ̣[ὸ]ν ἅπαντα χρόνον τὴν ὑπάρχουσαν ἡμῖν δο[ύ]λην χαμαίρετον τροφευθεῖσαν ὑ̣π̣᾽ ἐ̣μ̣ο̣ῦ̣ τ̣ῆ̣ς̣

5 προκειμένης γυναικὸς τῷ ἐμαυτῆς γάλακτι τιμῆς τῆς πρὸς ἀλλήλο̣υ̣ς̣ συνπεφ[ων]ημέ̣ν̣ης̣

6 δεσποτικῶν ἁπλῶν νεοχαράκτων νομισματίων δύο, (γίνεται) νο(μισμάτια) β, ἅ̣περ ἐδεξάμ[εθ]α παρὰ σοῦ διὰ χει-

7 ρὸς πλήρη ἐφ᾽ οἷς εὐδοκοῦμε̣[ν πᾶσι τοῖς ἐγγεγραμμένοις] πρὸς τὸ ἀπὸ τοῦ νῦν σε τὸν ὠνούμενον ἐπικρατεῖν

8 καὶ κυρ[ιεύ]ειν καὶ δεσπόζειν τῆς πεπραμένης σοι δούλης καὶ ἐξουσίαν ἔχειν διοικεῖν καὶ οἰκονομεῖν

9 περὶ αὐτῆς τρόπῳ ᾧ ἐὰν αἷρῃ, τῆς βεβαιώσεως ἐξακολουθούσης ἡμ̣ῖ̣ν τοῖς ἀποδομένοις διὰ παντὸς

10 ἀπὸ παντὸς τοῦ ἐπελευσομένου ἢ [ἀντιποιησομένου.] Κ̣υρία ἡ πρᾶσις δισσὴ γραφεῖσα ἐφ᾽ ὑπογραφῆς τοῦ

11 ὑπὲρ ἡμῶν ὑπογράφοντος βέβαια ἔστω κα̣[ὶ ἔν]νομος πανταχοῦ ἐπιφερομένη καὶ ἐπερωτη-

12 θέντες ὡ[μολογήσαμ]ε̣ν.

13 Ὑπατίας Μ̣αμερτίν̣ο̣υ καὶ Νε̣β̣ουιέ̣ττα τῶν λαμπροτάτων, Θὼθ καθ᾽ Ἕλλη(νας).

14 (M.2) Αὐρήλιος Ψάις Πεκύσιος καὶ Τατ̣οῦπ γυνὴ οἱ προκείμενοι πεπράκαμεν τὴν προκειμένην δούλην ̣ ̣ ̣ ̣

15 καὶ ἀπέσχομεν τὴν τιμὴν ἐν χρυσοῦ νομισματίοις δυσὶ καὶ βεβαιώσωμέν σοι πάσι βεβαιώσει ὡς πρόκειται

16 καὶ ἐπερωτ̣η̣θ̣έντες ὁμολ̣ο̣γήσαμεν. Ἔγραψα ὑπὲρ αὐτῶν γράμματα μὴ εἰδότων Αὐρήλιο[ς Τι]μ̣όθεος

17 Ἁρποκρατίωνος ἄρξ̣α̣ς̣ ἀξιωθίς̣.

18 (M.3) Αὐρήλιος Δημοσθένης Πολ[υ]κράτους ἀπὸ κώμης Κέλλεως μαρτυρῶ.
19 (M.4) [Αὐρήλι]ος Ὡρίων Τιμοθέου ἀπὸ κώμης Κέλλεως μα[ρτυρῶ.]

9 ἄν 13 Ὑπατείας, θωθ` Pap. 15 βεβαιώσομεν, πάσῃ 16 -τηθ- ex corr., ὡμολογήσαμεν 17 ἀξιωθείς

"The Aurelii Psais son of Pekysis, grandson of Palitous, and Tatoup his wife, both from the village of Kellis in the Mothite nome, resident in the hamlet of E---, to Aurelius Tithoes son of Petesis, carpenter, from the same village in the same nome, greetings. We agree that we have sold and conveyed to you from now for all time the slave girl belonging to us, raised from the ground and reared by me the aforementioned wife with my own milk, at a price agreed between us of two nomismatia of imperial, unalloyed, and newly minted gold, total 2 nomismatia, which we have received from you from your hand in full on all the terms written herein to which we give assent, in order that you the purchaser from henceforth possess, own and have proprietary rights over the slave girl sold to you and have the right to control and manage her in whatever way you choose, the guarantee resting on us the vendors throughout against every litigant or claimant. Let the sale, having been written twice under the signature of he who is subscribing for us, be authoritative, guaranteed and legal everywhere it may be produced and having been formally questioned we have assented. In the consulate of Mamertinus and Nevitta, *viri clarissimi*, Thoth, according to the Greek calendar."
(2nd hand) "We, the aforementioned Aurelii Psais son of Pekysis and Tatoup his wife, have sold the aforementioned slave girl ---- and we have received the price in two nomismatia of gold and we shall guarantee the sale for you with every guarantee as aforesaid and having been formally questioned we have assented. I, Aurelius Timotheos son of Harpokration, ex-magistrate, have written for them at their request since they do not know letters."
(3rd hand) "I, Aurelius Demosthenes son of Polykrates, from the village of Kellis, am a witness."
(4th hand) "I, Aurelius Horion son of Timotheos, from the village of Kellis, am a witness."

Aurelius Psais and his wife Tatoup from Kellis agree to the sale of a female slave to Aurelius Tithoes also of Kellis; the price paid for the slave was 2 solidi. The slave who is unnamed and was therefore probably still only a child is described as χαμαίρετος, 'taken from the ground', i.e. a foundling (see 4n.). This text seems to be the latest dated sale of a slave known from Roman Egypt which gives a price. The latest slave sale with price which is listed by I. Biezunska-Malowist, *L'esclavage dans l'Egypte gréco-romaine* (Warsaw 1974) 165-67, or J.A. Straus, ZPE 11 (1973) 289-95, is BGU I 316 = M.Chrest. 271 (359) in which a 14-year-old Gallic slave is sold in Askalon for 18 gold solidi; for an update of these lists, see P.Col. VIII 219 introd., and for other late-3rd and early 4th-century prices of slaves, where they are known, see

P.Nepheros 33, introd. In Archiv 3 (1906) 415ff. = SB XVIII 13174 (629?) one finds a 12-year-old female slave sold for 4 solidi.

A preliminary version of this text was presented by Whitehorne at the workshop on Greek documents at the 20th International Congress of Papyrologists (Copenhagen 1992); we are grateful to J.R. Rea, who chaired this session, and to our colleagues (particularly A. Jördens) for their comments upon problems of reading.

1. Neither Παλιτοῦς nor Ταταοῦπ is listed by F. Preisigke, *Namenbuch* or D. Foraboschi, *Onomasticon Alterum Papyrologicum*. The former name can be assimilated to indecl. Παλίτ, which is already represented by one hellenised declinable by-form Παλ(λ)ίτης (NB s.v.); on the other hand, however, cf. the name of the father of Αὐρήλιος Πεκῦσις in **13**.1, Ἀλίτου; Παλιτοῦς is, of course, a combination of the prefix Π(α)- + Ἀλιτοῦς and apparently we are dealing here with his grandson Αὐρήλιος Ψάις.
2. On the Mothite nome cf. **41**.4n.
4. χαμαίρετον: an *addendum lexicis* which should be compared with the more usual κοπρι(αν)αίρετος. The fact that the girl is not named but is described as a foundling who has been weaned by Tatoup herself and that no age is given for her suggest that she was little more than a toddler at the time of the sale. Cf. now P.Oxy. LX 4058 (158/9) in which a boy slave was bought at just a year old and resold twice by the time he was seven.
7. For the supplement cf. **39**.18-19 and **42**.36.
10. For the restoration of [ἀντιποιησομένου] cf. **38.a** and **38.b**.16.
13. For the consular formula cf. R.S. Bagnall a.o., *CLRE* s.a. 362. Unusually there appears no numeral after Θώθ. For this lack of a day numeral, see also **57**.4 and note ad loc. and cf. also P.Kellis inv. 93.60+71 (from House 4; 368; still unpublished). Surprisingly enough, in quite a few more or less completely preserved contracts from Kellis not only the day, but even the month is not indicated, viz. in **10**.16, **23**.30, **24**.9-10, **29**.1-2, **45**.24-26 and **48**.16-17 (see note ad loc.).
14. The traces after δούλην are too exiguous to confirm whether χαμαίρετον should also be read here.

9: PRIVATE AGREEMENT

(Later 4th century)

P.Kellis inv. A/2/99+100 (House 2, room 7, on bed). H. 16 x B. 10 cm. Top margin 2 cm. The writing runs parallel with the fibers, the verso is blank.

1 [Αὐρήλιος N.N.] Ὥρου Μέρσιος ἀπὸ κώμης Κ̣[έλλεως τοῦ Μωθίτου νομοῦ
2 [Α]ὐρηλίῳ Τιθοῆτι Πετήσιος ἀπ[ὸ τῆς αὐτῆς κώμης τοῦ
3 [αὐτοῦ νομοῦ] ̣ χαίρειν. Ἐπειδὴ ἐ̣γ̣ά̣μ̣η̣σ̣α̣ τ̣ὴν ἀδε̣λ̣[φήν σου
4 [ ]ιοντος καὶ πρὸς ὀλίγον χρόνον το ̣[
5 [ἀ]δ̣ιαθέτου καὶ τὴ̣ν̣ [ὁ]ρ̣μ̣ὴν ἐποίησ̣α̣ εἰς [
6 [ ]ν̣ ἐποίησα· ἐλθὼν δ̣ὲ̣ σ̣ή̣μερον εἰς Ὄ̣α̣σ̣[ιν
7 [ ] ̣ τῆς γυναικός μ[ο]υ τῶν κα[τ]αλιφθ[έντων
8 [π]ατρός σου `καὶ τῆς μη[τ]ρός σου´ καὶ παραδέδωκάς μοι εἰς λ̣[όγον
9 [ὁμολογῶ οὐδέ]να λόγον ἔχειν̣ [πρ]ὸς σὲ ἐντεῦθε̣[ν περὶ οὐδενὸς ἁπλῶς

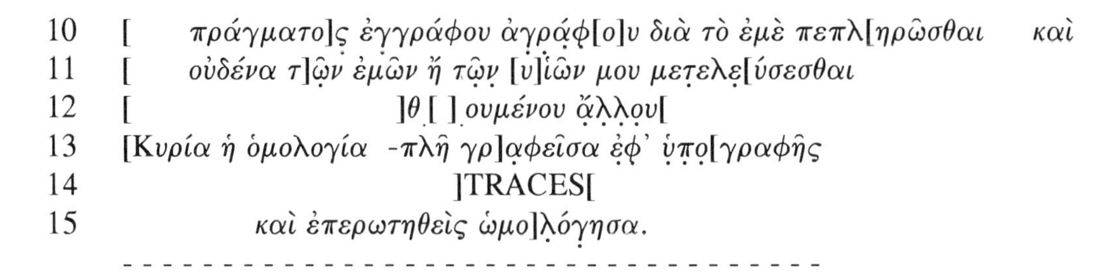

10 [πράγματο]ς̣ ἐγγράφου ἀγρά̣φ[ο]υ διὰ τὸ ἐμὲ πεπλ[ηρῶσθαι καὶ
11 [οὐδένα τ]ῶ̣ν ἐμῶν ἢ τῶ̣ν̣ [υ]ἱῶν μου μετ̣ελε̣[ύσεσθαι
12 [ ]θ̣[ ]̣ουμένου ἄ̣λ̣λ̣ο̣υ[
13 [Κυρία ἡ ὁμολογία -πλῆ γρ]α̣φεῖσα ἐ̣φ᾽ ὑ̣π̣ο̣[γραφῆς
14]TRACES[
15 καὶ ἐπερωτηθεὶς ὡμο]λ̣όγησα.

- -

3 Or read ἐγάμησας? 7 καταλειφθέντων 9 ἐντεῦθεν: first epsilon blotted 10 εγ᾽γραφου Pap. 11 υϊων Pap.

"Aurelius N.N. son of Horos son of Mersis, from the village of Kellis belonging to the Mothite nome, to Aurelius Tithoes son of Petesis, from the same village in the same nome. As I married your sister --- and for a short time --- intestate and I made my way to --- I made, and as I came today to the Oasis --- of my wife, of the bequeathed items --- of your father and your mother, and as you have handed over to me for ---, I agree that I have no claim against you henceforth concerning any matter written or unwritten because I am satisfied and that nobody of my family or of my sons will proceed against you ---. This agreement is authoritative, written in *n* copies --- and I have given my assent to the formal question."

It is unfortunate that this document is so much damaged. The situation can be reconstructed as follows: the author of the document issues a statement to the addressee (= his brother-in-law) in which he acknowledges that, as he had married the addressee's sister, and as she had died without a testament (cf. ἀ]διαθέτου, l. 5) during his absence (cf. l. 6, ἐλθὼν δ̣ὲ̣ σήμερον εἰς Ὄα̣σ̣[ιν]), he has now received from his brother-in-law (the) objects belonging to the inheritance (only that of his wife, or also of his parents-in-law [who also might have died during a long journey] ?) and that he has no further claims. The acknowledgement (and the situation) shows some vague resemblances to BGU II 405.

1. For (Aurelius) Horos son of Mersis, see also **34**.2,21; **38.a**.10; **38.b**.10; **51**.3; **52**.2 and **57**.5; apparently he lived in the earlier part of the 4th century, cf. **51**.3n. As there is reason to think that the present document was written at a later date (cf. l. 2n.) it seems more reasonable to think that this document was not written by Horos himself, but rather by a son.

For the name Mersis (= 'the red one') itself cf. G. Wagner, *Les Oasis d'Egypte* 241.

2. For Aurelius Tithoes son of Petesis, cf. **8**.2 (362); the date of that document gives some indication of the period when the present papyrus was written, i.e. ca. 350-375.

4. The phrasing ὁρμὴν ποιέω/ποιέομαι occurs in a number of papyri, cf. F. Preisigke, *Wörterbuch*, s.v. ὁρμή; add, e.g., P.Oxy. XLVIII 3440.21 and LIV 3771.6; P.Panop.Beatty 1.iv.90, viii.219.

8. The last trace of a letter visible at the end of the line is a λ or a χ.

13-15. One expects the regular formula in Kellis papyri: Κυρία ἡ ὁμολογία *n* γραφεῖσα ἐφ᾽ ὑπογραφῆς τοῦ ὑπὲρ ἐμοῦ ὑπογράφοντος καὶ βεβαία καὶ ἔννομος ὡς ἐν δημοσίῳ κατακειμένη καὶ ἐπερωτηθεὶς ὡμολόγησα, but we have not succeeded in identifying any of the expected words in the remaining traces in l. 14.

10: ORDER FOR PAYMENT

(Second half of 4th century)

P.Kellis inv. A/2/68 (House 2, room 2, roof collapse). H. 12.8 x B. 6.7 cm. The writing runs along the fibers. The papyrus was reassembled from a number of fragments. The text is complete except for the bottom margin. The back is blank. The text was mentioned earlier in JSSEA 17 (1987) 173; for organizational purposes the papyrus was previously referred to as 'P.Kellis 10'.

1 Κυρίῳ μου ἀδελφῶι
2 Τιθοεῖ
3 Ἀμμώνι[ος] χ[αίρ]ειν.
4 Ἀργυρίου τάλαντα
5 τετρακισχείλια ὑπὲρ
6 κριθῶν καγκ[έλ-]
7 λων πέ[ν]τε δὸς [
8 τῷ ἀδελφῷ Μακαρίῳ
9 ἀλλὰ πάντως καὶ
10 ὑπὲρ τοῦ ἄλλου ἑνὸς
11 καγκέλλου ὑπὲρ δα-
12 πάνης τάλαντα
13 ὀκτακόσια. ⟦δ..⟧ Ἐρρῶ-
14 σθαί σε εὔχομαι,
15 ἄδελφε.
16 ιβ´ ἰνδικ(τίωνος).

5 τετρακισχίλια 13 ἐρρῶ- written over ευχ (which is in a lighter ink).

"To my lord brother Tithoes Ammonios sends his greetings. Give four thousand talents of silver to brother Makarios for five *cancelli* of barley, but especially also eight hundred talents for the other one *cancellus* for expenses. I pray that you are well, brother. 12th indiction year."

This letter from a certain Ammonios to Tithoes authorising payment of 4000 talents to a certain Makarios for 5 artabas of barley + 800 talents for an extra artaba is written by a hand which resembles that of **11** (also written by an Ammonios); it seems, however, that both hands are not quite identical, but the difference may be explicable by the fact that they were written at different times.

5. The same amount of 4000 tal. (paid here for 5 *cancelli*, sc. artabas at 40 choenices; cf. for this measure P.Oxy. LV 3804.141-42n.), hence a price of 800 tal./*cancellus*, cf. ll. 10-13) is paid for 2 artabas of barley in **11** (also written by an Ammonios and probably dating from roughly the same time). Apparently the price of barley could fluctuate between 800 and 2000 tal./art. within a relatively short period of time. For barley prices in the 4th century cf. R.S. Bagnall, *Currency and Inflation in Fourth Century Egypt* (Chico 1985) 65; comparing his data with the price level found in this papyrus and in its counterpart **11** one gets the impression that this points toward a date somewhere in the second half of the 4th century; 353/4 is almost certainly too early for the price, and the 12th indiction referred to in l. 12 is thus probably 368/9 or 383/4.
9. For ἀλλὰ πάντως cf. **79**.11n.
11-12. The description in JSSEA (cf. above) has it that the δαπάνη tax is being referred to, but we fail to see the basis for that view; the word δαπάνη may refer to any expense made.
16. References to an indiction are not uncommon in the papyri from Kellis, but here one expects with it an indication of a month and a day (cf. **17**.4-5). Neither seems to have been present here, but the papyrus is broken off just below l. 16 and it is just possible that there was another line, now lost, which gave the month and the day; for a similar problem cf. **16**.6n. The description in JSSEA 17 (cf. above) states mistakenly that the text dates from Tybi (?) 12th.

11: ORDER FOR PAYMENT

(Second half of 4th century)

P.Kellis inv. A/2/61+64 (House 2, room 2, roof collapse). H. 13.4 x B. 8.4 cm. Written parallel to the fibers; the back is blank. The text was mentioned earlier in JSSEA 17 (1987) 172. For organizational purposes the papyrus was previously referred to as 'P.Kellis 32'.

1 Κυρίῳ μου ἀδελφῷ
2 Σαμοῦν Τιθοῆτος
3 τέκτονος Ἀμμώνιος
4 χαίρειν. Τὰς δύο ἀρτά-
5 βας κριθῶν τὰ<ς> παρὰ σοὶ
6 παράσχου τῷ πατρὶ
7 Δημοσθένει ἢ τὴν τιμὴν
8 ạὐτῶν ἐν ταλάντοις τετρα-
9 κισχιλείοις ἢ τὴν ἀρτά-
10 βην σιζύφου κατὰ τὴν συν-
11 ταγήν· ἀλλὰ μὴ ἀμελήσῃς.
12 Ἐρρῶσθαί σε εὔχομαι.

6 παράσχου: -χ- ex corr. 8 α̣ὐτῶν, α ex corr. ταλάντοις, -o- blotted (ex corr.? 8-9 τετρακισχιλίοις 10 ζιζύφου (2nd zeta ex sigma)

"To my lord brother Samoun son of Tithoes the carpenter, Ammonios sends greetings. Send to father Demosthenes the two artabas of barley which are with you or the price of them in four thousand talents, or the artaba of jujubes according to the arrangement; but don't be neglectful. I pray that you are well."

For the price of barley in this text (2 artabas of barley cost 4000 talents), see **10**. Evidently these 2 artabas are the equivalent of 1 artaba of jujubes. For the fruit of the jujube tree (having the size of a cherry, approximately), see P.Oxy. LIX 4006.2n.; apparently it was a quite common commodity in the region, as it is mentioned frequently enough in various other documents from Kellis. We have not been able to establish whether the fruit is still grown in the Oasis.

2-3. For the name Σαμοῦν in general cf. CdE 67 [1992] 173 on CPR X 8. It occurs also in other Kellis papyri and ostraka, cf. JSSEA 17 (1987) 163 and 173 on A/2/65 (= **12** Frag. I). For his father, the carpenter Tithoes, see the introd. to **8** - **12**. Ammonios is also the author of **10**.

12: FRAGMENTS OF A PRIVATE LETTER

(4th century)

The glass frame contains 4 fragments which apparently are thought to belong together.
Frag. I: P.Kellis inv. A/2/65 (House 2, room 2, level 2, low in Northeast corner). H. 10 x B. 8.4 cm. Margin at the top ca. 1 cm. The writing on both sides runs parallel to the fibers. Described in JSSEA 17 (1987) 163, 173.
Frag. II: P.Kellis inv. A/2/66 (House 2, room 2, level 2, low in Northeast corner). H. 6.7 x B. 5.2 cm. The writing runs parallel to the fibers.
Frag. III: P.Kellis inv. A/3/22 (Structure 4, room 1, North of levels 2 and 4). H. 4.8 x B. 4 cm. The writing runs parallel to the fibers.
Frag. IV: P.Kellis inv. A/2/63 (House 2, room 2, level 2, low in Northeast corner). H. 3.1 x B. 5.2 cm. The writing runs parallel to the fibers. Evidently this is part of the end of a letter (cf. the lay-out of the Ἐρρῶσθαι-formula).

It remains uncertain whether these fragments really all belong to the same letter. The handwriting is not quite consistently the same in all four fragments. While fragments I and IV may belong to the same letter, fragments II and IV cannot be placed next to each other (together they would be at least ca. 10.5 cm. wide, while Frag. I is 8.4 cm. wide), while the greeting formulas in ll. 20-21 and 31-32 do not go together as well. If, on the other hand, one tries to put Frag. II on top of Frag. IV, there is an interruption (ll. 29-30) in the series of greetings "Ἀσπάζομαι ...' (ll. 20ff., 31-32). Furthermore, the place of Frag. III is also doubtful. Whatever the merits of the arrangement of the fragments, the text is not without interest as it refers to a monastery and to the trade of linen-weaving. It seems slightly more economical to suppose that these activities took place in the Oasis, rather than that they should be located at some place in the Nile Valley (cf. ll. 18-19n.).

Frag. I:

1 Τῶι κυρίωι μου πατρὶ [Τιθοῆτι]
2 Σαμοῦν χαίρειν. Πρὸ πα̣[ντὸς]
3 πολλά σε ἀσπάζομαι εὐχόμε-
4 νός σε διὰ παντὸς <ὑγιαίνειν>. Ἀσπάζομαι
5 τὴν κυρίαν μου μητέραν καὶ τὴν̣
6 κυρία<ν> μου ἀδελφὴ<ν> Τσενπαμ̣ο̣ῦν̣
7 μετὰ τῶν υἱῶν μου. Ἀσπάζο-
8 μαι τὴν κυρίαν μου γυναῖκα
9 με<τὰ> τῶν κυρίων μου υἱῶν. Ποσά-
10 κις σοι ἐδήλωσα περὶ τῶν ὁλο-
11 [ca. 7 ω]ν καὶ οὐ̣[δε]μ̣ίαν̣ ἐπ[ι-]
12 [στολὴν] . . . . [

- -

Frag. II:

- -

13 [. . . . . ὁ]λονομισμάτιον
14 [. . . . .] . ἀντίγραψόν μοι διὰ
15 [πιστοῦ ἀν]θ̣ρώπου . . . αλ̣ω
16 [. . . . .] . σης τ̣ῶ̣ν̣ υ̣ἱῶν. Κα-
17 [θὼς ἐδήλωσ]ά σοι περὶ τὸν υἱὸν
18 [. . . . .]βάλε εἰς τὸ μονοστή-
19 [ριον ὅπου δι]δάσκι αὐτὸν λίν̣ο̣υ-
20 [φικὴν. Ἀσπά]ζ̣ομαι τὸν ἀ[δελ]φὸν
21 [. . . . .] . . ν καὶ τὴν ἀ[δ]ελ̣φὴ[ν]
22] TRACES

- -

Frag. III:

- -

23]πεπι . . . . [
24] . μοι μέρος πα[
25]ουσαν ἐτῶν π[εντ
26 κλ]ηρονόμους [
27]τούτου τοῦ ε . [
28] . δικ̣αίο̣υ . λ̣η[

- -

Frag. IV:

- -

29 ἐποιησ . [
30 ω ἵνα ἴδω τὸν Ἱλαρι̣[
31 τις. Ἀσπάζομαι Θατμε̣[μετὰ τῶν]
32 υἱῶν αὐτῆς καὶ τὴ<ν> ἀδ[ελφὴν

33 Ἐρρῶσθαί σε εὔχ[ομαι,
34 πάτερ, πολλοῖς [χρόνοις
On Verso of Frag. I:
35 τῶι κυρίωι μου \ / Τι[θοῆτι
36 πατρὶ / \ Σα̣μ̣[οῦν

2 Σαμοῦν ex corr. 7, 9 υἵων Pap. 17 τοῦ υἱοῦ 18]βαλε: see note 18-19 μοναστήριον 19 διδάσκει 30 ἵνα Pap. ἴδω (ἴδω Pap.) 31 θατ᾽με[Pap.

(Ll. 1-12) "To my lord father Tithoes, Samoun sends greetings. Before all I greet you very much while praying that you enjoy good health in all circumstances. I greet my lady mother and my lady sister Tsenpamoun together with my sons. I greet my lady wife together with my sons. How many times have I written to you concerning the solidi (?) and (you wrote) no letter ---."
(Ll. 16-21) "-- of the sons. As I indicated to you concerning my son ---, put him into the monastery, where it (one) teaches him the linen-weaving trade. I greet my brother N.N. and my sister --."
(Ll. 31-36) "--. I greet Thatme- with her sons and my sister N.N. I pray for your health, father, in many years. To my lord father Tithoes, Samoun."

1-2. For Tithoes and his son Samoun cf. **8** - **12**, introd.
4. A verb like ὑγιαίνειν should be supplied after the participle εὐχόμενος, cf. **64**.5, **68**.5 and **74**.4 (**72**.4-5 has ὁλοκληρεῖν).
5-6. For the addition of final -ν in μητέραν and the loss of final -ν in κυρία<ν> and ἀδελφῇ<ν> cf. F.T. Gignac, *Grammar*, I 111-112.
7ff. Given the fact that the author of the letter greets his sister Tsenpamoun and his 'sons' in l. 7 <u>and</u> his (anonymous) wife in l. 9 with his 'sons' it must be assumed that in the first case he is, after all, greeting her sons = his nephews.
9-12. It is a *topos* in epistolography to reproach a correspondent for not reacting to frequent earlier messages (cf. H. Koskenniemi, *Studien zur Idee und Phraseologie des griechischen Briefes bis 400 n.Chr.* [Helsinki 1956] 64-67. In the present case the writer may have written earlier about, e.g., money and one may think of restoring in ll. 10-11: ὁλο-[κοττίνω]ν (= *solidi*), but other subjects and words starting with ὁλο-/ὀλο- are also possible (cf. l. 13). In l. 12 one expects a verb like ἀντέγραψας, but the preserved traces do not match with any of the needed letters.
13. ὁ]λονομισμάτιον (an *addendum lexicis*) looks like a conflation of ὁλοκόττινος + νομισμάτιον.
15. For the supplement of πιστοῦ in the lacuna cf. **7**.10.
18-19. Is τὸ μοναστήριον the subject of διδάσκει? The monastery in question may have been the monastery at Tenida (cf. G. Wagner, *Les Oasis d'Egypte* 196); there is another reference to a monastery in a Coptic letter from House 2 (A/2/76+77) written by Tithoes to Samoun in which (ll. 5-7) it is communicated that Samoun's son Tithoes went to the monastery, together with father Pebok (we are grateful to I. Gardner for providing us with a provisional translation of this letter); it is, however, difficult to establish a connection between the events as transmitted in the Greek letter above and in the Coptic letter, as in each the names of the senders / addressees are reversed; only if one changes ἐδήλωσά σοι into ἐδήλωσα<ς> μοι (l. 17), or supplies something like ἡ μήτηρ ἔ]βαλε <αὐτὸν> does it seem possible to establish such a connection, but such a re-wording of the Greek text is not acceptable.

The supplement λινου- | [φικὴν presupposes a word like *τέχνην* ('the trade of a linen-weaver') understood. For the subject of linen-weaving according to the papyri cf. E. Wipszycka, *L'industrie textile dans l'Egypte romaine* (Warsaw 1965).
25. No doubt one finds here an indication of age, but it is uncertain whether it refers to a human being or to something else.
26. It is unclear what the *κλ]ηρονόμους*, 'heirs', are doing here.
28. It is just possible to read/restore: *κ̣λη[ρονομίας*, but many other alternatives are conceivable.
31. There are no names in Θατμ- listed in F. Preisigke, *Namenbuch* or in D. Foraboschi, *Onomasticon Alterum Papyrologicum*.

13: DIVISION OF PROPERTY

(335)

P.Kellis A/2/62+64+66+73+74+75 (House 2, roof collapse, room 2). The papyrus was reassembled from a number of fragments (in the top section of the same frame are 4 unplaced smaller fragments which may not belong to the document published here) and its central and right hand part are still incomplete; at least 20 - 30 letters are missing at line ends. The papyrus now consists of 4 main fragments:
Frag. I (at the left): H. 23 x B. 18 cm.
Frag. II (upper mid): H. 6.5 x B. 10.2 cm.
Frag. III (at the right): H. 19.5 x B 10.5 cm.
Frag. IV (lower mid): H. 3.8 x B. 2.6 cm.
The full breadth of the document as far as preserved is ca. 34 cm. The writing runs parallel with the fibers. Margins: at the top 3, at the left hand side 1, at the bottom 4 cm. The back is blank. The text was mentioned previously in JSSEA 17 (1987) 172-73. For organizational purposes the papyrus was referred to previously as 'P.Kellis 33'.

1 Αὐρήλιοι Πεκῦσις ᾿Α̣λ̣ιτου καὶ Πεβῶς ἀδελφὸς [αὐτοῦ καὶ Παχοῦμις ἄλλος ἀδελφὸς καὶ ῟Ωρος Σύρου καὶ Ταοῦπ N.N. οἱ πέντε ἀπὸ κώ-]
2 μης Κέλλεως τῆς Μωθ̣[ιτ]ῶ̣ν̣ πόλεως ἀλλήλοις[χαίρειν.
3 Βουλόμενοι {ἡμᾶς} διαιρ[εῖσθ]αι ` . α̣ς́ [κ]αὶ τὸν̣ ἕνα ἕκαστον̣ [ἡμῶν ἀπὸ τοῦ νῦν ἐπὶ τὸν ἅπαντα χρόνον] ̣ιδεμ ̣ ̣[ὁμολογοῦμεν κεκτᾶσθαι]
4 ἐγὼ μὲν Πεκῦσις κέλλαν [μία]ν̣ ἐν τῇ̣ δευτέρα̣ στέγῃ̣ τ[ῆς οἰκίας καὶ] κ̣α̣τ̣ά̣γα̣[ιον, - - ἐγ]ὼ δὲ ὁ Πεβῶς [ἑτέραν] κέλλαν τὴν̣ ̣[ἕως τῶν]
5 ὑπερῴ̣ων οὗ μῆκ̣[ος ̣ ̣ ̣ κ]α̣ὶ̣ σιτοβολῆα ὀνοικ̣[- -, ἐγὼ δὲ] Π̣εκῦσις ἕως τῶ̣ν̣ [ὑπ]ε̣ρῴ̣ων, ἐγὼ [δὲ Παχ]οῦμις ἑτέραν̣ [κέλλαν - - - πυ-]
6 λῶνα Πεβῶτος ἄ̣[χρι]ς ὑπερῴ̣ων· κἀγὼ̣ [- -] δὲ καὶ ὁ ῟Ωρος Σύρου σὺν ταῖς ἀδελφαῖς̣ κέλλαν τὴν ἐν̣[τὸς] τοῦ πυλῶνος ̣[κἀγὼ ἡ Ταοῦπ N.N.]

7 *τὴν κέλλαν τὴν ἐ̣ν̣ .[ ]λ̣ερίῳ̣ λεγομένην τε κ̣[αὶ σιτο]β̣ο̣λ̣ῖον δεδιφρον απτοιον ωνων και[. .]. . ἄχρις ὑπε̣[ρώῳ]ν̣ καὶ τη. . .[κοινὰ]*

8 *καὶ ἀδιαίρετα [ὄντα τοῖς] π̣έ̣ν̣τε συνκληρονόμ[οις . . . .]. καὶ ὁμολογοῦμεν συνπεπε̣[ῖσθαι τ]αύτῃ τῇ διαιρ[έσει] κ̣α̣ὶ̣ μ̣ὴ̣ ἔξεστα[ι ἡμῖν τήνδε τὴν ὁμολογίαν παραβαίνειν.]*

9 *Καὶ ἐάν τις ἡ[μῶν μὴ ἐπα]κ̣ολουθήσῃ τῇ [διαιρέσ]ε̣ι, ἀποκατασ[τή]σῃ ὑπὲρ λόγου̣ [προστ]ίμου τάλαντα .[χ]ίλι[α] διὰ τὸ ἑκου̣[σίως ἡμᾶς ἐπὶ τούτοις συντεθεῖσθαι.]*

10 *Κυρία ἡ ὁμολογία τῆ[ς διαιρ]έσεως πενταση γρα̣[φεῖσα ὁμο]τύπ̣ω̣[ς] π[ρὸς τὸ - -]σεσι εἶ[ναι μονα]χὸν πρὸς ἀσφάλ[εια]ν ἐφ' ὑπογραφῆς [τοῦ ὑπογράφοντος ὑπὲρ ἡμῶν]*

11 *ὑπογράφεως <καὶ> βέβαι[α ἔστω κ]αὶ ἔννομος ὡς ἐν δημ̣ο̣σ̣ί̣ῳ̣ κα̣[τακειμένη καὶ ἐπερωτ]ηθ(έντες) ὡμολογήσαμεν.*

12 *Ὑπατίας Ἰουλίου* Κωνστ[*αντίνο*]υ *πατρικίου ἀδελφοῦ τοῦ δεσπότ*[*ου ἡμῶν* Κωνσταντίνου Αὐγούστο]υ *καὶ* Ῥουφίου Ἀλβίνου *τῶν λαμπρο*[*τάτων*, Month, day ?]

13 (M.2) Αὐρήλιος Πεκῦσις *ὁ π*[*ροκεί*]*μενος ἐθέμην τήνδε τὴ*[*ν διαίρεσιν ἐφ' αἷς περιέχει δι*]*αστολαῖς πάσαις αἷς καὶ εὐδοκ*[*ῶ καὶ ἐμμενῶ ὡς πρόκειται*]

14 *καὶ ἐπερωτηθεὶς ὡ*[*μολό*]*γησα. Ἔγραψα ὑπὲρ αὐτοῦ γρά̣*[*μματα μὴ εἰδότος* Αὐρήλιος Στ]ώνιος Τεπνάχθου *ἱερεὺς ἀπὸ τ*[*ῆς αὐτῆς κώμης* Κέλλεως.

15 (M.3) Αὐρήλιος Πεβῶς *ὁ προκί̣*[*μενο*]*ς συνεθέμην τή*[*νδ*]*ε̣ τὴ̣ν διαίρεσιν* [*ἐφ' αἷς περιέχει διαστολαῖς πάσαις αἷς*] *ε̣ὐ̣δ̣οκῶ καὶ ἐμμενῶ ὡς πρόκειται καὶ* [*ἐπερωτηθεὶς ὡμολόγησα. Ἔγραψα ὑπὲρ αὐτοῦ*]

16 *γράμματα μὴ εἰδότ*[*ος* Αὐρή]λιος Σαράπαμμ̣[ων]. .*τος ἀπὸ* [*τῆς αὐτῆς κώμης* Κέλλεως.]

17 (M.4) Αὐρήλιοι Παχοῦμις *καὶ οἱ ἀδελφοὶ οἱ προκ(ειμενοι)*[*συνεθέ*]*μεθα τήνδ*[*ε τὴν διαίρεσιν ἐφ' αἷ*]*ς περιέχε*[*ι διαστολαῖς πά*]*σαις αἷς εὐδοκοῦμεν καὶ ἐνμενοῦμεν ὡς πρ*[*όκειται καὶ ἐπερωτηθέντες ὡμολογήσαμεν. Ἔγραψα*]

18 *ὑπὲρ αὐτῶν γράμμα̣*[*τα μὴ εἰδότω*]*ν̣* Αὐρήλιος Φο̣[ιβ]ά̣μ̣[μων *ὁ̣ κ̣α̣ὶ̣* Τριφιό[δωρος *ἀπὸ τῆς* Ἰβιτῶ]ν̣ *πόλεως*.

19 (M.5) Αὐρήλιος Ὧρ[ος *σὺν τοῖς ἀδ*]*ελφοῖς ὁ προκ̣εί*[*μεν*]*ος συνεθ̣*[*έμην τήνδε*] *τὴν δια*[*ίρεσιν*] *ἐφ' αἷς πε*[*ρι*]*έχει διασ̣τολαῖς πάσαις αἷς ε̣*[*ὐδοκοῦμεν καὶ ἐμμενοῦμεν ὡς πρόκειται*]

20 *καὶ ἐ̣π̣ε̣ρ̣ω̣τ̣η̣θ̣έ̣ν̣*[*τες ὡμο*]*λογήσαμεν. Ἔ̣γραψ*[*α ὑ*]*πὲρ αὐτῶ̣ν̣* [*γράμματα μ*]*ὴ ἰδόδῳ̣*[*ν* Αὐρή]λιος Ἡλι[ό]δωρος Ὥρου *ἀπὸ τῆς αὐτῆς* [*κώμης* Κέλλεως.]

21 (M.4) Αὐ̣ρ[ηλία] Ταοῦπ . .ι̣[. . *συνε*]*θ̣έμην* [*τή*]*νδε τὴν διαίρεσιν ἐφ' αἷς π̣*[*εριέχει διαστολαῖς πάσαις αἷς εὐδο*]*κῶ καὶ ἐ̣ν̣μενῶ ὡς πρόκ(ειται) καὶ ἐπερωτηθεῖ*[*σα ὡμολ(όγησα). Ἔγραψα ὑπὲρ αὐτῆς γράμματα*]

22 *μὴ εἰδυίης* Αὐρήλ̣[ιος Φοιβάμμων *ὁ κ*]*αὶ* Τριφιόδωρος *ἀπὸ* Ἰβιτῶν *π̣ό̣λ̣*[*εως*.

5 ὑπερωων Pap. σιτοβολεῖα; ἀνοικ.[? 8 συγκληρονόμ[οις 11 ὑπογραφευς Pap. 12 ὑπατιας Pap. (l. ὑπατείας), ϊουλιου 15 προκείμενος 17 ἐμμενοῦμεν 20 εἰδότων 21 ἐμμενῶ 22 ϊβιτων Pap.

"We, the Aurelii Pekysis son of Alitous and Pebos his brother and Pachoumis another brother and Horos son of Syros and Taoup daughter of N.N., the five from the village of Kellis belonging to the city of the Mothites, send greetings to one another. Wishing to divide and that each one of us (has) from now on for all time ... we agree that we have acquired ownership, viz. I, Pekysis, of one room on the second storey of the house and of a cellar ---, I, Pebos, another room -- as far as the upper chambers of which the size is -- and the granary ---, I Pekysis as far as the upper chambers, and I, Pachoumis, another room -- the gate of Pebos until the upper rooms. and I -- and the aforesaid Horos son of Syros jointly with his sisters a room inside the gateway, and I, Taoup daughter of N.N., the room said to be in the -- and the granary --- until the upper rooms and the -- being in joint and undivided ownership by the five joint-heirs and we agree that we are in accord with this division and that it shall not be permitted to us to offend against this agreement. And if any one of us does not comply with the division, let him/her pay by way of penalty *n* thousand talents since we have made the division on these terms voluntarily. Let the agreement of the division, written five times in identical copies for ... (each of us?) to have a single copy for surety under the hand of the *hypographeus* writing for us, be authoritative and guaranteed and legal as though deposited in a public office, and having been formally questioned we have agreed. In the consulate of Iulius Constantius, patrician, brother of our master Constantine *Augustus*, and of Rufius Albinus, *viri clarissimi* (month, day?).
(M.2) I, the aforesaid Aurelius Pekysis, have made this division on all the terms which it contains to which I both give my assent and by which I shall abide as aforesaid and having been questioned I have agreed. I, Aurelius Stonios son of Tepnachthes, priest, from the same village of Kellis, wrote on his behalf as he does not know letters.
(M.3) I, the aforesaid Aurelius Pebos, have concluded this division on all the terms which it contains to which I both give my assent and by which I shall abide as aforesaid and having been questioned I have agreed. I, Aurelius Sarapammon son of N.N., from the same village of Kellis, wrote on his behalf as he does not know letters.
(M.4) We, the aforesaid Aurelius Pachoumis and his brothers, have concluded this division on all the terms which it contains to which we assent and by which we shall abide as aforesaid and having been questioned we have agreed. I, Aurelius Phoibammon alias Triphiodoros, from the city of the Hibites, wrote on their behalf as they do not know letters.
(M.5) I, the aforesaid Aurelius Horos, with my brothers (*sic*), have concluded this division on all the terms which it contains to which we assent and by which we shall abide as aforesaid and having been questioned we have agreed. I, Aurelius Heliodoros son of Horos, from the same village of Kellis, wrote on their behalf as they do not know letters.

(M.4) I, Aurelia Taoup daughter of N.N., have concluded this division on all the terms which it contains to which I assent and by which I shall abide as aforesaid and having been questioned I have agreed. I, Aurelius Phoibammon alias Triphiodoros, from the city of the Hibites, wrote on her behalf as she does not know letters."

This papyrus contains a contract of division (*διαίρεσις*) of an inheritance (cf. l. 8. *τοῖς*] *π̣έν̣τε συνκληρονόμ*[*οις*) of a house property between five parties, the Aurelii Pekysis, Pebos, and Pachoumis, all the sons of Alitous (l. 1), Aurelius Horos son of Syros with his sisters (l. 6) or brothers (l. 19) and Aurelia Taoup daughter of N.N. (cf. l. 21n.). Since Taoup employed the same *hypographeus* as Pachoumis, she was perhaps a full sister to the three brothers, while Horos was perhaps a half-brother of the other four since all five are described as *συγκληρονόμοι* (l. 8). Unfortunately, due to the heavy mutilation of the papyrus it is impossible to reconstruct with great precision the allotments given to each of the five parties to the division. In addition it would be unwise to assume from its find place that **13** records a division of House 2 itself; the document may or may not relate to the building in which it was found.

For documents of this type, see O. Montevecchi, *La Papirologia*, 208-209, and the discusions by L. Mitteis, *Grundzüge* II 270f. and H. Kreller, *Erbrechtliche Untersuchungen* 77ff. J. Beaucamp, *Le Statut de la femme à Byzance (4e -7e siècle). II: Les pratiques sociales* (Paris 1992) 427-429 lists 9 Byzantine contracts of division in which women played a certain part, viz. P.Abinn. 62, P.Cair.Isid. 105 (+ BL VII 33), P.Lond. III 978 (+ BL I 291-2), P.Oxy.Hels. 44, P.Prag. I 42, PSI VI 698, P.Stras. 555, 672, and P.Ness. III 22.

1. Ἀλιτοῦς is otherwise unattested (although D. Foraboschi, *Onomasticon Alterum Papyrologicum*, lists an Αὐρήλιος Ἀλῖτις), but the name should be compared with the name Παλιτοῦς in **8**.1 (see note ad loc.); that document was issued in 362 by Aurelius Psais son of Pekysis (!) and grandson of Palitous, so that in the case of (Π)αλιτοῦς we are apparently dealing with the same person. For the names of other parties to the contract supplemented at line end, see ll. 5 and 17 (Pachoumis), 6 and 19 (Horos), 6 and 21 (Taoup).
2. For the relationship between the village of Kellis and the city of the Mothites cf. **20**.3-5n.
3. It is not possible to suggest a convincing reading for the first two letters of the interlinear word ̣ ̣α̣ς. **13** appears to diverge at this point from the parallels, which usually have *διῃρῆσθαι πρὸς ἑαυτούς* with or without *ἐξ εὐδοκούντων*, 'wishing to make a division with one another', cf. P.Oxy. III 503.4, P.Tebt. II 383.8, BGU I 234.5, II 444.6, IV 1037.5. But apart from the nu of *τὸν* the letters seems certain, and a reexamination of the original has confirmed that it is apparently not possible to read `*πρὸς*´ [*ἑ*]*αυτοῦ̣ς*.
5. After *μῆκος* an indication of length (e.g.: '*n* cubits') is expected, but the lacuna can have held only a symbol + a numeral. The papyri usually have the form *σιτοβολών*, for which see G. Husson, *OIKIA*, 253-54, rather than *σιτοβολεῖον* as here, and perhaps also in l. 7, where the letters are broken but reasonably certain. The plural *σιτοβολῆα* seems to rule out *ὃν οἰκο*[-. We reckon with the possiblity that *ὀνοικ*[may be a spelling error for *ἀνοικ*[, but it is impossible to go any further and suggest a convincing restoration of the full word.
5-6. For the restoration of *πυ*-] | *λῶνα* cf. the word *πυλῶνος* at the end of l. 6.
6. It is unclear how the lacuna between *κἀγὼ* and *δὲ καὶ ὁ Ὧρος Σύρου κτλ.* should be filled. For *Ὧρος Σύρου σὺν ταῖς ἀδελφαῖς* (fem.) cf. l. 19, where one finds Αὐρήλιος Ὧρ[*ος Σύρου σὺν τοῖς ἀδ*]*ελφοῖς* (masc.).

Possibly one should read: *τοῦ πυλῶνος κ̣[ἀγὼ ἡ* Ταοῦπ *κτλ*. The number of letters missing in the lacuna at the line end suggests that Taoup's name (restored from l. 21; see note ad loc.) was followed by her patronymic.

7. *ε̣ν̣* is broken but secure; what follows may be part of a tau. It is unclear what should be restored before]λ̣ερίῳ (or read *κελ*]λ̣α̣ρ̣ί̣ῳ? See G. Husson, *OIKIA* 147; but the alpha is really difficult to accept).

δεδιφροναπτοιονωνων: the reading of most letters seems clear (although we have considered *ἤτοι* for *αἀπτοι*-), but their division into words is quite uncertain. Assuming that it is the *σιτοβολῖον* which is being described, one might posit an otherwise unattested adj. *δεδίφρος* indicating that the granary was equipped with a bench or a seat, cf. BGU IV 1116, discussed by Huson, *op.cit.* 154, where λασανῖται *δίφροι* are perhaps latrines. *ονωνων* might then be taken as a part of an *ὀνών* (Gen. *ὀνῶνος*), again unattested but analogous to *βοών*, *μοσχών*, *οἰνών*, *περιστερεών*, *καμηλών*, etc. The word following *ονωνων* may be *και*[*νό*]*ν̣*, this being the customary term used of 'new' as opposed to abandoned or ruined constructions (see Husson, *op.cit.*, 197-99). Possibly read at end: *καὶ τὴν̣ δ̣ε̣σ̣*[*πο*-.

9. Τάλαντα ε̣[*πτ*]α̣ *χίλια* or ε̣[*ννε*]α̣ *χίλια* seem possible readings from a palaeographical point of view, but with multiples of 1000 one would expect at least a compound of the appropriate numerical adverb and *χίλια*, cf. F.T. Gignac, *Grammar* II 199 sub 16.a. For the line end, cf. P.Lips. 26.16.

10. *π*[*ρὸς τὸ* - -]*σεσι εἶ*[*ναι*: once again **13** appears to diverge from the parallels which usually have the formula *πρὸς τὸ ἑκατέρῳ/ἑκάστῳ* (with or without *μέρει*) *εἶναι μοναχόν*. Perhaps read *π*[*ρὸς τὸ ἅμα ταῖς διαιρέ*]*σεσι*, although this is unparalleled.

14. A pagan priest (*ἱερεύς*) Aurelius Stonios son of Tepnachthes is also mentioned in a number of papyrus fragments coming from the central village temple excavated at Ismant al-Kharab. His occurrence here proves that the local temple was still in use for the pagan cult as late as 335.

19. Aurelius Horos and his un-named brothers (or sisters?; cf. l. 6) are treated as a single party for the purposes of the *dihaeresis*, but are regarded as plural for the formal questioning and acknowledgement in l. 20.

21. Read the woman's name as Ταοῦπ Ἀ̣λ̣ι̣[*τοῦ*? But on the original the first letter hardly looks like an alpha, rather like a psi followed by an alpha, which suggests Ψ*ά̣ι̣*[*τος vel sim*. To be sure, it is not possible to read the woman's name as Τατοῦπ, cf. that name in **8**.1.

14: FRAGMENT OF AN AGREEMENT

(356)

P.Kellis inv. A/2/96+97+106 (inv. A/2/96+97 from House 2, room 7, understairs cupboard, on base of bed; inv. A/2/106 from room 3, level 1, found in cupboard in NE corner; parts mentioned in JSSEA 17 [1987] 173). H. 10 x B. 15.5 cm. The writing runs parallel to the fibers; the verso is blank. Margin at the bottom 5 cm. At 5 cm. from the left hand edge a join is visible.

1	[. Ὑπατείας τῶν δεσ-]
2	[ποτῶν ἡμ]ῶν Κω̣[ν]σταντίου Α̣[ὐγούστου τὸ η´ καὶ Κλα]υ̣δίου [Ἰου-]
3	[λιανοῦ Κα]ίσαρος τὸ α/ [Month, day]
4 (M.2)	[Αὐρήλιο]ς Ὡρίων ὁ προκείμενος ε̣θ̣έμην τὴν ὁμολογία̣[ν]
5	[ἐφ᾽ αἷς π]εριέχει διασ̣τ̣ολαῖς πάσαις ὡς π̣ρόκειται καὶ ἐπερωτηθεὶς
6	[ὡμολό]γη[σ]α̣. Ἔγραψα ὑπὲρ αὐτοῦ γρ̣ά̣μματα μὴ ε̣ἰδότος Αὐρήλιος
7	[ca. 5]ς Τιθοέους κωμογραμματέως τῆς αὐτῆς κ̣ώ̣μης.
8 (M.3)	[Αὐρήλ]ι̣ος Ἡρακλῆς Ψάιτος ἀπὸ κώμης Κε̣λ̣λ̣ε̣ω̣ς̣ μαρτυρῶ.

"--. In the consulate of our Lords Constantius *Augustus*, consul for the 8th time, and of Claudius Julianus Caesar, consul for the first time, [Month + day?]. I, the abovementioned Aurelius Horion, made this agreement with all the articles contained in it as written above and upon the formal question I have consented. I, Aurelius N.N. son of Tithoes, the village scribe of the same village, have written for him because he could not write. I, Aurelius Herakles son of Psais, from the village of Kellis, am witness."

All this badly mutilated end of a contract offers is a consular date and a few names of persons living in this village. Even so it is of some interest, as it presents us with an attestation of the function of a village scribe, presumably officiating at Kellis. For the office of village scribe (abolished in the 3rd century and re-emerging in the 4th century) cf. R.S. Bagnall, *Egypt in Late Antiquity* (Princeton 1993) 134 and CPR VII 18.16n.

1-3. This is the consulate of 356, cf. R.S. Bagnall a.o., *CLRE*, s.a. There is sufficient space in the lacuna at the end of l. 3 for restoring a month and a day, but it is also possible that, as more often in the Kellis papyri (cf. **8**.13n.), these were simply never written. Evidently (cf. the size of the lacuna at the left of these lines with the restorations of the lines 4ff.) there is not enough space to restore an (expected) epithet like, e.g., ἐπιφανεστάτου between Julian's name and title. For the same reason it seems necessary to assume that the consular dating formula started somewhere in the second half of a line, rather than that it began a new line.

4. It is not possible to identify this Aurelius Horion. An Aurelius Horion son of Timotheos occurs as a witness in **8**.19 (362), but he may be a different person.

5. For the phrasing ἐφ' αἷς περιέχει διαστολαῖς πάσαις cf. **13**.13ff., **31**.30ff. and **58**.6.

7. Should we correct κωμογραμματέως into κωμογραμματεὺς and assume that the office of village scribe belonged to the son rather than to the father? But one may expect the son of a village scribe also to be able to write by himself.

A Tithoes (for the name cf. **8** - **12**, introd.) was the father of an Aurelius Pebos in 352 (cf. **24**.13); therefore one might speculate about restoring [Πεβῶ]ς at the start of this line (according to other Kellis papyri an Aur. Pebos was able to write, cf. **42**.37f. [364] and **44**.23f. [382]; cf. also **43**.38f. [374?]), but notwithstanding some similarities in the handwriting here and in other subscriptions written by Pebos it remains a doubtful restoration, the more so as in the other documents Pebos writes his father's name in the genitive as Τιθοῆτος.

15: PUBLIC DECLARATION TO THE PRAESES THEBAIDOS

(357)

P.Kellis inv. A/2/79 (House 2, room 3, level 6, under the pots) + A/2/110 (room 5, level 3, NE corner of room). The papyrus now consists of 2 separate fragments. Frag. I: H. 27 x B. 3,5 cm. Frag. II: H. 14.5 x B. 8.5 cm. The writing runs parallel to the fibers; the verso of the papyrus is blank.

1 [Φλ]αυίῳ Δομ[ιτίῳ] Ἀ̣σκληπιάδῃ τῷ λαμ̣[π]ρ[ο]τά̣τῳ
2 [κό]μετι φλαυι̣[αλίῳ] ἡγεμό̣νι παρὰ Αὐρηλίου
3 [Ψά]ιτος Πετεμ̣[ίνιος ἀπ]ὸ κώμης Κέλλεως τοῦ Μω-
4 [θί]του νομοῦ [χαίρειν]. Οἵ τε ἀπαιτηταὶ καὶ οἱ ἐπικριταὶ
5 [τ]ο̣ῦ πραγματ[ευτικοῦ] χρυσαργύρου ὑποβάλλοντες
6 [δ]έ̣κα ἀπὸ τῆ[ς (αὐτῆς) κώμη]ς ὥστε τού̣τ̣ο̣ις ἐνχειρι̣σ̣θ̣ῆ-
7 [ν]α̣ι τὴν ἀπα[ίτησιν κ]α̣ὶ δι᾽ αὐτῶν γέν̣εσθ̣αι ἐ . ε̣-
8 [.] . ξαν καὶ το . [. . . . . . .]· ἐγὼ δὲ φυ̣λ̣αττόμενος
9 [μ]ή ποτε τι . [. . . . .] . οιντο καὶ εὑρέθω ἐγκαλού-
10 [μ]ε̣νος ἀλλότ[ριος παν]τελῶς τούτου τοῦ πράγμ[α-]
11 [τ]ος ἐγενόμ[ην, περὶ δὲ]τ̣οῦ πᾶσι τ̣ο̣ῦ̣το φανερὸν
12 [γ]ένεσθαι κα[ὶ . . . .]ἀν̣αίτιον̣ [μη]δ̣ὲ ὑπεύθυ-
13 [ν]ον δοκεῖ[ν δημοσίᾳ̣] π̣ρότιθη[μι ἀσ]φαλιζόμε-
14 [ν]ος καὶ ὑπ̣[. . . . .]ων ὅτι ο[. . . .] . . [. .] . .
15 [.]ου ἡ ἀπαίτ̣[ησις . . γέ]νηται ο[. . . .] κ̣εκοινώ-
16 [ν]ηκα τοῖ[ς . . . .] . σεις πρα[. . . .] . τὸ καθόλου̣.
17 [῾Υπα]τ̣ίας τῶν̣ [δεσποτῶ]ν ἡμῶν Κ[ωνσ]τ̣αντίο̣υ
18 [Α]ὐ̣γούστου τ[ὸ θ´ καὶ Κλαυ]δίου Ἰουλ̣[ιανοῦ]
19 [Κα]ίσαρος τὸ δ[εύτερον, Month day].

1 φλαυϊω Pap. 2 φλαυϊ[αλιω] Pap. 6 ἐγχειρισθῆ- 8 φυλατ᾽τομενος Pap. 17 ὑπατείας 18 ϊουλ[ιανου Pap.

"To Flavius Domitius Asklepiades, *vir clarissimus, comes, flavialis, praeses*, from Aurelius Psais son of Peteminis, from the village of Kellis belonging to the Mothite nome, greetings. The tax collectors and the *epikritae* of the tax in gold and silver levied on trades and businesses, who proposed ten (persons) from the village in order that the collecting of taxes would be entrusted to them and would take place through them, ---. But I, taking care lest they would --- and I shall be found being accused, was absolutely alien to that matter and in order that this becomes clear to all and I turn out to be guiltless and not responsible I bring (this) forward publicly while safeguarding myself and --- that --- the tax collecting --- in general. In the consulate of our lords Constantius *Augustus* consul for the 9th time and of Claudius Julianus *Caesar* consul for the second time, [Month, day]."

This papyrus contains a much damaged public declaration addressed to the governor of the Thebaid concerning a problem re the appointment of tax collectors. Though a number of details of the text's wording escape us (especially in ll. 14-16; probably the author of the document protested in public against errors made in the appointment procedure, as a consequence of which he might suffer personal damage), it is of considerable importance as it is the first papyrus giving an exact year (357) for Flavius Domitius Asklepiades, known as *praeses Thebaidos* only from the undated

BGU IV 1027 = W.Chrest. 424 (on the codex to which this text belongs cf. G. Poethke in Proceed. XVIth [1980] Internat. Congress of Papyrology, 457-462 at 459; in view of the date of this papyrus there is now reason to date the *BGU* codex to the 350's and early 360's rather than to the 380's); for a list of the 4th-century provincial governors of the Thebaid cf. J. Lallemand, *L'administration civile de l'Egypte de l'avènement de Dioclétien à la création du diocèse,* 249-256 (Asklepiades is # 24 in her list), and the addenda to that list by P.J. Sijpesteijn and K.A. Worp in Tyche 1 (1986) 193.

2. On the rank of *comes* (= 'count', a rank in the imperial government institutionalised by the emperor Constantine the Great and divided into three grades) cf. A.H.M. Jones, *The Later Roman Empire,* I 104-105; on the title of *flavialis* cf. *ibidem* 675 (the interpretation in *W.Chrest.* 424.9n. is not to be followed).
3. For the restoration of the name Πετεμῖνις as that of the father of Psais, cf. **23**.18 (353). As the space in the lacuna is rather short, his name may have been abbreviated or left undeclined.
3-4. On the *Μωθίτης νομός*, see **41**.4n.
4-5. For the office of *ἀπαιτηταί* cf. B. Palme, *Das Amt des ἀπαιτητής in Ägypten* (Wien 1989); *ἐπικριταί* as collectors of the *chrysargyron* also appear in P.Lips. 64 = W.Chrest. 281, 30-38. For the *chrysargyron* (a tax on trades and businesses, levied predominantly in towns and urban settlements) in general cf. R. Delmaire, *Largesses sacrées et res privata. L'aerarium impérial et son administration du IVe au VIe siècle* (Collection École franç. Rome [1989], 121) 354-374; cf. also R.S. Bagnall, *Egypt in Late Antiquity* 153f., Tyche 7 (1992) 15-17, P.Rain.Cent. 122 introd. and Pap.Lugd.Bat. XXV 65 introd.
5-6. *ὑποβάλλω* is a technical term used with liturgical officials meaning 'to propose, to nominate'; cf. N. Lewis, *The compulsory public services of Roman Egypt* (Firenze 1982) 63. It seems unusual Greek to find that before or after the numeral *δ]ἐ̣κα* no word like, e.g., *ἄνδρας* was written. In itself it is not unusual to find such a large number of tax collectors as the ten persons proposed here; cf., e.g., the ten *sitologoi* nominated in P.Amh. II 139 (350). On the other hand, it is a little surprising that for the collection of the chrysargyron in the village of Kellis apparently as many as 10 persons were nominated. This suggests a large number of resident craftsmen and merchants, such as one might expect in a metropolis (cf. in general R.S. Bagnall, *Egypt in Late Antiquity* 127-30); we may compare in this regard the considerable number of former magistrates from Mothis apparently living in Kellis. The large number of collectors probably reflects not so much the burdensomeness of collecting of the *chysargyron* as it does an official desire to distribute the burden of collective responsibility over a number of 'strong shoulders' in case of any defaulting tax payers.
7. The unread letter between the two epsilons at the end of the line seems to be a ny or a pi.
11. For the construction resulting from the restoration of *περί* + the articular genitive meaning 'so that ...' cf. B.G. Mandilaras, *The Verb in the Greek Non-Literary Papyri* (Athens 1973) § 859.
12. Restore *κα[ὶ ἐμαυτόν]*? At the end of this line *[μη]δ̣έ* is expected, but the delta is really uncertain.
13. For the publication of such complaints addressed to a provincial governor cf. **23**.31.
16. Perhaps one should restore something like *τοῖ[ς ἀπαιτ]ήσεις πρά[ττουσ]ι̣*?
17-19. Constantius Augustus IX and Claudius Julianus Caesar II were the consuls of 357, cf. R.S. Bagnall a.o., *CLRE,* s.a. It is slightly odd to see that the first iteration numeral was written as a letter/numeral (in the lacuna in the middle of l. 19 there is not enough of space for restoring the ordinal written out in full), while evidently the second iteration numeral was written out in full (note, that Julian was a second consul, which implies a date to either 356 [cos. I], 357 [cos. II] or 360 [cos. III]), but the reading of the δ of *δ[εύτερον* is certain.

It is possible that in this papyrus, as in other texts from Kellis (cf. **8**.13n.), the month and day (for which there is space enough in the lacuna) were never indicated.

16: BUSINESS NOTE

(4th century)

P.Kellis inv. A/2/63+108 (both from House 2, room 2; A/2/63 low in level 2, in NE corner of room, A/2/108 in level 5, in front of door to room). H. 13.3 x B. 7.2 cm. Margins: at the top 1.4, at the left 1, at the bottom 5.8 cm. Folded 1x horizontally, 4 (?) x vertically. On the verso there are some traces of ink (possibly just ink blobs?).

1 Κ̣υρίῳ̣ μου πατρὶ
2 [Γε]λ̣α̣σ̣ί̣[ῳ̣] Αἰωνιανὸς
3 χαίρειν. Δὸς τῷ̣ ἀδε̣λ-
4 φῷ̣ Πατ̣αϊᾶτ̣ι φοινίκ(ων)
5 ἀρτάβας τέσσαρας ἀλλὰ̣
6 μ̣[ὴ ἀμελ]ήσ̣ῃς γ ἰνδικτί(ονος).
7 [Ἐρρ]ῶσθαί σε εὔχομαι,
8 [κύρ]ιέ μου πάτερ.
9? Traces ?

"To my lord father Gelasios (?) Aionianos sends his greetings. Give to my brother Pataias four artabs of dates, but don't forget: of the 3rd indiction. I pray for your health, my lord father."

This small note from a certain Aionianos to a 'father' contains an order to hand over 4 artabs of dates to a 'brother' Pataias. In itself this does not seem to be a message of great importance, but nevertheless the text has a special interest, if it is compared with another text from Kellis, P.Kellis inv. 93.60+71 (still unpublished; from House 4; 368) in which an Aurelius Aionianos son of Gelasios, makes a contract with a veteran concerning the irrigation of a plot of land. As the personal name Aionianus is rare (it is listed neither in F. Preisigke's *Namenbuch* nor in D. Foraboschi's *Onomasticon Alterum Papyrologicum* and it is also lacking in Pape-Benseler's *Wörterbuch der griechischen Eigennamen*) it seems not unreasonable to assume that this Aionianus is the same person as the sender of this small letter; furthermore, though in l. 2 the reading of the name of the 'father' (who does not necessarily need to be a physical father) is uncertain, it seems just possible to recognize the name of Gelasius again here. This may induce us to think that at some moment Gelasios (the recipient of the message!) actually lived in House 2; on the other hand, there is also a papyrus referring to a Gelasios from House 3, viz. **29** (cf. below, 1-2n.).

1-2. For Gelasios cf. above and also SB XVIII 13852 (309) where a Gelasios is *στρατηγὸς ἤτοι ἐξάκτωρ* Ὀάσεως, and **29** (331), where a Gelasios occurs as a former logistes (ἀπὸ λογιστῶν); cf. also **7**.22n.

The name does not seem to be very common in the Oasis and in fact one may be dealing in these texts with the same person throughout.

As I. Gardner reminds us, it is possible that that the name Aionianos may have been inspired by Manichaean ideas.

4. For papyri illustrating *φοίνικες* = dates cf. N. Hohlwein, *Palmiers et palmeraies dans l'Egypte romaine*, Et.Pap. 5 (1939) 1-74.

The form Παταιᾶς is not listed in F. Preisigke's *Namenbuch* and D. Foraboschi's *Onomasticon Alterum Papyrologicum*, but it is presumably a variant of the names Παταᾶς and Παταγᾶς. Other instances of Παταιᾶς in the Kellis papyri are found in **7**.2,26 and **76**.33-34 (in both he is the father of a certain Gena) and in **24**.19 (brother of Psais).

6-7. We do not think that the reference to the 3rd indiction belongs to a dating formula without a month and a day being present. We compare the situation in **79** (cf. there l. 11n.) and think that here the reference to the 3rd indiction should be taken with the preceding and that the author means: '... Send four artabs of dates, but don't forget: (dates) of the 3rd indiction.'

9. Though the ink traces are ambiguous it does not seem to be excluded that in fact they may have contained part of a short dating formula, probably referring to an indiction year, a month and a day.

FROM STRUCTURE 4

17: END OF A LETTER

(4th century)

P.Kellis inv. A/3/26 (Structure 4, room 2, level 2). H. 6.2 x B. 5.5 cm. The writing on both sides runs parallel with the fibers. There are three vertical folds visible.

- -
1 TRACES (Partly smudged)
2 Λέωνι τῷ ἀπαιτη-
3 τῇ· ἀλλὰ πάντως.
4 Παχὼν ιγ τῆς
5 δ ἰνδικτίονος.
6 Ἐρρῶσθ[α]ί σε
7 εὔχομαι, κύριέ
8 μου ἄδελφε,
9 πολλοῖς χρό-
10 νοις.
Verso:
11 ἀδελ]φῷ Νεῖλος

"-- to Leon the *apaitetes*. But (do it) absolutely. Pachon 13 of the 4th indiction. I pray for your health, my lord brother, in many years."

The only information presented by this small fragment is to be found in the occurrence of an unknown *apaitetes* (= tax collector, cf. l. 2n.) Leon whose name is not found elsewhere in the Kellis papyri. Evidently it was the end of a personal or business letter (cf. ll. 6-10) written by a certain Neilos (not a common name in the Kellis papyri) to an anonymous 'brother' (or colleague?).

2. *Apaitetae* are also referred to in **15**.4 (see note ad loc.), where they collect the *chrysargyron*-tax. The term is generic ('tax collector') and here the *apaitetes* may have been collecting another tax.
3. ἀλλὰ πάντως: cf. **79**.11n.
4. Or read Παχὼν γ? Pachon 3 = 28.iv, Pachon 13 = 8.v. A fourth indiction year in the 4th century covers the years 315/6, 330/1, 345/6, 360/1, etc. (cf. R.S. Bagnall - K.A. Worp, *The Chronological Systems of Byzantine Egypt* [Zutphen 1978], Chaps. II and III), hence the date of the document is 29.iv/8.v.316, or 28.iv./8.v.330, 345, 360, 375 or 390.

18: FRAGMENT OF A LOAN OF MONEY

(Ca. 350)

P.Kellis inv. A/3/36 (Structure 4, room 6, level 1). H. 6.8 x B. 2.7 cm. Margin at the top 1.3 cm. Verso blank.

NB: a few fragments of a private letter mounted in the same frame do not belong to the papyrus fragment transcribed below.

1 Αὐρ(ήλιοι) Γεν]ᾶ Οὐώνσιος ̣[καὶ N.N. τοῦ]
2] ̣ου ἀπὸ κώ̣μ[ης Κέλλεως]
3 τοῦ Μωθ]ί̣του νομοῦ Α[ὐρ(ηλίῳ) N.N. τοῦ]
4 N.N. ἀπὸ] τ̣ῆς αὐτῆς το̣[ῦ αὐτοῦ νομοῦ
5 χαίρει]ν̣. Ὁμολογοῦ[μεν ἔχειν καὶ δε-]
6 δανεῖσθ]αι παρὰ σοῦ ε[ἰς ἰδίαν ἡμῶν καὶ]
7 ἀναγ]κ̣αίαν χρείαν [χρυσοῦ νομισμά-]
8 τιον ἕνα,] γί(νεται) νο(μισμάτιον) α, ἐφ' ᾧ̣[τε ἡμᾶς τοῦτο ἀπο-]
9 δοῦναί σ]οι τῷ καιρῷ τ̣[
10 τῆ]ς δωδεκάτ̣[ης ἰνδικτίωνος

— —

"The Aurelii Gena son of Ouonsis and N.N. son of N.N. from the village of Kellis in the Mothite nome to Aurelius N.N. son of N.N. from the same village in the same nome, greetings. We acknowledge that we have received and borrowed from you for our private and immediate need one gold *solidus*, total 1 sol., on condition that we repay this to you at the moment - - of the twelfth indiction - -"

Only the opening of a loan contract has been preserved. The loan concerns one *solidus* which may have to be repaid at harvest time (see 9n.). For bibliography on loans of money cf. below, the introduction to **40** - **47**.

1. For a man named Gena son of Ouonsis, cf. **23**.2 (353) and **24**.3n. (352); both papyri are from House 3, whereas this text, like **12** Fragm. III, comes from Structure 4. The restoration of his name is not certain, of course.

3. For the Mothite nome cf. **41**.4n.

9. A restoration of the clause concerning the repayment of the loan (cf. F. Preisigke, *Wörterbuch* I s.v. καιρός, col. 722) can be proposed only 'exempli gratia', e.g. τῷ καιρῷ τῆς τρύγης / συγκομιδῆς καρπῶν, *vel sim.*, although one expects such a phrasing in a loan of commodities, not of money (cf. the note to **45**.12ff.). Given the date assigned to this text a 12th indiction may be related to the years 353/4, 368/9, or perhaps earlier to 338/9.

FROM HOUSE 3

The occupants of House 3

In a number of papyri from House 3 dating from the early-4th century occurs an Aurelius Pamour(is) son of Psais. Moreover, in quite a few other papyri he is apparently referred to as father or grandfather. We have tried to construct a family tree of Pamour and his family members mentioned in papyri throughout the 4th century. For this purpose we used in the first place contracts (often bearing a more or less exact date) in which a person's family relations are described in terms of: 'X', son of (father) 'A' (sometimes followed by the name of the father and grandfather of 'A')) and (mother) 'B'. Furthermore, we suppose that, unless all documents were just 'imported' into House 3 after it had been deserted, at least a significant number of the documents found in House 3 were related (often enough: addressed) to members of a (or perhaps: *the*) family which occupied the house during the 4th century and kept these documents for some purpose; in a few cases (esp. with loans of money) one has to assume that a document was addressed to another party *by* a person connected with House 3, but living for some time elsewhere (i.c. in Aphrodite in the Nile valley), and that the document in question, after it had been received back, was taken to the house in Kellis (cf. **32**, **42**, **44**, and possibly **43**; **30** was also written in Aphrodite, but addressed to a person who came from Kellis).

It is probably impossible to put all addressees of documents found in House 3 into a neat coherent scheme. It may have been the case that the house was not always occupied by one single family, but that at any given time part of it was leased by one or more other persons; there is no clear evidence on that subject. From both the Greek and the Coptic personal letters one gets the impression that at times a rather complex family may have lived in it. Firstly the more obvious relations among members of the family of Aurelius Pamour(is) can be outlined as follows:

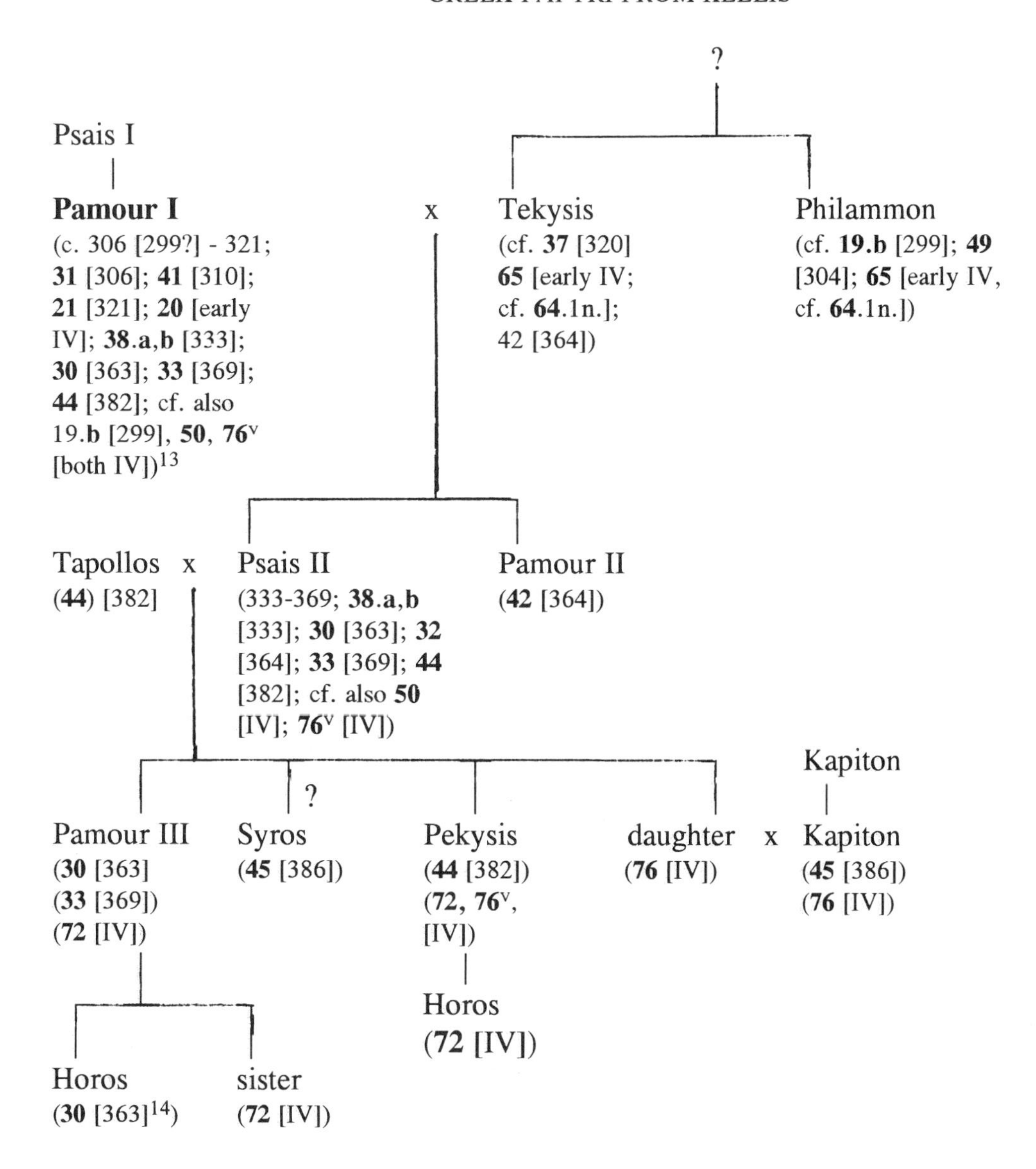

It should be stressed that much in this reconstruction is (still) hypothetical; especially letters in which people address each other as ἀδελφός/ἀδελφή (cf., e.g., **71**: 'To Psais, from his brother Pamour', and **73**: 'To Pamour, from his brother Psais [s.o.?] Tryphanes') or πατήρ (cf. **74**: 'To father Aron, from Psais the potter his son') cannot be used without great caution, as these terms should not always be taken literally (cf. **74**.14n. and 34n.). Moreover, letters which can be dated only by way of palaeographical or other 'indirect' criteria have been mostly left out of account.

Moreover, especially difficult to assess are the connections between persons mentioned in the Greek texts and people mentioned in the ± 70 Coptic letters from Kellis being prepared for publication by A. Alcock and I. Gardner. As long as a full edition of these texts is not available it must be considered possible (perhaps even: likely) that

13) For Pamour I son of Psais I see also **27**.2n.

14) It is conceivable that Horos had yet another brother or sister, cf. the note to **30**.8ff.

part of the family tree outlined above may have to be altered. We feel certain that this forthcoming publication will allow us to see things with greater clarity and that new details may be fitted into the whole scheme.

We assume therefore that at least a substantial part of the total documentation from House 3 can be seen as a kind of family archive consisting of documents addressed or at least related to various members/generations of the same family. Nevertheless, the problem remains that quite a few texts were addressed or refer to persons whose links with the family of Aurelius Pamour(is) are, to put it mildly, not obvious (see below). Were all of these texts 'intruders' blown into House 3 only after it was deserted? Or was the house used as a kind of 'storage place' when people made preparations to move from Kellis to another, unknown destination and collected at a suitable location things they wanted to take with them (the date of such a movement is unknown, but it is probably not much later than the latest datable document in this col lection of texts [**26**, ca. 389[15]], say between 390 and 400). The assumption, that documents found in House 3 were addressed/related to people living there, and the consequences drawn above for sketching the family relations of Aurelius Pamour, do not explain the presence of the following documents:[16]

a.1 To Aur. Horos, s.o. Mersis: **34** (315); **51** (320?); **52** (320)

a.2: By Aur. Horos, s.o. Mersis: **57** (332)

Comment: see the relationship between Horos and Psais son of Pamour as indicated in **38.a,b** and the plan of Houses 1 - 3, p. 5; a camel shed (now: Structure 4?) belonging to Horos son of Mersis was apparently almost adjacent to House 3, where Psais son of Pamour lived; maybe the presence of the Horos documents can be explained through that connection. For Horos son of Mersis, see also the family tree given in the introduction to **8** - **12** (from House 2), esp. **9**.

----

b.1: To Philammon, from Valerius: **64** (IV)

b.2: To Hilaria his slave, from Aur. Valerius s.o. Sarapion: **48** (355)

Comment: there seems to be no obvious connection between any of the addressees and the 'main' family of House 3; moreover, there is some reason to assume that there were two different persons named Philammon (cf. **64**.1-3n.). Furthermore, an identification of the authors of **48** and **64** is by no means certain and there is also no obvious relationship between any Valerius and the 'main' family of House 3, though it should be noted that a Valerius was the father of Aurelius Pausanias (for the latter, see under 'c' and **4**.1n. [from House 2]).

----

c.1: To Pisistratos and Pausanias (known from House 2, cf. sub 'b'), by N.N.: **63** (IV)

c.2: To Pisistratos (creditor) from Palammon (?) s.o. Palammon (?) (debtor): **46** (IV)

Comment: even if we identify both people named 'Pisistratos' with each other, there is no obvious relationship between any Pisistratos and the 'main' family of House 3. On the other hand, there is a Pausanias who has a kind of relationship with that family, (cf. **38.a,b**) and who seems to have lived in House 2 (cf. **4**, **5**, **6**; or were these documents were just blown into that house?).

----

[15]) To be sure, the earliest document in this volume which can be assigned to a more or less precise year is **1** (293 or 294), but there are at least two texts apparently dating from an even earlier period within the 3rd century (**28**, **62**).

[16]) As texts **22**, **28**, **53** - **56**, **59** - **62**, **82** - **86**, **88** - **90** contain no names of addressees we do not discuss here their presence in House 3.

d.1: To Elias, from his father Psais: **68** (IV)
d.2: To Elias, from Sabeinos: **81** (IV)
d.3: To Strategios, from Elias: **75** (late IV)
Comment: it is not certain that the 3 persons named 'Elias' are identical with each other, but even if they are, it is difficult to establish a convincing link between them and the 'main' occupants of House 3. The name Psais (in d.1) is not helpful, as the name seems common in Kellis (cf. the [still unpublished] ostraka coming from the excavations). For Strategios in 'd.3' cf. **26** (ca. 389), Fr. II, ll. 6-7.
----

e.1: To Kapiton, from his brother Psenamounis: **80** (IV)
e.2: To Aur. N.N. s.o. Kapiton (creditor), by Aur. Lilous (debtor): **47** (IV)
Comment: Maybe the full name of the addressee was in both cases: Aurelius Kapiton son of Kapiton, cf. **45**. The assumption, that that man was connected (through marriage) with the family of Pamour living in House 3, may explain the presence in House 3 of a few documents addressed to him. On the other hand it must be kept in mind that at some time Kapiton was apparently away from Kellis, cf. **76**.
----

f. To Aniketos (?), from Psais (?): **79** (IV)
Comment: both the name of the addressee and the name of the sender are read with considerable uncertainty. An apparent connection with the 'main' occupants of House 3 is lacking, though on the basis of the date of the handwriting there might be a link with Psais II (one would have to suppose that he received his original letter back from the addressee).
----

g. To Gelasios ex-logistes, through Riraus, from Aurelius Nikantinoos: **29** (331);
Comment: we see no connection with the 'main' occupants of House 3.
----

h. To Aur. Kleoboulos, logistes, and Philosarapis alias Mikkalos and Andromachos s.o. Apollo, from N.N.: **25** (IV)
Comment: we see no connection with the 'main' occupants of House 3.
----

i. To N.N. logistes, from Petechon s.o. Ammonios: **69** (IV)
Comment: we see no connection with the 'main' occupants of House 3.
----

j. To Psempnouthes, from Timotheos the carpenter: **70** (IV)
Comment: we see no obvious connection with the 'main' family of House 3, but the name Psem(p)nouthes occurs in the family tree of some of the occupants of House 2, see the stemma given in the introduction to **8** - **12**; furthermore, a Psempnouthes occurs in **74**.18 (where his relationship to the 'main' occupants of House 3 is also uncertain), see sub 'k'.
----

k. To Aron, from Psais the potter, his son: **74** (IV)
Comment: We see no direct relationship between 'Psais the potter' and Psais I or Psais II. In view of the handwriting of the letter Psais I is probably too early, and Psais II was the son of Pamour I. Should we assume that Pamour I had an alias name 'Aron' which is not given elsewhere?
----

l. To Serenus, *praepositus pagi* of Trimithis, from Valerius Herculanus (a high official): **27** (early IV)
Comment: we see no connection with the 'main' family of House 3.
----

m. To Theognostos, from N.N.: **67** (IV)
Comment: The name Theognostos is referred to in other Greek and Coptic documents found in House 3, but his relationship with the 'main' family living there is hard to define.

----

n. To the prefect, from Aur. Gena s.o. Ouonsis (petitioner): **23** (353)

Comment: we see no obvious relationship with the 'main' family living in House 3; a Gena son of Ouonsis occurs in **18** (from Structure 4).

----

o. To N.N. from Aur. Ploutogenes: **58** (337)

Comment: obviously, all possibilities re a connection between the addressee and the 'main' family of House 3 are open.

----

p. To Aur. Am- from Hibis, by Aur. N.N., s.o. Theodoros: **35** (IV)

Comment: again, we see no connection with the 'main' family of House 3.

----

q. To the office of the dux, by a number of individuals/subscribers, among which Pamour son of Psais (l. 15): **24** (352)

Comment: As many different hands of subscribers are to be found in the document it must be an original which should have been sent off. Nevertheless, Pamour son of Psais may be identical with Pamour III. Was the document kept (or, received back) by him?

----

r. To Psarapis, from Pamour: **66** (IV)

Comment: Was this Pamour perhaps identical with Pamour I or Pamour II (Pamour III seems unlikely in view of the date of the handwriting of the letter), and did he receive his own letter back?

----

s. To Psais, from his brother Pamour: **71** (IV)

Comment: Are we dealing with correspondence between Psais II and Pamour II, or between Psais III and Pamour III?

----

t. To Pamour, from his brother Psais [s.o.?] Tryphanes: **73** (IV)

Comment: are we dealing with Pamour II or with Pamour III? The relationship between Pamour [son of ?] Tryphanes (see **71**.39n.) and the 'main' family of House 3 is hard to define.

----

u. To Aur. Pebos s.o. Pamour (buyer), from Aur. N.N (seller): **39** (IV)

Comment: This addressee may be connected with the 'main' family, but was he the son of Pamour I or the son of Pamour II (probably not of Pamour III, as the handwriting does not seem to belong to the later part of the IVth century)?

----

v. Amulet worn by Pamour s.o. (mother) Lo: **87** (IV)

Comment: *If* it could be demonstrated that Lo should be identified with Tapollos, then this Pamour is identical with Pamour III.

NB: Of course, it is possible that some of the persons named 'Pamour' listed under 'r' - 'v' should be identified with each other, but it remains impossible to tell whether one is dealing with Pamour II or III.

19.a: PETITION TO THE PRAESES THEBAIDOS

(Ca. 299)

P.Kellis inv. P. 61.D (House 3, room 8, level 4). H. 12.5 x B. 6 cm. The text on the recto (**19.a**) is written parallel with the fibers, the text on the verso (**19.b**) runs across the fibers. The fragment shows a horizontal and a vertical fold (see below, **19.a**.Appendix).

1 [᾿Ιουλίωι ᾿Αθηνοδώρωι τῶι διασημοτάτωι] ἡγουμένωι Θηβαίδος
2 [παρὰ Αὐρηλί-- ἀ]πὸ κώμης̣ Κ̣έλλεως
3 [ ]ος, δέ̣σ̣π̣οτα̣ ἡγεμών,
4 [συνεπιπαρ]ό̣ντος καὶ συνευδο-
5 [κοῦντος Αὐρηλίου ᾿Απο]λ̣λ̣ο̣δώρου ἄρξαντος
6 [τῆς Μωθιτῶν πόλεως] ̣ι τὴν δούλην Σ̣ε̣νορ-
7 [ἐ]π̣ὶ χρόνον ἔτη δύο ̣[̣ ̣ ̣] ̣ ̣ ̣
8 [ ] ̣λ̣ε̣ια γενόμενοι
9 [ἀργυρί]ου καινοῦ τάλαντα
10 [ ]δούλης κατ᾿ ἔνγραφον
11 [᾿Ονό]μαστος υἱὸς κατ᾿ ἐξον
12 [ ]ς υἱὸς μετ᾿ ἑξάμην̣ο̣ν̣
13 [ ]ν δούλην γενόμενος α-
14 [ ]λ̣ῆναι περὶ τῆς προειρημέ-
15 [νης]κοψα̣ν ἄνθρωπος
16 [ ] ̣μ̣ε̣νος· ὅθεν ἐν̣τάξας
17 [ ] ̣σεδίου π̣ανδο ̣[̣] ̣ ̣η

- -

10 *ἔγγραφον* 11 *κατ᾿ εξον* ex corr. 12 *μεθ᾿* 13 *α-* ex corr.

This papyrus fragment contains part of a petition addressed to a *praeses Thebaidos*. The name of the addressee has not been preserved, but in view of the date on the verso of the papyrus (299; cf. below) one may restore it with some probability as that of Iulius Athenodorus the first known governor of the Thebaid (created in or shortly before 298) who was in office between 298-300 (see J. Lallemand, *L'administration civile de l'Egypte*, 249). If this restoration is correct, it follows that in l. 1 seventeen out of originally ± 49 letters have been preserved (some datives may have been written with iota subscriptum rather than with iota adscriptum), i.e. only the right-hand third part of the original petition would have been preserved. As this part is folded vertically, one might argue, then, that the text in its present state is broken on a similar vertical fold and that to the left of this fold there were at least 3 other folds, i.e. there were originally 6 foldings, each pair (I.a,b; II.a,b; III.a,b) being inscribed with ± 17 letters: [(margin) I.a ¦ I.b ¦ II.a ¦ II.b] ¦ III.a ¦ III.b edge

This reconstruction, however, yields a problem as regards the text on the verso (cf. below).

The content of the petition is difficult to reconstruct. Apparently we are dealing with a male petitioner, who submits a copy of an earlier document (cf. l. 16 *ἐν̣τάξας* and for its meaning F. Preisigke, *Wörterbuch* s.v. *ἐντάσσω*, 7). Possibly the complaint was directed against a woman who had been helped by a former magistrate Aurelius Apollodoros or his son (cf. l. 4-5, *συνεπιπαρ]ό̣ντος καὶ συνευδο-/[κοῦντος - - Αὐρηλίου Ἀπο]λ̣λ̣ο̣δώρου ἄρξαντος* and below, **19.a**, **Appendix**; it should be noted that in view of the size of the lacuna in l. 5 *Ἀπο]λ̣λ̣ο̣δώρου* could be a father's name rather than the name of the person himself, but cf. ll. 4-5 and 24 of the text in the **Appendix**). Reference is made in l. 6 to a female slave Senor- (cf. note ad loc.) who may have been sent out for learning something for a period of two years (cf. l. 7, *ἐ]π̣ὶ χρόνον ἔτη δύο*; for such *διδασκαλικαί* cf. the bibliography given by H.-A. Rupprecht, *Kleine Einführung in die Papyruskunde* [Darmstadt 1994] 125-126) in exchange for a certain amount of talents in 'new' silver (l. 9. *ἀργυρί]ου καινοῦ τάλαντα*; maybe the whole transaction was put in writing (cf. l. 10, *κατ' ἔνγραφον* and if she were taken (by her owner) or sent (by her teacher) back after a period of only 6 months (cf. l. 12, *μετ' ἑξάμηνον*), that could have been the reason for the other party for petitioning the governor. It is not clear, however, how a son Onomastos (l. 11; restore in l. 12 *ὁ προειρημένο]ς*?) fits in and for ll. 13-15 it is also difficult to devise a reconstruction. Starting with l. 16, *ὅθεν ἐν̣τάξας*, we may be dealing with the start of a formula regularly found at the end of the body of a petition: 'therefore, enclosing a copy of the (other document) I come to you, most benevolent *praeses*, in order that you may help me', *vel sim.*

4. For the restoration of *συνεπιπαρόντος* cf. **41**.25-26 and note ad loc.
5. The reading of the name *Ἀπο]λ̣λ̣ο̣δώρου* is not quite certain (as an alternative one might think of, e.g. *Σαρ]α̣π̣ο̣δώρου*), but cf. below, **Appendix**, ll. 4-5 and 24.
6. *Σ̣ε̣νορ-* (or read *Σ̣α̣νορ-* ?) is the beginning of an Egyptian woman's name like *Σενορσενοῦφις* / *Σενόρσις*.
7. Though the right hand part of the delta and the left hand part of the ypsilon have merged, *δύο* seems a more likely reading than *δέκ̣[α*.
8.] *λεια*: or read] *λεί̣α̣*? At first one might prefer reading *-λιεια*, but the 'iota' after the lambda is in fact the tail of the rho in the previous line.
11. *ἐξον*: possibly from *ἔξειμι* (accentuate *ἐξόν*), i.e. 'according to (her) capability', but it is also conceivable that *ἐξον* forms the first part of a much longer word.
14. Or read]*θῆναι* ?
16. *ἐντάξας*: cf. above, the introd.
17. A reading *ἐ̣ὰν δόξ[η] τ̣ῇ σ̣ῇ* does not seem convincing.

19.a, Appendix

Just before closing off the manuscript we came across a few papyrus fragments from House 3 which deserve to be published here, especially as the bottom of **19.a** may be connected with the top of the fragments now inventoried as P.Kellis inv. P. 61.T+W (House 3, room 8, level 4) + P. 65.C (room 8, level 3) [hereafter: **19.a**,

Appendix]. This combination of fragments apparently contains, after the opening of the document with a description of the parties (ll. 1-7), part of a contract of apprenticeship according to which a (female) slave owner has given a female house-born slave to a teacher for learning the weaver's trade (cf. ll. 8-11).

The question is whether **19.a**, **Appendix** forms the document which is referred to in **19.a**.16, *ἐντάξας*. Both texts came from the same room, but there is no physical join between **19.a** and **19.a**, **Appendix**. The dimensions of **19.a**, **Appendix** (H. 12.2 x B. 6.2 cm.; like **19.a** also folded horizontally and vertically; verso blank) are much similar to those of **19.a** and it could be argued that the vertical fold on **19.a** finds its continuation in **19.a**, **Appendix** and that the horizontal fold of **19.a** finds its parallel in **19.a**, **Appendix**. Furthermore, the subjects of both texts show certain mutual links (cf. below), while both texts were written in the reign of the emperor Diocletian (**19.a** dates from ca. 299; it is, however, impossible to propose a more precise year for **19.a**, **Appendix**). Furthermore, it is striking that in apparently both texts one finds an Aurelius Apollodoros who apparently acts as an assistant (*συνεπιπαρών*) for a woman.

On the other hand, the handwriting in **19.a**, **Appendix** is distinctly smaller (though not necessarily written by a *different* person); in favor of a physical combination of both texts one would have to argue that one or more lines written on the central horizontal fold of an originally ca. 25 cm. high papyrus sheet are lost, while in the second half of the same document the scribe would have used a much smaller writing. If so, did the scribe write much smaller, because he felt that he was running out of space, or in order to highlight the fact that in this lower part he was copying another document [cf. **19.a**.16, *ἐντάξας*]? Such a hypothesis may seem not very appealing and there is also another important argument militating against a close relationship between the two texts: in **19.a**.9 one finds an amount of money described as *ἀργυρί]ου καινοῦ τάλαντα*, while in **19.a**, **Appendix**.16-17 the wording *ἀργυρίου παλ]αίου Πτολεμαικοῦ νομίσμα[τος τάλαντα* is found; if we were dealing with the same case in both texts, the same description should have been used.

On balance a physical join between the two texts seems not likely. Moreover, as only 1/3 part of **19.a** has been preserved and as the writing of **19.a**, **Appendix** is much smaller than that of **19.a**, the loss of text must be even more sizable in the case of the papyrus transcribed below if compared with the loss of text in **19.a** (cf. also the note to ll. 21-22). The restorations now proposed in the lacunas at the left-hand side of each line pretend to be no more than 'exempli gratia' (see, e.g., l. 4-5n.) and it is disturbing that in some lines a distinctly longer restoration seems inescapable than in others; cf. the size of the restoration of 55 letters in l. 22 vs. the 41 letters in l. 4.

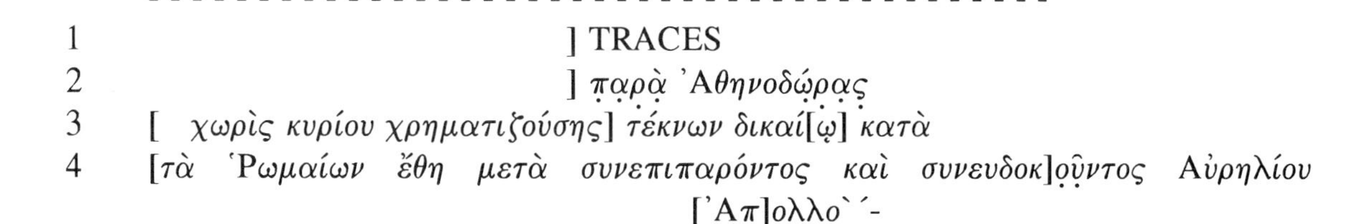

\- -

1] TRACES
2] π̣α̣ρ̣ὰ̣ Ἀθηνοδώ̣ρα̣ς
3 [χωρὶς κυρίου χρηματιζούσης] τέκνων δικαί[ω̣] κατὰ
4 [τὰ Ῥωμαίων ἔθη μετὰ συνεπιπαρόντος καὶ συνευδοκ]ο̣ῦ̣ντος Αὐρηλίου [Ἀπ]ολλο`.´-

5 [δώρου ἄρξαντος τῆς Μωθιτῶν] π̣[ό]λ̣εως τῆς Μεγάλ[ης] Ὀά̣σ̣εως
6 [to N.N.]̣τι Γερμανοῦ ἀπὸ [Κέ]λ̣λεως
7 [τῆς Μωθιτῶν πόλεως καταμένο]ν̣τι ἐνταῦθα ἐν κώμῃ
8 [N.N. τοῦ N.N. νομοῦ. Ὁ]μ̣ολογῶ δεδωκέναι σοι τὴν
9]κρίνουσαν πρὸς τ[ὸ] ἐνεστὸς
10 [ἔτος N.N. θυγατέρα τῆς οἰκ]ο̣γενοῦς μου δούλης
11 [N.N. πρὸς μάθησιν τῆς] γερδιακῆς τέχνης ἐπὶ
12 [χρόνον]Traces δύο καὶ α̣ὐ̣τ̣η̣ ̣ξο-
13]̣οσ̣ ̣ ̣ ̣ καὶ τρέφε̣[σ]θαι καὶ
14 τοῦ προδ]ηλουμένου χρόνο̣υ̣, οὐδὲ
15 [Ἐὰν δὲ N.N. θέλῃ τ]αῦτα παραβῆναι, δώσει τῷ μέρει
16 [τῆς Ἀθηνοδώρας ἀργυρίου πα]λαίου Πτολεμαικοῦ νομίσμα-
17 [τος τάλαντα *n* ὑπὲρ τοῦ] προδηλουμένου χρόνου
18 χ]ωρὶς Θεοῦ βίας. Ἐξεδόμην
19 [σοι τὴν ὁμολογίαν δισσὴν γραφεῖσαν, ἧς]̣ς ἑκάτερος ἡμῶν ἔσ̣χεν.
20 [ἀντίτυπον, κυρίαν ἐφ' ὑπογραφῆς τοῦ ὑπὲ]ρ ἡμῶν γράφοντος καὶ
21 [βέβαιαν καὶ ἐπερωτηθεὶς ὡμολόγησα. (Ἔτους) --] τῶν κυρίων ἡμῶν Διοκλητιανοῦ
22 [καὶ Μαξιμιανοῦ Σεβαστῶν καὶ Κωνσταντίου καὶ Μαξιμιανοῦ τῶν ἐπιφ]ανεστάτων Καισάρων, Ἐπεὶφ γ̄.
23 τὴν προγεγρ]αμμένην δούλην
24 Αὐρ]ήλιος Ἀπολλόδωρος ̣[
25 σ]υνευδοκῶ. [

"--- from Athenodora, acting without a guardian because of the *ius (trium) liberorum* according to the laws of the Romans, with the presence and agreement of Aurelius Apollodoros, former magistrate of the city of the Mothites in the Great Oasis, to N.N. son of Germanos from Kellis belonging to the city of the Mothis, residing here in the village of N.N. in the N.N. nome. I acknowledge that I have given to you the --- for the current year N.N. daughter of my house born slave N.N. for learning the weaver's trade, for a period of --- two and --- and to be feeded and --- for the aforementioned period, and that not ---. But if N.N. wants to offend against these (agreements), he shall give to the party of Athenodora --- *n* silver talents in old Ptolemaic money --- for the aforementioned period --- without an act of God. I have handed over to you the agreement written in two copies of which each of us received a copy, which is authoritative with the subscription of the person who is subscribing for us and which is legal and in answer to the formal question I have assented. Year -- of our lords Diocletianus and Maximianus *Augusti* and Constantius and Maximianus *nobilissimi Caesares*, Epeiph 3. --- the aforementioned female slave. --- Aurelius Apollodoros --- I agree."

3-4. For the χωρὶς κυρίου-formula found here cf. J. Beaucamp, *Le statut de la femme à Byzance (4ᵉ - 7ᵉ siècle* (Paris 1992) 198ff., form. 'A'.
4-5. For Apollodoros (cf. l. 24) and the participles preceding his name in the restoration cf. **19.a**.4-5; for the restored participle συνευδοκ]ο̣ῦ̣ντος cf. l. 25. It is unclear in what relation Apollodoros stood to Athenodora; apparently there is no place in the formula for an element like τοῦ ἐμαυτῆς ἀνδρός (it should have followed the participle συνευδοκοῦντος).
6-7. For the relationship between the village of Kellis and the city of the Mothites cf **20**.3-5n.
12. Does the numeral δύο refer to the number of years the apprentice contract was intended to last? Cf. **19.a**.7.
15. For the penalty clause starting in this line and parallels in contracts of apprenticeship cf. A. Berger, *Die Strafklauseln in den Papyrusurkunden*, 166
16-17. For the description of the kind of coinage used cf. **19.a**.9 (where ἀργυρί]ου καινοῦ τάλαντα are mentioned!).
18. χ]ωρὶς Θεοῦ βίας = 'an act of God excepted': as far as we can see, such a '*vis maior*'-clause is not used elsewhere in other contracts of apprenticeship, cf. W. Dahlmann, 'H Βία *im Recht der Papyri* (Diss. Köln 1968) 48ff.: 'Haftungsausschluß durch βία (θεοῦ)'.
18-19. For the formula as restored here cf. **31**.19ff.
19. Or read γραφεῖσαν] ἧς?
21-22. As a regnal formula after the *Augusti* Diocletian and Maximian and the *Caesars* Constantius and Galerius (293-305) is expected, their most common regnal formula may be considered for restoration (cf. R.S. Bagnall - K.A. Worp, *Regnal Formulas in Byzantine Egypt* [Missoula 1979] 10ff., form. 4). At the same time this shows how much of text is lost in the lacuna at the left-hand side of the fragment; at the start of ll. 22 at least 55 letters have now been restored (and one might add an extra τῶν κυρίων ἡμῶν [= 13 letters] before Κωνσταντίου), vs. 23 letters being preserved; compare the ratio 'letters lost' (55 or 68?) :: 'letters preserved' (23) with the calculated loss of text in **19.a** (cf. the introd. to that text). Epeiph 3 = 27.vi.
25. Perhaps one should restore something like ἄρξας τῆς Μωθιτῶν πόλεως συμπάρειμι (or συνεπιπάρειμι, cf. **19.a**.4) in the lacuna before σ]υνευδοκῶ.

19.b: FRAGMENT OF A PREFECTURAL HYPOGRAPHE

(Early 299)

Written on the verso of **19.a**.

(M.2)
1 παρὰ Αὐρηλίου Πα[μοῦρ Ψάιτος ?
2 καὶ Φιλάμμων[ος
3 (ἔτους) ιε´ καὶ ιδ[´ καὶ ζ´
4 Παχὼν[
5 ὁ στρατηγὸς πα[ρόντος τοῦ δια-]
6 δικοῦντος μέ[ρους μεταξὺ ὑμῶν δια-]
7 λήμψεται πε̣[ρὶ
8 τὴν οἰκίαν δ[
9 τὸ προσῆκον[

"To Pisistratos (?), from Aurelius Pamour son of Psais (?) and Philammon --. Year 15 and 14 and 7, Pachon [ ]. In the presence of the contending party the strategos will decide between you concerning the --- the house -- the fitting --."

After a date in ll. 3-4 (regnal year 15 [Diocletian]- 14 [Maximian] - 7 [Caesars] is 298/9; in this year the month Pachon according to the Greek calendar is 26.iv - 25.v, according to the traditional Egyptian calendar 6.ii - 15.iii; cf. D. Hagedorn - K.A. Worp in ZPE 104 [1994] 243-255) one is dealing in ll. 5-9 of this text with the contents of a ruling made by the provincial governor to the effect that a lawsuit will be decided by the local strategus. For a collection of such *hypographae*, see **22** introd. The precise relationship between this text and the petition written on the recto is unclear. Prefectural *hypographae* were usually added at the bottom of the petition, not on the verso of a document, and ll. 1-2 on the verso seem to form an alien element coming in between the petition on the recto and the hypographe. These lines mention the names of two or more senders of a document the contents of which followed in ll. 3ff. (i.c. the dated *hypographe*); it is not indicated to whom they sent that document.

1-2. The suggested restorations are meant only 'exempli gratia'. In view of the date of this text the Philammon mentioned in l. 2 may be identifiable with Philammon, the brother-in-law of Aurelius Pamour son of Psais, who is attested at the start of the 4th century (see the family tree given at p. 51); it is this supposed identification which suggests the restoration of the names in l. 1. The use of *παρὰ* + gen. could in itself suggest a previous mentioning of an addressee of the text on this side of the papyrus ('Τῷ A *παρὰ τοῦ* B'), but nothing has been preserved.
5-6. For the suggested restoration, see especially P.Cair.Isid. 74.22f. If this restoration is correct, it would mean that 10 - 14 letters at the beginning of each line are preserved, and though the papyrus is broken at this part straight down, 12 letters in l. 6 vs. 17 letters in l. 7 should be restored (for the restoration cf., e.g., CPR XVII.A 15.16 and SB XVIII 13780.4; or restore only *μέ[ρους ὑμῖν δια-]*, i.e. 11 letters?), i.e. on this side ± half of each line would have been preserved. This yields an odd discrepancy with the situation on the recto **19.a** of which it is assumed that only 1/3 of the original sheet is preserved. It is not easy to believe that 1/3 of the papyrus sheet was cut off, before the verso was inscribed.
8. It seems too daring to us to establish a link between the petition on the recto (**19.a**) and the *hypographe* here on the verso via a reading *τὴν οἰκ(ε)ῖαν δ[ούλην*.
10. The words *τὸ προσῆκον* remind us of similar phrasings found in the subscriptions of P.Col. VII 169.18, *τὴν προσήκουσάν σοι βοήθειαν*, and CPR XVII.A 15.16, *τὸν προσήκοντα ὅρον*.

20: PETITION TO THE PRAESES THEBAIDOS

(Ca. 300 - 320)

P.Kellis inv. P. 61.V+X + P. 63.A (all from House 3, room 8, level 4) + P. 65.B+C (House 3, room 8, level 3). The papyrus has been broken into 3 fragments. In the same frame there are some small scraps which do not necessarily belong to the same papyrus and which have not been transcribed. Fragm. I (upper left corner): H. 10 x B. 9 cm.; Fragm. II (upper right corner): H. 10 x B. 3.5 cm.; Fragm. III (ll. 16ff.): H. 4 x B. 8.5 cm. The papyrus has a margin at the left of 2 cm. and one at the top of 1.5 cm. The writing runs parallel with the fibers, the back is blank. There are traces of at least 7 vertical folds; as the foldings grow bigger from the right to the left, the papyrus was folded that way.

1 *Αὐρη[λίῳ̣] Ἡρώδῃ̣ τῷ̣ δ̣[ιασημο]τάτῳ̣ ἡγου-*
2 *μένῳ̣ Θηβα[ίδος.]*
3 *Παρὰ Αὐρηλίου Παμού[ριος Ψάι]τ̣ος ἀπὸ κώ-*
4 *μης Κέλλεως τῆς Μω̣[θειτῶ]ν πόλεως*
5 *τῆς Μεγάλης Ὀάσεως. [Ο]ὐ̣[δὲν] δεινότερον*
6 *οὐδὲ βιαιότερον, ἡγεμὼν [κύρι]ε̣, βίαν καὶ*
7 *πλεονεξίαν ἐν τοῖς τότ[ε ̣ ̣] κ̣ατασ̣τ̣ασίοις*
8 *καιροῖς ὑπὸ πολλῶν· ὁ̣ς̣ Ψα̣[̣ ̣ ̣]ς ἀπὸ τῆς αὐ-*
9 *τῆς Μωθειτῶν πόλεως̣, [ἄν]θρωπος με-*
10 *γάλα ἐπὶ τῶν τόπων δυνά[με]ν̣ος, βι̣αίως*
11 *καὶ τυραννικῶς ἥρπ̣α̣σ̣[εν] τ̣ὸν ὄνον*
12 *μου ἔτ̣ι ἀτελοῦς τότε τ̣[ῆς ἡ]λ̣ικ̣ίας κα̣ὶ*
13 *ταῖς ἐ̣ξ ἀνθρώπων ̣[̣ ̣ ̣] ̣ συν̣έ̣κ̣ο̣-*
14 *ψεν. Μ̣έτριος̣ ὢν καὶ [διὰ] ̣[̣ ̣ ̣ ̣ ̣]*
15 *μ̣ων μου τὰ πρὸς τὸ̣[ν βίον μου ποριζό-]*
16 *μενος ἀναγκαίως κα̣[ταφεύγω πρὸς σέ,]*
17 *δέσποτα, διὰ τῶνδε τῶ[ν βιβλιδίων ἀξι-]*
18 *ῶν κ̣αὶ δεόμενος κε̣[λεῦσαι*

— —

8 *ὡς*? 13 *ανθρώπων* Pap.

"To Aurelius Herodes, the most eminent *praeses* of the Thebaid from Aurelius Pamouris son of Psais, from the village of Kellis of the city of the Mothites of the Great Oasis. Nothing (was regarded) by many in those times of turmoil (?) more terrible or forceful, mylord *praeses*, <than to suffer> violence and arrogance. For Psa-s, from the same city of the Mothites, a locally powerful man, took my donkey away, forcefully and acting like a tyrant, while at that very moment I was still an adolescent, and he came into conflict with the --- from men. As I am a person of limited means and as through my --- I earn my living, I necessarily take refuge to you, my lord, through this petition, asking and begging you to order, that ...."

This papyrus contains the upper part of a petition sent by Pamouris, a villager from Kellis, complaining to the *praeses Thebaidos* about the theft of a donkey by an influential inhabitant of the city of Mothis. As the document is broken at the bottom, we do not know whether the *praeses* gave his reaction by way of a *hypographe* (for these subscriptions, see **19.b** and **22**). A list of such 4th-century petitions to the highest authorities in Egypt is printed in TYXH 2 (1987) 178-181 (addenda to that list are given in CPR XVII.A 16, introd.); for a more general list of 4th-century petitions, see ZPE 69 (1987) 155f. For various documents illustrating forms of criminal theft in Roman Egypt in general cf. H.-J. Drexhage, 'Eigentumsdelikte im römischen Ägypten', ANRW X.1 [1988] 952-1004 (for donkeys cf. esp. 959ff.). Apparently the incident about which Pamouris is complaining took place some time before he sent in this petition; cf. the notes to ll. 7 and 12.

1. For the *praeses Thebaidos* Aurelius Herodes cf. J. Lallemand, *L'administration civile de l'Egypte*, 254 # 22. Apparently he is attested thus far only in the undated P.Oxy. IX 1186 and our papyrus is helpful in establishing the date of his office more precisely, as a Pamour(is) son of Psais (cf. l. 3) occurs in many other Kellis papyri between 306 and 321, cf. in particular the family tree, p. 51. It follows that Aurelius Herodes probably officiated some year(s) within the first two decades of the 4th century.

3-5. The phrasing *ἀπὸ κώμης Κέλλεως τῆς Μωθειτῶν πόλεως* occurs frequently in the papyri from Kellis; a variant phrasing is *ἀπὸ κώμης Κέλλεως τοῦ Μωθίτου νομοῦ* (for the nome see **41**.4n.). This interchangeable use of *ἡ Μωθιτῶν πόλις* and *ὁ Μωθίτης νομός* illustrates the position of Kellis vis-à-vis the same territorial entity. In other words, Kellis formed part of the territory of the city of the Mothites, the metropolis of the Mothite nome. The phenomenon of such an interchangeability of metropolis and nome (cf., e.g., P.Grenf.II 72.2n.; P.Vindob.Worp 8.22n.) is also illustrated by, e.g., an addressee of a document being styled as a an official *τῆς Ὀξυρυγχιτῶν πόλεως* ('of the city of the Oxyrhynchites') by a sender of the document who styles himself as *Αὐρήλιος --- ἀπὸ κώμης --- τοῦ αὐτοῦ νομοῦ* ('from the village X of the same province'); in such cases (cf. P.Gron.Amst. 1.2-3;) the words 'the same province' can only refer to 'city of the Oxyrhynchites', i.e. the metropolis of the Oxyrhynchite province; a parallel for Hermopolis is found in, e.g., CPR V 6.4-6. Finally, compare phrasings like *ἀπὸ κώμης Πενεύτου τῆς Διοσπόλεως* (P.Corn. 13), *ἀπὸ κώμης Κράμμνου τῆς Ἀντιπύργου πόλεως* (P.Köln V 232.2) next to *ἀπὸ κώμης Πώεως νομοῦ τῆς αὐτῆς* (sc. *Ἀπόλλωνος*) *πόλεως* (P.Heid. IV 307.2-3) and *ἀπὸ κώμης Ταννυαίθεως νομοῦ Ἀπόλλωνος πόλεως Μικρᾶς* (P.Mich. XIII 670.4; P.Michael. 43.3, 44.3-4; P.Vat.Aphrod. 14.7), from which it appears that the use of a word *νομοῦ* before *πόλεως* was optional (our scribe *could* have written: *ἀπὸ κώμης Κέλλεως <νομοῦ> τῆς Μωθειτῶν πόλεως*).

5ff. For the opening sentences of such petitions, see Frisk's remarks in an excursus in P.Berl.Frisk, p. 81-91. Often enough the petitioners make some kind of general statement concerning the hardships of life, their weak sex (in the case of women), their feeble age or youth, or their poverty (*πενία*) or modest condition-of-life (*μετριότης*), etc.; for *μετριότης* referred to in such openings cf., e.g., P. Cair.Isid. 68.4ff., 69.25ff., 74.2ff.; SB XVI 12814.5; P.Mert. II 91.6f.,16f.; P.Oxy. I 71.i = M.Chr. I 62.3ff; VIII 1121.5ff.; XLIII 3126.ii.10f.; XLVIII 3394.3ff.; P.Panop.Köln III 27 = SB XII 11220.4ff.,19ff.; P.Sakaon 41 = P.Ryl. IV 659,7ff.; P.Sakaon 44 = P.Thead. 17 = P.Turner 44.14f.; PSI VII 769.1f. In its present form the text of our papyrus does not seem satisfactory and apparently the petitioner (led away by his emotions?) has left out some words; how, otherwise, should we explain the accusatives *βίαν καὶ πλεονεξίαν*? It is difficult to escape inserting a verb which governs these accusatives; insert, therefore, something like, e.g., *<ἢ παθεῖν>* before, e.g., *βίαν καὶ πλεονεξίαν* in l. 6-7 and interpret: 'Nothing is more terrible or forceful than to suffer violence and arrogance'? Compare, e.g., P.Cair.Isid. 68.7: *βίαν καὶ παρανομίαν πάσχω*, and cf. also the phrasing in SB IV 7464.3: *ὕβρεως οὐδὲν οὔτε δεινότερον οὔτε χαλεπώτερον*. Furthermore, it looks more likely that the element *ὑπὸ πολλῶν* should be connected with persons who share this opinion rather than that it should be related to the number of persons by whose hands violence and arrogance were caused (does it make any difference for a victim, whether he suffers hardship at the hands of many or at the hands of only one person?); but this presupposes that a verb like *ἐνομίζετο* has also been omitted. The imperfect seems necessary in view of *τότε* in l. 7 (see note ad loc.). There is no real gain, we think, in reading *ὑπὸ Πολλωνος*; for the merits of the letters read as *ος*, see l. 8n.

6. It is interesting to compare for *ἡγεμὼν κ[ύρι]ε* l. 17, where the *praeses* is addressed as *δέσποτα*. Obviously the author of this petition felt that there was no great difference between the words *κύριος* and *δεσπότης*; cf. D. Hagedorn - K.A. Worp, *Von κύριος zu δεσπότης*, ZPE 39 (1980) 165f., esp. 176-7.

7. Though the dotted tau in *καταστασίοις* betrays some uneasiness, a reading *κατασπασίοις* seems less likely, as the trace of ink to the left of the loop of the *α* is hardly compatible with the way a *π* is normally written by this hand. The adjective *καταστάσιος* (cf. also the adjectives *ἀντιστάσιος* and *προστάσιος* derived from the nouns *ἀντίστασις* and *πρόστασις*) is not listed in LSJ, but in the present context its meaning may be compared with *καταστασιαστικός* = 'factious' (cf. LSJ s.v.). After all, the late third/early fourth century was a period of political turmoil in the Roman Empire which did not leave Egypt undisturbed (for the revolt of Domitius Domitianus in 297, see J.D. Thomas in ZPE 22 [1976] 253-279). F. Preisigke, *Wörterbuch* s.v. *κατάστασις*, 3 translates: 'gerichtliches Streitverfahren'. It seems unlikely that we should translate 'those founding years of old' (cf. F. Preisigke, *Wörterbuch* s.v. *κατάστασις*, 2).

It looks as if the adverb *τότε* (= 'at that time, then', in past or future times, normally denoting the opposite of *νῦν* = 'right now, presently, to date'), was used here with the very meaning of *νῦν*. After all, it is more natural that in a general statement concerning the hardships of life, 'Nothing --- more terrible or forceful ...', reference should be made to a present situation rather than to a situation in the past. But it must be admitted that the obstacles against such an interpretation are too serious to translate safely here: 'in these times of turmoil' and it seems more likely that Pamour referred to general views held since a long time. There may be space in the lacuna after *τότ[ε* for restoring a short particle like *ἤδη*.

8. The reading of the damaged letters in the middle as *ὸς* seems the most likely, but they do not make any sense unless the omikron is changed into *ὡς*. After that one might restore the name as *Ψά[ει]ς* (l. *Ψάις*) or read *Ψά[ις τι]ς*.

12. For the phrasing *μου ἔτι ἀτελοῦς τότε τῆς ἡλικίας* = 'while I was at that moment still an adolescent' cf. BGU I 168.5 = M.Chrest. 121. It should, however, be remarked that one finds there the accusative *τὴν ἡλικίαν* instead of the genitive. For the compound *ἀτελής* cf. F.M.J. Waanders, *The History of* Τέλος *and* Τελέω *in Ancient Greek* (Diss. Amsterdam 1983) § 167ff.

13-14. The verb *συγκόπτω* normally governs an accusative, but here it should apparently be associated with the preceding dative *ταῖς ἐξ ἀνθρώπων [ ]*. We have adopted (not without some doubts) an interpretation *συγκόπτω τινί* = 'to come into conflict with', i.e. postulated an intransitive use of the verb, though such a use is not common, cf. LSJ s.v. We have not been able to read the noun (in the dative) governed by the verb; if our interpretation of *συγκόπτω* is correct, one may perhaps conjecture, e.g., *δ[ικαῖ]ς*.

ἐξ ἀνθρώπων seems to mean here: 'man made'. In itself there exists an adjective *ἐξάνθρωπος* (cf. LSJ s.v. II: 'inhuman'), but the gen.plur. ending *-πων* prevents its being connected with the previous dative *ταῖς*. Only if one changes the reading into *ἐξανθρώποις*, an interpretation <*με*> *συνέκοψεν ταῖς ἐξανθρώποις π[ληγαῖ]ς* = 'he beat me up with savage blows' becomes conceivable, but then the use of the article *ταῖς* is slightly remarkable.

14ff. For the phrasing restored here in l. 15 cf. P.Oxy. XII 1557.11-12: *μετρίῳ ὄντι καὶ ἐξ αὐτῶν* (sc. *κτήνων*) *τὸ ζῆν πορίζομένῳ*. For the meaning of the adjective *μέτριος* in general cf. P.Herm. 19.13n. As the my at the start of l. 15 is strangely written, but fairly certain, one cannot read *[διὰ] τ[ῶν κτή-]/νων κτλ*.

17-18. For the combined use of the two verbs *ἀξιόω* and *δέομαι* cf. H. Zilliacus, *Zur Abundanz der spätgriechischen Gebrauchssprache* (Helsinki 1967) esp. p. 37f.: 'Synonyme, wirkliche und scheinbare'.

21: PETITION TO A FORMER MAGISTRATE

(6.i.321)

P.Kellis inv. P. 61.R+T+V+W+X+Y (House 3, room 8, level 4) + P. 65.D (House 3, room 8, level 3). H. 27.6 x B. 19.5 cm. Margins: at the top 1, at the left 3.3, at the bottom 6.5 cm. The writing runs parallel to the fibers, the verso is blank. There are several horizontal folds, while the papyrus was folded vertically at least 7 times. A much more fragmentary copy 'B' of the same text has been preserved in P.Kellis inv. P. 17.Q (House 3, room 10, level 3) + P. 18 (House 3, room 10, level 1)+ P. 20 (House 3, room 10, level 3) + P. 63.B (House 3, room 8, level 4).

1 [Αὐρηλίῳ Φαυσ]τιανῷ ἄρξαντι Μωθ̣ιτῶν πόλεως τῆς Μεγάλης Ὀάσεως
2 [ἐ]κδίκῳ χώρας.
3 [Παρὰ Αὐρηλίου] Παμούριος Ψάιτος ἀπὸ κώμης Κέλλεως τῆς Μωθιτῶν
4 [πόλεως. Εἰ] ἑ̣κάστῳ προχωρήσει τὰ τῆς αὐθαδίας καὶ εἰ μὴ ἡ τῶν
5 [νόμων ἐπιστ]ρέφεια ἐπακολουθεῖν εἴωθεν, ἀβίωτος ἂν ἡμῖν τοῖς
6 [. . . . .]ς̣ χρόνος ἐγείνατο. Σόις τοίνυν Ἀκούτ̣ι̣ο̣ς κώμαρχος
7 [τῆς αὐτῆς κ]ώ̣μης Κέλλεως ἀεὶ ἐπιβουλεύων μοι ὁσημέραι
8 [. . . . .] ̣ μοι παρ' ἕκαστα τοὺς π̣αρεπιδημοῦντας στρατιώ-
9 [τας καὶ ὀφ]φικιαλίους καὶ ἐκσπούν̣κτορας ἐπικωμάζων τῇ συμ-
10 [βίῳ μου καὶ] ἐπιφυόμενός μοι. Τῇ γὰρ χθὲς ἡμέρᾳ̣ κατ' ἀπ[ο]υ̣σίαν μου
11 [. . . . . . .]ν̣ θύραν κα̣τασχίσας πελυκίῳ ἐπισελθὼν ἅμα υἱῷ Ψενα-
12 [μούνιος] τέκτονος [ἀ]πὸ Πμοῦν Παμω, μήτε ὢν λ̣ιτουργὸς̣ μήδ' α̣ὐ̣
13 [. . . κω]μ̣ήτης μ[ο]υ τυγχάνων, ἐπελθὼν τῇ συμβίῳ μου
14 [μεθ' οὗ εἶ]χεν ῥωπ̣ά̣λῳ πλη[γ]αῖς αὐτὴν συνέκοψεν, ὡς αἱ πλη-
15 [γαὶ φαίν]ονται ἐπὶ [σ]ώματος αὐτῆς, ὡς μὴ ὑποκείμενοι νόμοις.
16 [Οὕτως τ]οίνυν οὔ[σ]ης τῆς τῶν προειρημένων τ̣οῦ τε κωμά̣ρ̣-
17 [χου καὶ το]ῦ υἱοῦ Ψ̣ε̣ναμούν̣[ιο]ς [δι]α̣νοίας, ο̣ὐ̣ δ̣υ̣νάμ̣ε̣νος
18 [δι' ἡσυ]χίας ἄγειν̣, ἐπιδίδωμι τῇ σῇ ἐπιεικείᾳ̣ τάδε τὰ βιβλία
19 [ἀξιῶν α]ὐ̣τὰ ταῦτα μηνυθῆναι τῇ ἀνδρείᾳ̣ τοῦ κυρίου μου
20 [διασημ]οτάτου ἡγε̣μόνος Οὐαλερίου Οὐικτωρι<νι>ανοῦ
21 [πρὸς τὸ] δύνασθαι τὸ τετολμημένον τυχεῖν τῆς προση-
22 [κούσης] ἐκδικείας. Διευτύχει.
23 [Μετὰ τὴ]ν̣ ὑ̣π̣ατίαν [τ]ῶν δεσποτῶν ἡμῶν Κωνσταντίνου
24 Σεβαστοῦ τὸ ϛ̅ καὶ Κωνσταντίνου τοῦ ἐπιφανεστάτου
25 Καίσαρος τὸ α̅, Τῦβι ια̅. (M. 2) Αὐρ(ήλιος) Παμοῦρις Ψάιτος ὁ προκ(είμενος)
26 ἐπιδέδωκα. Ἔγραψα ὑπὲρ αὐτ(οῦ) μὴ εἰδ(ότος) γράμματα Αὐρ(ήλιος) Φιβίων
27 ἄρξας Ἑρμοῦ πόλεως.

3 ψαϊτος 6 ἐγένετο 9 ἐξπούγκτορας 11 ἐπεισελθὼν 12 λειτουργὸς 13 τυγ'χανων Pap. 14 ῥοπάλου 20 ουϊκτωριανου Pap. 22 ἐκδικίας 23 ϋπατιαν Pap. (l. ὑπατείαν) 25 ψαϊτος Pap. 26 ϋπερ Pap.

Copy B, as far as preserved, offers the variant reading *τῆς αὐτῆς* Μωθιτῶν in l. 3.

"To Aurelius Faustianus, former magistrate of the city of the Mothites in the Great Oasis, *defensor* of the country. From Aurelius Pamouris son of Psais, from the village of Kellis of the city of the Mothites. If for everybody deeds of wilfulness will have success and if the severity of the laws would not usually follow, these times would be unsupportable for us ---. Now Sois son of Akoutis, comarch of the same village of Kellis, who is constantly plotting against me, (is harrassing ?) me every day in violation of everything, stirring up the locally present soldiers and *officiales* and *expunctores* against my wife and being a constant pain in the neck for me. For yesterday, during my absence, he burst the --- door open with an axe, went in with the son of Psenamounis (or: with his son Psenamounis?) the carpenter from Pmoun Pamo, though being neither a liturgist nor happening to be a (fellow?-)villager of mine, he assaulted my wife with a club and he beat her up with blows so that these are visible on her body, as if they are not subject to the laws. As such is the mentality of the said comarch and the son of Psenamounis (or: his son Psenamounis?), and because I cannot live in peace, I present this petition to your clemency and I ask that these things be relayed to the braveness of my lord the *praeses* Valerius Victorinianus *vir perfectissimus*, in order that their reckless act get a fitting vindication. Farewell. After the consulate of our lords Constantinus *Augustus* consul for the 6th time and Constantinus *nobilissimus Caesar* consul for the 1st time, Tybi 11. (M.2) I, the aforementioned Aurelius Pamouris son of Psais, have submitted (the petition). I, Aurelius Phibion, ex-magistrate of Hermopolis, have written on his behalf because he is not able to write."

This petition addressed to a former magistrate of the city of Mothis (modern Mut) and *defensor civitatis* of the whole *chora* contains a complaint from Aurelius Pamouris son of Psais, about physical violence committed by a certain Sois son of Akoutis, comarch of Kellis, and an apparently anonymous son of Psenamounis the carpenter (cf., however, the note to l. 11-12) against the petitioner's wife; while the petitioner himself was absent, she was beaten up severely. Such cases of violent crime occur frequently enough in the papyri, cf., e.g., the recently published CPR XVII.A 23 and W. Dahlmann, Ἡ Βία *im Rechte der Papyri* (Diss. Köln 1968). **23** is another complaint about assault.

1. The name Φαυστιανός (restored from copy B where it has been fully preserved) occurs also in other documents from Kellis like the famous Harvest Account Book, though in view of the date assigned to that text (probably the last quarter of the fourth century) the persons can hardly be identical.
2. Unless another title (e.g.: *βουλευτῇ*) or *γενομένῳ* preceded *ἐ*]*κδίκῳ*, this line was indented; for the office of *ἔκδικος* (= '*defensor civitatis*') cf. the full discussion by B. Kramer in Pap.Flor. XIX.1 (1990) 305-329; apparently this is now the earliest attestation of the title (cf. Kramer, *op.cit.*, 307) *and* the earliest occurrence of the official acting alone. The meaning of the word *χώρα* is not quite clear. Like in **23**.29 (*τῷ στατιωναριῷ τῆς χώρας*) it is used in an official's title, but *χώρα* can indicate regions of every

size ranging between a simple village and a large part of Egypt like the Thebais (cf. F. Preisigke, *Wörterbuch* s.v., 1). If Kramer is right in stating that normally a *defensor civitatis* was competent only for a metropolis and adjacent province, it follows that χώρα indicates here the Mothite province. At the same time one wonders why the scribe did not simply write: Αὐρηλίῳ Φαυστιανῷ ἄρξαντι ἐκδίκῳ Μωθιτῶν πόλεως τῆς Μεγάλης Ὀάσεως, cf. e.g. P.Stras. 296 verso 2-3 (# 21 in Kramer's list).

3-4. For Aurelius Pamouris son of Psais, see the family tree at p. 51. For the relationship between the village of Kellis and the city of the Mothites cf. **20**.3-5n.

4. For such general opening statements, see **20**.5ff. note (this petition was also sent by Pamouris).

6. At the start of this line a qualifying adjective like, e.g., [μετριωτάτο]ις is expected.

For comarchs in general cf. N. Lewis, *The Compulsory Public Services of Roman Egypt* (Firenze 1982) 36-37 s.v. and **23**.2n.

8. One expects at the start a verb governing the dative μοι and meaning something like 'to obstruct, to harrass, to attack', *vel sim.* It was probably more or less synonymous with the verb ἐπιβουλεύω, cf. the participle in l. 7. In itself it is conceivable that the verb also governed the following accusatives τοὺς παρεπιδημοῦντας στρατιώ- | [τας καὶ ὀφ]φικιαλίους καὶ ἐκσπούνκτορας (cf. below, l. 9n.), but in that case one would expect the acc.pl. ἐπικωμάζοντας rather than the nom.sg. ἐπικωμάζων.

9. For the office of an *expunctor* (an army official who removed soldiers' names from the lists of soldiers on active duty) cf. the meaning of the Lat. verb *expungo* discussed in P.Oxy. IX 1204.6n and Rom.Mil.Rec. 47 i.16n. The noun *expunctor* is not yet listed in the Oxford Latin Dictionary (nor, for that matter, its graecisized form in LSJ). The same officials seem to occur in **77**.13. In general cf. also S. Daris, *Il Lessico latino nel Greco d'Egitto* (Barcelona 1991[2]) 45.

The use of the verb ἐπικωμάζω τινά + dat. meaning something like 'to stir up someone against ...' is not normal; more regularly the verb is used intransitively with the meaning 'to make a riotous assault', cf. LSJ s.v.; as, however, the papyrus does not read ἐπικωμάζοντας (to be connected with στρατιώτας etc.) it is difficult to see what other meaning can be assigned to it at this place (cf. also above, l. 8n.).

11-12. In itself one might prefer reading Ψενα-/[μούνει] at the start of l. 12 and assume that Psenamounis was the son of Sois, but τέκτονος should then be changed into τέκτονι (such a mix of cases is not uncommon) and one would have to assume that the Psenamounis was living apart from his father.

12-13. The village Pmoun Pamo occurs also in the still unpublished P. Kellis inv. 93.60+71 verso, l. 3 (House 4); its exact location is unknown. For toponyms in the Oasis starting with an element Πμοῦν- = 'water' cf. G. Wagner, *Les Oasis d'Egypte*, passim, esp. 159ff.

The reading λιτουργός poses a small riddle as to its meaning. If we take μήτε ὢν λιτουργός as meaning simply 'neither being a liturgist' there is the obstacle that according to, e.g, the testimony of **23** the office of a comarch in Kellis was a liturgical one. Should we take μήτε ὢν λιτουργός to mean within the context of this petition that Sois was not 'on duty' and therefore had nothing to seek in Pamour's house?

Probably one should restore συγκω]μήτης or ὁμοκω]μήτης at the start of l. 13. If so, one would accentuate the letters αυ in l. 12 as the particle αὖ (for its meaning after a negation cf. F. Preisigke, *Wörterbuch*, s.v. 1). As Sois, however, was comarch of the same village the petitioner Pamour lived in, it seems more likely that the writer means to describe Psenamounis, who came from Pmoun Pamo and held no official position; in that case one must change ὢν λιτουργὸς into ὄντι λιτουργῷ and κω]μήτης ... τυγχάνων into κω]μήτῃ ... τυγχάνοντι.

15. As a consequence of his emotions the petitioner forgets to keep using the singular and writes ὑποκείμενοι (after all, there were two assailants).

16. A restoration of τοιαύτης in the lacuna at the start would probably be just too long. For εἰμί + adverb see R. Kühner - B. Gerth, *Grammatik der Griechischen Sprache, II: Satzlehre*, I 38.

20. For the starting date of Victorinianus' tenure in 321 cf. CPR XVII.A 15 introd. The present papyrus is even earlier than that text, as its date (see note to l. 23ff.) is 6.i.321, while the Vienna papyrus con tains a petition mentioning an earlier subscription given by Victorinianus on 22.ii.321 in response to a previous other petition. Victorinianus' name was apparently too difficult for the scribe to spell correctly; his error amounts to the loss of the syllable -ni-.

23ff. For the consuls of 320 and their postconsulate in 321, see R.S. Bagnall a.o., *CLRE* s.a.; Tybi 11 = 6.i.
26-27. It is interesting to see a former magistrate of Hermopolis Magna here subscribing for a person living in the Great Oasis. It seems most likely that the present text was written in the Oasis, rather than in Hermopolis, and apparently Aurelius Phibion resided at least temporarily in the Oasis.

22: PART OF A DATED PREFECTURAL (?) HYPOGRAPHE

(5 - 12.ii.324)

P.Kellis inv. P. 56.F # 1 (House 3, room 9, level 3, Western doorway) + P. 61.W (House 3, room 8, level 4). H. 12 (in part 9.3) x B. 11.5 cm. Margins: at the left: 2.5, at the bottom 6 cm. Between lines 1 and 2 is a space of 3 cm. The verso is blank.

- -
1 . . .[

2 Τέταρτον μέλλουσιν ὑπάτοι[ς, πρὸ ———]
3 Εἰδῶν Φεβραρίων· με[τ' ἀνάγνωσιν τῶν]
4 ἐνγεγραμμένων συννόμῳ[ς ὁ Title]
5 διαλήμψεται. Κολλ(ήματος) ρ̣[τόμ(ου) -]

4 ἐγγεγραμμένων

" . . . Under the future consuls for the fourth time, on the *n*th day before the Ides of February. After reading the written text the ... will take a decision in accordance with the laws. Sheet 100+, Roll --."

No more can be said about this papyrus than that it obviously contains a part of a dated *hypographe* (= a written decision) given by some higher judicial authority (possibly the provincial governor) in response to a petition, remnants of which are preserved only in the scanty fragments of line 1. Apparently the case was referred to a lower judicial authority for further decision; for such practice, see **19.b** and CPR XVII.A, p. 79-80, where other such *hypographai* occurring in 4th-century petitions to the provincial governor and references in there to κόλλημα = 'sheet'-numbers are printed.

1. It is difficult to tell whether this line and lines 2-5 were written by a different hand. If not, one is probably dealing with a copy of an original.

2-3. This is the consulate of 324, cf. R.S. Bagnall a.o., *CLRE* s.a.; add **56**.3 and P.Nepheros 48.1 (cf. ZPE 78 [1989] 135). The document was evidently written between 5 - 12.ii.324. It seems probable that there was a numeral indicating the number of days before the Ides and given the size of the lacuna it seems likely that it was written out in full. For the use of Roman months in the papyri from Egypt, see in general P.J. Sijpesteijn in ZPE 33 (1979) 229-240 and P.Mich. XV 720.8n.
4. The adverb *συννόμως* is not listed in F. Preisigke's *Wörterbuch* and subsequent supplements, but cf. LSJ s.v. If this text is the *hypographe* of a provincial governor, one expects at the end of this line before the verb *διαλήμψεται* as its subject the indication of a lower-ranking official (e.g.: the *strategus* [cf. **19.b**.5], the *logistes* or the *exactor civitatis*) who was appointed to make a decision in court.

23: PETITION TO THE PRAESES THEBAIDOS

(353)

P.Kellis inv. P. 78.G+J+K (House 3, level 3). H. 24.5 x B. 33.5 cm. Margins: at the left ± 2, at the top 2, at the bottom (before l. 31 was filled in) 1, and at the right 2 - 3 cm. The writing runs parallel with the fibers, but the fibers in the left-hand margin of the recto run vertically, hence this must have been part the so-called 'protocollon' (cf. **44**, description). The verso is blank.

1 [Φ]λαουίῳ Φαυστίνῳ τῷ διασημοτάτῳ ἡγεμ̣ό̣νι

2 παρὰ Αὐρηλίου Γενᾶ Οὐώνσιος κωμάρχου κώμης Κέλλεως [τ]ο̣ῦ Μωθ̣ίτου νομοῦ. Κώμαρχος

3 κ̣[λ]η[ρ]ωθείς, κύριε, τῆς ἡμετέρας κώμης μετὰ τῶν ἄλλων λ̣ιτουργῶν̣ ὑπὸ παρουσίᾳ τοῦ διαδόχου

4 τ̣ο̣ῦ̣ ἐ̣ξ̣άκτορος καὶ τῶν ἐν τέλει ἁπάντων κατὰ τὸ σύνηθες ἐποίησα τοὺς λιτουργοὺς πάντας τὴν

5 τ̣ύ̣χην ἑαυτῶν τῇ στρατηγικῇ τάξει διδόναι κατὰ τὸ ἔθος καὶ ἕκαστ̣[ος ἡμῶν κα]θεξῆς ἐκληρώθη <εἰς>

6 [λ]ι̣τ̣ο̣υργίας, μόνον δὲ Ταα τινα τοὔνομα κληρωθέντα μεθ' ἡμῶν̣ `[ ]την´ ο̣ψ̣ω̣ν̣ι̣α̣στὴν ὄντα Ἁρπο-

7 [κ]ρ̣α̣τ̣ί̣ωνος ἄρξαντος μετῆλθον ὥστε καὶ αὐτὸν προσκαρτερεῖν τῇ δημοσίᾳ χρείᾳ μετὰ τῶν

8 [σ]υ̣λ̣λ̣ε̣ιτουργῶν. Ὁ δὲ θαρρῶν τῇ δυναστίᾳ τοῦ αὐτοῦ Ἁ̣ρ̣π̣ο̣κ̣ρατίωνος πολλῇ οὔσῃ ἐπὶ τῶν τό-

9 [πων] ἧττον̣ ἐφρόντισεν τῆς ἐμῆς μετριότητος. Κατασχεθέντος δὲ ὑπ' ἐμοῦ καὶ τοῦ κοινωνοῦ

10 [μ]ου Γενᾶ τοῦ ἄλλου κωμάρχου ὁ προειρημένος Ἁρποκρατίων πολλῇ τυραννίᾳ χρώμενος ἐπὶ

11 τ̣ῶν τόπων συμμάχους τοὺς ἑαυτοῦ παρέβαλέν μοι μετὰ ῥοπάλων, οἵτινες ἐπῆλθόν μοι

12 ὡ̣ς ἐν πολέμῳ μέσῳ πληγαῖς θανασίμοις συνκόψαντές με καὶ τὸν δημόσιον λιτουργὸν

13 π̣αρ' ἡμῶν ἀπέσπασαν τόν τε ἀριστερὸν ὀφθαλμὸν ἔπληξαν καὶ τὰς πλευρὰς συνέκοψαν· ἔτι πρὸς θα-

14 ν̣ά̣τ̣ο̣υ̣ ὢν ἐπὶ τήνδε τὴν τῶν λιβέλλων ἐπίδοσιν ἦλθον μὴ ⟦τι⟧ ἀνθρώπινόν τι παθῶ πρὸ τῆς ἐκδικίας

15 καὶ ἀνεκδίκητός μου εἰ̣ν̣`αι´ ὁ φόνος. Καὶ γὰρ Τιμόθεος ὁ τούτου παῖς ἑκάστοτε μεταχειρίζεται τῇ τυραννίᾳ̣

16 [± 12]. ἐντεθυμ̣[εῖ]ται π̣ο̣ι̣ε̣ι̣.[ ]μενος τοὺς χοίρους ἡμῶν ⟦καὶ⟧ προῖκα κατασωτευόμενος

17 [αὐθαιρ]έτως `δὲ´ καὶ τὰ οἰνάρια κ̣λ̣επ[τ]φ̣ό̣νου τὸν χοῖρον τοῦ ἀδελφοῦ μου ὑφειλάμενος ὡς καὶ ἐλ̣ε̣γ-

18 χ̣θ̣ε̣ὶ̣ς̣ ὑπὸ Ψάιτος Πατ̣εμίνιος κ[α]ὶ̣ Ψ̣[ε]κ̣ῆτος Ψεννούφιος· κ̣αὶ π̣άντα καὶ ταῦτα οὐκ ἠρκέσθη [αὐτ]ῷ̣, ἡ το̣ῦ̣ χοίρου

19 ε̣υ̣ηλ̣ . . ία, ἀλλὰ αὐτὸν τὸν ἄθλιόν μου ἀδελφὸν ἐξέδυσεν τῆς ἐσθῆτος δημοσί[ᾳ̣ κ]α̣ὶ̣ ἐφυγάτευσε̣ν̣

20 α̣ὐ̣τὸ̣ν̣ ε̣ἰ̣ς Αἴγυπτον ὡς . . . ωσδε καὶ ὑπερπήδησας εἰς τὴν οἰκίαν μου νυκτὸς ὑφεῖλ[εν] τὰ οἰνάρια ἅπερ

21 ἀ̣π̣ὸ̣ [τῆ]ς̣ ἑ̣αυτοῦ οἰκίας δ̣η̣μ̣ο̣σ̣ί̣ᾳ̣ ἐξήν̣εγκα̣, πρὸς δὲ σκ̣έ̣πασιν καὶ ἔλεγχο̣ν̣ τῆς κα̣[τ'] ἐ̣μοῦ γενομέ-

22 ν̣ης ὕ̣βρεως ὑποβάλ̣λω Πεβῶν Τιθοῆτος Χηνου ὁ ν̣ῦν ἔχων τὰς ῥοπαλους ἐπὶ τῆς οἰκίας

23 α̣ὐ̣τ̣ο̣ῦ̣, ἃς ἀπέ̣λαβεν παρ̣ὰ̣ τ̣ῶν συμμάχων ὧν τὰ ὀνόματα Τρόδα, Ψενπνούθης, Πορφύριος,

24 Θ̣ε̣ό̣τιμος, Λέων, Σαπ̣ . . ς, Κ̣όρα[ξ,]. Παχοῦμις .[.].ιτος Λαβουα̣τ̣[ο]υ̣· μάρτυς δὲ τῆς ἐφόδου

25 Ὠ̣ρί̣[ω]ν̣ Τιθοῆτος Χηου, [μ]ά̣ρτυρ[ες δὲ]⁻ θυγάτηρ Γενᾶ Π[α]κ̣ύ̣σιος, Σαραπόδωρος Ἔρωτος· ὅθεν ταῦ-

26 [τα] τ̣ὰ̣ ἔ̣γγραφα ἐπιδίδ[ωμι Ἑ]ρ̣μ̣[ογ]ένει τῷ̣ διαδόχῳ̣ `τ̣ο̣ῦ̣´ ἐξάκτ̣ορος ἀξιῶν καὶ ἐξορκίζων αὐτὸν

27 [κατὰ] τ̣ὴ̣ν̣ θείαν καὶ οὐράνιον τ[ύ]χην̣ τῶ̣[ν π]ά̣ντα νικώντων δ̣εσπο̣τ̣ῶ̣ν̣ ἡμῶν Ἀγούστου τε καὶ Καίσαρος `ἀνενεγκ̣ε̣ῖ̣ν̣´ ἐπὶ

28 τ̣ὴ̣ν̣ ὄ̣ψιν τοῦ ἐμοῦ κυρί[ου N.N.]. πρὸς ἣν ἤδη κ̣α̣τ̣αφε̣ύ̣ξ̣ομαι ἐκδικίαν αἰτησόμενος ὧν κα-

29 κ̣ῶ̣ν̣ πέπονθα, τούτω[ν δὲ ἀντίγραφον ἐπι]δέδωκα Ἀμμωνίῳ τῷ̣ στατιωναρ̣ε̣ίῳ̣ τῆς χώρας.

30 [Ὑ]π̣α̣τ̣ε̣ί̣α̣ς̣ τῶν δεσπο̣τῶν [ἡμῶν Κωνσταν]τίου Ἀγούστο̣υ̣ τὸ [ϛ] κ̣αὶ [Κ]ωνσταντίου τοῦ ἐπιφανεστάτου Καίσαρος τὸ β/.

31 (M.2) [Α]ὐ̣ρ̣ήλ̣ι̣ος Γενᾶ Οὐ[ώνσιος κώμαρ]χου ὁ προκ[είμενος] δημοσίᾳ̣ προῦθηκα.

3 *λειτουργῶν* 4 *λειτουργούς* 5 *κα]θεξῆς*: -εξ- ex corr. 6 *λειτουργίας* 7 *προσκαρτερεῖν* corrected into (or from?) *προσοκνεῖν* 8 *ὁ* Pap., *δυναστείᾳ* 9 *ἧττον*: at the inside of the second vertical hasta is an ink blob 11 *συμμάχους*: 2nd upsilon

drawn 2x, μοι: -ο- corr. ex -ε- 12 συνκόψαντες: -ες ex -αις- corr., l. συγκόψαντες, λειτουργόν 15 εἶναι: ny ex eta? μεταχεϊρiζεται Pap. 16]μενος: -ος ex -ους corr. 17 ἀδελφοῦ: -φ- ex corr. 18 καὶ: κ- ex corr. (ex μ?) or drawn 2x 20 ἐφυγάδευσεν 22 τὸν νῦν ἔχοντα τὰ ῥόπαλα (-α- in ῥόπαλ- ex corr., from η?) 23 ἀπέλαβεν: -εν ex -ον corr. τροδα: -δ- ex τ or vice versa 26 αὐτὸν: the ending -τον was added afterward 27 (and 30) Αὐγούστου 29 στατιωναρίῳ 31 κώμαρχος

"To Flavius Faustinus *vir perfectissimus*, *praeses*, from Aurelius Gena son of Ouonsis, comarch of the village of Kellis in the Mothite nome. Appointed by lot, my lord, as comarch of our village, together with the other liturgists in the presence of the vice-*exactor* and all the other officials according to custom I made all the liturgists declare their status to the office of the strategus according to custom, and each one of us was appointed by lot to his liturgy consecutively, but I had to go after only a certain fellow named Taa, appointed by lot together with us ..., who is a an employee of the ex-magistrate Harpokration, in order that he, too, would stick to the public service together with our fellow-liturgists. But he, confident in the influence of the said Harpokration (which is considerable at the local level) despised my modest circumstances. And when he was held by me and my colleague Gena, the other comarch, the aforementioned Harpokration with great display of tyrannous conduct put some local assistants of his own armed with clubs in my way; they attacked me as if in open war, striking me with deadly blows, and drew the public liturgist away from us and they hit my left eye and my side. Now, while I am still on the verge of death, I have come to sending in this written complaint in order that I shall not die before the avenging takes place and my death goes unpunished. For Timotheos, his boy, also has a hand every time in ... the brutality -- he has planned (?) -- our pigs while squandering freely -- and stealing (?) the wine -- taking away the pig of my brother, as also convicted by Psais son of Pateminis and Psekes son of Psennouphis. And even all these things were not enough for him, i.e. the theft (?) of the pig, but he robbed in public my poor brother of his clothing and chased him away to Egypt --- and forcing his way into my house he stole the wine which I had brought away from his home in public and for corroboration and proof of the violence done to me I mention Pebos son of Tithoes, the ..., who now has the clubs (?) at his home which he took from the assistants whose names (are): Troda, Psenpnouthes, Porphyrios, Theotimos, Leon, Sap..s, Korax, N.N., Pachoumis, N.N. son of Labouates (?), and witness of the assault were Horion the son of Tithoes the ..., and witnesses a daughter of Gena son of Pakysis and Sarapodoros son of Eros. Therefore I send in this document to Hermogenes the deputy of the *exactor*, asking and conjuring him by the divine genius of our Lords the all-victorious *Augustus* and *Caesar* to bring him before our lord N.N in whom I now take refuge begging for retribution for the evil deeds I have suffered and a copy of this petition I have given to Ammonios, the *stationarius* of the countryside. In the consulate of our Lords Constantius *Augustus* consul for the 6th time and of Constantius *nobilissimus Caesar* consul for the 2nd time. I, the aforementioned Aurelius Gena son of Ouonsis, have put this on public display."

In general, the contents of this petition are clear enough. The petitioner, a comarch from Kellis, lodges a complaint in public (cf. l. 31, *δημοσίᾳ πρὸθηκα*) about an assault made on him and his fellow-comarch by a man who had been selected for liturgical duty but tried to dodge his obligations. During a fight, in which his opponent had been helped by a number of other people in the service of a local potentate, the petitioner himself had suffered badly, wine and pigs had been stolen (l. 17), his colleague had also been molested and even chased away to Egypt (= the Nile valley), in short: the comarch had a lot of reasons to lodge a complaint. The petitioner claims that he has a number of witnesses to back up various details of his story and states that he has sent copies of his complaint to the deputy-*exactor* and to the local *stationarius*. As usual in such petitions, he asks in no unambiguous terms to bring up the culprits and to give him redress of his suffering. As the middle part of the petition is damaged, some details of its wording unfortunately escape us. For another text from Kellis containing a complaint about assault, see **21.**

Especially interesting is the information given in the opening lines (ll. 2ff.) concerning the appointment procedure of liturgical comarchs of Kellis in the middle of the 4th century: they were stil drawn by lot (cf. l. 3, *κληρωθεὶς*) in the presence of a high official (here, the deputy-*exactor*, ll. 3-4) and other civil servants, and after the comarch had been appointed, he took the necessary steps in order that the other liturgists to be appointed would report their status and fortune (cf. l. 5, *τύχη*) to the office of the strategus; apparently the strategus still played some role in the Mothite Nome at this time. For appointment procedures of liturgists in Roman Egypt in general, see N. Lewis, *The Compulsory Public Servies of Roman Egypt* (Firenze 1982) 83ff., esp. 88-89: 'The Late Third and Fourth Centuries'.

1. A *praeses Thebaidos* Flavius Faustinus officiating ca. 353 is not otherwise attested. It seems just possible that he may be identical with the *rationalis Aegypti* Faustinus mentioned by Athanasius in 356, cf. PLRE I 326.
2. Is this Gena son of Ouonsis, also mentioned in **18**.1 (from Structure 4)? Cf. also **24**, ll. 3,]Ọὐώṇσιο[ς], and 8, Γενᾶ.

For the office of comarch, see H.E.L. Missler, *Der Komarch* (Diss. Marburg 1970). We learn from l. 9-10, that Kellis was administrated by two comarchs. Cf. also **21**.6 and the note ad loc.

3-4. For the name of the representative of the *exactor* cf. l. 26, Hermogenes; for the office of *exactor*, see J.D. Thomas, *Strategus and Exactor in Fourth-Century Egypt: a Reappraisal*, forthcoming in CdE (1994).
4. For the expression Οἱ ἐν τέλει cf. F.M.J. Waanders, *The History of* Τέλος *and* Τελέω *in Ancient Greek* (Diss. Amsterdam 1983) 18-19.
5. The word *τύχην* refers to the status or condition of the liturgists, cf. F. Preisigke, *Wörterbuch* s.v. 2 and 3. In practice the comarchs were supposed to inform the office of the provincial strategus of the (free-born) legal status of the liturgists and their *πόρος* (= personal assets).

For the office of the strategus in the 4th century cf. the article by J.D. Thomas referred to supra, l. 3-4n.

6. The word *ὀψωνιαστής* is found to date only in P.Lips. 97 cols. v.13, xii.8 and xiv.1. LSJ offers the translation 'caterer', but F. Preisigke, *Wörterbuch* s.v. translates it with 'Lohnempfänger'.
11. For a comprehensive survey of the role of the *σύμμαχοι* in the papyri cf. A. Jördens in ZPE 66 (1986) 105-118 and 92 (1992) 219-231.

15. Is *παῖς* intended to mean 'child' or 'slave'? On the question cf. in general G. Stanton in Proceedings XVIIIth [1986] International Congress of Papyrology, I (Athens 1988) 463-480. It would seem slightly more attractive to assume that Timotheos is Harpokration's own son rather than a mere slave.

It is not quite clear precisely what Timotheos is accused of doing, but he may have had a hand in driving away pigs belonging to Gena (cf. l. 16, *τοὺς χοίρους ἡμῶν*), so squandering his dowry, and in stealing a pig belonging to his colleague/brother Gena (cf. l. 17, *τὸν χοῖρον τοῦ ἀδελφοῦ μου ὑφειλάμενος*). Furthermore he publicly tore the clothing from Gena's body and chased him away 'to Egypt', i.e. away from the Dakhleh Oasis (cf. **81**.5n.).

As the verb *μεταχειρίζομαι* always governs an accusative, it must be assumed that the dative *τῇ τυραννίᾳ* should be taken with a lost participle like *χρώμενος* (cf. l. 10).

16. LSJ lists the verb *κατασωτεύομαι* = 'squander on profligate living' with only one attestation, Josephus' Bellum Judaicum 4.4.3.

19. At the start of this line a word like *ἀπελασία* may be expected, but the preserved ink traces do not seem to allow this reading. The letter before the ending *-ια* may be either kappa or eta.

20. After Αἴγυπτον one cannot read *ὡσαύτως*.

22, 25: It is unclear what *χηνου* / *χηου* should mean. Is it an Egyptian name or a profession?

23. The name Τρόδα is not listed in the regular onomastica.

25. It is unclear whether the horizontal dash coming out of the lacuna before *θυγάτηρ* could belong to the epsilon of *δέ* (print δ]έ̣?).

26. *αὐτὸν* at the end apparently goes with *ἀνενγκεῖν* at the end of l. 27.

28. In the lacuna after *κυρί[ου* a name (e.g. that of the *exactor*) is expected.

πρὸς ἣν probably refers back to *τὴν ὄψιν* at the start of this line.

29. For the (military) rank of a *stationarius* cf. the remarks in CPR V 12.1n. and the attestations given by S. Daris, *Il lessico Latino nel Greco d' Egitto*[2] (Barcelona 1991) 107.

For the word *χώρα* in an indication of an official's sphere of competence cf. **21**.2n.

30. The consuls are those of 353, cf. R.S. Bagnall a.o., *CLRE*. As more often (cf. **8**.13n. and **48**.16-17n.) the month and a day are not indicated.

24: OFFICIAL DECLARATION TO THE OFFICE OF THE DUX

(352)

P.Kellis inv. P. 59.B+E (House 3, room 3, level 3) + P. 60.A (House 3, room 9, level 4) + P. 81.B (House 3, room 6, level 4). The papyrus consists now of three separate fragments, Fragm. I: H. 10.3 x B. 7.2 cm.; Fragm. II: 8.9 x B. 3.7 cm.; Fr. III: H. 18.3 x B. 20.1 cm. The original dimensions were H. 18.3 x B. ± 31.5 cm. Traces of at least 9 vertical folds are visible; the foldings grow bigger from right to left. The writing runs parallel to the fibers, the back is blank. For organizational purposes fragments of the papyrus were referred to previously as 'P.Kellis 81' and 'P.Kellis 83'.

1 [Τῷ δεῖνι τάξε]ως τοῦ̣ [κυ]ρί̣ο̣υ̣ μου̣ διασημ̣ο̣τάτου δουκὸς
παρὰ τῶν

2 [ἐξῆς ἀπὸ κώμης Κέλλεως τοῦ Μωθ]ίτου νομ[ο]ῦ. Ἐ̣π̣εὶ κα̣τ᾽ ἀπέχθε̣ι̣αν καὶ
κατ᾽ ἔχθ̣ραν Ἁ[τ]ρ̣ῆς

3 [± 24]Ο̣ὐώ̣ν̣σιο[ς] π̣ρ̣ε̣σβυ̣[τ]έρου καθ[ο]λικῆς
ἐκκλησίας ὢν δι`ε´-

4 [± 24] μεν τοῦτο οὐκ ἐγένετο, ὁμολογοῦμεν ὄμνυντες τὸν
5 πα[ντοκράτορα Θεὸν καὶ τὴν ε]ὐσέβειαν τῶν πάντα νικώντων αἰωνίων δεσποτῶν·
6 ἀπ[οστάντες τ]ῆς ἀ[πο]νοίης μη[δ]ὲ ἀκούσαντ[ές] ποτε εἶναι ἐπὶ τῆς ἡμετ[έ]ρας κώμης ἐπ[αγ]γέλ-
7 λομεν ἡμεῖς τὸν [..]ἀσφαλισμὸν πρὸς τὸ μηδεμία[ν ὄ]χλησιν παθεῖν ἀλόγως ὁ προειρημέ-
8 νος Γενᾶ ἐν τῇ εὐμ[εν]ίᾳ τῶν ε[ὐ]τυχεστάτων τούτων καιρῶν.
9 Ὑπατίας τῶν δεσποτ[ῶν] ἡμῶν Κωσταντίου Αὐγούστω τὸ ε̄´ καὶ Κωσταντίου τοῦ ἐπιφανεστάτου
10 Καίσαρος τὸ α/.

11 (M.2) Αὐρήλιοι Παμῖνις πρ[εσβύτ]ερος καὶ Πκουρ[..]ς διάκονος κ[αὶ Χ]ῶλ[ο]ς ἄλ[λο]ς καὶ Ψενπνοῦθης [..]ϊ κ[αὶ] Ψάις Τ[ρ]υφάνους
12 καὶ Τιμόθεος Λούδω[νος] καὶ Λούδων Λ[. Ἔ]γραψα ὑπὲρ αὐτῶν [γρά]μμ[ατ]α μὴ εἰδότων Α[ὐρ]ή[λιος]
13 Σαραπάμμων Ψάιτος ἀ[πὸ τ]ῆς αὐτῆς κώμη[ς. Αὐρηλιοι N.N. κ]αὶ Πεβῶς Τιθοῆτ[ο]ς κ[αὶ]ρίων ἀδελφὸς κα[ὶ N.N.]
14 Τιθοέους καὶ Τιθοῆς ἀ[δελ]φὸς καὶ Γενειλο[ς . .]νος κ[αὶ N.N.] Βησᾶτος Ψάιτος καὶ Ἀμπέλι[ο]ς Ἀκο[υ]τίου. Ἔγραψα ὑπ[ὲ]ρ αὐτῶν
15 [γ]ράμματα μὴ εἰδ[ότων] Αὐρήλιος Πα[μοῦρ]ις Ψάιτος ἀπὸ τῆς αὐτῆς κώμης. Αὐρήλιος Κ[απ]ίτων Κόρακος καὶ Ὧρος
16 [N.N. Ἔγραψεν ὑπὲρ αὐτῶν μὴ εἰδότ]ων γράμμα<τα> Αὐρήλιος Τιμόθεος Τιμοθέου ἀπὸ τῆς αὐτῆς
17 [κώμης. N.N. son of N.N. κ]αὶ Μάρων ἀδελφὸς καὶ Κλώδιος (ὁμοίως) καὶ Ψενοῦφις (ὁμοίως) ὁ καὶ Βῆσας
18 [καὶ N.N. son of N.N. καὶ N.N. καὶ Τι]θοῆς Σπου[.]μ( ) καὶ Πινοῦτα Γενᾶ Χώλου Ταα καὶ Τιθοῆς
19 [son of N.N. καὶ N.N. ὁ καὶ Π]αταιᾶς κα[ὶ] Ψάις ἀδελφὸς καὶ Πεβῶς Καλικλέως. Ἔγραψα ὑπὲρ
20 [αὐτῶν γράμματα μὴ εἰδότων Αὐρήλιος] Σῦρος Βησᾶτος ἀπὸ κώμης Κέλλεως.

Verso (at upper left hand side):

21] τινος ἐπιδεδώκαμεν [
22] Αὐρήλιος Τῖς.

At the lower left bottom of the verso there are traces of 1 or 2 letters.

1 κυρίου, διασημοτάτου: -ου ex -ω corr. 6 ἀπονοίας, ἀκούσαντ[ες]-: ακ- ex corr. 7-8 τὸν προειρημένον 8 εὐμενείᾳ 9 Ὑπατείας, Κωνσταντίου (2x), Αὐγούστου 11 [..]ϊ Pap. 13 ψαῑτος Pap. 14 αμ·πε- Pap. 19 παταϊας Pap., Καλλικλέως

The details of this mutilated declaration sent by a number of inhabitants of the village of Kellis presumably to an official (name lost) employed in the bureau of the provincial *dux* of the Thebaid escape us. At the left hand side in ll. 1-4 ± 24 letters are lost. After the address (ll. 1-2) and a very fragmentarily preserved introduction, in which the reasons for making the declaration are explained (ll. 2-4: apparently because a certain Hatres had acted out of hatred and enmity against one or more fellow-villagers), the subscribers to the document (for their number, see ll. 11-20n.) make a statement confirmed by an imperial oath (ll. 4ff.) that they are staying aloof from the folly (cf. ἀποστάντες τῆς ἀπονοίης, l. 6; apparently due to Hatres' actions, cf. l. 2), that they had never heard about this (?: cf. l. 6n.) and that they send off this act of surety (ἐπαγγέλλομεν τὸν [δι-?]ἀσφαλισμόν, ll. 6-7), in order that a fellow-inhabitant of the village, a certain Gena (l. 8; perhaps the son of Ouonsis, l. 3), who apparently had been bothered by Hatres, will not suffer any further hardship (ll. 7-8, πρὸς τὸ κτλ.).

1. On the military/judicial competence of the *dux Thebaidos* (= the military commander of the whole Thebaid), see J. Lallemand, *L'administration civile de l'Egypte* (Bruxelles 1964) passim; a list of 4th-century *duces* is given by R. Rémondon in CdE 40 (1965) 186f., where the following should be added:
a. P.Oxy. XLV 3261.10 mentions a διασημότατος δοὺξ Βάρβας in Oxyrhynchus, 324;
b. sub 7, Valacius, add now CPR V 10 (337-345) and P. Oxy. LV 3793 (340).
c. For the date of Fl. Eleutherius (385 according to Remondon) cf. now most recently J.R. Rea in ZPE 56 (1984) 86, who argues for 399-400 (the critical remarks re Remondon's dating of the Vienna papyrus made earlier by Bagnall and Worp in BASP 18 [1981] 50 were partly vindicated, partly superseded by Rea's new findings); maybe the predecessors of Fl. Eleutherius mentioned in the Vienna Papyrus, Fl. Pulcher and Fl. Heraclianus, were also *duces*.
For a list of papyrological attestations of the word δούξ cf. S. Daris, *Il lessico Latino nel greco del Egitto*[2] (Barcelona 1991) 41-42.
2. For the restoration of ἑξῆς at the start of this line cf. F. Preisigke, *Wörterbuch* s.v., 2.

For the Mothite nome cf. **41**.4n.

κατ' ἀπέχθειαν καὶ κατ' ἔχθραν: cf. for such a dicolon H. Zilliacus, *Zur Abundanz der spätgriechischen Gebrauchssprache* (Helsingfors 1967) Ch. III, esp. p. 48ff.

A Hatres is mentioned in the Greek Kellis papyri only here.
3. The name Οὐῶνσις (= 'Wolf', as Mr. O. Kaper reminds me; cf. G. Wagner, *Les Oases d'Egypte*, 241) is connected as a father's name with the name Γενᾶ in **23**.2 (353), where a Γενᾶ Οὐώνσιος is a komarch of Kellis (for the same combination of names cf. also **18**.1). In fact, in ll. 7-8 below reference is made to the προειρημέ-/νος Γενᾶ, so that person must have been mentioned earlier in the text. Even so, it might seem a bit rash on that basis to restore the name of Γενᾶ here in the lacuna at the start of the line.

A 'priest of the catholic church' also occurs in **58**.8 (337); cf. also **48**.20n. (355) and **32**.21. (364); below in l. 11 the word πρεσβύτερος is not followed by ἐκκλησίας καθολικῆς (for the meaning of this term see now E. Wipszycka, ΚΑΘΟΛΙΚΗ *et les autres Épithètes du nom* ΕΚΚΛΗΣΙΑ, JJP 24 (1994) 191-212. It is unclear whether this function of 'priest' goes here directly with Οὐώνσιο[ς, or with a [lost] preceding name.

ὤν may be taken to be a participle of εἰμί going with Ἀ[τ]ρῆς (l. 2), but it is conceivable that one should accentuate ὧν and take this as the gen.pl. of the relative pronoun. δι`ε´- at the end could form part of a historical tense of a verb.
4-5. For the (not previously attested) oath formula found here cf. in general the list of formulas given in ZPE 45 (1982) 199ff. The earliest invocations of the παντοκράτωρ Θεός known to date are from the

joint reign of the emperors Honorius and Theodosius II (408-423), but cf. the incompletely preserved oath formula in PSI VIII 951.10 (388?) where Θεὸν παντοκράτορα *vel sim.* may already be restored at the start.

5-6. Due to the mutilation of the text its grammatical construction is not quite clear. After ὁμολογοῦμεν ὄμνυντες - δεσποτῶν (l. 4-5) one would expect in l. 6 one or more infinitives (the first of which should govern the genitive ἀ[πο]νοίης), but clearly there is none. Therefore it must be assumed that immediately after the first main clause ὁμολογοῦμεν ὄμνυντες another main clause 'ἀποστάντες ...... μηδὲ ἀκούσαντές ... ἐπαγγέλλομεν' follows, cf. the construction in P.Char. 26.3: ὁμολογῶ· οἱ γεωργοὶ ἐσοῦ οὐ δεδώκασιν, κτλ.

7. Neither the word ἀσφαλισμός nor a compound like [δι]ασφαλισμός is listed in any dictionary, but cf. ἀσφάλισμα = 'surety, pledge'. The purpose of the pledge is to make certain that Gena will not be bothered without good reason (ἀλόγως).

8. The phrasing ἐν τῇ εὐμ[εν]ίᾳ τῶν ε[ὐ]τυχεστάτων τούτων καιρῶν is a rather solemn reference to the current reign of the emperor Constantius II Augustus and Constantius Gallus Caesar; for a much similar phrasing cf. PSI VII 767.32.

9. For the consuls of 352 cf. R.S. Bagnall a.o., *CLRE* s.a. Once again an indication of the month and the day is lacking; for this phenomenon cf. **8**.13n. and **48**.16-17n.

11-20. We find here a listing of a considerable number of male inhabitants of Kellis, led by a priest and 2 deacons, who by their subscription pledge that the preceding statement is correct. Altogether at least 33 persons seem to have subscribed; they are grouped in four clusters and it is at least conceivable that this list contains a more or less complete listing of all family heads (or even of all male inhabitants?) of the village at the time of drawing up this document; the situation in this text reminds us of a vaguely similar situation in P.Haun. III 58 from 439, cf. R.S. Bagnall, *Egypt in Late Antiquity*, [Princeton 1993] 138; see, however, J.R. Rea in ZPE 99 [1993] 89-95 for a new interpretation of that text. The clusters are to be distinguished as follows:

ll. 11-13: 1 priest (Aurelius Paminis), 2 deacons (Pkoureus [?] and Cholos) and at least 4 private persons (Psenpnouthes son of N.N.; Psais, son of [?] Tryphanes [cf. **71**.39-40n.]; Timotheos son of Loudon; Loudon, son of N.N.) followed by the name of the person who subscribed for them, viz. Aurelius Sarapammon son of Psais.

ll. 13-15: 8 persons (Aurelius N.N.; Pebos son of Tithoes [cf. **23**.22 from 353, **42**.37 from 364 and **44**.23-24 from 382]; N.N. his brother; N.N. son of Tithoes; Tithoes his brother; Geneilos son of N.N.; N.N. son of Besas son of Psais; Ampelius son of Akoutis) followed by the name of the person who subscribed for them, viz. Aurelius Pamouris (III), son of Psais (II; for him, see the family tree at p. 51).

ll. 15-16: probably 2 persons, Aur. Kapiton son of Korax and Horos son of N.N., followed by the name of the person who subscribed for them, viz. Aurelius Timotheos son of Timotheos.

ll. 17-20: apparently at least 12 persons (N.N. son of N.N.; Maron his brother; Klodios son of Klodios (?); Psenouphis son of Psenouphis (?), alias Besas; N.N. son of N.N.; N.N. son of N.N.; Tithoes son of Spou...; Pinoutas son of Gena [cf. **3**.9. mid-IV]] son of (?) Cholos son of Taa; Tithoes son of N.N.; N.N. alias [?] Pataias; Psais his brother; Pebos, son of Kallikles), followed by the name of the person who subscribed for them, viz. Aurelius Syros son of Besas.

11. Χῶλος is a regular personal name in the papyri, occurring among the Kellis papyri also in **65**.41; ἄλλος refers to the office of διάκονος going with his colleague whose name may be restored perhaps as Πκουρ[εύ]ς (= 'the barber', i.e. formed from the Egyptian prefix Π- + κουρεύς; for the formation of such names cf. BASP 27 [1990)]109).

12. The name Λούδων is not attested in the regular papyrological onomastica. It is certainly possible that his father's name was also Λούδων.

14. A name Γενειλος is not attested in the regular papyrological onomastica

17. Following the names Κλώδιος and Ψενοῦφις a sinusoidal curve crossed by a diagonal rising dash has been written; it bears some resemblance to the symbol for (ὑπέρ) found in texts from late-Byzantine Egypt. As, however, it does not make sense taking the symbol as standing for (ὑπέρ) and as most names in the list of subscribers are followed by their patronymic, we have resolved it as (ὁμοίως), Κλώδιος

(ὁμοίως) being the equivalent of 'Κλώδιος Κλωδίου', i.e. 'Klodios son of Klodios'. A variant attempt to interpret it might be 'likewise as Maron', i.e. 'also a brother'. Maybe, however, one is dealing here with a variant manifestation of the symbol for (αὐτός) found frequently in 4th-century papyri from the Hermopolite nome (though one would at least expect, then, an article <τοῦ> preceding (αὐτοῦ)).

Under all circumstances the alias name following Ψενοῦφις, viz. ὁ καὶ Βῆσας, is 'mal-placé', as one would expect it immediately after Ψενοῦφις, i.e. without the sinusoidal curve + diagonal rising dash intervening. In general it should be noticed that alias names in documents from Kellis are not frequent.

18. Πινοῦτα Γενᾶ Χώλου Ταα: is Πινοῦτα a variant form of Πινούθης (a son of a certain Gena in **3**.9 [also from the mid-IVth century])? It is not clear what is intended after Γενᾶ; earlier in this list of subscriptions one finds a person's name followed by a profession/title or a patronymic, but here one might have as many as four (!) generations enumerated: 'Pinoutas son of Gena, grandson of Cholos, great grandson of Taa'; it is, however, also possible to accentuate χωλοῦ and interpret: 'Pinoutas son of Gena the lame, grandson of Taa'; even so, it is already exceptional to find a grandfather's name listed.

19. We have taken Π]αταιᾶς as an alias name (cf. 17n.), i.e. restored ὁ καὶ Π]αταιᾶς, rather than as an undeclined patronymic.

25: ADDRESS OF AN OFFICIAL DOCUMENT

(4th century)

P.Kellis inv. P. 17.N (House 3, Room 10, level 3). H. 4 x B. 11.2 cm. Written across the fibers; the other side of the papyrus is blank. In the same frame are 3 small fragments which seem to belong to the same papyrus, but their exact placing vis-à-vis the opening lines cannot be established and they do not seem to contain any interesting words or names, hence they are not published here.

1 [Α]ὐρηλίοις Κλεοβο[ύλ]ῳ λογιστῇ Ὀάσεω ς̣
2 [Με]γάλης καὶ Φιλοσ̣α̣ρά[πι]δι τῷ καὶ Μικκάλῳ̣
3 [ἄρ]ξαντι προέδρῳ Μω[θι]τῶν πόλεως κ̣α̣ὶ
4 [᾿Αν̇]δρομάχῳ ᾿Απόλλ̣ω̣ν[ο]ς ἄρξ(αντι) συνδίκ̣ο[ις]
5 Traces [ ] Traces [ ]
- -

"To the Aurelii Kleoboulos, *logistes* of the Great Oasis, and Philosarapis alias Mikkalos, former magistrate and president (of the town council) of the city of the Mothites, and Andromachos son of Apollon, former magistrate, syndics ---".

In itself this fragment does not contain more than the opening lines of a document with a mention of its addressees. Still, as the addressees are high-ranking officials, i.e. the *logistes* (= an imperial official) of the Great Oasis and the president of the town coun-cil of Mothis, the fragment has some interest of its own. The date of this document is problematic; on the one hand one might be tempted by prosopographical considerations (cf. l. 1n.) to assign it to the second half of the 4th century, but palaeographical considerations seem to militate against that, as the handwriting (a small, very regular cursive, slightly tilted towards the right) seems to point rather in the direction of the early first half of the 4th century. Also the apparent occurrence of two syndics (cf. l. 4n.) points in that direction.

1. The name Aurelius Kleoboulos (one more instance of these classical Greek names frequently attested in the Great Oasis, cf. G. Wagner, *Les Oasis d'Egypte* 224ff.) reminds us of a homonymous person mentioned a few times in documents from the Great Oasis, cf. P.Lips. 36 (= M.Chrest. 77).2, 64 (= W.Chrest. 281).58 and P.Lips.inv. 348 = M.Chrest. 78.2 (376-78); in these texts he is referred to as a *πολιτευόμενος Ὀάσεως μεγάλης /[Ἰβιτ]ῶν πόλεως*. Is he perhaps the same man as in our document and should one restore [Μωθιτ]ῶν πόλεως in M.Chrest. 78.2? For a *γεοῦχος* Κλεόβουλος in the Hibite nome living some time during the second half of the 4th century, see O.Douch III 339 and O.Ain Waqfa 31-36, 38, 43, 46, 47 and 70.

For the office of *logistes* (first attested in Egypt in 303) cf. B.R. Rees in JJP 7-8 (1954) 83-105; for lists of known *logistae* cf. P.Oxy. LIV pp. 222-229 and Pap.Flor. XIX.2 (1990) 518ff.

2-3. Philosarapis alias Mikkalos is the first president of the town council of Mothis known to us. For the role of the president of a town council in Roman Egypt in general cf. A.K. Bowman, *The Town Councils of Roman Egypt* (Toronto 1971) Ch. III.

3. For municipal syndics (a plurality of these officials is still attested in 326) cf. B. Kramer in Pap.Flor. XIX.1 (1990) 305-329. No syndics for Mothis (Mut) were known before. In itself it is an interesting question, whether (a) all three persons were syndics of Mothis, or (b) only the latter two of them, or whether (c) there was only one syndic (read in l. 4: *συνδίκ̣ῳ̣*). Before 326 a city in the Nile Valley regularly had 2 syndics (cf. Kramer, 307; cf. also **21**.2n.), and it is not normal, perhaps even impossible, for a *logistes* to be a syndic simultaneously (in Oxyrhynchus one finds a few syndics who had been *logistae* previously, cf. the careers of Fl. Julianus and Fl. Hermias). At the same time, however, one would expect, then, that the text would have said more clearly that only the latter two persons in the address were addressed as syndics by inserting the word *ἀμφοτέροις* before *συνδίκο[ις]*; though in P.Oxy. XXXIII 2673 the document is addressed to (a) the president of the town council and (b) to two syndics, it is unclear whether both offices could not be held by one person simultaneously (cf. P.Oxy. XLIV 3186 introd. for the conjunction of the offices of syndic and designate-prytane). On the other hand, the reading *συνδίκο[ις]* seems slightly preferable to a singular *συνδίκ̣ῳ̣*.

26: REPORT OF JUDICIAL PROCEEDINGS

(Ca. 389)

P.Kellis inv. P. 78.D (House 3, room 6, level 3) + P. 90.A (House 3, room 6, level 4, West wall) + P. 92.35.G (House 3, room 11, level 4) + P. 93.B+D (House 3, room 6, level 4). The papyrus consists now of 2 complexes of fragments; Fragm. I: H. 8 x B. 15 cm.; writing parallel to the fibers, verso blank. Fragm. II: H. 4.5 x B. 6.7 cm. + H. 13.3 x B. 9.5 cm.; writing parallel to the fibers, verso blank. The exact relationship of each fragment to the other is uncertain, but the second hand of Fragm. II seems to be identical with the hand which wrote the Greek lines of Fragm. I.

Fragm. I: -

1]. . Septimius Euṭṛ[o]pi[u]ṣ [v(ir)] c(larissimus) pres(es) Theba(idos) ei ḍ(ịx̣ịṭ)· ἡ συνε̣ Traces

2 (M.2)]αδδ( ) ἔσισεν συνεργοὺς ἔχων· [τ]ε̣τ̣ακται ἐν τοῖς π̣ρ̣ο̣τ̣έρ̣ο̣ι̣[ς

3]. . Septimius Eutropius ṿ(ir) c(larissimus) pres(es) Tḥ[eba(idos) ei d(ixit)] Traces[

4 (M.2)] πρὸς αὐτὸν κατέλαβεν στρατιώτ[ης

5]. Septimius Eutropius v(ir) c(larissimus) pres(es) Theba(idos) ei ḍ(ixit)[

6 (M.2)] εἰς λόγον δίκης δ̣ε̣δώκαμεν ἀλλ̣[

7]. Septimius Eutropius [v(ir) c(larissimus) pres(es) Theba(idos) ei d(ixit)

8] Traces [

- -

1, 3, 5, 7 praes(es) 2 ἔσεισεν

Fr. II: -

1 (M.1)]Latin

2 (M.2) ο]υ ὁ τοῦ παιδίου τούτου πατὴρ̣[

3]ε[.]τ̣ος ἐμβέβληται .[

4]νειν εἰ μὴ οἱ σε οἰκ[

5]β̣ληθῆναι V A C A T

6 Στρα]τήγιός τις καὶ ἑτερ̣[

7]τ̣η̣ Στρατηγιο.[

8 (M.3)]τοὺς προστυγχάνον[τας

9]ε̣[α]υτὸν κακῶς ἀπῆλ̣[θεν] ἕνεκεν προφάσεως[

10 (M.2)].νθεισι. ὁ δὲ συναγορευόμε̣ν̣[ος -] π̣α̣ρ̣ε̣[σ]κ̣ε̣ύ̣[α]σεν αὐτὸν ὅλα τριάκοντ[α

11 (M.3)]βοηθὸς ἐν τοῖς .[ ].ης καταβ̣λ̣ηθεν̣τ̣[

12] Traces [ ] Traces [

- -

11 καταβληθεντ[corr. (ex καταβληθεῖσαι ?)

The precise contents of these tantalizing fragments of what looks like a bilingual report of court proceedings (esp. as regards Fragm. I) cannot be reconstructed; for such reports, see the discussion and list in P.Oxy. LI p. 46-47[17]. Nevertheless, the papyrus is of extra interest, as to date it is the latest approximately datable papyrus from Kellis (cf. l. 1n.).

Fragm. I:

1. Septimius Eutropius was *praeses* of the Thebaid on 26.xii.389, cf. J. Lallemand, *L'administration civile*, p. 254 # 18. His predecessor, Fl. Eutolmius Arsenius, is known in office on 14.vi.388, while his

[17]) In the unpublished P.Kellis inv. A/1/77 and A/2/98 other remains of bilingual Greek-Latin texts are preserved, but we cannot find any links between these texts and the text published above.

successor Fl. Asclepiades Hesychius had already come into office before 20.x.390. The term of office of Eutropius was, therefore, restricted to ± 2 years. We owe the reading of 'Theba(idos) ei d(ixit)' to J.D. Thomas who referred us for this (instead of reading 'Thebaeid(os)' as one word) and for the use of Greek in the governor's speech to remarks made by J.R. Rea in ZPE 41 (1981) 282. In fact, there is no clear sign of abbreviation visible on the papyrus after 'Theba' and a spelling -eid- for -id- should be no reason for great consternation. Nevertheless, it seems preferable to follow the suggestion made by Rea, *loc.cit.*

At the end of this line read perhaps *συνε̣τ̣ω̣σ̣ε̣ ̣[*

2. We have not been able to devise a convincing resolution of the word ending on *αδδ(*); moreover, though in general the papyrus seems to present an alternation of lines in Greek and in Latin, it does not seem excluded that after all one should read Latin here, i.e. print:]add( ). Maybe one should resolve, then, the abbreviation as add(ixit). The use of the verb *σείω* (= 'to blackmail' cf. LSJ s.v. I.4) suggests that this line is part of an accusation brought against a defendant. The reading of the last word on this line, *π̣ρ̣ο̣τέρ̣ο̣ι̣ς*, especially its ending, is highly dubious.

4. Perhaps a soldier came to a person (for the meaning of the verb *καταλαμβάνω* cf. **68**.23n.); did he do so in order to fetch the defendant in this process?

Fragm. II:

1. The reading of the Latin is difficult. J. Kramer (Trier/Siegen) proposes (by letter from 8.v.1994) with reservations: ']̣ iustitia cu['.

4. Or should we read *οἷς ἐοικ*[?

5. Cf. l. 11n.: restore here *κατα]βληθῆναι* (cf. l. 11) or *ἐμ]βληθῆναι* cf. ll. 3, 5.

6-7. A Strategius occurs also in the private letter **75**.3, 34-35. Is there a connection between these homonymous persons?

10. *ὁ συναγορευόμενος* indicates the client of an advocate, cf. LSJ s.v. *συναγορεύω*.

For the construction of *παρασκευάζω* cf. P.Vindob.Worp 13.17-19n. Should one restore at the end of the line a word like *νομισμάτια* and speculate that the issue of litigation was about a full payment of 30 *solidi*?

11. Some form of the partic.Aor.Pass. of *καταβάλλω* = 'to pay' seems intended here; cf. also l. 5.

27: OFFICIAL DOCUMENT

(4th century)

P.Kellis inv. P. 97 [from P. 90.B + (House 3, room 6, level 4, West wall) + P. 92.A+B (House 3, room 6, level 4, South wall) + P. 92.14 (House 3, room 1a, level 1) + P. 92.18 (House 3, room 1a, level 2)]. H. 26.5 x B 34.5 cm. Margins: at the top (reckoned from line 2 upward) 3.5, at the right 7, at the bottom 7 cm. Folded vertically at least 10 times (left hand edge, where papyrus is broken on a fold, included). The space between each fold was approximately 3.5 cm. wide. Sheet joins: 13 cm. from the left hand edge and on the right hand edge. Verso blank.

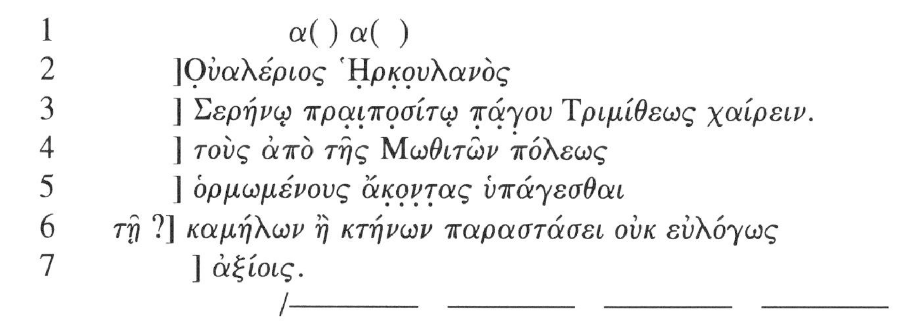

1 α( ) α( )
2]Ο̣ὐαλέριος Ἡ̣ρκο̣υλανὸς
3] Σερήνῳ πρα̣ι̣πο̣σίτῳ π̣άγου Τριμίθεως χαίρειν.
4] τοὺς ἀπὸ τῆς Μωθιτῶν πόλεως
5] ὁρμωμένους ἄκ̣ο̣ν̣τας ὑπάγεσθαι
6 τῇ ?] καμήλων ἢ κτήνων παραστάσει οὐκ εὐλόγως
7] ἀξίοις.
/———— ———— ———— ————

"--. Valerius Herculanus to -- Serenus, *praepositus pagi* of Trimithis, greetings. --- the people from the city of the Mothites, unwilling (?) to appear at the production of camels or small cattle without good reason, -- with fitting ---."

Unfortunately this document, written in surprisingly large handwriting on an impressively large sheet of papyrus and almost certainly emanating from a high level in the provincial administration of the Thebaid (the taxpayer would have to pay for whatever amount of papyrus the government used!), is preserved only incompletely. It raises various problems:

(a) Its exact date cannot be established. The use, however, of the gentilicium Valerius (l. 2) may lead one towards supposing that the papyrus was written before or at least not much later than 324 (cf. for this particular year's significance re nomenclature J.G. Keenan in ZPE 11 [1973] 46); for a possible connection with a governor of the Thebaid in 309 cf. below, l. 2n.

(b) The text seems to come from the office of governor of the Thebaid, especially in view of the size of the papyrus sheet (for a recent discussion of papyri issued by provincial governors and their sheet sizes cf. P.Oxy. L 3577 introd.). The text has been written by a trained scribe who wrote an experienced cursive handwriting; the text, however, is not written in the style of writing known as the 'chancery hand' (cf. **1** introd.). It should be observed that, though there is sufficient space in the bottom margin of our document, a personal signature by Valerius Herculanus (like, e.g., the *ἐρρῶσθαί σε εὔχομαι*-formula added by the prefect Subatianus Aquila in the famous text SB I 4639 or the *ἔρρωσθε* of the *praeses* Ausonius in P.Oxy. L 3577.8; for him, see R.S. Bagnall in Tyche 7 [1992] 9ff., esp. 11) is missing here. One might assume, therefore, that Valerius Herculanus, who clearly was Serenus' superior, wrote the whole of the text by himself, but this idea is not easily reconciled with the idea of an order issued by a provincial governor or by, e.g., his chief-of-staff (cf. below).

(c) An important question, furthermore, concerns the amount of papyrus lost at the left. Before each line there was probably some amount of blank margin (not necessarily a margin as generously wide as the margin at the right) and as part of the initial omikron of Ọὐαλέριος in l. 2 is lost in the lacuna at the left, it may be inferred that at least one strip of papyrus between the original left hand edge of the papyrus sheet and a first fold [= now the left hand edge] is lost; hence it may be inferred that an element like Αὐρήλιος or Φλ(άουιος), perhaps written out in full, preceded in this line. Similarly, some (abbreviated?) name may have preceded in l. 3 (cf. the note ad loc.). Furthermore, it should be noticed that in l. 6 one expects at least the article *τῇ* with *παραστάσει*. On the other hand, however, there is no loss of text expected between *τοὺς ἀπὸ τῆς* Μωθιτῶν *πόλεως* (l. 4) and *ὁρμωμένους* (l. 5). Under all circumstances, furthermore, a verb governing the accusative *τοὺς* ... *ὁρμωμένους* is needed and though we have tried to devise a construction based on the assumption, that one should read *ἀξιοῖς* and take this as the 2nd ps.sing.praes.ind./subj. of *ἀξιόω*, on balance such an approach does not seem is really successful (cf. below, l. 7n.; for one thing, one would expect an aorist rather than a praesens; furthermore, one would rather expect the verb *καταξιόω*, but the amount of uninscribed papyrus before *αξιοις* suggests that this was not part of a compound).

On the basis of these considerations only a very tentative reconstruction of the general line of the document's content can be ventured: a sender Valerius Herculanus seems to request an addressee Serenus (for his function cf. l. 3n.) to do something with an unspecified number of inhabitants of the city of the Mothites (ll. 4-5, *τοὺς ἀπὸ τῆς Μωθιτῶν πόλεως ... ὁρμωμένους*), who had been unwilling (l. 5, *ἄκọṇṭας*) to appear at an occasion at which camels or other animals (like goats and sheep) were to be produced (ll. 5-6, *ὑπάγεσθαι* [*τῇ* ?] *καμήλων ἢ κτήνων παραστάσει*), while having no good reason to do so (l. 6, *οὐκ εὐλόγως*). Maybe Serenus was ordered to go after them with a fitting punishment (cf. l. 7, *ἀξίοις*)?. At any rate, the form of the document is different from that found in 4th-century orders for arrest (cf. ZPE 84 [1990] 207-210); at best it vaguely reminds of SB XIV 11975, a document concerning an order issued by a *centurio ordinatus/princeps* of the praefectural staff of the governor of the Thebaid to send up certain persons who are referred to nominatim.

Finally, it remains mysterious how this document (which was probably sent to Trimithis!) arrived at Ismant-el-Kharab. Did Serenus retire to Kellis and did he take the document with him?

1. The abbreviation *α*( ) *α*( ) seems to be unknown. If the large sheet and the sizable handwriting should be interpretated as indications that the text were to be displayed in public (cf l. 7n.), it may be proposed that perhaps one is dealing here with an *ἀ(ντίγραφον) ἀ(ντιγράφων)*, i.e. a new copy of Herculanus' letter made from other copies made earlier, but this interpretation seems rather dull. We have also considered resolving *ἀ(ντίγραφον) α(ὐθεντικόν)*, but this seems problematic as these words seem to be conflicting with each other qua meaning (cf. F. Preisigke, *Wörterbuch*, s.v. *αὐθεντικός*, 2).

2. A Valerius Herculanus does not appear to have occurred earlier; he clearly was his correspondent's superior-in-rank. *If* the name of the *praeses Thebaidos* -]lanus in the unpublished Kellis papyrus inv. P. 17.A.1 (adressed to him by Aurelius Pamour, son of Psais and dated: Ὑπατείας τ]ῶν δεσ̣[ποτ]ῶν ἡμῶν Λι[κι]ννιανοῦ̣ / [Λικιννίου σε]βαστου̣ κ̣[αὶ Φ]λαουίου Οὐαλ[ε]ρίου / [Κωνσταν]τ̣ί̣ν̣[ου υἱ]οῦ Αὐγούστων τὸ ι/ [sic!; cf. 'Diocletianus pater Augg. cos. X' in the consular formula for 308]) were to be expanded into Hercu]lanus, it would follow that Herculanus was the governor of the Thebaid in 309. On the basis, however, of SB XIV 11975 referred to above (not a complete parallel, but at least a comparable text), one might also infer that in our text Valerius Herculanus was also a *princeps*.

3. Should one restore in the lacuna at the left Αὐρηλίῳ, Οὐαλερίῳ̣ or Φλαουίῳ̣ (on these names as status designations cf. J.G. Keenan in ZPE 11 [1973] 33ff. and 13 [1974] 283ff.)? If Serenus were a military person, and if the document had been written after 324 (but cf. l. 2n.), the name Flavius would seem most likely.

The reading of the word after *πρα̣ι̣π̣ο̣σίτῳ* is not quite certain. We have adopted the reading *π̣ά̣γου*, rather than *τ̣ό̣π̣ου*, and it is excluded, then, that we are dealing with the military commander (*praefectus*) of the military unit stationed at Trimithis (for this place cf. S. Timm, *Das Christlich-koptische Ägypten* VI 2846), i.e. the Ala I Quadorum (cf. Not.Dign., Or. XXXI 56)[18]. Even so, one

[18]) In itself a reading *τ̣ό̣π̣ου* cannot be ruled out with certainty; though a *πραιπόσιτος τόπου* = a *praefectus* in charge of a village seems to be unattested, the career of Fl. Abinnaeus (*praefectus* of the military camp at Dionysias, who also exercised a variety of duties on the civilian level) may be compared. The indication, however, of a military camp by the Greek word *τόπος* seems unparalleled and on balance the reading *π̣ά̣γου* looks slightly better.

may still wonder what the function '*praepositus pagi*' with the following genitive Τριμίθεως means precisely; are *pagi* in the Dakhleh Oasis named after the central village of the *pagus*, while elsewhere in Egypt they are usually numbered (for a named pagus in the Nile valley see P.Oxy. XLVI 3307.1)?
5. The reading of ἄκ̣ο̣ν̣τας is not very convincing (read instead ἀβ. .τ̣ας?), but we see no good alternative.
6. The precise purpose of the presentation of camels and small cattle referred to here is not indicated, but one may reckon with, e.g., requisitions for the military or an inspection tour of the provincial governor (cf. N. Lewis, *Life in Egypt under Roman Rule* 176).
7. For ἀξίοις cf. above. This cannot be taken as (part of) the optative form of the verb ἀξιόω / καταξιόω (in general cf. B.G. Mandilaras, *The Verb in the Greek Non-Literary Papyri* [Athens 1973], p. 270ff., esp. § 620), especially not as the more regular formula of request found in Byzantine documents uses the subjunctive καταξιώσῃ(ς) or the imperative καταξίωσον, cf. H.A. Steen, *Les clichés épistolaires dans les lettres sur papyrus grecques* (Classica & Mediaevalia 1 [1938] 119-176, esp. 146). Though the following interpretation (put forward by R.P. Salomons) has the merit of being extremely ingenious, we do not really think that one should interpret the text on the basis of a construction: οὐκ εὐλόγως ἀξιοῖς τοὺς ἀπὸ τῆς Μωθιτῶν πόλεως -- ὁρμωμένους ἄκ̣ο̣ν̣τ̣ας ὑπάγεσθαι τῇ καμήλων ἢ κτήνων παραστάσει, i.e. 'you require without good reason that the people coming from the city of the Mothites be made subject against their will to (appearing at) a presentation of camels and small cattle', and that we should combine this translation with a notion that such a message was to be displayed in public as a matter of public record.

28: ADMINISTRATIVE ACCOUNT

(3rd century ?)

P.Kellis inv. P. 31 (House 3, room 3, level 1) + P. 52.C (House 3, room 9, level 3). H. 7.8 x B. 9.5 cm. Margin at the top 1.5, at the left 1 cm. The writing on the front runs parallel with the fibers, on the back across these.

- - - - - - - - - - - - - - - - - - - -

1] πόλεως vacat [
2] κωμητῶν (δραχμ.)[
3 γί(νονται) αἱ προει(ρημέναι), ὧν
4 προσόδου· Θέων (δραχμὰς) ιε χδ πρ(ὸς) .[
5 Μεσοβή, κωμητ̣ῶν (δραχμὰς) ʼ.σμγ (πεντώβολον) (ἡμιωβέλιον)

- -

Verso:
6 ʼΑμούν(εως)
7 Traces

In itself this fragmentarily preserved papyrus does not yield much information. Obviously one is dealing with some kind of account listing amounts of drachmae paid (as tax?) on various categories of land (?; cf. l. 4 n.) occasionally owned perhaps by villagers (cf. κωμητῶν in ll. 2 and 5). Μεσοβή in l. 5 is the name of a geographical district, in which land owned by villagers was situated for which an amount of several thousands of drachmas + 243 drachmas + 5.5 obols was paid.

1. Probably a reference to the nome metropolis, i.e. *ἡ Μωθιτῶν πόλεως*.
2 (and 5). For the term *κωμητῶν* = 'villagers' (not common in papyri and ostraka generally) cf. the remarks by H.C. Youtie, *Scriptiunculae*, II (Amsterdam 1973), 921, 924 and by H. Cadell in Ktema 12 (1987) 19ff., esp.23-24.
3. For the expression *αἱ προειρημέναι* / *προκείμεναι* in accounting practice (closing off an account, after the total has already been given at the beginning) cf. H.C. Youtie, *Scriptiunculae* I 54, II 817, 819, 837 n.72.
4. For *προσόδου* (sc. *γῆ*) as a kind of domain land cf. S.L. Wallace, *Taxation in Egypt* 3-5; the general meaning of the word is, of course, 'revenue'.

We take *θεων* to stand for the personal name Θέων (who paid, then, 15 dr. and 4 chalkoi [=0.5 obol]; it is remarkable that in l. 5 the symbol for *ἡμιωβέλιον* is used), rather than for the genitive plural *θεῶν*, as an interpretation of *προσόδου* (sc. *γῆ*) *θεῶν* as '*prosodos*-land (in the hands) of the gods' seems unlikely (for this category of land, comparable to domain land, but leased at an extra high rental see S.L. Wallace, *Taxation in Roman Egypt from Augustus to Diocletian* [Princeton 1938] 3ff.). 'For revenue of the gods' would make, perhaps, better acceptable sense, but given the general impression of the fragment as preserved it looks somewhat doubtful whether this was ever intended.

The use of drachmae, obols and chalkoi (which strongly suggest a date to ca. the mid-3rd century or even earlier; obols occur as late as the the date of the archive of Heroninus [ca. 250-270], see D. Rathbone, *Economic Rationalism and Rural Society in Third-Century A.D. Egypt* [Cambridge 1991], passim; it remains to be seen whether the editor's date of O.Mich. II 753.2 [Late III/early IV] is correct) and the palaeographical characteristics of the handwriting (which also suggest a 3rd-century date) make this papyrus stand out in opposition to most of the papyri from House 3 which are dated to the 4th century; cf. also the relatively small amounts of drachmae mentioned in the wooden board **62** and the remark made in **66**.19-20n.
5. The geographical name Μεσοβῆ is not listed in A. Calderini - S. Daris, *Dizionario Geografico*, but it occurs in other documents from Kellis (cf., e.g., the [still unpublished] ostrakon O.Kellis ^{31}/420 D.6-1/D/1/142 [294/5] as the name of a toparchy and in P.Kellis inv. P.93.60+71.^{verso} [still unpublished]) as the name of a *μερ*( ), an abbreviation which may be resolved into *μέρ(ος)* or *μερ(ίς)*; for the meaning of the latter term one may compare the division of the Fayum into 3 *μερίδες*. It remains to be seen whether in the Dakhleh Oasis the term *μερ*( ) has a fiscal meaning, like the *μερίδες* occurring in documents from the Hermopolite nome (for these cf. ZPE 97 [1993] 119-121).
6. We do not know whether Ἀμούν(εως) should be taken here as a personal or as a geographical name.

29: RECEIPT FOR THE COST OF TRANSPORTATION OF STATUES

(331)

P.Kellis inv. P. 92.B (House 3, room 6, level 4, South wall) + P. 92.7 (House 3, room 2, level 3). The papyrus now consists of 2 fragments, viz. one large Fragm. I (H. 9.3 x B. 11 cm) and, forming the lower left corner, a smaller Fragm. II (H. 4.7 x B. 3.7 cm). Margins: at the top 1.7, at the bottom 2, at the left 2.7, at the right 2 cm. A join is visible on the left hand edge of the fragment. On both sides of the sheet the writing runs parallel with the fibers.

1 [Μετὰ τ]ὴν ὑπατίαν Φλαυίου Γαλλικανοῦ καὶ
2 [Αὐρη]λίου Συμμάχου τῶν λαμπροτάτων.
3 [Διέγρ]αψεν Γελάσιος ἀπὸ λογιστῶν δ(ιὰ) Ῥιραῦτος
4 ὑ[πὲρ] φορέτρου ἀ̣νδρε̣[ι]ά̣ντων ἀ̣π̣οσ̣τ̣ε̣λ[λ]ομέ-
5 νων̣ [εἰς] Ἀλεξάνδρειαν ἀ̣[ρ]γ̣υρίου ἐν τετραχρύ-
6 σῳ̣ ν[ομ]ι̣σματι τάλαντα ἐ̣ννέα, γ(ίνεται) (τάλαντα) θ. Ἔγραψα
7 τὴν̣ [ἀπο]χὴν Αὐρήλ̣ι̣ος Νικαντίνοος ἀποδέκτης.
Verso:
8 Ἀποχὴ φορέτρο]υ [ἀ]ν̣δριάν(των) Τριμ̣ί̣θ̣(εως)
9 γρα]φεῖσα ὑπ̣ὸ̣ Ν̣ι̣κ̣α̣ν̣[τινόου.

1 ὑπατείαν

"After the consulate of Flavius Gallicanus and Aurelius Symmachus, *viri clarissimi*. Gelasius, former-*logistes*, has paid through Riraus for costs of transportation of statues to be sent to Alexandria nine talents of silver in 'four-gold' coinage, total 9 talents. I, Aurelius Nikantinoos, *apodektes*, have written the receipt." (Verso) "Receipt for transportation costs of statues of Trimithis (?) --- written by Nikantinoos (?)."

This papyrus contains a short receipt for the payment of 9 talents by a former logistes Gelasius as his contribution towards the defrayment of costs of the transportation of an unspecified quantity of statues to Alexandria. It must remain an interesting but speculative question, what kind and number of statues were actually involved. It is not easy to believe that, e.g., there was a factory of (imperial ?) statues operating in the Western part of the Dakhleh Oasis and that statues manufactured here went regularly all the way to Alexandria, first by camel or donkeys right through the desert to the Nile, then further downstream by boat. Moreover, if this were the case, the (composite?) statues involved would need to be relatively small for transport first by animals. Furthermore, to our knowledge there was in this part of the Oasis no important quarry for rare, high-quality stone and it seems hardly conceivable that one is dealing here with a regular transport of statues made from local, relatively cheap stone to the city of Alexandria; already the costs of transportation would be prohibitively high and if people in Alexandria really needed such imports, they could have found manufacturers closer by. Therefore, as these considerations seem to exclude any idea of statues made from stone in the Oasis, one is tempted towards assuming that one is dealing here with either (a) a general levy on inhabitants of the Mothite nome towards the transport cost of statues made from stone and shipped from elsewhere, or with (b) a transport of smaller (more expensive/lucrative?) statues made in the Oasis itself from faience or metal (bronze ?), *vel sim.*; their transportation, moreover, may have been an exceptional event[19] and in any case it seems telling that a former *logistes* is entrusted with

[19]) Dr. Alcock speculates that they might have been terracotta statues sent for the festivities attending the inauguration of Constantinople in 330.

(partly) defraying the costs. For a recent discussion of various aspects re the subject of statues in Graeco-Roman Egypt cf. Th. Pekáry und H.-J. Drexhage, *Zur Behandlung und Restaurierung von Bildwerken in der Antike*, in: ΜΟΥΣΙΚΟΣ ΑΝΗΡ. *Festschrift M. Wegner zum 90. Geburtstag* (Bonn 1992) 343-355.

1-2. For the consuls of 330 cf. R.S. Bagnall a.o., *CLRE* s.a. Datings to their post-consulate must have been written very early in 331 (the earliest consular dated papyrus from that year is P.Sakaon 69 from 14.i). The form of the name of the second consul found here (in full: Aurelius Valerius Tullianus Symmachus) occurs also in SB V 7666.9 (Panopolis).

For the lack of an indication of a month and a day cf. **8**.13n. and **48**.16-17n.

3. For Aurelius Gelasius (already known as a *strategus/exactor* of the Great Oasis) in 309 cf. G. Bastianini- J.E.G. Whitehorne, *List of Strategi and Royal Scribes of Egypt* 83 [the text referred to there is now SB XVIII 13852]; he is not yet known to have held the post of a *logistes* (for a recent list of these cf. *Miscellanea Papyrologica* II 518-520).

The name Ῥιραῦς is not yet listed in F. Preisigke's *Namenbuch* or in D. Foraboschi's *Onomasticon Alterum Papyrologicum*. Despite the fact that an interchange *ου/αυ* is not frequently attested in the papyri (cf. F.T. Gignac, *Grammar* I 217) one may be dealing with a variant form of the name Λιλοῦς occurring frequently in papyri from the Thebaid (for λ/ρ in the papyri cf. C. Milani in *Studi O. Montevecchi* 221-229).

It is slightly remarkable to see the name Αὐρήλιος being omitted with the names of both Gelasius and Riraus.

5-6. In the phrasing ἀ̣[ρ]γυρίου ἐν τετραχρύσῳ ν[ομ]ί̣σματι τάλαντα one finds a terminological novelty; adjectives like τετράχρυσος / τετραχρύσους are not listed in the standard Greek dictionaries and their precise meaning here is not clear. According to the list of 4th-century gold prices compiled by R.S. Bagnall (*Currency and Inflation in Fourth-century Egypt* 61) ca. 330 the gold price hovered around the 2500 Tal./lb. level and in some papyri one finds the price of a solidus (coined at 72 to the pound, each solidus being τετραγραμματιαῖος, i.e. weighing 4 γράμματα) as exactly 36 Tal. (cf. SB XIV 11591-11592). A payment of 9 talents in early 331 would represent, then, exactly the value of a quarter of a solidus and it seems theoretically possible that in practice the '9 silver talents' could go over the counter in the form of one τετράχρυσον (or, for that matter, τετραχρύσουν) νόμισμα = 1 small 1/4 sol. gold coin containing 1 γράμμα of gold; we have not found any evidence for the existence of such a coin. It is tempting to try establishing a link between the adjective τετραγραμματιαῖος and the adjectives τετράχρυσος / τετραχρύσους, but such a link is difficult to explain semantically. Likewise, one may wish to speculate about an error of τετράχρυσος for τετράδραχμος, but we see not much gain in supposing such an error; tetradrachms were hardly current ca. 330. On the other hand, it must be recalled that in a few other Kellis papyri (cf. **30**.39-40, **34**.7 and **41**.8) amounts of (silver) talents are stated to have been paid out actually ἐν νούμμοις. One wonders, therefore, whether there is a connection between the qualification ἐν τετραχρύσῳ ν[ομ]ί̣σματι and the qualification ἐν νούμμοις; we see, however, no obvious connection. It is, of course, also possible that these 9 talents were just part of a larger sum of money which Gelasius had to pay and that the rest of the money he owed was sufficient to let him pay a full solidus[20].

7. An ἀποδέκτης (= tax collector; for literature concerning the office cf. P.Herm.Landl. F.433 note) Aurelius Nikantinoos is not known to us from elsewhere.

9. The readings in this line are far from certain.

[20]) We are grateful to R.S. Bagnall (New York) for kindly discussing this subject with us by letter.

30: EXCHANGE OF OWNERSHIP RIGHTS

(22.v.363)

P.Kellis inv. P. 71 (room 6, level 3) + P. 52.A+C (room 9, level 3) + P. 56.F (ibidem, Western Doorway) + 'Unnumbered # 2' (House 3, provenance not stated). The papyrus consists now of two combinations of fragments. Fragm. I: H. 25 x B. ± 24.2 cm.; Fragm. II: H. 25 x B. 2.5 cm. The margins are: at the top 1.5, at the left 3, at the bottom 3 and at the right ± 1 cm. On both sides the writing runs parallel with the fibers.

1 Ὑπατείας τοῦ δεσπότου ἡμῶν Ἰ̣ο̣υ̣λ̣ι̣α̣νοῦ του αἰων[ίου Αὐγούστου τὸ δ/ κ]α̣ὶ Φ̣λ̣α̣ο̣υ̣ΐ̣[ου Σαλλουστίου τοῦ λαμπροτάτου ἐπά]ρ̣[χου]
2 τοῦ ἱεροῦ πραιτ̣[ωρ]ί̣ο̣υ̣ Παχὼν κζ ζ´´ νέας ἰνδ[ι]κτίονος [ ] ἀντ̣ι̣κ̣α̣τ̣α[λλαγή
3 Αὐρήλιος Ψεν̣π̣ν̣ούθης Παχουμῶν̣τος μητρὸς Ἀγάπης ὡς ἐτῶν νε̣ [οὐλὴν] ἔχων ἐπ̣[ὶ]ης̣
4 ἀριστερο̣ῦ̣ π̣ο̣δ̣[ὸ]ς̣ [ἀπὸ] κ̣ώ̣μης Συνορίας τοῦ Π̣ανοπολίτου κατ̣α̣[μένων ἐ]ν κώμῃ [Ἀ]φ̣[ροδίτης τοῦ Ἀνταιοπολίτου νομοῦ] Α̣ὐρηλίῳ
5 Ὥρῳ Παμοῦρ διὰ τ̣[οῦ] α̣ὐτοῦ πάππου κατὰ πα[τ]έρα Αὐρηλίου Ψάιτος Π[α]μοῦρ μητρὸς Τεκύσιος ὡ̣[ς ἐτῶν π οὐλὴν ἔχοντος ἐπὶ] πλα-
6 γίας ἀντικνήμης ἀρ̣ιστεροῦ ποδὸς ἀπὸ κώμης Κέλλεως τῆς Μωθιτῶν πόλεως Ὀάσεως Μ[εγάλης χρηματίζοντος ὑπὲρ τοῦ] υἱωνοῦ
7 Ὥρου καὶ τοῦ υἱοῦ Παμοῦρ Αἰ̣γ̣υ̣πτ̣ί̣ω̣ν̣ λ̣εγομένῳ̣[ν ἐπ]ιδημήσ̣αντος τῇ αὐτῇ κώμῃ Ἀφροδίτης τοῦ [αὐτοῦ νομοῦ ἀλλήλοι]ς χαίρειν.
8 Ὁμολογοῦμεν ἀντικατ̣ηλλάχθαι πρὸς ἀλλήλου[ς ἀπὸ τοῦ] ν̣ῦ̣ν̣ ἐ̣πὶ τ̣ὸ̣ν̣ [ἅπ]αντα χρόνον τὸ ἐλθὸν [εἰς σὲ ± 10 ἀπ]ὸ̣ κληρο-
9 νομίας τῆς μητρός [σ]ου, ἀπόντος σοῦ δε καὶ [τοῦ πατρός σο]υ Παμοῦ̣[ρ ἐν τ]ῇ̣ Ὀάσι τυγχάνοντες χ̣[ρηματιζόντων διὰ τοῦ] πάππου
10 Ψάιτος μέρος ἕκτον ἐπ̣α̣ύλεως ὃ̣ν̣ σὺν τῇ [ ]....... ἐ̣ν̣ τοῖς νοτίνοις μέρεσι κ[ώμης Ἀφροδίτης κατ]ὰ κοινω-
11 νίαν ἐμοῦ τοῦ Ψενπνούθου· γίτονες δ̣ὲ̣ τῆ[ς ἐπαύλ]ε̣ω̣ς ἴσης ἡμισεία[ς Νότο]υ χωρήματ[α, Βορρᾶ ῥύμη δημοσία ἐν] ῇ̣ ἀνέ-
12 ῳ̣γεν ἡ θύρα καταν̣τικρ̣ὺ τῆς α̣ὐτῆ̣ς ο̣ἰ̣κία̣[ς, Ἀπηλιώτου] Π̣αχουμίου μ̣α̣ύρου ἔρκοι´´, Λ̣ι̣β̣ὸ̣ς η[± 15 οἰκόπ]εδα̣
13 Βήσιος ἀποπουλεως ἢ οἳ [ἂ]ν̣ ὦσι γ̣ί̣τονες π̣ά̣ν̣[τοθεν].. ἐγὼ δὲ ὁ Ψενπνούθης ...[ἀντικατηλλά]χθαι

14 τὸ ἐλθὸν εἰς ἐμὲ ἀπ̣ὸ̣ δ̣ι̣κ̣α̣[ίου] πράσεω̣ς̣ .[ ] MANY TRACES [κατὰ τὴ]ν γεγε-

15 νημένην διαίρεσι[ν] π̣ρ̣ὸ̣ς̣ ἕκ̣α̣σ̣τ̣ον ...[ ] TRACES ματι καὶ ....ρίοις ..[γείτονες] δὲ καὶ

16 τῆς ὅλης οἰκίας κ̣α̣ὶ̣ τοῦ χωρήματος ...[ ] ῥ̣ύμη δ̣ημ[οσ]ία ...ην ὀ̣π[ί]σω TRACES [σὺ]ν̣ τῇ

17 παλαιᾷ̣ οἰκίᾳ̣ Ἡρ..νίου Θεοδώρου Λ̣ι̣β̣[ὸς χω]ρήματα̣ ἄλλων ἢ οἳ ἂ̣ν̣ ὦσ̣ι̣ γ̣ί̣τ̣ο̣ν̣ε̣ς̣ [πρὸς τὸ ἀπεντε]ῦθεν

18 ἕκαστον ἡμῶν κ[υρ]ιεύειν καὶ δυ̣ν̣[ασ]τεύειν καὶ δε̣σ̣π̣ο̣τ̣εύειν καὶ οἰκο[ν]ομεῖν τ̣ῶ̣ν̣ κατ̣η̣λ̣λ̣[αγμένων καὶ ἀν]οικοδο-

19 μεῖ̣ν̣ καὶ βεβαιώσο̣[με]ν̣ ἀ̣λ̣λήλοις πά̣σ̣ῃ̣ [β]εβα̣ιώσει ἀπὸ παντ[ὸς] τοῦ ἐπ[ελε]υ[σο]μένου ἐ̣μ̣ο̣ὶ̣ [τε καὶ τοῖς ὑπὲρ ἐμο]ῦ̣ ἀπο-

20 στήσειν ἐξ ἰδίο[υ] ἀναλώματος, τὸν δὲ TRACES τοῖς τοῦ .αμ..[ ] καὶ ἐν-

21 μένειν̣ πᾶσι τοῖς ἐγγ̣[ε]γραμμένοις ὡς π[ρόκ]ε̣ι̣τ[αι. Ἡ] καταλλαγὴ [ ]π̣λ̣ῆ̣ γραφεῖσα{ν} ὁμότυπος κυρ[ία καὶ βεβαία καὶ ἐπερωτηθεὶς ὡμολόγησα.]

22 Αὐρήλιος Ὧρος Παμ[ο]ῦρ δι' ἐμοῦ τοῦ πάππου [κα]τὰ πατέρα Αὐρηλίου Ψάιτος Παμοῦρ ὁ προκ(είμενος) ἀντικ[α]τή[λλαξα τὸ ἕκτον μ]έρος

23 ἐπαύλεως σοι Ψενπνούθ̣ῃ̣ καὶ ..... βεβαιώσω̣ [σ]οι πᾶσι τοῖς ἐγγεγραμμέν[οι]ς ὡς [πρόκειται. Αὐρήλιος --]δ̣ης

24 Σαρμάτου ἀπὸ Ἀφρ̣[οδί]τ̣η̣ς̣ ἔγραψα ὑ̣π̣ὲ̣ρ̣ [αὐτοῦ γράμματα μὴ εἰδότος. (M. 2) Αὐρ̣ήλιος Ψενπν[ούθης Παχουμῶντος ὁ πρ]οκ(είμενος) κατή-

25 λαξα καὶ βε̣β̣[α]ι̣[ώσω σοι π]ά̣σ̣ῃ̣ β̣ε̣βα̣[ι]ώσι καὶ εὐδ̣ο̣κ̣ῶ̣ πᾶσι [τ]οῖς ἐ̣γ̣γ̣ε̣γ̣ρ̣α̣μ̣μ̣έ̣ν̣[οις ὡς πρόκει]τε. Ἀ̣ξιω(θεὶς)

26 ἔγραψα ὑπ̣[ὲρ αὐτοῦ γράμματα] μ̣ὴ εἰδότο[ς] Φλάυιος Κολλο[ῦθος καὶ μαρ]τ̣υρῶ.

Verso:

27 Traces of one line with probably a summary of the contents of the document.

2 ϊερου, ϊνδικτιονος Pap. 5 παμουρ', ψαϊτος Pap. 6 υϊωνου Pap. 9 τε, Ὀάσει, τυγχάνοντος or τυγχανόντων(?) 10 ψαϊτος Pap. 11 γείτονες, ϊσης Pap. 13,17 γείτονες 20 ϊδιου Pap. 20-21 ἐμμένειν 23 ἐπαύλεως: -αυ- ex corr. 24-25 κατήλλαξα 25 πρόκειται

"In the consulate of our lord Julianus perpetual Augustus, consul for the 4th time, and of Flavius Sallustius *vir clarissimus*, prefect of the imperial *praetorium*, Pachon 27 of the 7th new indiction. Exchange --. Aurelius Psenpnouthes son of Pachoumon and mother Agape, about 55 years old, with a scar on the -- of the left leg, from the village Synoria in the Panopolite nome, residing in the village of Aphrodite in the Antaiopolite nome, to Aurelius Horos son of Pamour, who is represented by his paternal grandfather Aurelius Psais son of Pamour and mother Tekysis, about *n* years old, with a scar on the flank of the shin of the left leg, from the village of Kellis belonging to the city of the Mothites in the Great Oasis, acting on behalf of his grand-son Horos and his son Pamour named 'Egyptians', residing in the same village of Aphrodite in the same nome, greetings to each other. We agree that we have exchanged with each other from now onwards for ever the sixth part of a farm stead which has come to you (Horos) from an inheritance of your mother, while you and your father were away, happening to be in the Oasis, acting through your grandfather Psais, (a sixth part of a farm stead) which is situated together with the -- in the Southern parts of the village of Aphrodite, under joint ownership with me, the aforementioned Psenpnouthes; the neighbours of the farm stead are, for the equal half, at the South: plots of land, at the North: a public street in which the door of the opposite house opens, at the East: the enclosure walls of Pachoumios the black (or: son of Mauros?) at the West: -- fields of Besis --, or whoever the neighbours at all sides are; -- and that I, the aforesaid Psenpnouthes -- have exchanged the -- coming to me by right of sale -- according to the contract of division which has come to each -- and the neighbours of the whole house and the plot of land are -- public street, (behind which?) at the backside -- with the old house of Her-nios son of Theodoros, at the West plots of lands of others, or whoever the neighbours are, in order that from now onwards each of us may be the owner and proprietor and manager of the exchanged properties and may build and we shall guarantee to each other with every guarantee from every person who wants to raise a claim against me and those who are acting for me (and we agree) that we shall reject these at our own cost, and that the -- and that we shall stand by all clauses written in this document as stated above. The contract of exchange, written in *n* identical copies, must be authoritative and legal and in answer to the formal question I have assented. I, thc aforementioend Aurelius Horos son of Pamour represented by my paternal grandfather Aurelius Psais son of Pamour, have given in exchange the sixth part of a farm stead to you Psenpnouthes and -- I shall guarantee to you (with every guarantee and I agree) with all clauses written in the document as stated above. I, Aurelius -des son of Sarmates from Aphrodite, have written for him because he does not know letters. (M. 2) I, the aforementioned Aurelius Psenpnouthes son of Pachoumon, have exchanged and I shall guarantee to you with every guarantee and I agree with all clauses written in the document as stated above. I, Flavius Kollouthos, have written for him (Psenpnouthes) at his invitation, because he does not know letters, and I am witness."

In this document an exchange of property rights (ἀντικαταλλαγή) is recorded between Aurelius Psenpnouthes from the Panopolite nome and Aurelius Horos from Kellis concerning immovables in the middle-Egyptian village of Aphrodite. For similar documents cf. O. Montevecchi, *La Papirologia*, 232 (where add, e.g., P.Stras. 556 and CPR XIV 13; cf. also P.Mich. XI 612.11; P.Oxy. XVI 1917.48,50,90; XIX 2243A.82; LV 3805.v.65; P.Princ. II 78.7; P.Panop.Köln 21.ii.15; PSI I 34.11). Unfortunately the description of the immovables subject to the exchange is very much damaged. Horos gives the sixth part of a farm in the Southern part of Aphrodite, which he had inherited from his mother; apparently she was a co-owner with Aurelius Psenpnouthes. The precise location of the immovables brought in by Psenpnouthes is unclear, but we are apparently dealing with a house, cf. l. 16 , where the description of the boundaries of the house are indicated. Even so, the document is of considerable interest especially because of the description of family of the addressee of the document, Aurelius Horos son of Pamour, represented by his grandfather Aurelius Psais son of Pamour and Tekysis (cf. 4-5n.).

1-2. For the consuls of A.D. 363 cf. R.S. Bagnall e.a., *CLRE*, s.a.; Pachon 27 = 22.v;

For the expression 'New indiction' in datings in Greek documentary papyri cf. R.S. Bagnall - K.A. Worp, *The Chronological Systems of Byzantine Egypt* (Zutphen 1978), Chapt. 5. In this papyrus the element 'new' seems to be the equivalent of 'just started' (presumably the indiction year started in the Dakhleh Oasis, like elsewhere in the Thebaid, on Pachon [May] 1). For new attestations of *νέα ἰνδικτίων* published since CSBE, see O. Waqfa 61.2 (372/3 or 387/8?; 1st ind.; past?), P. Prag. I 44.13 (IV; 5th ind.; future ref.); ZPE 100 (1994) 275.14 (7th ind.; 31.xii.347; future ref.); P.Oxy. LV 3803.10,20 (16.viii.411; 11th ind.; future crop); P.Laur. IV 162.11 (354; 13th ind.; collected crop).

3-4. A man named Αὐρήλιος *Ψενπνούθης* son of Παχουμῶν/Παχουμῶς and Ἀγάπη does not seem to be attested elsewhere. For the name *Ψενπνούθης* see **24**.11, for a woman Ἀγάπη see **74**,6-7; probably these people are not to be identified with the persons referred to in this document. There is a problem with the father's name Παχουμῶντος (gen.); was the nominative Παχουμῶς (genitive usually: -ῶτος) as attested in F. Preisigke, *Namenbuch*, or Παχουμῶν (genitive usually: -ῶντος)? The second nominative seems thus far unattested; for both forms cf. F.T. Gignac, Grammar, II 61.ix, x.

ἐπ[ι]ης: one expects a phrasing like *ἐπὶ πλαγίας ἀντικνήμης ἀριστεροῦ ποδός* in ll. 5-6.

A *κώμη Συνορίας* in the Panopolite nome seems unattested. We have thought about printing *συνορίας* and interpreting the phrase *ἀπὸ κώμης συνορίας Πανοπολίτου* as 'from a village in the borderland of the Panopolite nome' (for the term *συνορία* cf. P.Pheretnouis, p. 7) but in that case one would have to assume that the village name was not given; such an omission, however, would be quite irregular, and in itself we fail to see why *Συνορία* could not be a village name. The Panopolite nome is not frequently referred to in the Kellis documents; for another instance of connections between this nome and people from Kellis, see JSSEA 17 (1987) 167, where a wooden board from Area 'B' is mentioned; at some moment the board was used to record the transfer of a house from one occupant of Kellis to another, while the house is stated to be situated in the Nile Valley at Akhmim/Panopolis.

For the village of Aphrodite cf. the note to **32**.3ff., where its links with people from Kellis (cf. below, l. 7) are discussed. Here one is dealing with a person from a village in the Panopolite nome who resided at Aphrodite. There he met with people from Kellis who also resided at Aphrodite.

4-5. For Αὐρήλιος Ὧρος son of Παμοῦρ (III) (cf. also ll. 7, 9, 22) and for Horos' paternal grandfather Aurelius Psais (II) son of Pamour (I) and Tekysis see the family tree, p. 51, and **37**.1n.. In this transaction the grandfather Aurelius Psais clearly acted on behalf of (a) his grandson Horos and (b) his son Pamour, who apparently were absent (cf. l. 9). Though it is tautological, of course, to find here a phrasing 'Αὐρηλίῳ Ὥρῳ κτλ. (l. 4-5) *διὰ* ... Αὐρηλίου *Ψάιτος κτλ.* (l. 5-6) [*χρηματίζοντος ὑπὲρ τοῦ*] *υἱωνοῦ* Ὥρου *καὶ τοῦ υἱοῦ* Παμοῦρ *κτλ.* (l. 6-7)', we fail to see how the words *υἱωνοῦ* | Ὥρου *κτλ.* (6-7) can be connected with the preceding description of Aurelius Psais (which is still continued in l. 7, cf. the participle *ἐπιδημήσαντος* which still belongs to Aurelius Psais) otherwise than via a restoration of *χρηματίζοντος ὑπὲρ τοῦ*] in l. 6. A similar form of tautology must be assumed in l. 9-10 where we also restored *χ[ρηματιζόντων διὰ τοῦ] πάππου Ψάιτος* in order to establish a meaningful phrasing.

It is regular to find a full description of a person's physical characteristics (here, those of Aurelius Psais), if and when he is acting on behalf of another party, cf. P.Flor. I 75.6ff. (cited by G. Hübsch, *Die Personalangaben als Identifizierungsvermerke im Recht der gräko-ägyptischen Papyri* [Berlin 1968; =

Berliner Juristische Arbeiten, 20] 68-69). At the same time it is always slightly remarkable to find such a description (quite normal in documents from Roman Egypt) in a document from Byzantine Egypt, cf. Hübsch, *ibidem*, 68.

6. The form *ἀντικνήμη* occurs only rarely, cf. LSJ Suppl.; more regular forms are *ἀντικνήμιον* and *ἀντικνημία*.

For the relationship between the village of Kellis and the city of the Mothites cf. **20**.3-5n.

7. We are not certain what is meant precisely by the phrase *Αἰγύπτιων λεγομενω[ν*; are they nicknamed 'the Egyptians'? For *λεγόμενος* + Name following a person's name cf. R. Calderini in Aegyptus 21 (1941) 239f.

8. The object to be brought into the transaction from Horos' side (as in l. 13 follows the description of the immovables owned by Psenpnouthes, we must be dealing here with Horos' side of the deal, hence the restoration of [*εἰς σε*, l. 8, and [*σ*]*ου*, l. 9) comes from an inheritance by Horos from mother whose name is unknown.

9. The precise relationship between the words *ἀπ*]*ọ̀ κληρο-* | *νομίας τῆς μητρός* [*σ*]*ου* and the following *ἀπόντος σοῦ δε* (l. *τε*) *καὶ* [*τοῦ πατρός σο*]*υ Παμοῦ̣*[*ρ ἐν τ*]*ῇ* '*Οάσι τυγχάνοντες* (l. 9) is not quite clear. Should we read *τυγχάνοντος* (for confusion between -*ος* and -*ες* cf. F.T. Gignac, *Grammar* I 289), to be related only to Horos' father Pamour, who then would have been absent from Aphrodite because of a journey to the Oasis [to Kellis ?], while the precise whereabouts of Horos would not have been stated, or should the participle be related to both Horos *and* his father and changed from nom.pl. into gen.pl., i.e. read *τυγχανόντων*? It looks as if Horos' mother died while her son and husband were absent; in the meantime Horos' grandfather would have represented his grandson's interests, because Horos' father (probably the first person to represent his son) was also absent. There is, of course, no objection against assuming that both the father (Pamour III) and his son (Horos) were in the Dakhleh Oasis; one wonders whether they were members of a family of cameldrivers (headed by Psais II and Pamour II, with Psais' son Pekysis joining as well? Cf. their relationship with Aphrodite borne out by **32**, **42**, **44**) who made regular trips between Kellis and Aphrodite and had a 'pied-à-terre' in Aphrodite part of which could be let (**32**). Similar traffic between Kellis and the Nile Valley (Hermopolis) is attested by **51**, **52**.

The object concerned is a sixth part of a farm house (*ἐπ̣ạύλεως*, cf. G. Husson, *OIKIA. Le vocabulaire de la maison privée en Égypte d'après les papyrus grecs* [Paris 1983] 77-80) with appurtenances (*σὺν τῇ* [ ]........) situated in the Southern part of Aphrodite and co-owned by Psenpnouthes (*ὃν ... ẹ̀ṿ τοῖς νοτίνοις μέρεσι κ*[*ώμης* '*Αφροδίτης κατ*]*ὰ κοινω-* | *νίαν ἐμοῦ τοῦ Ψενπνούθου*).

11f. *γίτονες δ̣ὲ̣ τῆ*[*ς ἐπαύλ*]*ẹω̣ς ἴσης ἡμισεία*[*ς*]: It looks as if the farm house was owned for 50 % by Horos' mother and for 50 % by Psenpnouthes, cf. *κατ*]*ὰ κοινω-* | *νίαν ἐμοῦ* in the preceding line. If Horos, while inheriting a sixth part of the farm house, received an equal part of the mother's inheritage and if there were no other goods to divide, the mother should have had three children. In fact, two of them, Horos and his sister (cf. the family tree, p. 51) are attested in the available documentation. We take *ἴσης ἡμισεία*[*ς*] (which seems to refer to *κατ*]*ὰ κοινω-* | *νίαν* in the preceding line) as a (slightly superfluous) kind of apposition to the immediately preceding words.

The indication of the neighbours does not present many questions: To the South are *χωρήματα* (cf. F. Preisigke, *Wörterbuch* II, s.v.; according to Husson, *op.cit.*, 78 and 294 one might think of a plot of land not built upon), to the North a public street in which the door of the house opposite the farm-house opens (for *θύρα* cf. G. Husson, *op.cit.*, 93-107), to the East the enclosure walls of Pachoumios 'the black' (or should we print *Μαύρου* and interprete 'Pachoumios son of Mauros'?); only the indication of the neighbours at the West is lost beyond recognition.

12. The word *ἕρκος* is not regularly used in the papyri. The two diagonal dashes seem to be intended as a kind of marker/separator.

13. It is unclear what the genitive *ἀποπούλεως* means: an indication of a profession, a patronymic or an indication of origin? In the latter case one may separate *ἀπὸ* | *Πούλεως* or *ἀπ'* | '*Οπούλεως*, but neither place name seems known. It is not safe to regard it as a writing error for *ἀπόπολις*, gen. *ἀποπόλεως* meaning 'far away from the city, banished' (cf. LSJ s.v.), the more so as the word seems too poetical to have been used in a documentary text.

Starting with l. 13 Psenpnouthes starts the description of the object he brings in. He had acquired ownership of it 'ἀπὸ δικαίου πράσεως', i.e. by buying it from a person who maybe had received it earlier as part of a division of an inheritance (*κατὰ τὴν γεγενημένην διαίρεσιν*, l. 15; for such a *διαίρεσις* cf. **13**). The object probably was a house and further appurtenances, cf. ll. 15-17, where a description of the neighbours is given.
16-17. Most of the indications of the neighbours of the house are gone; in itself one reckons with the same order of neighbours as in the preceding case (l. 11-12): 'South, North, East, West'. after *ῥ̣ύμη δ̣ημ[οσ]ία* one expects perhaps *μ̣ε̣θ'* *ἣν κτλ.* but we have not been able to read this.
18-19. The use of the verb *δυναστεύειν* (rare in the papyri) in the phrasing *ἕκαστον ἡμῶν κ[υρ]ιεύειν καὶ δυ̣ν̣[ασ]τεύειν καὶ δε̣σ̣π̣ο̣τεύειν καὶ οἰκο[ν]ομεῖν τ̣ῶ̣ν̣ κατ̣η̣λ̣λ̣[αγμένων καὶ ἀν]οικοδομεῖ̣ν̣* is remarkable.
19. One expects *ἡμῖν*, *ἡμῶν* rather than the singular *ἐμοί*, *ἐμοῦ*, but the wording may reflect here the position of only Psenpnouthes rather than that of both him and Horos.
21. Probably at least 2 copies of the document were written, one for Horos (whose copy we have here, after he took it with him back from Aphrodite to Kellis), the other for Psenpnouthes; but even more copies may have been made for other interested parties.
22-26. Both parties cannot write their own subscriptions by their own hand and make use of a *hypographeus* (for him, see **56** introd.). For the party of Aurelius Horos as represented by his grandfather Aurelius Psais son of Pamour subscribes an Aurelius -des son of Sarmatos from Aphrodite, for Aurelius Psenpnouthes subscribes a Flavius Kollouthos. These people do not occur elsewhere in the Kellis papyri. Flavius Kollouthos also acts as a witness to the whole transaction.
In l. 23, after *βεβαιώσω σοι* the subscriber should have written *πάσῃ βεβαιώσει* and he might have had in mind to continue with *καὶ εὐδοκῶ πᾶσι τοῖς ἐγγεγραμμένοις* (cf. l. 25). Probably he was confused by *πάσῃ* / *πᾶσι* (which sounded similar) and the result was a mixed-up formula.

31: LEASE OF A HOUSE (?)

(27.iv.306)

P.Kellis inv. P. 68.A+E (House 3, room 6, level 3) + 61.L (House 3, room 8, level 4). H. 34.5 x B. ca. 13 cm. Margins: at the bottom 4, at the left 1 cm. The writing runs parallel with the fibers. The verso is empty.

1-16: These lines contain only line beginnings consisting of 1 or 2 letters (not transcribed).
17 νου τῶν[
18 καὶ εἴ τι ἀλ̣λ̣[
19 ὄντων [. Ἥδε ἡ ὁμολογία τῆς]
20 μισθώσ̣[εως κυρία ἔστω δισσὴ γραφεῖσα, ἧς]
21 ἀντίτυπο[ν ἐξεδόμην σοι εἰς ἀσφάλειαν]
22 ἐφ' ὑπογρα̣[φῆς ἐμοῦ, καὶ βεβαία]
23 καὶ ἔνν[ομος ὡς ἐν δημοσίῳ κατακείμενη]
24 καὶ ἐπερ[ωτηθεὶς ὡμολόγησα.]
25 (Ἔτους) ιδ´ [τῶν κυρίων ἡμῶν Κωνσταντίου]
26 καὶ Μαξιμια̣[νοῦ Σεβαστῶν κα]ὶ̣ [(ἔτους) β´ τῶν κ]υ̣ρίων̣
27 ἡμῶν Σεου̣[ήρ]ο̣υ̣ καὶ Μα̣ξ̣[ιμίνου τῶ]ν̣ ἐ̣πιφανεστάτων

28 Καισάρων V A C A T Παχὼ̣ν̣ β-
29 (M. 2) Αὐρήλιο̣[ς] Πετεχῶ̣ν̣ ὁ̣ π̣ροκείμε[νος]
30 μισθω[το]ῦ̣ με̣μίσθωκα τὴν̣
31 προκει[μένην] μίσθωσιν ἐφ' [αἷς]
32 περιέχε[ι διαστο]λ̣α̣ῖ̣ς̣ πάσαις
33 ὡς πρό̣[κειται] κα̣ὶ ἐπερωτη-
34 θεὶς ὡμ̣[ολό]γησα.
35 (M. 3) ιδS´ καὶ β̣S´ [month] β̣· ἔσ̣χον παρὰ σ̣[ο]ῦ
36 Παμοῦρ̣ ̣[ ] ̣ ̣ ὑπὲρ μισθώσε̣ω̣[ς]
37 μίας ἀ̣ρ̣[γυ]ρ̣ί̣ο̣υ̣ τ̣ά̣λ̣α̣ν̣τα περὶ ἡμε-
38 ̣ ̣ ̣ ̣ ̣[ ]ροσ ̣ ̣τ̣ο̣υ̣ ὑπὲρ γενήματος
39 τοῦ αὐ[το]ῦ̣ ἔτους̣ ἀ̣ργυρίου ἐν νούμ-
40 μοις τά[λα]ν̣τα ἐ̣ν[ν̣έ]α̣ ὡς πρόκειται.

41 (M. 2) Αὐρή[λι]ος Πετ̣ε̣χῶν ὁ προκείμε-
42 νος μ[ισ]θ̣ωτὸ[ς] σ̣ε̣σημίωμαι.

30 *μισθωτός* 31 *ἐφ'*: *φ* ex corr. 40 *πρόκειται*: *-κει-* ex corr. 42 *σεσημείωμαι*

(Ll. 19ff.) "This agreement of lease must be authoritative, written in two copies of which I gave one copy to you for your surety with my signature, and guaranteed and legal as if deposited in a public archive and in answer to the formal question I have replied positively. Year 14 of our lords Constantius and Maximianus *Augusti* and year 2 of our lords Severus and Maximinus *nobilissimi Caesares*, Pachon 2. (M. 2) I, the aforementioned lessor Aurelius Petechon, have let the aforementioned lease under all the conditions which are in it as written above and in answer to the formal question I have replied positively. Year 14 and 2, [month], 2. (M. 3) I have received from you, Pamour --, for the single lease -- silver talents (?) concerning our --- for the revenue of the same year nine silver talents in *nummi* as written above. (M. 2) I, Aurelius Petechon, the aforementioned lessor, have signed."

The fragmentarily preserved papyrus contains a lease contract (*μίσθωσις*), probably for (part of?) a house; for other such leases from Kellis cf. also **32** and **33** (remarkably enough, we have no evidence for leases of land in/near Kellis). For the subject of rents and leases of houses, rooms, and other similar objects in general, and for an analysis of the various clauses found in such contracts, cf. H. Müller, *Untersuchungen zur* ΜΙΣΘΩΣΙΣ *von Gebäuden im Recht der gräko-ägyptischen Papyri* (Köln 1985); on rent levels in the fourth century, cf. also R.S. Bagnall, *Currency and Inflation in Fourth Century Egypt* 71 and K.A. Worp in Tyche 3 (1988) 273-275. The main part of this contract containing a detailed description of the parties concerned, the object leased, the term of the lease and the rent, is mostly lost; starting with lines 19ff. we seem to be dealing with the final clauses of the contract itself, containing the usual formulas concerning the authoritativeness of the contract and a stipulation formula (l. 24) which precedes a date in ll. 25-28 (regnal year '14 = 2' covers the year 305/6; Pachon 2 = 27.iv). In ll. 29-34 one finds the subscription of the lessor, Aurelius Petechon; one might have expected to find here also the subscription of the lessee, but this is not necessary and in fact his name seems to occur only in the last part of the document, ll. 35-40, in which a payment by a certain Pamour of nine talents, actually paid in *nummi* (i.e., with the *nummus* at 25 Den./*num.* in the early fourth century, in 540 *nummus*-coins) is recorded. It is not absolutely clear whether these 9 talents covered the rent for a whole year, but in view of the amount of money involved this looks at least likely; it looks equally likely, then, that the whole rent was paid already early in the term of the lease (in September 306 a new regnal year would have started, but cf. ll. 35ff. with ll. 25ff.). The receipt is closed off (ll. 41f.) by a signature of the lessor, Aurelius Petechon.

It seems well possible that the Pamour in this document (l. 36) should be related to Pamour son of Psais, who is known from many other papyri from House 3 (*flor.* ca. 310-321; cf. the family tree at p. 51; cf. also **29**.2n.). It could be a payment of rent for the house he actually lived in, but it is also possible that the papyrus refers to, e.g., a house he had occupied earlier before he moved into House 3.

19ff. It is not normal to find the word ἀντίτυπον = 'copy' at this place of a lease contract. In fact, to date it occurs in papyri from the Nile Valley only in cases in which a later-made copy of an earlier written document is being referred to (cf. P.Oxy. XII 1470.6; XXIV 2408.7; XLIII 3129.6; L 3578.4,5; P.Ryl. IV 652.9; P.Turner 45.1, 13, 24; SB XVI 12692.19; the editor's restoration in P.Harr. I 131.3-4 has now been cancelled, cf. ZPE 101 [1994] 97-98). There seems, however, to be no way of changing its reading here and the restoration of ll. 19-21 is suggested by the wording of **13**.10 and the remnants of the formula in the following ll. 22-24. For the κυρία-formula, see also the remarks ad **37**.12ff.; it must be admitted that the suggested restoration of l. 22 is a bit short, but there is no point in reading ἐφ' ὑπογρα̣[φῆς τοῦ ὑπὲρ ἐμοῦ ὑπογράφοντος καὶ βεβαία (which is, moreover, much too long), as the subscription (ll. 29-34) has been written by one of the contracting persons himself rather than by someone else who acted as a hypographeus.

30. It is clear that Aurelius Petechon is the lessor (cf. μεμίσθωκα), but the Greek word used in this line (and cf. l. 42) for 'lessor', μισθωτός, seems unattested with this meaning (cf. LSJ s.v.). One would have expected ὁ προκείμενος μισθώσας.

35. The month the rent at nine talents was paid in could be, but does not need to be restored as Pachon (cf. l. 28, where the same date occurs in the main part of the contract itself); one has a choice between months in the range Pachon - Epagomenon.

36-38. Lines 37-38 are extremely difficult to read. Does ὑπὲρ μισθώσ̣ε̣ως μίας refer to a lease term of one year, or does μίας introduce the description of the object leased, e.g. μίας οἰκίας (the word οἰκίας, however, cannot be read; moreover, one would rather expect ὑπὲρ μισθώσ̣ε̣ως οἰκίας μίας). Silver talents are not expected to have been mentioned twice (ll. 37, 39-40) and the reading in l. 37 is very doubtful. After ἡμε- in l. 37 one would expect at the start of l. 38 τερ- but that reading seems impossible. For a list of receipts of rent payments cf. H.-A. Rupprecht, *Studien zur Quittung im Recht der graeco-ägyptischen Urkunden* (München 1971), 30 Anm. 19. It is well-known that the word γένημα has more meanings than 'crop'; here a translation 'revenue' seems better applicable.

32: LEASE OF A ROOM

(28.x.364)

P.Kellis inv. P. 83 (House 3, room 6, level 4). H. 26 x B. 14 cm. Writing (with brown ink, by a very clumsy hand) parallel to the fibers. There is a join visible on the left hand edge of the sheet. The verso is blank.

1 Ạὐρηλία Μ̣άρσις VACAT
2 ἀπὸ κώμης Κέλλεως τῆς Μω-
3 θιτῶν πόλεως καταμέ-
4 νουσα ἐν κώμῃ Ἀφρο-
5 ⟦ο⟧δίτῃ τοῦ Ἀνταιοπολίτου
6 νομοῦ Αὐ̣ρηλίῳ̣ Ψάιτι Παμούριος
7 ἀπὸ τῆς αὐτῆς καταμένον-
8 τι ἐν τῇ αὐτῇ κώμῃ χαίρειν.
9 Μ⟦αι⟧μ`ε´μίσθωμαι παρὰ σοῦ σήμερο̣ν̣
10 πρὸς μόνον τὸ ἐνεστὸς ἔτος
11 κέλλαν̣ μίαν ἐπὶ τῆς οἰκίας <σ>ου
12 καὶ δώσω σοι ὑπὲρ ἐνοικείου
13 ταύτης τοῦ ὅλου ἐνιαυτοῦ
14 σίτου ἀρτάβας δύο. Ἡ
15 μίσθωσις κυρία καὶ ἐ-
16 περωτηθεῖσ<α> ὡμολόγ<ησ>α.
17 Ὑπατείας Ἰουανοῦ καὶ Βαρωνιανοῦ
18 παιδὸς αὐτο̣ῦ̣, Ἁθὺρ α̅. (M.2?) Αὐρηλία
19 Μάρσις ἡ προκειμένη μ⟦αι⟧`ε´μίσθωμαι
20 ὡς πρόκειται. Αὐρήλιος Ἰακῶβ Βήσιος
21 πρ(εσβυτέρου) ἀναγνώστης καθολικῆς ἐκε̣λησίας
22 ἔγραψα ὑπὲρ αὐτῆς γράμματα μὴ
23 εἰδυίης.

1 Αὐρηλία: Α- ex Ο-? 4-5 Ἀφροδίτης 5 Ἀνταιοπολίτου: -αι- ex -ου- 6 ψαϊτι Pap. 9 μεμίσθωμαι 12 ἐνοικίου (first omikron ex corr.) 17 ϋπατειας Pap., Ἰωουιανοῦ, Βαρω- ex παρω- 20 ϊακωβ Pap. 21 ἐκκλησίας

"Aurelia Marsis from the village of Kellis belonging to the city of the Mothites, now resident in the village of Aphrodite in the Antaiopolite nome, to Aurelius Psais son of Pamouris from the same village now resident in the same village, greetings. I have leased from you today for only the current year one room in your house and I shall give you as rent for this for the whole year two artabs of wheat. The lease contract is authoritative and in answer to the formal question I have assented. In the consulate of Iovianus and Varronianus his son, Hathyr 1. (M.2) I, the aforesaid Aurelia Marsis, have leased as stated above. I, Aurelius Iakob son of Besis the priest, reader of the catholic church, have written on her behalf as she is not able to write by herself."

In Byzantine times the rent for houses or rooms to live in is normally paid in money, while in a few contracts payments in kind are made for renting storage rooms etc. (cf. H. Müller, *op.cit.* 330). As the rent in the present contract is paid in kind and as a *κέλλα* can denote both a room for living and a room for storage (for a thorough discussion of the various uses of *κέλλαι* cf. G. Husson, *OIKIA. Le vocabulaire de la maison privée en Egypte d'après les papyrus grecs* [Paris 1983] 136-142) it seems most probable that the lessor used the object for the latter purpose, e.g. for keeping wheat (cf. also the discussion of rent payments for renting storage rooms in Roman Egypt by H.-J. Drexhage, *Preise, Mieten/Pachten, Kosten und Löhne im römischen Ägypten* [St. Katharinen 1991] 78, 90, 92-96 and esp. 106; from his discussion it becomes clear that in Roman Egypt, too, such rents were paid in kind often enough, whereas rents for houses and living rooms were always paid in money).

1. An Aurelia Marsis does not occur in any of the Greek papyri from Kellis. Dr. I. Gardner, however, informs us that the name Marsis is frequent in the Coptic papyri from the site.
2-3. For the relationship between the village of Kellis and the city of the Mothites cf. **20**.3-5n.
3ff. This papyrus yields an instance of persons born in Kellis and residing in Aphrodite at the moment the contract was written; cf. **42** (364), **43** (374 or 387?), **44** (382), and also **30** (363). Apparently, Psais took the contract back to Kellis at some later moment. For such migration movements cf. also **35**.2-3n. The references here and in **42** (also from 364) to the village of Aphrodite in the Antaiopolite nome are relatively early, but cf. P.Col. VIII 235 from 312 (?). It is well-known from the 6th-century Dioscorus archive (for the village cf. the long entry in A. Calderini - S. Daris, *Dizionario Geografico* I.2. 302ff. and the remarks in REG 105 [1992] 235-6).
10. In fact, as a date to Hathyr 1 (l. 18) falls 2 months after the start of the Egyptian civil year on Thoth 1, the term of the rent contract cannot have been a full year.
12. For the indiscriminate use of the terms *ἐνοίκιον* and *φόρος* next to each other in papyri from Byzantine Egypt cf. H. Müller, *op.cit.* 218.
14. An amount of two artabs of wheat may have represented in the fourth century the average purchasing power of ca. 0.25 solidus, cf. R.S. Bagnall, *Currency and Inflation in Fourth Century Egypt* 6. This figure cannot be compared easily with other rents paid in 4th-century papyri, as most of these give indications in talents or myriads of *denarii*; one must be on one's guard, moreover, against comparing with each other prices paid for different objects at different locations. A rent level to the amount of some fraction of a *solidus* is found in some 6th-century papyri, cf. H. Müller, *op.cit.* 335f.
17-18. For the consulate referred to here cf. R.S. Bagnall et al., *CLRE*, s.a. 364; add P.Lips. 13 (cf. ZPE 100 [1994] 203) and the Michigan papyrus published in ZPE 105 (1995) 247.1, with the formula 'D.N. Iovinianus [sic!] perp. Aug. I & Varronianus nobilissimus' (in Greek); Hathyr 1 = 28.x. Like the authors of the other papyri the present writer has garbled the emperor Iovian's name which should have been spelled correctly as Ἰωουιανοῦ or Ἰωβιανοῦ; the name of his son Varronianus has been dealt with slightly better, but here, too, the spelling is irregular; in view of this text and the papyrus published in ZPE 105 it does not seem excluded that one should restore something like *τοῦ ἐπιφανεστάτου παιδὸς αὐτοῦ* (cf. the formula '*nobilissimus filius*' found in many Western inscriptions) in CPR X 107.10.
21. On the *ἀναγνῶσται* ('readers of the Holy Scripture and martyrologies in the church') and their role in the papyri see E. Wipszycka in JJP 23 (1993) 194-205. For the meaning of the term *καθολικὴ ἐκκλησία* cf. **24**.3 n.

33: LEASE OF A ROOM

(21 [?].xi.369)

P.Kellis inv. P. 17.L+W (House 3, room 10, level 3) + P. 50 (House 3, room 6, level 1). H. 21 x B. 8 cm. Margin at the top 1.5 cm. On both sides the writing runs parallel with the fibers.

1 Αὐρήλιος Ψ̣άις Ψ̣ύ̣ρου τέκτω̣ν̣

2 ἀπὸ κώμης Κέλλεως τοῦ Μωθ[ί-]

3 του νομοῦ Αὐρηλίῳ̣ Παμοῦρ[

4 Ψάιτος Παμοῦρ ἀπὸ τῆς αὐτῆς̣

5 κώμης τοῦ αὐτοῦ νομοῦ

6 χαίρειν. Ὁμολογῶ μεμισθῶ-

7 σθαι παρὰ σοῦ τὴν ὑπάρχου-

8 σάν σοι κέλλαν ἐπὶ τῆς οἰκί-

9 α̣[ς τ]ῆς ̣ ̣[̣ ̣ ̣ ̣ ̣]ἐ̣π̣ὶ τῷ̣ μ ̣ ̣[

10 [καὶ ἀποδώσω σοι ὑπὲ]ρ ἐνοικίου

11 [ἑκάσ]του ἐν̣ι̣αυτ[οῦ]

12 [ἀργυ]ρ̣ί̣ου τάλαντα δια[κό-]

13 [σι]α καὶ ἀποκαταστήσ̣[ω]

14 σοι̣ τὴν αὐτὴν [κέλλαν ὥσ-]

15 π̣ερ ἔλαβον ὁ π ̣[ca. 6]

16 ἀνυπερθέτως κ[αὶ ἄνευ]

17 ἀντιλογίας. Κυρ[ία ἡ μίσθω-]

18 σις ἁπλῆ γραφ[εῖσα ἐφ' ὑπο-]

19 γρα̣φῆς τοῦ ὑπὲ̣ρ [ἐμοῦ]

20 ὑπογράφοντος <καὶ> βε̣β̣[αία]

21 ἔστω καὶ ἔννομος καὶ ἐ̣[περω-]

22 τηθεὶς ὡμολ[ό]γησα. [

23 [Ὑ]πατίας τῶν δεσ[πο]τῶν ἡ[μῶν]

24 Οὐαλεντ[ι]νια[νο]ῦ Νέο[υ]

25 τοῦ ἐπιφανεστά̣[τ]ο̣υ κ[αὶ Φλ(αουίου)]

26 Οὐίκτορος τοῦ λ[α]μ̣προτ̣[άτου,]

27 Φαμενὼθ κατ' Αἰγυπτίο[υς] τῆς τρ[ίτης].

28 (M. 2?) Αὐρήλιος Ψάις ὁ [π]ροκ(είμενος) ἐθέ̣[μην]

29 τὴν μίσθ̣ωσι[ν ὡς π[ρό]κ̣(ειται).

Verso:

30 Μίσθωσ(ις) Ψάιτος (ὑπὲρ)[

23 Ὑπατείας τοῦ δεσπότου 27 τῇ τρίτῃ ?

"Aurelius Psais son of Psyros, carpenter, from the village of Kellis in the Mothite nome, to Aurelius Pamour son of Psais and grandson of Pamour, from the same village in the same nome, greetings. I acknowledge that I have leased from you the room belonging to you at the house of --- and I shall pay you for rent each year two hundred silver talents and I shall return the same room to you as I (the aforementioned?) received it without delay and without protest. This lease contract, written as a single copy (and) provided with the signature of the person who is subscribing for me must be authoritative and guaranteed and legal and in answer to the formal question I have assented. In the consulate of our lord Valentinianus Iunior *nobilissimus* and of Fl. Victor, *vir clarissimus*, Phamenoth according to the Egyptian calendar, on the 3rd (?). (M.2) I, the aforementioned Aurelius Psais, have made this lease as stated above."

This contract deals with the lease of a room in a house in Kellis for an amount of 200 talents per year. For general bibliography on lease contracts, see the introduction to **31**.

2-3. For the Mothite nome as a separate province, see **41**.4n.
3-4. For Aurelius Pamour son of Psais and grandson of Pamour, see the family tree at p. 51.
8-9. After *ἐπὶ τῆς οἰκί-/α̣[ς τ]ῆς* something like, e.g., *μ̣η[τρὸς* may be expected, but the traces before the lacuna are too exiguous to allow such a reading to be put into the text itself.
12. 200 talents paid in 369 as annual rent for a room does not seem an extraordinary amount of money; for 4th-century rents cf. R.S. Bagnall, *Currency and Inflation in Fourth Century Egypt*, 71; H. Müller, *op.cit.* 350ff. K.A. Worp in Tyche 3 (1988) 273-275.
14-15. We cannot read *ὡς παρέλαβον*.
15. Restore something like *ὁ πρ̣[οκείμ(ενος)]*? We cannot read *ὁ Ψ̣ά̣[ις* (which, moreover, is too short to fill the lacuna completely).
19-20. The phrasing *ἐφ' ὑπο-] | [γ]ρ̣α̣φῆς τοῦ ὑ̣π̣[ὲρ ἐμοῦ] ὑπογράφοντος* is well-paralleled, but in the present case it does not make much sense, as in ll. 28-29 Aurelius Psais apparently subscribes by his own hand (cf. l. 28-29n.) rather than that he uses the services of a *hypographeus*; for a similar problem cf. the note to **31**.19ff.
23-26. For the consulate found in these lines cf. R.S. Bagnall a.o. *CLRE* s.a. 369 and the new formula 'Valentinianus iunior nobilissimus filius D.N. Valentis perpetui Augusti et Fl. Victor v.c. magister' published in ZPE 79 (1989) 200.
27. Phamenoth 3 according to the Alexandrian calendar = 27.ii; here, however, the date is stated to be according to the Egyptian calendar which in the span of years 367-371 preceded the Alexandrian/Greek calendar by 98 days, cf. D. Hagedorn and K.A. Worp in ZPE 104 [1994] 243-255. As the document was written in the julian year 369, it follows that one should count 98 days backwards from 27.ii in the year 370 (!), in order to arrive at the julian date of this lease contract, viz. 21.xi.369. The use of the genitive *τῆς τρ[ίτης]* for indicating the day numeral is irregular (one expects the dative, cf. already E. Mayser, *Grammatik der griechischen Papyri aus der Ptolemäerzeit*, II.2 (Berlin-Leipzig 1934) 224 sub 2.b.α), but we see no other option. A date to 21.xi.369 would fall within the 13th indiction, but the available space in the lacuna is certainly not sufficient for restoring *τῆς τρ[ισκαιδεκάτης ἰνδ(ικτίονος)] vel sim.*
28-29. We would expect that in the subscription to this contract a different hand would become visible (cf. 19-20n.), but in fact that does not seem to be the case; there is not much of difference in ink and writing between these lines and the preceding part of the document. On the other hand, if the whole document had been written by Aurelius Psais, his wording in l. 19-20 is plainly wrong and he might have used here a phrasing *ἐθέμην ... ὡς πρόκ(ειται) <ὁ καὶ τὸ σῶμα γράψας>*.

34: SALE OF HALF OF A FOAL

(27.xi.315)

P.Kellis inv. P. 52.B+C+D+H (House 3, room 9, level 3) + P. 56.A+C (ibidem, Western doorway) + P. 61.D (House 3, room 8, level 4). H. 25.3 x B. 20.2 cm. Margin at the left 3, at the top 2, and at the bottom 5 cm. The writing runs parallel with the fibers on both sides of the sheet. On the verso there is a long black band under the line of writing.

1 Αὐρήλιος Τ̣[οῦ Βησαπώ]νυκος ἀπὸ̣ κώμης Κεραμίων τῆς Μωθι-
2 τῶν πόλεω̣[ς Αὐρηλί]ῳ Ὥρῳ Μ̣έρσιος ἀπὸ κώμης Κέλλεως τῆς
3 αὐτῆς πόλ[εως χαίρε]ι̣ν. Ὁμολογῶ πεπρακέναι σοι ἀπὸ τοῦ νῦ̣ν̣
4 ἐπὶ τὸν ἅπ[αντα χρόνο]ν τὴν ὑπάρχουσάν μοι ἡμίσιαν πώλου λε[υ-]
5 κὸν το̣ῦ̣τ̣[ον τοιοῦτον] ἀναπόρε̣ι̣φον καὶ ἀνεπίλημπτον ἐλθόν-
6 τα εἰς ἐμ[ὲ ἀπὸ . . . . . .]γε̣ννήσ[αν]τι ἐμοῦ τιμῆς τῆς συμπεφω-
7 ν̣ημένη[ς ἀλλήλοις ἀρ]γυρίου Σεβα̣σ̣τῶ̣ν νομίσματος ἐν νούμμοις [τά-]
8 λ̣α̣ν̣τα δύ̣[ο (δραχμὰς) 'Γ, (γίνεται)] (τ̣ά̣λ̣α̣ν̣τ̣α̣) β (δραχμαὶ) 'Γ, ἅπερ ἄπεσχον παρὰ σοῦ σήμερο[ν]
9 [δι]ὰ χειρὸ[ς ἐκ πλήρου]ς. Εὐδοκῶ καὶ πέπισμαι καὶ βεβαι[ώ]σω̣
10 [π]ά̣σῃ βεβα̣[ιώσει πρὸς τ]ὸ̣ ἀπὸ τοῦ ν̣ῦ̣ν̣ σ̣ε̣ ἐπικρατεῖν καὶ κ̣υ̣ρ̣ι̣[εύειν]
11 [τὸ]ν ὠνούμ̣[ενον τοῦ π]επραμένο̣υ̣ σο̣ι̣ ὑπ᾽ ἐμοῦ ἡμίσ[ια]ν πώλου ν̣[
12 [ ] . αλλην . [ ] . [. .]ν̣ ὑπὲρ τοῦ μέρους σου τὸ προκείμε[νον]
13 [μέ]ρος καὶ ἐ[ξουσίαν ἔχειν] δ̣ιοικεῖ̣ν̣ καὶ ἐπιτελεῖν περὶ αὐτοῦ . [
14 [ῷ ἐ]ὰν αἱρῇ τ[ρόπῳ, τῆς βεβαι]ώσεως ἐξακολουθούσης μοι τῷ ἀ[πο-]
15 [δο]μένῳ δ[ιὰ παντὸς ἀπὸ πα]ν̣τὸς τοῦ ἐπελευσομένου. Κυρία ἡ π[ρᾶ-]
16 [σις -πλῆ γραφεῖσα ἐ]φ᾽ [ὑπογραφ]ῆ̣ς̣ τ̣ο̣ῦ̣ ὑ̣πὲρ ἐμοῦ ὑπογρ[ά]φοντος ἔ[στω]
17 κα̣ὶ̣ βεβαία ὡς ἐν δημοσίῳ κατακειμένη καὶ ἐπερωτηθεὶς
18 ὡμολόγησα.
19 Ὑ̣πατείας τῶν δεσποτῶν ἡμῶν Κωνσταντίνου καὶ Λικιννίου
20 Σ̣εβαστῶν τ̣ὸ δS/ Μεχεὶρ κε κ̣ατ᾽ Αἰγυπτίους.
21 Αὐρήλιος Τ̣οῦ Βησαπώνυκος Αὐρηλίῳ Ὥρῳ τῷ προκειμένῳ·
22 πέπρακ̣[ά σ]οι τὴν ἡμίσιαν πώλου καὶ ἄπεσχον τὴν τιμὴ̣ν̣ ταλάν-
23 τα δύο [ἥ]μ̣ισυ ἐν νούμμοις νομίσματος, (γίν.) (τάλαντα) β (δραχμαὶ) 'Γ καὶ βεβ̣α̣ι̣-
24 ώσω̣ σοι ὡ̣ς πρόκειται καὶ ἐπερωτηθεὶς ὡμολόγησα ὡ̣ς π̣ρ̣ό̣κ̣(ειται). [Ἔγρα-]
25 ψε̣ν̣ ὑπὲρ [α]ὐτοῦ γράμματα μὴ εἰδότος Αὐρήλιος Ψάϊς . . δ[. .]ιος
26 [ἀπὸ κώμ]ης Κέλλεως.

Verso:

27 Πρᾶσις ἡμίσι{σι}αν πώλου Τοῦ Βησα̣π̣ώ̣ν̣υ̣κ̣ο̣ς

1 Βησεπωνύχου, Κεραμείων 4 ἡμίσειαν 4-5 λευκοῦ 5 ἀναπόρριφον 6 γεννήσαντος μου 7 νούμμοις 9 πέπεισμαι 11 ἡμίσεως 14 ἄν 21 Βησεπωνύχου 27 ἡμίσεως, Βησεπωνύχου

"Aurelius Tou son of Beseponychos, from the village of Kerameia belonging to the city of the Mothites, to Aurelius Horos son of Mersis, from the village of Kellis belonging to the same city, greetings. I acknowledge that I have sold to you from now on for always the half part belonging to me of a white foal, exactly as it is right now, irrevocable and unassailable, coming to me (from) ... of my father, for the price agreed upon between us of Imperial silver money in *nummi*, i.e. two talents, 3000 drachmae, in sum 2 tal. 3000 dr., which I received from you today in cash in full. I agree and I am satisfied and I shall guarantee with all guarantee in order that from now on you, the buyer, may possess and own the half foal sold to you by me - - - - and that you have the right to dispose of and manage concerning it in whatever way you may wish, while upon me, the seller, rests in all circumstances the duty of eviction against every person making a claim. Let the contract of sale written in *n* copies, with the signature of the person subscribing on my behalf, be authoritative and guaranteed as if deposited in a public record office and in answer to the formal question I have agreed. In the fourth consulate of our lords Constantinus and Licinnius the *Augusti*, Mecheir 25 according to the Egyptians. Aurelius Tou son of Beseponychos, to Aurelius Horos the aforementioned: I have sold to you the half part of a foal and I have received the price, two and a half talents, in *nummi*-money, in sum 2 tal., 3000 dr., and I shall guarantee for you as stated above and in answer to the formal question I have agreed as stated above. Aurelius Psais son of ..., from the village of Kellis, has written for him as he does not know letters." (Verso) "Sale of half of a foal by Tou son of Beseponychos."

This papyrus (not written in entirely irreproachable Greek) contains a contract from 315 regarding the sale of half a share in the ownership of a πῶλος. This noun indicates a young animal (i.e. a foal) and it is used especially for indicating the age of donkeys, camels or horses. As the price of only half an animal may have been (at least slightly) depressed, the foal in question would have been worth at least ca. 5 Talents. In 315 this amount of money seems compatible with the price of a young donkey, cf. the list of 4th-century donkey prices in CPR VI.1, p. 24 and R.S. Bagnall, *Currency and Inflation in Fourth Century Egypt* 67-68; on the other hand, horses were traded at about the same prices as donkeys (cf. H.-J. Drexhage, *Preise, Mieten/Pachten, Kosten und Löhne im römischen Ägypten* [St. Katharinen 1991] 301), and a camel of unknown age was sold in P. Grenf. II 74 (302) for 9 Talents, hence it is difficult to be certain what kind of animal was sold in this contract. We know, however, from **51**.3 that the buyer in this contract, Aurelius Horos son of Mersis, was a cameldriver and one would therefore expect him to buy a young camel rather than a donkey or a horse. The price (2 tal., 3000 dr. = 3750 *denarii*) was paid in *nummi* (cf. ll. 7, 23) and as in this period the *nummus*-coins were the equivalent of 25 *denarii* (cf. R.S. Bagnall, *op.cit.*, 24), this means that in fact 150 such coins went over the counter (it may be that, e.g., 100 of them were packed in a small bag, a kind of 'mini-follis' [on the *follis* cf. the remarks in Bagnall, *op.cit.*, 17]).

1. For the personal name Τοῦ cf. the name Πτοῦ in **46**.31f.

It is not quite certain whether behind Βησαπώνυκος there are one or two names. The ending -ωνυκος at the place of an expected genitive suggests a nominative -ωνυξ, but the single instance of such a name, Σενεπώνυξ, found through F. Dornseiff - B. Hansen, *Rückläufiges Wörterbuch der griechischen Eigennamen* and W. Pape - G.E. Benseler's *Wörterbuch der griechischen Eigennamen*, in a London papyrus turns out to be an error for the well-known name Σενεπώνυχος (cf. O. Masson in ZPE 104 [1994] 205-210); the form Βησαπώνυκος probably consists, therefore, of a personal name Βῆς + the per sonal name Ἐπώνυχος (for this name cf. W. Crönert in SPP II p. 41; for the development ε>α and χ>κ cf. F.T. Gignac, *Grammar*, I 283ff. and 92). It is more difficult to establish whether after all one is dealing here with a really new composite (undeclined) name Βησεπώνυχος, or with two individual names which should, in principle, be kept separate from each other; in that case Βῆς should be the name of the father, Ἐπώνυχος the name of the grandfather of Τοῦ. Given the fact, however, that the article τοῦ, which regularly precedes a grandfather's name, is lacking after Βῆς (this form is regularly undeclined, though cf. P.Vindob.Worp 3.14 n.) and that in general composite names tend to become more and more popular in later Roman Egypt, it seems preferable to regard Βησαπώνυκος as a slightly misspelled form of a single name Βησεπώνυχος.

The village of Τὰ Κεραμεῖα in the Mothite Nome has not occurred before; there is a homonymous district in the Theban area.

2. For Horos son of Mersis cf. **9**.1n. and **51**.3n.

2-3. For the relationship between the village of Kellis and the city of the Mothites cf. **20**.3-5n.

4-6. One may explain the accusatives λε[υ-]/κὸν τοῦτ[ον τοιοῦτον] ἀναπόρειφον καὶ ἀνεπίλημπτον ἐλθόν-τα most simply by assuming that the scribe apparently thought that he had earlier written: τὸν ὑπάρχοντά μοι ἥμισυν πῶλον.

For the *τοῦτον τοιοῦτον ἀναπόρριφον καὶ ἀνεπίλημπτον*-clause frequently occurring in such sale contracts cf. the literature given by H.-A. Rupprecht, *Kleine Einführung in die Papyruskunde* (Darmstadt 1994) 117.

6. The interpretation of γεννήσ[αν]τι and, connected with this, the restoration of the preceding lacuna is problematic; one might expect, e.g., ἐλθόντα εἰς ἐμ[ὲ κατὰ δωρέαν τοῦ] (14 letters) or εἰς ἐμ[ὲ ἀπὸ διαθήκης τοῦ] (15 letters), but both supplements are too long for the lacuna containing ca. 10 letters (subtracting the ε of ἐμ[ὲ and the article τοῦ, only ca. 6 letters are left for filling out this lacuna with a preposition and a noun); moreover, both approaches presuppose an error of the dative γεννήσ[αν]τι for the genitive γεννήσαντος. Nevertheless, it is attractive to suppose that the seller Tou got his half part of the animal from his father (= ὁ γεννήσας).

7. For the use and value of the *nummus* cf. R.S. Bagnall, *Currency and Inflation in Fourth Century Egypt* 12-15; cf. also the introduction above.

12. It is unclear how the remains of this line should be interpreted and what should be restored in the lacuna; there does not seem to be a parallel for the phrasing found here.

14. [ᾧ ἐ]ὰν αἱρῇ τ[ρόπῳ is restored here after **36**, Frag. 1.6; cf. also **8**.9, **38.a**.14, **38.b**.14, **39**.13-14, in which documents the word order is slightly inverted (τρόπῳ ᾧ ἐὰν αἱρῇ).

16. It is uncertain how many copies of the document were made; maybe only one, but cf. below, the appendix.

19-20. For the consuls of the year 315 cf. R.S. Bagnall et al., *CLRE* s.a. As in the 4 years between 315-319 there was a difference of 85 days between the Egyptian wandering year and the Alexandrian year (cf. D. Hagedorn & K.A. Worp in ZPE 104 [1994] 243-255), and as the year 315/316 was a leap year, Mecheir 25 according to the Egyptian (wandering) calendar is the equivalent of Hathyr 30 (= 27.xi) in the Alexandrian calendar.

34, Appendix

With the text published above one may compare the small fragment P.Kellis inv. P.77.A (H. 5.5 x B 2.5 cm.; margin at the top 1.5 cm.; verso blank); it may be just a duplicate of **34**.

1 [Αὐρήλιος N.N. son of N.N. ἀπὸ κώμης N.N. τοῦ Μωθίτο]υ νομοῦ
2 [Αὐρηλίῳ N.N. son of N.N. ἀπο κώμης Κέλ]λεως
3 [τῆς αὐτῆς πόλεως χαίρειν. Ὁμολογῶ πεπρακέναι] σοι ἀπὸ
4 [τοῦ νῦν ἐπὶ τὸν ἅπαντα χρόνον Animal] λευκὸν
5 [Further description τιμῆς τῆς] συμπε-
6 [φωνημένης ἀλλήλοις ἀργυρίου Σεβαστῶν νομίσματος] τάλαν-
7 [τα
- -

35: SALE OF A HEIFER

(4th century)

P.Kellis inv. P. 17.S+AA+BB (House 3, room 10, level 3). Two strips of a vertically folded papyrus have been preserved, measuring H. 13.7 x B. ca. 3 cm. each, while the margin at the top measures 2 cm. The writing runs parallel with the fibers; the verso is blank.

1 Αὐρήλιος N.N.] Θεοδώρο̣[υ . . . .]υ̣ε̣ι ἐ̣κ μ̣ητ̣[ρὸς N.N.
2 ἀπὸ κώμης . . .]μ̣ησῃ τῆ̣ς Μ[ωθιτῶν πό]λεως κατα[μένων ἐν
3] . τ Πακέβκ̣[. . . . Αὐρ]ηλίῳ Ἀμ . [. . . . .
4]ἀπὸ Ἴβει[τῶν πόλεω]ς χαί[ρειν. Ὁμο-
5 λογῶ πεπρακέν]αι σοι ἀπὸ [τοῦ νῦν ἐ]πὶ τὸν ἅπα̣[ντα ἑξῆς
6 χρόνον τὴν ὑπ]άρχουσάν̣ [μοι ἡμισεί]αν δαμά̣[λεως
7 λευ]κοχρώμου̣ [τιμῆς τῆ]ς σ̣υ̣μπεφ[ωνη-
8 μένης πρὸς ἀλλ]ή̣λους ἀργ[υρίου . . .] . . . νομεί[σματος
9 ca. 12] . ω τάλλα̣[ντα ἑκατ]όν, γί(νεται) (τάλαντα) ρ, α . [
10 ca. 12 σ]ήμ̣ερον δ[. . . . . . . ἀ]ρ̣ιθμῃ πλῆρ[ες
11 ca. 12] . ι καὶ βεβ[αιώσω σοι] πάσι βεβαι[ώσει
12 ca. 11 π]αντὸς τ̣[οῦ . . . . .]σουμένου . [
13 `κα]ὶ τῆς βεβα̣ι̣[ώσεως μοι ἐξακολ]ουθούσης δι[ὰ παντὸς´
14 ἀπὸ παντὸς τοῦ] ἐ̣πε̣[λευσομένο]υ̣ κυριευθ̣ . [
- -

4 ἴβει[των Pap., l. Ἰβι[τῶν 8 νομίσματος 9 τάλαντα 11 πάσῃ l. 13 is squeezed in between ll. 12 and 14

"Aurelius N.N. son of Theodoros (?) son of -- (?), and N.N. being his mother (?), from the village of --mese belonging to the city of the Mothites, residing in --, to Aurelius Am- -- from the city of the Hibites, greetings. I agree to have sold you from now on for ever the half part of a heifer belonging to me -- white-coloured, for the mutually agreed price of hundred talents in silver -- money -- today -- in full (?) -- and I shall guarantee you with every guarantee -- from every --, and the right of eviction falling to me in all circumstances against every person who shall make a claim --".

This papyrus is very mutilated and many details of the original wording of this contract remain unclear. As to the original form of the papyrus it may be supposed that the strips now preserved (each containing 6 - 8 letters) are the result of its being broken along the folds and that the original had (a) at least two more such strips (together ca. 12 letters, cf. ll. 5, 8) before the preserved left-hand strip, (b) one strip between the preserved strips, and (c) one more strip joining to the right of the second preserved strip (if it had a little blank space at its right-hand edge, this strip would have contained less than the 6 - 8 letters written on the other strips), viz.:

[I] | [II] | III | [IV] | V | [VI].

If these assumptions are correct, it may be supposed that the original sheet was first folded vertically in the middle, then folded twice, i.e. one time from each side toward the center.

After an opening of the 'A to B *χαίρειν*' type (ll. 1-4) we are dealing with a sale of half part of a heifer (ll. 4ff.) for 100 talents. The scribe (who, judged by his handwriting, was not doing a first-class job) possibly committed various spelling errors and used an irregular formula (see l. 10n.). Even so, the papyrus remains of interest, as sales of cows are hardly attested for early Byzantine Egypt, cf. R.S. Bagnall, *Currency and Inflation in Fourth Century Egypt* 68; the situation is not better in later times, cf. A.C. Johnson - L.C. West, *Byzantine Egypt* (Princeton 1949) 212 (add there CPR VIII 67, VI/VII: young bulls sold at very much diverging prices) and the recent remarks by A. Jördens in ZPE 98 (1993) 266. For documentation concerning the sales of cows in Roman Egypt cf. H.-J. Drexhage, *Preise, Mieten/Pachten, Kosten und Löhne im römischen Ägypten* (St. Katharinen 1991) 301-02. It is also worthy of note that the seller seems to come from a village in the Mothite nome but is residing now somewhere else (maybe in Kellis, where the document was found?), while the buyer comes from the town of Hibis. Finally, it should be noted that some of the suggested restorations may be transferred from the end of a line to the beginning of the next line.

1-4. Much is uncertain at the start, but it is reasonable to suppose that one is dealing with an opening 'A son of ..., provenance, to B son of ..., provenance, *χαίρειν*'. If Αὐρήλιος in the first lacuna in l. 1 was written out in full (cf. l. 3) there is only little space for restoring his personal name (cf. above, the calculations about the amount of text lost at the left); restore, e.g., Ὧρος?. Θεοδωρο̣[seems to belong to the father's name.

After the second lacuna in l. 1 much is uncertain; instead of]υ̣ε̣ι ἐ̣κ μ̣ητ̣[ρὸς one might perhaps also think about reading] κ̣α̣ὶ 'Α̣κμ̣ητ̣[, but it remains to be seen whether that produces more satisfactory

results, the more so as the lacuna is too large for containing, e.g., only an article *τοῦ* preceding] *κ̣α̣ὶ* (resulting in Theodore's being provided with an alias-name).
2. A village name in -*μησῃ* is unknown in the region. On the other hand, if one reads *κώ*]*μης* one seems to be stuck with a superfluous eta (unless the rest of the restoration of this line is wrong).
2-3. We have assumed that one is dealing here with the rather regular phenomenon of a person's place of birth (his *ἰδία*) being different from his present habitat (for relations between, e.g., Kellis and the village of Aphrodite in the Nile valley cf. **32**.3n.; in general, see also the word index s.v. *καταμένω, οἰκέω*); for migration movements within Byzantine Egypt cf. H. Braunert, *Die Binnenwanderung* (Bonn 1964) 293ff.

It does not seem excluded that at the start of l. 3 one should take some letters of the present reading] ̣*τ* (from *κτῆμ*]*α̣τ*( ), but without abbreviation marking?) *Πακέβκ̣*[*εως* together and read *Τπάκε* (in the Mothite nome, cf. **52**.1); the doubtful kappa, moreover, could be changed into an eta. It is, however, uncertain what *βη*[would indicate; was there something like a village *Τπάκε βῆ*[*τα*? Against this whole idea it could be argued that there is a small spacing between the tau and the pi and it does not solve the problem what more could have stood between *βῆ*[*τα* and *Αὐρ*]*ηλίῳ* (only 5 letters restored in a lacuna of ca. 8 letters).
6-7. One may expect before the indication of the color an indication of the animal's age, but *δάμαλις* itself already indicates a young cow and the restoration of a word like *ἐνκύου* (gen. of *ἔγκυος* = 'in calf') is also possible, cf. P.Köln I 55.6.
7-8. The restoration at the end of l. 7 is very short, but we see no alternative.
8. The word *Σεβαστῶν* might be expected between *ἀργ*[*υρίου* and *νομεί*[*σματος*, but we have not been able to identify its last letters with the traces preserved before *νομεί*[*σματος*.
9. At the end one may wish to read, e.g., *ἄπ̣*[*ερ* (cf. **34**.8), but the letter trace after the alpha does not clearly belong to a pi.
10. At the end, *πλῆρ*[*ες* (partly restored) seems to suggest that the price has been paid in full, but it remains uncertain what preceded this; *ἀ*]*ριθμη* may be an error for *ἀριθμῷ*; it seems less likely to interpret this as *ἀριθμή*(*σεως*).
12. One expects some form of a guarantee clause containing a future participle, but]*σουμένου* seems to come from *πε*]*σουμένου*, the future participle of *πίπτω* or a compound of it, and we do not know of any formula containing this element. Is a spelling error made here, i.e. read *ἐπελευ*]*σομένου* (but cf. the same participle restored in l. 14)?
14. *κυριευθ̣* ̣[: we do not know how to fit this form into a known formula.

36: FRAGMENTS OF A CONTRACT OF SALE

(308)

P.Kellis inv. P. 17.BB (House 3, Room 10, level 3) + P. 63.A (House 3, Room 8, level 4). Frag. I: H. 6 x B. ca. 5.5 cm.; there are no margins. Frag. II: H. 10.5 x B. 5 cm.; there is on this fragment a lower margin of 4.5 and an upper margin of 1.5 cm., but this 'upper margin' may be in fact only the open space between the body of the contract and the dating formula underneath it. The writing on both fragments runs parallel with the fibers, the versos are blank.

Frag. I:

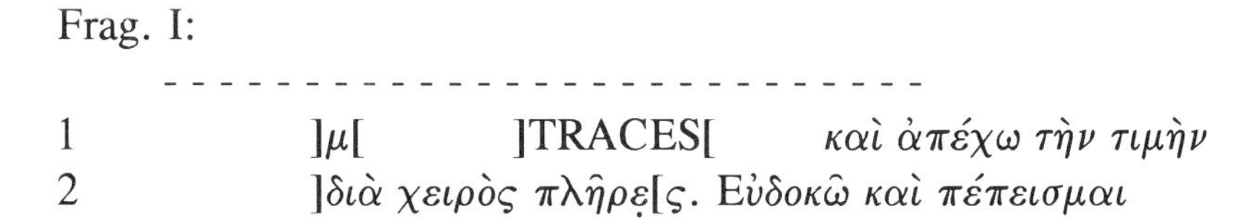
- -
1]μ[ ]TRACES[καὶ ἀπέχω τὴν τιμὴν
2]διὰ χειρὸς πλῆρε̣[ς. Εὐδοκῶ καὶ πέπεισμαι

3 καὶ βε]βαιώσω σοι πάσι β[εβαιώσει πρὸς τὸ ἀπὸ τοῦ νῦν
4 ἐπικ]ρατεῖν καὶ κυριεύε[ιν σε τὸν ὠνούμενον τῶν πεπραμένων
5]καὶ ἐξ[ο]υσίαν ἔχε[ιν διοικεῖν καὶ ἐπιτελεῖν περὶ αὐτῶν
6 ᾧ ἂν αἱρ]ῆται τρόπῳ, τῆς [βεβαιώσεως ἐξακολουθούσης μοι
7 τῷ ἀποδ]ομένῳ [ἀπὸ παντὸς τοῦ ἐπελευσομένου
- -

Frag. II:

- -
11 Ὑπατε[ίας τῶν δεσποτῶν ἡμῶν Διοκλητιανοῦ πατρὸς τῶν βασιλέων]
12 τὸ ι´ κ[αὶ Γαλερίου Οὐαλερίου Μαξιμιανοῦ Σεβαστοῦ τὸ ζ´]

13 Αὐρήλιο[ς ὁ προ-]
14 κείμενο[ς πέπρακα Object ὡς πρόκειται καὶ ἐπερωτηθεὶς]
15 ὡμολόγη[σα. Ἔγραψεν ὑπὲρ αὐτοῦ γράμματα μὴ εἰδότος]
16 Αὐρήλιος[N.N. ἀπὸ N.N.]

3 πάσῃ

(Frag. I) "--- and I have received the price --- in cash in full. I agree and I am satisfied -- and I shall guarantee with all guarantee in order that from now onwards you the buyer may be owner and master of the sold items and have the opportunity to dispose of them and manage them in whatever way it may be wished, the duty of eviction under all circumstances resting upon me, the seller, against every person who shall lay a claim --." (Frag. II) "In the consulate of our lords Diocletian *pater Augustorum* consul for the 10th time and of Galerius Valerius Maximianus *Augustus* consul for the 7th time. I, the aforementioned Aurelius N.N, have sold the --- as stated above and I have answered the formal question. I, Aurelius N.N. from ---, have written for him as he does not know letters."

These fragments are related to a contract of sale, but the precise object of the sale has not been preserved; in itself it can have been anything, e.g. immovables, a slave, or an animal. For the restorations suggested above in the lacunas in Frag. I cf. the contracts **4**, **8**, **34**, **35**, **38.a**,**b** and **39.**

11-12. These are the consuls of 308, cf. R.S. Bagnall a.o., *CLRE* s.a.

37: SALE OF PART OF A HOUSE

(320)

P.Kellis inv. P. 17.O (House 3, room 10, level 3). Frag. I: H. 7.3 x B. 3.8 cm. Top margin 1.5 cm.; Frag. II: H. 9 x B. 10 cm. Bottom margin: 2 cm. The writing runs parallel with the fibers. The verso is blank.

Frag. I:

1	[Αὐρηλία Τακῦσις	ἀπὸ] κώμης
2	[N.N.	Αὐρ]ηλίῳ
3	[N.N.	ἀπὸ τῆς] ạὐτῆς κώ-
4	[μης νῦν οἰκοῦντι ἐν	] χαίρειν.
5	[Ὁμολογῶ πεπρακέναι σοι	ἀπὸ τοῦ] ν̣ῦν ἐπὶ τὸν
6	[ἅπαντα χρόνον ἀπὸ τῶν ὑπαρχόντων μοι	μέρ]ο̣ς τετάρτου
7	[οἰκίας ἐν τοῖς ἀπὸ	μ]έρ̣εσι τῆς
8	[κώμης διὰ τῆς (?)	]τ̇ραπέζης
	[	\`Ἀ]γ̣αθος´
9	[	ἀ]πὸ Αὐρηλίων
10	[	]σίδο̣υ ἄρξαν̣τος̣
11	[	] . . ίου̣

- -

Frag. II:

- -

12	[Κυρία ἡ πρᾶσ]ις δ[ισσὴ γραφεῖσα ἐφ᾽ ὑπογραφῆς τοῦ ὑπο-]
13	[γρά]φοντος ὑπὲρ ἐμο̣ῦ̣ [καὶ βεβαία ὡς ἐν δημοσίῳ κατακει-]
14	[μέν]η καὶ ἐπερωτηθεῖ[σα ὡμολόγησα.
15	[Ὑπα]τίας τῶν δεσποτῶ[ν ἡμῶν Κων]σ̣ταν̣[τίνου Αὐγούστου]
16	[τὸ] ϛ¯ καὶ Κωνσταντ[ί]νου τοῦ ἐπιφανεστά̣[του Καίσαρος τὸ α´]
17	Παχὼν κ— κα[τ᾽
18	[Αὐ]ρηλία Τακῦσις [ἡ] προκει\`μέ´νη πέπρα[κα τὸ προκεί-]
19	[με]νον μέρος τέτα[ρτ]ον οἰκοίας καὶ ἀ̣\`πέ´σχο̣[ν τὴν τιμὴν ἐν]
20	[τα]λ̣ά̣ντοις δύο, γ(ίνεται) [(τάλαντα)] β, πλύ̣ρη ὡς πρό[κ(ειται) καὶ βεβαιώ-]
21	[σω] π̣άση̣ β̣α̣ιβέω̣[σει καὶ] ἐπερωτηθεῖσ[α ὡμολόγησα. Ἔγρα-]
22	[ψα] ὑπὲρ αὐτῆς γ[ράμμα]τα μὴ εἰ\`δ̣υ̣ί̣´ης Αὐρήλ[ιος N.N. ἀπὸ τῆς]
23	[αὐ]τῆς κώμης κ̣[αὶ ἐσωμάτι]σα. (M.2) Αὐρήλιος Ψάις̣ [
24	[. .] ἐμ̣αρτύρησα τ̣ὰ̣ [πάντα ὡ]ς̣ π̣ρ̣ό̣κ̣(ειται).

6 τέταρτον 15 Ὑπατείας 18 Αὐρηλία: -α ex -ος corr. 19 τέταρτον: τ- ex δ- corr., οἰκίας 20 πλήρη 21 βεβαιώσει

(Ll. 1-8) "Aurelia Takysis (daughter of N.N. and N.N.) from the village of N.N. - - - to Aurelius N.N. (son of N.N. and N.N.) from the same village, now living in (?)

- - -, greetings. I agree to have sold to you from now onwards for all time from my belongings - - -a fourth part of a house - - - in the - - - part of the village - - - through the bank of N.N. (?) ---. (Ll. 12-24) The sale contract is authoritative, written in two copies with the signature of the person who is subscribing for me, and guaranteed and legal as though deposited in a public record office and having been formally asked I have agreed. In the consulate of our lords Constantine *Augustus* consul for the 6th time and Constantine *nobilissimus Caesar* consul for the 1st time, Pachon 20, according to the - - - (calendar). I, the aforementioned Aurelia Takysis, have sold the aforesaid fourth part of a house and I have received the price consisting of two talents, total 2 tal., in full, as mentioned above, and I shall guarantee the sale with every guarantee and having been formally asked I have agreed. I, Aurelius N.N., from the same village, have written for her, as she does not know letters, and I have written the body of the contract. I, Aurelius Psais - - - was witness to everything as described above."

Sales of (parts of) houses are quite a common phenomenon among the Greek papyri from Egypt; the most recent comprehensive survey of the pertinent (extensive) literature is given by B. Kramer and J.C. Shelton in their introduction to P.Nepheros 29. Among the Kellis papyri, however, this is to date the only such contract of a house sale. An extra point of interest is the fact that the owner/seller of the ¼ part of a house is a woman, Aurelia Takysis, who was the wife of one of the main occupants of House 3, Aurelius Pamour(is) son of Psais (cf. the family tree at p. 51); for female property owners in Roman Egypt cf. D. Hobson in TAPA 113 (1983) 311-321.

One may wonder, whether the ¼ part of the house sold in this document refers to House 3 itself; in that case one is dealing with the copy of the contract going to the buyer who kept it in House 3. It is, however, also possible that one is dealing with the seller's copy; did Takysis, living in House 3, perhaps sell a ¼ part of another house belonging to her in another part of Kellis?

For the prices fetched for house property in the Nile Valley, see H.-J. Drexhage, *Preise, Mieten/Pachten, Kosten und Löhne im römischen Ägypten* (St Katharinen 1991) 74ff.; R.S. Bagnall, *Currency and Inflation in Fourth Century Egypt* (Chico 1985), 70-71.

1. The name of the seller, Aurelia Takysis, is restored from l. 18; the same name occurs also in **30**.5, **42**.2 and in **65**.1, though in slightly different spellings (Τεκῦσις, Τακοσε, Τεκοσε).
4. The restoration of *νῦν οἰκοῦντι ἐν* (to be followed by a place name) is inspired by the thought that a restoration of the obvious phrasing after *ἀπὸ τῆς*] *ạὐτῆς κώ-*/[*μης* , viz. *τοῦ αὐτοῦ νομοῦ*, certainly would not fill the lacuna before *χαίρειν* (for its length cf. ll. 5-6 and the note to l. 5) sufficiently.
5. The restoration of only [*Ὁμολογῶ πεπρακέναι σοι ἀπὸ τοῦ*] is too short in comparison with the average line length of ll. 12ff., but the restoration of [*Ὁμολογῶ πεπρακέναι σοι καὶ καταγεγραφέναι σοι ἀπὸ τοῦ*] (cf. **8**.3, 362) is not really warranted (and in fact too long).
7. One expects here an indication of the precise position of the house within the village; cf. F. Preisigke, *Wörterbuch*, s.v. *μέρος* 1.e and f.
8ff. Among the Greek documents from Kellis this seems to be the only reference to a bank. Unfortunately, the context is damaged and the name of the bank is lost. In itself one might be inclined to

think of a restoration of, e.g., *κατὰ διαγραφὴν διὰ τῆς ... τραπέζης*, but this formula is usually given with the indication that the price was paid. However, that part of the standard formula of a sale contract should appear only later on, i.e. after the indication of the neighbours of the house, and it would seem more likely that ll. 9-11 contained part of the neighbour's description (one of whom apparently was a former magistrate, cf. *ἄρξας* in l. 10).

12ff. The printed restoration of the *kyria*-formula (for further literature also the note on **4**.13f.) follows a regular pattern in Kellis documents; the length of the lacuna in l. 13 does not allow a restoration of the words *καὶ ἔννομος*, too, and one finds the shorter formula in, e.g. **34**.15ff. (315), **38**.17ff. (333), **41**.16ff. (310) and **49**.10ff. (304). In itself this might make one wonder whether the longer *κυρία καὶ βεβαία καὶ ἔννομος*-formula could be a later development, but one finds it already early in, e.g., **31**.20ff. (306) and P.Grenf. II 75.15 (308). For regionalisms in such *kyria*-formulas cf. CPR XIV 2.18n.

15-16. These are the consuls of 320, cf. R.S. Bagnall a.o., *Consuls of the Later Roman Empire*, s.a.

17. Restore Ἕλληνας or Αἰγυπτίους? For the use of the 'Greek' vs. the 'Egyptian' calendar in documents from Egypt cf. D. Hagedorn - K.A. Worp in ZPE 104 (1994) 243-355. Pachon 20 'according to the Greeks' = 20.v, 'according to the Egyptians' = 19.ii.

21-23. For the formula used here Ἔγραψα *ὑπὲρ αὐτῆς* - - - Αὐρήλιος N.N. *καὶ ἐσωμάτισα* cf. **41**.29-30 (310), **44**.24-26 (382) and **45**.35-36 (386): *ἔγραψα* Αὐρήλιος N.N. - - - *ὁ καὶ τὸ σῶμα γράψας*.

24. Or read *ἐμαρτύρησα τα[ύτῃ τ]ῇ π̣ρ̣ά̣σ̣ε̣ι̣*?

38.a: GRANT OF A PLOT OF LAND

(28.x.333)

P.Kellis inv. P. 52.F (House 3, room 9, level 3). H. 24 x B. 22 cm. The margin at the top measures 2 cm., at the left 4.5 cm., and at the bottom 4 cm. The papyrus sheet was folded vertically several times. The writing on the sheet runs parallel with the fibers, the back is blank.

1 Αὐρήλιος Π̣α̣υ̣σ̣α̣ν̣ίας Οὐαλερίου ἄρξα[ς Μωθιτῶν πόλεως]
2 Αὐρηλίῳ [Ψά]ι̣τι Παμοῦρ ἀπὸ κ̣ώ̣μ̣η[ς Κέλλεως τῆς]
3 αὐτῆς Μ̣ω̣θ̣ι̣τ̣ῶ̣ν̣ π̣ό̣λεως [χαίρειν.]
4 [Ὁ]μολογ̣[ῶ κεχαρ]ί̣σ̣θαι σοι χάριτι αἰ̣ω̣ν̣ί̣α̣ [καὶ ἀναφαιρέτῳ]
5 ἀ̣π̣ὸ̣ τοῦ ν̣ῦ̣[ν ἐπὶ] τ̣ὸν ἅπαντα χρόνον ἀ̣[πὸ τῶν ὑπαρχόν-]
6 των μοι [ἐ]δ̣α̣φῶν ἐξ Ἀπηλιώτ̣ου κώμη[ς Κέλλεως τόπον]
7 πρὸς ἀνοι[κ]ο̣δομ̣ὴ̣ν̣ Νότου καὶ Βορρᾶ [πηχέων τεκτονι-]
8 κῶν δεκ̣[απ]έ̣ν̣[τε], Ἀπηλιώτου καὶ Λιβὸ̣ς̣ [πηχέων πέντε <καὶ> εἴκο-]
9 σι. Γείτονες· Ἀ̣π̣η̣λιώτου ἐδάφη ἐμοῦ Πα̣[υσανίου, Λιβὸς καμη-]
10 λῶν Ὥρο[υ] Μ̣έρσ̣ι̣[ο]ς, Νότου οἰκία σου [καὶ υἱοῦ καὶ ......]
11 σου, Βορρᾶ ῥύμη δημοσία, ἢ οἳ ἐὰν ὦσι̣ [γείτονες πάντοθεν,]
12 πρὸς τὸ̣ ἐξεῖν̣[αί σοι] ἐ̣π̣ικρατεῖν καὶ κυριε[ύειν αὐτοῦ καὶ]
13 διοικεῖν καὶ οἰκονομεῖν περὶ τοῦ χαρισθ[έντος σοι τόπου]
14 ἑκουσίῳ γ̣ν̣ώμ̣η̣ τρόπῳ ᾧ ἐὰν αἱρῇ, τῆς β[εβαιώσεως]
15 ἐξακολουθο̣ύ̣σ̣ης μοι διὰ παντὸς ἀπὸ παντὸς[τοῦ ἐπελευσομέ-]
16 νου ἢ ἀντιπ̣ο̣ιησομένου. Κυρία ἡ χάρις ἁπ[λῆ γραφεῖ]σ̣α̣ ἐφ᾽
17 ὑπογραφῆς μου ἔστω καὶ βεβαία ὡς ἐν δημ̣[οσίῳ] κ̣α̣τ̣α̣κ̣ειμ̣έ̣νη

18 καὶ ἐπερωτηθεὶς ὡμολόγησα.
19 Ὑπατείας Φλαυίου Δελματίου ἀδελφοῦ τοῦ δ[εσπότ]ου ἡμῶν
20 Κωνσταντίνου Αὐγούστου καὶ Δομεττέου [Ζην]οφίλου [τ]ῶν
21 λαμπροτάτων Ἀθὺρ α-.

22 (M. 2) Αὐρήλι[ο]ς Πausανίας Οὐαλερίου ἄρξας κεχάρισ[μαι]
23 τὸν προκείμεν(ον) ψιλὸν τόπ[ον] ὡς πρόκειτται καὶ ἐπερ[ωτηθεὶς]
24 ὡμολόγησα.

2 ψαῖτι Pap. 11 ἄν 14 ἑκουσίᾳ, ἄν 23 πρόκειται

"Aurelius Pausanias son of Valerius, former magistrate of the city of the Mothites, to Aurelius Psais son of Pamour, from the village of Kellis belonging to the same city of the Mothites. I acknowledge that I have granted to you as a perpetual gift which cannot be withdrawn, from now onwards for ever, from the plots of land belonging to me in the Eastern part of the village of Kellis a plot for building, at the South and the North being fifteen carpenter's cubits long, at the East and at the West being twenty five cubits. The neighbours are, (1) at the East: land belonging to me, Pausanias; (2) at the West: a camel-shed belonging to Horos son of Mersis; (3) at the South: the house of you and your son and -- of you; (4) at the North: a public street, or whoever they (i.e. these neighbours) may be on every side, in order that you may be able to possess it and to be master and to dispose and to manage as regards the plot given to you according to your own free will and as you wish, while the duty of eviction rests on me in all circumstances against every person who wants to contest or to lay a claim. Let this grant provided with my signature be authoritative and guaranteed as if it has been deposited in a public record office and in answer to the formal question I have assented. In the consulate of Flavius Delmatius, brother of our lord Constantine *Augustus*, and of Domitius Zenophilus, *viri clarissimi*, Hathyr 1. (M.2) I, Aurelius Pausanias son of Valerius, former magistrate, have granted the aforementioned vacant plot as stated above and in answer to the formal question I have assented."

This remarkable papyrus contains a grant of a small plot of land in the Eastern part of Kellis; especially interesting is the fact that it contains a precise indication of the dimensions and neighbours of the donated object. The land was given by Aurelius Pausanias to Aurelius Psais son of Pamour; both persons are known from other documents from Kellis. It is rare, if not unique, that we are able to study such a document found during controlled excavations and that possibly the plot of land may be found back on the archaeological map of Kellis, cf. the note to ll. 6ff.; many of, e.g., our sales of houses were removed by illegal excavators from their archaeological context and we are no longer able to connect such documents to a specific object. For grants in general cf. R. Taubenschlag, *The Law of Graeco-Roman Egypt* (Warszawa 1955[2]) 399-401 and P.Col. X 274 introd.

It is also remarkable that, though according to l. 16 only a single copy of this document was written (cf. the phrasing 'Κυρία ἡ χάρις ἁπ[λῆ γραφεῖσα'), apparently a copy of the same text is found in **38.b**. For this curious situation we cannot find a better explanation than the idea (in fact a counsel of despair) that a scribal error must be at stake and that the scribe wrote ἁπλῆ where he should have written διπλῆ. Or, as **38.b** contains a writing error (cf. the critical apparatus on l. 8), should we assume that the same document was written again after the earlier copy had already been signed by Pausanias, while the earlier copy was not destroyed?

1. An Aurelius Pausanias is also mentioned in **4**, **5**, and **6** (all from House 2) and in **63** (from House 3, a Greek private letter to Pisistratos and Pausanias). In all cases we may be dealing with the same person. He was the son of a Valerius who may have been the author of **48** (a manumission of a female slave; 356) and **64** (a 4th-century private letter from Valerius to Philammon).
2. For Aurelius Psais son of Pamour cf. the family tree at p. 51.
2-3. For the relationship between the village of Kellis and the city of the Mothites cf. **20**.3-5n.
4. For the phrasing *χάριτι ἀ̣ἰ̣ω̣ν̣ί̣ῳ* [*καὶ ἀναφαιρέτῳ*] cf. **38.b**.4 and P.Grenf. II 71.11ff. Elsewhere one finds, e.g., *χάριτι ἀναφαιρέτῳ καὶ ἀμετανοήτῳ* (P.Grenf. II 68.4; 70.7).
6ff. The plot of land described here seems to be identical with the plot of land situated to the North of House 3.
The following arguments can be adduced in favour of this identification:

(a) The grant was found in House 3 where the beneficiary of the donation, Aurelius Psais son of Pamour, had been living;

(b) the text states clearly (l. 10) that to the South of the plot now given away is 'the house of you (= the beneficiary) and ...';

(c) to the North of the plot should be a 'public street' and in fact there is a street running North of the excavated 'Area A';

At the same time this identification clearly suggests that the '*καμηλών* (camel-shed) of Horos son of Mersis' was situated to the West of the plot. A man of this name occurs in papyri both from House 2 (**9**) and House 3 (**34**; **38.a,b**; **51**; **52**; **57**) and he is known to have been a camel-driver; it makes sense to connect a camel-driver with a camel-shed and if Horos ever lived in House 3 at some particular moment, he may have 'parked' his camels not too far away; it is, however, more problematical, as C.A. Hope (the site director) remarks, that the only building adjacent to the west of the plot given away in this document is Structure 4 (its precise nature is unclear) and that this could hardly have been used as a camel-shed, cf. its ground plan on the plan of Houses 1 - 3 (p. 5).
7-9. For the size of the 'carpenter's cubit' (= 45 cm.) cf. **4**.5-7n.; 15 such cubits (the dimensions of the plot at the South and at the North) = 6.75 m, 25 cubits (at the East and at the West) = 11.25 m. The whole plot measured almost 76 m^2. It is remarkable that these dimensions do not match with the size of the area adjacent to the North of House 3 (cf. the plan, p. 5). In fact, it looks as if the scribe used the dimensions of the East and West side while indicating the dimensions of the North and South side, and the dimensions of the North and South side for the West and East side.

In itself it does not seem very likely that the scribe would have forgotten to write *καὶ* in the lacuna at the right of l. 8; moreover, the (regular) form of the cardinal '25' should have been *εἴκοσι πέντε*, cf. **38.b**.8. On the other hand it should be noted that (a) it is impossible to read the first two letters in **38.a**.9 as *τε* (a reading *σι* seems to impose itself), (b) there is simply not enough of space for *καὶ* in the lacuna, and (c) next to *εἴκοσι πέντε* the Greek form *πέντε καὶ εἴκοσι* still occurs in later Greek, cf. F.T. Gignac, *Grammar*, II 196 (12).
14. For *ἑκουσίῳ γνώμῃ* instead of *ἑκουσίᾳ γνώμῃ* cf. F.T. Gignac, *op.cit.* II 111.
16. Cf. above, the introduction.
19f. These are the consuls of 333, cf. R.S. Bagnall a.o., *CLRE* s.a. Hathyr 1 according to the Alexandrian calendar = 28.x, but if the date were calculated according to the Egyptian calendar, it

would fall 89 days earlier, viz. on 1.viii.333. For the persistent use of the traditional Egyptian calendar next to the Alexandrian calendar cf. D. Hagedorn - K.A. Worp in ZPE 104 (1994) 243-255.

38.b: GRANT OF A PLOT OF LAND

(28.x.333)

P.Kellis inv. P. 52.H (House 3, room 9, level 3) + P. 65.L (House 3, room 8, level 3). H. 24 x B. cm. The writing runs parallel with the fibers, the back is blank.

1 [Αὐρ]ήλιο[ς Πανσανίας Οὐ]ạλερίου [ἄρ]ξας Μωθιτῶν πόλεως
2 [Αὐρηλί]ῳ Ψ[άιτι Πα]μ̣[ου]ρ[ίος ἀπὸ] κ̣ώ̣[μη]ς Κέλλεως τῆς αὐτῆς
3 [Μωθι]τ̣ῶ̣ν̣ πόλεως χ[α]ί̣ρειν.
4 [Ὁμολογῶ κε]χαρ[ίσθαι σοι χ]ά̣ρ̣[ιτι αἰ]ω̣[νί]α̣ καὶ ἀναφαιρέτῳ ἀπὸ
5 [τοῦ ν]ῦ̣ν ἐπὶ τὸν ἅπαντα χ[ρό]ν̣ο̣ν̣ ἀ̣πὸ τῶν ὑπαρχόντων
6 [μοι ἐ]δ̣αφῶ̣[ν ἐξ Ἀπ]η̣λ̣ί̣τ̣ο̣υ̣ κ̣ώ̣μ̣ης Κέλλεως τόπ[ο]ν
7 [πρὸς] ἀ̣νοικ̣[οδομὴ]ν̣, Νότο̣υ̣ καὶ Βορ[ρ]ᾶ πηχέων τεκτον[ι]κῶν
8 [δεκαπ]έντε, Ἀ̣[πηλιώ]τ̣ου κα̣ὶ̣ Βορρᾶ [πη]χέων εἴκοσι πέντε.
9 [Γείτ]ονες· Ἀπ̣[ηλιώ]του ἐδ̣ά̣φη ἐμο[ῦ Π]αυσανίου, Λ̣ι̣β̣ὸ̣ς̣ κ̣αμη-
10 [λὼν] Ὥ̣ρου Μέρσι[ος, Νό]του οἰκία σου κ[αὶ] υ̣ἱ̣ο̣ῦ̣ κ̣α̣ὶ̣ . . [.] . ν σου,
11 Β̣ο̣ρρᾶ ῥύμη δ[η]μοσία, ἢ οἳ ἐὰν ὦσ̣ι̣ γείτονε[ς πάντοθ]εν,
12 πρὸς τὸ ἐξεῖναί σοι ἐπικρα̣τεῖν κα̣ὶ̣ [κυριεύειν αὐτο]ῦ̣ καὶ
13 ἐξουσίαν ἔχειν διοικεῖν καὶ οἰκονο̣μ̣ε̣ῖ̣ν̣ περὶ τοῦ χ[αρισθέν]τος
14 σοι τόπου ἑκουσίῳ γνώμῃ τρόπῳ ᾧ ἐὰν α[ἱρῇ τῆς β]ε̣βαι-
15 ώσεως ἐξακολουθούσης μοι διὰ π̣α̣ν̣τ̣[ὸς ἀπὸ πα]ν̣τ̣ὸ̣ς̣ τοῦ ἐ̣πε-
16 λευσομένου ἢ ἀντιποιησομένου. Κυρί̣[α ἡ χάρι]ς ἁπλῆ γραφεῖσα
17 ἐπ' ι' ὑπογραφῆς μ̣ο̣υ̣ ἔσ̣τ̣ω κ̣α̣ὶ̣ β̣ε̣β̣α̣ί̣α [ὡς ἐν] δημοσίῳ κατα-
18 κειμένη καὶ ἐπερωτηθεὶς ὡμολόγησα.
19 Ὑπατείας Φλαυίου Δελματίου ἀδελφοῦ τοῦ δ[εσπότο]υ ἡμῶν
20 Κωνσταντίνου Αὐγούστου καὶ Δομιττίου Ζηνοφί̣λ̣[ου τῶ]ν λαμπροτάτων
21 [Ἁ]θὺρ α.
22 (M. 2) Αὐρήλιος Πανσανίας Οὐαλερίου ἄρξας ὁ προκείμενος ἐχ̣α̣ρισ̣ά̣-
23 μην τὸν προκείμενον ψιλὸν τόπον ὡς πρόκειται καὶ ἐπερωτη-
24 θεὶς ὡμολόγησα.

6 Ἀπηλιώτου 8 Βορρᾶ error for Λιβός! 9 ἐμοῦ: ἐμ- ex corr. (σ-?) 11 ἐὰν ex corr., l. ἄν 14 ἑκουσίᾳ, ἄν

For an introduction and commentary to this text (a copy of **38.a**) cf. above, **38.a**; a comparison of **38.a** and **38.b** yields the following result:

38.A 1 Αὐρήλιος Π̣α̣υ̣σ̣α̣ν̣ίας Οὐαλερίου ἄρξα[ς Μωθιτῶν πόλεως]
38.B 1 [Αὐρ]ήλιο[ς Παυσανίας Οὐ]α̣λερίου [ἄρ]ξας Μωθιτῶν πόλεως

38.A 2 Αὐρηλίῳ [Ψά]ι̣τι Παμοῦρ ἀπὸ κ̣ώ̣μ̣η̣[ς Κέλλεως τῆς]
38.B 2 [Αὐρηλί]ῳ̣ Ψ[άιτι Πα]μ̣[ου]ρ̣[ίος ἀπὸ] κ̣ώ̣[μη]ς Κέλλεως τῆς αὐτῆς

38.A 3 αὐτῆς Μ̣ω̣θ̣ι̣τ̣ῶ̣ν̣ π̣ό̣λ̣εως [χαίρειν]
38.B 3 [Μωθι]τ̣ῶ̣ν̣ πόλεως χ[α]ί̣ρειν.

38.A 4 [Ὁ]μολο̣γ[ῶ κεχαρ]ί̣σ̣θαι σοι χάριτι α̣ἰ̣ω̣ν̣ί̣α̣ [καὶ ἀναφαιρέτῳ]
38.B 4 [Ὁμολογῶ κε]χαρ[ίσθαι σοι χ]ά̣ρ̣[ιτι αἰ]ω̣[νί]α̣ καὶ ἀναφαιρέτῳ̣ ἀπὸ

38.A 5 ἀ̣π̣ὸ̣ τοῦ ν̣ῦ̣[ν ἐπὶ] τ̣ὸν ἅπαντα χρόνον ἀ̣[πὸ τῶν ὑπαρχόν-]
38.B 5 [τοῦ ν]ῦ̣ν ἐπὶ τ̣ὸν ἅπαντα χ[ρό]ν̣ο̣ν̣ ἀ̣π̣ὸ τῶν ὑπαρχόντων

38.A 6 των μοι [ἐ]δ̣α̣φῶν ἐξ Ἀπηλιώ̣του κώμη[ς Κέλλεως τόπον]
38.B 6 [μοι ἐ]δ̣αφῶ̣[ν ἐξ Ἀπ]ηλ̣ί̣τ̣ο̣υ̣ κ̣ώ̣μης Κέλλεως τόπ[ο]ν

38.A 7 πρὸς ἀνοι[κ]ο̣δ̣ομὴν̣ Νότου καὶ Βορρᾶ [πηχέων τεκτονι-]
38.B 7 [πρὸς] ἀ̣νοικ̣[οδομὴ]ν̣, Νότο̣υ̣ καὶ Βορ̣[ρ]ᾶ πηχέων τεκτον[ι]κῶν

38.A 8 κῶν δεκ̣[απ]έ̣ν̣[τε], Ἀπηλιώτου καὶ Λιβὸ̣ς̣ [πηχέων πέντε <καὶ> εἴκο-]
38.B 8 [δεκαπ]έντε, Ἀ̣[πηλιώ]του κα̣ὶ̣ Βορρᾶ [πη]χέων εἴκοσι πέντε.

38.A 9 σι. Γείτονες· Ἀ̣πηλ̣ιώτου ἐδάφη ἐμοῦ Πα̣[υσανίου, Λιβὸς καμη-]
38.B 9 [Γείτ]ονες· Ἀπ̣[ηλιώ]του ἐδ̣ά̣φη ἐμο[ῦ Π]αυσανίου, Λ̣ι̣β̣ὸ̣ς̣ κ̣αμη-

38.B 10 λὼν Ὥρο[υ] Μ̣έρσ̣ι̣[ο]ς, Νότου οἰκία σου [καὶ υἱοῦ καὶ ......]
38.B 10 [λὼν] Ὥ̣ρου Μέρσι[ος, Νό]του οἰκία σου κ[αὶ] υ̣ἱ̣ο̣ῦ̣ κ̣α̣ὶ̣ ..[.].ν σου,

38.A 11 σου, Βορρᾶ ῥύμη δημοσία, ἢ οἱ ἐὰν ὦσι̣ [γείτονες πάντοθεν,]
38.B 11 Β̣ο̣ρρᾶ ῥύμη δ[η]μοσία, ἢ οἱ̣ ἐὰν ὦσ̣ι̣ γείτονε[ς πάντοθ]εν,

38.A 12 πρὸς τ̣ὸ ἐξεῖν̣[αί σοι] ἐ̣π̣ικρατεῖν καὶ κυριε[ύειν αὐτοῦ καὶ]
38.B 12 πρὸς τὸ ἐξεῖναί σοι ἐπικρα̣τεῖν κα̣ὶ̣ [κυριεύειν αὐτο]ῦ̣ καὶ

38.A 13 διοικεῖν καὶ οἰκονομεῖν περὶ τοῦ χαρισθ[έντος σοι τόπου]
38.B 13 ἐξουσίαν ἔχειν διοικεῖν καὶ οἰκονομ̣ε̣ῖ̣ν̣ περὶ τοῦ χ[αρισθέν]τος

38.A 14 ἑκουσίῳ γ̣ν̣ώ̣μ̣η̣ τρόπῳ ᾧ ἐὰν αἱρῇ, τῆς β[εβαιώσεως]
38.B 14 σοι τόπου ἑκουσίῳ γνώμη τρόπῳ̣ ᾧ ἐὰν α[ἱρῇ τῆς β]εβαι-

38.A 15 ἐξακολουθο̣ύ̣σ̣ης μοι διὰ παντὸς ἀπὸ παντὸς[τοῦ ἐπελευσομέ-]
38.B 15 ώσεως ἐξακολουθούσης μοι διὰ π̣α̣ν̣τ̣[ὸς ἀπὸ πα]ν̣τ̣ὸ̣ς τοῦ ἐ̣πε-

38.A 16 νου ἢ ἀντιπ̣ο̣ιησομένου. Κυρία ἡ χάρις ἁπ[λῆ γραφεῖ]σ̣α̣ ἐ̣φ'
38.B 16 λευσομένου ἢ ἀντιποιησομένου. Κυρ̣ί̣[α ἡ χάρι]ς ἁπλῆ γραφεῖσα

38.A 17 ὑπογραφῆς μου ἔστω καὶ βεβαία ὡς ἐν δημ̣[οσίῳ] κατα̣κ̣ειμέ̣ν̣η
38.B 17 ἐπ`ὶ´ ὑπογραφῆς μ̣ο̣υ̣ ἔ̣σ̣τ̣ω κ̣α̣ὶ̣ β̣ε̣β̣α̣ί̣α [ὡς ἐν] δημοσίῳ κατα-

38.A 18 καὶ ἐπερωτηθεὶς ὡμολόγησα.
38.B 18 κειμένη καὶ ἐπερωτηθεὶς ὡμολόγησα.

38.A 19 Ὑπατείας Φλαυίου Δελματίου ἀδελφοῦ τοῦ δ[εσπότ]ου ἡμ̣ῶν
38.B 19 Ὑπατείας Φλαυίου Δελματίου ἀδελφοῦ τοῦ δ[εσπότο]υ ἡμῶν

38.A 20 Κωνσταντίνου Αὐγούστου καὶ Δομεττ̣έ̣ο̣υ̣ [Ζην]οφί̣λ̣ου [τ]ῶ̣ν̣
38.B 20 Κωνσταντίνου Αὐγούστου καὶ Δομιττίου Ζηνοφί̣λ̣[ου τῶ]ν λαμπροτάτων

38.A 21 λαμπροτ̣ά̣τ̣ων Ἁθὺρ α⁻.
38.B 21 [Ἁ]θὺρ α.

38.A 22 (M. 2) Αὐρήλι[ο]ς Πανσαν̣ί̣α̣ς Οὐαλερίο̣υ ἄρξας κ̣ε̣χ̣ά̣ρισ̣[μαι]
38.B 22 (M. 2) Αὐρήλιος Πανσανίας Οὐαλερίου ἄρξας ὁ̣ προκείμενος ἐχ̣αρισ̣ά-

38.A 23 τὸν̣ προκεί̣μ̣ε̣ν(ον) ψιλὸν τόπ̣[ον] ὡ̣ς π̣ρ̣ό̣κειττα̣ι καὶ ἐπερ[ωτηθεὶς]
38.B 23 μην τὸν προκείμενον ψιλὸν τόπον ὡς πρόκειται καὶ ἐπερωτη-

38.A 24 ὡμολό̣γησα.
38.B 24 θεὶς ὡμολόγησα.

The more important divergences between the two copies are in l. 8 (where **38.b** is incorrect in the indication of the neighbours, while **38.a** uses an slightly unusual form for the numeral 'twenty five') and l. 13 where **38.b** inserts ἐξουσίαν ἔχειν. In l. 22 **38.b** adds an extra-element ὁ προκείμενος.

39: SALE OF PART OF AN ORCHARD

(4th century)

P.Kellis inv. P. 92.15 (House 3, room 1.a, level 2). In the frame are two fragments. Frag. I: 12.3 x B. 9 cm. Margin at the top 2, at the right ca. 1 cm. At least 3 vertical folds are preserved, while the fragment has broken on a fold at the left. Frag. II: H. 7.5 x B. 3.2 cm. Margin at the left 7.5, at the bottom ca. 2 cm. The verso is blank.

NB: the two fragments may not belong together.

Frag. I:

1 [Αὐρήλιοι N.N. καὶ N.N. sons of -]υς ἀπὸ κώμης Κέλλεως
2 [τῆς Μωθιτῶν πόλεω]ς Αὐρηλίῳ Πεβῶτι Παμοῦρ
3 [ἀπὸ τῆς αὐτῆς (?) χαίρειν.]
4 [Ὁμολογοῦμεν πεπρακέναι σοι] ἀπὸ τοῦ νῦν ἐπὶ τὸν ἑξῆς
5 [ἅπαντα χρόνον - - - - - τὸ ἕβδ]ομον μέρος κηπίου ὕπαρχον
6 [ἡμῖν· γείτονες Νότου ψιλὸς ἡμ]ῶν, Βορρᾶ ψιλὸς ἡμῶν πάλιν,
7 [Λιβὸς - - - - - - - - -. Ἀπηλιώ]του ψιλὸς Ἠλία ἐλθόντος εἰς ἡμᾶς
8 [ἀπὸ κληρονομίας (?) τιμῆς] τῆς συμπεφω[νημέ]νης
9 [ἀργυρίου Σεβαστ- ταλάντων πεντα]κισχιλία, γί(νεται) (τάλ.) Ε-,
10 [καὶ εὐδο]κοῦμεν καὶ πεπεί-
11 [σμεθα πρὸς τὸ ἀπὸ τοῦ νῦν σε ἐπι]κρατεῖν τοῦ πραθέν-
12 [τος σοι μέρους] μετὰ τοῦ μέρους τῶν[
13 [καὶ ἐξεῖναί σοι διοικεῖν καὶ ἐπιτελ]εῖν περὶ αὐτοῦ τρόπ[ῳ]
14 [ᾧ ἐὰν αἱρῇ,] TRACES

- -

5 ϋπαρχον Pap. 9 πεντα]κισχιλίων 14 ἄν

Frag. II:

- -

15 προσ[
16 ἀγουσι[
17 κυρία[
18 Ἱερακ[εὐδοκῶ πᾶσι τοῖς ἐγγε-]
19 γραμμ[ένοις ὡς πρόκειται.]
20 Αὐρή[λιος N.N. ἀπὸ - - - - - - - - -]
21 ἔγραψ[α ὑπὲρ αὐτ- γράμματα μὴ εἰδότ-.]

18 ϊερακ Pap.

(Ll. 1-14) "Aurelius N.N., from the village of Kellis belonging to the city of the Mothites, to Aurelius Pebos son of Pamour, from the same village, greetings. I agree that I have sold (?) to you from now on for all of the future the seventh part of an orchard which belongs to us. Its neighbours are: to the South an empty plot of land belonging to us, to the North an empty plot of land belonging to us again, to the West ---, to the East an empty plot of land belonging to Elias. The plot has come to us from an inheritance ...; the price agreed upon is five thousand Imperial silver talents, 5000 (tal.). -- and we agree and we are satisfied with regard to your henceforward owning the share (?) which has been sold to you --- with the part of the --- and that you may dispose and manage it in whatever way you prefer - -."

This incompletely preserved papyrus contains a contract of sale (cf. l. 4) of a seventh part of an orchard. The situation of the orchard within the territory of the village of Kellis is rather precisely indicated and it is worth noticing that both at the South and at the North empty plots of land (ψιλοί, sc. *τόποι*) adjacent to this orchard are owned by its sellers. The size of the orchard sold is unknown and five thousand talents paid for only a 7th share in such an orchard may seem at first sight a lot of money; on the other hand, the precise date of this transaction is now lost and especially during the 2nd half of the 4th century 5000 talents did not buy very much (in PSI VIII 959 [ca. 385-388], e.g., wine was sold at 4000 Tal./knidion and in P.Oslo III 88 [ca. 360-375] the price of gold was 15,000 Tal./solidus, cf. R.S. Bagnall, *Currency and Inflation in Fourth Century Egypt* 66 [wine], 62 [gold]).

1. We must be dealing with a plurality of persons, cf. l. 4n. It is likely that the name of the father ended in the genitive on -ο]υς; restore, e.g., Πλουτογένους or Τιθοέους (these names are frequent enough in the onomasticon of Kellis).

2. For the reading cf. **20**.3-5n. The length of the restoration at the left (15 letters) does not allow the restoration of an extra word like κώμης in the lacuna at the left of l. 3 (now already 18 letters).

4. The phrasing ἀπὸ τοῦ νῦν ἐπὶ τὸν ἑξῆς ἅπαντα χρόνον indicates that one must be dealing here with a sale; cf. also l. 11ff., where future property rights are being described. The restoration of the plural Ὁμολογοῦμεν should be compared with l. 6, ἡμῶν, l. 7, ἡμᾶς, and with the plurals in ll. 10-11, εὐδο]κ̣οῦμεν καὶ πεπεί-[σμεθα.

5. For κῆποι = 'orchards' in the Oases cf. G. Wagner, *Les Oasis d'Egypte* 116 and 289. They are not often referred to elsewhere in the Greek papyri from Kellis. According to the description of the neighbours of the present orchard it was situated in the middle of some empty plots of land (maybe on the outskirts of the village?).

The structure of the text in this and the following lines is not altogether clear. On the basis of parallel documents one expects τὸ ὑπάρχον ἡμῖν ἕβδομον μέρος κηπίου, ὧν γείτονες κτλ., but there is not enough space to restore ὑπάρχον ἡμῖν in the lacuna in l. 5 (dropping the superfluous stop-gap word ἅπαντα could remedy this), and its restoration would seem tautological in view of the preserved ὕπαρχον at the end of the line.

6. The use of πάλιν is a bit unusual. More often one finds in such an enumeration of owners of adjacent plots, where an owner owns similar property at more than one side, some form of the word ἄλλος used (i.c.: ἄλλος ψιλὸς ἡμῶν).

7-8. The phrasing ἐλθόντος εἰς ἡμᾶς (= 'coming to us') found after the indication of some property indicates the source of the present ownership (cf. **34**.6n.), i.e. its coming from, e.g., an inheritance. For that reason we have tentatively restored ἀπὸ κληρονομίας in the lacuna; after that one would expect an indication of a deceased person ('father', 'mother', etc.), but one may, of course, prefer restoring, e.g., [ἀπὸ δικαίου ὠνῆς = 'by right of sale'. It should be noted that here the genitive ἐλθόντος goes apparently with κηπίου (l. 5), though it might seem more logical to see the words τὸ ἕβδ]ο̣μον μέρος in that same line being followed by a accusative participle, sc. ἐλθὸν εἰς ἡμᾶς. There is no reason to think that ἐλθόντος εἰς ἡμᾶς should be taken with Ἠλία.

9. Restore either Σεβαστοῦ or Σεβαστῶν.

10-14. For the phrasing restored here cf. **34**.9ff.

14. It seems just possible to read at the end of this line]δ̣ι̣ὰ̣ [π]α̣ν̣ i.e. part of the formula τῆς βεβαιώσεως ἐξακολουθούσης μοι] διὰ παν- | (14.a) [τὸς ἀπὸ παντὸς τοῦ ἐπελευσομένου κτλ., cf. **34**.14-15.

15ff. It is uncertain whether this fragment really belongs to the same text as ll. 1-14. Given the extant remains of restorable text it looks likely that somewhere in ll. 17-18 a second hand started writing the subscription for the selling party, after a professional scribe had written the body of the contract itself. Indeed, it seems not excluded that one may connect the writing of ll. 1-14 with the writing preserved in ll. 15-17, but there is little material for a thorough palaeographical comparison.

21. Should one read αὐτοῦ, εἰδότος or αὐτῶν, εἰδότων (cf. the plural in ll. 1, 10) ?

40 - **47**: LOANS OF MONEY

On the subject of loans of money in general there is a considerable bibliography; for the principal works, see now H.-A. Rupprecht, *Kleine Einführung in die Papyruskunde* (Darm-stadt 1994) 118ff., 127f.

In general the loan contracts from Kellis follow the phrasings found in loan contracts from the Nile valley. No contract has been cancelled by way of *chiasmos*, while **40**.10, **41**.15, **42**.26 and **45**.18 state in unambiguous terms that the contract had been drawn up in a single copy (cf. also **43**.28 and **44**.16); some of the loans (**42**, **44**; possibly also **43**) concern money apparently borrowed in the village of Aphrodite by members of the family living at Kellis in House 3 who had moved (at least temporarily) to the Nile valley. In order to explain the presence of these texts at Kellis in this house it must be assumed that the original contracts were just returned by the creditor to the debtor after his repayment of the loan; the debtor then took the original with him back to Kellis.

An interesting phenomenon in these loan contracts from Kellis is the fact that the interest rate mentioned in them is sometimes considerably higher than the legal interest rate (in Roman times regularly 12% / year, cf. H.E. Finckh, *Das Zinsrecht der gräko-ägyptischen Papyri* [Diss. Erlangen 1962], §§ 6, 7). An investigation into interest levels found in other 4th-century loan contracts yields the remarkable result that in virtually all short-term loans from this century the interest rate can be calculated as having been significantly higher than the legal rate. The following table and discussion will be instructive:

Reference	*Amount*	*Term*	*Interest*
P.Amst. I 44 (314)	]9 Tal., - Dr.	8? months	?
BGU III 941 (376)	2 sol.	?	?
BGU III 943 (389)	1 sol.	?	?
P.Bad. II 27 (316)	]3 Tal., 400 Dr.	8 months	- %/month
P.Bad. II 28 (331)	373 Tal., 2000 Dr.	?	?
P.Charite 33 (346/7?)	1300 Tal.	?	?
P.Charite 34 (348?)	640 Tal.	?	- % p.month
P.Coll.Yout.II 82 (337)	500 Tal.	7 months	10 T./month or 16 T.,4000 dr. for penalty
P.Gen. I 12 (383)	1 sol.	?	?
P.Giss. I 53 (IV)	4 sol.	?	?
P.Grenf. II 72 (308)	2 Tal.	?	?
P.Haun. III 56 (IV/V)	15 sol.?	-	?
P.Laur. III 76 (IV)	?	?	?
P.Lips. 12 (IV)	60 Tal.	?	?
P.Lips. 13 (364)	2 sol.	?	$^1/3$ *gramma* gold/month
P.Lips. 14 (391)	850 Tal.	?	?
P.Lond. II 153 (p.318; IV)	1000 Dr.	?	?
P.Lond.III 870 (p.235; IV)	5 sol.	?	?
P.Mich. XV 728 (IV/V)	2 sol.	'undetermined'	?

Reference	Amount	Term	Interest
P.Nepheros 32 (344)	80 Tal.	4 months	?
P.Oslo II 41 (331)	53 T.,1000 Dr.	1 month	?
P.Oxy. VII 1041 381)	4200 Myr.Den.	1.5 month	?
P.Oxy. X 1318 (308)	5000+ Dr.	?	?
P.Oxy. XII 1495 (IV)	ca. 40 Tal.	?	?
P.Oxy. XIV 1714 (IV)	110? Tal.?	?	?
P.Oxy. XIV 1716 (333)	300 Tal.	?	?
P.Panop Köln 21 (315)	11 Tal., 300 Den.	6 months	'Without interest'
P.Sakaon 64 (307)	3.5 Tal.	1 month	- % /month
P.Sakaon 65 (328)	78 Tal.	3 months	- % /month
P.Sakaon 66 (328)	340 Tal.	2 months	- % /month
P.Sakaon 96 (303)	4320 Dr.	1 month	- % /month
P.Select. 7 (314)	6.5 Tal.	1 month?	- % /month
PSI III 215 (339)	?	?	?
PSI VII 841 (IV)	400 Dr.	?	?
PSI IX 1078 (356)	4000 Tal.	?	?
P.Stras. 278 (316)	- Tal., 200 Dr.	1 month	?
P.Stras. 817 (340)	?	?	?
P.Wash.Univ. I 23 (IV/V)	1 sol.	?	?
SB I 4652 (304)	1 Tal.	?	?
SB IV 7338 (300)	3000 Dr.	?	?
SB VI 9191/9270 (337)	87 or 7 Tal.	1-8 months	?
SB X 10655 (IV)	1120 Myr.Den.	?	?
SB XIV 11385 (326)	35 Tal.	8 months	11 Tal., 4000 Dr.
42 (364)	5000 Tal.	?	500 Tal./month
44 (382)	1 sol.	?	7200 Tal./year
46 (IV)	1 Myr.Tal.	?	?

To be excluded from this list is P.Ant. II 102 [ed. 390, but cf. BL VIII 9: 445], a loan of an unknown number of solidi for an unknown period at an interest of 5+ myr.den.

Repayment in kind for loans of money is promised in the following loan contracts which cannot easily be used for calculating interest rates:

Reference	Amount	Term	Repayment
P.Rain.Cent. 86 (381)	5 sol.	?	5 bundles of flax
P.Col. VII 177 (326)	7 Tal.	6 months	1 Art.vegetable seed
P.Col. VII 184 (372)	3600 Tal.	6? months	6 Art. barley
SB XIV 12088 (346)	50 Tal.	3-4 months	1.5 --- vegetables
41 (310)	2 Tal., 3000 Dr.	?	To be repaid by performing services
45 (386)	1 sol.	<6? months	5 *maria* of oil
47 (IV)	1 Myr.Tal.	?	1 Art. wheat

Now, if (1) for the following discussion those documents are excluded beforehand in which a number of gold coins (*solidi*) are borrowed without any further specification of interest to be paid and if we restrict ourselves to amounts of money indicated in (billon) talents with or without an additional amount of drachmas, and if (2) we restrict ourselves to short term loans (in fact, there are not many long term loans in the list printed above), and if (3) we assume that (3.a) in the amounts of billon currency borrowed the (concealed) interest is included (i.e. that the amounts were actually paid out with a certain amount of money for interest deducted beforehand) and that (3.b) in a specific situation a 'logical' round sum (e.g.: 350 talents) was actually borrowed (rather than, say, 351 Tal., 3527 Dr.), it seems possible to make some calculations for reconstructing interest levels which are presented below in ascending order:

Reference	*Amount*	*Term*	*Interest*
P.Bad. II 27 (316)	]3 Tal., 400 Dr.	8 months	- % / month

The (relatively small) amount of 400 drachmae suggests to us that the number of talents borrowed was 3 rather than [1]3, [2]3, etc. If the principal sum borrowed were 3 Tal. (= 18,000 Dr.) and interest was to be paid at 400 Dr. / 8 months > 600 Dr./year, the interest rate would be 3.333 % / year; this is very low. If, however, the principal sum = 2 Tal., 4000 Dr. (= 16,000 Dr.) and interest = 2,400 Dr., the interest rate = **15**% / 8 months > **22.5**% / year. With a principal sum of 2 Tal., 3000 Dr. and an interest of 3,400 Dr./8 months > 5,100 Dr./year the interest rate would be **34**% / year. Such rates are definitely better, though these percentages are not paralleled (cf. below).

P.Panop.Köln 21 (315)	11 Tal., 300 Den.	6 months	-

If the principal sum borrowed were 10 Tal. and interest was to be paid to the amount of 1 Tal., 300 Den., then interest at 7,200 Dr. for 6 months > 1,200 Dr./month, i.e. 2% / month = **24**% / year. N.B. The document itself states that the loan was 'without interest' (cf. P.W. Pestman, *Loans without Interest?*, JJP 16/17 [1971] 7ff.), but that statement was not taken seriously by the editors.

P.Coll.Youtie II 82 (337)	500 Tal.	7 months	10 Tal. / month, 16 Tal., 4000 dr. / month

On the basis of the interest sums indicated in the document itself it is easy to calculate that normal interest was 2% / month = **24**% / year, while the penalty interest stood at **40**% / year.

44 (382)	1 sol.	?	7200 Tal. / year

If 1 sol. has a value of 30,000 Tal. (see the note to l. 9), then the interest rate was **24**% / year.

P.Stras. 278 (316)	[1] Tal., 200 Dr.	1 month	?

Given the amount of 200 drachmae (cf. above ad P.Bad. II 27) we calculate that the principal sum borrowed was 1 Tal. (the editor did not restore the numeral for the amount of talents), the interest for 1 month being 200 drachmae; this yields an interest level of **40**% per year; cf. the next item. With a principal sum of 2 or even more Tal., 200 dr., it becomes virtually impossible to calculate a sensible interest rate.

P.Oxy. VII 1041 (381) 4,200 Myr.Den. 1.5 month ?
If the principal sum borrowed was 4,000 Myr.Den. and interest to be paid was 200 Myr.Den., then interest = **40**% / year.

SB XIV 11385 (326) 35 Tal. 8 months 11 Tal., 4000 Dr. (= 11 1/3 Tal.)
The interest level in this text stands at exactly **50**% / year; 11 1/3 Tal. interest for 8 months > 17.5 Tal. / year.

P.Lips. 13 (364) 2 sol. = [48 Ker.] ? 1/3 gr. [= 2 Ker.] / month.
Interest was evidently **50**% / year. For the date of the document, see C. Zuckerman in ZPE 100 (1994) 203.

P.Lips. 14 (391) 850 Tal. ? ?
Was the principal sum lent 800 Tal. and the interest 50 Tal. for a loan of 1 month? If so, the interest level would be 6.25% / month > **75**% / year; but if the loan actually ran for 3 months (see the next item), the interest level would be **25**% / year.

P.Sakaon 65 (328) 78 Tal. 3 months ?
If the principal sum lent were 65 Tal. and the interest for 3 months were 13 Tal., the interest rate is 20% / 3 months > **80**% / year.

P.Sakaon 66 (328) 340 Tal. 2 months - % / month.
If the principal sum lent were 300 Tal. and the interest for two months was 40 Tal., then the interest rate was **80**% / year.

P.Bad. II 28 (331) 373 Tal., 2000 Dr. ? ?
If the principal sum lent were 350 Tal. and the interest was 23.3333 Tal., then the interest = 6 2/3 % of the principal sum. If, furthermore, the term of the loan is 1 month (cf. the next item), then the interest level was **80**% / year. If, however, the term of the loan actually was 2 months, the interest level would drop to 40% / year.

P.Charite 34 (348?) 640 Tal. incl. ? - % / month
It is stated in the text that the 640 Tal. included interest. Was the principal sum lent 600 Tal. and was the interest 40 Tal.? If so, then interest is, again, 6 2/3% of the principal sum and if the term of the loan was 1 month, then the interest level was **80**% / year. If, however, the term of the loan actually was 2 months, the interest level would drop to **40**% / year.

P.Oslo II 41 (331) 53 Tal., 1000 Dr. 1 month ?
If the principal sum borrowed was 50 Tal. and if the interest were 3 Tal., 1000 Dr., then interest = **76**% / year. The reading of '1000 Dr.', however, seems doubtful; we wonder whether the original reads (δρ.) 'Γ rather than (δρ.) 'Α (1000 Dr. in this context seems odd). Hence, if the interest is 3.5 Tal. / month, then the interest rate is 7% / month > **84**% / year.

P.Sakaon 96 (303) 4320 Dr. 1 month -/
If the principal sum borrowed were 4000 dr. and if the interest were 320 dr., then the interest rate was 8% / month > **96**% / year.

P.Select. XIII 7 (314) 6.5 Tal. 1 month? - % / month
If the principal sum borrowed were 6 Tal. and the interest were 0.5 Tal. for 1 month, then the interest rate was exactly **100**% / year.

P.Nepheros 32 (344) 80 Tal. 4 months ?
If the principal sum borrowed were 60 Tal. and the interest were 20 Tal., then the interest rate was **100**% / year. We fail to see an alternative ratio (here 3::1) between the principal sum and the interest which would result into an acceptable rate of interest.

942 (364) 5000 Tal. ? 500 Tal. / month
The interest rate is clearly **120**% / year.

P.Sakaon 64 (307) 3 Tal., 3000 Dr. 1 month - % / month
If the principal sum borrowed were 3 Tal. and interest was 0.5 Tal., then the interest rate was even as high as **200**% / year. If, on the other hand, the principal sum borrowed were 20,000 Dr. (3 Tal., 2000 Dr.), 1000 Dr. / month for interest would have represented an interest rate of 5% / month = **60**% / year.

Certain patterns in these rates can be observed: interest rates of 24, 84, 96 and 120% are all multiples of 12 % / year). Likewise, 200% = 2 x 100 %, while 50% = 100% ÷ 2 and 75% is 1.5 x 50%, while 80% = 2 x 40% (or, for that matter, 40% = 80% ÷ 2) and 60% is 1.5 x 40%. The only interest rates which stand out are the 22.5% or 34% found in P.Bad. II 27, but they are close enough to 24% or 40 % to be acceptable. Though it may be objected that some of the calculations seem rather artificial, there is in our opinion no good reason to look generally with great suspicion at interest rates in 4th-century documents which are much higher than the usual 12%. In times of inflation people may have wanted to limit the risks of money lending by demanding considerably higher interest rates than the legal rate. Moreover, in some places and at certain times capital may have been short. It may be interesting to chart the various years of the documents just discussed and the reconstructed interest rates calculated:

303: 96%
307: 60 % or 200%?
314: 100%
315: 24%
316: 22.5% or 34%?, 40%
326: 50%
328: 80%, 80%
331: 80%, 84%
337: 24, 40% (penalty interest)
344: 100%
348?: 80 or 40%?
364: 50%, 120%
381: 40%
382: 24%
391: 25 or 75%?

In concluding we wish to observe that nowadays short term loans for, e.g., bridging finance are usually at a higher % annualised than long term loans. Was the same practised in Antiquity?

40: FRAGMENT OF A LOAN (?)

(306/307)

P.Kellis inv. P. 51.E # 1 (House 3, room 9, level 3, East wall). H. 22 x B. 4.8 cm. Margins: at the left 2, at the bottom 2.5 cm. The writing runs parallel with the fibers, the verso is blank.

1 Αὐρήλιọ[ι καὶ Ταψάις]
2 ἀμφότε[ροι ἀπὸ κώμης N.N. Ὁμολογοῦμεν ἐσχηκέναι παρὰ σοῦ εἰς ἰδίαν καὶ ἀναγκαίαν]
3 ἡμῶν χ[ρείαν]
4 διὰ τῆς χạ[ ]
5 καὶ μηδε.[ ]
6 ὅλον απạ[ ]
7 λων τῶṿ[ ]
8 ἐὰν δέ τις[ ]
9 τοῦ ἀνα[. Κυρία ἡ ὁμολο-]
10 γία ἁπλ̣[ῆ γραφεῖσα καὶ βεβαία καὶ ἔννομος καὶ ἐπερω-]
11 τηθέντẹ[ς ὡμολογήσαμεν.
12 (Ἔτους) ιεS// καὶ [γS// καὶ αS// τῶν κυρίων ἡμῶν Μαξιμιανοῦ]

13 καὶ Σεου[ήρου Σεβαστῶν καὶ Μαξιμίνου καὶ Κωνσταντίνου τῶν]
14 ἐπιφαν[εστάτων Καισάρων, Month, day.]
15 Αὐρήλι[οι καὶ]
16 Ταψάις[ ]
17 ἐσχή[καμεν]
18 φ̣[ ]
19 καὶ ἐπ[ερ(ωτηθέντες) ὡμολ(ογήσαμεν). Ἔγραψεν ὑπὲρ αὐτῶν γράμματα μὴ εἰδό-]
20 των Αὐ[ρήλιος N.N. ἀπὸ N.N.]

Though this fragmentarily preserved papyrus does not contain many clues for establishing its precise nature there is some reason to regard it as the remains of a loan contract, cf. ll. 9-10, ὁμολο-]γία and l. 17, ἐσχή[καμεν (in the subscription by what we take to be the lending parties; for the plural cf. ἀμφότε[ροι in l. 2); hence we restore in ll. 2-3: [- -. Ὁμολογοῦμεν ἐσχηκέναι παρὰ σοῦ εἰς ἰδίαν καὶ ἀναγκαίαν] / ἡμῶν χ[ρείαν, 'we acknowledge that we have borrowed from you for our private and immediate use' (for formulas found at the start of loans of money cf. in general P.Sta.Xyla p.47 (some of the formulas, however, listed there do not have anything to do with loans). The restorations of 36 letters in l. 10, 32 letters in l. 12, 42 [!] letters in l. 13 and 36 letters in l. 19 are all modelled after parallels in other Kellis papyri. At the same time they show that the restoration as printed in the lacuna of l. 2 (58+ ? letters) is much too long and that some shorter, though similar phrasing must have been written there originally. Unfortunately it does not seem possible to propose further suggestions for a complete and convincing restoration of the original text of the papyrus.

1. For the restoration at the end of this line cf. ll. 15-16.
8. Is this perhaps the start of a penalty clause?
9-11. For the *kyria*-formula as restored here cf. **37**.12f. note.
12-14. For this much restored regnal formula of the emperors Galerius, Severus and the Caesars Maximinus and Constantinus (apparently the standard formula in use under their reign) cf. R.S. Bagnall & K.A. Worp, *Regnal Formulas in Byzantine Egypt*, Missoula 1979 (BASP Suppl. 2) 31. Should we, in order to shorten the formula, omit Σεβαστῶν, like in **2**.6?

41: LOAN OF MONEY WITH PARAMONE CLAUSE

(12.vii.310)

P.Kellis inv. P. 61.AA+L+M (House 3, room 8, level 4). H. 25 x B. 17 cm. Margins: at the top 2.5, at the left 3, at the bottom (in which line 31 was written) 3 cm. Dark-brown papyrus, inscribed with brownish ink. The sheet was folded 6x vertically and 3x horizontally. A join is visible on the right hand margin. The verso is blank. For organizational purposes the papyrus was previously referred to as 'P.Kellis 64'.

1 Αὐρηλ̣ί̣α̣ Ε̣ἱερακείενα Τασηχθισος Καπίτ[ω]νι
2 ἀπὸ Μωθιτῶν πόλεως κατ̣αμένουσα ἐν ἐποικίῳ
3 Πμοῦν Τ̣άμετρα Αὐρηλίῳ Παμοῦρ Ψάιτος
4 ἀπὸ κώμης Κέλλεως τοῦ Μωθίτ[ο]υ νομῷ
5 χαίρει̣[ν]. Ὁ̣μολογῶ ἐσχηκα̣ίναι καὶ̣ δ̣εδανῖσθαι
6 παρὰ σ[ο]ῦ διὰ χειρὸς εἰς ἰδίαν μου καὶ ἀνανκαία̣ν
7 χρείαν ἀργυρίου Σεβαστῶν νομίσματος ἐν
8 νούμ̣μ̣οις τάλαντα δύο καὶ δραχμὰς τρισχ[ει]λίας
9 ἐφ᾽ ᾧ μ̣αι παραμῖναί σοι ἐργασομέν̣η<ν> ἀντὶ τῷν
10 τόκου καὶ ὑπηρουτημένου ὑπὸ σοῦ κατὰ τ̣ὰ [ἐσ]τ̣α-
11 μένα ἀντὶ τῶν τόκου ἄχρι ἀποδώσεως τ[οῦ π]ρ̣ο-
12 κειμένου καιφαλέου ἢ ὁπότον θέλ̣ῃ̣ς ἀπ̣οκα-
13 ταστ̣ήσω σοι ἀνυπερθέτως καὶ χωρὶς {ης} εὐ-
14 ροσιλ̣ογίας ἀνακομισοσμένῳ ταῦτά μου τ̣ὰ
15 γρά̣μ̣ματα ἁπλᾶ γρ̣αφέντα ἐφ᾽ ὑπογραφῆς
16 το[ῦ π]αρανεκθέντας ὑπ̣᾽ ἐμοῦ κ̣α̣ὶ̣ κάτ[ω ὑπογρά-]
17 φ̣ο̣ντας ὑπὲρ ἐμοῦ ὑπογραφέως φίλου, ἅπερ
18 κύριε ἔστω καὶ βαίβεα ὡς ἐν δημοσίῳ κ̣α̣τα-
19 κειμένη καὶ ἐπερωτηθ̣εῖσα ὡμολόγη[σ]α̣.
20 Ὑπατείας Στατίου Ἀνδρονίκου καὶ Πομπηίου Πρόβου
21 τῶν λαμπροτάτων ἐπάρχων τοῦ ἱεροῦ πρ̣α̣ιτορίου,
22 πρὸ δ̄ Εἰδῶν Ἰουλίων ὅ ἐστιν Ἐφὶφ ιη̄ κατ᾽ Ἕλ̣λην̣(ας).
23 Α̣ὐρηλία Εἰερακείενα ἡ προκειμένη Αὐρηλίῳ Παμοῦρ
24 τῷ προκειμένῳ ἐτανεισάμην παρὰ σοῦ τὰ τ̣οῦ ἀργυ-
25 ρίου τάλαντα δύο καὶ δραχμὰς <τ>ρισχειλίας συνεπιπα-
26 ρούσης μοι Σεμνῆς γυναικὸς Σιβιτύλλου ἀπὸ Μωθι-
27 τῶν πόλεως καὶ ἐθέμην τὴν ὁμολογίαν αὐτῶν
28 ἐπὶ τοῖς προκειμένοις ὅροις καὶ ἐπερωτηθε̣ῖ̣σ̣α̣ ὡ̣μο-
29 λ̣όγησα. Ἔγραψα ὑπὲρ αὐτῆς Αὐρήλιος Πι[ ]
30 ἴωνο̣ς ἀπὸ Μωθι̣τῶν πόλεως ὁ καὶ τὸ σῶμα γ̣ρ̣ά̣ψ̣α̣ς̣.
(In bottom margin):
31 Φαῶφι ιη̄ κατὰ Ἐγυπτίους.

1 (and 23) Ἱερακίαινα, Καπίτωνος 4 νομοῦ 5 ἐσχηκέναι, δεδανεῖσθαι (-θαι ex corr.?) 6 ἀναγκαίαν 8 (and 25) τρισχιλίας 9 με παραμεῖναι, ἐργασομένη<ν>: -η- ex corr. 9-10 τοῦ τόκου or τῶν τόκων 10 ὑπηρετουμένην ὑπό σε 11 τοῦ τόκου, ἀποδόσεως 12 κεφαλαίου, ὁπόταν 13-14 εὑρησιλογίας 14 ἀνακομιζομένῳ 15 ὑπογραφῆς: -ης oddly written (corr. from -αι?) 16 παρενεχθέντος, ὑπ᾽: -π ex -ε 17 -φοντος 18 κύρια, βέβαια 18-19 κατακείμενα 21 πραιτωρίου 22 Ἐπεὶφ 24 ἐδανεισάμην 27 καὶ ex corr. 30 ἴωνος Pap. 31 Αἰγυπτίους

"Aurelia Hierakiaina alias (or: daughter of?) Tasechthis, daughter of Kapiton, from the city of the Mothites, residing in the hamlet of Pmoun Tametra to Aurelius

Pamour son of Psais, from the village of Kellis in the Mothite Nome, greetings. I acknowledge that I have received and borrowed from you in cash for my private and immediate use of silver Imperial money in *nummi* two talents and three thousand drachmae on condition that I shall stay with you working instead of (paying) interest and being at your service according to the standing agreements instead of (paying) interest until repayment of the aforementioned principal sum or whenever you wish I shall refund you without delay and without looking for pretexts if you hand over this document of mine drawn up in a single copy signed by a friend/signer who was invited by me and who signed on my behalf. Let this document be authoritative and guaranteed, as if it were deposited in a public archive, and having been asked the formal question I have assented. In the consulate of Statius Andronicus and Pompeius Probus, *viri clarissimi*, praefects of the imperial *praetorium*, on the 4th day before the Ides of July, which is the 18th Epeiph according to the Greeks. I, the aforementioned Aurelia Hierakiaina, to the aforementioned Aurelius Pamour: I have borrowed from you the two silver talents and three thousand drachmae, while at the same time Semne, the wife of Sibityllus from the city of the Mothites, was present for me, and I have made the agreement about these (sc. 2 Tal., 3000 dr.) on the aforementioned conditions and having been asked the formal question I have assented. I, Aurelius Pi- son of -ion from the city of the Mothites, have written on her behalf, as I have also written the body (of the contract)."

1. It is difficult to believe that Aurelia Hierakiaina really was a Greek woman (as the name Hierakiaina itself might suggest) rather than an Egyptian woman; the name 'Hierakiaina' may have been a calque into Greek of an Egyptian theophoric name The name Τασηχθισος itself seems to point to Egyptian connections (note the prefix Τα-), but it is unclear what the element -σηχθισος in the (undeclined?) name stands for. Was Τασηχθισος an alias of Hierakiaina, though without the usual ἡ καὶ *vel sim.* intervening (on alias-names in Kellis cf. **24**.17n., **71**.39-40n.)? In that case Kapiton must be regarded as her father's name. It is, however, also conceivable that Hierakiaina had no legal father and that only the name of her mother (= Τασηχθισος) was indicated. If that idea is correct, Kapiton must have been her grandfather (despite the dative Καπίτ[ω]νι he cannot be the addressee of the document, cf. l. 3).
3. The village Πμοῦν Ṭάμετρα is also mentioned in the Harvest Account Book from Kellis, l. 345 (ed.princ.: Πμ(ουν) Ταμυρα). For Πμ(οῦν) = 'the water'= cf. G. Wagner, *Les Oasis d'Egypte*, 29, 180, et alibi; Mr. O. Kaper who is studying place names in the Dakhleh Oasis (cf. his article in BIFAO 92 [1992] 117-132) informs me, that the second element Ṭάμετρα is probably related to the goddess Demeter. He compares T3mtr in E.Bresciani, *l'archivio demotico del tempio di Soknopaiu Nesos*, I (Milano 1975) 16-17 # 16.

For Aurelius Pamour(is) son of Psais, see the family tree at p. 51.
4. This is the earliest attestation of a separate Mothite province. In the three centuries of Roman government of Egypt the Dakhleh Oasis was a province apparently administered by the provincial strategus (στρατηγὸς Ὀάσεως Θηβαΐδος) residing in Hibis; his right-hand man, the 'basilikos grammateus', may have resided in the Dakhleh Oasis (cf. G. Wagner, *Les Oasis d'Egypte*, 254); if so, he may have had his office in Mothis. Among the papyri from Kellis one finds the following references either to a Μωθίτης νομός or a Μωθιτῶν πόλις (for the 'equivalence' of these indications cf. **20**.3-5n.):

Μωθίτης νομός
41 (310); 24 (352); 23 (353); 15 (357); 8 (362); 33 (369); 45 (386); 3 (mid IV); 18 (mid IV); 9 (later IV; in restoration)

Μωθιτῶν πόλις:
41 (310); 34 (315); 52 (320); 21 (321); 4 (331); 38.a,b (333); 13 (335); 48 (355); 30 (363); 32 (364); 42 (364); inv. P.93.60+71 (368; House 4; unpubl.); 44 (382); 20 (early IV); 27 (early IV); 25 (IV); 35 (IV); 39 (IV)

Furthermore, one finds the following attestations outside the Kellis papyri:

Μωθίτης νομός
P.Duke inv. G.9 (383, cf. BASP 25 [1988] 129f.)

Μωθιτῶν πόλις:
P.Grenf. II 75 (308); P.Genova I 20 (319); P.Genova I 21 (320); P.Bodl. I 33 (ca. 300-310); SB XVI 12754 (early IV); Possibly to be restored in: M.Chrest. 78.2 (376/378?), cf. 25.1n.?

On the other hand, one finds in **2** (301) and in P.Grenf. II 74 (302) a reference to the Hibite Nome; it looks, therefore, as if at some moment before 301 the Great Oasis was split up into two separate provinces, the Hibite and the Mothite nomes. Perhaps this administrative reorganization was linked to the reorganization which caused the separation of the Thebaid from Northern and Central Egypt shortly after 297 (for a discussion of the chronology cf. J.Lallemand, *L'administration civile* 44f.; A.H.M. Jones, *The Later Roman Empire* I 43; cf. also **19.a**).

7-8. The principal sum borrowed (2 Tal., 3000 drachmas = 15,000 Dr.) was actually paid out in *nummi* and as the value of that coin was at this time 25 Den. = 100 Dr./*nummus* (cf. R.S. Bagnall, *Currency and Inflation in Fourth Century Egypt* 24), 150 *nummus* coins actually went over the counter; cf. for the same phrasing also **31**, introd. and **34**, introd.

9-12. Instead of paying interest for the principal sum lent (*ἀντὶ τῶν τόκου* [l. *τοῦ τόκου*] Hierakiaina promises to stay with her creditor and work for him until the moment of repayment of the loan, a date for which is not set (*ἐφ' ᾧ μαι παραμῖναί* [l. *με παραμεῖναί*] *σοι ἐργασομένη*<*ν*> -- *καὶ ὑπηρουτημένου ὑπὸ σοῦ* [l. *ὑπηρετουμένην ὑπό σε*] --- *ἄχρι ἀποδώσεως* [l. *ἀποδόσεως*] *τοῦ προκειμένου καιφαλέου* [l. *κεφαλαίου*], *ἢ ὁπότον θέλῃς ἀποκαταστήσω σοι ἀνυπερθέτως κτλ.*). It is not stated in the text that the 2.5 talents should be regarded as an advance payment (*προχρεία*) for services still to be rendered. Furthermore, it should be noted that in this contract no agreements are made about Hierakiaina being provided with food and clothing etc. during her stay with Aurelius Pamour, though such agreements are normal in the case of a *παραμονή*-contract. The loan simply runs for an indefinite period of time without a specified 'Tilgungsplan'. As ca. 310-320 male (!) laborers earned 300 drachmas/day (CPR XVII.A 9.a) the repayment of an amount of 2 talents, 3000 drachmas (= 15,000 drachmas) would have taken at least some 50 days. As females earned probably less, it may have taken Hierakiaina at least 2 months to pay back the money she borrowed.

For similar papyri from Byzantine Egypt with similar undertakings to perform work instead of paying interest, see in general P. Heid. V, Chapt. VII (p. 271ff.), 'Arbeitsverpflichtungen und Darlehen'.

15-17. The formula found here concerning the authority of the document being connected with its being signed by a *hypographeus* is unique among the Kellis papyri; for the *hypographeus* and his role, see **56**, introd.

20-22. These are the consuls of 310, cf. R.S. Bagnall a.o., *CLRE*, s.a.; the first name of the first consul should have been spelled 'Tatius'; 4 Id. Jul. (= 12.vii) = Epeiph 18 'according to the Alexandrian calendar'; cf. also l. 31, where one finds a new date to Phaophi 18 'according to the Egyptian calendar'. This date is in fact incorrect, as in 310 Epeiph 18 'according to the Alexandrian calendar' equals Phaophi 6 rather than Phaophi 18 (in 310 the Egyptian calendar was 83 days ahead of the Alexandrian calendar). One cannot escape the impression that in l. 31 the numeral '18' with Phaophi was copied mistakenly from Epeiph 18 in l. 22. On the use of the traditional Egyptian and the Alexandrian calendars cf. D. Hagedorn - K.A. Worp in ZPE 104 (1994) 243-255.

25-26. In these lines one encounters the remarkable phenomenon that apparently a woman (Semne, the wife of a certain Sibityllos) is assisting Hierakiaina, rather than a male as expected (a female *συνεστώς* occurs also in P.Stras. 142 = SB V 8024.4-5, 23, where a mother assists a daughter involved in a divorce procedure). Furthermore, the verb *συνεπιπάρειμι* (not listed in LSJ) is an *addendum lexicis*; cf. also its restoration in **19.a**.4. For recent discussions of the role of a *συνεστώς* or *συμπαρών*, see E. Kutzner, *Untersuchungen zur Stellung der Frau im römischen Oxyrhynchos* (Diss. Münster 1987), Frankfurt/Main 1989, 79ff., esp. 93-94, and J. Beaucamp, *Le Statut de la Femme à Byzance* (4e - 7e siècle), II: *Les pratiques sociales* (Paris 1992) passim, esp. 251 - 257. After the Constitutio Antoniniana the terms *συνεστώς* and *συμπαρών* begin to appear; their function seems to have been more or less similar to that of a *κύριος* (= 'guardian'; for him cf. in latest instance H.A. Rupprecht, *Zur Frage der Frauentutel im römischen Ägypten*, Festschrift A. Kränzlein [Graz 1986] 95-102), but their status was not identical. Obviously, in our contract Semne cannot have had the function of a legal *κύριος* of Hierakiaina, but must have been present only for moral support (she does not even subscribe for Hierakiaina, cf. below ll. 29-30n.). On the other hand, it is not stated that Semne acted as a witness to the contract, otherwise one would have expected a formula like '*Σεμνὴ ἡ προκειμένη ἐμαρτύρησα*'.

The name Semne does not occur frequently and the name Sibityllos is an *addendum onomasticis papyrologicis*.

29-30. For the statement that a *hypographeus* also wrote the body of the contract cf. **37**.23, **44**.26 and **45**.36.

42: LOAN OF MONEY

(15.ii.364)

P.Kellis inv. P. 59.D (House 3, room 3, level 3) + P. 60.B (House 3, room 9, level 4). H. 26.3 x B. 12.5 cm. Writing parallel with the fibers. Margins: at the top 0.5, at the left and at the bottom 1 cm. The papyrus was folded 4 times horizontally, 3 times vertically.

1 Αὐρήλιος Παμ̣[οῦρ Π]α̣μ̣[ο]ύ̣ρι[ο]ς [μητρὸς]
2 Τακοσε ἀπ[ὸ] κ̣ώ̣[μ]ης Κ̣έλλ̣ε̣ω̣ς τῆς [Μω-]
3 θ[ι]τῶν πόλεως τ̣[ῆ]ς̣ Μεγάλ̣ης Ὀ̣ά̣σ̣ε̣ω̣ς
4 νυνὶ οἰ̣κῶν ἐν κ̣ώμῃ Ἀ̣φροδίτη[ς το]ῦ
5 Ἀνταιο̣[π]ο̣λ̣ίτου μελανχέτ̣ης κολ̣[ο]β̣ὸ̣ς̣
6 Αὐρηλ̣ί̣α̣ Σ̣ο̣φ̣ί̣α̣ Βησᾶ μητ̣ρὸς Τα ̣ ̣ ̣ς
7 ἀπὸ τῆς αὐτῆς κώμης Κέλλεως ν̣ῦ̣ν̣
8 διατριβούσῃ ἐπ̣ὶ̣ τῇ (αὐτῇ) κώμῃ Ἀφρο̣δ̣ί̣τ̣η̣ς̣ χαίρειν.
9 Ὁμολογῶ ἐσχηκέναι καὶ δεδανεῖσθαι
10 παρὰ σοῦ ἐντεῦθεν εἰς ἰδίαν μου καὶ
11 ἀναγκαίαν χρ[εί]αν καὶ ἠριθμῆσθαι διὰ
12 χειρὸς ἀργυρίο[υ Σ]εβαστῶν νομίσματος
13 τάλαντα πεν[τ]ακισχείλια, γί(νεται) ἀργ(υρίου) (τάλαντα) Ἐ´
14 κεφαλα[ίου καὶ π]α̣ρ̣έ̣ξω σοι ὑπ̣ὲ̣ρ̣ ἐ̣π̣έ̣ργ[ο]υ̣
15 τούτων ἀποτάκτου κατὰ μῆ̣να ἕκαστον
16 ἀργυρίου τάλαντα πεν[τ]ακόσια, (γίν.) (τάλ.) φ,
17 ἀπὸ τῆς ἐνεστώσης ἡμέρας τοῦ ὄντος
18 μηνὸς Μεχεὶρ κ¯ τῆς παρούσης ϛS´´

19 *ἰνδικ(τίωνος) ἄχρις ἀποδόσεως τοῦ κεφαλαίου*
20 *καὶ ὁπόταν βουλήθῃς ἀπολ[ύε]ι̣ν̣ παρ'*
21 *ἐμοῦ τὸ κεφάλαιον ἀποκαταστήσω σοι*
22 *μετὰ τοῦ συναγομένου ἀποτάκτου ἤτοι*
23 *ἐπέργου ἀνυπερθέτως καὶ ἀναμφιλόγως̣*
24 *τῆς πάσης μου εὐπορείας ὑποκειμέ-*
25 *νης σοι ἕως ἂν ἀποδῶ τὸ ὄφλημα.* Τὸ *δὲ*
26 *χειρόγραφον τοῦ̣το ἁπλοῦν σοι ἐξεδόμην*
27 *πρὸς ἀσφάλειαν κύριον καὶ βέβαιον καὶ*
28 *ἐπερωτηθ(εὶς) ὡμ̣[ο]λόγ(ησα).* Μετὰ <*τὴν*> *ὑπατείαν*
29 Ἰ̣ο̣[υλιανοῦ] *τὸ δṢ κ̣αὶ* Φλαυίου Σαλουστίο[υ]
30 *τοῦ λ[α]μ̣π̣ρ̣ο̣τάτου ἐ̣πάρχου τοῦ ἱεροῦ πραιτωρίου*
31 Μεχεὶρ *κ-.* (M. 2) Αὐρήλιος Παμοῦρ Παμούριος
32 *ὁ πρ̣ο̣κείμενος ἔσχον καὶ ὀφείλω τὰ τοῦ*
33 *ἀργυρίου κεφαλα̣ί̣ου τάλαντα πεντακισχίλεια*
34 *καὶ ἀποδώ̣σω με̣τ̣ὰ̣ τοῦ συναγομένου ἐπέργου*
35 *κατὰ μῆνα ἀργυρίου τάλαντα πεντακόσια*
36 *καὶ εὐδ̣ο̣κ̣[ῶ πᾶσ]ι̣ τοῖς ἐγγεγραμμέ̣νοις ὡς πρό-*
37 *κειται.* Αὐρήλ̣ι̣ο̣ς Πεβῶς Τιθοῆτος *ἀπὸ τῆς αὐτῆς*
38 *κώμης* Κ̣ε̣λ̣λ̣ε̣ω̣ς *ἔγραψα ὑπὲρ αὐτοῦ γράμματα*
39 *μὴ εἰδότος.*
Verso:
40 Παμοῦρ Παμοῦρ *ἀπὸ* Κέλλεως *ἀργ(υρίου) (τάλαντα)* ,Ε.

5 *μελαγχαίτης* 10 *ϊδιαν* Pap. 13, 33 *πεντακισχίλια* 24 *εὐπορίας* 29 *ϊουλιανου* Pap. 30 *ϊερου* Pap. 34 *συναγομένου* partly blotted 35 *ταλάντων πεντακοσίων* 40 *παμοῦρ' παμοῦρ'* Pap.

"I, Aurelius Pamour son of Pamour and Takose, from the village of Kellis (in the territory) of the city of the Mothites in the Great Oasis, now living in the village of Aphrodite of the Antaiopolite Nome, with black hair, stocky, to Aurelia Sophia, daughter of Besas and Ta---, from the same village of Kellis, now residing in the same village of Aphrodite, greetings. I acknowledge that I have received and borrowed from you henceforth for my private and immediate use and that I have been paid in cash five thousand silver talents of money of the emperors, total 5000 silver Tal., as principal sum, and I shall provide you as fixed interest for these five hundred silver talents per every month, total 500 Tal., from the current day of the current month of Mecheir 20 of the current 7th indiction, until the repayment of the principal sum, and whenever you wish to receive the capital back from me, I shall return this to you together with the accumulated fixed amount or interest, without delay and without dispute, while my whole private wealth is sequestered for you until I repay my debt. I have handed over this contract, written in one copy, to you for your surety, while it is authoritative and guaranteed and in answer to the formal question I have assented. After the consulate of

Julian for the 4th time and of Fl. Sallustius *vir clarissimus*, praefect of the imperial *praetorium*, Mecheir 20. I, the aforementioned Aurelius Pamour son of Pamour, have received and owe the five thousand silver talents as capital and I shall repay (them) together with the accumulated interest, five hundred silver talents per month, and I agree with all the clauses of the contract as written above. I, Aurelius Pebos son of Tithoes from the same village of Kellis, have written for him as he does not know how to write." (Verso) "Pamour son of Pamour, from Kellis, 5000 silver Tal."

2. The name Τακοσε is listed neither in F. Preisigke, *Namenbuch*, nor in D. Foraboschi, *Onomasticon Alterum Papyrologicum*, but it is probably just an undeclined variant of the well-known female name Τεκῶς/Τεκῦσις, cf. W.C. Till, *Datierung und Prosopographie der koptischen Urkunden* 214 s.n. Tecôše; cf. also W. Spiegelberg, *Ägyptische und griechische Eigennamen aus Mumienetiketten der römischen Kaiserzeit*, Leipzig 1901 [repr. Chicago 1978] 26* Nr 190, Πεκῦσις = 'the Ethiopian'.
2-3. For the relationship between the village of Kellis and the city of the Mothites cf. **20**.3-5n.
4. On Aphrodite, see also **30**, the notes to **32**.3ff. and **44**.3 and the introduction to **43**.
5. The adjective *μελαγχαίτης* is not yet listed in the papyrological dictionaries, but cf. LSJ s.v. (apparently the word was used predominantly by poets). For physical descriptions of persons as given in the papyri in general J. Hasebroek, *Das Signalement in den Papyrusurkunden* (Berlin-Leipzig 1921) is still authoritative; cf. also A. Caldara, *I connotati personali nei documenti d'Egitto dell età greca e romana* (Milano 1924). The adjective *κολοβός* has been translated here as 'stocky' (=short, undersized) but other translations are conceivable, cf. LSJ s.v.: was Pamour perhaps clubfooted?
14. The meaning 'interest' of the word *ἔπεργον* seems to be new, cf. LSJ s.v. (the translation, however, given there for IG XII (7) 62.15 [Amorgos]: '*work done in addition* to payment of rent' is not necessarily correct).
15ff. The interest of 500 Tal. / month paid on a principal sum of 5000 Tal. (at this time worth about 1/3 sol., cf. R.S. Bagnall, *Currency and Inflation in Fourth Century Egypt* 61-61) amounts to an interest rate of 120 % / year. This is much higher than what is commonly found as the legal interest rate in Roman Egypt (1 % per month, cf. H.E. Finckh, *op.cit.*.).
18. The 7th indiction covers the year 363/4.
20. The use here of the verb *ἀπολύω* in the sense of 'to receive back' is not common (cf. LSJ s.v.), but cf. Xenophon, *Hist.Graec.* IV 8.21.
22. For the use of *ἤτοι* in the papyri cf. P.J. Sijpesteijn in ZPE 90 (1992) 241ff. Here it coordinates *ἀποτάκτου* and *ἐπέργου*.
28. For the consuls of 363 and their postconsulate in 364 cf. R.S. Bagnall a.o., *CLRE* s.aa. (it is probably no more than sloppiness which made the scribe omit the article *τὴν* before *ὑπατείαν*); it is noteworthy that here, too, *τοῦ δεσπότου ἡμῶν* is not given before Julian's name (cf. *CLRE* p. 68 n. 14); at the moment this text was written the emperor Julian was no longer alive (he died on 26.vi.363) and he was therefore no longer to be spoken of in terms of 'Dominus Noster'.
31. Mecheir 20 in 364 (a leap year) = 15.ii.
37. Aurelius Pebos son of Tithoes, also occurs in **44**.24 (382), where he also acts as a *hypographeus* for one of the contracting parties. There he has written even the whole body of the contract which is evidently not the case in this papyrus; cf. also **43**, introd.

43: LOAN OF MONEY WITH MORTGAGE

(374 or 387?)

P.Kellis inv. P. 1 (House 3, room 6, level 1) + P. 43 (House 3, room 5, level 3). H. 25.2 x B. 6 cm. The writing runs parallel with the fibers, the verso is blank. The papyrus is folded horizontally twice and at least once vertically. It may have been broken at the left on a fold; the second and the third folding are preserved, while the fourth folding is lost ([I] | II | III | [IV]).

\- -

1] .[.] ἀπὸ [κώμης
2] . κ̣α̣τ̣α̣μ̣[ένοντι ἐν κώμῃ Ἀφ-
3 ροδίτης το]ῦ̣ Ἀ̣ν̣ταιοπο[λίτου χαίρειν.
4 Ὁμολογῶ ἐ]σχηκένα[ι καὶ δεδανεῖσθαι παρὰ
5 σοῦ εἰς ἰ]δίαν μου̣ κ̣[αὶ ἀναγκαίαν χρείαν
6 ἀργυρίου] τ̣αλάν̣τ[ων μυριάδα
7] .ια κεφα̣λ̣[αίου καὶ παρέξω σοι ὑπὲρ
8 λόγου ἐ]π̣ικ̣ερδίας [τούτων κατὰ μῆνα ἕκαστον
9 ἀργυρίου] τ̣άλαντα υ̣[
10]ντων ἀργυ̣ρ̣[
11 πρὸς] τ̣ὸ π̣ά̣ρον η̣ .. [λογιζομένου τοῦ χρόνου ἀπὸ μηνὸς --
12 τῆ]ς ἐνεστώσ̣[ης ORDINAL ἰνδικτίονος
13 ἄχρι ἀπο]δόσεως το[ῦ κεφαλαίου, ἃ καὶ ἀπο-
14 δώσω χωρ]ὶ̣ς τινος ὑ̣π̣[ερθέσεως καὶ πάσης ἀντι-
15 λογίας ὁ]πόταν [βουλήθῃς
16] TRACES[
17 μυ]ριάδ̣ας [.].[
18] γ̣ί̣(νεται) (τ̣α̣λ̣ά̣ν̣τ̣ω̣ν̣) (μυριάδες) δ̣ .[
19] .ησομ̣έν̣ω̣ν[
20 τοῦ] χρόνου ὑποτίθε̣[μαι
21] .ον μέρος ἐπιβα[λλ
22]ρου ἐγγὺς τῆς ο̣ἰκί[ας
23]α καταντικρὺ ἐ̣μ̣[οῦ
24 ἐλθὸν] ε̣ἰς ἐμὲ ἀπὸ κληρονομ̣[ίας τῆς ἀπογενο-
25 μένης μο]υ̣ γυναικὸς Ταύριο̣ς[
26 ἐπ' ἀ]σ̣φα̣λ̣ίας τῆς ὀφιλῆ[ς̣ ca. 5 τῶν προ-
27 κειμένω]ν̣ ἀργυρίων σου. Τόδε τ̣[ὸ χειρόγραφον
28 ἐξεδόμην] σ̣οι πρὸς σὴν ἀσφάλει[αν κύριον -πλοῦν γρα-
29 φὲν καὶ βέ]βαιον καὶ ἔννομον [ἐφ' ὑπογραφῆς
30 τοῦ ὑπὲρ ἐ]μ̣οῦ ὑπογράφοντ̣ος [καὶ ἐπερωτηθεὶς
31 ὡμολό]γησα.
32 Ὑπατείας τοῦ] δεσπότου ἡμῶν [
33 τοῦ αἰωνίου] Αὐγούστου τὸ γ κ[αὶ Φλ. τοῦ
34 λαμπροτάτ]ου, ἰνδικτίονος [

35 Αὐρ. Ν.Ν ὁ] π̣ρ̣ο̣κ̣ε̣ίμενος ἔ̣σ̣[χον
36] ταλάντων μυρι[άδα
37]τ̣α̣χου καὶ ἀποδ̣ώ̣[σω ὡς πρόκειται.
38 Ἔγραψε]ν̣ Α̣[ὐ]ρήλιος Πε[βῶς ἀπὸ κώμης
39 Κέλλεως οἰ]κῶν [ἐ]ν Ἀφροδίτ[ης κώμῃ
40 ἀξιωθεὶς ὑπὲρ] α̣ὐτοῦ γρ̣ά̣μ̣ματα μ[ὴ εἰδότος.

25 ταϋριος Pap. 26 ἀσφαλείας, ὀφειλῆς

"-- from the village of -- residing in the village of Aphrodite in the Antaiopolite nome, greetings. I acknowledge that I have received and borrowed from you for my private and immediate use *n* myriad(s?) of silver talents -- as a principal sum and I shall provide you on account of interest for these 400 (?) silver talents -- while the term (of the loan) is calculated from the month of -- of the current *n*th indiction until the repayment of the principal sum, which I shall pay back without any protest of delay whenever you wish -- total 4 (?) myriads of talents -- I give in hypothec the *n*th part -- near the house -- opposite me -- which came to me from an inheritance of my deceased wife Taüris -- for security of the debt -- of the aforementioned money of you. I have given you this contract for your security, which is authoritative in *n* copies and guaranteed and legal with the signature of the person who is signing for me and in answer to the formal question I have agreed. In the consulate of our lord N.N. the eternal Augustus for the 3rd time and of N.N., *vir clarissimus*, indiction *n*. I, the aforementioned N.N., have received -- *n* myriad(s?) of talents -- and shall pay back as written above. Aurelius Pebos from the village of Kellis, residing in the village of Aphrodite has signed for him at his request, as he does not know letters."

This badly damaged papyrus contains a loan of money which is secured by a mortgage. Among the early Byzantine papyri this type of loan (cf. the discussion by R. Taubenschlag, *Law*[2] 277) is apparently not very common, but a parallel case is offered by P.Lond. III 870 (p. 235; Panopolis, 4th cent.); cf. also P.Flor. III 313 (Hermopolis, 449). The structure of the text (many of the proposed restorations are only tentative) can be analyzed as follows:

ll. 1-3: opening of the contract, probably according to the scheme 'A to B, χαίρειν', with an indication of the provenance of the parties concerned. Party 'B' (the creditor?) apparently resided in a village situated in the Antaiopolite nome. Apparently the contract was taken from Aphrodite back to Kellis. This situation may be compared with **30** [363], **32** [364], **42** [364] and **44** [382], all mentioning contract parties living in the village of Aphrodite in the Antaiopolite nome (especially **44** offers in many respects a good parallel for our text, cf. also below, ll. 38ff.); on this basis we have restored the same village name here;

ll. 4-7: start of the loan contract with an indication of the amount of money borrowed;

ll. 8-19: indication of the interest to be paid + indication of the moment the loan will have to be repaid (cf. **44**.10ff.); after specification of further provisions concerning repayment follow

ll. 20-27: start of the mortgage-part of the contract + description of the object given as mortgage (some kind of immovables, e.g. a house), which came into the present owner's hands through an inheritance from his deceased wife Taüris;

ll. 27-31: closing lines of the contract ending with the *stipulatio*-formula.

ll. 32-34: consular dating + indiction; the dating formula referred to a consulate held by an emperor who was consul for the 3rd time and by a private person. When we take 382 (the date of **44**) as a point of departure (cf. below ad ll. 35-40), such a situation occurred 8 years earlier in 374 (Gratianus Aug. III & Fl. Equitius), 5 years later in 387 (Valentinianus Aug. III and Eutropius) or 11 years later in 393 (Theodosius Aug. III & Fl. Abundantius). In view of the space available in the lacuna to the right of l. 33 it looks more likely that one should restore between Φλ(*αουίου*) and *τοῦ* the name Ἐ*κυτίου* (7 letters) or Εὐ*τροπίου* (9 letters), rather than Ἀ*βουνδαντίου* (12 letters). If, however, Φλ(*αουίου*) and *τοῦ* were never written (cf. **45**.24-26n.) the situation is different. The year 374 was covered partly by the 2nd, partly by the 3rd indiction, while the year 387 was covered partly by the 15th, partly by the first indiction;

ll. 35-40: signature of the debtor, written in fact (ll. 38-40) by his *hypographeus* (Αὐ*ρήλιος* Πε[ ) who may be the same person as the one who wrote **44**.23ff., Αὐ*ρήλιος* Π*εβῶς*; it deserves attention that in both texts Pebos apparently wrote both the corpus of the contract *and* the subscription (though in the present text there is not enough room for restoring a formula [*ὁ καὶ τὸ σῶμα γράψας*] after l. 40 of this text. It also deserves attention that the handwriting of **43** and **44** is not obviously identical.

1-3. At the end of line 2 / start of l. 3 we have restored Ἀ*φ*-] | *ροδίτης το*]ῦ Ἀ*νταιοπο*[*λίτου*, but it is uncertain, that one should restore the village name in the lacuna of l. 1-2 as Κ*έλλεως τοῦ* Μ*ωθίτου νομοῦ* / *τῆς* Μ*ωθιτῶν πόλεως*.

6. It is uncertain how many myriads of talents were borrowed; cf. l. 18 in which mention is made of 4 (?) myriads of talents (= 40,000 Tal.) in an uncertain context; comparing l. 9, in which 400 (?) Tal. are mentioned in an indication of interest one wonders whether the interest rate in this text was 1 % per month (400 Tal. = 1 % of 40,000 Tal.).

44: LOAN OF MONEY

(26.iv.382)

P.Kellis inv. P. 62.C (House 3, room 6, level 3). H. 28 x B. 17.5 cm. Margins: at the left 3, at the bottom 4, and at the top 1.5 cm. On both sides the writing runs parallel with the fibers, but the direction of the fibers in the margin at the left of the recto is vertical. Apparently, this is part of the first leaf of the original papyrus roll, the 'protocollon'; on this, see E.G. Turner, *The Terms 'recto' and 'verso'. The Anatomy of the Papyrus Roll* (Brussels 1978) 20f.

1 Αὐρήλιος Πεκῦσις Ψάιτο[ς] Παμούρις μ̣ητ̣[ρὸς Τ]απολλῶς
2 ἀπὸ κώμης Κέλλεως τῆς Μ̣ωθιτῶν πόλεως τῆς Με-
3 γάλης Ὀάσεως Αὐρηλίῳ Ἀ̣ν̣τωνίνος ἀπὸ [τ]ῆς αὐτῆς
4 κώμης τοῦ αὐτοῦ νομοῦ οἰκῶν ἐν κώμης Ἀφροδίτης
5 τοῦ Ἀνταιοπολίτου χαίρειν. Ὁμολογῶ ἐσχηκέναι
6 καὶ δεδανῖσθαι παρὰ σοῦ ε̣ἰς ἰ̣δίαν μου καὶ ἀνανκαίαν
7 χρε[ί]αν χρυσοῦ δοκίμο[υ ν]ομισμάτιον ἓν κεφαλαίο̣υ
8 γί(νεται) χρυσοῦ νο(μισμάτιον) α καὶ παρέξ[ω] σοι ὑπὲρ λόγου ἐ̣πικερδίας
9 τούτων κατὰ μ̣ῆ̣ν̣α ἕκαστο̣ν̣ ἀργυρίου τάλ̣[α]ντα ἑξακό-
10 σια, γί(νεται) τάλ(αντα) χ̣̅, λογιζομέ̣νου τοῦ χρ̣όνου ἀπὸ
11 τοῦ ὄντος μη[ν]ὸς Παχ̣ὼ̣ν α̅ τῆς [ἐ]νεστώσης
12 ἐν̣[δε]κάτης ἰνδικτίονος ἄχρι ἀποδ[ό]σεως
13 το[ῦ] κ̣εφαλαίου ἄνευ πάση[ς] ἀντιλογί̣α̣ς καὶ ὑπερ-
14 θέσ̣ε̣ως {ενευ} πάσης τῆς παντο[ί]α̣ς μου εὐπο-
15 ρίας κατεχομ̣ένης ὑπὸ σ̣ο̣ῦ, ἐπ̣άν σε πληρώσω.
16 Τ[ὸ γρά]μ̣μα τοῦτ̣ο̣ κ̣[ύριο]ν̣ ἐ̣[ξ]ε̣δόμην̣ [σο]ι πρὸς `σὴν´ ἀσφάλει-
17 α̣ν̣ ἐ̣φ' ὑ̣πογ[ρα]φῆς τοῦ ὑπὲρ ἐμ̣οῦ ὑ̣[πογρ]άφοντος
18 καὶ ἐπερωτηθεὶς ὡμολόγησα.
19 Μετὰ τὴν ὑπατίαν Εὐχερίου καὶ Συ{ν̣}αγρίου [τ]ῶν λαμπροτάτ[ων]
20 Παχὼν α̅.
21 Αὐρήλιος Πεκῦσις Ψάιτος ὁ προκείμενος ἔσχον
22 {τὰς} τὸ χρυσοῦ νομισμάτιον ἓν κεφαλαίου καὶ
23 ἀποδ[ώσ]ω σὺν τῷ τόκῳ ὡς [π]ρόκειται. [Α]ὐ̣ρήλιος
24 Πεβ[ῶς] Τιθοῆτος ἀ̣πὸ τῆς αὐτῆς κώμης οἰκῶν
25 ἐν κῷ[μ]η {ώμη} Ἀφροδίτης ἀξιωθεὶς ἔγρα̣ψα ὑπὲρ αὐ(τοῦ)
26 γράμ[μα]τα μὴ εἰδότ̣ος ὁ καὶ τὸ σῶ[μα γρ]άψας.

Verso:

27 χειρ(όγραφον) Πεκῦσις Ψάιτος χρυσοῦ νο(μισμάτιον) α.

1 ψαῖτο[ς] Pap., Παμούριος 3 Ἀντωνίνῳ 4 οἰκοῦντι, κώμῃ 6 δεδανεῖσθαι, ἀναγκαίαν 9 τούτου 12 ϊνδικτιονος Pap. 13 ἄνευ: -ν- ex -π- corr. 15 ϋπο Pap. 19 ὑπατείαν, Συαγρίου 21 ψαϊτος Pap. 27 Πεκύσιος

"Aurelius Pekysis son of Psais, the son of Pamouris, and of Tapollos, from the village of Kellis belonging to the city of the Mothites in the Great Oasis, to Aurelius Antoninus from the same village in the same nome, living in the village of Aphrodite in the Antaiopolite nome, greetings. I acknowledge that I have received and borrowed from you for my private and immediate use one *solidus* of gold in legal tender as principal sum, total 1 sol. of gold, and I shall provide you on account of interest for this six hundred talents for each month, total 600 Tal., while the term of the loan is calculated from Pachon 1 of the current month of the current eleventh indiction until the repayment of the capital without any protest or any delay, while all of my wealth of every kind is held by you (until) when I shall repay you in full. I have handed over to you for your surety this contract as being authoritative, provided with the signature of the person who is subscribing for me, and in answer to the formal question I have agreed. After the consulate of Eucherius and Syagrius, *viri clarissimi*, Pachon 1. I, the aforementioned Aurelius Pekysis son of Psais, have received the single *solidus* of gold as principal sum and I shall repay this together with the interest as stated above. I, Aurelius Pebos son of Tithoes, from the same village (Kellis), (now) living in the village of Aphrodite, after having written the body of the contract, have signed for him at his request as he does not know letters." (Verso) "Contract of Pekysis son of Psais, 1 sol. of gold."

1. For Aurelius Pekysis son of Psais and Tapollos, grandson of Pamouris, cf. the family tree at p. 51.
2-4. For the relationship between the village of Kellis and the city of the Mothites cf. **20**.3-5n.
3. Aurelius Antoninus occurs only here. The fact that he was born in Kellis, but lived now in the village of Aphrodite in the Antaiopolite nome finds parallels in other Kellis documents, cf. **32**.4-5 (lease of a room); **42**.4 (cf. note ad loc.), 8; **43**.39 (cf. introd.) [both loans of money]; cf. also the description of the parties in **30**. Apparently the contract was taken from Aphrodite back to Kellis.
8. For the term *ἐπικερδία* = 'interest' cf. also **43**.8 and **90**.2; for the terminology concerning 'interest', see in general H.E. Finckh, *op.cit.* 6.
9ff. The plural *τούτων* at the start of l. 9 is not correct, as only 1 *solidus* is lent. If the interest on a principal sum of 1 *solidus* is 600 Tal. / month, and if the interest level were 1 % per month, then the ratio bronze :: gold would be 100 x 600 = 60,000 Tal. / *sol.* In fact, the gold price in this period is ca. 2,160,000 Tal. / lb or (÷ 72) 30,000 Tal. / *sol.* (PSI VIII 959-960, cf. R.S. Bagnall, *Currency and Inflation in Fourth Century Egypt*, 62) Our conclusion must be, then, that the interest agreed in this loan was 2% / month, i.e. 24% / year.
11-12. Pachon 1 = 26.iv, the 11th indiction = 382/3; apparently we are dealing with an indiction year starting on Pachon 1 without this being indicated by way of a term like ἀρχῇ. For the start of the indiction year cf. R.S. Bagnall - K.A. Worp, *The Chronological Systems of Byzantine Egypt* (Zutphen 1978), Chapt. IV.
14. The letters *ενευ* are superfluous. Maybe the scribe was reminded of *ἄνευ πάσης* in l. 13.
15. *ἐπάν* means 'when', but here one would expect 'until' ('My whole property is held by you, until I shall repay you').
16. A reading ἀ̣[πλοῦ]ν̣ instead of κ̣[ύριο]ν̣ is not to be excluded, cf. **42**.26 and **43**.28ff. On loan contracts drawn up in single copies cf. the introduction to **40** - **47**.
19-20. For the (post-)consulate of Fl. Eucherius and Fl. Syagrius cf. R.S. Bagnall a.o., *CLRE*, s.a. 381, 382; for Pachon 1 cf. ll. 11-12n.
23f. An Aurelius Pebos son of Tithoes may also occur in the subscription of **43**; cf. also the subscription in **42** (364) and cf. **24**.13 (352); though this is not indicated in **42**.37, one might argue that he had already moved from Kellis to Aphrodite before 364, as that contract was concluded between two persons stating to be living in Aphrodite. It is, however, possible that they went back to Kellis temporarily for some other purpose and had that loan of money subscribed there by Aurelius Pebos.

45: LOAN OF MONEY

(386)

P. Kellis inv. P. 62.A (House 3, room 6, level 3) + P. 77.B (House 3, room 6, level 4 East wall) + P. 79 (House 3, room 6, level 3) + P. 81.D+E + P. 93.B (all from House 3, room 6, level 4). H. 27 x B. 9 cm. Margins: at the top and at the left 1, at the bottom 2 - 3 cm. On both sides the writing runs parallel with the fibers.

1 [Α]ὐρήλιο[ς] Κ̣απίτων Καπίτωνος
2 [ἀ]πὸ κώμης Κέλλεως κ̣αταμένον
3 [ ] ἐν ἐπ̣ο̣[ι]κ̣ίῳ̣ Θιῳ τοῦ Μωθίτου
4 νομοῦ Αὐρηλίῳ Σύρῳ Ψάιτι
5 {[Σ]ύρῳ} ἀπὸ τῆς αὐτῆς̣ τοῦ αὐτοῦ
6 [ν]ομοῦ χαίρειν. Ὁμολογῶ
7 [ἐσ]χηκ[έν]αι καὶ δεδ̣α̣νῖσθαι
8 [π]αρὰ σοῦ̣ [εἰς] ἰ̣δ̣ίαν μου καὶ ἀναγκαί-
9 [αν] χρεί̣[αν] χρυσοῦ ν̣ομισμά-
10 [τιο]ν̣ ἕ̣[ν], γί̣(νεται) νο(μισμάτιον) α, ἐφ' ᾧ̣ με
11 [παραδώσ]ω σοι ὑπ[ὲρ τι]μῆ[ς]
12 [αὐτοῦ κα]ι̣ρῷ τῆς [. . .] ους ιε̣S
13 [ἰνδικ(τίονος) Ἐ]πεὶφ ν[εο]μηνίᾳ̣
14 [ἐλαίου μάρ]ια π̣έ̣ντε, γί(νεται)
15 ἐ̣λαί[(ου)] μ̣ά̣ρ(ια) ε̣ τῷ̣ Ἰβι[τι]κῷ̣ χοεῖ
16 τῆς̣ πεντεκαιδεκά̣τ̣ης ἰνδ̣ι̣κ̣τίο-
17 νος χ̣ω[ρὶ]ς ἀντιλογίας. Κυρία̣
18 ἡ ἀσφάλε[ια] ἁπλῆ γρ̣αφεῖσα ἐφ' ὑπ̣[ο-]
19 γραφῆς τοῦ ὑπὲρ ἐμοῦ ὑπογρά-
20 φοντος κ̣α̣ὶ βεβα̣[ί]α καὶ ἔ̣ν̣-
21 νομος [ὡς ἐν δημοσίῳ] κ̣α̣τ̣α̣-
22 κειμέ̣ν̣[η καὶ ἐπερω]τ̣η̣θεὶς
23 ὡμολόγ[ησα.
24 Ὑπατίας το[ῦ δεσπότου ἡ]μ̣ῶ̣ν̣
25 Ὀνωρίου̣ [τοῦ ἐπιφανεστ]ά̣τ̣ο̣υ̣
26 Καίσαρος κ[αὶ Εὐοδίου λαμ]π̣ροτάτου.
27 Αὐρήλιο[ς Καπίτων ὁ] προκ(είμενος)
28 ἔσχον τὸ [χρυσοῦ νομισμά]τιον
29 ἐφ' ᾧ̣ με π̣[αραδώσω . . . .] σοι ὑπὲρ
30 τιμῆς α̣[ὐτοῦ ἐν μηνὶ Πα]ῦνι τῆς
31 $\overline{\iota\epsilon}$ ἰνδικ(τίονος) ἐ̣[λαίου μάρια πέν]τε,
32 γί(νεται) μ̣ά̣ρ(ια) ε, κ̣[αὶ ἐπερω]τ̣ηθεὶς
33 [ὡ]μ̣ο̣λόγ[ησα. Ἔγραψα ὑπ]ὲρ αὐτ̣(οῦ)
34 γράμ̣μ̣α̣[τα μὴ εἰδότος Α]ὐ̣ρήλιος
35 Ἀνδρέας̣ [κωμογραμματεὺς (?) τ]ῆς

36 Κελλεω̣̣[ς ὁ καὶ τὸ σῶμα γρ]άψας
37 ἀξιωθε̣ί̣ς̣.[
Verso:
38 Α̣ὐ̣ρ̣ή(λιος) Κ̣α̣πίτ(ων) (ὑπὲρ) ἐλαί(ου) μαρ(ίων) ε

2 *καταμένων* 4 Ψ*άιτος* 7 *δεδανεῖσθαι* 11 *παραδώσειν* 15 *ϊβιτικω* Pap. 24 Ὑ*πατείας*

"Aurelius Kapiton son of Kapiton, from the village of Kellis, residing in the hamlet of Thio- belonging to the Mothite nome, to Aurelius Syros son of Psais, from the same village from the same nome, greetings. I acknowledge that I have received and borrowed from you for my private and immediate use one solidus of gold, total 1 sol., on condition that in return for its price I shall provide you at the time of the - - 15th indiction on the first day of Epeiph with five *maria* of oil, total 5 *mar.* of oil, measured with the chous-measure of Hibis of the fifteenth indiction, without protest. This document is authoritative, written in one copy and signed by the person who is subscribing for me, and guaranteed and legal as if deposited in a public archive and I have answered the formal question positively. In the consulate of our lord Honorius *nobilissimus Caesar* and of Euodius *vir clarissimus*. I, the aforementioned Aurelius Kapiton, have received the solidus of gold on condition that I shall provide you in return for its price in the month of Pauni of the 15th indiction five *maria* of oil, total 5 *mar.*, and I have answered the formal question positively. I, Aurelius Andreas, village scribe (?) of Kellis, after having written the body of the contract, have signed for him at his request as he does not know letters." (Verso) "Aurelius Kapiton for 5 *maria* of oil."

In this document a loan of 1 *solidus* is recorded. Instead of repaying this gold coin with interest, the debtor promises to deliver 5 *maria* of oil. The term of the loan is problematic, cf. the note to l. 12ff. For loans of money to be repaid in kind cf. in general R.S. Bagnall in GRBS 18 (1977) 85-96 and A. Jördens in ZPE 98 (1993) 263-282. Cf. for such documents from the 4th century also the introduction to **40** - **47**.

1. An Aurelius Kapiton son of Kapiton does not occur in other exactly dated Greek papyri from Kellis, but there seems to have been a family relation between him and other members of the main family living in House 3, cf. **76**.

3. A hamlet Θ(ε)ιος/Θ(ε)ιον is apparently still unknown in this region, cf. G. Wagner, *Les Oasis d'Egypte* 188-196.

This papyrus offers a late attestation of the existence of the Mothite Nome; cf. **41**.4n.

4-5. [Σ]ύρῳ in l. 5 seems to repeat mindlessly Σύρῳ in l. 4, unless it is intended to indicate the grandfather's name belonging to Syros son of Psais (in that case one should read here Σύρου).

10-11. The construction here is irregular, as one expects an infinitive rather than an indicative after ἐφ' ᾧ με (the same irregularity seems to occur in **46**.9). After με the papyrus apparently has another letter, but a reading μέν̣ does not seem to make sense.

12ff. A combination of *καιρῷ τῆς -- ἰνδικτίονος* is unusual (cf. F. Preisigke, *Wörterbuch* s.v. *καιρός*) and the reading of this passage is really uncertain; the word *ἰνδικ(τίονος)* itself has been restored at the start of l. 13, the preceding numeral is not very certain, and the word preceding that is much damaged; for *καιρῷ τῆς* --- cf. also **18**.9n.

The 15th indiction (l. 16, cf. l. 31) covers the year 386/387; as elsewhere in Upper Egypt the indiction year in the Dakhleh Oasis started probably on Pachon (May) 1 (cf. **44**.11-12n., 19-20n.), but in light of the consular date of this document and of what we know about consular dating elsewhere in Egypt (cf. below, l. 24-26n.) there is a serious problem. Repayment of the loan of 1 *solidus* by way of a delivery of five *maria* of oil should take place in the month of Pauni (v-vi) of the 15th indiction (ll. 30-31), at any rate before the first day of the month Epeiph (25.vi.; cf. l. 16); with an indiction year starting on Pachon 1 that means 'repayment before 25.vi.386'. If, however, the contract was written up some time áfter 26.vi.386, it follows that the delivery of oil in Pauni/before Epeiph would take place only in the summer of 387, i.e. at the start of the *1st* indiction; the term of the loan would have covered at least 6 months (which seems regular in such loans), possibly even a full year. It is also worth noticing that the phrasing of the repayment in ll. 12ff. differs from the phrasing in Kapiton's subscription, ll. 30-31. Furthermore, it is remarkable that the 15th indiction in l. 16-17 is separated by two lines from 'Ε]πεὶφ ν[εο]μηνίᾳ, l. 13, though these chronological indications seem closely connected with each other. Maybe, however, we should link the 15th indiction in l. 16 to the Hibite *Chous*-measure in l.15.

14-15. For *μάριον* as a measure of capacity of liquids like oil and wine cf. now O.Douch III 245.5n. and O.Ain Waqfa 19.4n; it is stated to be a diminutive form of *μάρις* (cf. LSJ s.v.). According to F. Hultsch, *Griechische und römische Metrologie*[2] [Berlin 1882] 564, 574, one Macedonian *maris* was 1/20 of a Babylonian *maris* of ca. 30 liter, i.e. ca. 1.5 liter, while one *maris* in Pontos = 30 ÷ 2 = ca. 15 liter). 5 *maria*, therefore, would be either ca. 7.5 or ca. 75 liter. On the other hand, according to the *Fragmentum Eusebianum* (ed. F. Hultsch, *Scriptores Metrologici* I [1864, repr. 1971] 277.12) 1 *maris* = 20 *sextarii* (cf. W.E. Crum, *Coptic Dictionary* 183 s.v. ΜΑΥΡΕϹ: 1 *marion* = 19 *sextarii*) and as 1 *sextarius* = ca. 0.5 liter, this would yield 1 *marion* = ca. 10 liter > 5 *maria* = ca. 50 liter (i.e. 33% less than ca. 75 liter). Finally, one finds in Polyaenus 4.3.32 that 1 *maris* = 10 *choes*; with 1 *chous* = ca. 3 liter (cf. below) 5 *maria* would be the equivalent of ca. 150 liter.

There should be, of course, a relationship between the value of the borrowed 1 *solidus* and the quantity of oil to be delivered (5 *maria*), and as it happens we know that 4 years later than this papyrus, in 390, 2 *solidi* were paid for the price of 80 *sextarii ἐλαίου χρηστοῦ* = ca. 40 liter of 'first-quality' oil (P.Oxy. XIV 1753.2-3); 1 *solidus*, therefore was sufficient to buy ca. 20 liter of such oil. If in our papyrus 1 *solidus* was borrowed at an interest level of, say, 100 % per year (cf. above, the introduction to **40** - **47**) and ran for a whole year, one would expect that after a year 2x the amount of oil to be bought for 1 *solidus* had to be returned. With the situation in 390 as a point of departure one would think, then, that after a year 40 liter of oil had to be returned upon an initial investment of 1 *solidus*. Using this approach it can be ruled out that 5 *maria* were the equivalent of ca. 150 or even ca. 75 liter, while 7.5 liter of oil would be far too little; an amount of ca. 50 liter of oil returned for a loan of 1 *solidus* seems the best acceptable quantity, though even so it may seem rather large (and the interest level very high).

The 'Hibite *chous*'-measure occurs here for the first time in the papyri; no doubt it was based on a local standard measure. Unfortunately, we do not know exactly what precise capacity this measure had, but in general a *chous* contained ca. 3 liter.

24-26. This is the consulate of 386, cf. R.S. Bagnall a.o., *CLRE* s.a.; the latest attestation of a post-consulate in 386 in the Nile Valley dates from 26.vi (Oxyrhynchus, SB XVIII 13916), the first attestation of a consulate from 29.viii (Oxyrhynchus, P.Oxy. XXXIV 2715). It looks improbable that in the Dakhleh Oasis one would have had much earlier knowledge of the consular formula for this year than in Oxyrhynchus and we must conclude that our document was written some time after 26.vi.386; cf. also above, note to ll. 12ff.

It is remarkable that the formula in this text refers to Honorius as a Caesar, whereas the standard formula found in inscriptions and papyri from this year (cf. also the postconsular formula given in *CLRE* s.a. 387) refers to him as *nobilissimus puer*; it is also remarkable that the lacuna does not seem sufficiently large for restoring the expected Φλ(αουίου) and *τοῦ* (cf. also the note on **43**.32-34 in the introduc-

tion to that text). For the phenomenon of a lacking indication of the exact month and day, see **8**.13n., **48**.16-17n.
35. The restoration of the function of Andreas as that of a village scribe is only 'exempli gratia' (cf. **14**.7 and note ad loc.); the restoration of a short patronymic followed by *ἀπὸ τῆς αὐτ]ῆς* is also possible.

46: LOAN OF MONEY

(Second half of the 4th century)

P.Kellis inv. P. 68.D + E (House 3, room 6, level 3). H. 28 x B. 8 - 6 cm. The sheet tapers down towards the bottom. On both sides the writing runs parallel with the fibers and the original sheet was folded 3 times vertically and at least 9 times horizontally.

1 Τῶι δεσπότῃ μου
2 Πισιστράτωι
3 Παλάμμων Παλάμμωνος
4 χαίρειν.
5 Ἔχεις παρ' ἐμοὶ ὑπὲρ
6 λόγου πρ[ο]λοίπου τῆς τι-
7 μῆς ἁμάξης ἀργυρίου
8 τάλαντα μυριάδαν μί-
9 αν, γί(νεται) ταλ(άντων) (μυριὰς) α, ἐφ' ᾧτέ
10 με παρέξω σοι αὐτὰ τῇ
11 λ [τοῦ] μην{ὶ}`ὸς´ Τῦβι κατ' Αἰ-
12 [γυπτίο]υς χωρὶς ἀντι-
13 λογίας καὶ ἄνευ πάσ[η]ς
14 εὑρεσιλογίας καὶ ἐξεδό-
15 μην σοι ταύτην μου
16 τὴν ἐπιστολὴν πρ[ὸ]ς
17 ἀσφάλειαν. Ἐὰν δ[ὲ ἀ]με-
18 λεία γείνεται τῆς ἀπο-
19 δόσεως τῇ ὡρισμένῃ
20 προθεσμίᾳ τὰ αὐτὰ ἀρ-
21 γύρια ἐν ταλάντοις
22 λογί[σο]μαι [σὺν] τόκ[ῳ]
23 ..[..]..ρα.[.]ῳ κατὰ
24 τὸ ἐπιχώριον ἔθος
25 ἄχρι ἀποδόσεως τοῦ
26 προκειμένου μυρι-
27 άδαν μίαν ταλάντων.
28 Ἐρρῶσθαί σε εὔ-
29 χομαι, δέσποτά μου,

30 πολλοῖς εὐτυχοῦν-
31 τα χρόνοις.
32 Ἔγραψα ὑπὲρ αὐτοῦ γράμ-
33 ματα μὴ εἰδότος Φλάυ-
34 ιος Μακάριος Πτοῦ
35 [ἱ]ππεὺς ἀξιωθ[ε]ίς.
Verso:
36 τῷ δεσπότῃ μου \ / Πισ[ιστράτῳ] Παλάμμων
37 / \ Παλ[άμμωνος] ταλ(άντων) (μυρ.) α

8 ταλάντων μυριάδα 9 τε at end blotted 10 παρέξειν 14 εὑρησιλογίας 17-18 ἀμελία γίνηται 22 ἀποδώσω 25-27 τῆς προκειμένης μυριάδος μίας

"To my lord Pisistratos, Palammon son of Palammon (?) sends greetings. You have on loan from me on account of the balance of the price of a waggon one myriad of silver talents, total 1 myr. Tal., on condition that I shall give them (back) to you on the 30th of the month of Tybi according to the Egyptian calendar without dispute and without looking for pretexts and I have handed over this letter to you for your surety. If, however, on the fixed time I turn out to be careless as regards the repayment I shall pay the said money in talents with - - - interest according to the local custom until the repayment of the said one myriad of talents. I pray for your health, my lord, enjoying prosperity for many years. I, Flavius Makarios son of Ptou, have signed for him at his request because he does not know how to write."

This loan of money is quite remarkable in that it is not drawn up as regular contract, but phrased rather in terms of a letter (cf. l. 12-13 ταύτην μου τὴν ἐπιστολὴν); we have not found a parallel for this aberration of normal Greek loan contracts, but Dr A. Alcock informs us that in Coptic there are parallels, cf. ΟΥΝΤΑΚ ΕΡΟΙ and W.E. Crum, *A Coptic Dictionary* (Oxford 1939) 481.b (the business letter P.Oxy. 3979 is also a credit note for the transfer of funds, but it does not offer a complete parallel for the situation in the Kellis papyrus). At the same time the letter form explains the lack of a dating formula, as already by the 2nd century letters tend to be undated. At first sight the amount of money borrowed (10,000 talents) may seem quite substantial, but it depends on the decade within the 4th century whether this is really the case; there seems no problem with dating this papyrus to the middle or even the second half of the 4th century, by which time 10,000 talents (= 1500 myr. den.) were no longer a very large amount of money (ca. 340 it would be the equivalent of 1 *solidus*). Unfortunately, there do not seem to be any exactly datable prices for carts etc. available from 4th-century Egypt (R.S. Bagnall, *Currency and Inflation in Fourth Century Egypt*, does not list any in his chapter [IX] on prices classified by object). Given the letter form of the document it looks as if Palammon stood to Pisistratos in a kind of client/patron relationship and that Pisistratos had given the said amount of money to Palammon in order to pay for the price of a waggon.

1. In the course of the 4th century the words δεσπότης and κύριος got to be used rather indiscriminately in addresses of letters, but δεσπότης expresses a greater respect of a letter's sender towards the addressee, cf.D. Hagedorn - K.A. Worp in ZPE 39 (1980) 165ff., esp. 177.
2. The name Pisistratos is one of those classical names which occur so remarkably frequently in the Oasis, cf. G. Wagner, *Les Oasis d'Egypte* 225. The name occurs also in **63** and in another still unpublished Kellis document from House 4 (P.Kellis inv. P.93.59, cf. the report on the 1992/93 excavations); maybe we are dealing with the same person. For the name Παλάμμων cf. G. Wagner, *op.cit.* 231f.
5. As far as we have been able to ascertain through the Duke Data Bank on Documentary Papyri (PHI disk # 6), the phrasing ἔχεις παρ' ἐμοί meaning 'you have out with me' > 'I owe you' is unique for the Greek papyri; for Coptic parallels cf. above, the introduction.
9. At the end τε is blotted.
10. Apparently the scribe completely lost the correct syntax (requiring an infinitive rather than an indicative after ἐφ' ὥτ̣ε̣ με); cf. also **45**.10.
11-12. Obviously the reading λ̣ [τοῦ] μην{ὶ}`ὸ̣ς´ ̣ Τῦβι (= Tybi 30) is not very certain and one may consider reading ν̣[εο]μηνί̣α̣ Τῦβι (= Tybi 1) instead. For the use of the Egyptian calendar in Roman and early Byzantine papyri cf. D. Hagedorn - K.A.Worp in ZPE 104 (1994) 243-255.
21-23. Apparently the phrasing κατὰ τὸ ἐπιχώριον ἔ̣θ̣ος should be related to the percentage of the interest to be paid in case of Palammon's failure to repay the amount lent on the date agreed upon; on local customs in this respect cf. R. Taubenschlag, *Opera Minora*, II 91-106, esp. 96; on the meaning of the word ἔθος in the papyri in general cf. H.D. Schmitz, *Τὸ ἔθος und verwandte Begriffe in den Papyri* (Diss. Cologne 1970). At the same time the phrasing of the text suggests to us that Palammon was not obliged to pay interest for the 10,000 talents he had borrowed, as long as he paid these back to Pisistratos on the prearranged date; cf. also **47**.11ff.
31f. A cavalry-man Flavius Makarios son of Ptou(s) is otherwise unknown. He may have belonged to the *Ala I Quadorum* stationed at Trimithis = modern Amheida (Not.Dign., Or. § xxxi.56); on the modern identification of Trimithis, see C.A. Hope in Mediterranean Archaeology 1 [1988] 169 n.35.

On the name Flavius as a status designation regularly found with military men since 325 cf. J.G. Keenan, ZPE 11 (1973) 49-50.

The name of Makarios' father is uncommon. The genitive Πτοῦ may be a short form of Πτουτός, the genitive of Πτοῦς. Is this name a composition of the Egyptian masc. prefix Π- + Τοῦς? Cf. F. Preisigke, *Namenbuch*, s.n.; for other such combinations of names with a prefix Π- (or fem. T-) cf. **66**.1n. and the names 'Αλιτοῦς (**13**.1) / Παλιτοῦς (**8**.1), 'Αγάπη (**74**.6) / Ταγάπη (**74**.25). For such short genitives, see the remarks by P.J. Sijpesteijn in ZPE 64 ([1986) 119-120; as, however, in **34**.1 the name Τοῦ seems to occur in the nominative, one may also argue that Πτοῦ (Π- + Τοῦ) is just an undeclinable name.

47: LOAN OF MONEY

(Second half of the 4th century?)

P.Kellis inv. P. 85.A # 4 (House 3, room 6, level 4, Southeast corner). H. 12.5 x B. 4.3 cm. Margins: at the left 1, at the bottom 1.5, at the top 1 cm. The writing runs parallel with fibers, the verso is blank. Some letters seem to have been retraced or corrected.

1 Αὐρήλιος Λιλο[ῦς τοῦ Ν.Ν. ἀπὸ κώμης]
2 Τουπ̣χα Αὐρ[ηλίῳ Ν.Ν.]
3 υἱὸς Καπίδων[ος ἀπὸ κώμης Κέλλεως.]
4 Ὁμολογῶ ἐσχηκ̣[έναι παρὰ σοῦ σή-]
5 μερον εἰς ἰδίαν [μου καὶ ἀναγκαίαν]
6 χρείαν ταλ̣άν̣τ̣[ων μυριάδα]
7 μίαν, καὶ μ̣ε̣τ̣[. . . . ., γίνεται τα-]
8 λάντων (μυριὰς) α̣[. . . . . ἐπὶ μη-]
9 νὰ<ς> δύο μόνον ἀ̣[πὸ τοῦ ὄντος μηνὸς]
10 Παοπις ἕως [τοῦ ἐλθόντος μη-]
11 νὸς Χοιὰκ .[. . . . . Καὶ μετὰ]
12 τὴν προ̣θε̣σ̣[μίαν ταύτην, ἐὰν]
13 μὴ ἀποδῶ τ[ὴν μυριάδα ταλάν-]
14 τ[ω]ν, ἑτοίμ[ω]ς̣ [ἔχω ἀποδοῦναί σοι]
15 τὸν δόκον, [τουτέστιν ἀρτάβην]
16 μίαν σίτου κα̣[θαροῦ
17 ὑπὲρ ταλά̣[ντων
18 των. Ἡ ἀσφά̣[λεια κυρία ἐφ᾽ ὑπογρα-]
19 φῆς τῶν̣ ὑ̣[πὲρ ἐμοῦ ὑπογράφοντος. (M.2?) Ἔγραψα ὑπὲρ αὐτοῦ]
20 μὴ εἰδότος̣ [γράμματα Αὐρ(ήλιος) Ν.Ν. ἀπὸ Ν.Ν.]

3 υἱῷ Καπίτων[ος 5 ἴδιαν Pap. 10 Φαῶφ̣ι 15 τόκον 19 φῆς: φ- ex corr.; τοῦ

"Aurelius Lilous son of N.N. from the village of Toupcha (?) to Aurelius N.N. son of Kapiton from the village of Kellis. I agree that I have received from you today for my private and immediate use one myriad of --- talents and ---, totals 1 myr. --- for only two months from the current month of Phaophi until the coming month of Choiak ---. And after this term, if I do not repay the myriad of talents, I am prepared to pay you the interest, i.i. one araba of clean wheat ---. for talents ---. This pledge is authoritative with the signature of the person who is subscribing for me. (M. 2?) I, Aurelius N.N. from N.N. has written for him, as he does not know letters."

Evidently we are dealing with a loan of money, i.e. of a myriad (= 10,000) of talents (cf. ll. 6ff.). The loan was concluded in Phaophi (l. 10) and the money has to be repaid 2 months later, i.e. in (or before the end of?) Choiak (l. 11); no particular provision for interest payment seems to have been made, but if the lender does not repay the principal sum in time, at least the interest will be repaid through the delivery of an artab of wheat; other 4th-century money loans to be repaid in kind are listed in the introduction to **40** - **47** (some of them come from other regions and all show formulas different from the one apparently used in this text). The level of interest in this loan (one artab of wheat as interest for borrowing 10,000 talents during 2+ months) may point to a date after ca. 350 (for wheat prices in the 4th century cf. R.S. Bagnall,

Currency and Inflation in Fourth Century Egypt, 64). It is remarkable that the contract itself was evidently undated.

It is not certain that the amount of text lost at the right in the lacuna is restricted to the ca. 13-17 letters now restored in many lines (cf. ll. 4-5, 13-14, 18). If the proposed tentative restorations are plausible, the sheet may have broken along the central vertical fold.

1-2. One expects a formula 'A son of N.N., provenance, to B son of N.N., provenance, *χαίρειν*'; if necessary, one can also use the 'To A, B *χαίρειν*'-formula (one cannot have a nominative form both in l. 1 [start of the description of person 'A'] and in l. 3 [part of description of person 'B']. If the size of the lacuna is indeed ca. 13 letters the father's name expected after Λιλο[ῦς must have been a short one.

2. If the restoration at the end of l. 1 is correct, one expects at the start of this line a village name, but a village Τουπχα is not known. In itself it is possible that one should read, e.g., *τοῦ* Πχα (instead of reading a pi a ny or an eta may be considered), but this is not more illuminating.

4-5. The element *σήμερον* at this place of the 'I have from you'-formula is not usual in loan contracts; cf., however, for a similar indication of 'I have received today' the sale contract **34**.8 and the phrasing 'I have leased today' in **32**.9.

7. We do not know what to expect with *με̣τ̣[. . . . .*

10. As there is no numeral marking, it is probably better not to read Παοπι (l. Φαῶφι) ϛ.

11. Before Χοιάκ there is a small space possibly indicating that the name of the month was filled in at some later moment.

19. The restorations in this line are, if compared with ll. 4-5 and 18, much too long. We have restored the full wording of the regularly used formula, but probably many words were originally abbreviated; it may even be that the scribe left out the words *ὑπὲρ ἐμοῦ* and that one should read *ὑ̣[πογράφοντος* but even then the restoration remains too long (NB: *τῶν* seems to indicate that the scribe may have reckoned mistakenly with two [!] *hypographeis*).

48: MANUMISSION OF A FEMALE SLAVE

(355)

P.Kellis inv. P. 56.C (House 3, room 9, level 3, Western doorway) + P. 61.F+G+U+V (House 3, room 8, level 4) + P. 65.F+J (House 3, room 8, level 3). H. 24.8 x B. 16.7 cm. There is a join at 2 cm. from the right hand margin. On both sides of the sheet the writing runs parallel with the fibers. The sheet was folded 7 times vertically and 3 times horizontally. The upper right side is extremely fragile.

1 Ἀ(*ντίγραφον*) *ἀ̣[πελευθερώσεως.*
2 Αὐρήλιος Οὐα̣λέρι[ο]ς Σαραπ̣ίωνος *ἄρξας [τῆς]*
3 Μωθιτῶν *πόλεως* Ἱλαρίᾳ̣ *ἰδίᾳ̣ μου χαίρειν.*
4 Ὁμολογῶ *δι᾽ ὑπερβ̣ολὴν χ[ρι]στιανότητ̣ο̣ς̣ ἀ̣πε-*
5 *λευθερωκέν̣αι σε ὑ̣π̣ὸ* Δία Γῆν Ἥλιον *μετὰ κα[ὶ] τοῦ*
6 *πεκουλίου σ̣ου κα̣ὶ εὔνοιαν τὴν̣ πρὸς μ̣ὲ̣ πρὸ̣ς̣ τ̣ὸ̣*
7 *ἐντεῦθέν σ̣ε̣ ἔ̣χει̣ν τὴν ἐλευ̣[θερία]ν̣ ἀν̣επί[λη-]*

8 πτον ἀπὸ π̣[αντὸ]ς̣ ἐ̣π̣ιλημψο̣μ̣έ̣[νου] σοι ε[ἰς]
9 ταύτην τὴ[ν] ἀ̣π̣ε̣λευθέρωσιν̣ δ̣[ι]ὰ̣ τ̣ο̣ῦ̣ α̣ἰδε[σιμω-]
10 τάτου πατ̣ρ[ὸς ἡμῶν] Ψ̣εκῆτ̣[ος]
11 ναχων .[. . .] . . .[ ] . . .[ ] TRACES[
12 κα γένεσθ[αι] . .[. .]βουλε̣ι̣ . . .[. .]θ̣έ̣τ̣ως ἐξ .[. .] . .
13 σεαυτῆς χ[. .] .[. .]ν̣η. Ἡ ἀπελευθέρωσις [αὔ]τ̣η
14 κυρία ἔστω [κ]αὶ βεβαία καὶ ἔννομο̣ς πανταχοῦ [ἐπ]ι̣φε-
15 ρομένη κ[αὶ] ἐ̣περωτηθ(εὶς) ὡμολόγησα.
16 Μετὰ τὴν ὑπατείαν Κωνσταντίου Αὐγούστου τὸ ζS/
17 καὶ Κωνσταντίου τοῦ ἐπιφανεστάτου Καίσαρος τὸ γS/.
18 Αὐρ(ήλιος) Οὐαλέριος ἄρξας ὁ προκ(είμενος) ἐθέμην τὴν ἀπελευ-
19 θέρωσιν ὡς πρόκ(ειται) καὶ ἐπερωτηθ(εὶς) ὡμολόγησα.
20 (M. 2?) Αὐρ(ήλιος) Ψεκῆ[ς] πρ( ) ὁ προκ(είμενος) παρὼν μαρτυρῶ.

Verso:

21] Ἀ(ντίγραφον) ἀπελευθερώ̣σεως X

3 ϊλαρια ϊδια Pap.

"Copy of a deed of manumission. Aurelius Valerius son of Sarapion, ex-magistrate of the city of the Mothites, to my own Hilaria, greetings. I acknowledge that I have set you free because of my exceptional Christianity, under Zeus, Earth and Sun, together also with your *peculium*, and (because of) your loyalty towards me, in order that from hereonwards you shall have your freedom unassailed by anyone who shall try to lay a claim upon you with regard to this deed of manumission (made?) through the most reverend father Psekes - - -. (13ff.) Let this deed of manumission be authoritative and guaranteed and lawful wherever it is produced and in response to the formal question I have answered positively. After the consulate of Constantius *Augustus* consul for the 7th time and of Constantius *nobilissimus Caesar* consul for the 3rd time. I, the afore-mentioned Aurelius Valerius, ex-magistrate, have drawn up the deed of manumission as written above and in response to the formal question I have answered positively. (M. 2?) I, the aforementioned Aurelius Psekes, pr(iest?), am present and witness." (Verso) "Copy of a deed of manumission."

This fragmentarily preserved papyrus contains the copy of a deed of manumission of a female slave Hilaria by her master Aurelius Valerius, former magistrate of the city of the Mothites. Notwithstanding its rather lacunose state of preservation the document is of outstanding interest, as we have only few slave manumissions from Roman Egypt and even fewer from Byzantine Egypt (cf. J. Straus, "L'esclavage dans l'Egypte romaine", ANRW X.1 [1988] 841-911, O. Montevecchi, *La Papirologia*[2] [Milano 1988], 201-202, 567, and most recently J. Farr's publication of a manumission from A.D. 116 in the form of a *donatio mortis causa*, BASP 30 [1993] 93-104). The most complete list of actual deeds of manumissions and references to other documents related to manumission (e.g.: testaments) is found in I. Biezunska-Malowist, *La schiavitú nell' Egitto greco-romano* [Roma 1984] 293-4, n. 133 (cf. also her *L'esclavage dans l'Egypte romaine*, II [Warsaw 1977] 145 n. 151); add there the 6th-century documents referred to below. For various forms of manumission found in the papyri, i.e. *per vindictam, inter amicos* and *per epistulam* cf. *eandem*, *La schiavitú* 281; in general, see A. Berger, *Encyclopedic Dictionary of Roman Law* [Philadelphia 1953] 575-77). The only other such 4th-century deed of manumission known to date is the famous P.Edmondstone = M.Chrest. 361 (from Elephantine and also from the year 355, cf. BL VII 123) considered by Biezunska-Malowist as a '*manumissio per epistulam*' (but cf. the cautious remarks by Mitteis in his introduction; he reckons also with a '*manumissio inter amicos*'); cf. also the 4th-century petition PSI V 452, in which manumission is referred to. Furthermore there is now a 6th-century manumission published in P.Köln III 157 (589); earlier published were the 6th-century '*donationes mortis causa*' P.Cair.Masp. III 312,99ff. (567) and P.Gron. I 10 (probably VI, cf. BL V 39) and the certificate (in 2 copies) of a female servant's free status in P.Cair.Masp I 67089 = III 67294 (cf. now SB XVIII 13274). Due to the lack of pertinent parallel texts it is impossible to restore the new text completely; ll. 10-13 especially are severely affected. Nevertheless, it is certainly remarkable to notice the phrasing in ll. 4-5 where the 'preeminence (i.e. an extraordinary degree) of Christianity' (*ὑπερβολὴ χριστιανότητος*, cf. LSJ s.v. *ὑπερβολή*, 5) is effortlessly combined with the traditional formula *ὑπὸ Δία Γῆν Ἥλιον* 'under Zeus, Earth and Sun' (for this formula, see P.M. Meyer, *Juristische Papyri*, Nr 6., Einl.); this combination offers a nice illustration of the amalgam of Christian and pagan elements sometimes occurring next to each other in 4th-century documents; in ll. 7-8 of the Edmondstone papyrus the wording *ὑπὸ Γῆν καὶ Οὐρανόν* is used in combination with the *εὐσεβία τοῦ πανελεήμονος Θεοῦ*.

D. Hagedorn (P. Köln III 157, p. 154) has already highlighted the problems in applying a specific juridical label to the manumission document he published. In our papyrus there is a similar problem: we are probably not dealing with a '*manumissio per epistulam*' (used when a slave lived at some distance from his master) or a '*manumissio inter amicos*' (for which five witnesses were required, whereas here we encounter only one). Furthermore, there seems no reason to think of a '*manumissio per vindictam*' and the idea of a '*manumissio testamento*' is also not applicable. If the witness Aurelius Psekes were a priest (cf. l. 21n.), one might be tempted to think of a '*manumissio in ecclesia*', 'in the church' (for this form of manumission, see W.W. Buckland, *The Roman Law of Slavery* [Cambridge 1908] 449-50; Berger, *op.cit.* 576 and F. Fabbrini, *La manumissio in ecclesia* [Milano 1965]); there are, however, important obstacles here against such an approach in both the Cologne papyrus and in our document; see Hagedorn's observations, *loc.cit.*:

(1) The bilateral character of the papyrus stands in opposition to the *manumissio in ecclesia* as a 'negozio giuridico unilaterale', and

(2) any indication that a bishop and a religious community were present, while the *manumissio* was being effected, is lacking.

At the most we have one witness who may have been a priest; that does not seem enough for a *manumissio in ecclesia* (but cf. l. 11n.).

1. ἀ( ) for ἀ(ντιγραφον) (cf. also the verso, l. 21) is a rather common abbreviation, cf. O. Montevecchi, *La Papirologia*[2], 471; cf. also P. Turner 45.1n. The alpha of ạ[πελευθερώσεως is rather uncertain and in itself an omega could be read; but ω̣[μολογίας would contain a spelling error, and ἀπελευθερώσ̣εως on the verso (l. 21) is clear enough.
4. Remarkably enough the substantive χριστιανότης does not seem to be attested yet, i.e. it is not listed in G.W.H. Lampe's *Patristic Greek Lexicon*.
6. For references in the papyri to the *peculium* of slaves (i.e. their private money and other property) cf. especially BGU I 96.14, PSI IX 1040.18 (both III) and P.Princ. II 85.13 (V ?); for papyrological attestations of the word in general, see S. Daris, *Il Lessico latino nel Greco d'Egitto*[2] (Barcelona 1991) 88-89. For the nature of the *peculium* as a slave's own cash cf. W.W. Buckland, *op.cit.* 187ff.
9. Or should one read ε̣[π]ι̣ rather than δ[ι]ạ?
10ff.. Unfortunately enough, substantial parts of these lines are much damaged and the lack of parallel texts prevents the text from being restored with confidence. Certainly the Psekes in l. 10 is the same person as the witness Psekes occurring in l. 20 (hence the use of ὁ προκ(είμενος) = 'the afore-mentioned' in that line), but the details about his role in this passage remain hidden. The letters πατ̣ρ̣[in l. 10 and length of the lacuna seem to suggest the word πατρὸς (ἡμῶν is only a stop-gap), but if this idea is correct, Psekes was, of course, not Valerius' physical father (who was Sarapion, l. 2). For the use of the epithet αἰδεσιμώτατος cf. O. Hornickel, *Ehren- und Rangprädikate in den Papyrusurkunden* (Diss.Giessen 1930); there seem to be no instances of its use as a honorific epithet for clergy and for that reason it is doubtful whether 'father' refers here to a priest (cf. l. 20n. for Psekes' position in society). For another attestation of an αἰδεσιμώτατος πατήρ cf. SB XIV 12085.2, but there we are probably dealing with a 'physical' father.
11. ναχων may suggest a restoration of μο-]ναχῶν, 'monks' (especially if the text were a '*manumissio in ecclesia*'), but their precise role would also remain problematic (for monks in 4th-century papyrus documents cf. E.A. Judge in *Proceedings of the XVI Congr. of Papyrology* [Chico 1981] 613-620). If some monks were present during the manumission, they apparently did not subscribe as witnesses.
12. ἀνυπερ]θέτως is probably too long for the restoration of the word ending with -]θ̣ε̣τ̣ως.
14. For this form of the *kyria*-clause including the element καὶ ἔννομος cf. the note to **37**.12ff.
16-17. The consuls mentioned here are those of the year 354, their postconsulate occurring in 355, cf. R.S. Bagnall a.o., *CLRE* s.a. It is interesting to note that, as happens rather frequently in the papyri from this region, an indication of a month + day is lacking in this text; cf. the remarks at **8**.13n. and cf. P.Duke inv. G.9, published by J.F. Oates in BASP 25 (1988) 129-135 (as Worp observes on a photo of the Duke papyrus kindly put at his disposal by P. van Minnen, it is difficult to accept the reading of l. 22 suggested in BASP 28 [1991] 65).
20. Remarkably enough there is only one witness to this manumission deed; in P.Edmondstone (cf. the introduction above) there are 5 witnesses. As this document is a copy (cf. ll. 1, 21: ἀντίγραφον) one would expect the whole document to have been written in one hand. Still, it looks as if the writing of this line is slightly different from ll. 1-19.

A resolution of the abbreviation following Aurelius Psekes' name as into πρ(εσβύτερος) may be most attractive (cf. **32**.21n. and E.A. Judge, *loc.cit.*, 619), but other resolutions like πρ(ύτανις)/πρ(όεδρος), πρ(αιπόσιτος), πρ(ονοήτης), πρ(αίκων) *vel sim.* seem also conceivable; cf. also ll.10-13n.
21. There is a rather large X-shaped cross at the end of this line; its function may be compared with that of the well-known crosses and designs found on the back of ordinary papyrus letters, which were intended as a precaution against unauthorized opening (for these cf. P.Oxy. XLVIII 3396.32n., CPR XIV 50, introd. and K. Vandorpe, *Breaking the Seal of Secrecy: Sealing Practices in Greco-Roman and Byzantine Egypt* [Leiden 1995] 12ff.); its occurrence here, however, does not seem sufficient reason to label the manumission as one given '*per epistulam*'.

49: LOAN OF OIL

(2.vi.304)

P.Kellis inv. P. 61.GG (House 3, room 8, level 4). H. 23 x B. 10 cm. The writing runs parallel with the fibers. Margins: at the top 1.5, at the left hand side also 1.5, and at the bottom 3 cm. For organizational purposes the papyrus was referred to previously as 'P.Kellis 67'.

1 [Αὐρήλιος Πιπέ]ρισμι ἀπὸ Τριμιθει-
2 τῶν πόλε̣ω̣[ς] καταμένων ἐν κώμῃ
3 Πμοῦν Κε̣( ) Αὐρηλίῳ Φιλάμωνι
4 ἀπὸ κώμης Κέλλεως χαίρειν.
5 Ὁμολογῶ ἐσχηκένα̣ι παρὰ σοῦ
6 εἰς ἰδίαν μ̣ου χρεία̣ν̣ ἐλαίου κερά-
7 μιον ἓν τῷ μέτρῳ τὴν κώμην
8 καὶ ἀποδώσω σοι τὴν προκειμέ-
9 νην ἐλαιοποιείας ἐν πεντα-
10 χοείαις τῷ καιρῷ. < Ἥδε ἡ ἀποχὴ > κυρία ἁπλῆ
11 γραφεῖσα ἔστω καὶ βεβαία
12 ὡς ἐν δημοσίῳ κατακειμένη
13 καὶ ἐπερωτηθεὶς ὡμολόγησα.

14 (ἔτους) κ, ιθS´ καὶ (ἔτους) ιβ· τῶν κυρί-
15 ων ἡμῶν Διοκλητιανοῦ καὶ
16 Μαξιμιανοῦ καὶ Κωνσταν-
17 τίου καὶ Μαξιμιανοῦ Σεβαστῶ[ν]
18 τῶν ἐπιφανεστάτων Καισάρων
19 Πα̣ῦ̣νι η̄.
20 Αὐρήλιος Πιπέρισμι Αὐρηλίῳ
21 Φιλάμμωνι τῷ προκειμένῳ· <Ὁμολογῶ>
22 ἐσχηκέναι παρὰ σοῦ εἰς ἰδίαν
23 μου χ[ρ]είαν ἐλαίου κεράμιον
24 ἓν τῷ μέτρῳ τὴν κώμην.
25 Ἔγραψα ὑπὲρ αὐτοῦ γράμμα-
26 τα μὴ ε̣ἰδότος Αὐρήλιος
27 Ἑρμοκλῆς ἀξιωθείς.

1-2 Τριμιθιτῶν 3 read Πμουνκεμ̣^{o} or Πμουνκελ̣´? Φιλάμμωνι 7, 24 τῆς κώμης 8-9 τὸ προκείμενον 9-10 πενταχόῳ? Cf. note ad loc. 20 Αὐρήλιῳ: υ ex corr. 21 προκειμένῳ: 2nd epsilon ex corr.

"Aurelius Piperismi from the city of the Trimithites, resident in the village of Pmoun Ke(llis?), to Aurelius Philammon, from the village of Kellis, greetings. I acknowledge that I have received from you for my own private use one *keramion* of oil by the measure of the village and I will pay back the aforementioned (*keramion*) at the time of the pressing of oil in a five-chous measure at the appointed time. Let this receipt which is written in a single copy be authoritative and guaranteed as though deposited in a public record office, and having been formally asked I have agreed. Year 20-19-12 of our lords Diocletian and Maximian and of Constantius and Maximianus the *Augusti nobilissimi Caesares*, Pauni 8. Aurelius Piperismi to the aforementioned Aurelius Philammon. I acknowledge that I have received from you for my own private use one *keramion* of oil by the measure of the village. I, Aurelius Hermokles, have written for him at his request since he does not know letters."

A receipt for one *keramion* of oil which Aurelius Piperismi from Trimithis currently resident in Pmoun Ke(llis?; perhaps a subdivision of Kellis?) has borrowed from Aurelius Philammon. It is of interest that this is apparently the first reference to Trimithis as a 'city' rather than as a village. We have had the benefit of a preliminary transcript of this text made by Dr. R.G. Jenkins of the University of Melbourne.

1. The name Πιπέρισμι is not listed by F. Preisigke, *Namenbuch*, or D. Foraboschi, *Onomasticon Alterum Papyrologicum*. It is clearly a variant of Πιπέρ (cf. *Namenbuch* s.n.), which is already represented by the by-forms Πιπᾶς, Πιπερᾶς and fem. Πιπεροῦς; we do not know, however, how to explain the second part of the name -ισμι.

1-2. Although broken the reading πόλεως is secure. Although an important settlement (there was a Roman army unit, sc. the *Ala I Quadorum*, stationed there, cf. Not.Dig., Or. xxxi.56), it had hitherto been thought that Trimithis had the status of only a κώμη. For this place (which should now be identified with Amheida in the Western part of the Dakhleh Oasis, cf. C.A. Hope in Mediterranean Archeology 1 (1988) 169 n.35) cf. G. Wagner, *Les Oasis d'Egypte*, 191-92; S. Timm, *Das Christlich-koptische Ägypten*, VI 2846; A. Calderini - S. Daris, *Dizionario Geografico* V 30. The same designation ἡ Τριμιθιτῶν πόλις occurs in a very mutilated contract of sale of an unknown object (P.Kellis inv. P. 85.D + P.93.C; 4th century, not published) in the description of one of the parties. In **27** reference is made to a πραιπόσιτος πάγου Τριμίθεως. Finally, we refer to the wall painting from Amheida (published by L.M. Leahy, '*The Roman Wall-paintings from Amheida*' in JSSEA 10 (1980) 351-54 and Pl. XXXIII.a; reference courtesy of A.J. Mills) which includes the seated figure of a woman which is labelled 'POLIS'. Could this perhaps refer to Trimithis itself, as Leahy has suggested?

3. For geographical names starting with Πμοῦν cf. Wagner, *op.cit.*, 29. In itself two readings seem possible (cf. above, the app.crit.). If the latter is chosen, one may think about resolving Πμουνκέλ̣(λεως). It is, however, not quite clear what the difference between Πμουνκέλλις and Κέλλις is; if there is no difference one would then expect ἀπὸ τῆς αὐτῆς in l. 4.

8-9. Other occurrences of ἐλαιοποίεια (cf. SB VI 9406.172, P.Ryl. II 393A) suggest that the word is used of the act or occasion of the oil pressing, not the product. We take the genitive as a temporal genitive, but it is conceivable that one should take ἐλαιοποιείας ... τῷ καιρῷ together.

9-10. The word πενταχοείαις (dat.pl.) is problematic, as no substantive πενταχοεία is known; the scribe may have been influenced by the form of ἐλαιοποιείας in the preceding line. Cf. the adjective πεντάχοος = "containing 5 choes" in P.Ent. I 34.3, P.Teb. III 793 xii.19 and 888.3f. (where it defines κεράμια). Perhaps one should correct πενταχοείαις into πενταχόῳ (sc. κεραμίῳ)? After all, Piperismi has borrowed only 1 *keramion* of oil, and it is difficult to see in what alternative measure related to 5 choes (1 *chous* = ca. 3 liter, cf. **61**.3n.) he can return this amount of oil. For measures of liquids in the papyri, see U. Wilcken's fundamental remarks in WO I 757ff.

14-19. For the slightly aberrant form of the regnal formula in this papyrus cf. R.S. Bagnall - K.A. Worp, *Regnal Formulas of Byzantine Egypt* (Missoula 1979) 10ff., form. 4 (with the element Σεβαστῶν added wrongly after the second Μαξιμιανοῦ instead of after the first) and p. 15 form. 5 (with an extra element τῶν ἐπιφανεστάτων Καισάρων). Year 20-19-12 = 303/4, Pauni 8 = 2.vi; hence the date would be 2.vi.304, but at that date it is unusual to find regnal year 19 still mentioned at this time in the year (the earliest attestion of regnal years 20-12 dates from 16.xii.303 [O.Mich. II 900 from the Fayum, cf. CdE 46, 1971, 174-75, 178] and according to SB I 4652.8 regnal years 20-12 were already in use in the Oasis on 15.ii.304.
26-27. Aurelius Hermokles seems otherwise unknown.

50: RECEIPT FOR VARIOUS OBJECTS

(4th century)

P.Kellis inv. P. 61.S+V (House 3, room 8, level 4) + P. 65.D+G (House 3, room 8, level 3). H. 10 x B. 13.8 cm. Margins: at the bottom 2.5, at the left hand side 1.5 cm. The Greek text on the 'front' is written across the fibers, the summary on the 'back' runs parallel with the fibers; the sheet was folded at least 4 times horizontally. On the 'back' of the sheet a (faded) Coptic letter has been written, also across the fibers. Parts of the address of this Coptic letter are visible on the 'front' of the sheet, where the Greek text appears. It is difficult to tell which text was written first.

1 Κυρίῳ μου πατρὶ Ψάιτι Παμοῦρ
2 Ψά̣ι̣[ς] Τ̣ρ̣υ̣φάνης χαίρειν. Ἔσχον πα-
3 [ρὰ] σ̣οῦ κατ' ἐντολὴν Ψάιτος Κέλε
4 Πατ̣σῖ[ρε] χαλκοῦ̣ ̣δ̣ ̣ ̣σ̣ιον ἓν καὶ
5 λυχον καὶ ἠθμὸν κα̣ὶ τρίχουν ἀ-
6 πὸ ὑάλων καὶ ἐ̣[ξεδό]μην σοι ταύ-
7 την τὴν [ἀπ]ο̣χὴν π̣ρ[ὸ]ς ἀσφάλειαν.
8 Ἔγραψα ὑπὲρ αὐτοῦ γράμματα μὴ εἰδότος
9 Αὐρήλιος Τιθέριος Ὡρπατῶτος ἀπὸ τῆς α̣ὐ̣τ̣ῆ̣ς
10 κώμης Κέλλεως.
Verso:
11 Ἀποχὴ Ψάιτ(ος) Τρυφά-
12 νης ὑπὲρ Ψάιτος Κέ-
13 λε Πατσῖρε.

4 ε̅ν̅ Pap. 6 ϋαλων Pap.

"To my lord father Psais son of Pamour, Psais Tryphanes greetings. I have received from you according to an order from Psais, the son of Kele and grandson of Patsire --- of bronze --- and a --- and a sieve and a three-chous measure made from glass and I have handed over to you this receipt for your surety. I, Aurelius Titherios son of Horpatos, from the same village Kellis, have written for him as he does not know letters. Receipt of Psais Tryphanes on behalf of Psais son of Kele, grandson of Patsire."

This papyrus contains a receipt for a number of utensils used for, e.g., housekeeping or perhaps in the local cult (for lists of temple properties preserved on papyrus, see P.Oxy. XLIX 3473 introd.). If the latter use was intended, it may be assumed that the recipient of the utensils, Psais Tryphanes (cf. the verso), was involved with the local cult. On the other hand it seems worthwhile to note that according to l. 8ff. he could not write by himself and needed the assistance of a *hypographeus* (for whom cf. **56**, introd.).

1-2. On the basis of the text on the verso it may be assumed that (a) here Παμοῦρ must be an undeclined father's name going with Ψάιτι and that (b) the name of the sender was Ψ̣ά̣ι̣[ς] Τ̣ρ̣υ̣φάνης; in itself, considerations of space would not rule out a reading Ψ̣ά̣ι̣[τος] in l. 2 going with Παμοῦρ (l. 1) as a nominative = the name of the sender of the document. The name Τρυφάνης and its relationship to Παμοῦρ is problematic (cf. **71**.39-40n.).
3-4. We assume that one is dealing with Psais son of Kele and grandson of Patsire, but it cannot be excluded that one of the names is in fact an alias (on the problem of alias-names in documents from Kellis cf. **24**.17n. and **71**.39-40n.).
5. A word λυχον (acc.) does not occur in LSJ or in the papyrological dictionaries; the reading is certain. Of course, one wonders whether an error for λύχνον (= 'lamp') is involved.
9. The name Τιθέριος is not listed in the papyrological onomastica, but it may be an error for Τιβέριος, unless it is another theophoric name based on the locally prominent cult of Tithoes (cf. **8** - **12**, introd.). The name Ὡρπατῶς is a combination of the Egyptian names Ὥρ (undeclined) + Πατῶς. It seems, however, unlikely here that one should separate both elements from each other, as it is apparently not common to find a grandfather's name in the subscription of a *hypographeus* (for his role cf **56**, introd.); on the other hand, the combination of two individual names into a new combination is a well-known phenomenon, cf., e.g., the name Ὡραπόλλων.

51: TRANSPORTATION RECEIPT

(1.x.320?)

P.Kellis inv. P. 7.A (House 3, room 6, level 2). H. 9.3 x B. 6.4 cm. Bottom margin 1 cm. Writing parallel with the fibers, verso blank. Probably the papyrus has broken off on a central fold.

In the same glass frame there is a small fragment which may be related to the main fragment, as the handwriting seems similar. Apparently it contains part of a dating formula: *Σεβαστο]ῦ τὸ ϛ´´ καὶ Κωνσ̣τ̣[αντ*, referring to the consulate of either 320 (Constantinus Augustus VI & Constantinus Caesar I) or 353 (Constantius Augustus VI & Constantius Caesar II). If the restoration of the name of Aurelius Horos son of Mersis below in l. 3 is correct (cf. the note ad loc.), the earlier date is preferable. There remains, however, a question where this consular dating formula might have occurred in the document; it cannot have stood before Φ]α̣ῶφι δ‾ in l. 8 and it does not seem likely that it stood somewhere below l. 10. The only logical place for it can be somewhere above the present l. 1; on the basis of that assumption the common phrasing *ὑπατείας τῆς προκ(ειμένης)* has been restored in l. 8 before Φ]α̣ῶφι.

- -

1 [   ]..[.].[τ]ῆ̣ς Ἑρμοῦ πόλεως
2 [τῆς μεγάλης ἀναγραφόμενος] ἐπ̣' ἀμφόδου Πόλεως Ἀπη-
3 [λιώτου Αὐρηλίῳ̣ Ὥρῳ̣ Μέρσ]ι̣ος καμηλίτῃ̣ ἀπὸ Ὀάσ̣εως.
4 [Ὁμολογῶ παρειληφέναι] παρὰ σοῦ γόμον καμήλ̣ο̣υ
5 [ἕνα .... καὶ ἰσχ]άδας καὶ σταφίδας καὶ ὀθό-
6 [νια καὶ ....]ι̣ον ἓν καὶ σ[π]υ̣ρίδιον.
7 [Ἐξεδόμην σοι τὴν ἀποχὴν εἰ]ς ἀσφάλιαν κ̣[α]ὶ̣ ἐπερωτηθ(εὶς)
8 [ὡμολ(όγησα). Ὑπατείας τῆς προκ(ειμένης), Φα]ῶ̣φι δ‾.
9 [Αὐρήλιος N.N.   ὁ καὶ   ]..χίδημος ἔγρ̣α̣ψ̣[εν]
10 [ὑπὲρ αὐτοῦ γράμματα] μ̣ὴ εἰ̣δ̣(ότος).

7 ἀσφάλειαν

"--- of Hermopolis Magna, registered in the 'East City' quarter, to Aurelius Horos son of Mersis, camel-driver, from the Oasis. I acknowledge that I have received from you one camel load (consisting of) --- dried figs and dried grapes and fine linen and ---, one, and a basket. I have issued this receipt for your surety and having been formally questioned I have assented. In the aforementioned consulate, Phamenoth 4. Aurelius N.N. alias Archidemos has written for him because he does not know letters."

The damaged papyrus (the restorations of the lacunas at the left count 18 - 23 letters) contains a receipt issued by N.N. from Hermopolis, to Aurelius Horos (?) son of Mersis (?), a camel driver from the Oasis, concerning a camel load of various commodities (ll. 5-6: dried figs, dried grapes, fine linen, a basket) which N.N. has taken over from Horos. For a similar text mentioning a camel driver Horos son of Mersis, see **52** and cf. below, l. 3n.

1-2. Contacts between Kellis and Middle Egypt in general are illustrated by the fact that several people are stated to come originally from Kellis, while they are now living in the village of Aphrodite in the Antaiopolite Nome (cf. **30**, **32**, **42**, **44** cf. also **43**). An inhabitant from Hermopolis occurs also in **21**.26-27, while **52** was evidently written there (cf. l. 4, *ἐνταῦθα ἐν τῇ Ἑρμοῦ πόλει*). Furthermore, cf. the mention of Antinoopolis in **71**.16 and **77**.30 and that of an inhabitant of a Panopolitan village in **30**.

In l. 1 one might supply either a simple *ἀπὸ τῆς Ἑρμοῦ πόλεως* or, e.g. a function indication + *τῆς Ἑρμοῦ πόλεως*. The stop-gap phrase *τῆς μεγάλης* is sufficient as a restoration of the word(s) in the lacuna preceding the participle *ἀναγραφόμενος* in l. 2.

2-3. The quarter of Hermopolis called 'East City' is well-known, cf. A. Calderini - S. Daris, *Dizionario dei nomi geografici e topografici dell' Egitto greco-romano* II.3 (Milano 1975) 169f.

3. For the camel-driver Aurelius Horos son of Mersis, see also **34**.2 (315), **38.a**,**b**.10 (333), **52**.2 (320) and **57**.5 (332); a son of his may be referred to in **9**.1 (n.d.; see note ad loc. for the name *Μέρσις*). For a

list of camel-drivers mentioned in the papyri in general cf. CPR XIII p. 106-109. Cf. also A. Leone, *Gli animali da trasporto* (Rome-Barcelona 1988). While Horos' provenance is given here simply as 'from the Oasis', he is stated to be 'from the village of Kellis' in **52**.3; indeed in various Kellis documents the village is being referred to as *κώμη* Κέλλεως *τῆς* Μωθιτῶν *πόλεως τῆς* Μεγάλης Ὀάσεως = 'the village of Kellis which belongs to (the territory of) the city of the Mothites in the Great Oasis' (cf. **20**.3-5n., **42**.2-3, **44**.2-3; cf. also **21**.1,3).

If the papyrus were written in 320 (see the description above), it seems likely that this text, like **52**, was written and handed over to Aurelius Horos in Hermopolis on 1.x (**52** is also dated to *Φαῶφι δ* = 1.x in that year). Apparently he was on that date in Hermopolis (with a kind of small caravan?) and handed over various commodities to various persons.

5. *ἰσχάδες* are dried figs (for these s. M. Schnebel, *Die Landwirtschaft im hellenistischen Ägypten* [München 1925] 300), *σταφίδες* are dried grapes.

5-6. For *ὀθόνια* (= fine linen) in the papyri cf. S. Bartina in Stud.Pap. 4 (1965) 27-38.

6. For baskets in the papyri, see R.M. Fleischer, *Measures and Containers in Greek and Roman Egypt* (unpubl. Diss. New York University 1956) 53ff., for *σπυρίδιον* esp. 60-62.

7. For the restoration in the lacuna at the left of this line, see **52**.6-7.

8. Phaophi 4 = 1.x; cf. also above, l. 3n.

9. One is tempted to read the name as Ἀ̣ρ̣χίδημος, but the first two letters are too poorly preserved to warrant the reading Ἀ̣ρ̣-.

52: TRANSPORTATION RECEIPT

(1.x.320)

P.Kellis inv. P. 35.B (House 3, room 6, level 1, North end). H. 12 x B. 10.2 cm. Margins: at the top 1.2, at the bottom 6 cm. The writing runs parallel with the fibers; the verso is blank.

1 [Αὐρήλιος . . . σο]π ἀπὸ κώμης Τ̣π̣άκε τῆς Μωθειτῶν
2 [πόλεως Αὐρηλί]ῳ̣ Ὥρωι Μέρσει καμηλείτῃ ἀπὸ κώ-
3 [μης Κέλλεως τῆ]ς αὐτῆς [π]όλεως χαίρειν. Ὁμο̣λ̣ο̣γ`ῶ̣´
4 [παρειληφέναι π]αρὰ σοῦ ἐνταῦθα ἐν τῇ Ἑρμοῦ πόλει ὀνι-
5 [κοὺς γόμους ἐλ]αιῶ̣ν̣ θαλλ̣ί̣ω̣ν̣ κουκίων, ἵνα παράσ-
6 [χω τῷ δεσπότῃ] μ̣ου γεο̣[ύ]χῳ̣. Ἐξεδόμην̣ σ̣οι τὴν ἀπο-
7 [χὴν εἰς ἀσφάλειαν] καὶ ἐπε̣ρ̣[ω]τ̣ηθεὶς ὡμολόγησα.
8 [Ὑπατείας τῶν δεσ]ποτῶν ἡμ̣ῶ̣ν Κωνσταντίνου Σεβαστοῦ
9 [τὸ ς καὶ Κωνσταντί]ν̣ου τοῦ ἐπιφανεστάτου Καίσαρος τὸ α̅,
10 [ ] Φαῶφι δ̅.
11 [Αὐρήλιος . . . . .]σοπ ὁ προκείμενος παρείληφα τοὺς
12 [προκειμένους γό]μ̣ους ὡς πρόκειται. Ἔγραψα ὑπὲρ αὐτοῦ
13 [γράμματα μὴ εἰδό]τος Αὐρήλιος Ψεναμοῦνις Πετοσίριος
14 [ἀπὸ τῆς Ἑρμοῦ πόλ(εως).]

1]π` Pap., Μωθιτῶν 2 Μέρσιος, καμηλίτῃ (καμ- απο ex corr.) 5 ]αιων̣: -ϊ- Pap., -ω- ex α; κουκί<ν>ων (?; cf. ll. 4-5 n.) ϊνα Pap., ϊ- ex corr. 11 σοπ`, ὄ προκειμενος Pap.

"Aurelius -sop, from the village of Tpake (?) belonging to the city of the Mothites, to Aurelius Horos son of Mersis, camel-driver, from the village of Kellis belonging to the same city, greetings. I acknowledge that I have received from you here, in Hermopolis, -- donkey loads of olives in(?) sacks of palm fibers (?), to hand them over to my lord the landowner. I have issued this receipt to you and having been formally questioned I have assented. In the consulate of our lords Constantine *Augustus* consul for the 6th time and of Constantine *nobilissimus Caesar* consul for the 1st time, Phaophi 4. I, the aforementioned Aurelius -sop, have taken over the aforementioned loads as stated above. I, Aurelius Psenamounis son of Petosiris from Hermopolis (?), have written on his behalf, as he does not know letters."

Like **51** this text contains a receipt for the transportation of certain commodities. The receipt was issued in the Middle-Egyptian town of Hermopolis by a villager from Tpake in the Mothite nome to the camel-driver Aurelius Horos son of Mersis, from the village of Kellis in the same nome; both persons were, therefore, far away from their own homes (the distance between the Mothite nome and Hermopolis is ca. 300 km 'as the crow flies'). Unfortunately it remains unclear whether Horos had brought his cargo from the Oasis to Hermopolis or had transported the goods from elsewhere in the Nile valley to Hermopolis, before he travelled back to the Oasis (and took this receipt with him back to Kellis); in the latter case one would have had a better idea about the overall range of Horos' transport activities. Moreover, we do not know whether the anonymous landlord (*γεοῦχος*) lived in Hermopolis or in the Dakhleh Oasis. It looks probable that the issuer of the receipt and Horos only met in Hermopolis and that they did not cover the distance Dakhleh Oasis — Hermopolis or *vice versa* simultaneously.

1. Or read the place name as Π̣ι̣ακε? The village apparently does not occur elsewhere in the Kellis papyri (cf., however, **35**.2-3n.) and is not mentioned by G. Wagner in his discussion of the names of places in the Dakleh Oasis (*Les Oasis d'Egypte* [Cairo 1987] 188-196). For the relation between villages in the Mothite nome and the metropolis 'the city of the Mothites' cf. **20**.3-5n.

2. For the camel-driver Aurelius Horos son of Mersis, see **51**.3n.

4-5. These lines are somewhat problematic; in itself one does not expect 'donkey loads' (ὀνι-/[κοὺς γόμους) after a reference to a camel-driver, but ὀνι- definitely suggests the adjective ὀνικός (cf. LSJ on words starting with ὀνι-) and one needs as an object a noun like γόμον in **51**.4[21]; in fact,]μους in l. 12 makes γόμους virtually inescapable. Maybe the 'donkey loads' were a description of what they represented to the recipient, because the donkey was what he used to transport these loads. Thereafter one would expect a numeral followed by an indication of the nature of the cargo (in the genitive; e.g.: 'two donkey loads of ...'). As there is hardly space for a written-out numeral, it must be concluded that this was indicated by a single letter, e.g. β = 2; . . .]αίων̣ (gen.pl.) could, then, be a substantive of the commodity transported and ἐλ]αιῶν (suggested by Mr. I. Poll) is a most fitting word. θαλλ̣ί̣ων, gen.plur. of θαλλίον = 'sack' (cf. the discussion by H.I. Bell in *Wadi Sarga* [Copenhagen 1922] 20f.), could refer to the container the olives were packed in and, as κοῦκι = 'palm', one might think that such containers were made of palm leaves or fibers; there is, however, a problem in that one would probably need to correct κουκίων into κουκί<ν>ων (gen.plur. of an unattested adjective κούκινος = 'made from palm fibers'), as a

[21]) That the full text originally had a plural form is borne out by l. 11, παρείληφα τούς.

θαλλίον κουκίων would denote a 'sack of (filled with) palms'. Moreover, it is unclear how the genitive plural *θαλλ̣ί̣ων κουκί<ν>ων* should be construed with the preceding *ὀνι-/[κοὺς γόμους ἐλ]αιῶν*.
8-10. For the consuls of 320 cf. R.S. Bagnall a.o., *CLRE* s.a.; Phaophi 4 = 1.x. **51** was written the same day, cf. l. 8n.
13. The name of Aurelius Psenamounis son of Petosiris, does not seem to occur elsewhere in the Kellis papyri, but it must be kept in mind that in view of the place the document was issued we are probably dealing here with an inhabitant of Hermopolis, unless one prefers to assume that the issuer of the receipt, who could not write, was accompanied by person who also came from the Dakhleh Oasis; for another inhabitant of Hermopolis in a papyrus from Kellis cf. **21**.26-27. For identification purposes the name of Psenamounis was probably followed by an indication of his provenance or of his profession, cf. the other Kellis papyri with formulas used by such *hypographeis*.

53: LIST OF EXPENSES

(4th century)

P.Kellis inv. P. 17.D+T (House 3, room 10, level 3). H. 15 x B. 7.2 cm. Margins: at the top 2.7, at the left hand side 1.5, at the bottom 2.2 cm. Written parallel with the fibers; verso blank.

1 Λόγ(ος) ἀναλωμ[άτων
2 Ἡρωδιανὸς [
3 Πτολεμαῖος [
4 Ἐ̣χεύς [
5 μαξιλλάριο<ς> `.´[
6 ἐβρέκων [
7 πρίνκιπος [
8 χάρτης [
9 ἐπιστολὴ [
10 ὑπομνήματα [
11 ἑρμηνία [
12 μισθ[ὸς] καθηκη<τοῦ>
13 χωρὶς ναύλου πλοίου
14 τάλ(αντα) ια (δραχμαὶ) Βχ.

6 *εβρεκων*: *ε*- ex *ι*; l. *πραίκων* ?   7 *πρίγκιπος*   11 *ἑρμηνεία*   12 *καθηγητοῦ*

"List of expenses [ ]; Herodianos [ ]; Ptolemaios [ ]; Echeus (?) [ ] Maxillarius (?) [ ]; a herald [ ]; of the *princeps* [ ]; papyrus roll [ ]; a letter [ ] memoranda [ ]; translation [ ]; for wages of a teacher not including costs of transportation by boat, 11 tal(ents), 2600 dr(achmae)."

According to its first line this is a list of expenses and as such it may be compared especially with **54**. It is not without interest that both lists share a number of the same kind of expenses (cf. **54**.4, 6, 13, 16, 21, 22 with this text ll. 6-10) but there are also differences; here two personal names are registered (ll. 2-3: Herodianus, Ptolemaios) while in the parallel document personal names do not occur; for the expenses in ll. 11ff. there are no parallels in **54.** In itself it is striking that many entries are given in the nominative, whereas one might expect, especially in the case of commodities, genitives denoting expenses made 'because of/for ... '.

2,3. These persons do not occur elsewhere in the Greek papyri from Kellis.
4. Apparently a Greek personal name Echeus does not exist; on the other hand, for palaeographical reasons a reading *ọχεύς* = 'a kind of receptacle' (cf. LSJ s.v.) seems less likely.
5. A personal name Μαξιλλάριο<ς> is unknown to us. The word form reminds one of Latin rather than Greek and there are more Latin words in this text (cf. ll. 6,7). Lat. *maxilla*, however, means 'jaw, jawbone' (see the OLD s.v. and cf. the adjective *maxillaris*) and it is not easy to see what the concept of 'jaw' would do here together with personal names (ll. 2-3), indications of offices (cf. ll. 6-7) and words in the sphere of writing (l. 8ff.). One can only speculate whether there is a connection with **54**.4-5; if so, should we read <ἁ>μαξιλλάριο<ς> (= 'waggon driver'?) ?
6. It looks very attractive to cancel the initial epsilon and to regard the remaining letters *βρέκων* as an attempt to transliterate the Latin word *praeco* = 'crier, herald, auctioneer' into Greek (for *π/β* cf. F.T. Gignac, *Grammar* I 84), the more so as the spelling *βρέκων* is found in P.Ryl. IV 644.9 and the concept of expenses made 'for a herald' make good sense; cf. also **54**.6.
7. *πρίνκιπος* (l. *πρίγκ-*), which must be related to the Lat. word *princeps*, may refer here the 'Chief of staff' of a provincial governor, cf. P.Mich. XI 613.2n.; for other attestations of the word, see S. Daris, *Il lessico latino nel greco d'Egitto*[2] (Barcelona 1991) 94 s.v.; cf. also **54**.4.
8. For *χάρτης* = 'papyrus roll' cf. N. Lewis, *Papyrus in Classical Antiquity* (London 1974) 70ff.; idem, *Papyrus in Classical Antiquity. A Supplement* (Bruxelles 1989) 34.
11. On the practice of translation in 4th-century Egypt cf. R.S. Bagnall, *Egypt in Late Antiquity*, (Princeton 1993) 233 and W. Peremans, *Les EPMHNEIC dans l'Egypte romaine*, in: *Das römische Ägypten. Akten des internationalen Symposions, 26-30 September 1978 in Trier.* (Mainz 1983; = Aegyptiaca Treverensia, 2) 11-17, esp. p. 16 + n.63 (where attestations of the word *ἑρμηνεία* = 'translation' in the papyri are listed). Are we are dealing with costs made for a translation into Greek of a text written originally in, e.g., Syriac, Coptic or Latin, or *vice versa*?
12-14. The word starting with the letters *καθηκη* does not seem to have been abbreviated. *Καθηκη* is not the regular beginning of a normal Greek word and though it may seem a high-handed procedure to assume a spelling error *-ηκη-* for *-ηγη-* in order to obtain a recognizable word (and only the start of it) we see no other alternative herefore (for the interchange of *γ/κ*, see F.T. Gignac, *Grammar*, I 77-80).

As the right hand bottom edge of the papyrus seems to have been preserved, we take ll. 12-14 together and think that the scribe registered expenses made for the wages (*μισθός*) of a teacher who had to come from afar. The phrasing *χωρὶς ναύλου πλοίων* = 'not including costs of transportation by boat' (cf. l. 13n.) suggests that the teacher came from somewhere in the Nile valley and covered part of the distance by a boat.
13. For the phrasing *χωρὶς ναύλου πλοίων* cf. especially ZPE 64 (1986) 117-118. Many of the documents referred to there [P.Mich. VI 399-417; SB VI 9436; O.Mich. I 171-172] contain Fayumic receipts for deliveries of amounts of wheat.
14. The symbol used for indicating the numeral 2000 is, as more often, a 'latin' b with a horizontal bar drawn through the upper part of the vertical hasta, b.

54: LIST OF EXPENSES

(4th century)

P.Kellis inv. P. 51.E # 2 (House 3, room 9, level 3, East wall). H. 25 x B. 5 cm. Margin at the bottom: 6.5 cm. The writing runs parallel with the fibers, the verso is blank.

1 Λόγ(ος) ἀν̣[αλωμάτων
2 Τ̣ῷ ῥήτορι [τάλαντ- Number]
3 καὶ διζ[ύφων μάτ(ια) Number]
4 τῷ πρίγκιπ̣[ι καὶ τῷ ἀ-]
5 μαξηλ[άτῃ
6 πρέκω̣[νι
7 μ̣ι̣σθοῦ κ̣[τάλαντ- Number]
8 τῷ ῥη ̣ ̣ ̣[
9 εἰ̣ς ̣[
10 κ ̣ ̣[
11 ἐπιστολη[φόρῳ τάλαντ- Number
12 καὶ διζύ[φων μάτ(ια) Number]
13 μισθοῦ ὑπομν̣[ηματογράφου καὶ ἐκ-]
14 σκέπτωρ[ος τάλαντ- Number]
15 καὶ διζύφω̣[ν μάτ(ια) Number]
16 τὴν ἐπιστολὴ[ν τοῦ στρατη-]
17 γοῦ καὶ τοῦ πολ̣[ιτευομένου τάλαντ- Number]
18 καὶ διζύφ[ων μάτ(ια) Number]
19 μισθοῦ εἰς Ἑρμ[- ὑπο-]
20 μνημα̣[τογράφου τάλαντ- Number]
21 τιμ(ῆς) χά<ρ>του β̅[τάλαντ- Number]
22 καὶ μισθοῦ ὑπομ̣[νηματογράφου τάλαντ- Number]
23 (γίνεται) ἐπὶ τὸ αὐτὸ τά̣[λαντα Number]
24 ἐπιστολεὺς ̣[διζύφων]
25 μάτ(ια) δ- [
26 (γίνεται) ἐπὶ τὸ αὐτὸ δ[ιζύφων μάτ(ια) Number]

3, 12, 15, 18, 26 ζιζύφων 8 read ῥή[τ]ο̣ρ[ι ? 21 χαρτῶν?

Unfortunately this papyrus is seriously damaged. It shows certain resemblances to **53**. Apparently one is dealing with a list of expenses (l. 1, Λόγ(ος) ἀν̣[αλωμάτων), in which payments of amounts of talents for wages (μισθός, ll. 7, 13, 19, 22; cf. l. 23, where the total amount of talents was recorded) and deliveries of jujubes (ζίζυφος, cf. ll. 3, 12, 15, 18, 24-25 and l. 26, where the total amount of jujubes was recorded) to various officials were registered. It may be assumed that in principle wages were paid in money, supplemented sometimes by an amount of the fruit of the jujube tree. This tree and its fruit were apparently an important commodity in the region, as frequent reference is made to it in other (still unpublished) Kellis papyri. For the fruit (approximately the size of a cherry), see P.Oxy. LIX 4006.2n., where extensive further literature is given. See also V. Täckholm, *Students Flora of Egypt*[2] (Beirut 1974) 344-345. From l. 25 it may be gathered that the jujube fruits were measured in *μάτια* (cf. the Coptic 'maaje', a dry measure of capacity); for its size cf. K. Maresch and P.J. Sijpesteijn in ZPE 99 (1993) 64-65: depending on whether the decimal or the duodecimal system was used, a *μάτιον* is the equivalent of 1/10th or 1/12th of an artaba. 10 *μάτια* therefore would be 1 or 0.83333 artaba, in itself a rather sizable amount of jujube fruits. In **11**.9-10, too, reference is made to an artaba of jujubes.

The main interest of this text is found in its mention of a number of titles and professions about which we would have liked to know more especially in their relationship with Kellis , viz. the *ἀμαξηλάτης* (l. 4-5) *ἐπιστολήφορος* (l. 11; on this office [a liturgy in Roman times] cf. P.Petaus 84), *ἐκσκέπτωρ* (l. 13-14; cf. H.C. Teitler, *Notarii et exceptores* Diss. Utrecht 1983), *ἐπιστολεύς* (l. 24), *πολιτευόμενος* (l. 17; cf. H. Geremek in Anagennesis 1 [1981] 231-247), *πρέκων/πραίκων* (l. 6; cf. S. Daris, *Il Lessico Latino nel Greco d'Egitto*[2] [Barcelona 1991] s.v.), *πρίγκεψ* (l. 4; cf. **53**.7n.), *ῥήτωρ* (l. 2; cf. l. 8), *στρατηγός* (?; l. 16-17) and the *ὑπομνηματογράφος* (l. 13, 19-20, 22; on the municipal *hypomnematographoi* in Roman Egypt cf. J.E.G. Whitehorne in Aegyptus 67 [1987] 101-125). As some of these titles were given to municipal or government officials, it may be assumed that the payments were of an official rather than of a private nature; maybe the burden of defraying expenses made by/for these people fell upon the village of Kellis?

4-5. Cf. **53**.5n.; in itself it is possible that *μαξηλ[* contains an error for *μαξιλ[*; as there are no Greek words beginning with *μαξηλ-/μαξιλ-*, we suppose that the scribe wrote the initial alpha of *ἀ-*] | *μαξηλ[άτη* in the lacuna at the end of line 4.

9. Or read *ἐξ̣ ̣[* ?

16. It is remarkable that there is no preposition like, e.g., *εἰς* or *πρός* governing the accusative *τὴν ἐπιστολήν*. The restoration of *τοῦ στρατη-]* at the end of this line is uncertain, of course; in view of the context, however, it seems a decent guess.

19-20. Probably Ἑρμ[forms the start of a personal name like Hermes, Hermodoros, *vel sim.*, rather than that of (some form of) the name of the city Ἑρμοῦ πόλις.

Maybe one should restore the accusative *ὑπο-]* | *μνημα̣[τογράφον* (going with the preceding name) rather than the genitive *ὑπο-]* | *νημα̣[τογράφου* (going with *μισθοῦ*).

21. Cf. **53**.8n.

55: LIST

(4th century)

P. Kellis inv. P. 61.D (House 3, room 8, level 4). H. 13 x B. 3.5 cm. The bottom margin measures 5, the left hand margin 1 cm. The writing runs parallel with the fibers; the verso is blank.

1 Λόγ(ος) κτη[
2 κριθῆς [
3 ἄχυρον .[
4 ὁ ἄλλος .[
5 προβολὴ [
6 ἕως εἰστọ[
7 .οις τρ[
8 προβọλὴ [
9 ἕως τῆς [
10 ἀργυ(ρίου) ἐν ṿ[ούμμοις
11 ποτιστρ[

The precise purpose of this list (cf. l. 1, Λόγ(ος)) is uncertain, as the word after it has been preserved only incompletely; one could restore, e.g., κτή[ματος (= 'of an estate'), κτη[νῶν (= 'of animals') or κτή[σεως (= 'of property'); various other restora tions may be conceivable as well.

A coherent general interpretation of the fragment cannot be proposed with certainty; in principle it could be the remains of a list of amounts of money received or spent for various purposes in connection with, e.g., running a farm or feeding animals. After the heading in l. 1 one finds in ll. 2 and 3 two kinds of farm produce (barley and chaff), used e.g. for feeding animals and for which money could have been spent. In the following lines, however, apparently a change of subject is made and it is not clear, what exactly entries like ὁ ἄλλος (= 'the other', l. 4) or προβολή (ll. 5, 8) would mean within the context of a farm (for the various meanings of the word προβολή cf. LSJ s.v.). As the word ἕως in l. 9 seems to function as a preposition followed by the genitive, it may have that same function already in l. 6, but what is εἰστọ[(l. ἱστọ[?) ? The entry in l. 7 remains also enigmatic while the restoration in l. 10 is suggested only 'exempli gratia'; an alternative may be, e.g., ἐν ṿ[ομίσματι (cf. **29**.5-6 and note ad loc.). Finally, the word ποτίστρα (cf. l. 11) means 'watering-place, conduit, channel' and it may be that espenses for construction or maintenance of these were recorded.

56: SUBSCRIPTION TO A DOCUMENT

(324)

P.Kellis inv. P. 92.11 (House 3, room 11, level 1). Frag. I: H. 2.7 x B. 4.8 cm.; Frag. II: H. 6.5 x B. 5 cm. At the bottom of Frag. II there is a margin of 2.8 cm. On both sides the writing runs parallel with the fibers.

Frag. I:

- - - - - - - - - - - - - - - - -

1]̣ρος
2]μεν καὶ ἐπερωτηθεὶς
3 [ὡμολογήσα. Τέταρτον] μέλλουσιν ὑπά̣τ̣ο̣ις

- - - - - - - - - - - - - - - - -

Frag. II:
(M.2) - - - - - - - - - - - - - - - - -
4 [Αὐρ(ήλιος) N.N. ὁ προκε]ίμενος τέθιμαι
5 [ταύτην τὴν ὁμολογία]ν ἐφ' αἷς περιέχει
6 [διαστολαῖς πάσαις ὡς πρό]κειται καὶ ἐπερω-
7 [τηθεὶς ὡμολόγησα.] Ἔγραψα ὑπὲρ αὐτοῦ
8 [Αὐρήλιος]̣ων Ἀπολλωνίου
9 [Κέλλε]ως.
Verso:
10 Ὁμολογία [

4 τέθημαι

(Frag. II): "I, the above-mentioned N.N., have lodged this agreement under all of the conditions which it contains as mentioned above and I have answered the formal question. I, Aurelius --on son of Apollonios, --- of Kellis (?), have written for him."

These papyrus fragments contain the end of the body of a contract, including the consular dating formula, and the subscription to probably the same contract. As the contracting person was not able to write his subscription by himself he made use of a *hypographeus*. For this type of agent cf. the articles by H.C. Youtie in ZPE 17 (1975) 201-221 and 19 (1975) 101-108 = *Scriptiunculae Posteriores* I (Bonn 1981) 179ff., 255f.

3. This is the consulate of 324, cf. R.S. Bagnall, *CLRE*, s.a.; add **22**.2 and P.Nepheros 48.1 (cf. ZPE 78 [1989] 135).
9. Of course, the restoration of the name of an office + the toponym Kellis (e.g. [κωμογραμματεὺς Κέλλε]ως) can be proposed only 'exempli gratia' and in itself the restoration of a stop-gap formula like, e.g., [ἀπὸ τῆς αὐτῆς Κέλλε]ως is also conceivable. The 'same' village has not been mentioned earlier in the subscription but it may have been referred to already in the body of the text.

57: FRAGMENT OF A DATED SUBSCRIPTION

(26.ii - 26.iii.332)

P.Kellis inv. P. 17.Y (House 3, room 10, level 3). H. 3.7 x B. 2.5 cm. The writing runs parallel with the fibers; the verso is blank.

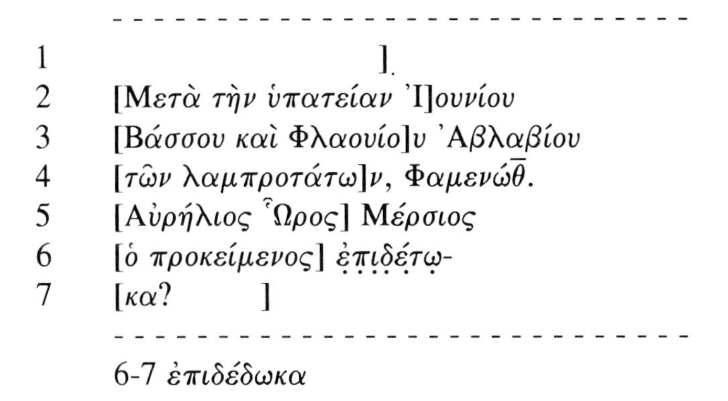

\- -

1]̣
2 [Μετὰ τὴν ὑπατείαν 'Ι]ουνίου
3 [Βάσσου καὶ Φλαουίο]υ 'Αβλαβίου
4 [τῶν λαμπροτάτω]ν, Φαμενῶθ̅.
5 [Αὐρήλιος Ὧρος] Μέρσιος
6 [ὁ προκείμενος] ἐ̣π̣ι̣δ̣έ̣τ̣ω̣-
7 [κα?]

\- -

6-7 ἐπιδέδωκα

"--. After the consulate (?) of Iunius Bassus and Flavius Ablabius, *viri clarissimi*, Phamenoth. I, the aforementioned Aurelius Horos son of Mersis, have submitted (?)."

The mutilated fragment published above contains only a mutilated dating + a subscription, but even so it is not without some interest of its own, as to date it may be the first papyrological attestation of a postconsulate of the consuls of 331 in 332 (cf. R.S. Bagnall e.a., *CLRE* s.a.). Phamenoth = 26.ii-26.iii and if we were to read Φαμενὼ(θ) θ̅, the exact date of the papyrus would be 5.iii.332. But often in papyri from Kellis the numeral for a day is simply not indicated; cf. **8**.13n.

2. The size of the lacuna in the following lines 3 and 4 allows the restoration of 'Μετὰ τὴν ὑπατείαν'; restoring only ''Ὑπατείας' would presuppose that the dating formula started right in the middle of the line. Though there are certainly parallels for this, it seems more likely to us that the scribe started the dating formula on a new line.
5. The restoration of Horos' name is inspired by the fact that in the papyri from House 3 we know of no other sons of a man called Mersis; for Horos son of Mersis, cf. **51**.3n. For the name Mersis, see **9**.1n.
6-7. The reading of the verb is all but certain; its restoration does not militate against normal practice. If it is correct, it probably closed off a document sent to a government official (e.g.: a petition).

58: FRAGMENT OF AN AGREEMENT

(337)

P.Kellis inv. A/5/4 (House 3, room 1, level 1, in Southeast corner). H. 11.6 x B. 10.3 cm. There is a margin at the bottom of 5.2 cm. The writing runs parallel with the fibers; the back is blank.

- -

1]ἐ̣κ̣ λο̣ . . [

2]θ̣ήκης κυρια̣σ̣τ̣ισης καὶ ε̣[

3 [καὶ ἐννομο. ὡς] κατακειμένης ἐν [δημοσίῳ καὶ ἐπερωτηθεὶς ὡμολόγησα.]

4 [Ὑπατείας Φλαυίου Φ]ηλικιανοῦ καὶ Τεττίου Τιτιανο̣[ῦ τῶν λαμπροτάτων]

5 [Month, day. (M.2) Αὐρήλιος Πλο]υ̣τογένης ὁ προκείμενος ἐθέ[μην τὴν ὁμολογίαν]

6 [ἐφ' αἷς περιέχει διασ]τολαῖς πάσαις καὶ εὐδοκῶ. [Ἔγραψεν ὑπὲρ αὐτοῦ]

7 [γράμματα μὴ εἰδότος] Αὐρήλιος Πολυκράτης Ὥρο[υ ἀπὸ ca. 11 letters)

8 (M. 1) [ca. 5. Αὐρήλιος Ἁρπ]ο̣κράτης πρεσβύτερος καθολικῆς ἐκκλησ̣[ίας μαρτυρῶ.

3 κατακειμένη (?)

"(L. 3ff.) -- and legal as if deposited in a public archive and in answer to the formal question I have replied positively. In the consulate of Flavius Felicianus and Tettius (!) Titianus, *viri clarissimi* - - -. I, Aurelius Ploutogenes the aforementioned, have lodged the agreement under all of the conditions which it contains and I agree. Aurelius Polykrates son of Horos, from --, have written for him as he does not know letters. I, Aurelius Harpokrates, priest of the catholic church, am witness."

This badly mutilated fragment of a Greek contract does not contain sufficient elements to establish its original nature precisely (cf. ll. 2-3n.). Nevertheless, it is interesting as it contains an aberrant consular dating formula (cf. ll. 4-5n.).

1. Something like ἐ̣κ̣ λόγο̣υ̣ or ἐ̣κ̣ λοι̣π̣ or ἐ̣κ̣λογῆ̣ς could be read; but the readings are rather uncertain and they do not suggest a particular formula.

2-3. Evidently we are at the end of the body of a contract; following these lines one finds the dating formula (ll. 4-5) and the signatures of one of the contracting parties (written by his representative, cf. ll. 5-7) and that of a witness (l. 8) The precise nature of the contract is not clearly preserved, but one might think about restoring a word like παρα(κατα)]θήκη = 'deposit of money' at the start of l. 2 (for this type of document cf. the literature cited by O. Montevecchi, *La Papirologia*, 230). Ll. 2-3 might contain a *kyria*-formula found often enough in contracts from Kellis (cf., e.g., **41**.18-19; cf. also the note to **37**.12ff.). Problematic, however, is the fact that apparently genitives (cf.]θ̣ήκης, κατακειμένης) have been used instead of the expected nominatives and that the word order in l. 3 is slightly irregular. Moreover, the reading of the word starting with *κυρι-* is also problematic; the three letters preceding the copula *καὶ* are to be read as *-σης* (cf. earlier in this line the ending of *]θ̣ήκης*), while the letter preceding this looks like *-ι-* (iota coming down with a long tail, like in l. 4, Τι-). It is, however, less certain, what comes in between *κυρι-* and *-ισης*; the writing looks like two omikrons connected with each other + a connecting stroke towards the iota. We have also considered reading *κυριε̣υ̣ο̣υ̣σης*, but we feel to see how its meaning (cf. F. Preisigke, *Wörterbuch*, s.v. *κυριεύω*) can be fitted into the context.

4-5. The garbled form of the consular formula makes it interesting. The consuls of 337 were Flavius Felicianus and Fabius Titianus (cf. R.S. Bagnall e.a., *CLRE* s.a.); the nomen Tettius going here with the second consul belongs to the second consul of 336, Tettius Facundus (in office with Virius Nepotianus). Though in principle such an error could have been made at all times, it seems more plausible that it was committed soon after a change in the consular formula. As the consuls of 336 were still being referred to in Egypt (via their post-consulate) as late as March 4, 337 (cf. Bagnall e.a., *CLRE* s.a. 337), this document might have been written soon afterwards.

5-6. Among the Kellis papyri there are several parallels for the formula restored here, cf. **14**.4-5, **31**.31f. and **56**.5-6.

7-8. Ca. 15 letters in the lacuna at the end of l. 7 and ca. 16 letters at the start of l. 8 are missing in Aurelius Polykrates' fairly large writing. This means that there is enough of space at the start of l. 8 for restoring something that still belongs to the signature of Polykrates, e.g. an indication of his origin.

8. At the start one might also reckon with another name ending in *-κράτης* like, e.g., Πολυκράτης (cf. l. 7), but this man cannot have been the same person as the priest of l. 8 as the handwriting is completely different. The occurrence here of a priest of the 'catholic' church in the year 337 is interesting, as it is the earliest occurrence in the Kellis papyri and early in the papyri in general. For the meaning of the term *καθολικὴ ἐκκλησία* (also in **24**.3 and **32**.21) cf. now E. Wipszycka, ΚΑΘΟΛΙΚΗ *et les autres Épithètes du nom* ΕΚΚΛΗΣΙΑ, JJP 24 (1994) 191-212, esp. 209ff.; in connection with villages it would often mean 'most important church, permanently in use for religious service'. It remains, of course, to be seen, what the nature of that church in Kellis was: Christian or Manichaean? Dr. Alcock informs me that the Coptic documents P. Kellis inv. 92.10 and inv. P. 92.18 refer to the 'Holy Church' which seems to refer to some Manichaean variety and thus distinguish it from the 'catholic' church.

59: CONSULAR DATE

(27.iii - 26.iv.328)

P.Kellis inv. P. 68.B (House 3, room 6, level 3). H. 5.5 x B. 7.5 cm. The papyrus has broken off at the top, at the bottom there is a margin of 2.5 cm. The writing runs parallel with the fibers; the verso is blank.

- -

1 Ὑπατ̣ί̣α̣ς̣ Φλ(αουίων) Ἰανουαρί̣ν̣ου κ̣α̣ὶ̣
2 Οὐου[εττί]ο̣υ̣ [Ἰούσ]τ̣ου τ̣[ῶ]ν̣ Traces (?)
3 λαμπ[ροτάτων], Φαρμ̣[οῦθι] ̣-.

1 Ὑπατείας, ϊανουαρινου Pap. 2 ϊουστου Pap.

For the consulate of Fl. Ianuarinus and Vettius Iustus in 328 cf. R.S. Bagnall a.o., *CLRE* s.a., where add SB XVIII 13260.29 (4.iv). The month of Pharmouthi covers the period 27.iii-26.iv.

2. The diaeresis on top of the iota of [Ἰού]στου is still visible, while the iota itself is lost.

60 - 62: WOODEN TABLETS FROM HOUSE 3

One of the most striking aspects about the whole corpus of inscribed material found at Kellis is the relatively large amount of wooden tablets with some form of writing upon them; it is common knowledge that in Egypt wood was, after all, a commodity which certainly was not used for writing as frequently as papyrus or potsherds. The newly found tablets range from a few more or less complete multi-page codices (among which the most spectacular are the Isocrates Codex and the Harvest Account Book, both still to be published), via individually preserved boards, to small fragments of boards with only minimal traces of writing preserved. Tablets appear to have been used in Kellis for several purposes: administration, astrology, liturgy and religious affairs in general, and for school exercises. A useful survey of the use of wood for various writing purposes and a list of publications of wooden tablets known from Graeco-Roman Egypt was published by W.M. Brashear and F.A.J. Hoogendijk in Enchoria 17 (1990) 21-54 (add now to the list, e.g, the tablets published in P.Brook. 27-31 and the astronomical T.Amst. inv. 1, published in CdE 52 [1977] 301ff. and recently discussed in CdE 68 [1993] 178f.; add also Bodl.Gr.Inscr. inv. 4, cf. Pack[2] 2710); for the subject in general cf. also E. Lalou, *Les tablettes à écrire de l'Antiquité à l'époque moderne* (Turnhout 1992), where P. Cauderlier gives (p. 63-96) another list of published tablets and where J.L. Sharpe discusses (p. 127-148) codicological aspects of the Isocrates Codex and the Harvest Account Book from Kellis. For the manufacture of wooden tablets at Kellis cf. **67**.

Several wooden tablets with administrative texts found in Kellis in Area A, House 2, and in Area B are to be published by R.G. Jenkins and G. Wagner. Other wooden tablets from House 3 published hereafter are **82**, **84**, **88** and **90**.

60: LIST OF NAMES

(Late 3rd / early 4th century)

T.Kellis inv. A/5/91 (House 3, room 7a, level 2). H. 13.5 x B. 5.2 cm. Thickness of the wood 6 mm. The upper margin measures 3.1, the bottom margin 4.5 cm. The writing runs across the grain of the wood. There are no holes, the verso is blank. For organizational purposes the tablet was referred to previously as 'T.Kellis 17'.

1 Ψάις Ψ̣εναπολλῶτος
2 ῾Ω̣ρος υἱὸς Τιβερίος
3 Ψάις Εὐτυχῆ Φαριᾶ
4 Βῆς Δημητρίου
5 Καλλικλῆς Σύρου
6 τέκτον(ος)
7 Μύρων Πεβῶτ(ος) Σαρᾶ
8 Ψάις Τειμοθέω
9 Ψάις 'Αλεξάνδ(ρου) παραχύτ(ος)
10 Τιθοῆς Σαβείνος
11 Τιθοῆς 'Ḥλία

2 Τιβερίου 8 Τιμοθέου 9 Παμουθ(ίος) 10 Σαβείνου 11 ηλϊα Tab.

"Psais son of Psenapollos; Horos son of Tiberius; Psais son of Eutyches son of Pharias (?); Bes son of Demetrios; Kallikles son of Syros the carpenter; Myron son of Pebos son of Saras; Psais son of Timotheos; Psais son of Alexander, *parachytos*; Tithoes son of Sabinus; Tithoes son of Elias."

The purpose of this list giving the names of ten males with their fathers' names (sometimes also a grandfather's name [ll. 3, 7, 9] or a profession [l. 5-6, 9]) is not stated; it could be, of course, a *decania*-list (for literature cf. O.Cair.GPW 133-137, introd.), but the characteristic sign for the δεκανός himself is absent on the board. Though many of the names on this board are known from other Kellis texts, none of these persons occurs elsewhere in the Greek documents from Kellis; several names (Senapollos, Eutyches, Pharias, Bes, Demetrios, Myron, Alexander) apparently occur only here. The dating of the board is not quite certain. For palaeographical reasons a dating to the later 4th century seems unlikely. Furthermore, most names are pagan Egyptian, Greek and Latin names and they seem to point to an earlier period; only the fathers' names Timotheos and Elias (ll. 8, 11), may be related to the spreading of Christianity (unless they were borne by Jews, cf. **61**, introd.). Given the fact that none of the persons here mentioned seem to occur elsewhere in the Greek papyri from Kellis one may be tempted to think that perhaps the board belongs to another, slightly earlier period. On the other hand, our evidence from Kellis for the first decade of the 4th century or even earlier is rather slender and there is no palaeographical obstacle against dating the text to ca. 300 - 310 rather than ca. 290 - 300. Under these circumstances a general dating to the late 3rd/early 4th century seems the most fitting.

2. In itself it was not necessary to indicate the father/son relationship by the use of *υἱός*. Should we take it that in fact Horos was the son of Psais, (l. 1), while Tiberius was his alias-name? But this is not clearly indicated. One finds *θυγ(άτηρ)* used for expressing a father/daughter relationship below in **61**.12, but there it may have been used on purpose, as the daughter's name (now partially lost in a lacuna) may have been abbreviated.

3. *Φαριᾶ* (gen.) looks like a grandfather's name, rather than an alias-name or the indication of some (unknown) profession. Cf. ll. 7, 9 for other (names of) grandfathers. A masculine name *Φαριᾶς* seems to be an *addendum onomasticis*; for the female *Φαρία* cf. F. Preisigke, *Namenbuch*, s.n. It does not seems very likely that here both the father and the mother of *Ψάις* were mentioned and that we should read *Φαρία*<*ς*>.

4. The short name *Βῆς* occurs only here. Several names, however, in *Βησ-* were current in Kellis.

9. For another occurence of the word *παραχύτος* cf. **3**.9n.

61: LIST OF MONEY ARREARS

(4th century)

T.Kellis inv. A/5/106 (House 3, room 3, level 1). H. 22.9 x B. 6.3 cm. Thickness of the wood 3 mm. The bottom margin is 13.5 cm. wide. The writing runs across the grain of the wood. There are 2 x 2 holes visible on the left hand edge (they are partly incomplete, where the board has broken). The verso is blank. For organizational purposes this wooden board was known previously as 'T.Kellis 18'.

1 ἔχθε̣σ̣(ις) ἀργυ(ρίου) ἐν πορφ(ύρα̣)
2 Ἰ̈α̣κῶβ κεραμέως
3 ἐλαίου χο(ῦς) S/
4 Κοπρία χο(ῦς) S/
5 Ῥαχῆλ κόμμεως μ(ετρητὴς ?) α
6 Θ̣ε̣ρμοῦθ(ις) Παπν(ου)θ(ίου) ἐρεοξ(ύλου) μν(ᾶς) S/
7 Κατα̣ΐ̣( ) Ἀπολλ( ) χαλκ(έως) τάλ(αντα) ϡ
8 Π̣αταΐ δι(ὰ) Παπνουθ(ίου) τάλ(αντα) χ
9 Ναρ̣σ̣[.]( ) Ἀπολλῶς Ἀφροδι( )
10 τάλ(αντα) ω
11 Μαρ[.]α Ἀπόλλων(ος) κρ(ι)θ(ῆς) μ(όδιοι) ε
12 Ἰσι̣[δώρα] θυγ(άτηρ) Ἰωά̣ν̣ν̣(ου) τάλ(αντα) σ
13 Ἰσιδ̣(ωρ-) Π̣απνουθ(ίου) τάλ(αντα) σ.

1 ἔκθεσ(ις) 7 καταϊ Tab. 12 ϊσι-, ϊωανν Tab. 13 ϊσι- Tab.

"Arrears of money in purple. From Jacob the potter, ½ *chous* (of oil); Kopria, ½ *chous* (of oil); Rachel, 1 *metretes* (?) of gum; Thermouth(is) daughter (?) of Papnouthios, ½ *mna* of cotton; Katai( ) son of Apoll( ), the bronzesmith, 900 tal(ents).; Patai through Papnouthios, 600 tal.; Nars( ) son (?) of Apollos son of Aphrodi( ) (?), 800 tal.; Mar.a daughter of Apollon, 5 *modii* of barley; Isidora daughter of John, 200 tal., Isid( ) son of Papnouthios, 200 tal."

According to l. 1 this board contains a record of arrears of money owed, ἔχθεσ(ις) ἀργυ(ρίου); apparently these arrears were connected with purple dye (cf. ἐν πορφ(ύρᾳ)) and it looks probable that the amounts of money owed were to be converted into amounts of purple dye as that was probably a more stable commodity than steadily depreciating 'silver' money (cf. for deliveries or payments 'ἐν πορφ(ύρᾳ)' the remark in P.Hamb. I 90.10n. and P.Giss. 103 = M. Naldini, *Il Cristianesimo in Egitto* # 43.9-14 [also from the Great Oasis]). It is remarkable, however, that in the following ll. 2-13 one finds entries registering either (*a*) amounts of some commodity other than purple (oil [ll. 3, 4], gum [l. 5], cotton [l. 6] and barley [l. 11]) or (*b*) sums of talents. Are the first registrations indications of commodities bought with money which also should be recompensed in purple dye? Also remarkable is the fact that this wooden board contains a certain concentration of 'Jewish' names, cf. Ἰακῶβ (l. 2), Ῥαχῆλ (l. 5), and Ἰωάννης (l. 12); cf. also Μάρ[θ]α / Μαρ[ί]α in l. 11. These names are probably connected with the christianization of the village of Kellis during the 4th century and the concomitant introduction of Biblical names used by the Christians, as there seems no good reason to think that there was a kind of 'Jewish quarter' in the village or in its neighbourhood. The size of the amounts of talents (200 - 900) is compatible with a date to ca. 350 or slightly later.

1. For the subject of 'purple' in the ancient and Arabic world there is a vast literature; see M. Reinhold, *History of Purple as a Status Symbol in Antiquity* (Coll. Latomus 116); see also, e.g., J. Balfour-Paul, 'Indigo in the Arab World', Hali 61, pp.98-105 and 140 (we owe this reference to the kindness of Dr. A. Alcock). Dr. Alcock informs us that the term for purple dye also occurs fairly commonly in the Coptic texts from Kellis, alone and in connection with wool.
2. For a list of potters occurring in the papyri published until 1987 cf. CPR XIII, pp. 109-14. For other potters in the Kellis documents cf. **66**.22; **74**.2, 35 (?); cf. also the village name κώμη Κεραμείων in **34**.1.
3. For the resolution of χο( ) into χο(ῦς) (= ca. 3 liter) cf. **90**.7n.
4. For the name Κοπρία cf. the remarks by S.B. Pomeroy, *Copronyms and the Exposure of Infants in Egypt*, in: *Studies in Roman Law in Memory of A.Arthur Schiller* (Leiden 1986), 147-162.
5. We have resolved μ(ετρητής), but a resolution like, e.g., μ(άτιον) or μ(άριον) can perhaps not be excluded.
6. Though it is true that in l. 12 the father/daughter relationship is clearly expressed by θυγ(άτηρ), almost all names in Θερμουθ- are borne by women, hence the idea that one is dealing here with a daughter rather than with a son of Papnouthios. One wonders whether this father Papnouthios is the same person as the Papnouthios in ll. 8 and 13. For the subject of cotton in the Great Oasis cf. G. Wagner, *Les Oasis d'Egypte* 291-93 (P.Mich. VIII 500.7 also contains a reference to cotton).

7. The name Κατα̣ΐ̣( ) seems to be an *addendum onomasticis*. A resolution of χαλκ( ) into χαλκ(έως) rather than into χαλκ(οῦ) is indicated by the fact that in this period there are no χαλκ(οῦ) τάλαντα in use any longer. In itself one may prefer to take the indication of the trade as going with the son rather than with the father, hence resolve χαλκ(εύς).
8. The name Π̣αταϊ is apparently unabbreviated and as such it seems to be an *addendum onomasticis*; but cf. names like, e.g., Πατάις and, in Kellis, Παταιᾶς.
9. The reading of Ναρσ̣⟦ ̣⟧( ) is uncertain; is Ἀπολλῶς Ἀφροδι( ) intended to mean 'Apollos son of Aphrodi(sios)' *vel sim.*, or should one resolve Ἀφροδι(τοπολίτης) and take the meaning as 'Apollos from Aphrodite'?
11. Both Μαρ[ί]α and Μάρ[θ]α are possible.
12. For the use here of θυγ(άτηρ) cf. above **60**.2n.

62: LIST OF RENT PAYMENTS

(Late 3rd / early 4th century)

T.Kellis inv. A/5/194 (House 3, room 8, level 4). H. 26 x B. 9.5 cm. Thickness of the wood 5 mm. The bottom margin measures ca. 4 cm. The writing runs across the grain of the wood. On the verso are scattered traces of text (mostly gone). There are several holes in the wood, 2 x 2 drilled ones at the right hand side (diameter: .5 cm) and various other ones caused by worms. For organizational purposes the board was previously known as 'T.Kellis 9'.

1 ẸS´´ Χοιὰκ ιβ̅· ἔδ̣ω̣κ̣ε̣ν̣
2 Ἱενᾶ Φιλυς ὑπὲρ φόρου χωρίου
3 Πανέους ἀργυρίου δραχμὰς
4 ἕκατον, γ(ίνονται) (δραχμαὶ) ρ. Ἔδωκεν
5 [τ]ὴν ἀπο̣χὴν Φ̣ι̣λούμεν[ος].
6 Φαρμοῦθ(ι) ̣—· ὁ αὐτὸς ἔδωκεν
7 ὑπὲρ τοῦ α̣ὐ̣τ̣ο̣ῦ̣ φόρου [ἀρ]γυρίου
8 δραχμὰς διακοσίας δώδε-
9 κα, γ(ίνονται) (δραχμαὶ) σιβ. Ἔδ̣ωκεν [τ]ὴ[ν]
10 ἀποχὴν Φιλούμενος.
11 Παχὼν ε̅· ἔδωκεν ὁ αὐτὸς
12 ἄλλας δραχμὰς ἑξήκοντα ὀκτ[ώ],
13 (γίνονται) (δραχμαὶ) ξη. Ἔδωκεν τὴν ἀποχὴν
14 Φιλούμενος.
15 Θὼθ— ιγ·
16 ἔδωκεν Γενᾶ Φιλυς ὑπὲρ φόρ(ου)
17 χωρίου Πανέους ἀργυρίου
18 δραχμὰς ἕκατον, γ(ίνονται) (δραχμαὶ) ρ. Ἔδωκεν
19 τὴν ἀποχὴν Φιλούμενος
20 Φαῶφι κ̅· ἔδωκεν ὁ αὐτὸς
21 ἄλλας δραχμὰς διακοσίας εἴκο-

22 σι τέσαρες, γ(ίνονται) (δραχμαὶ) σκδ. Ἔδωκεν
23 τὴν ἀποχὴν Φιλούμενος.
24 Ἀθὺρ κ̄· ἔδωκεν Γενᾶ Φιλυς
25 ὑπὲρ τοῦ αὐτοῦ φόρου ἄλλας
26 ἀργυρίου δραχμὰς ἕκατον, (γίνονται) (δραχμαὶ) ρ.
27 Ἔδωκεν τὴν ἀποχὴν Φιλούμενος
28 Τῦβι κ̄· ἔ̣δ̣ω̣κ̣ε̣ν̣ ὑπὲρ τοῦ αὐτοῦ
29 φόρου ἄ̣λλας ἀ̣ργυρίου δ̣ρ̣α̣χμὰς
30 ἕκατον τριάκοντα δύο, (γί̣νονται) (δραχμαὶ) ρλβ·
31 ὁμοίως ἄλλας δραχμὰς
32 εἴκοσι τέσαρες, γ(ίνονται) (δραχμαὶ) κδ. Ἔδω-
33 κεν τὴν ἀποχὴν Φιλούμενος.

2 ϊενα Pap. 20 φαωφι' Pap. 22 τέσσαρας 24 αθυρ' Pap. 28 τυβι' Pap. 31 τέσσαρας

"Year 5, Choiak 12. Iena son of Philus (?), has paid for rent for the farm of Panes a hundred silver drachmas, 100 dr. in total. Philoumenos has issued the receipt. Pharmouthi -. The same person has given for the same rent two hundred and twelve silver drachmas, 212 dr. in total. Philoumenos has issued the receipt. Pachon 5, the same person has paid another sixty eight drachmas, 68 dr. in total. Philoumenos has issued the receipt. Thoth 13. Gena son of Philus (?), has paid for rent for the farm of Panes a hundred silver drachmas, 100 dr. in total. Philoumenos has issued the receipt. Phaophi 20. The same person has paid another two hundred and twenty-four drachmas, 224 in total. Philoumenos has issued the receipt. Hathyr 20, Gena son of Philus (?), has paid for the same rent another hundred silver drachmas, 100 dr. in total. Philoumenos has issued the receipt. Tybi 20. He has paid for the same rent another hundred and thirty-two silver drachmas, 132 dr. in total. Likewise, another twenty-four drachmas, 24 dr. in total. Philoumenos has issued the receipt."

This wooden board contains a series of rent payments made by a certain Iena (Gena). Two of the payments (ll. 1-5, 15-19) record specifically that he paid 'for the farm of Panes', and it may be assumed that indeed all receipts refer to the same purpose of payment. It is, however, not clear what was paid for: the rent of, e.g., a farm house, or of a small plot of land? The payments (which all have been recorded by a certain Philoumenos) can be tabulated as follows:

Ll.	*Month #*	*Month Name*	*Drachmas*
1-5	IV	Choiak 12	100
6-10	VIII	Pharmouthi [-]	212
11-14	IX	Pachon 5	68
15-19	I	Thoth 13	100
20-23	II	Phaophi 20	224
24-27	III	Hathyr 20	100
28-30	V	Tybi 20	132
31-33	(idem)	(idem)	24

The total amount paid was 960 drachmae paid in 8 instalments covering a period of 13 months, i.e. more than 1 year. At the same time it should be noticed that there is no change indicated from a 5th year (cf. l. 1 and note ad loc.) to a next, 6th year. It is also remarkable that there was no fixed monthly rent payment; the average payment per month was $^{12}/_{13}$ x 960 = 89.25 dr. (= ca. 3 drachmas a day), but the rent was paid apparently at irregular times and in irregular amounts (all amounts of drachmas, however, are multiples of 4 and this points to actual payments of tetradrachms). Given the use of drachma-coinage and the fact that the total amount of 960 drachmas for rent for a period of more than 1 year is relatively small (slightly more than the price of an artab of beans for future delivery in 308, cf. R.S. Bagnall, *Currency and Inflation in Fourth Century Egypt* 65 [P.Cair.Isid. 87, 88, 89]), it may be assumed that this wooden board should probably dated to the first decade of the 4th century or else to the preceding period (cf. line 1n.).

1. It is not stated clearly what the numeral ε̣S´´ refers to, but it looks like a numeral for a year. There are, then, two possibilities:
a. a regnal year, or
b. an indiction year.

If it is a regnal year, one is almost forced to assume that 'regnal year 5' refers to a reign preceding that of the emperor Diocletian (for the argument cf. BASP 16 [1979] 221ff.: 'Single Year Dating under Diocletian and his Successors'); the latest possible year 5 of a single ruler is that of the emperor Probus, i.e. 279/80; but then one cannot rule out, of course, year 5 of Aurelian, 273/4.

If it is an indiction year numeral, there are, again, two possibilities:
(1) it may be connected with the system of 5-year cycles of tax levies (ἐπιγραφαί, διατυπώσεις, ἰνδικτίωνες) operating between 287-302 (for this system cf. J.D. Thomas, BASP 15 [1978] 133-45 and R.S. Bagnall - K.A. Worp, *The Chronological Systems of Byzantine Egypt* [Zutphen 1978], Ch. I), or
(2) it may be connected with the well-known system based on a cycle of 15 years (these years being numbered 1-15, the cycle itself NOT being numbered) which was operating in Egypt from 313 onwards (with indiction year 1 of the first cycle = 312/3, cf. Bagnall-Worp, *op.cit.* and CPR XVII.A 2 introd.).

As the first system was never used for simple dating purposes (only to indicate tax levies), this option may be discarded, but 'year 5' may be related to the 5th indiction in 316/7 (for other considerations of dating this text cf. above).

Instead of reading the numeral as ε̣ a reading δ̣ cannot be excluded. If so, the years in the Julian calendar are either 278/9 or 272/3, resp. 315/6.

2. It is remarkable that the scribe's spelling fluctuates between Ἰενᾶ (here) and Γενᾶ (ll. 16, 24), apparently reflecting an Egyptian [j]-sound (for similar fluctuations cf. F.T. Gignac, *Grammar*, I 73f.). A personal name Φιλυς is not listed by F. Preisigke, *Namenbuch*, of D. Foraboschi, *Onomasticon Alterum Papyrologicum*.
3. A Χωρίον Πανέους (gen. of Πανῆς) is not known from elsewhere, but Πανῆς is known as a personal name.
5. Philoumenos is the person who signed the receipt, but he may have been only a rent collector, while another person owned the object for which Iena/Gena paid rent. The name does not turn up elsewhere in the Greek texts from Kellis.

63: MANICHAEAN LETTER

(First part of 4th century)

P.Kellis inv. P. 87 (House 3, room 6, level 4, South wall). H. 28 x B. 11.3 cm. The upper margin is 1.5 cm. wide, at the left there was originally a margin of 1 cm. left free, but it has been inscribed. The text was written parallel with the fibers on both sides of the sheet.

1 Κ̣[υ]ρίοι̣ς καὶ π`ο´θ̣ε̣ι̣ν̣ο̣τάτο[ι]ς υ[ἱο]ῖς
2 κ̣αὶ ἡμῖν ἐρασμ̣ι̣ωτάτ̣ο̣ι[ς] Πανσα̣νί̣α̣
3 [κ]αὶ Πισι[σ]τράτῳ [ ] . . [ ]
4 ἐν Θεῷ χαί[ρ]ε̣ιν.
5 [Π]ολλ̣ῆς κα̣ὶ ἀπεί̣[ρο]υ οὔσης ἔν τ̣ε̣ δ̣ι̣α-
6 νοία̣ καὶ στόμα̣[τι] ἡμῶν τῆ̣ς ὑ̣μ̣ε̣[τ]έρ̣[α]ς
7 ε̣ὐ̣φημία̣ς̣ [β]ο̣ύ̣λ̣ομαι διὰ] γραμ̣μ̣ά̣τ̣[ω]ν̣
8 ταύτην ἐ̣π̣ὶ̣ τ̣ο̣σ̣ο̣ῦ̣τ̣ον ἐ̣κφᾶναι κ̣[α]ὶ̣
9 ἐπε̣κ̣τε̣ῖναι· τῷ γὰρ ἐ̣ν ὑμ̣[ῖ]ν ε̣ἰλι[κρι-]
10 ν̣ε̣σ̣τ̣άτῳ ν̣ῷ τ̣ο̣ῦ̣το ἀναγέγρ[α]π̣ται κα̣ὶ̣
11 μ̣εμ̣α̣ρτύ̣ρηται· Ὅμως κ̣α̣ὶ̣ τ̣ὸ γράμμα
12 μ̣ετ̣ρίως εὐ̣φραί̣ν̣ε̣ιν ἐπιστάμ̣ε̣νοι
13 ἐ̣π̣ε̣ι̣γό̣μεθα κ̣[α]ὶ̣ τ̣[ο]ύ̣τ̣ῳ σ̣υνεχῶ̣ς χρᾶ-
14 σ̣θ̣αι καὶ ὧν ἔνδ[ο]ν πρὸς τὴν ὑμετ̣έ̣-
15 ρα̣ν φέρομεν θ[ε]ο̣[σ]ε̣βῆ δ̣ι̣[ά]θεσιν̣ κυη-
16 [μάτων] θ̣ε̣ίων ε[ἰ]ς̣ τ̣οὺς [. .]α̣ν[. . .]ασωδι-
17 . σ̣ί̣α̣ς̣ ἐ̣κπέ̣μπειν· πάνυ γὰρ ἡδ̣όμεθα
18 κ̣α̣ὶ̣ χ̣α̣ί̣ρομεν κομιούμ[ε]νοι τὰ̣ [τ]ῆς ὑμ̣ε-
19 [τ]έρας εὐνοίας τεκμήριά̣ τ̣ε κ̣α̣ὶ̣ ἀσμ̣έ̣-
20 ν̣α̣ ὑ̣μῶν γράμματα, λέγω [. .] ν̣· κ̣[α]ὶ̣
21 ν̣ῦν ἀπ̣ο̣λαύομεν πνευ̣μ̣α̣τικῶν
22 ὀ̣λ̣ί̣γων καρπῶν, ἀ̣πολ̣αύ[ο]με̣ν̣ δ[ὲ] π̣ά-
23 λιν κα̣ὶ τῶν ψυχικῶν τῆς ε̣ὐ̣σ̣εβο̣ῦ̣ς
24 . . φ̣ο̣ρα̣ς̣ δηλονότι· καὶ ἀμφοτέρ[ω]ν
25 π̣επλησμ̣[έ]ν̣οι πᾶσαν ε̣ὐλογίαν̣ σ̣π̣[ε]υ-

26 σό̣μεθα πρὸς τὴν φω̣τινο̣τά̣τη[ν] ὑ-
27 μῶν ψυχὴν καθ̣᾽ ὅσον ἡμῖν ε[στι] δ̣υ̣να̣-
28 [τὸν . . .]. Μόνος γὰρ ὁ δ[ε]σπότης ἡμ̣ῶ̣ν
29 [ὁ] π̣[α]ρ[άκ]λητος `ἱκανὸς´ ἐπαξί̣ως ὑμᾶς εὐ̣λο̣γῆσα[ι]
30 κ̣[α]ὶ̣ τ̣[ῷ̣] δέοντι καιρῷ̣ ἀνταμείψα̣[σ]θ̣αι·
31 κ̣ε̣κ̣ο̣μ̣ί̣σμεθα μὲν ο̣ὖ̣ν̣ τ̣ὸ̣ σπυρίδιον καὶ
32 [π]ρ[οσ]ομολογοῦμεν τῇ εὐσ̣ε̣βεστάτῃ̣ ὑ-
33 [μ]ῶν π̣ροαιρέσει καὶ τὰ πρὸς τὸν κ̣ύριον
34 . . ρυλλο̣ν δεδ̣ώκαμεν· ὁμ̣οίως κ̣αὶ τὸ̣
35 [. . .]λιον̣ εἰλήφαμεν· διαμένο̣ιτ̣ε
36 ἡμῖν τοιοῦτοι εὐχομένο̣ις· τ[ο]ὺς
37 π[άν]των π[ρ]οσ . . . α . . . α̣ξ̣ιώ̣σ̣ατ̣ε
- -

In the left hand margin:

38 ο̣ἱ̣ ἀ̣δελ̣φοὶ ὑμῶν πολλ̣ὰ̣ [ὑμᾶς] πρ[ο]σ[αγο]ρ[ε]ύ̣ο̣υσιν TRACES
39 καὶ . . ελιος

Verso:

40 - - - - - ἐρασ]μιω- \ /
41 τάτο[ις Π]ισ[ι]σ[τράτῳ] / \

6 ὑ̈μετερας Pap. 9 επεκτειναι· Pap. 11 μεμαρτυρηται· Pap. 14 ὡν Pap. 16 θεϊων Pap. 24 δηλονοτι· Pap. 26-27 ϋμων Pap. 30 ανταμειψασθαι· Pap. 32 ϋ- Pap. 34 δεδωκαμεν· Pap. 35 ειληφαμεν· Pap. 36 ευχομενοις· Pap.

"To my lords sons who are most longed-for and most beloved by us, Pausanias and Pisistratos, N.N. sends greetings in God. Since your good reputation is great and without limit in our mind and in our speech, I wish to reveal this as much as possible and to extend it through this letter. For this has been recorded and testified to by the most sincere mind in you. And yet, knowing that this letter will gladden (you) in due measure, consequently we hasten to make use of this and to send off to the --- word of the divinely generated conceptions which we cherish inside towards your pious character. For we are most pleased and rejoice when (or: that?) we shall receive both the indications of your sympathy and the welcome letter of yours, I mean ...; and now we benefit from a few fruits of the spirit and (later) again we benefit also from the fruits of the soul of the pious ...., of course; and filled with both we shall set going every praise towards your most luminous soul inasmuch as this is possible for us. For only our lord the Paraclete is competent to praise you as you deserve and to compensate you at the appropriate moment. We have received the basket and we give in to your most pious preference and we have given the objects destined for the lord -ryllos. Likewise, we also received the ---. May you remain so helpful for us as we pray; ..."

The background situation of this letter seems to be the following: Pausanias and Pisistratos had solicited a kind of letter of recommendation from their correspondent (whose name is lost, unfortunately); now he replies to their request in a letter with elegant phrasings which are quite uncommon in ordinary Greek private letters; at the same time he confirms receipt of a few commodities.

To our knowledge this is the second Greek papyrus letter which may be connected with or attributed to Manichaeans; the first such letter was published first by J.H. Harrop in JEA 48 (1962) 133-140, later republished by E.G. Turner as P.Oxy. XXXI 2603 and by M. Naldini, *Il Cristianesimo in Egitto* # 47, but its character and background have been described as 'Christian' rather than 'Manichaean' (cf. now the remarks by S.N.C. Lieu, *Manichaeism in Mesopotamia and the Roman East* (Leiden 1994) 98 n.316.

Dr. I. Gardner comments about this exceptional letter: "The Manichaean beliefs held by the letter's author, and presumably shared by Pausanias and Pisistratos, are made evident by the reference to 'our lord the Paraclete' (l. 27-28). Mani claimed to have been the recipient of direct revelation from his divine Twin-Spirit, which being was understood to have been the 'Paraclete' foretold by Jesus (Jn. 14:16); and with whom Mani became 'one body and one spirit' (*Kephalaia* 15.23-24). This reference here in **63**, and two amongst the Coptic personal letters (P. 84, line 9, and P. 88, line 27), answers a long running discussion among scholars as to whether the community directly identified their founder with the Paraclete (in catholic Christianity identified as the Holy Spirit), or otherwise in some sense held the divine and human apart. It would seem that, at this popular level at least, the identification became complete.

Once the Manichaean authorship is noted various other distinctive features in the letter's terminology can also be understood with reference to the community's doctrine. In particular, the 'most luminous soul' (ll. 26-27) must be related to teachings about the Living Soul. This figure is the collectivity of the divine light that has become trapped and entwined in the natural world; which is equally the history of each individual. The divine psyche is awakened to salvation and truth by the Light Nous; as incarnated in the apostles, the true church, and the individual made anew. Here, the author praises the purity and enlightenment of those whom he is addressing."

3. For a man named Pausanias in Kellis cf. **4** (331), **5** (IV), **6** (IV) [all three found in House 2], and **38.a,b** (333) [from House 3], esp. **38.a**.1n.; we think that we are dealing here with the same person, and this letter's handwriting forms no palaeographical obstacle against the hypothesis that it was written somewhere in the first part of the 4th century; it is impossible to determine a more precise date. The fact, that we have two documents issued by Pausanias in the 330's, should not make us exclude a slightly earlier date for this letter, but it is equally possible that it dates from, e.g., ca. 345. A Pisistratos occurs also on an otherwise insignificant [undated] scrap in P. 17.V.

21-24. We are not certain how to understand the author's wording *ν̣ῦν ἀπο̣λαύομεν πνευ̣μ̣α̣τικῶν* | *ὀ̣λ̣ί̣γων καρπῶν, ἀ̣πολ̣αύ[ο]με̣ν̣ δ[ὲ] π̣ά-* | *λιν κα̣ὶ τῶν ψυχικῶν τῆς ε̣ὐ̣σ̣ε̣βο̣ῦ̣ς* | *. . .φο̣ρα̣ς̣ δηλονότι·* (the stop occurring on the papyrus after *δηλονότι* prevents us from taking this word with the following passage). The word *καρπῶν* goes also with *τῶν ψυχικῶν*, but what these *πνευματικοὶ* and *ψυχικοὶ καρποί* exactly are (they are clearly distinct from each other, cf. in ll. 24-25 *καὶ ἀμφοτέρ[ω]ν* (sc. *καρπῶν*) *π̣επλησμ̣[έ]ν̣οι*), is all but clear.

34. We have not been succesful in reading the first letters of the name (that of another member of the Manichaean community in Egypt) and in fact there are several possibilities for restoration.

64: PRIVATE LETTER

(Mid 4th century)

P.Kellis inv. P. 82.C (House 3, room 6, level 4, in Southeast corner). H. 27 x B. 6.2 cm. Margins: at the top 1.5, at the bottom 7, at the left 0.5 cm. Writing parallel with the fibers on both sides. The papyrus was folded 2x vertically and 1x horizontally.

1 [Κυ]ρίῳ μου ἀδελφῶι
2 Φιλάμμωνι
3 [Οὐ]αλέριος χαίρειν.
4 Ἀσπάζομαί σε πολλὰ εὐ-
5 χόμενος ὑγιαίνειν. Θαυ-
6 μάζω ὅπως ἔμεινας
7 παρὰ σοί, ὡς δὲ ἐδηλώ-
8 σας περὶ τοῦ υἱοῦ, ὡς
9 ὅτι {ε} ἐδέξατό \`τι´ παρὰ τοῦ
10 ἀδελφοῦ Ἀρσενίου. Οὐ-
11 δὲν οὖν ἔσχεν παρ᾽ αὐτοῦ
12 οὐδὲ ὡμείλησεν αὐτῷ
13 περὶ φορέτρου, ἀλλὰ σὺ
14 λαβὼν παρ᾽ αὐτοῦ \`δύο νομισμάτια´ δέδω-
15 κας τῷ αὐτῷ υἱῷ. Ὅπως
16 μὴ θελήσῃς ἀφοδιώσεσι
17 χρήσασθαι, ἀλλὰ ποιήσῃς
18 με τ̣ὸ̣ν̣ τ[ο]ύ[τ]ων λόγον σου.
19 Ἰδοὺ γὰρ ἐδήλωσα αὐ-
20 τῷ περὶ τούτου. Μέμνη-
21 σο δὲ ἐνεγκεῖν μοι τοὺς
22 ἐννέα ξέστας μέλιτος
23 οὓς χρεωστεῖς μοι ὑπὲρ
24 τοῦ τότε λόγου \`τῆς ἐπιστολῆς σου´· ἀλλ᾽ ἐν
25 καλῷ μέλιτι. (M.2) Ἐρρῶσθαί
26 σε εὔχομαι πολλοῖς
27 χρόνοις εὐτυχοῦντα.

Verso:

28 Κυρίῳ μου ἀδελφῷ \ /
29 Φιλάμμωνι / \ Οὐαλέριος

7 υἵου Pap. 12 ὡμίλησεν 14 υἵω Pap. 16 χρήσασθαι: first alpha ex corr. 18 μοι ? (cf. note ad loc.)

"To my lord brother Philammon, Valerius, greetings. I greet you sincerely praying for your health. I wonder why you stayed at home and why you sent a message concerning your son, that he had received something from brother Arsenios. He [the son] received nothing from him [Arsenios] and he did not speak with him about the transportation costs, but you got two *solidi* from him [Arsenios] and gave them to him [the son]. Avoid using ...., but give me your account of these. For you see, I have sent him [Arsenios?] a message about this matter. Please remember to bring me the nine *sextarii* of honey, which you owe to me because of the earlier account (of your letter), but [send them] in good honey. I pray for your health while you are successful for many years." (Verso) "To my lord brother Philammon, Valerius."

This private letter deals with the transfer of money and the conveyance of some honey.

1-3. Philammon (l. 2) is probably the same person as one of his namesakes occurring in **19.b**.2 (299); **49**.3, 21 (304); **65**.1, 51; **71**.36, 49; **72**.39 and **79**.6 (all IV). A distinction, however, can be made (cf. **79**, introd.) between two homonymous persons, one living at the start of the 4th century (**19.b**, **49**, **65**), the other ca. 350 (**71** and **72**). A similar distinction between two different Philammons seems possible in the case of the Coptic papyri (information kindly provided by I. Gardner). We are inclined to identify the Philammon occurring here with the second bearer of that name (**71**, **72**; possibly also **79**). In this connection we wonder, furthermore, whether Valerius (l. 3) is the same person as the Aurelius Valerius who manumitted his female slave Hilaria in 355 (cf. **48**) and the father of Aurelius Pausanias (cf. **38.a** and **38.b** from 333). From a palaeographical point of view there seems to be no obstacle against dating the letter to the middle of the 4th century and there is an argument in favour of a date after ca. 325-330, cf. l. 14n.

5. A construction θαυμάζω ὅπως ... ὡς δὲ ... (For θαυμάζω ὅπως/ὡς cf. R. Kühner - B. Gerth, *Grammatik der griechischen Sprache. Satzlehre* II 370 Anm. 2.) seems more attractive than a construction θαυμάζω ὅπως ..., followed by a new phrase starting with Ὡς δὲ ..

8-9. Ὡς in ὡς ὅτι is superfluous, cf. F. Blaß - A. Debrunner, *Grammatik des N.T. Griechisch*[12] (Göttingen 1965) § 396.

10. An Arsenios is mentioned only here in the Greek papyri from Kellis.

13. If Philammon were identical with the homonymous driver of dromedaries in **79**.6-7 (cf. above, l. 1-3n.), the word φόρετρον used here (= 'expenses of transport') would apply to Philammon's occupation.

14. The earliest precisely dated use of the word νομισμάτιον = '*solidus*' seems to be P.Stras. 9 from 352, but the word also occurs in some undated texts which may be ca. 2 decades earlier, cf. R.S. Bagnall, *Currency and Inflation in Fourth Century Egypt* 16.

15f. For the construction of ὅπως μή + subj. Aor. indicating a prohibition cf. W.W. Goodwin, *Syntax of Greek Moods and Tenses* (repr. London 1965) § 283, 364.

16. ἀφοδιώσεσι: Is this a new word ἀφοδίωσις, meaning something like 'pretext'? LSJ does not list it and it is at least conceivable that one is dealing with a misspelling of another, known word. Following that line of thought there are at least two candidates, both not unproblematical, viz.

(a) ἀποθείωσις (from τὸ θεῖον = sulphur) = 'fumigation', cf. LSJ. Though one can adduce parallels for the change of $\pi > \phi$, of $\theta > \delta$, and of $\epsilon\iota > \iota$, this does not seem an attractive supposition, the more so as never before the word has appeared in the papyri. The only reference given in LSJ, to Onasander 10.28 in the Loeb-edition, makes one wonder why the translation given in LSJ should be applicable there; the Loeb-editor of Onasander translates 'deification' and obviously takes *ἀποθείωσις* to be synonymous with *ἀποθέωσις*. Anyway, in the context of the papyrus both 'fumigation' and 'deification' seem inapplicable.

(b) *ἀφοσίωσις* = 'doing as a matter of form', cf. LSJ s.v., 2. In fact this word does appear in at least one papyrus (P.Oxy. XXXIII 2666 ii.3) and the translation seems better applicable here, but the problem of 'explaining' the erroneous spelling *ἀφ-οσ-ίωσις* > *ἀφ-οδ-ίωσις* remains unsolved.

18. Many letters in this line are read doubtfully; it is possible to read *μεγαν* instead of *με τον*, but it is unclear what a *μέγας λόγος* would mean here. On the other hand the accusative *με* is difficult to accept; one would rather expect a *dativus commodi* *μοι*.

21. A *ξέστης* = Lat. *sextarius* contains ca. 0.5 liter, cf. A. Segré in Aegyptus 1 (1920) 321; the total amount of honey referred to here is ca. 4.5 liter, possibly packed in 9 jars of 0.5 liter each. For honey in the papyri cf. H. Chouliara-Raios, *L'abeille et le miel en Egypte d'après les papyrus grecs* (Ioannina 1989; = ΔΩΔΩΝΗ, 30). The writer stresses that the honey he wants to receive should be of first-class quality.

65: PRIVATE LETTER

(Early 4th century)

P.Kellis inv. P. 61.Z (House 3, room 8, level 4). H. 23.5 x B. 8.5 cm. There is a kollesis ca. 1.5 - 2.0 cm. from the righthand edge of the front which the writer has avoided as far as l. 16. After writing, the papyrus was turned vertically from top to bottom and the letter was continued on the bottom back across the fibers. It was then folded top to bottom across the middle and the address was written along the fibers on the bottom lefthand side of the back before the letter was rolled up. For organizational purposes the papyrus was referred to previously as 'P.Kellis 65'.

1 [Φιλ]ά̣μ̣μ̣[ων]{ι} Τεκοσε τῇ
2 ἀ̣[δ]ελφῇ μ[ο]υ πολλὰ χαίρειν.
3 Θαυμά[ζ]ω πῶς οὐκ ἔγρα-
4 ψάς μοι μίαν ἐπιστολὴν περὶ
5 οὐδενὸς ἁπλῶς. Ἔγραψά σοι
6 πρὸ τούτου ὅτι 'Τήρησον τὸν
7 τόπον μου ὅ ἐστιν ἐπὶ μισθῷ
8 ὄν'. Τοίνυν οὖν καλῶς ποιή-
9 σ̣ε̣ι̣ς λάβε ἀνθρώπου<ς> καὶ ἴκα-
10 σον τὰς ἐλαίας. Ἐὰν δὲ
11 ὁ Θεὸς κελεύει σ' ἀπολῦσαι
12 ἡμᾶς καὶ ζήσωμεν, ἐγὼ
13 πληρώσω σοι τὴν χάριν
14 σου, ἐὰν δὲ μὴ ὁ Θεός,
15 δίδωμί σοι τὴν χάριν.
16 Πάντως γὰρ καὶ σὺ ἤκουσας

17 τὰ̣ περὶ ἡμῶν ἐγένετο ἐνθά-
18 δε. Ἁπλῶς δὲ περὶ πάντων
19 πιστεύσω σοι τὸν ἐμὸν τό-
20 πον, ἵνα τηρήσῃς σὲ αὐ-
21 τόν. Καὶ τὸ μικκὸν ἐλά-
22 διον ἣν {ε}ἄγῃς παρὰ σὲ, π̣ώ̣-
23 λησον αὐτὰ καὶ ταχέως
24 πέμψῃς τὴν τιμὴν διὰ πιστοῦ
25 ἀνθρώπου, ἐπὶ χρείαν αὐ-
26 το<ῦ ἔχω> ἐνθάδε, ὅτι πολλὰ ζημία
27 ἐγὼ ἐδόθη ἐνθάδε. Καὶ
28 τὸν πῶλον, πώλησον
29 αὐτὰ καὶ πέμψῃς τὴν
30 τιμήν. Θαυμάζω δέ·
31 ἔγραψά σοι ὅτι 'Πέμψῃς τὸ
32 μαρφόρτιόν μου καὶ ⟦ουκε⟧
33 τὸ χιτώνιον' καὶ οὐκ ἠμέ-
34 λησέ σοι· πέμψῃς μοι. οἶδες
35 καὶ σὺ ὅτι ἐγὼ μνημονεύ-
36 εις. Διὰ τί καὶ ἡμεῖς οὐκ ἐ-
37 μνημονεύεις, ἀλλὰ λή-
38 θαργός σοι; Ἀσπάζομαι τὸν
39 υἱόν σου Ψάιν καὶ τοὺς
40 ἀδελφοὺς αὐτοῦ. Ἀσπάζο-
41 μαι Χῶλος, ἀσπάζομαι
42 Ἀμμ̣ώ̣νιον.

Back at the bottom, across the fibers:

43 Τοίνυν οὖν βλέπεις τὴν μη-
44 τέραν μου. Ὅσα ἔχεις ἐγώ,
45 τήρησον αὐτὰ ὅτι οὔπω
46 ἔμαθες τὰ περὶ ἡμῶν ἐν-
947 θάδε.
48 Ἐρρῶσθαί σε
49 εὔχομαι πολλοῖς
50 χρόνοις.

Back, along the fibers:

51 Τεκοσε ἀδελ- \ / π(αρὰ) Φιλάμμων{ι}
52 φῇ μου{ι} / \

7 ὅς 8 ὤν 9-10 εἴκασον (ἴκασον Pap.) 17 ἅ 20 σύ 23 αὐτὸ 25 ἐπεὶ 27 μοι 29 αὐτὸν 32 μαφόρτιον 33-34 ἐμέλησε 35-36 μνημονεύω 36 ἡμᾶς 36-37 ἐμνημόνευες or μνημονεύεις 38 συ 39 ψαϊν Pap. 41 Χῶλον 43 βλέπῃς 44 μοι for ἐγώ? 45 αὐτὴν 46 ἔμαθε 51 Φιλάμμωνος

"Philammon to my sister Tekose, many greetings. I am amazed that you have not written me a single letter about anything at all. I wrote to you before this: 'Look after my plot which is out to rent'. So therefore please get some fellows and estimate the olives. And if God bids you to save us from trouble and we survive, I shall repay you your favour in full. And (even) if God does not, I shall do you the favour. For doubtless even you have heard what happened to us here. In short I shall entrust my plot to you in everything for you to look after it. And if you take the little bit of olive oil to your place, sell it on your own responsibility and quickly send me the price via a trustworthy fellow since I have need of it here, because I have incurred much loss here. And as for the foal, sell it and send the price. I am amazed that I wrote to you: 'Send my cape and my tunic' and you did not bother. Send them to me. You know too that I am mindful of you. Why weren't you mindful of us too, but forgetful? I greet your son Psais and his brothers. I greet Cholos, I greet Ammonios. Now, look to my mother. As much as you can, look after her for me, since she has not yet learnt what has happened to us here. I pray that you are well for many years." (Verso) "To my sister Tekose from Philammon."

This papyrus contains a letter from Philammon (cf. **64**.1-3n.; probably to be identified with the Philammon of **49** [304] which has the same find spot) to a 'sister' Tekose who may be identifiable with Aurelia Takysis in **37**.1, 18 [320] and Takose, the mother of Aurelius Pamour, in **42**.1-2, 31 [364]. The writer, who was in financial difficulties, instructs her to collect the rent due on a plot of land out on lease, to estimate the olive crop, and to realise the price of a small amount of olive oil and a foal to help cover a substantial financial loss. The nature of the great *ζημία* (l. 26; = financial loss) for which Philammon was liable is unknown. Dr. A. Alcock kindly refers to the Coptic P.Kellis inv. 68.G (b) in which a certain Philammon complains to Theognostos / Loui Shai (cf. **67**.2n.) of losses that he has sustained (*'Let him therefore send five pairs of cloth to me, because you ... you of/for the losses which he caused me to sustain'*; unfortunately the person causing the loss is difficult to identify). In preparing this text we had the benefit of a preliminary transcript by Dr. R.G. Jenkins.

1. The reading of the writer's name ending in -*μωνι* is confirmed by its repetition, undamaged, in the address on the back. Neither F. Preisigke, *Namenbuch*, nor D. Foraboschi, *Onomasticon Alterum Papyrologicum* list this form, but in light of the many variants throughout this text it may be no more than a (Copticised ?) form of *Φιλάμμων*. Coptic names in general often end in -*ε* or in -*ι*. Μου on the back, in the address, also seems to have an unnecessary iota added to it.

5. Despite its use as an adverb with the verb *πιστεύω* in l. 18-19, *ἁπλῶς* most probably belongs here to *οὐδενὸς* rather than to *ἔγραψα* cf. F. Preisigke, *Wörterbuch* s.v. *ἁπλοῦς*, 6.

7-8. For the periphrastic present of *εἰμί* + pres.part. which seems to be more common in New Testament Greek than in the papyri, see F. Blass - A. Debrunner - R. Funk, *Grammar of New Testament Greek*, § 353, and F. Gignac, *Grammar of the Greek papyri of the Roman and Byzantine periods* II 284; for periphrastic constructions in general, see also W.J. Aerts, *Periphrastica. An investigation into the use of εἶναι and ἔχειν as auxiliaries or pseudo-auxiliaries in Greek from Homer up to the present day* (Diss. Amsterdam 1965).

8. According to the Duke Data Bank on Documentary Papyri (PHI CD-ROM # 6) *τοίνυν οὖν* is found at the start of a main clause in P. Oxy. XII 1591.7, PSI VII 830.4 and P.Stras. 233.6; due to the mutilated transmission of the text the situation in SB VI 9590.4 is far from clear, but it seems attractive to regard it there, too, as the start of a main clause.
20-21. The writer's meaning is clear even if the grammar is not. It seems simpler to read *σε αὐτόν* as two words with *σε* = *σὺ*, than to construe *σεαυτόν* = *σεαυτοῦ* for *σεαυτῆς*.
32. For *μαφόρτιον*, a short cape covering the neck and shoulders which was usual worn by women, see P.Oxy. LIX 4004.15 n. with reff. A *χιτώνιον* was also more properly a woman's dress or shift, cf. LSJ s.v.

66: PRIVATE LETTER

(Early 4th century)

P.Kellis inv. P. 61.EE (House 3, room 8, level 4). H. 25.5 x B. 8.5 cm. Margins: at the left 1, at the top 1.4 and at the bottom 3 cm. The writing runs parallel with the fibers, the verso is blank.

1 Παμοῦρ Ψαράπι τ[ῷ χαίρειν.]
2 Πρọ̀ παντὸς πολλά σε ἀσ[πάζεται N.N. καὶ - - -]
3 αὐ[τ]οῦ. Πολλά σε ἀσπάζομ[αι. Ἔλαβον - - - -]
4 γόμ̣ο̣ν ἕ̅ν̅α̅ καὶ διὰ Ψάιτος [χιτώνια]
5 δύ[ο]. Δὸς αὐτῷ τάλαντ[- *n* καὶ δραχμὰς --ισχι-]
6 λείας ὑπὲρ φολετροῦ ̣[
7 ἐπά̣νω τοῦ γόμου ἐπεμ[ψ
8 ἐπάνω τοῦ γόμου· μαθ̣[εῖν σε θέλω ὅτι — — —]
9 ὧν̣ τρὶς τὴν τιμὴν ἔπ̣[εμψά σοι, ἀπέσχηκα.]
10 Ἀ[γό]ρασόν μοι ἐριδίων [ca. 17]
11 Μὴ ἀμελήση̣ς ταχέω[ς γράψαι μοι καὶ περὶ]
12 ὧν θέλεις κε̣λ̣ε̣υέ μοι ἡ[δέως ἔχοντι.
13 Ἐρρῶ[σθαί σε εὔχομαι]
14 VACAT [
15 VACAT [
16 ἔ̣λαβε διὰ̣ ̣ρ TRACES[
17 δέδωκα ἅμ̣α̣ τινί· οὐδὲν ἔλαβες· Ζ[ήτησον πάντο-]
18 θεν δέρματα πέντε καὶ ἀγόρασ̣[ον αὐτά μοι]
19 καὶ πέμψον μοι. Μαθεῖν σε θέλω [ὅτι οὐδέν σοι]
20 κ̣ρύπτω οὐδὲ δίχαλκον· ἔλαβες τι ̣[ca. 10]
21 μ̣ενει εἰς Ἑρμοῦ πόλιν καὶ Ψάις ἑρμ̣[ca. 10]
22 [̣] ̣ κεραμέας· πάλιν οὐδὲ̣ν ἔλαβες ̣[ca. 10]
23 π̣ερὶ οὐδένος. Γείνου πρὸς Σεν ̣[ca. 10]
24 ̣ι αὐτῇ χιτώνια γυνὴ καὶ πώλη[σον ca. 7]
25 [τ]ιμὴ τὰ δύο χιτώνια ἐπάνω τ̣ο̣[ῦ αὐτοῦ γόμου]

26 Πεβῶτι Σαᾶ. Μὴ ἀμελήσῃς ..[ca. 10]
27 [Ὥ]ρου Ἡλιοδώρου καὶ ἀπαίτησον τ[ὰς αὐτὰς δρα-]
28 [χ]μᾶς τριχιλείας· ἐὰν κρατῇς ου[ca. 10]
29 [.]ν αὐτόν, εἰ μή, λαβὲ σ[VACAT?

1 Παμουρ) Pap. 6 -λίας, φορετροῦ 10 ἐριδίων: -ω- corr. 17 Or read ἅμα, or, e.g., Ἅμα Τινί ? 22 οὐδέν: -δ- partly written over -υ- 23 γίνου 24 αὐτῇ: -η ex corr.? 26 σαᾱ Pap. 28 τρισχιλίας, κρατῇς: -ατ- ex corr., or simply smudged?

"Pamour sends greetings to Psarapis his -- . Before all N.N. and his -- send you many greetings. I send you many greetings. I received one load of -- and through Psais two other laods. Give him *n* talents and *n*000 drachmas for costs of transport of these -- on top of the load -- have sent -- on top of the load. I want you to known that I have received the -- of which I sent you the price three times. Buy me -- of wool --. Don't forget to write quickly to me and send me your orders about your wishes which I am pleased (to carry out). I pray for your health. (l. 16ff) He received through -- I have given together with someone; you have received nothing. Look everywhere for five skins and buy them for me and send them to me. I want you to know that I don't hide even a dichalkon from you (?). You received -- for -menes to Hermopolis and Psais -- potters. Again you received nothing -- concerning (for?) nothing. You must be with Sen-- to her chitons -- and sell -- price (?) the two chitons on top of the same load to Pebos son of Saas. Don't forget to -- of Horos son of Heliodoros and claim the three thousand drachmas. If you can -- him, if not, take --."

Despite its damaged state and the rather conventional information passed on by the text as far as it has been preserved, this letter is of some interest as its format is unusual. After a first letter of 12 lines closed off by the regular Ἐρρῶσθαί σε εὔχομαι-formula in l. 13 the author adds a postscript which is even longer (14 lines) than the original letter.

The papyrus is broken in such a way that, while 3 folds are preserved in the upper part of the letter, viz.:

margin, te | xt | text | [text | text]

an extra fold is preserved in the lower part at the right (l. 16ff.), while the margin at the left is lost, viz.:

] | text | text | text | [text]

It may be assumed, therefore, that the upper part of the letter was broken on the central vertical fold. The precise length of each line and the size of the lacunas in the first part of the letter may be calculated from l. 11 (see note ad loc.; 17 letters lost out of a total of 32 letters); as for the second part of the letter cf. l. 17, where the total number of letters seems to have been ca. 37 letters, 11 of which are lost.

1. The name Ψαρᾶπις (not listed in the regular papyrological onomastica) may be a combination of the masc. prefix Πα- + Σαρᾶπις, cf. Ψύρος < Π- + Σύρος in **33**.1; for such combinations cf. also the note to **46**.31f. and **74**.25.

2-3. The order of persons who send their greetings is remarkable. Normally a letter starts by conveying the author's personal greetings to the addressee; after that it is often stated that other persons greet the addressee as well. Here the normal order is reversed. In the lacuna at the end of l. 2 restore, e.g. *τὰ τέκνα*] or *ἡ σύμβιος*]. At the end of l. 3 an indication of the nature of the cargo (*γόμος*) is expected.

4-5. For the restoration at the end of l. 4 cf. l. 25, where (again?) two chitons are mentioned.

5-6. Either one single talent, or an unknown number of talents is at stake. For the amount of drachmae perhaps restore the same numeral as in l. 28, i.e. [*τρισχι-*]/*λείας* (l. -*λίας*)? The numeral must be lower than six thousand drachmas (= 1 talent).

7. *ἐπάνω τοῦ γόμου*: for *ἐπάνω* = 'on top of, added to' cf., e.g., P.Genova I 20.7 (=P.Genova II App. 1) and 21.9 (see note ad loc.).

8-9. For the restoration of *μαθ̣*[*εῖν σε θέλω* cf. l. 19. After the restored *ὅτι* an indication of an object (plural, cf. *ὧν*, l. 9) is expected.

10. Wool as a commodity is also mentioned in three other letters from Kellis, **71**.46, **72**.38 and in **73**.30. After *ἐριδίων* one expects an indication of the measure, e.g. *σάκκους* = 'bags' (cf. BGU III 812 i.3) and the number of the containers.

11. The amount of the text lost in the lacuna (17 letters) is about the same as that of the preserved text (15 letters). Apparently the papyrus was broken here into two halves, possibly on the central vertical fold.

13-15. It is conceivable that after Ἐρρῶ[*σθαί σε εὔχομαι* in l. 13 the formula continued in ll. 14-15 with *πολλοῖς χρόνοις εὐτυχοῦντα κύριέ μου vel sim.* As in ll. 14-15 the left hand part of the surface of the papyrus has been preserved, while the right hand part of the surface has peeled off, it must be assumed that these lines were indented and that all of these 'extra' words started at the same place as Ἐρρῶ[*σθαί* in l. 13.

19-20. The restorations are, of course, uncertain and instead of Μ*αθεῖν σε θέλω* [*ὅτι οὐδέν σοι*] *κ̣ρ̣ύπτω οὐδὲ δίχαλκον· ἔλαβες τι̣* [one could read, e.g., Μ*αθεῖν σε θέλω* [*ὅτι* N.N. *οὐκ ἐστίν ἐν* Αἰ]*γύπτῳ̣* and continue thereafter with *οὐδὲ δίχαλκον ἔλαβε στι̣* [.

A dichalkon was the smallest unit used in Roman Egypt for the calculation of taxes and J.G. Milne identifies the smallest bronze coins from Nero's times with the dichalkon (cf. L.C. West - A.C. Johnson, *Currency in Roman and Byzantine Egypt* [Princeton 1944] 17f.). It is remarkable to find dichalkoi still being referred to at this (late) time in the 4th century, as the value of the coins must have been utterly insignificant. Perhaps one is dealing here with some kind of reproachful proverbial expression ('You/he did not receive even a dichalkon')? Cf. the use of 'farthing' and 'halfpenny' in colloquial English.

21. One may accentuate -*μ̣ένει* and regard it as the dative of a name on -*μένης*.

Read *ἑρμ̣*[or Ἑρμ̣[?

22. Read at the start [*εἰ*]*ς*? For a list of potters mentioned in the papyri cf. CPR XIII p. 109ff.

23. It is difficult to find a meaningful interpretation for *γυνή*. Probably it goes too far to suppose an error for *γυναικεῖα* (going with the *χιτώνια*).

24-26. Is something meant like 'sell for the same price the two chitons on top of the same load to Pebos son of Saas', i.e. read *πώλη*[*σον τῇ αὐτῇ*] / [*τ*]*ιμῇ τὰ δύο χιτώνια ἐπάνω τ̣ο̣*[*ῦ αὐτοῦ γόμου*] Π*εβῶτι* Σ*αᾶ* ? But one would expect a genitive (*τῆς αὐτῆς τιμῆς*) rather than the dative.

25. For the restoration here cf. ll. 7, 8.

26. Is Σαᾶ an error for Σαρᾶ? For a man named Pebos son of Saras, cf. **60**.7.

27-28. The same amount of drachmae may have been mentioned before in ll. 5-6, cf. the note ad loc. Under the present circumstances the restoration of *αὐτὰς* is nothing more than a stop-gap.

29. It is hard to tell whether one should read the last letter in this line (with its upper horizontal bar prolonged to the right) as a sti (= 6) or as a sigma (= 200).

67: PRIVATE LETTER

(Early to mid 4th century)

P.Kellis inv. P. 17.D+N+EE (House 3, room 10, level 3). Frag. I: H. ca. 7 x B. ca. 5 cm; Fragm. II: H. ca. 9 x B. ca. 7.6 cm. The writing on both sides runs parallel with the fibers. On the back a name written in Syriac was initially read as 'Pekysis' by R.G. Jenkins (who also made a preliminary transcript of the text), but M. Franzmann tells us that this is 'Loui Shai', see. l. 2n. For organizational purposes the papyrus was previously referred to as 'P.Kellis 63'. *Ed.princ.* (with incorrect indication of the dimensions and some readings which cannot stand any longer) in the *Proceedings of the 20th International Congress of Papyrology, Copenhagen 1992* (1994) 277-83.

1 Τῶι ἀγαπητῶι υ̣[ἱῶι
2 Θεογνώστωι ο̣[
3 ἐν Θ̣ε̣ῷ̣[ι χαίρειν.
4 Εἰ μὲν παρὰ σοί ἐ̣[στιν ὁ ἀδελ-]
5 φός σου Ψάις κ̣[
6 προσέχετ̣ε ἑαυτ[οὺς
7 σης νήψεως κα̣[ὶ ἐπιστο-]
8 λ̣ὰ̣ς ταύτας λ̣αβό[ντες

- -

(several lines missing)

- -

9]ῶ̣ν̣ ἐστιν
10]ν̣ παρ' ὑμῖν
11 [ἐσ]τίν .μ̣.α̣.[ ]. καὶ ὄ̣ψε-
12 ται. Ἀσπάσασθε πάντας
13 κατ' ὄνομα. Οἱ ἀδελφοὶ ὑ-
14 μῶν ἀσπάζονται ὑμᾶς.
15 Ἐρρῶσθε ἐν Θεῶι
16 ὑ̣μ̣ᾶ̣ς εὔχομαι, ἀ̣[γαπη]τοί.
17 (M.2) Πινακίδιον εὔμετρον καὶ
18 ἀστῖον δέκα πτυχῶν πέμ-
19 ψον τῷ ἀδελφῷ σου Ἰσίωνι.
20 Ἑλληνιστὴς γὰρ γέγονεν
21 καὶ ἀναγνώστης συναγτικός

- -

Down left hand margin, also in 2nd hand:

22 Μαθέτω ὁ υἱὸ[ς] πρὸ τοῦ δοθῆναι αὐτήν.

5 Ψαϊς Pap. 10 υμϊν Pap. 15 Ἐρρῶσθαι 18 ἀστεῖον 21 συνακτικός

(Ll. 1-7) "To my beloved son Theognostos, from ..., greetings in God. If your brother Psais is with you, take heed (concerning) your sobriety and ----" (Ll. 12-21) "Greet all by name. Your brothers greet you. I pray that you are well in God, beloved (friends)". (Second hand) "Send a well-proportioned and nicely executed ten-page notebook for your brother Ision. For he has become a user of Greek and a comprehensive reader." (Margin) "Let the son (of N.N.?) learn that ... before she was given (as wife?).

Although the change from one addressee in the first fragment (ll. 1-3) to several in the closing formula in the second fragment (ll. 13-16) is unusual and there is no secure join between the two pieces of the text R.G. Jenkins has confirmed that an examination of the papyrus under the microscope shows that all fragments derive from the same sheet. The suggestion made in the *ed.princ.* that the fragments may have come from two separate letters written in the same hand may therefore be ignored.

2. The name Theognostos occurs also in two other Greek letters among the Kellis papyri, esp. in **71**.9 and **72**.9; both letters are reminiscent of similar Manichaean letters from Kellis written in Coptic. I. Gardner informs us that in the Coptic letter P. 68.G.a the same person is called both Theognostos and Loui Shai and if the reading of the Syriac by M. Franzmann is correct, evidently we are dealing with the same man in this letter. On the name Loui Shai see also **71**.1-3n.
5. Kappa is better at line end than *ψ*.
6. For *ἑαυτοὺς* instead of the expected *ὑμᾶς αὐτούς* cf. P.Vindob.Worp 13.13n.
6-7. Restore as *περὶ τῆς] σῆς νήψεως*? But one would expect *ὑμετέρας* rather than *σῆς*.
11. *ἄ̣ψεται* or *ἔ̣ψεται* is not likely.
16. Apparently this is a variation on a regular closing formula in Christian private letters, cf. P.Oxy. LVI 3857 introd. *ἀ̣[δελ]φοί* is not possible.
17ff. For the request for a 10-page tablet book cf. P.Fouad 74.10-12 (also of the 4th century). For codices in general, see C.H. Roberts - T.C. Skeat, *The Birth of the Codex* (London 1983) and the introduction to **60** - **62**.
21. For writing Greek cf. LSJ s.v. *ἑλληνίζω*; the word *Ἑλληνιστής*, 'speaker/writer of pure Greek' (cf. LSJ s.v. and W. Bauer, *Wörterbuch zum N.T.* 1971[5] s.v.) has apparently not yet occurred in the papyri. Likewise, the word *συνακτικός* seems to be new in the papyri, but cf. LSJ s.v. where its principal rendering is given as 'able to bring together'; it is not quite clear what a 'reader able to bring together' would mean precisely; we think that the wording must refer to an accomplished/comprehensive reader.

68: PRIVATE LETTER

(4th century)

P.Kellis inv. P. 17.E (House 3, room 10, level 3). The papyrus consists now of 2 fragments both measuring H. 12.2 x B. 8.5 cm. each. The writing runs parallel with the fibers, the verso is blank.

1 Κυρίῳ̣ μου υἱῷ̣ Ἠλίᾳ̣
2 Ψάις χαίρειν. Ἀσπάζομαί

3 σε πολλὰ κ[αὶ] τὰς κυρίας μου
4 θυγατέρα̣ς̣ μετὰ τῆς μητρὸς
5 αὐτῶν ε̣ὐ̣χόμενος ὑγιαίνει̣ν̣,
6 γράμματά̣ [σ]ου μὴ δεξάμενος
7 διὰ τοσούτου χρόνου διὰ
8 τὸ ἀνῆκόν σοι πρᾶγμα
9 περὶ Πακ̣ύ̣σ̣ι[ο]ς. Καὶ τελέως
10 ὁ ἄλλος ἀπήλλαξέν σε. Θαυ-
11 μάζω ὅ[πως] μὴν ἐσχόλα-
12 σας ἀπ̣[ελθεῖν εἰς] Μ̣ε̣σ̣ο̣βὴ
13 [. .]ιοισ̣ .[ ]ν̣ οἰκοδ[ο-]
14 [μ]ησα̣[ ]TRACES

- -

15 TRACES[ ] .λε̣ίου
16 [. . .] . .[ ]ανεσ̣[
17 . [ ] κ [. . . . . .]μὴ ἀφα-
18 [νί]σθη[. . . . .] . ξύλο[υ] σ̣χιστοῦ
19 ὡς καὶ ἐξ[. . .]επει ασαν.
20 Μὴ ἀμελή[ση̣ς] τῶν ἐν τοῖς
21 ν̣ο̣τ̣ί̣ν̣ο̣[ις π]ράγμασι καὶ νο-
22 μίζω ὅτι σὺν Θεῷ ὑμᾶς
23 καταλαμβάνω. Εἰ γράμματα
24 λάβοιμι τ̣οῦ κυρίου μου γεούχου
25 ἢ ἐὰν μὴ γράψῃ ὡς χρείαν
26 μου μὴ ἔχοντος, ἐλε̣[ύ]σομαι.
27 Περὶ ὧν θέλεις γράφε μοι. Ἐρρῶ-
28 σθαί σε εὔχομαι πολλοῖς χρόνοις.
29 Ἐν συστά̣[σει] ἔ̣χε τοὺς ἀδελφούς σου.

"To my lord son Elias, Psais greetings. I greet you very much and the ladies my daughters together with their mother, while I pray for (your) health, after I had received no letter from you for so long a time because of the matter which concerned you as regards Pakysis. The other has released you completely indeed! I wonder how really you had time to go to Mesobe --- (l. 20) don't forget about what is in the Southern property and I think that with God's help I come to you. If I should receive a letter from my lord the landowner, or if he does not write, as he has no need for me, I shall come. Write to me about what you want. I pray for your health for many years. Take care of your brothers."

This letter, now broken into two pieces which perhaps do not join completely (cf. ll. 14 - 15), is badly damaged in its central part where the text might contain some bits of real information on building activities (cf. l. 18n.). After a standard opening ('To B,

A χαίρειν'; cf. F.X.J. Exler, *The Form of the Ancient Greek Letter. A Study in Greek Epistolography* [Diss.Washington 1923] 60ff., 67) most of the remaining text contains a series of standard phrases concerning the conveyance of greetings, wishes for good health, etc. It is interesting, however, that the author of the letter (a certain Psais who cannot be identified any further) refers to his firm intention to come over to his correspondent Elias and his family, regardless of whether he gets a letter from his landlord urging him to do so, or not. The phrasing in the final line (29), *τινα ἐν συστάσει ἔχειν*, is not common in the documentary papyri.

1. A 'son' Elias is also the addressee of another private letter (**81**), but that papyrus was written by a certain Sabeinus. It is conceivable, of course, that not too much of importance should be attached to the word *υἱός* = 'son' (on its 'affectionate' use, see F. Preisigke, *Wörterbuch*, s.v.) and that in fact one is dealing in both cases with the same addressee (it may be noted that in both documents reference is made to a *γεοῦχος*). On the other hand, in **75** a certain Elias is the author of a letter to a certain Strategios; that document, however, seems to have been written much later than the other two documents (possibly it is dating from the second or third quarter of the 4th century ?).

9. Καί stresses *τελέως*, cf. J.D. Denniston, *The Greek Particles*[2], 317. For the meaning of *τελέως* = 'absolutely, completely' cf. F.M.J. Waanders, *The History of* ΤΕΛΟΣ *and* ΤΕΛΕΩ *in Ancient Greek* (Diss. Amsterdam 1983) § 210.

10. Does ὁ ἄλλος mean another person named Pakysis (cf. the preceding line)?

12. 'Mesobe' is the name of a district in the Mothite nome, cf. **28**.5.

13-14.]ν̣ *οἰκοδ[ο-]* | *[μ]ησα̣[*: or should one read *ἀ]ν̣οικοδ[ο-]* | *[μ]ησα̣[*?

15.]ε̣λα̣ίου seems a conceivable, though slightly more 'daring' reading.

18. *ξύλο[υ] σ̣χιστοῦ* = 'split timber' seems to be related here to building activities, cf. *οἰκοδ[ο-]* | *[μ]ησ-α̣[* in l. 13-14.

19. Maybe one should read *-επειρασαν*; is one dealing with a composite form of the verb *πειράω*?

21. Despite the damaged state of the letters the reading at the beginning of this line seems fairly certain, but it is less clear whether the interpretation of *νότινα πράγματα* as 'Southern property', i.e. 'property (e.g. a farm) situated in the Southern part of the region' is correct.

23. For the meaning of the verb *καταλαμβάνω* ('to come over to') cf. the remarks by W. Döllstädt, *Griechische Papyrusprivatbriefe in gebildeter Sprache aus den ersten vier Jahrhunderten nach Christus* (Diss. Jena 1934) 44.

23ff. For the use of *εἰ* + optative (*εἰ .. λάβοιμι*) or *ἐάν* + subjunctive (*ἐὰν μὴ γράψῃ*) in the protasis with a future indicative (*ἐλε̣[ύ]σομαι*) in the apodosis cf. B.G. Mandilaras, *The Verb in the Greek Non-Literary Papyri* (Athens 1973) §§ 401, 403, 650.

25-26. It is regular Greek to find a genitive absolute with a participle the subject of which is identical with the subject of the main verb, cf. R. Kühner - B. Gerth, *Ausführliche Grammatik der griechischen Sprache* II 2, p. 110-11; Mandilaras, *op.cit.*, § 910.1. Here the subject of *μὴ ἔχοντος* must be looked for in *τ̣οῦ κυρίου μου γεούχου* (l. 24), while at the same time this landlord is the subject of *ἐὰν μὴ γράψῃ*.

69: PRIVATE LETTER

(4th century)

P.Kellis inv. P. 56.F # 2 (House 3, room 9, level 3, Western doorway). H. 14 x B. 8 cm. There is a margin at the bottom of ca. 1.5 cm.; the writing runs parallel with the fibers on both sides of the papyrus. The letter was folded 3x vertically and at least 3x horizontally (the sheet is broken on a fold at the top).

	- -
0	[τε-]
1	*θαυμακέν̣αι. Περὶ δ̣ὲ̣ τ̣[οῦ]*
2	*ἄλλου τοῦ πρὸς τὸν πατέρα*
3	*᾿Αγαθήμερον· μέχρι τοῦ*
4	*παρόντος οὔπω δέδω-*
5	*κεν προσδοκῶν*
6	*τὰ γράμματα τοῦ δεσπό-*
7	*του μου Ἡρακλείου καὶ*
8	*ἦ̣ ὥρα̣ ἐὰν δώσῃ πάλιν*
9	*γράφω· π̣ε̣[ρ]ὶ̣ δ̣ὲ̣ ὧ̣ν̣ β̣ό̣υ̣-*
10	*λει κέλευέ [μοι ἡδέως]*
11	*ἔχοντ[ι]*
12	*᾿Ερρ[ῶσθαί σε]*
13	*εὔχομαι πολ̣[λοῖς]*
14	*χρόνοις*
15	*εὐτυχοῦντα,*
16	*δέσποτά μου.*
Verso:	
17	] Χ *λογ̣ισ̣τῇ Πετεχῶν ᾿Αμμωνίου*
18	*διδασκάλου*

"-- to have been astonished. And concerning the other (sent) to father Agathemeros: until now he has given nothing, as he is awaiting the letter of my lord Heraclius, and the moment he shall give (it) I write again. Give me your order about your wishes, which I am pleased (to carry out). I pray, my Lord, for your health, being well for many years."(Verso) "To N.N. the *logistes* (from) Petechon son of Ammonios the teacher."

This fragment of a letter does not seem to contain any information of particular relevance except for the address on the verso. Among the Kellis papyri another *logistes* (Kleoboulos) is found in **25**.1 and a former *logistes* (Gelasius) in **29**.3, but it remains uncertain whether the addressee of this letter should be identified with either of these persons. On the other hand the indication of *Πετεχῶν ᾿Αμμωνίου διδασκάλου* raises the question whether Ammonios was a school teacher. As Dr. I. Gardner reminds us, a *διδάσκαλος* was a title or grade in the Manichaean church. The Coptic equivalent term (P-sah) is found a few times in the Coptic letters from Kellis (e.g. in P. 70.49, where it seems to have this technical meaning). It is well-attested in the Manichaean literary sources (e.g. the Kephalaia). For the complete list of the 6 grades of the Manichaean church in Greek (5 of the elect + catechumens = 'hearers'), see S.N.C. Lieu, *An Early Byzantine Formula for the Renunciation of Manichaeism*, JAC 26 (1983) 178-9, 199.

6. The name Agathemeros occurs among the Greek papyri from Kellis only here.

70: BUSINESS LETTER

(Second half of the 4th century)

P.Kellis inv. P. 79.1 (House 3, room 6, level 3). H. 14.7 x B. 10 cm. The papyrus appears to be a palimpsest. There are traces of lines of writing at the bottom of the sheet and similarly, across the fibres, down the right hand side. For organizational purposes the papyrus was referred to previously as 'P.Kellis 68'.

1 Τῶι κυρίῳ μου ἀδελφῶι Ψ̣εμπνούτῃ
2 Τιμόθεος τέκτων χαίρειν.
3 Πρὸ παντὸς πολλά σε ἀσπάζομα̣ι̣
4 μετὰ τῶν σῶν πάντων. Θαυμάζω
5 ὅτι μετὰ τοσοῦτον χρόνον οὐκ ἠθέλη-
6 σας δοῦναι τὰ ἀργύρια. Τοίνυν, ἐὰν
7 ἤλθε`ι´ πρὸς σὲ Παχοῦμις, παράσχου
8 αὐτῷ τὰ τρισχίλεια τάλαντα· ἤδη
9 γὰρ ἔσχον παρ' αὐτοῦ. Μάθε γὰρ
10 ὅτι ἐὰν μὴ θελήσῃς δοῦναι αὐ-
11 τῷ, ποιῶ σε ἀπαιτηθῆν̣αι ὑπὸ
12 στρατιωτῶν. Ὅρα μὴ ἀμελήσῃς.
13 Ἐρρῶσθαί σε εὔχομαι
14 πολλοῖς χρόνοις.

Verso:

15 Τῶι̣ κυρίῳ μου \ / [Τι]μ̣ό̣θ̣εος̣ τέκτων
16 Ψ̣ε̣νπνοῦτ̣ῃ / \

4 *μετατων* Pap. 7 *ἔλθῃ* 8 *τρισχίλια* 11 *ὕπο* Pap. 16 *Ψεμπνούτῃ*

"To my lord brother Psempnoutes, Timotheos the carpenter sends greetings. Before all I send you many greetings along with all your family. I am surprised that after such a long time you have not been willing to pay the money. Therefore, when Pachoumis comes to you, give the three thousand talents to him, for I have already received them from him. For be informed that if you are unwilling to give them to him, I will get them dunned from you by soldiers. See to it that you are not neglectful. I pray that you are well for many years." (Verso) "To my lord Psenpnoutes, Timotheos the carpenter."

A somewhat threatening letter from a carpenter regarding the non-payment of a debt; there is no indication that the debt regarded tax arrears rather than that it had a private background; it may well be that in our case soldiers would have been called in by Timotheos, as they provided some kind of police assistance in the Oasis. For extortion by army personnel in the Late Empire, see A.H.M. Jones, *The Late Roman Empire* II 644, 676, and R. MacMullen, *Corruption and the Decline of Rome* (New Haven 1988) 131-2, 145-6, 160-1 and 185. See also R.S. Bagnall, 'Official and Private Violence in Roman Egypt', BASP 26 (1989) 201-216, and *Egypt in Late Antiquity* (Princeton 1993) 172ff., esp. 180. Was it intended irony to add after the threat, that soldiers may collect the debt, the wish: 'I pray that you are well for many years'?

1. Elsewhere in the Kellis papyri one finds a spelling Ψενπνούθης (cf. **23**.23, **24**.11, **74**.18; cf. also the Psemnouthes (for Ψεμ<π>νούθης?) in a Coptic document from House 2, see the introd. to **8** - **12**); it remains uncertain whether these persons are all identical.
2. For τέκτονες in the Kellis papyri, see **5**.29n.
4. It seems not excluded that the line above μετατων comes in fact from the text written previously (cf. the palaeographical description of the papyrus).
7. For ἐάν + indic. (ἦλθε) instead of the subjunct. cf. A. Jannaris, *A Historical Greek Grammar* (London 1897; repr. Hildesheim 1968) § 1987. It looks as if Timotheos has tried to correct this (cf. the correct use of ἐάν in l. 10, ἐὰν μὴ θελήσῃς), but his correction has not been complete.

71: PRIVATE LETTER

(Mid 4th century)

P.Kellis inv. P. 57.B (House 3, room 9, level 3, Northern doorway). H. 26 x B. 8 cm. Folded 3 x or 4 x vertically, 1 x horizontally. Originally the left hand margin measured 1 cm. On both sides the writing runs parallel with the fibers; there is also perpendicular writing downwards in the left hand margin on the front. Faint traces of the address (in a second hand) are visible on the back, along the fibers on the top half of what was the left hand side of the front. For organizational purposes the papyrus was referred to previously as 'P.Kellis 76'.

1 Κυ̣[ρ]ί̣ῳ̣ τιμιωτάτῳ καὶ ὡς ἀληθῶς
2 π[οθ]εινοτάτωι ἀδελφῶι Ψάιτι
3 Π̣α̣μοῦρις ἐν Θεῷ χαίρειν.
4 Προηγουμένως πολλὰ τὴν σὴν εὐ-
5 λάβειαν προσαγορεύομεν ἐγὼ
6 καὶ ἡ σύμβιος καὶ οἱ υἱοὶ κατʼ ὄ̣-
7 νομα, εὖ ἔχοντες τ̣έως προ-
8 νοίᾳ τοῦ Θεοῦ. Προσε[ί]πατε ἡμῖν
9 τ[ὸ]ν κύριον ἀδελφὸν Θεόγνωστον
10 καὶ [τ]ὸν υἱὸν Ἀνδρέαν· περὶ
11 τῆς σῆς πρὸς ἡμ[ᾶ]ς ἀφί̣ξ̣ε̣ω̣ς,
12 [τ]ιμιώτατε, ὁσημέραι {κ} π̣ροσ̣δ̣ο-
13 κ̣ο̣ῦμεν ἐκ πάλαι, ἐξ ὅτου γεγρά-
14 φηκας. Καὶ νὴ τὸν Θεὸν διὰ
15 σὲ ἐνθαδὶ παρέμεινα μὴ ἀ̣π̣ελ-
16 θὼν εἰς τὴν Ἀντινόο̣υ ἀναγκαί-
17 ας χρείας ἕνεκεν μετὰ τοῦ ἀ[δε]λ-
18 φοῦ Πεκυσίου. Ἀλλὰ ἰδού, πολλά-
19 κις με̣τεπέμψατό με ἐκεῖ, ἀ̣[λλʼ]
20 ἐπειδή σε προσδοκῶ, οὐκ ἀ[πῆλ-]
21 θον. Αὐτὸ δὴ τοῦτο καὶ αὐτῷ [ἔ-]
22 γραψα{ς} ὅτι τὸν ἀδελφὸν μετ[ὰ]
23 [τ]ῶν παι[δ]ίων προσδοκῶ ἐ[ν-]
24 ταῦθα. Διὸ μὴ ἀμελήση̣ς ἐ[λ-]
25 θεῖν. Φέρε μοι μετά σου πελύ-
26 κιον καὶ βατέλλιον χαλκοῦν
27 κλιβανωτόν. Πρόσειπέ μοι
28 ἕκαστον κατʼ ὄνομα. Τεθα[ύ-]
29 μακα δὲ πῶς, τοσούτων ἐλ̣-
30 θόντων πρὸς ἡμᾶς, οὐδὲ
31 κἂν γράμματος ἡμᾶς κατ[η-]
32 ξιώσατε διὰ τοσούτου χρόνου,
33 ἀλλὰ κἄγω ἤμην κρίνας̣
34 μὴ γράψαι καὶ ὅμως οὐκ ἐδ[υ-]
35 νήθην βαστάξαι, μάλιστα [ὅτ]ι
36 Φιλάμ̣μων ἐστίν· ἢ οὐκ οἴ-
37 δατε ὅτι διψῶμεν τῶν ὑμ[ε-]
38 τέρων γραμμάτων; πρόσε[ι-]
39 πέ μοι Καπίτωνα καὶ Ψάις
40 Τροφάνους μετὰ συμβίων καὶ τέ-
41 κνων. Πολλά μοι πρόσειπε τὴ[ν]
42 μητέρα Μαρίαν καὶ τὴν μικρὰν
43 Τσεμπνούθην. Πέμψον μοι, ἀξι-
44 ῶ, τὴν κόραν. Ἐγὼ δίδω τὸ φολε-

45 τρὸṿ καὶ καθ' ἕκαστον ἐνιαυτὸν
46 χạρ[ί]ṣω σοι ἐρέαν εἰς ἱμάτιον τοῦ
47 μισθọῦ αὐτῆς. Ἔρρωσό μοι, κύριε.

Left hand margin, downwards:

48 Ἀξιῶ δέξαι παρὰ Καμὲ τοὺς δέκα στατῆρας στήμονος καὶ δὸς Ψάι{ς} Τρυφάνους. Θαυμάζω, μήτερ Μαρία, πῶς οὐκ ἔγραψάς
49 μοι ὅτι ἐδεξάμην τὸ παρακρεμάṣιον παρὰ Ψάιτος· δέξαι τοῦτο τὸ ἄλλον παρὰ Φιλάμμωνος καὶ κυθρίδιον ἰχθύων.

Verso, upwards on the bottom half of what was the right hand side of the recto:

50 ἀξιῶ, μήτηρ Μαρία, πέμψον μοι τὸ βατẹλ̣[λ]ιον καὶ τὸ κρί-
51 κιον τὸ σιδηροῦν, ὅτι θέλω αὐτὰ βαλεῖν εἰς τὸν ἱστόν.
52 Ἐγὼ Μαρία προσαγορεύω τὴν κυρίαν μου τὴν μητέρα
53 καὶ τὴν ἀδελφὴν μετὰ τέκνων. Προσαγορεύει ὑμᾶς
54 καὶ τὰ τέκνα μου. Ἐρρῶσθέ μοι.

Traces of the address (in a second hand) are visible on the verso, on the top half of what was the left hand side of the recto.

2, 39, 48, 49 ψαϊ- Pap. 10 ανδρεαν· Pap. 13-14 γεγραφηκας· Pap. 18 ϊδου Pap. 24-25 ελθειν· Pap. 36 εστιν· Pap. 39 Ψάιν 40 Τρυφάνους 44-45 φορετρόν 46 ϊματιον Pap. 49 ϊχθυων Pap. 50 μήτερ 51 αὐτό

"To his most honoured and truly most longed-for lord brother Psais, Pamouris sends greetings in God. First of all I and my wife and sons each individually send many greetings to your reverence, being well up until now through the providence of God. Greet for us our lord brother Theognostos and his son Andreas. About your coming to (?) us, most honoured one, every day we -- from long ago since you wrote. And, I swear by God, it was on your account that I remained here, not departing for Antinoopolis to transact pressing business with my brother Pekysis. But look, he summoned me there many times and since I was expecting you, I did not leave. Indeed I wrote this very thing to him too that 'I am expecting my brother and his children here'. So don't neglect to come. Please bring with you a small hatchet and a bronze oven dish. Please greet each by name for me. I am amazed that, while so many have come to us, you have not deemed us worthy of even a letter for such a long time; but I myself, too, had decided not to write, and yet I was unable to endure, particularly since Philammon is here. Or don't you know that we are thirsting for your letters? Greet Kapiton for me and Psais, the son of Tryphanes, with their wives and children. Give many greetings for me to mother Maria and the little Tsempnouthes. Please send the girl to me. I am giving you her travel money and each year I will give you a present of wool for a cloak as her hire. Farewell, my lord."
(Left hand margin downwards) "Please get ten loom weights from Kame and give them to Psais, the son of Tryphanes. I wonder, mother Maria, why you have not written to me: 'I received the hanging (?) from Psais'. Accept this other one from Philammon and a little pot of fish."

(Back, upwards along the fibers on the bottom half of what was the right hand side of the front) "Mother Maria, please send me the dish and the iron ring because I want to put it on the loom. I Maria greet my lady mother and sister along with her children. My children also greet you. Farewell."

Pamouris writes a soulful letter to Psais who has neither visited nor written to him. Whereas other Greek letters from Kellis are almost uniformly mundane (cf., however, the exceptional character of **63** as a letter with a Manichaean background), this well preserved letter is much less businesslike in tone and content. In view of the letter's provenance in House 3 which has produced all of the 21 Coptic letters identified to date by I. Gardner as Manichaean, a Manichaean connection may be suggested. But although both writer and addressee appear also in a number of the Coptic letters from House 3, as do several of the others mentioned in this text (references, which we owe to Dr. Gardner, are listed in the notes), there does not seem to be anything distinctively 'Manichaean' in the tone or content of the present letter.

A preliminary transcript of this text was presented by Whitehorne at the workshop on Greek documents at the 20th International Congress of Papyrologists; we are grateful to our colleagues, particularly N. Lewis and J.D. Thomas, for their comments upon problems of reading and interpretation.

1-3. For the brothers Psais and Pamour, see the family tree at p. 51.

Among the Coptic texts from House 3 Dr. Gardner has noted:

(1) P. 91.A/B (Room 6, level 5) written by Pamour to his brothers Psais and Theognostos and relaying greetings also to his father Pshai (Ψάις), Kapiton and son Lammon (= Φιλάμμων ?); 'mother Maria' is also mentioned in an underlying Coptic letter.

(2) P. 45 (Room 5, levels 1+3+4 and room 9, level 3) written by Pamour to his brothers Pekosh (Πεκῦσις), Pshai (Ψάις), Andreas, and Θεόγνωστος/Loui Shai (on the latter name see the article by O. Kaper and K.A.Worp forthcoming in the Revue d'Egyptologie); there are also other personal names mentioned, including father Pshai (Ψάις), brother Kapiton, Maria, Philammon etc. Both these texts are identified by Gardner as Manichaean.

Ἐν Θεῷ of itself is not enough to indicate that the writer was an orthodox Christian (cf. M. Naldini, *Il Cristianesimo* 12-13 and 41); as *nomina sacra* appear in 'Manichaean' papyri from Kellis like in numerous Christian texts from elsewhere, the fact that Θεός is not abbreviated as a *nomen sacrum* cannot be used as an argument for assigning this letter to more specific religious background.

4. The first line of the letter proper is offset ca. 0.5 cm. to the left. J.D. Thomas remarks that although this happens regularly in Vindolanda texts, it is apparently unparallelled in Greek letters on papyrus.

4-5. It should be noted that in later Greek the honorific abstract εὐλάβεια (used here by Pamouris for addressing Psais) is frequently (but not exclusively) used for clergy; cf. H. Zilliacus, *Untersuchungen zu den abstrakten Anredeformen und Höflichkeitstiteln im Griechischen* (Helsingfors 1949) 68, 89.

5. A Theognostos occurs also in **67** (as the addressee) and in **72**.9. Among the Coptic material a Theognostos occurs in P. 68.G.a (as Loui Shai / Θεόγνωστος; apparently he bore both names), P. 92.19 and P. 52.G (information kindly provided by Dr. Gardner).

10. Andreas occurs in the Coptic P.inv. 17.V.i, along with Pshai, Pekosh and Kapiton, and in P. 92.19 (information kindly provided by Dr. Gardner).

11. After the alpha of ἀφ̣ί̣ξ̣ε̣ω̣ς there is a horizontal split across the middle of the word. The alpha itself is secure, but the other letters are broken and abraded.

26. For other occurrences of the word *βατέλλιον* (cf. Lat. 'patella'), see S. Daris, *Il Lessico Latino nell Greco d'Egitto*[2] (Barcelona 1991) 33 s.v.
31. *κἄν*: for its regular use in later Greek as a stronger equivalent of *καί* cf. LSJ s.v., I.3.
33. *ἤμην κρίνας*: for the periphrastic pluperfect active, see B.G. Mandilaras, *The Verb in the Greek Non-Literary Papyri* (Athens 1973) 233f.
36. The reason for Pamouris' change of heart becomes apparent from l. 49, from which it is clear that Philammon was the bearer of the letter to Psais as well as the gifts to Maria.
37. For the meaning of *διψάω* = 'to be very eager to receive' cf. W. Bauer, *Wörterbuch zum Neuen Testament*[5] (1971), s.v., 3.
39. The name Kapiton as that of a living person occurs also in in **45** (386) and in the undated letter **80**; cf. also the undated letter **76** referring to a possibly deceased person of that name. Although the name is sufficiently common to make one hesitate about identifying them, some of the Coptic material from House 3 has also produced the name in association with several of the other names mentioned in this letter, cf. 1n., 10n.
39-40, 48. The name *Τρυφάνης* seems to be unknown in the papyri, but cf. the genitive *Τροφανηο(ῦτος)* in P.Mich. II 121^{V}.x.3 (1st cent.; a genitive *Τροφανηο(ῦτος)* would come from a nominative *Τροφανηοῦς* rather than from *Τροφανῆς*, as listed in the indices and in D. Foraboschi, *Onomasticon Alterum Papyrologicum*; but it is possible, of course, that one should resolve the genitive into *Τροφανήο(υς)*, cf. genitives like *Ἡρακλήους*, *Διοκλήους*, *Αὐνήους* *Φατρήους* etc.; in our text one finds in l. 40 the spelling *Τροφάνους*, in l. 48 the spelling *Τρυφάνους*. Furthermore a Psais son of (?) Tryphanes, (*Ψάις* T[*ρ*]*υφάνους*) is found as a subscriber to an official document in **24**.11. On the other hand, in **50** the receipt opens with:

1 *Κυρίῳ μου πατρὶ Ψάιτι Παμοῦρ*
2 *Ψάι[ς] Τρυφάνης χαίρειν*.--- [cf. the verso, (11-12): *Ἀποχὴ Ψάιτ(ος) Τρυφά-/νης*]

and in **73** the letter opens with:

1 *Κυρίωι μου ἀδελφῶι Παμοῦρι*
2 *Ψάις Τρυφάνης χαίρειν*. -- (similarly the address on the verso, l. 33).

The latter two instances give the impression that, though this has not been indicated as such by way of *ὁ καί vel sim.*, *Τρυφάνης* is a kind of alias going with *Ψάις*. **73**, however, also provides us with the information (ll. 9-10) that a certain 'Psais Tryphanes' had a son Tryphanes (*ἀπέστειλά σοι τὸν υἱόν μου Τρυφάνην*); in case the latter was named after his grandfather, one would have to take *Ψάις Τρυφάνης* as 'Psais son of Tryphanes' while assuming that Psais was sloppy in using a nominative *Τρυφάνης* rather than a genitive *Τρυφάνους*. The address *Κυρίῳ μου πατρὶ Ψάιτι* in **50**.1 does not need to be taken literally, as 'Psais son of Tryphanes' cannot have had two fathers (viz. Tryphanes ánd Psais son of Pamour) simultaneously; one may be dealing here with a kind of 'affectionate' loose language (for a similar situation cf. **74**.6-7n., 14n.). Finally, a Psais son of (?) Tryphanes (Pshai Tryphane), is found in the Coptic P. 92.19, along with Andreas, Theognostos, Pamour, Philammon, and others (cf. above, notes to ll. 3, 5, 10). As to the etymology of the name *Τρυφάνης* it may be remarked that the name looks Greek rather than Egyptian, cf. names like *Τρύφων* and its feminine counterpart *Τρυφαῖνα*; the second half of the name should be compared with the (many) Greek names in -*φάνης*.
42. For 'mother Maria' cf. the Coptic P. 91.A/B and P. 45 (see above, l. 1-3n.).
43. For a woman with the name Tsempnouthes cf. the Coptic papyrus A/2/101-102 in JSSEA 17 (1987) 173 (for its male counterpart see **70**.1n.)
46. Or should one read *χ̣ο̣ρ[η]γῷ*?
48. The recognition that these 'staters' are loom weights, not coins, is owed to J.D. Thomas.
49. The word *παρακρεμάσιον* is a puzzling *addendum lexicis*. Except for -*σ*- the reading is secure. The word is most easily derived from (*παρα*)*κρεμάννυμι* but what sort of object it was and what it hung beside is unknown.

72: PRIVATE LETTER

(Mid 4th century)

P.Kellis inv. P. 85.B # 1 (House 3, room 6, level 4, Southeast corner). H. 27 x B. 8.5 cm. Margins: at the top 0.5 cm., at the left occupied. The papyrus was folded horizontally several times, probably 3 times vertically. The writing on both sides of the sheet runs parallel with the fibers.

1 Κυρίῳ μο̣υ̣ ἀ̣δε̣[λφῷ Παμοῦρι]
2 Πεκῦσ̣[ι]ς̣ ὁ ἀ[δελ]φ̣[ός σου.]
3 Πρὸ πάντος πο̣[λ]λ̣ά̣ σε πρ[οσα-]
4 γορεύω ε̣[ὐ]χόμενο̣ς ὁλοκ̣[λη-]
5 ρεῖν. Πρ[οσ]αγορεύ̣ει σε ἡ σύμ-
6 βιός σου καὶ ὁ υἱός σου ῾Ωρος
7 καὶ ἡ μικρὰ α̣ὐτοῦ ἀδελφή. Ἀσπά-
8 ζεταί σε ὁ ἀδελφός σου ῾Ωρος
9 καὶ Θε[όγ]νωστος καὶ Ψάις καὶ πάν-
10 τες ο̣ἱ̣ ἡμέτεροι καὶ ἐρρωμέ̣ν̣οι
11 ἐσμὲν πάντες Θεοῦ χάρ̣ι̣τ̣ι.
12 Ἴσως μὲν ἠκούσθης π̣ε̣ρ̣ὶ
13 τοῦ υἱοῦ ἡμῶν ῾Ωρου ὅτι λι-
14 τουργεῖ ἄρτ̣ι καὶ π̣ά̣ντως δ̣ι̣ὰ̣ τ̣ο̣ῦ-
15 το οὐκ ἠθελήσας πρὸς ἡμᾶς
16 ἐλθεῖν πρ[ο]ορώ̣μ̣ενος τὴν
17 τῆς λιτουργ̣ε̣ί̣α̣ς̣ [πίμ]π̣ληστι̣ν̣. Ἐλ-
18 θέ συ, καὶ χρείαν σ̣ο̣υ̣ οὐκ ἔχε̣ι̣ εἰς τοῦ-
19 το. Θαυμάζω δὲ πῶς οὐκ̣ ἐ̣-
20 πέστειλάς μοι κἂν̣ ποκά̣ρι[ο]ν
21 ἓν εἰδῶς ἡμᾶς μὴ ἄλλο ἔ-
22 χοντας ἐν χερσί̣. Οὔτε ἐμ̣[οὶ]
23 ἔπεμψας οὔτε τῷ υἱῷ σου.
24 Οὐ μόνος γὰρ αὐ̣τ̣ὸς σχολά̣ζει
25 εἰς τὴν ὑπηρεσίαν τῆς λειτουρ-
26 γίας, ἀλλὰ ἐγὼ αὐτὸς σχολὴν
27 πρὸς μίαν ὥρ[α]ν οὐκ ἔχω ἀ-
28 πὸ τῶν τοιούτω̣ν̣· ἐκπλήττομαι
29 δέ σου τὸ ἀμέριμνον περὶ ἡ-
30 {η}μ`ῶ´⟦α⟧ν. Εἰ γὰ̣ρ ἠγόρασας τὴν
31 μικρὰ̣ν̣ [πορ]φύραν καὶ μό-
32 νον διὰ̣ σάκκον, οὐκ ἔπεμ-
33 ψας. Θαυμαστόν· ἐδύνου γὰρ
34 σαβάνιον ἀγοράσαι καὶ βαλεῖν
35 αὐτὴν εἰς [α]ὐτὸ καὶ ἀποστεῖλαί
36 μοι. Ἀξιω[θ]εὶς δὲ καλόχρω-

37 μου ἀγόρασόν μοι τὸ μικρὸν
38 ἐρίδιον. Πρόσειπέ μοι τὸν ἀ-
39 δελφὸν Φιλάμμῳνα, εἰ παρὰ
40 σοί ἐστι. Ὃ ποιεῖς ποίησον. Ἐρ-
41 ρῶσθαί σε εὔχομαι πολλοῖς
42 χ[ρ]όνοις εὐτυχοῦντα.

In the left hand margin:

43 καὶ καταλαμβάνω ὑμᾶς ταχέως ἐπὶ το[ῦτο, ὡς] γὰρ βαρυκέφαλος ἐφάνης.

Verso:

44 Ἐλυπηθήμεν δὲ πάνυ MANY TRACES μὴ
45 δεξάμενοι διὰ τῶν πρὸς ἡμᾶς νυνὶ ἐληλυ-
46 θότων, Νεστόριον δὲ λέγω καὶ Βησᾶν Σύρου.
47 ὅλην γὰρ τὴν ἡμέραν ἐν ᾗ εἰσεληλύθα-
48 σιν ἔτι ἠξέφαινεν TRACES θέσεως
49 TRACES
50 ἔρρωσαι

51 Κυρίῳ μου ἀδελφῶι \ / Πεκῦσις
52 Παμοῦρι / \

11 χαριτι. Pap. 12 ϊσως Pap. 13-14 λειτουργεῖ 14 τουρ- ex τυρ- 17 λειτουργίας 19 το. Pap. 21 ἐν Pap. 26 -ος ex -ου 28 τοιουτων˙, εκπλητ᾽τομαι Pap. 30 ημ`ω´⟦α⟧ν. Pap. 33 θαυμαστον˙ Pap. 40 εστι. Pap. 47 ή Pap.

"To my lord brother Pamouris, Pekysis your brother. Before all I greet you very much, praying for your health. Your wife greets you and your son Horos and his little sister. Your brother Horos greets you and Theognostos and Psais and all our family and we are in good health thanks to God's grace. Perhaps you heard about our son Horos that he is a liturgist just now and for that very reason you did not want to come to us, in view of the performance of the liturgy. So come, and he does not need you for that. I wonder why you have not sent me even one fleece, though you know that we had no other one in hand; you did not send it, neither to me nor to your own son. For not only he himself has no spare time for the service of the liturgy, but I myself have no spare time for even an hour because of such things. I am baffled by your carelessness towards us. For if you had bought the small amount of purple dye and only by sack, you did not send this. Remarkable: for you could buy a linen cloth and put it (the purple) in there and send that off to us. Please buy for me the little amount of nicely coloured wool. Greet for me my brother Philammon, if he is with you. Do what you are doing. I pray for your health and well-being in many years to come." (In left-hand margin) "And I'll come to you quickly for this, because you appeared heavy-headed." (At verso) "And we were very sorry not receiving ... through the persons who now have come down to us, I mean Nestorios and Besas, the son of Syros. For the whole day on which they arrived he (?) still showed....."

9. *Θεόγνωστος*: possibly the same person as in **67**.2 and **71**.9.
17-19. The precise meaning of the phrase and its connection with the preceding lines is not very easy to grasp; we have considered a supplement of <*εἰ*> between *καὶ* and *χρείαν* ('So come, even if he [= the liturgist] does not need you for that [= the performing of the liturgy]').
20. For *κἄν* cf. **71**.31n.
29. More normal than *τὸ ἀμέριμνον* would have been *τὴν ἀμεριμνίαν*.
32. *διὰ̣ σάκκον*: this reading seems preferable to *δὶς σάκκον* (= 'twice a sack') or *δίσ̣σακκον* (= 'a double sack'?; the word as such is not attested, but cf. *δισάκκιον*).
44-45. One expects something like *Ἐλυπηθήμεν δὲ πάνυ γράμματα παρὰ σοῦ μὴ/ δεξάμενοι*, but between *πάνυ* and *μὴ* most of the writing has been abraded.
46. *Νεστόριον*, *Βησᾶν Σύρο̣υ̣*: these persons seem to be mentioned only here, but it is not said that they lived in Kellis.
48. *ἠξέ̣φ̣α̣ι̣ν̣εν*: from *ἐκφαίνω*; for the double augment cf. F.T. Gignac, *Grammar*, II 253.

73: PRIVATE LETTER

(4th century)

P.Kellis inv. P. 85.B # 2 (House 3, room 6, level 4, Southeast corner). Frag. I: H. 7 x B. 7 cm. Frag. II: H. 6.5 x B. 7 cm. The writing on both sides of the sheet runs parallel with the fibers.

1 Κυρίωι μου ἀδελφῶι Παμοῦρι
2 Ψάις Τρυφάνης χαίρειν. Προηγου-
3 μένως πολλά σε προσαγορεύω.
4 Ἀσπάζεταί σε πάνυ ὁ ἀδελφός
5 σου καὶ τὰ τέκνα καὶ ἡ μήτηρ
6 αὐτῶν. Ἀσπάζεταί σε ἡ σύμβ̣ι̣-
7 ώς <σ>ου καὶ τὰ τέκνα σου καὶ πάν-
8 τες οἱ ἐν τῇ οἰκε̣ίᾳ̣ ὅλοι. Ἰδοὺ
9 οὖν, ἀπέστειλά σοι τὸν υἱόν
10 μου Τρυφάνην μετὰ τὰ̣ εἴδη
11 μου, ἵνα ποιήσῃς τὴν σπου-
12 δὴν κ̣α̣ὶ̣ σ̣υ̣ν̣ά̣γεις μετ᾽ αὐτοῦ
- -
13 [ ]μ̣ου καὶ π̣ρ̣ι̣[. . . . .]-
14 κα μετ᾽ αὐτοῦ ἐν κ̣α̣λ̣[. . .]
15 . . μῃ καὶ, ἐὰν ποιήσῃς
16 δέκα ἡμέρας ἢ εἴκοσι με-
17 τ᾽ αὐτοῦ ἕως πιπράσκεις
18 τὰ εἴδη μου, ἑτοίμως ἔχω
19 παράσχειν σοι τὸν μισθόν
20 σου τέως. Μὴ κατέχῃς
21 τὸν υἱόν μου παρὰ σοί· ἵνα ἐλ̣-

22 θῇς μετ' αὐτοῦ πρὸς τὸν και-
23 ρὸν τοῦ γλεύκους. Οἶδα γὰρ
24 τὴν σὴν σπουδήν. Ἐρρῶ-
25 σθαί σε εὔχομαι πολ-
26 λοῖς χρόν̣[οις].
In left hand margin downward:
27 ἀξιωθεὶς πὰν ποίησον, ἐὰν δ[ύνῃ, ἀποστεῖλαί] μοι τὰ ἔργα TRACES
28 αὐτοῦ τ̣ῶν̣ ἀγρῶν ἐκεῖ μ[ ] TRACES
Verso:
29 τὸ δὲ πρόλοιπον τῶν τριάκον̣[τα] . . ων πορφυρῶν
30 δὸς αὐτὰ ὑπὲρ ἐριδίων σπου̣[δ] TRACES
31 ενος καὶ ἀπόστειλόν μοι[ ] .

32 Κυρίωι μου ἀδελφῷ \ / Παμοῦρι
33 / \ Ψάις Τρυφάνης

6-7 σύμβιος 8 οἰκίᾳ 10 τῶν εἰδῶν? See note 12 συνάγῃς 17 πιπράσκεις: first -ι- ex omikron 28 τ̣ῶν̣: ῶ̣ ex α, ν clumsy; the Pap. has a dash over the omega of αγρων

(Ll. 1-12, 15-27) "To my lord brother Pamouris Psais son of (?) Tryphanes sends greetings. Before all I greet you many times. Your brother greets you very much and his children and their mother. Your wife greets you and your children and all present at home. Look now, I have sent you my son Tryphanes with (?) my goods in order that you make an effort and together with him bring together ... (l. 15) and if you spend ten or twenty days together with him, while you are selling my goods, I am prepared to give you your salary in the meantime. Don't keep my son with you; go with him in view of the season of the sweet new wine. For I know your zeal. I pray for your health for many years. At my request please do everything, if you can, to send me the work -- ."

A fragmentary letter from Psais son of (?) Tryphanes (cf. **71**.39-40n.) to his brother Pamour. Palaeographical considerations do not speak against the assumption that the letter was written somewhere in the middle of the 4th century; for the addressee, see the family tree at p. 51. The contents of the letters are as to be expected: the conveyance of greetings and the order to perform certain services. An item of interest is the reference to the sweet young wine in l. 23 which was produced probably within the Oasis (for another reference to viticulture cf. **23**.17, 20).

8. ὅλοι is redundant after πάντες, but it seems conceivable that one is dealing with a iotacistic spelling for ὅλῃ.

10. Or should one read *μετὰ τοῦ εἴδη* (l. *εἴδους*)?
15. For the meaning of *ποιέω* = 'to spend' cf. LSJ s.v., VII.
23-24. It seems that the words Οἶδα *γὰρ τὴν σὴν σπουδήν* = 'For I know your zeal' should be inderstood in relation to the preceding statement in l. 20f.: Μὴ *κατέχῃς τὸν υἱόν μου παρὰ σοί*, 'don't keep my son with you'. It is, however, conceivable that it should be taken with the adhortation "*ἵνα ἐλθῇς μετ' αὐτοῦ*" = 'go with him'; the author may have tacitly omitted a thought like, e.g., 'I know that I can make this appeal to you, for I know your zeal', etc.
29ff. It is difficult to make a coherent combination of the text on the verso with the text on the recto. Apparently there is a question of purple-dyeing (cf. l. 29, *πορφυρῶν*; are the remainder [*τὸ πρόλοιπον*] of 30 weighing units, e.g. 'pounds' or 'sacks', meant?) and wool (cf. l. 30, *ὑπὲρ ἐριδίων*), but the lacuna between the two fragments is large enough to prevent us from understanding the text satisfactorily. Wool and purple are also found together in **72**.30f., 37f.; the same combination is found frequently among the Coptic texts from Kellis (information kindly provided by Dr. A. Alcock).

74: PRIVATE LETTER

(Mid 4th century)

P.Kellis inv. P. 62.B (House 3, room 6, level 3). H. 25.5 x B. 10.8 cm. The writing runs parallel to the fibers on both sides of the sheet. For organizational purposes the papyrus was previously referred to as 'P.Kellis 72'.

1 Κυρίῳ μου πατρὶ Ἄρωνι Ψάις
2 κεραμεὺς ὁ υἱὸς χαίρειν.
3 Ἀσπάζομαί σε πολλὰ τὸ πρὸ πάντων
4 καὶ ὑγιαίνειν εὔχομαι. Ἡ μήτηρ μου
5 καὶ οἱ ἀδελφοὶ κατ' ὄνομα πολλά σε
6 ἀσπάζονται καὶ τὴν μητέρα Ἀγά-
7 πην πολλὰ ἀσπάζομαι καὶ τὴν θυγα-
8 τέρα αὐτῆς· ἀξιωθεὶς κατὰ τὴν
9 συνταγὴν πέμψον μοι τὸ ὀλί-
10 γον πορφύρας εἰς χιτώνιον τῆς
11 μητρός μου καὶ τῆς ἀδελφῆς μου,
12 ἐπεὶ χρεία ἐστὶν καὶ κεῖται τὰ
13 σύνεργα ἕως πέμψῃς ταχέως
14 τὴν πορφύραν. Μάθε δὲ ὅτι ἦρκεν
15 τὰς ἐλαίας ὁ πατὴρ Κλωδιανὸς καὶ
16 δέδωκεν ἡμῖν τὸ μέρος τοῦ ἐπικει-
17 μένου καρποῦ, δέδωκεν δὲ τὰς ἐλαί-
18 ας Ψενπνούθῃ, καὶ ὡς ἄρτι οὔπω
19 ἐσχήκαμεν μισθούς. Ὅπως δηλώ-
20 σῃς ἡμῖν εἰ θέ[λεις] λαβεῖν εἰ μ[ή].
21 Μάθε δὲ ὅτι TRACES [ ]

22 ησαν ἡμῖν οἱ κ̣λ̣η TRACES [ ]
23 λου χάριν τῆς [πορφ]ύ̣ρ[ας] . . [ca. 8]
24 μὴ διστάξῃς τ[ὸ] γράψ̣α̣ι̣ μ̣ο̣ι τῇ[
25 μητρὶ Ταγάπῃ [ὑπ]ο̣δεικ̣νύων̣
26 \`ὅτι´ ''Ἀπέστη ἀπὸ τῆς οἰκίας Πετεμ̣[ίνιος?]
27 καὶ ἐνοχλεῖ μοι σ̣υνεχῶς ὡς σοῦ
28 χρεωστούσης αὐτῷ̣. Εἰ μὲν οὖν
29 χρεωστεῖς αὐτῷ̣ τί ποτε, ὑπό-
30 δειξόν μοι καὶ ἐκπλέξω αὐ-
31 τόν'. Ἀξιωθ̣εὶς δέ,
In left hand margin:
32 ὦ ἄδελφε Ἄρων, σπούδασον καταλαβεῖν ἡμᾶς, ἐπεὶ πάνυ χρείαν σου ἔχομεν.
33 Ἐρρῶσθαί σε εὔχο̣μ̣α̣ι̣ κ̣ύ̣ρ̣ι̣έ̣ μ̣ου δέσποτα.
Verso:
34 Κυρίῳ̣ μου πατρὶ ἀδελφῷ
35 Ἄρωνι ἐ̣ν̣ Κ̣ε̣λ̣[λει] Ψάις κ̣ε̣ρ̣α̣μ̣(εύς)

1 ψαϊς Pap. 2 χαῖρειν Pap. (supplied later by 2nd hand?) 6-7 γάπην corr. into Ἀγάπην 9 ολι- ex ολο- corr. 20 ἤ 28 χρεωστοῦντος (?)

"To my father Aron, Psais the potter, his son, sends greetings. I greet you very much in the first place and pray for your health. My mother and brothers each greet you very much by name and I greet my mother Agape very much and her daughter. As requested according to the order send me the small amount of purple-dye for the garment of my mother and (that) of my sister, as I need it and as all work has stopped until you quickly send the purple-dye. Be informed that father Claudianus has plucked the olives and that he has given us our share of the present harvest and he has given the (other) olives to Psenpnouthes and that recently we had not yet received our wages. Indicate to us whether you want to take them (i.e. the olives) or not. Also be informed that the ... to us ... because of the purple. Don't hesitate to write for me to my mother Tagape indicating that 'Peteminis (?) has gone away from the house and he bothers me constantly, as if you owe him something. Now if you owe him something, indicate this to me and I'll set him free'. But please, brother Aron, make haste to come to us as we need you very much. I pray for your health, my lord, very much." (Address) "To my lord father brother Aron in Kellis, Psais the potter (?)."

This letter contains, as usual, greetings from the sender and the persons around him to the addressee and those who are with him. Furthermore, instructions are given concerning the dispatch and receipt of various commodities like olives and purple-dye.

1. For possibly Jewish names, see **61**. The name Aron does not occur elsewhere in the Greek Kellis documents and we wonder whether we should not aspirate Ἅρωνι and regard it as another Horos-name. Though the regular papyrological onomastica do not list a name Ἅρων, such Horos-names starting with an element Ἁρ- are common enough.
2. For potters, see **61**.2n. and **66**.22n. In itself one might be tempted to read *κεραμεὺς* {ς} *υἱός*, but this reading does not make much sense; *χαίρειν* may have been added by a second hand (did the scribe first abbreviate *χαίρ(ειν)*, then add the ending as yet?).
6-7. It is remarkable to see that Psais greets his 'mother' Agape (cf. l. 25, Tagape), as if she is with his father Aron, whereas from l. 4 one gets the impression that Psais' mother is with Psais himself. Only one of the two can have been his real mother, whereas in the other case the word 'mother' is used in conformity with epistolary usage.
10. For the use of purple-dye in Kellis cf. **61**.1, **72**.31 and **73**.29.
14ff. For the translation of *ἀείρω* = 'to pluck' cf. LSJ s.v., I.2. Apparently Clodianus (the word 'father' is possibly used here again in conformity with epistolary usage, cf. ll. 6-7n., 34n.; so much is certain that Psais cannot have had two fathers, Aron and Clodianus) has plucked the olives and has given part of the harvest to Psais himself, part to Psenpnouthes.
18-19. *καὶ ὡς .. ἐσχήκαμεν* seems to form the continuation of *μάθε δὲ ὅτι* (l. 14). It seems less likely to regard *ὡς* here as synonymous with *ἕως* = 'until', but cf. LSJ s.v., A.d.2.
20. We assume that 'olives' are to be understood as the object of λαβεῖν.
23. In itself *χάριν* may be taken with the preceding genitive in -λου or with the following genitive *τῆς πορφυρᾶς* (on purple see **62**.1n.).
24. The reading of the central part of this line is not very convincing and the construction *μὴ διστάξῃς* + object in the form of an articulate infinitive = 'don't hesitate to ...' is all but regular (cf. LSJ s.v. *διστάζω*).
25. Is 'mother' Tagape the same person as 'mother' Agape in ll. 6-7, now with the Egyptian fem. article T- prefixed? For such prefixes cf. the notes to **46**.31f., **66**.1.
28. *χρεωστούσης* (fem.) refers, of course, to Tagape, not to the addressee of this letter.
30. The context requires that 'I'll set him free' should be understood as 'I'll pay him off' *vel sim.*.
34. The combination of 'father' and 'brother' used next to each other for addressing one person shows nicely what actual value these terms have, if one tries to establish a family tree.
35. Read *Ψάις κ̣ε̣ρ̣α̣μ̣(εύς)* or *Ψάις υ̣ἱ̣ό̣ς̣*?

75: PRIVATE LETTER

(Later [?] 4th century)

P. Kellis inv. P. 96.B (House 3, Room 6, level 4, South wall). H. 27 x B. 5.2 cm. Writing on both sides parallel with the fibers. There are two horizontal and two vertical folds. The papyrus was found rolled and tied up with a piece of papyrus string.

1 Κυρίῳ μου ἀ-
2 δελφῷ
3 Στρατηγίῳ
4 Ἠλίας χ<αί>ρειν.
5 Προηγουμέ-
6 νως πολλά σου τὴν

7 φιλαδελφί̣αν
8 προσαγορεύω
9 εὐχόμενός σε
10 προσκυνεῖν ἐν
11 τάχει. Πολλὰ
12 προσαγορεύ-
13 ω τὸν κύρι-
14 όν μου πατέρα
15 Βημοφάνη̣`ν´
16 καὶ τὸν τιμιώ-
17 τατον ἀδελ-
18 φὸν Ψάιν τὸν̣
19 μέγαν καὶ
20 τὸν ἄλλον
21 Ψάιν καὶ
22 Πλου`υ´τογέ-
23 νην καὶ ⟦.⟧
24 ῾Ωρα.
25 ἐρῶσσθαί
26 σε εὔχο-
27 μαι πολ-
28 λοῖς
29 χρόνοις,
30 ⟦α⟧ δέσ-
31 {σ}ποτα
32 ἄδελ-
33 φε ⟦.⟧.

Verso

34 (M.2) κυρίῳ μου \\ // (M.1)Στρατη-
35 ἀδελφῷ // \\ γίῳ Ἠλ<ί>α`ς´

7 *φιλαδελφίαν*: first -*α*- ex *η* corr. 16 *τὸν*: the scribe started writing *τι*- (from *τιμιώτατον*), then continued with -*ον* 17 *ἀδελ*-: -*δ*- ex corr. 22 Πλου`υ´τογέ-: the scribe first wrote *πλοτω*-, then added a supralinear ypsilon (*πλο`υ´τω*-), then cancelled the supralinear ypsilon and converted his tau + omega into an upsilon written at line level and wrote a new tau + omikron after that 25 *ἐρρῶσθαί* 26 *ευχο*- ex *αιχο*- ? 27 *μαι* ex *με* 33 *φε* ex *φαι*

"To my lord brother Strategios, Elias sends greetings. Before all I greet your brotherliness very much, while I am hopeful that I shall embrace you soon. I greet my lord father Bemophanes very much and my most esteemed brother Psais 'the great' and the other Psais and Ploutogenes and Hor. I pray for your health for many years, my lord brother. (Address) To my lord brother Strategios, Elias."

This letter, written by a rather clumsy hand featuring all the traits of a βραδέως γράφων (on such slow writers, see H.C. Youtie in GRBS 12 [1971] 239-61 = *Scriptiunculae* [Amsterdam 1973], II 629-651), conveys no other message than the greetings of a certain Elias to his father Bemophanes and his five 'brothers' Strategios (actually the addressee of the letter), Psais, a younger Psais, Ploutogenes and Hor. Such letters (which hardly pass on any further information) are frequent enough among the papyri; cf. in general H. Koskenniemi, *Studien zur Idee und Phraseologie des griechischen Briefes* (Helsinki 1956). The names Psais and Ploutogenes are well known in Kellis, the other names occur more or less rarely.

15. The name Βημοφάνην seems to be unique, but a correction into a better known name, Δημοφάνην, is not warranted. The writer seems to have left the final ν unfinished (writing only the first part) and then supplied this letter in full above the line.
18-21. Apparently there were two homonymous brothers (real brothers or spiritual brothers or colleagues?) named Psais, who were distinguished either by their size or their age (cf. LSJ s.v. μέγας I.b).
24. Apparently we are dealing here with the (declined) accusative form ῟Ωρα of the (normally undeclined) Egyptian name ῟Ωρ; for this declension of Egyptian names cf. F.T. Gignac, *A Grammar of the Greek Papyri of the Roman and Byzantine periods* II (Milano 1981) 103, who, however, lists no parallel for the accusative form ῟Ωρα. To be sure, one could also be dealing with an irregular accusative of the name Ὡρᾶς, cf. Gignac, *op.cit.* II 16, 18.

76: PRIVATE LETTER AND SURETY

(Second half of the 4th century)

P.Kellis inv. P. 81.E+F + P. 93.B (all from House 3, room 6, level 4). H. 29 x B. 6.4 cm. Written along the fibers. There is an upper margin of 1.8 and a bottom margin of 2.5 cm. For organizational purposes the papyrus was referred to previously as 'P.Kellis 61'.

1 Κυρίωι μου ἀδελφῶι
2 Σαράπιδι
3 Πεκῦσις χαίρειν.
4 Ἐπειδὴ ἐβουλήθης μετ-
5 ελθεῖν τῇ ἀδελφῇ μου
6 τῇ γυναικί τινος λεγο-
7 μένου Καπίτωνος, βου-
8 λόμενον ἀπαιτῆσαι αὐ-
9 τὴν ὑπὲρ αὐτοῦ μυριάδα
10 μίαν ἥμισυ, γί(νεται) (μυριὰς) α (ἥμισυ), ὑπὲρ
11 τῆς ἀπαιτήσεως τοῦ χρυσ-
12 αργύρου αὐτοῦ, ἀγνοοῦμεν
13 δὲ αὐτὸν τὸν ἄνθρωπον
14 ἐν σ̣ώματι εἶ[ναι] μέχρι τοῦ

15 πάροντος χρ[ον]ίσαντα ἐν τῇ
16 [Αἰ̈γ]ύπτῳ̣, δ[ιὸ] π̣αρέχῳ̣
17 [σοι] αὐτὴν τ̣[ὴν] ἐπι̣σ̣τ̣ο̣λὴν
18 εἰς ἀσφάλειαν καὶ πίστ[ιν],
19 ὁμολογῶν σοι ἑτοιμότ[α-]
20 τα {τα} ἔχειν σε πληρῶσαι
21 αὐτὴν τὴν μυριάδα μίαν̣
22 καὶ ἥμισυ ἀναμφιβόλως,
23 ἐὰν ἔλθῃ ἐκεῖνος ὑγιαίνων̣.
24 Εἰ δὲ ἀνθρώπι<ν>όν τι `ἔ´παθεν̣
25 καὶ ἀκούσωμεν ἀκριβῶς
26 αὐτὸν λυθῆναι τοῦ σώμα-
27 τος, οὐκ ἔξεσταί σοι ζητεῖν
28 ἢ ἀπαιτῆσαι ἡμᾶς ὑπὲρ
29 αὐτοῦ, μηδὲν κοινὸν ἔχοντα
30 πρὸς αὐτὸν ἐν οὐδένι. Ἐρρῶσ-
31 θαί σε εὔχομαι πολ-
32 λοῖς χρόνοις.
33 (M.2) Αὐρήλιος
34 Γενᾶ Παταιᾶτος
35 μαρτυρῶ.
Verso:
36 Κυρίωι μου ἀδελφῶι Χ Σαράπιδι Πεκῦσις Ψάιτ(ος) Παμούρ(ιος).

7-8 βουλόμενος 9 μυριάδα: -α corr. ex -η 20 σοι, ἔχειν: -ει- ex -ω- corr. 24 εἰ ex ἐὰν corr., `ἔ´παθεν̣ ex παθη corr. 29 εχοντα: -α- through -τ-, l. ἔχοντας 35 μαρτυρῶ: -υ- corr. ex -ω-

"To my lord brother Sarapis, Pekysis sends greetings. Since you have wanted to make a claim against my sister, who is the wife of a certain so-called Kapiton, wishing to demand from her on his behalf one and a half myriads, total 1½ myriads, for the collection of his (dues of) *chrysargyron*, and as we do not know whether the man himself is still alive, as he resided up to the present in Egypt, therefore I provide you with this letter as a guarantee and surety, acknowledging to you that I am most ready to pay you the one myriad and a half unambiguously if that person comes here in good health. But if he has suffered some mortal affliction and we hear for sure that he has died, it will not be possible for you to make any enquiry or demand from us on his behalf, since we have no common interest with him in any respect. I pray that you are well for a long time. (M. 2) I, Aurelius Gena son of Pataias, bear witness." (Verso) "To my lord brother Sarapis, Pekysis son of Psais, grandson of Pamouris."

The writer Pekysis offers a surety for a tax debt for which the addressee Sarapis is dunning Pekysis' sister, the wife of a certain Kapiton. According to Pekysis it is uncertain whether Kapiton is still alive; only if he turns up alive, is Pekysis willing to pay up (apparently expecting to reclaim the money from his brother-in-law); if, however, Kapiton has died, Pekysis rejects any responsibility for taxes due by Kapiton. For the persons, see the family tree at p. 51.

6ff. *τῇ γυναικί τινος λεγομένου Καπίτωνος* may be taken in apposition to *τῇ ἀδελφῇ μου* in l. 5. Given the way he indicates his brother-in-law, Pekysis was apparently on not too friendly terms with Kapiton; cf. also ll. 29-30, where Pekysis claims that he and his sister are *μηδὲν κοινὸν ἔχοντα<ς> πρὸς αὐτὸν ἐν οὐδένι* = "having nothing in common with him [Kapiton] in any respect" although of course they had a family relationship with Kapiton; for him see **45**.1n.). It looks as if Kapiton and his wife had separated and that Kapiton had left the Dakhleh Oasis more or less permanently (cf. ll. 14-16).

The construction with the accusative participle *βουλόμενον ἀπαιτῆσαι*, rather than the expected nominative *βουλόμενος* (going with *ἐβουλήθης*, l. 4), is due to Pekysis' mistakenly continuing his letter as if he had written something like *ἠκουσάμην σε βούλεσθαι μετελθεῖν κτλ. vel sim.* at the start.

11-12. For the *chrysargyron*-tax on trades and businesses, see **15**.4-5n.

14. For the phrase *ἐν σώματι εἶναι* = "to be alive" (cf. ll. 26-27, *λυθῆναι τοῦ σώματος* = "to die") cf. Bauer-Arndt-Gingrich, *Greek-English Lexicon of the NT* 806-807, s.v. *σῶμα* 1.b.

15-16. For the meaning of the verb *χρονίζω* = "to reside" cf. LSJ s.v., I,4; for 'Egypt' = the Nile Valley cf. **81**.5 and P.Genova II Appendix I.9n. (p. 75).

16. The use of *διό* here is not quite regular (after a protasis introduced by *ἐπειδή* [l. 4ff.] one would expect the apodosis to start with *διὰ τοῦτο*) but cf. already E. Mayser, *Grammatik der griechischen Papyri aus der Ptolemäerzeit*, II.3 74 § 157.b, P.Teb. I 44.20; for a much later example of the construction cf. P.Apoll. 72.1-2.

17. The lacuna is not large enough for restoring [*σοι τ*]*αύτην*. For the use of the personal pronoun rather than the demonstrative cf. F.T. Gignac, *A Grammar of the Greek Papyri of the Roman and Byzantine Periods* II 174, 3.d.

33. The addition of the witness's subscription gives a quasi-legal patina to what otherwise looks like a simple letter.

33-34. The second hand has all the characteristics of a 'slow writer', i.e. the letters are large and clumsily formed; for such slow writers cf. **75** introd. For this person cf. **7**, a letter written by Harpokration to Γενᾶ son of Παταιᾶς. For the name Gena in connection with House 2 cf. also the name of the addressee of **6** and the author of **5**.

77: FRAGMENT OF A LETTER

(Later 4th century)

P.Kellis inv. P. 41 (House 3, room 7.a, level 2) + P. 78.D (House 3, room 6, level 3) + P. 92.A (House 3, room 6, level 4, South wall). Large fragment (P. 41 + 92.A): H. 26 x B. 4.5 cm.; smaller fragment (P. 78.D): H. 9.5 x B. 2 cm. Margins preserved in Frag. I: at the top 2, at the bottom 5 cm. On both sides of Frag. I the writing runs parallel to the fibers; the back of the small fragment is blank.

Frag. I:

1] ̣οι καὶ σφόδρα [
2] ̣των μετριω̣[
3]δρωτων̣ τὸ ζ̣[
4] ̣η τῇ ἡμετέρα̣[
5]έχομεν μητ[
6] ̣ν κεῖσθαι κ[
7] ̣ιν̣ διὰ κτήνω̣[ν
8 ὀ]λ̣ι̣γῶν ὑδάτω[ν
9] ̣ι ἐξ ὤμων κα[
10]πάσχομεν παρ[
11 ἐ]ν̣ Ὀάσει Μῶθις τ̣[
12]ν̣ τοῦ βασιλικο[ῦ
13]σ̣ιαν ἐκσφουγ[κτορ-
14] ̣ χώραν δημ[
15 ο]υ̣ς καμηλάται[ς
16 ἡ]μ̣ισίας σχεδὸν̣ [
17]ειτοις αὐτῶ[ν
18] ἡμ̣ι̣σίας απα̣[
19]αλλας̣ τὰς δυ[
20]κομ̣[ι]δὴν τῶν̣[
21]ε̣ ἴσθ̣ι τὴν σὴν [
22] πρὸς τὴν ὑπη[ρεσίαν
23] ̣ τῶν ἄ̣λλων̣[
24]ησδεβ[̣ ̣] ̣ησε̣[
25]αι δυν̣[α
26]χρεία ὑπ[
27]ηλατοις καὶ[
28] μόνω̣ βαρουμ̣[

Frag. II: - - - - - - - -

31]ε ̣[
32]υτα ̣[
33]οχε[
34]εισιεν[
35]πορι ̣ ̣[
36]ρειτη[
37]εαυτα̣[
38]δ̣εχοντ̣[
39]ριοιον[
40]νκαια ̣[
41]εισιπολ[
42]κατακ[
43] ̣α̣λλη ̣[
- - - - - - - - -

Verso of Frag. I:

- -

29 TRACES] ̣[
30 τεταγμ̣ε̣[ ] VACAT μεθ' ἃ Ῥωμαικά· προσετέθη ἐν Ἀντινόου, Ἐπεὶφ κ.

16, 18 ἡμισείας 21 Or read]ε̣ισε̣ι? 30 προετέθη ?

These fragments apparently contain the remains of a letter of a (semi-)official character. Obviously the two strips result from a folded papyrus sheet which is now broken on its folds. Many lines contain a series of letters which allow of more than one word division and it seems tedious to give a listing of all conceivable restorations, as the original wording of the letter will still remain virtually unintelligible. Under the circumstances only two passages seem to warrant some further discussion, viz. ll. 11-15 and l. 29-30 (on the verso).

In l. 11 one is obviously dealing with a reference to the city of Mothis (at line end restore π̣[όλις?) situated in the (Great) Oasis, but it is less clear what the genitive *τοῦ βασιλικο*[*ῦ* (= 'the imperial'?) in l. 12 is referring to. In l. 13 a declined form of the noun *ἐξπούγκτωρ* (for this army official cf. **21**.9n.) is found, while in l. 15 one encounters camel-drivers, *καμηλάται* (also in l. 27?). It is uncertain in what relation the text on the verso stands to the text on the recto and which side was inscribed first. It is conceivable that there is no connection at all and that one is dealing with completely independent texts. On the verso one might be dealing with an official document, the uninscribed back of which was used later for a private letter, i.c. with the end of a copy of an official document (e.g.: a proclamation or a report of juridical proceedings) written and/or published (read *προετέθη*? Cf. l. 30n.) in Antinoopolis on Epeiph 20 = 14.vii in an unknown year. Apparently the original text had a passage written in Latin which was not taken over.. Normally such public notices would be on display in the metropolis only, cf. P.Oxy. XXXIII 2664.9n., where the use of Latin phrasings in such texts is also discussed.

29-30. Restore, e.g., *κατὰ τὰ προσ-*]/*τεταγμέ̣*[*να*, i.e. 'according to the orders'.
30. In view of parallel texts (cf. F. Preisigke, *Wörterbuch*, s.v. *προτίθημι* 1.a) it might seem attractive to correct *προσετέθη* into *προετέθη*. On the other hand, it is not inconceivable that the original text started at this place with a quotation: '---(do so) according to the orders' and that it continued with 'after which (= Greek text) Latin (text) was added; in Antinoopolis on Epeiph 20'.

78: BUSINESS LETTER

(Second half of the 4th century)

P.Kellis inv. P. 17.A (House 3, room 10, level 3). H. 9.7 x B. 10.8 cm. Margins: at the top 0.7, at the bottom 2.0 cm. The writing runs parallel with the fibers. Three vertical folds are still visible. For organizational purposes the papyrus was previously referred to as 'P.Kellis 70'.

1 Κυρίῳ μου ἀδελφῷ Εὐμαθίῳ Σ[ῖρι]ς
2 χαίρειν. Αὐτῆς ὥρας λαβών μου̣
3 τὰ γράμματα ἀπαίτησον ἀπὸ γεω̣[ρ-]
4 γῶν ὑπὲρ κριθῶν, φ[ο]ινίκων ἀ[ργ]υ-
5 ρίου τάλαντα δισχείλια, γί(νεται) τάλ(αντα) ͵β,
6 καὶ δὸς τῷ ἀδελφῷ Ἠλίᾳ. Ἀλλὰ μὴ
7 ἀμελήσῃς· δὸς αὐτῷ. Ἐρρῶσθαί σ' ε̣ὔ-
8 χομαι, ἄδελφε,
9 πολλοῖς χρόνο̣ι̣[ς].
10 Παχὼν ϛ ε ἰνδ(ικτίωνος).

Verso:

11 Κυρίῳ μο[υ] ἀδελφῷ Χ Σῖρις
12 Εὐμαθίῳ

5 δισχίλια

"To my lord brother Eumathius Siris sends greetings. Immediately after receiving my letter collect from the farmers for barley and dates two thousand talents of silver, 2000 tal. in total, and give them to brother Elias. But don't be neglectful; give them to him. I pray for your health, brother, for many years. Pachon 6, 5th indiction."

1. The names Eumathios and Siris do not occur in the other Greek papyri from House 3.
4. The asyndeton between κριθῶν and φ[ο]ινίκων is remarkable.
6. One finds persons named Ἠλίας in **39**.7, **68**.1, **75**.4, 35 and an Ἠλίας s.o. Σαβεῖνος in **81**.2.
10. Pachon 6 = 1.v; a 5th indiction in the second half of the 4th century covers the years 361/2, 376/7 or 391/2.

79: BUSINESS LETTER

(Mid 4th century)

P.Kellis inv. P. 85.A # 3 (House 3, room 6, level 4, Southeast corner). H. 12.2 x B. 5 cm. Margins: at the left 0.5, at the bottom 1.5 cm. Writing parallel with the fibers. The verso is blank.

1 [Κυρί]ῳ μ[ου ἀ]δ̣ε̣λ̣φῷ
2 Ἀν]ι̣κ̣ήτ̣ῳ
3 [. . . .] Ψάι̣ς̣ χ̣α̣ίρ̣ε̣ι̣ν.
4 Πέμψο̣ν̣ ε̣ἰ̣ς̣
5 Κ̣ελλι[ν] τῷ
6 ἀδ̣ε̣λ̣φῷ Φιλάμμ(ωνι)
7 τ[ῷ] δ̣ρομοδαρίῳ
8 κριθῶν δημοσίῳ
9 μέτρῳ ἀρτάβας
10 τρῖς ἥμισυ, γί(νονται) (ἀρτ.) γS´,
11 ἀλλὰ πάντως ϛ ἰνδ(ικτίωνος).
12 Ἐρρῶσθαί σε
13 εὔχομαι, κύριέ μου
14 ἄδελφε, πολλοῖς χρό-
15 νοις.

7 δρομεδαρίῳ 10 τρεῖς

"To my lord brother Aniketos ... Psais, greetings, Send to Kellis to my brother Philammon the *dromedarius* three and a half artabas of barley (measured) by public measure, total 3.5 art., but absolutely (barley) of the 6th indiction. I pray for your health, my lord brother, for many years."

The upper part of this short letter is damaged; therefore it is not certain that the name of the addressee was indeed Aniketos and we cannot tell in what relationship he stood to the better known occupants of House 3; to date this name is not attested elsewhere in the Kellis documents. On the other hand, as Psais is a common name in Kellis, that does not help further in the matter of placing this letter into a context. Furthermore there seem to be at least two persons named Philammon known in Kellis; in view of the handwriting of this text the Philammon mentioned here is probably not to be identified with the Philammon who occurs in Kellis texts from ca. 300 (cf. **19.b**.2, **49**.3, 20-21 and **65**.1, 51) the family tree at p. 51), but he might be identical with the Philammon who occurs a few times in papyri dating probably from later in the same century (ca. 350), viz. **71**.36, 49, and **72**.39; cf. also **64**.2 and 13n.

7. For attestations of *dromedarii* in the papyri cf. S. Daris, *Il lessico Latino nell' greco d'Egitto*[2] (Barcelona 1991) 42 s.v.. Most attestations are connected directly with the military.

11. ἀλλὰ πάντως: cf. texts **10**.9, **17**.3 and in general F. Preisigke, *Wörterbuch* s.v. πάντως.

There is no good reason to think that one should take ἀλλὰ πάντως separately as meaning 'but (do it) absolutely' (more commonly expressed by phrasings like μὴ ἀμελήσῃς) and that the 6th indiction would be a date of this letter, though without an indication of month and day. If we were dealing with a dating one would expect this after the closing formula, ll. 12-15 (cf. **16**.6-7n.).

80: BUSINESS LETTER

(4th century)

P.Kellis inv. P. 85.F (House 3, room 6, level 4, Southeast corner). H. 10.4 x B. 8 cm. Writing parallel with the fibers, written on the back of a letter written previously and now very much faded.

1 Κυρίῳ μου ἀδελφῷ Κα-
2 πίτω(νι) Ψεναμοῦνις χαίρε̣ι̣ν̣.
3 Μὴ ἀμελήσῃς· δὸς τῷ μο-
4 [̣]ητ ἐλαίου μάρι α, ἓν, κα<τὰ>
5 τὴν συνταγὴν, ἵνα παρά-
6 `σ̣´χῃ Συρίῳ, ἢ δὸς αὐτῷ
7 ἀποσταλέν<τι> τὰς ἐπ̣ι̣σ̣τ̣ο̣λ̣ά̣[ς].
8 Ἐρρῶσθαί σε εὔχο̣μ̣α̣ι̣.

8 Ἐρρῶσθαι: σ ex θ.

"To my lord brother Kapiton sends Psenamounis greetings. Don't be neglectful; give to the mo... 1 *mari* of oil, one, according to the order, in order that he may give it to Syrios, or give the letters to him, after he has been sent. I pray for your health."

This short note, written in a rather clumsy hand by a certain Psenamounis to his 'brother' Kapiton, concerns only the conveyance of one *mari* of oil via another person who in turn has to give it to a certain Syrios, who cannot be identified.

3-4. The two letters before ἐλαίου in l. 4 can be read as ητ, but no abbreviation is visible; it is unclear what is behind μο-/[̣]ητ which must be regarded as a dative after τῷ̣.
4. For the μάριον-measure used here cf. **45**.14-15n. we have followed the following line of thought for reading the text as it is:
(a) The accusative τὴν συνταγὴν should be preceded by a preposition; as one finds κατὰ τὴν συνταγὴν in **11**.10-11 and in **74**.8-9, κα at the end of l. 4, must be part of κα<τὰ>;
(b) It is regular to find after a measure a repetition of the numeral indicating the quantity, i.e. written out as a full word and written as a letter/cipher (or, for that matter, vice versa). Now, a reading μάρια (plural) ἓν (singular) would produce an incongruity. The word μάριον may be of non-Greek origin with a Greek ending added.
5-6. Due to a scribal error, the sigma of παρά-`σ´χη at the start of line 6 was apparently first omitted, then added later on, though at the level of the preceding 5th line, where remains of a letter are still visible in the margin before τήν.

81: BUSINESS LETTER

(4th century)

P.Kellis inv. P. 92.35.D+F+G (House 3, room 11, level 4). H. 14.1 x B. 6,5 cm. Margins: at the top 1, at the left 0.5, at the bottom 2 cm. Written across the fibers; the other side of the sheet is blank. The papyrus was folded 3x vertically and horizontally.

1 Κυρ[ί]ῳ̣ μου υἱῶι
2 Ἠλίᾳ̣ Σαβεῖνος
3 χαίρειν. Τοῦ κυρίου μου
4 γαιούχου ἐλθόντος
5 ἀπὸ τῆς Αἰγύπτου
6 καὶ μὴ συνχωρή-
7 σι μο̣ι τὴν προσθήκ̣ην
8 τῆς μία̣ς̣ ἡμέρα̣ς τῆς
9 [. . .]φυλ̣ακίας μου,
10 [παρ]έξω σοι τῇ̣ προσ-
11 [. . .] . . . . . . ο̣ί̣ο̣υ̣ μ̣ί̣σ̣θ̣ . .

12 [τῶν] γεωργῶν πάντων.
13 Ἐρρῶσθαί σε
14 εὔχομαι, κ[ύ]ριέ
15 μου, πολλοῖς
16 χρόνοις.

4 γεούχου 6-7 συγχωρήσῃ 7 προσθήκην: -κ- ex corr. (or is this letter rather a clumsily written xi?)

"To my lord son Elias, Sabinus sends greetings. When my lord the landowner has come from Egypt and (if) he does not allow me the single additional day for my -- guardship, I'll provide you with --- of all the farmers. I pray for your health, my lord, for many years."

The papyrus contains a short business note from a 'father' Sabinus to his 'son' Elias in which the latter is informed about some developments related to the coming of the landlord from the Nile valley.

3ff. The syntax is confused; after an absolute genitive the writer continues with a copula καὶ followed by the subjunctive aorist συνχωρήσῃ (the spelling συνχωρήσι is only a matter of iotacism); an expected conjunction, however, (e.g., ἐὰν) is lacking, though it should have introduced a protasis before the main verb παρέξω σοι, κτλ. (l. 10).
5. For 'Egypt' cf. above **76.**16n.
9. The lacuna holds apparently only three letters, but it may be just possible to restore [ἀγρο]φυλακίας, if one assumes that gamma + rho were written in ligature; an alternative like [ὑδρο]φυλακίας may be just a bit too long.
11 This line is heavily corrected; at the end one might expect an accusative μισθόν, but the two final letters cannot be read safely.

82 - 88: MAGICAL TEXTS FROM KELLIS

82: CALENDAR OF GOOD AND BAD DAYS

(4th century)

T.Kellis inv. A/5/2 (House 3, room 1, level 1). H. 21.7 x B. 9 cm. Thickness of the board 7 mm. The writing runs across the grain of the wood. Two holes have been drilled through the right side of the board's lower part; a parallel set of holes was probably drilled through the lost part of the upper right side. Moreover, on the right hand side there are traces of collational marks on the spine edge incised at 8.4 and 11.2 cm from the bottom (for such marks, see J.L. Sharpe's discussion of wooden codices from

Kellis in E. Lalou, *Les tablettes à écrire de l'Antiquité à l'Époqe Moderne* [Turnhout 1992] 127-148, esp. 132-133 and figs 4, 5 and 13. Probably this board formed part of a codex; the fact that the text at the front side seems to start *mediis in rebus* can be explained by assuming that preceding text was written on a codex page now lost. On the left hand edge the letters AIΩ have been written; they do not show any obvious connection with the text on the front or the back of the board. Traces of more, mostly effaced text are still visible at the lower frontside of the board on the part now uninscribed. The blackened back is also inscribed, but the text does not seem to be related directly to that of the frontside. Furthermore, on this back two half circles have been carved opposite to the holes just referred to; from these carvings it may be inferred that this board was the last page of a codex and that the carvings were intended as a kind of decoration. The tablet was mentioned first in the Bulletin of the Australian Centre for Egyptology 2 (1991) 42.

Front:

1 Τῶν ἡμερῶν· τῆς Κυριακῆ[ς day numeral betw. 1 - 4, quality]
2 ε κακή, ζ σαπρά, ιβ παρατηρ(ήσεως) [·]
3 Σελήνη<ς> β σαπρά, δ κακή, θ κ̣[ακή,]
4 ιβ παρατηρ(ήσεως)· Ἄρεως α παρατ[ηρ(ήσεως),]
5 η {η} ἀνεπιτήδειος· Ἑρμοῦ[day numeral betw. 1- 5]
6 σαπρά, ϛ κακή, ι σαπρά, ιβ σα[πρά·]
7 Διὸς β σαπρά, ζ παρατηρ(ήσεως), θ παρα[τηρ(ήσεως)]
8 Ἀφροδίτης δ κακή, ϛ σαπρά, ια κακή·[. . .]
9 Κρόνου α σαπρά, γ παρατηρ(ήσεως), θ κακή, ι [σα-]
10 πρά.

11 Σεληνοδρόμιον·

12	α καλή	κγ καλή
13	β καλή	κδ καλή
14	γ κακή	κε καλή
15	δ καλή	κϛ καλή
16	ε κακή	κζ καλή
17	ϛ καλή	κη καλή
18	ζ καλή	κθ καλή
19	η καλή	λ κακή
20	θ καλή	
21	ι κακή	
22	ια καλή	
23	ιβ καλή	
24	ιγ κακή	
25	ιδ καλή	
26	ιε κακή	
27	ιϛ καλή	
28	ιζ καλή	
29	ιη καλή	
30	ιθ καλή	
31	κ καλή	
32	κα κακή	
33	κβ καλή	

Back:
34 (M.2) ΚΝΑΞ ΖΒΙΙΧΘΥ
35 ΠΤΗΣ (M.3) ΦΦΕ
36 (M.4) Προσκυνῶ καὶ ὑ-
37 μνῶ ἐκ καθαρᾶς καρ-
38 δίας καὶ εὐλ̣

(180° turned)
39 (M.2) ΚΝΑΞ̣[
40 Κ
41 (M.3) ΑΒΙΧΘ̣ΥΟΣ

"(Ll. 1-10) Of the days: Sunday, ..., 5th: bad, 7th: evil, 12th: (a matter) of observation. Monday, 2nd: evil, 4th: bad, 9th: bad, 12th: (a matter) of observation. Tuesday, 1st: (a matter) of observation, ..., 8th: unfitting. Wednesday, *n*th: evil, 6th: bad, 10th: evil, 12th: evil. Thursday, 2nd: evil, 7th: (a matter) of observation, 9th: (a matter) of observation. Friday, 4th: bad, 6th: evil, 11th: bad; Saturday, 1st: evil, 3rd: (a matter) of observation, 9th: bad, 10th: evil."

The front of this text contains:
(a) a calendar of bad weekdays, i.e. days which were unsuitable for practising certain magical actions like, e.g., consulting an oracle, etc.
(b) a calendar of good and bad days within an unspecified month. For such lists of good and bad days (cf. **83**) in Pharaonic Egypt cf. Lexikon der Ägyptologie VI 154-156, s.v. Tagewählerei; T. Hopfner, *Griechisch-ägyptischer Offenbarungszauber* I[2] (Amsterdam 1974) § 829ff. discusses the only parallel text (from London) found among the Greek papyri published to date (PGM II vii.272-284; cf. also ibidem, ll. 155-168, where the phrasing δι' ὅλης ἡμέρας (cf. **83**.4) is connected with the 8th, 10th, 12th, 13th, 15th, and 27th - 29th days as being suitable for practising magical actions. Cf. also the remarks on Petronius' *Cena* cap. 30, in H. Gerstinger - O.Neugebauer, *Eine Ephemeride für das Jahr 348 oder 424 n.Chr.* [=Pack[2] 2037] 6.

Ll. 1-10 on this wooden board (evidently used for more permanent consultation) present the following distribution of weekdays 1 - 12 within (probably the first half of) a month while various qualifications have been added. (NB: not all day numerals and qualifications have been preserved):

1	if Tuesday:	παρατηρ(ήσεως)		if Thursday:	παρατηρ(ήσεως)
	if Saturday:	σαπρά	8	if Tuesday:	ἀνεπιτήδειος
2	if Monday:	σαπρά	9	if Monday:	κακή
	if Thursday:	σαπρά		if Thursday:	παρατηρ(ήσεως)
3	if Saturday:	παρατηρ(ήσεως)		if Saturday:	κακή
4	if Monday:	κακή	10	if Wednesday:	σαπρά
	if Friday:	κακή		if Saturday:	σαπρά
	if Sunday:	κακή	11	if Friday:	κακή
6	if Wednesday:	κακή	12	if Sunday:	παρατηρ(ήσεως)
	if Friday:	σαπρά		if Monday:	παρατηρ(ήσεως)
7	if Sunday:	σαπρά		if Wednesday:	σαπρά

The adjectives for days: σαπρά (= 'evil'), κακή (= 'bad'), παρατηρ(ήσεως) (= '(a matter) of observation' i.e. depending from the actual situation as found on the day indicated), ἀνεπιτήδειος ('unfitting') are used with the following day numerals + name of the weekday:

σαπρά	κακή	παρατηρ(ήσεως)	ἀνεπιτήδειος
1 if Saturday	4 if Monday or Friday	1 if Tuesday	8 if Tuesday
2 if Monday or Thursday	5 if Sunday	3 if Saturday	
6 if Friday	6 if Wednesday	7 if Thursday	
7 if Sunday	9 if Monday or Saturday	9 if Thursday	
10 if Wednesday or Saturday	11 if Friday	12 if Sunday or Monday	
12 if Wednesday			

It remains a question why in ll. 1-10 only days 1 - 12 would have been paid attention to; no numerals higher than 12 have at least been preserved (cf. the notes to ll. 2 [maybe a numeral higher than 12 + a qualification was lost?], 8). In itself one would expect an indication of the quality of days either during the first half of a month (days 1- 15), or during the first 10 days. If, however, within the first half of a month days 13-15 were always favorable, there would be no reason to mark them in a list like this which gives only the less favorable or bad days.

1. In the lacuna there is space for the indication of one or two day numerals (preceding a 5th day, l. 2) + qualification.

2. It is just possible (but not certain) that after the indication of a 12th day and its qualification another day numeral + qualification followed in the lacuna. It is, however, also possible that the end of the line was just left open (for such an open line cf. 8n.).

3-4. It is not certain whether after the 9th day and its following [lost] qualification an another day numeral + qualification preceded the indication of the 12th day. Probably there is not enough of space for the restoration of a qualification <u>and</u> a numeral + qualification.

4-5. It is not certain whether after the 1st day another day numeral + qualification preceded the indication of the 8th day. It may be just possible to restore: παρατ[ηρ( ) (numeral betw. β-ϛ) κακή], but space in the lacuna is a bit short.
5-6. At the end of l. 5 one expects at least one day numeral between 1-5 preceding the qualification σαπρά at the start of l. 6; there may be, however, space for a numeral + κακή + another numeral preceding σαπρά. At the end of l. 6 the line may have been left open after σα[πρά, like in l. 2.
8. The end of this line may have been left uninscribed, as there is not enough of space for the restoration of both a numeral and a qualifying adjective after κακή.
10. After πρα there is a sign intended to close off this part of the text.
11. The word σεληνοδρόμιον = 'moon orbit' is an *addendum lexicis*.
12-33. These lines list days 1 - 30 within an unspecified month with their qualifications: days 3, 5, 10, 13, 15, 21, and 30 are κακή (= 'bad'), all others are καλή (= 'in order, suitable').
34-35, 39. Apparently these are attempts to write the beginning of the well-known κναξζβιχθυπτηςφλεγμωδροψ, a nonsense word for which all letters of the Greek alphabet are used; for further literature, see ZPE 50 (1983) 98.
36-38. Apparently these lines contain the start of an invocation of a god, a daemon vel sim. ("I greet you and I praise you from a pure heart and I ..."). For the use of καθαρός = 'pure', related to a person's conscience, cf. G.W.H.Lampe, *A Patristic Lexicon*, s.v. E.2. Perhaps εὐλ̣ formed the start of εὐλογῶ (fitting well after ὑμνῶ καὶ --), but the word seems to break off all of a sudden and the last letter looks like the Coptic letter SCHAI. At the same time letters of the word from l. 41 are written through that last letter.
41. Should one separate ΙΧΘ̣ΥΟΣ from the preceding AB?

83: CALENDAR OF GOOD AND BAD DAYS

(4th century)

P.Kellis inv. P. 92.22 + P. 92.35.E+G (all from House 3, room 11, level 4). H. (tapering towards the right) 6.5 x B. 17.5 cm. (approximately; the papyrus is broken between Col. I and Col. II and the exact width of the original strip cannot be established precisely). Margins: at the left 1.5, under Col. IV 2.8 cm. The writing runs parallel with the fibers. Verso empty.

Col. I

1 α´ καλή
2 β ἕως ϛ
3 γ´ ἀπ(ὸ) ϛ ἕως [ι]β
4 δ´ δι' ὅλης
5 ε καική
6 ϛ κακή

Col. II

7 ζ̄ κα̣[.]ή
8 θ καλή
9 ιβ καλή
10 ιδ καλή

Col. III
11 $\overline{\iota\varsigma}$ κ̣αλή
12 ιθ καλή
13 κα΄ καλή
15 κε καλή

Col. IV
16 $\overline{\kappa\varsigma}$ καλή
17 κθ καλή

———

V A C A T

Without any doubt this papyrus also contains a list of good and bad days, cf. **82**. While according to that text (ll. 12-33) days 3, 5, 10, 13, 15, 21, and 30 are *κακή* and all others are *καλή*, in this papyrus only days 5 and 6 are *κακή*, while the other days mentioned (1, 2, 3, 4, 9, 12, 14, 17, 19, 21, 25, 27 and 29) are completely or at least for part of the time *καλή* (the 2nd day only until the 6th hour, the 3rd day only after the 6th until the 12th hour); due to the loss of one letter the quality of day 7 is unknown. It is unclear why in this text a number of days (days 8, 10, 11, 13, 15, 16, 18, 20, 22-24, 26, 28 and 30) have been simply disregarded.

4. For the meaning of δι' ὅλης (sc. ἡμέρας) cf. **82**, introd.

84: GREEK HOROSCOPE

(373)

T.Kellis inv. A/5/198+263) is broken into three pieces. Two of them (together = # A/5/198) were found in House 3, room 6, under three meters of sand (level 3); inv. # A/5/263 came from House 3, room 1, above the floor near top step, and was covered by two meters of sand. The dimensions are H. 33 x B. 10.7 cm. Two pairs of holes have been drilled through the wood at the left hand side of the text; apparently this board formed part of a kind of notebook or was intended to do so. Thickness of the wood: 4 mm. The margin of 7 cms at the bottom contains various decorations. There are vague traces of some kind of coating of the wood, but much of the text was written directly on the wood itself. The other side of the board contains a Coptic text (to be published separately by I. Gardner and A. Alcock). For organizational purposes the Greek text published below was previously referred to as 'T.Kellis 11.A'.

1	Γ$\overline{\text{ένεσι}}$[ς] V A C A T	"Birth.
2	ΠθS/ Διοκλητιανοῦ {Θὼθ}	Year 89 of Diocletian, Thoth
3	ἀπογόμενος $\overline{\alpha}$ κατ' Αἰγυπτίους	Epagomene (?) 1, according to the Egyptians,

4	ἥ ἐστιν καθ' Ἕλληνας Παχὼν κα,	which is according to the Greeks Pachon 21,
5	ὥρα̣ ια̣ ἡμέρας·	at the 11th hour of the day.
6	ὡροσκόπος Ζυγῷ, οἶκ(ος)	Horoscopos in Libra, the House
7	Ἀφροδίτη<ς> ὁρίοις Ἑρμοῦ ,	of Venus in the terms of Mercury,
	μ(οῖραι) κβ	22 degrees;
8	Ἥλιος Ταύρῳ, οἶκ(ος) Ἀφροδί(της)	the Sun in Taurus, the House of Venus
9	ὁρίοις Ἄρεως μ(οῖραι) η,	in the terms of Mars, 8 degrees;
10	Σελήνη Λέοντι, οἶκ(ος) Ἡλίου	the Moon in Leo, the House of the Sun
11	ὁρίοις Σελήνης μ(οῖραι) ιβ,	in the terms of the Moon, 12 degrees;
12	Ἄρης Σκορπίῳ, οἶκ(ος) Ἄρεως	Mars in Scorpio, the House of Mars
13	ὁρίοις Διὸς μ(οῖραι) θ,	in the terms of Jupiter, 9 degrees;
14	Ζεὺς Καρκίνῳ, [ο]ἶκ(ος) Σελήνη[ς]	Jupiter in Cancer, the House of the Moon
15	ὁρίοις Κρόνου μ(οῖραι) ε̣,	in the terms of Saturn, 5 (? or 9?) degrees;
16	Ἀ̣φροδίτη Λέοντι, οἶκ(ος) Ἡλίου	Venus in Leo, the House of the Sun
17	ὁρίοις Ἑρμοῦ μ(οῖραι) ι,	in the terms of Mercury, 10 degrees;
18	Κρόνος Ὑδρηχόῳ, οἶκ(ος) Κρόνου	Saturn in Aquarius, the House of Saturn
19	ὁρίοις Διὸς μ(οῖραι) ιδ,	in the terms of Jupiter, 14 degrees;
20	Κλῆρ(ος) Τύχ(ης) Σκορπίῳ, οἶκ(ος)	the Lot of Fortune in Scorpio, the House of
	Ἄρεως	Mars
21	ὁρίοις Διὸς μ(οῖραι) ζ	in the terms of Jupiter, 7 degrees;
22	Ἑρμῆς Διδύμοις, οἶκ(ος) Ἑ̣ρμοῦ̣	Mercury in Gemini, the House of Mercury
23	ὁρίοις Σελήνη̣ς μ(οῖραι) [ ]	in the terms of the Moon, [-] degree(s)."

3 Or ἀπα̣γόμενος, l. ἐπαγομένη ? Numeral α ex corr. (λ?), or drawn 2x? 4 κα drawn 2x 15 or θ̣ at end? 22 Ἑρμῆς: the horizontal bar of the final sigma is much prolonged to the right, possibly drawn 2x

A first publication with a full discussion of the various problems connected with this new Greek horoscope appeared in ZPE 106 (1995) 235ff.[22] We summarize:
(a) to our knowledge it is the only Greek horoscope written on a wooden board;
(b) there is a problematic conflict between the dating according to the Alexandrian *and* the Egyptian calendar;
(c) the astronomical and astrological data given in the text present difficulties of interpretation.

22) For the subject of Greek horoscopes in general see O. Neugebauer and H. Van Hoesen, *Greek Horoscopes*, Philadelphia 1959. (Mem. Am. Philos. Soc., 48); D. Baccani, *Oroscopi Greci, Documentazione papirologica*, Messina 1992 (Ricerca papirologica, 1). See also H.G. Gundel, 'Horoskop' in Reallexikon für Antike und Christentum, XVI (Stuttgart 1993) 598-662.

Ad (a): We do not know of any other ancient horoscope written on a wooden board.[23] See ZPE, *loc.cit.* 236 and *ibidem* fn. 2.
Ad (b): Year 89 of the era of Diocletian[24] (l. 2.) '*καθ' Ἕλληνας*', i.e. according to the Alexandrian calendar, runs from 29.viii.372 - 28.viii.373; Pachon 21 (l. 4) according to the same calendar = 16.v, hence the date of the horoscope according to the *Alexandrian* calendar is **16.v.373**.

On the other hand, year 89 of the Diocletian era (l. 2.) '*κατ' Αἰγυπτίους*', i.e. according to the traditional Egyptian calendar,[25] covers the period Thoth 1/22.v.372 - Epagomene 5/21.v.373.

The dating on the board: *Θὼθ ἀπογόμενος* $\overline{α}$ (ll. 2-3) is remarkable; *ἀπογόμενος* $\overline{α}$ strongly reminds us of *ἐπαγομένη* (sc. *ἡμέρα*) *α*, the first of the five epagomenal days which are added traditionally to the month of Mesore (preceding Thoth![26]).

Some kind of error in our text seems probable.[27] If Thoth 1 'Egyptian style' (= 22.v.372) should be the equivalent of Pachon 21 'Greek style' (= 16.v.373), there would be a remarkable conflict between the Egyptian and the Alexandrian calender in

[23]) A useful survey of the use of wood for various writing purposes and a list of publications of wooden boards known from Graeco-Roman Egypt was published by W.M. Brashear and F.A.J. Hoogendijk in Enchoria 17 (1990) 21-54 (add now to the list, e.g., the tablets published in P.Brook. 27-31, and the astronomical T.Amst. inv. 1, published in CdE 52 [1977] 301ff. and recently discussed in CdE 68 [1993] 178f.; add also Bodl.Gr.Inscr. inv. 4, cf. Pack^2 2710); for the subject in general cf. also E. Lalou, *Les tablettes à écrire de l'Antiquité à l'époque moderne*, Turnhout 1992 (Bibliologia, 12), esp. 127-149, where J.L. Sharpe III discusses the Dakhleh Tablets and gives some codicological considerations. The excavations at Ismant-al-Kharab have yielded many wooden boards and fragments thereof (see, besides Dr. Sharpe's article, also the photos in JSSEA 17 [1987] pl. XXI-XXIII.a; JSSEA 19 [1989] pl. II and BACE 2 [1991] pl. 8), i.e. in Area A House 1 yielded one board, House 2 yielded two complete codices [an Isokrates codex and the so-called 'Harvest (earlier: Farm) Account Book' (see Sharpe, *loc.cit.*)] and six boards, while House 3 produced two books (one [inv. A/5/53B] of five boards, with only one board [= two pages] inscribed; see the remarks in BACE 2 [1991] 42-43 and the publication by I. Gardner in Orientalia 62 [1993] 36-59) and 32 (partly fragmentarily preserved) boards; from House '4' came 39 (partly fragmentarily preserved) boards. Finally, Area B yielded one board (described JSSEA 17 [1987] 167 + Pl. XXIII.a), while Area D produced four boards.

[24]) Cf. R.S. Bagnall - K.A. Worp *The Chronological Systems of Byzantine Egypt*, Zutphen 1978, Chapt. 7 (Studia Amstelodamensia ad epigraphicam, ius antiquum et papyrologicam pertinentia, VIII); cf. also L.S.B. MacCoull & K.A. Worp, *The Era of the Martyrs*, in "*Miscellanea Papyrologica in occasione del bicentenario dell' edizione della Charta Borgiana*" (edd. M. Capasso, G. Messeri Savorelli, R. Pintaudi), Firenze 1990, 375-408. (Papyrologica Florentina XIX 2). A list of addenda and corrigenda to this article will be published in Analecta Papyrologica.

[25]) For the survival of this calendar into Roman Egypt and its use until ca. A.D. 400 cf. D. Hagedorn - K.A. Worp, *Das Wandeljahr im römischen Ägypten*, ZPE 104 (1994) 243-255; in the period A.D. 371-375 the Egyptian calendar was 99 days ahead of the Alexandrian calendar.

[26]) In numerous cases one encounters the phrasing *Μεσορὴ ἐπαγομένων* + numeral between '1' - '5' ('6' only in an Egyptian leap year). We do not know of any authoritative modern source according to which the Egyptian year is supposed to start with the epagomenal days rather than with Thoth, but cf. the expression *Θὼθ ἐπαγομένων* + numeral, found only in a few ostraka from Upper Egypt, i.e. O.Sarga 209, 349-354 = SB XVIII 13403, 13531-13536 (we owe these references to the kindness of D. Hagedorn); the editor of these texts does not express an opinion on the remarkable phenomenon.

[27]) Note that in SB XVIII 13531.3 *Θὼθ* was cancelled.

our horoscope. Under normal circumstances, at any rate, ἐπαγομένη α in year 89 of the Diocletian era would be, then, according to the *Egyptian* calendar the equivalent of **17.v.373** in our calendar.

It must be admitted that a radical cancelling of Θώθ in our text and the assumption of a spelling error ἀπο- for ἐπα- and a gender error -γόμενος for -γομένη are, especially if taken together, rather irritating and that, even if one accepts this, there would be still a discrepancy of 1 day left between 17.v.373 'Egyptian style' and 16.v.373 'Alexandrian style'; on balance, however, we regard that as less problematic than a discrepancy of more than a full year, the more so as we have other reasons to assume that the author of this text was not very competent.

ad (c): For a discussion of the more technical aspects of **84**, see ZPE, *loc.cit.* 237ff., where it is argued that the technical astronomical skill of the author of the horoscope was, to say the least, limited.

From a comparison of the planetary positions in **84** with those calculated for 16.v.373 A.D. (see the Table) it is clear that the agreement is quite poor. As there is hardly any reason to assume that the date given in **84** is not the correct one, one must assume that the author of this text was not very competent.

TABLE:[28] Planetary positions of **84** compared to positions calculated for the date in the text

	84	16.v.373, 4 pm
Sun	8 Taurus	25 Taurus
Moon	12 Leo	4 Virgo
Mercury	-- Gemini	8 Taurus
Venus	10 Leo	3 Cancer
Mars	9 Scorpio	21 Taurus
Jupiter	5/9 Cancer	5 Pisces
Saturn	14 Aquarius	9 Aquarius
Horoscopus	22 Libra	22 Libra

[28]) Dates are Julian dates and time is Mean Local Time. Positions are calculated for a location at longitude 30 degrees East of Greenwich and geographical latitude 25 degrees North.

85.a, 85.b: TWO FRAGMENTS OF A MAGICAL FORMULARY

(Fourth century)

P.Kellis inv. P.92.35.B, Frr. I and II (House 3, room 11, level 4). Two fragments of the same physical appearence, both written by the same semi-literary hand along the fibers on the recto (versos blank), both containing short magical prescriptions. The pieces were found together and have virtually identical dimensions. So we must be dealing with remnants of the same roll or folded sheet.

It seems very likely that the amulet **87** was copied directly from the prescription **85.b**.17ff. Everything but the heading of the fragmentary charm in the formulary occurs also in the amulet — most notably the elsewhere unattested *vox magica* *Σεσεμφθα* at the beginning. Furthermore, if **85.b**.17-18 are restored with the wording of the amulet, equal length of line results. It is hardly due to mere chance that both papyri were found in the same room 11 in House 3, the findspots differing only in that the formulary is from level 4, the amulet from level 3.

Applied charms were regularly copied from formularies: *Suppl.Mag.* I 46 - 51, e.g., are all applied love charms that resemble PGM IV 335-433, though none of them was copied from the Great Paris Magical Handbook itself, but rather from similar exemplars. Thanks to the controled excavation at Ismant al-Kharab/Kellis we have the unique situation of an applied amulet turning up next to its physically same formulary exemplar.

85.a. P.Kellis inv. P.92.35.B, Frag. I: H. 11.5 x B. 2.8 cm. Margins: at the left 0.7, at the bottom 0.8 cm. Writing parallel with the fibers, verso blank. Parts of three magical prescriptions. Of the first, survives only the end consisting of magical characters. The second probably began with π̣[ρός in esthesis (l. 2), as does the third (l. 6).

1 Figurae magicae

2 ̣[
3 *λαβὼν π[*
4 *γράψον ἐν ζ̣[*
5 *τὸν δῖ(να) ὃν ἔτε̣[κεν ἡ δῖ(να)*

———

πρ[ὸς
7 *σεραμικκη[*
8 *κοπ̣φιη [*
9 Βηλ Βηλ *ια* ̣[
10 *κ·κν·φθη[*
11 Figurae magicae

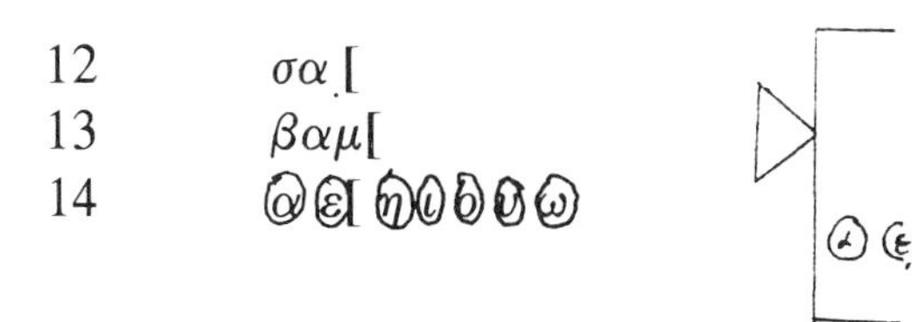

12 σα̣[

13 βαμ[

14

15 ἀπάλλαξον [

16 τοῦ μεγάλ[ου

5 δεῖνα bis 10 κ·κν·φθη Pap.

2. Probably π̣[ρός, unless the surviving stroke is from a magical sign in the preceding line. If so, the prescription began further to the right.

3-4. λαβὼν π[- - - | γράψον ἐν ζ̣[: perhaps λαβὼν π[ιττάκιον - - - | γράψον ἐν ζ̣[μυρνομέλανι. Cf. PGM XXXVI 264-267 λαβὼν αἷμα νυκτιβαοῦτος καὶ ζ μ υ ρ ν ό μ ε λ α ν, ὁμοῦ τὰ δύο μίξας, γράφε καινῷ καλάμῳ τὸ ζῴδιον, καθὼς περιέχι, εἰς π ι τ τ ά κ ι ο ν καθαρόν. Perhaps π[ιττάκιον was qualified with an adjective such as καθαρόν (PGM XXXVI 267, just cited) or ἱερατικόν (PGM IV 3142, VII 412). For ἐν ζ̣[μυρνομέλανι 'with ink', cf. PGM IV 3199 σκευῇ μέλανος, ἐ ν ᾧ δεῖ γράφειν and VIII 69-73 ἔστι τὸ μέλα[ν], ἐ ν ᾧ γράφεις - - - ἐ ν τ ο ύ τ ῳ γράφε. On instrumental ἐν, see Blass-Debrunner-Funk, *A Greek Grammar of the New Testament* § 219.

5. τὸν δῖ(να) ὃν ἔτε̣[κεν ἡ δῖ(να): 'N.N., whom (mother) N.N. bore'. On this standard formula, see D.R. Jordan, Philologus 120 (1976) 127-132. Cf. below, note on l. 15, and **85.b**.19n.

9. Βηλ Βηλ: grecized 'Baal, Baal'. Cf. PGM IV 1010 Βαλ Βηλ and *Suppl.Mag.* I 39.9 Βηλ Βαλ.

ιᾳ: the last letter probably not an omega; perhaps a damaged δ.

12-14. A *tabula ansata* enclosed three probably short lines consisting of *voces magicae* and, probably, the seven vowels. To the right of the *tabula ansata* may have been text or *figurae magicae*. On the use of the *tabula ansata* in magical texts, see R. Kotansky, Getty Museum Journal 11 (1983) 175-176; cf. *Suppl.Mag.* I 10.3-7.

12-13. σα̣[| βαμ[: possibly the familiar pair σαλ̣[αμαξα | βαμ[εαζα or variants; cf. C. Bonner, *Studies in Magical Amulets Chiefly Graeco-Egyptian* (Ann Arbor 1950) p. 96 and D 50, 192, 271, 284, 286, 396; A. Delatte - Ph. Derchain, *Les entailles magiques gréco-égyptiennes* (Paris 1964) 322-324; *Suppl.Mag.* I 10.3-5.

14. The seven Greek vowels represented the seven planets (see, e.g., H.G. Gundel, *Weltbild und Astrologie in den griechischen Zauberpapyri* [Münchener Beiträge 53, 1968], 41-52). The circles in which the vowels are drawn probably represent the planetary spheres (σφαῖραι, κύκλοι); see *Der Kleine Pauly* IV s.v. Planeten [E. Boer], esp. col. 883; also F. Boll - C. Bezold - W. Gundel, *Sternglaube und Sterndeutung* (Leipzig/Berlin 1931[4]), pp. 44, 118-119.

15. ἀπάλλαξον [: probably ἀπάλλαξον [τὸν δῖ(να) ὃν ἔτεκεν ἡ δῖ(να), then possibly mention of the ailment from which the patient should be healed. Parallels for ἀπαλλάσσειν in magical formularies and applied charms are gathered in R. Kotansky, *Greek Magical Amulets. The Inscribed Gold, Silver, Copper and Bronze Lamellae* I (Pap.Col. XXII.1, 1994) 52.116-17 commentary

16. τοῦ μεγάλ[ου: certainly a divine epithet. Perhaps from ὅτι δοῦλός ἐστι] | τοῦ μεγάλου θεοῦ, as in **87**.3-4. It could also be that a verb of swearing (ὁρκίζω or a compound) was followed by κατὰ | τοῦ μεγάλ[ου and then, e.g., θεοῦ (with or without a qualifier such as τοῦ ἐν οὐρανῷ) or one or more names of the deity.

85.b. P.Kellis inv. P.92.35.B, Frag. II: H. 11.7 x B. 2.7 cm. Margins: at the top: 1, to the left 0.5 cm. Parts of two prescriptions separated by paragraphus at ll. 15-16. The writer also used paragraphus at ll. 3-4 and 19-20, but in these places apparently not to indicate the beginning of a new charm, but rather to separate sections of the same charms. Only the purpose of the first prescription is preserved, *πρὸς ῥιγοπ[ύρετον*. The accusative object that followed certain or likely *πρός* in **85.a**.2,6 and in **85.b**.16 probably also indicated an ailment, though one cannot exclude mention of a bodily organ (*Suppl.Mag.* II 94.22, *πρ(ὸς) ὀφθαλμούς*), the patient(s) (*Suppl.Mag.* II 94.17, *πρ(ὸς) δαιμονιαζομένου[ς*, 96 A.48: *πρὸς γενοῦσαν*) or the goal (*Suppl.Mag.* II 94.7, *πρ(ὸς) εὐτ[ο]κίαν*).

1 πρὸς ῥιγοπ[ύρετον
2 ἐν ἡμέρα̣ ̣[
3 εαε [

————

4 ηηη ̣[
5 ιιι ̣[
6 ooooo ̣[
7 υυυυυυ [
8 ωωωωωωω [
9 ωυοιηε [
10 υοιηεω [
11 οιηυ̣ε [
12 ωοιη [
13 ωυο [
14 ωυ [
15 ω ̣[

————

16 πρὸς [
17 Σεσεμφθα ̣[
18 θον δαίμονα [
19 ἀπάλλαξον τ̣ο̣[

————

20 λιθαβιοχ[
21 υιεδ ισαχ σ ̣[

21 *υιεδ* ex *γυεδ* ?

1. *ῥιγοπ[ύρετον* or, less likely, *ῥιγοπ[υρέτιον*, cf. *Suppl.Mag.* II, Index V, p. 309 s.vv.
1-15. There was text to the right of the narrow column of vowels in ll. 3-15, where the papyrus breaks off, leaving only a few traces of initial letters at the edge. It might have consisted of a continuation of the Greek text in lines 1-2. The traces in ll. 3-15 could also be from magical vowels, words or characters.
3-15. For the various vowel combinations given here cf. *Suppl.Mag.* II, Index IX.
2. *ἐν ἡμέρα̣ ̣[*: before the break is a curve that suits omikron, sigma or omega, but hardly the belly of an alpha. If the prepositional phrase can be understood without what preceded or followed, it probably means 'by day' and refers either to an affliction that occurs by day or to a iatromagical procedure that should be carried out by day.

16-19. For commentary, see **87**, which was probably copied from this prescription (see introd. to **85.a** - **b**). What is preserved in lines 17-19 corresponds to **87** as follows: Σεσεμφθα ὑποκάτω ζωτρα Θερμοῦθιν σαρχαθον δαίμονα ὑποκάτω τῶν σπερμάτων ιαηγαρ | ἀπάλλαξον τὸν Παμοῦριν ὃν ἔτεκεν ἡ Λο ὅτι δοῦλός ἐστιν τοῦ | μεγάλου θεοῦ. This suggests for the formulary:

17 Σεσεμφθα ὑ̣[ποκάτω ζωτρα Θερμουθιν σαρχα-]
18 θον δαίμονα [ὑποκάτω τῶν σπερμάτων ιαηγαρ]
19 ἀπάλλαξον τὸ̣[ν δῖ(να) ὃν ἔτεκεν ἡ δῖ(να) ὅτι δοῦλός ἐστιν τοῦ]
19a? [Vacat μεγάλου θεοῦ]

There is ample space between extant lines 19 and 20 for τοῦ μεγάλου θεοῦ to have been written far to the right of the *paragraphos*. An indented l. 19a, rather than forcing the issue, might explain why τοῦ μεγάλου θεοῦ is indented far to the right in **87**.4, where the writer had sufficient space at normal line beginning.

17-18. --- | θον δαίμονα: if not σαρχα | θον δαίμον, then the copyist of **87** made a mistake and the formulary might have had well-known Ἀγα | θὸν Δαίμονα, on whom see *PW-RE Suppl.* III, coll. 37-59, s.v. Agathosdaimon (J. Fischer); D. Wortmann, Bonner Jahrb. 166 (1966) 87-90; *Lexikon der Ägyptologie* I, col. 94 s.v. Agathos Daimon (P. Derchain).

19. [- - - ἡ δῖ(να) - - -]: probably the papyrus had an angular *spiritus asper* above the eta, cf. **87**.3, ἡ λο.

20. λιθαβιοχ: there is some space between θ and α, so perhaps λιθ αβιοχ. But since the amount of space is not decisive, perhaps one should separate βιοχ, cf. PGM XIX.a.34 β̣ι̣ω̣χ βιωχ.

21. ισαχ: perhaps Ἰσαχ = Ἰσακ: there is space on either side, and the preceding magical word may have been punctuated with a high point; cf. **85.a**.10. The biblical name is certain and common in magical texts when accompanied by Abraham and Jacob (cf. e.g. PGM XII 287 τὸν Ἀβρααν, τὸν Ἰσακ, τὸν Ἰακκωβι, and see J.M. Rist, *The God of Abraham, Isaac and Jacob. A Liturgical and Magical Formula*, Journal of Biblical Literature 57 (1938) 289-303; R. Kotansky, *Greek Magical Amulets*, I 52.71-73n.). Here we would have an instance of Isaac either alone or in less direct connection with Abraham and/or Jacob, cf. PGM I 219-220 Ἀβρααμ θαλχιλθοε ελκωθωωηη αχθωνων σα Ἰσακ, IV 1216 σαησι· ἴσαχ χοη, IV 1376-1377 Ἀωθ Ἀβαωθ βασυμ Ἰσακ Σαβαωθ Ἰαω Ἰακωβ (cf. *Suppl.Mag.* II 87.10-11 and note ad loc.).

After Ἰσαχ either σε̣[or σθ̣[.

86: FEVER AMULET

(4th century)

P.Kellis inv. P. 78.H (House 3, room 6, level 3). H. 16.6 x B. 12.2 cm. The upper margin measures 2.5 cm. The writing is faded. The main text is inscribed along the fibers, but angels' names and magical signs are written in the margins against the fibers. The papyrus was folded horizontally in the middle (where it is now broken) and four times vertically. A series of cracks along the right side suggest that the papyrus might also have been rolled. The verso is blank.

The text contains a detail of linguistic interest. The word τελετή, which normally means 'rite', is used for the amulet itself.[29] This provides a parallel for the semantic development of *τέλεσμα* from 'rite' to 'amulet',[30] from which (probably through Arabic *ṭilsam*) we have the modern word 'talisman'.[31]

1 ω ω ω̣ ω [ω] ω ω
2 υ [υ] υ̣ υ̣ υ̣ υ
3 ο ο ο ο ο
4 ι [ι ι ι]
5 η [η η]
6 ε [ε]
7 α
8 Θ Α Ν Α̣ `Λ̣´ Β̣ Λ̣ Α Ν Α Θ
9 α
10 ε ε
11 η η η
12 ι ι ι ι
13 ο ο ο ο ο
14 υ υ υ υ υ υ
15 ω ω ω̣ ω ω {`ω´} ω ω

16 ἀπάλλαξον ᾿Ε̣λα̣ κην τὴν̣ φοροῦσαν
17 τὴν ἁ̣γί̣αν τα̣ύ̣την τελετὴν τριταίῳ̣
18 τεταρταίῳ̣ ἀμφημερινοῦ νυκτερινοῦ.

17 *τὴν*: -*η*- ex *υ* corr., *τριταίου* 18 *τεταρταίου*

In the left margin: ΡΑΦΑΗΛ, ΜΙΧΑΗΛ (at 180°).
In the right margin: ΟΥ̣Ρ̣Ι̣ΗΛ, ΓΑΒΡΙΗΛ (at 180°), figurae magicae.

3. Between the 4th and 5th omikron is a stain, stray ink or a deletion.
8. Θ Α Ν Α Λ Β Λ Α Ν Α Θ: cf. the common magical name and palindrome ᾿Αβλαναθαναλβα (on which see *Suppl.Mag*. I 9.1-7 comm.).
16. Ε̣λα̣ κη or perhaps Α̣λα̣ κη: the unread letter is γ, λ, or τ. The name does not seem to be attested in House 3 and it may be new altogether. For the phrasing *τὴν φοροῦσαν κτλ*. cf. the similar phrasing in the mostly illegible magical amulet P.Kellis inv. 92.35.b (House 3, room 11, level 4; H. 6.3 x B. 14 cm.) which reads in ll. 5ff.: *φέρον̣τα̣ το̣ῦ̣τ̣ο̣ Πα̣μ̣ο̣ῦ̣ρ ὃν ἔτεκ̣ε̣[ν* | *ἀ̣π̣ὸ̣ τ̣ρ̣ι̣τ̣α̣ί̣ο̣υ̣ α* TRACES *ου ἀπὸ κα̣[* | *ἤδη ἤδη ταχὺ ταχύ*.
17. *τελετὴν*: see the remarks in the introduction to this text with fn. 1.
17-18. *τριταίου, τεταρταίου, ἀφημερινοῦ, νυκτερινοῦ*: for the ellipsis of *πυρετοῦ* cf., e.g., LSJ s.vv. *τριταῖος, τεταρταῖος*.

87: FEVER AMULET

(4th century)

P.Kellis inv. P.92.191 (=A/5/284; House 3, room 11, level 3). H. 2.5 x B. 17.3 cm. The papyrus has been evenly cut away at the top and both sides, while it is unevenly torn away at the bottom. The writing runs parallel with the rough fibers on what is apparently the true verso. The smoother back (the true recto) is blank.

This applied charm is strikingly similar to **85.b**.17ff. and might have been copied directly from that part of that formulary (see intr. and comm. to **85.b**). As **85.b**.17-19 might have continued into ll. 20-21, it could be that the present amulet, which is torn away along the bottom, continued for a line or two on a now lost strip of the papyrus. It is also possible that the papyrus, as now preserved, is complete. In this case, the amulet's dimensions (about 7:1) would be comparable to a number of other extremely oblong amuletic papyri (see *Suppl.Mag.* I 31 introd.).

1 *Σεσεμφθα ὑποκάτω ζωτρα̣ Θερμουθιν σαρχαθον δαίμονα ὑ-*
2 *ποκάτ̣ω τῶν σπερμάτων· ιαηγαρ*
3 *᾿Απάλλαξον τὸν Παμοῦριν ὃν ἔτεκεν ἡ Λο, ὅτι δοῦλός ἐστιν τοῦ*
4 V A C A T [..] *μεγάλου θεοῦ̣*

3 *ἡ* Pap. 4 *θεου*: -*ε*- ex corr. (*υ*?)

1. *Σεσεμφθα*: attested only here and in **85.b**.17; perhaps from Egyptian sšm-Ptḥ = 'image of Ptah' (H.J. Thissen). The element *σεσεμ*- calls to mind the beginning of magical *Σεσενμενουρες* (*Suppl.Mag.* I 45.27) and of frequently occurring magical *Σεσενγερ Βαρφαραγγης* (cf. *Suppl.Mag.* I 10.2n.; II Index VI, s.v.).

ὑποκάτω ζωτρα̣· 'below *zotra*'? Cf. 1-2 *ὑποκάτω τῶν σπερμάτων*. As *zotra* is probably not an Egyptian equivalent of *τῶν σπερμάτων*, it may be a non-Greek (presumably Egyptian) word for a place or a place-name.

Θερμοῦθιν: this is grecized Renenutet, an Egyptian goddess of fertility and vegetation who was depicted as a snake or as a woman with a snake's head; see H. Bonnet, *Reallexikon der ägyptischen Religionsgeschichte* (Berlin 1952) pp. 803-805 s.v. Thermuthis; *Lexikon der Ägyptologie* V 232-236, s.v. Renennutet (C. Beinlich-Seeber). In PGM IV 2387 and VII 782, *θερμοῦθις* appears to be used as a common noun for a snake. As a personal name *Θερμοῦθις* occurs a number of times among the Greek documentary Kellis papyri (cf. the index nominum).

σαρχαθον δαίμονα: cf. **85.b**.17-18 comm.

1-2. *ὑποκάτω τῶν σπερμάτων*: 'below the seeds'. Apparently there is no parallel for this. The phrase might suit Thermouthis as goddess of vegetation.

2. It is just possible that one should read *ιαηγαρα̣*, though we might be dealing with discoloration rather than ink at the end of the line.

3. *ἡλο*: *spiritus asper* almost certainly copied from the formulary.

4. The personal name *Παμοῦρ(ις)* occurs frequently in Kellis (specifically in at least two generations of inhabitants of House 3, cf. the family tree at p. 51), but mother Lo cannot be fitted into the family tree as yet. As Dr. I. Gardner informs us, the name 'Lo' is borne by women in at least two Coptic letters from Kellis, P. 9 and P. 45. The name *Λο* may occur in P.Aberd. 72.A, recto.6 (*Λο Δανιηλ*, if the proposal in

BL 3 p. 2 is correct), where the sex is not certain. The similar Λω is a woman's name in SB III 6200 (*ἅμα* Λω *bis*) and a man's name in P.Erl. 127 (*ἄπα* Λω).

3-4. *ὅτι δοῦλός ἐστιν τοῦ μεγάλου θεοῦ*: the same formula is perhaps to be restored in **85.a**.15-16. Cf. PGM XII 71 *ὅτι δοῦλός εἰμι τοῦ ὑψίστου θεοῦ*, XIII 637 *ὅτι δοῦλός εἰμι σὸς καὶ ἱκέτης*, P. 5a.10-11 *ὅτι δούλη ἐστιν τοῦ θ(εο)ῦ τοῦ ζῶντος*.

88: CHRISTIAN AMULET

(4th century)

T.Kellis inv. A/5/193 (House 3, room 8, level 4, North wall). H. 23.8 x B. 9.8 cm. For organizational purposes the board was referred to previously as 'T.Kellis 10'.

The surviving prayer occupies one side of the present board (side A). The writing has faded away in most of ll. 1-5. Side A also shows traces of an earlier text that was washed away before the prayer was written. *After* the prayer was written, the right-hand side of the tablet was bored with two pairs of drill holes (each 0.5 cm).[32] On the same right-hand side are two V-shaped collational marks on the spine edge incised at 9.7 cm and 14.8 cm from the top. The pairs of holes and the collational marks suggest that the tablet was to be attached to one or more others so as to form a small notebook.[33]

Also side B bore writing, but nothing is legible now. Perhaps, as on side A, a text was washed away, and the writer of the prayer regarded side B as blank. It is also possible that the writer of side A also wrote on side B, but that here the writing has faded away almost entirely, just as it has in most of the first lines of side A. The position of the holes to the right of the surviving text suggests that the prayer is the back of the tablet if we imagine it in a notebook.

1 χει TRACES
2 δεσπότας TRACES
3 θ(εὸ)ς αἰ̣ώνιος TRACES
4 κ(υρίο)υ TRACES
5 θες τ̣ὴν̣ χ̣ε̣ῖ̣ρ̣ά̣ σ̣ο̣υ̣ τ̣ὴν̣
6 κραταιάν/, τὸν βραχί̣ο̣-
7 νά σου τὸν ὑψηλό̣ν̣, τ̣ὸ̣ν̣
8 πλήρη ἰάσεως/ καὶ ὁλο-
9 κληρίας/, τὸν πλήρη
10 δυνάμεως/ καὶ ζωῆς·
11 χώρισον ἀπ' αὐτοῦ/ πᾶ-
12 σαν νόσον/ καὶ πᾶ-
13 σαν μαλακίαν/ καὶ
14 πᾶν πν(εῦμ)α ἀσθενίας/,
15 ὅπως τοῦ ἐλαίου<ς> σου

16 τυχόντες/ δυνήθω-
17 σιν/ τὰς ἡμέρας τῆς ζω-
18 ῆς αὐτῶν/ σοι λατρεῦ-
19 σαί/, σοὶ εὐχαριστῆσαι/, ὅ-
20 τι σὺ εἶ ὁ σωτὴρ ἡμῶν/
21 καὶ καταφυγὴ/ καὶ β<ο>ηθ<ὸς>
22 τῆς ἀντιλήμψεως
23 ἡμῶν/, ὅτι δέδοτ̣α̣ι̣
24 καὶ ὑψῶται/ τὸ παν̣άγι̣<ον> [ὄ-]
25 νομά σου εἰς τοὺς αἰῶνας
26 τῶν αἰώνων.

8 ϊασεως Tab. 14 ἀσθενείας 15 ἐλέους 23 ὅτι ex corr. 24 ὕψωται Tab.

"(Ll. 2ff.) Masters - - - eternal God - - - of the Lord - - - your mighty hand, your lofty arm, full of healing and well-being, full of power and life. Keep away from him every disease and every infirmity and every spirit of illness, so that having received your mercy men can worship and thank you (all) the days of their lives. For you are our Savior and refuge and helper of our assistance, for your all-holy name has been given and is exalted for ever and ever."

The use of Old and New Testament passages characterize this as a 'Christian' (rather than a specifically 'Manichaean') text. The text is a protective amulet against disease for a single individual, cf. ll. 11-14 χώρισον ἀπ' αὐτοῦ πᾶσαν νόσον κτλ. The command is linked to a *captatio benevolentiae* consisting of an appeal to God's own interests:[34] "so that having received your mercy men can worship and thank you for all the days of their lives" (ll. 15-19).

The prayer ended with the concluding "for ever and ever" formula in ll. 25-26 (with a short line 26). The first lines of side A, however, are not necessarily the beginning of the prayer: it might have continued from illegible side B.

For prayers such as the following one, see C. Wessely, *Les plus anciens monuments du Christianisme* II, (Patrologia Orientalis XVIII.3, [Paris 1924; repr. Turnhout 1974]) Chapt. IV (pp. 424-450) and the list of J. van Haelst, *Catalogue des Papyrus littéraires juifs et chrétiens* (Paris 1976), Chapt. VII (pp. 263-330, nos. 720 - 1063; cf. esp. the wooden tablets nos. 744, 860, 1037). See also the Christian texts in PGM II pp. 209-232 and in *Suppl.Mag.* I 20-36.

Oblique strokes separate phrases of various length as in a number of other Christian literary texts; see Pap.Flor. XVIII 9 introd. and G. Bastianini, *Wiener Studien* N.F. 18 (1984) 196-199.

Why was the amulet written on a board of a notebook? As the person to be protected will not have worn it like a normal amulet (see the remarks made by W.M. Brashear in Enchoria 17 [1990] 23), some possible explanations are: (i) the formula was to be recopied onto a sheet of papyrus and then worn; (ii) the amulet was supposed to serve its protective function in the notebook itself, wherever the owner took it; (iii) the board was separated from the notebook and fastened to the wall of a room.

An immediate link between the board and the inhabitants of House 3 cannot be established; it does not provide sufficient evidence to maintain that the inhabitants of this house were 'Christians' rather than 'Manichaeans'.

NB: Just before going to print we received the new publication by R. Roca-Puig, *Anàfora de Barcelona: I altres pregàries* (Barcelona 1995), where p. 99 a text much similar to our **88** is printed. We hope to explore the consequences of this identification elsewhere.

5. *θες*: *θὲς* (imp.) or compound thereof? (In view of the Barcelona text probably *ἐπίθες*).
5-7. *τ̣ὴ̣ν̣ χ̣ε̣ῖ̣ρ̣ά̣ σ̣ο̣υ̣ τ̣ὴ̣ν̣ κραταιάν, τὸν βραχί̣ο̣ | νά σου τὸν ὑψηλό̣ν̣*: cf. e.g. LXX Deut. 3.24 *τὴν χεῖρα τὴν κραταιὰν καὶ τὸν βραχίονα τὸν ὑψηλό̣ν̣*, and Hatch-Redpath, *Concordance* I s.v. *βραχίων*. For the hand and arm of God as symbols of his might, see Kittel, *ThWbNT* I and IX s.v. *βραχίων* and *χεῖρ*.
7-9. *τ̣ὸ̣ν̣ πλήρη ἰάσεως καὶ ὁλοκληρίας*: cf. e.g. Just.Mart., *De Resurr.* 590C (Corp.Apol. 3, p. 222 Otto) *τὰς ἀσθενείας τῆς σαρκὸς ἰάσατο καὶ ὁλόκληρον ἐποίησε τὸ σῶμα*.
9-10. *τὸν πλήρη δυνάμεως καὶ ζωῆς*: for the collocation of *δύναμις* and *ζωή*, cf. e.g. Greg.Nyss., *Contra Eunomium* III.1, 49 (vol. 2, p. 18 Jaeger). *ἀλλ' ὁ ἐν τῇ ἀϊδιότητι τῆς πατρικῆς θεότητος εἶναι νοούμενος ἀεὶ ἐν αὐτῷ ἐστι, δύναμις ὢν καὶ ζωὴ καὶ ἀλήθεια καὶ φῶς καὶ σοφία καὶ τὰ τοιαῦτα*.
11-13. *πᾶσαν νόσον καὶ πᾶσαν μαλακίαν*: NT Matth. 4.23 (*θεραπεύων πᾶσαν νόσον καὶ πᾶσαν μαλακίαν ἐν τῷ λαῷ*) is used also in the Christian amulets PGM P4 ii.14-iv.4; P5.b.25-27; *Suppl.Mag.* I 30.3 (see comm.); 31.2; 33.2-4.
14. *πὰν πν(εῦμ)α ἀσθενείας*: cf. NT Luc. 13.11, *γυνὴ πνεῦμα ἔχουσα ἀσθενείας*, and see Kittel, *ThWbNT* I s.v. *ἀσθένεια* esp. p. 491.
15. *ἐλαίου<ς> σου*, r. *ἐλέους σου*: standard Judaeo-Christian 'mercy' (*ἔλεος*) is probably obscured by simple phonetic mistakes. It is not likely that the reading of the board is correct and that one should understand metaphorical *ἔλαιον* as a play on *ἔλεος* (cf. G.W.H. Lampe, *Patristic Greek Lexicon*, s.v. *ἔλαιον*, II.K,4).
15-19. *τυχόντες δυνήθωσιν τὰς ἡμέρας τῆς ζωῆς αὐτῶν*: the unexpressed plural subject is 'men' (*οἱ ἄνθρωποι*); see Blass-Debrunner-Funk, *A Greek Grammar of the New Testament* § 130 (2).
16-18 *τὰς ἡμέρας τῆς ζωῆς αὐτῶν σοὶ λατρεῦσαι*: cf. Greg.Naz., *Liturgia Alexandrina* (ed. Migne, Patrol.Graeca 36, col. 701) *ἀξίωσον ἡμᾶς ἐν καθαρῷ συνειδότι λατρεῦσαί σοι πάσας τὰς ἡμέρας τῆς ζωῆς ἡμῶν*.
19-23. *ὅτι σὺ εἶ ὁ σωτὴρ ἡμῶν καὶ καταφυγὴ καὶ β<ο>ηθ<ὸς> τῆς ἀντιλήμψεως ἡμῶν*: this is reminiscent of Psalm 17.3, *κύριος στερέωμά μου καὶ καταφυγή μου καὶ ῥύστης μου, ὁ θεός μου βοηθός μου, καὶ ἐλπιῶ ἐπ' αὐτόν, ὑπερασπιστής μου καὶ κέρας σωτηρίας μου, ἀντιλήμπτωρ μου* and Psalm 90.2, *ἀντιλήμπτωρ μου εἶ καὶ καταφυγή μου* (+ *ὁ θεός μου, βοηθός μου*). The addition in Psalm 90 is found in several manuscripts and most of the papyri that contain it (see R.W. Daniel, *Vigiliae Christianae* 37 [1983] 403, comment to l. 7). Due to its contents, Psalm 90 was the most frequently used Psalm in protective amulets, see Supp.Mag. I 26.6-8 comm. In the present passage *β<ο>ηθ<ὸς> τῆς ἀντιλήμψεως ἡμῶν*, 'helper of our assistance', seems to be redundant and unparalleled. Perhaps the writer or his source was freely adapting Scripture.

89: MEDICAL PRESCRIPTION

(4th century)

P.Kellis inv. P. 61.B (House 3, room 8, level 4). H. 9 x B. 11. cm. Margins: at the right hand side 5, at the left hand side 1, at the top 2, and at the bottom 2.8 cm. The writing runs parallel with the fibers, the verso is blank.

1	Traces	(ο̣ὐ̣γ̣κ̣ί̣α̣) α̣
2	*π̣ι̣π̣έρ̣εως*	(ο̣ὐ̣γ̣κ̣ί̣α̣) α̣
3	TRACES	(οὐγκία) α
4	*ζμύρνης*	(οὐγκία) α
5	*καδμείας*	(οὐγκία) α̣

The papyrus is extremely fragile, but the occurrence of cadmia and myrrh seems to suggest that these ingredients were intended for an eyesalve. For the subject of Greek medical prescriptions preserved on papyrus, see H. Harrauer - P.J. Sijpesteijn, *Medizinische Rezepte und Verwandtes* (Vienna 1981; = MPER N.S. XIII); for eyesalves and their ingredients, see especialy *ibidem*, texts ## 3, 4, 5 and 8; cf. also BASP XVIII (1981) 1ff. and M.-H. Marganne. *L'ophthalmologie dans l'Egypte gréco-romaine d'après les papyrus littéraires grecs*, Leiden 1994 (=Studies in Ancient Medicine, 8). For the Coptic documentation on eye salves, see W.C. Till, *Die Arzneikunde der Kopten* (Berlin 1951) 14-19.

90: SCHOOL EXERCISE

(4th century)

T.Kellis inv. A/5/220 (House 3, room 6, level 4). H. 5.3 x B. 5.8 cm. Thickness 3 mm. The writing on both sides stands perpendicular to the grain of the wood. Most of the coating on the backside has gone and a considerable part of the writing has gone as well.

Frontside:

1	Ἀργυρ(ίου) ταλ(άντων) (μυριὰς) α
2	(ὧν) ἐπικερ(δίας)
3	τάλ(αντα) ασ
4 (M.2)	Μῆνας δύο·

2 L: Pap.

"1 Myriad (=10,000) tal(ents) of silver, of which for interest 1200 tal(ents); two months."

Backside:

5 ἔσχον ....
6 Χοιὰκ δ̣——
7 ἐλαίου χ( ) β̣.

"I received ... Choiak 4 -- 2 ch(ous?) of oil."

While the backside of this wooden board seems to contain only a short statement concerning receipt of a certain quantitity of oil, its front side contains a calculation exercise: a pupil is asked to calculate, how much of time is needed for obtaining an interest at 1200 Talents from a capital of 10,000 Talents. The answer '2 months' presupposes that the interest level used here was 6 % per month or 72 % per year. This is significantly higher than the interest rate assumed to be normal in the 4th century; for this subject cf. also **40** - **47**, introd.

2. A resolution of the symbol 'L:' as '(ῶν)' is abundantly paralleled.
4. This line was written between two lines incised into the wood. Apparently these lines indicated the place where the pupil was supposed to write his answer. There is a third, spare line incised at a lower level; in the present case this serves no particular function.
7. Apparently the abbreviation χ( ) indicates a container of liquids. One may think of resolving χ(οῦς), but maybe also of χ(ῶρον) (for this measure cf. words like *μονόχωρον*, *δίχωρον*, *τρίχωρον*, *τετράχωρον*); for questions of metrology as far as measures of liquids are concerned, still see U. Wilcken's fundamental remarks in WO I 757ff.

WORD INDICES

I: EMPERORS

Probus or Aurelian?
(A.D. 273/4 or 279/80?)
εS´´: **62**.1

Diocletian, Maximianus, Constantius, Galerius
(A.D. 293/4)
Τοῦ κυρίου ἡμῶν Γαίου Αὐρηλίου Οὐαλερίου Διοκλητιανοῦ καὶ τοῦ κυρίου ἡμῶν Μάρκου Αὐρηλίου Οὐαλερίου Μαξιμιανοῦ Αὐτοκρατόρων Καισάρων Γερμανικῶν μεγίστων Σαρματικῶν μεγίστων καὶ τῶν κυρίων ἡμῶν Φλαουίου Οὐαλερίου Κωνσταντίου καὶ Γαλερίου Οὐαλερίου Μαξιμιανοῦ ἐπιφανεστάτων Καισάρων Εὐσεβῶν Εὐτυχῶν Σεβαστῶν: **1**.1-7 (yrs 9-8-1 or 10-9-2)

τὴν οὐράνιον τύχην τῶν κυρίων ἡμῶν Διοκλητιανοῦ καὶ Μαξιμιανοῦ <*Σεβαστῶν*> *καὶ Κωνσταντίου καὶ Μαξιμιανοῦ τῶν ἐπιφανεστάτων Καισάρων*: **2**.5-6

(A.D. 298/9)
(ἔτους) ιε καὶ ιδ καὶ ζ: **19.b**.3

(A.D. 303/4)
(ἔτους) κ, ιθS´ καὶ (ἔτους) ιβ τῶν κυρίων ἡμῶν Διοκλητιανοῦ καὶ Μαξιμιανοῦ καὶ Κωνσταντίου καὶ Μαξιμιανοῦ Σεβαστῶν τῶν ἐπιφανεστάτων Καισάρων: **49**.14-18

(A.D. 293-305)
(ἔτους) - τῶν κυρίων ἡμῶν Διοκλητιανοῦ καὶ Μαξιμιανοῦ Σεβαστῶν καὶ Κωνσταντίου καὶ Μαξιμιανοῦ τῶν ἐπιφανεστάτων Καισάρων: **19.a.App**.21-22

Constantius I, Galerius, Severus, Maximinus
(A.D. 305/6)
(Ἔτους) ιδ´ τῶν κυρίων ἡμῶν Κωνσταντίου καὶ Μαξιμιανοῦ Σεβαστῶν καὶ (ἔτους) β´ τῶν κυρίων ἡμῶν Σεουήρου καὶ Μαξιμίνου τῶν ἐπιφανεστάτων Καισάρων: **31**.25-28

ιδS´ καὶ βS´: **31**.35

Galerius, Severus, Maximinus, Constantinus I
(A.D. 306/7)
(Ἔτους) ιεS// καὶ γS// καὶ αS// τῶν κυρίων ἡμῶν Μαξιμιανοῦ καὶ Σεουήρου Σεβαστῶν καὶ Μαξιμίνου καὶ Κωνσταντίνου τῶν ἐπιφανεστάτων Καισάρων: **40**.12-14

Constantius II, Constantius III (Gallus)
(A.D. 352)
τὸν παντοκράτορα Θεὸν καὶ τὴν εὐσέβειαν τῶν πάντα νικώντων αἰωνίων δεσποτῶν: **24**.5-6
τὴν θείαν καὶ οὐράνιον τύχην τῶν πάντα νικώντων δεσποτῶν ἡμῶν Αὐγούστου *τε καὶ* Καίσαρος: **23**.27

II: CONSULS

(A.D. 293)
Ὑπατείας Διοκλητιανοῦ *τὸ ε´ καὶ* Μαξιμιανοῦ *τὸ δ´* Σεβαστῶν: **1**.7-8 (see n.)

(A.D. 301)
Ὑπατείας Ποστουμίου Τιτιανοῦ *καὶ* Οὐιρίου Νεπωτιανοῦ: **2**.1

(A.D. 308)
Ὑπατείας *τῶν δεσποτῶν ἡμῶν* Διοκλητιανοῦ *πατρὸς τῶν βασιλέων τὸ ι´ καὶ* Γαλερίου Οὐαλερίου Μαξιμιανοῦ Σεβαστοῦ *τὸ ζ´*: **36**.11-12

(A.D. 310)
Ὑπατείας Στατίου Ἀνδρονίκου *καὶ* Πομπηίου Πρόβου *τῶν λαμπροτάτων ἐπάρχων τοῦ ἱεροῦ πραιτωρίου*: **41**.20-21

(A.D. 315)
Ὑπατείας *τῶν δεσποτῶν ἡμῶν* Κωνσταντίνου *καὶ* Λικιννίου Σεβαστῶν *τὸ* δS/: **34**.19-20

(A.D. 320)
Ὑπατείας *τῶν δεσποτῶν ἡμῶν* Κωνσταντίνου Σεβαστοῦ *τὸ ς´ καὶ* Κωνσταντίνου *τοῦ ἐπιφανεστάτου* Καίσαρος *τὸ α´*: **37**.15-16; **52**.8-9; cf. also **51**, palaeographical descr.
ὑπατείας τῆς προκειμένης (A.D. 320?): **51**.8

(A.D. 321)
Μετὰ *τὴν ὑπατείαν τῶν δεσποτῶν ἡμῶν* Κωνσταντίνου Σεβαστοῦ *τὸ ς´ καὶ* Κωνσταντίνου *τοῦ ἐπιφανεστάτου* Καίσαρος *τὸ α´*: **21**.23-25

(A.D. 324)
Τέταρτον *μέλλουσιν ὑπάτοις*: **22**.2; **56**.3

(A.D. 328)
Ὑπατείας Φλαουίων Ἰανουαρίνου *καὶ* Οὐεττίου Ἰούστου *τῶν λαμπροτάων*: **59**.1-3

(A.D. 331)
Μετὰ τὴν ὑπατείαν Φλαυίου Γαλλικανοῦ *καὶ* Αὐρηλίου Συμμάχου *τῶν λαμπροτάτων*: **29**.1-2
Ὑπατείας Ἰουνίου Βάσσου *καὶ* Φλαουίου Ἀβλαβίου *τῶν λαμπροτάτων*: **4**.17-18

(A.D. 332)
Μετὰ τὴν ὑπατείαν Ἰουνίου Βάσσου *καὶ* Φλαουίου Ἀβλαβίου *τῶν λαμπροτάτων*: **57**.2-4

(A.D. 333)
Ὑπατείας Φλαυίου Δελματίου *ἀδελφοῦ τοῦ δεσπότου ἡμῶν* Κωνσταντίνου Αὐγούστου *καὶ* Δομεττίου Ζηνοφίλου *τῶν λαμπροτάτων*: **38.a**.19-21; **38.b**.19-20

(A.D. 335)
Ὑπατείας Ἰουλίου Κωνσταντίνου *πατρικίου ἀδελφοῦ τοῦ δεσπότου ἡμῶν* Κωνσταντίνου Αὐγούστου *καὶ* Ῥουφίου Ἀλβίνου *τῶν λαμπροτάτων*: **13**.12

(A.D. 337)
Ὑπατείας Φλαυίου Φηλικιανοῦ *καὶ* Τεττίου Τιτιανοῦ *τῶν λαμπροτάτων*: **58**.4

(A.D. 352)
Ὑπατείας *τῶν δεσποτῶν ἡμῶν* Κωσταντίου Αὐγούστου *τὸ ε´ καὶ* Κωσταντίου *τοῦ ἐπιφανεστάτου* Καίσαρος *τὸ α*/: **24**.9-10

(A.D. 353)
Ὑπατείας *τῶν δεσποτῶν ἡμῶν* Κωνσταντίου Αὐγούστου *τὸ ς´ καὶ* Κωνσταντίου *τοῦ ἐπιφανεστάτου* Καίσαρος *τὸ β*/: **23**.30

(A.D. 355)
Μετὰ τὴν ὑπατείαν Κωνσταντίου Αὐγούστου *τὸ ζS*/ *καὶ* Κωνσταντίου *τοῦ ἐπιφανεστάτου* Καίσαρος *τὸ γS*/: **48**.16-17

(A.D. 356)
Ὑπατείας *τῶν δεσποτῶν ἡμῶν* Κωνσταντίου Αὐγούστου *τὸ η´ καὶ* Κλαυδίου Ἰουλιανοῦ Καίσαρος *τὸ α*/: **14**.1-3

(A.D. 357)
Ὑπατείας *τῶν δεσποτῶν ἡμῶν* Κωνσταντίου Αὐγούστου *τὸ θ´ καὶ* Κλαυδίου Ἰουλιανοῦ Καίσαρος *τὸ δεύτερον*: **15**.17-19

(A.D. 362)
Ὑπατείας Μαμερτίνου *καὶ* Νεβουιέττα *τῶν λαμπροτάτων*: **8**.13

(A.D. 363)
῾Υπατείας τοῦ δεσπότου ἡμῶν ᾿Ιουλιανοῦ του αἰωνίου Αὐγούστου τὸ δ/ καὶ Φλαουίου Σαλλουστίου τοῦ λαμπροτάτου ἐπάρχου τοῦ ἱεροῦ πραιτωρίου: **30**.1-2

(A.D. 364)
Μετὰ <τὴν> ὑπατείαν ᾿Ιουλιανοῦ τὸ δ´ καὶ Φλαυίου Σαλουστίου τοῦ λαμπροτάτου ἐπάρχου τοῦ ἱεροῦ πραιτωρίου: **42**.28-30
῾Υπατείας ᾿Ιουανοῦ καὶ Βαρωνιανοῦ παιδὸς αὐτοῦ: **32**.17-18

(A.D. 369)
῾Υπατείας τῶν δεσποτῶν ἡμῶν Οὐαλεντινιανοῦ Νέου τοῦ ἐπιφανεστάτου καὶ Φλαουίου Οὐίκτορος τοῦ λαμπροτάτου: **33**.23-26

(A.D. 374?)
[῾Υπατείας τοῦ] δεσπότου ἡμῶν [Γρατιανοῦ? τοῦ αἰωνίου] Αὐγούστου τὸ γ κ[αὶ Φλ. ᾿Εκυτίου ? τοῦ λαμπροτάτ]ου: **43**.32-34

(A.D. 382)
Μετὰ τὴν ὑπατείαν Εὐχερίου καὶ Συαγρίου τῶν λαμπροτάτων: **44**.19

(A.D. 386)
῾Υπατείας τοῦ δεσπότου ἡμῶν ῾Ονωρίου τοῦ ἐπιφανεστάτου Καίσαρος καὶ Εὐοδίου τοῦ λαμπροτάτου: **45**.24-26

(A.D. ?)
-- τοῦ λαμπροτάτου κόμιτος: **3**.6
ὑπατείας τῆς προκειμένης (A.D. 320?): **51**.8

III: MONTHS, DAYS AND HOURS

(a) Months

῾Αθὺρ α — **32**.18; **38.a**.21; **38.b**.21
῾Αθὺρ κ — **62**.24
τῇ πρὸ -- Καλανδῶν — **1**.8-9
πρὸ —] Εἰδῶν Φεβραρίων — **22**.2-3
πρὸ δ Εἰδῶν ᾿Ιουλίων, ὅ ἐστιν ᾿Επεὶφ ιη κατ᾽ ῞Ελληνας — **41**.22
᾿Επείφ νεομηνία — **45**.13
᾿Επεὶφ γ — **19.a.App**.22
᾿Επεὶφ ιη κατ᾽ ῞Ελληνας — **41**.22

Ἐπεὶφ κ **77**.30

Θὼθ καθ' Ἕλληνας **8**.13

Θὼθ ιγ **62**.15

Μεσορή **2**.9

Μεχεὶρ κ **42**.18, 31

Μεχεὶρ κε κατ' Αἰγυπτίους **34**.20

Παῦνι η **49**.19

Παῦνι **45**.30

Παχὼν α **44**.11, 20

Παχὼν β **31**.28

Παχὼν ε **62**.11

Παχὼν ς **78**.10

Παχὼν ιγ (?) **17**.4

Παχὼν κ κα[τ' **37**.17

Παχὼν κζ **30**.2

Παχὼν - **19.b**.4

Τῦβι β **4**.18

Τῦβι ια **21**.25

Τῦβι κ **62**.28

Τῦβι λ κατ' Αἰγυπτίους **46**.11-12

Φαμενὼθ [γ?] κατ' Αἰγυπτίους **33**.27

Φαμενώθ **57**.4

Φαρμοῦθι - **59**.3; **62**.6

Φαῶφι δ **51**.8; **52**.10

Φαῶφι ς **47**.10

Φαῶφι ιη κατ' Αἰγυπτίους **41**.31

Φαῶφι κ **62**.20

Χοιὰκ δ **90**.6

Χοιὰκ ιβ **62**.1

Χοιὰκ - **47**.11

[month] β **31**.35

(b) Days

Ἄρεως **82**.4

Ἀφροδίτης **82**.8

Διός **82**.7

Ἑρμοῦ **82**.5

Κρόνου **82**.9

Κυριακή **82**.1

νεομηνία **45**.13; **46**.11 (?)

Σελήνης **82**.3

Days by numeral only:

α **82**.12; **83**.1
β **82**.13; **83**.2
γ **82**.14; **83**.3
δ **82**.15; **83**.4
ε **82**.16; **83**.5
ς **82**.17; **83**.6
ζ **82**.18; **83**.7
η **82**.19
θ **82**.20; **83**.8
ι **82**.21
ια **82**.22
ιβ **82**.23; **83**.9
ιγ **82**.24
ιδ **82**.25; **83**.10
ιε **82**.26
ις **82**.27
ιζ **82**.28; **83**.11
ιη **82**.29
ιθ **82**.30; **83**.12
κ **82**.31
κα **82**.32; **83**.13
κβ **82**.33
κγ **82**.12
κδ **82**.13
κε **82**.14; **83**.14
κς **82**.15
κζ **82**.16; **83**.15
κη **82**.17
κθ **82**.18; **83**.16
λ **82**.19

(c) Hours

ς **83**.2, 3
ιβ **83**.3

IV: INDICTIONS

γ ἰνδικτίων **16**.6
δ ἰνδικτίων **17**.5
ε ἰνδικτίων **78**.10

ϛ ἰνδικτίων	**79**.11
ζ ἰνδικτίων	**30**.2 (νέα); **42**.18-19
ια ἰνδικτίων	**44**.12
ιβ ἰνδικτίων	**10**.16; **18**.10
ιε ἰνδικτίων	**45**.12-13, 16-17, 31
- ἰνδικτίων	**43**.12, 34

V: PERSONAL NAMES

br. = brother of; ch. = child of; d. = daughter of; f. = father of; grf. = grandfather of; grs. = grandson of; s. = son of; w. = wife of; w/o = without

Ἀγαθήμερος	**69**.3
Ἄγαθος	**37**.9.a
Ἀγάπη	**74**.6-7 (cf. also s.n. Ταγάπη)
Ἀγάπη, w. Παχουμῶν, m. Αὐρ. Ψενπνοῦθης	**30**.3
Ἀθηνοδώρα	**19**.**a**.**App**.2, 16
Ἀθηνόδωρος	cf. s.n. Ἰούλιος Ἀθηνόδωρος
Αἰωνιανός	**16**.2
Ἀκοῦτις, f. Σόις	**21**.6
Ἀκοῦτις, f. Ἀμπέλιος	**24**.14
Ἀλέξανδρος, f. Ψάις	**60**.9
Ἀλιτοῦς, f. Αὐρ. Πεκῦσις, Πεβῶς, Παχοῦμις	**13**.1 (cf. also s.n. Παλιτοῦς)
Ἀμμώνιος	**10**.3; **11**.3; **23**.29; **65**.42
Ἀμμώνιος f. Πετεχῶν	**69**.17
Ἀμοῦν(ις)	**28**.6
Ἀμπέλιος, s. Ἀκοῦτις	**24**.14
Ἀνδρέας	**71**.10; cf. also Αὐρήλιος Ἀνδρέας
Ἀνδρόμαχος	cf. Αὐρήλιος Ἀνδρόμαχος
Ἀνίκητος	**79**.2
Ἀνου( )	**7**.23
Ἀντωνῖνος	cf. Αὐρήλιος Ἀντωνῖνος
Ἀπολλ.[	**1**.16
Ἀπολλ( ), f. Καταϊ( )	**61**.7
Ἀπολλόδωρος	cf. Αὐρήλιος Ἀπολλόδωρος
Ἀπόλλων, f. Αὐρ. Ἀνδρόμαχος	**25**.4
Ἀπόλλων, f. Μαρ[ ]α	**61**.11
Ἀπολλώνιος, f. Αὐρ. -ων	**56**.8
Ἀπολλῶς, s.(?) Ἀφροδι( ), f. Ναρσ( )	**61**.9

Ἁρποκράτης	cf. Αὐρήλιος Ἁρποκράτης
Ἁρποκρατίων, f. Αὐρ. Τιμόθεος	**8**.17
Ἁρποκρατίων	**7**.3, 25; **23**.6-7, 8, 10
Ἀρσένιος	**64**.10
Ἄρων	**74**.1, 32, 35
Ἀσκληπιάδης	cf. s.n. Φλάουιος Δομιτιος Ἀσκληπιάδης
Ἁτρῆς	**24**.2
Αὐρηλία Ἱερακίαινα Τασηχθισος, d.(?) Καπίτων	**41**.1, 23 (w/o Τασηχθισος, Καπίτων)
Αὐρηλία Μάρσις	**32**.1, 18-19
Αὐρηλία Σοφία, d. Βησᾶς & Τα....ς	**42**.6
Αὐρηλία Τακῦσις	**37**.1, 18 (cf. also s.nn. Τακοσε, Τεκοσε)
Αὐρηλία Ταοῦπ	**13**.1, 6, 21
Αὐρηλία Τατοῦπ, w. Αὐρ. Ψάις	**8**.1, 14
Αὐρηλία Ταψάις	**40**.1, 16
Αὐρήλιος Ἀμ.[.....]	**35**.3
Αὐρήλιος Ἀνδρέας	**45**.34-35
Αὐρήλιος Ἀνδρόμαχος, s. Ἀπόλλων	**25**.4
Αὐρήλιος Ἀντωνῖνος	**44**.3
Αὐρήλιος Ἀπολλόδωρος	**19.a**.5; **19.a.App**.4-5, 24
Αὐρήλιος Ἁρποκράτης	**58**.8
Αὐρήλιος Βησᾶς	**6**.11
Αὐρήλιος Γενᾶ, s. Οὐῶνσις	**18**.1; **23**.2, 31
Αὐρήλιος Γενᾶ, s. Παταιᾶς	**76**.33-34
Αὐρήλιος Γενειλος ....ν	**24**.14
Αὐρήλιος Δημοσθένης, s. Πολυκράτης	**8**.18
Αὐρήλιος Ἑρμοκλῆς	**49**.26-27
Αὐρήλιος Ἡλιόδωρος, s. Ὧρος	**13**.20
Αὐρήλιος Ἡρακλῆς, s. Ψάις	**14**.8
Αὐρήλιος Ἡρώδης	**20**.1
Αὐρήλιος Ἰακὼβ, s. Βῆσις	**32**.20
Αὐρήλιος Καλλικλῆς	**3**.10
Αὐρήλιος Καπίτων, s. Καπίτων	**45**.1, 27, 38
Αὐρήλιος Καπίτων, s. Κόραξ	**24**.15
Αὐρήλιος Κλεόβουλος	**25**.1
Αὐρήλιος Λιλοῦς	**47**.1
Αὐρήλιος Νικαντίνοος	**29**.7, 9 (w/o Αὐρήλιος)
Αὐρήλιος Οὐαλέριος, s. Σαραπίων	**48**.2, 18
Αὐρήλιος Π[..........	**4**.2
Αὐρήλιος Παμῖνις	**24**.11
Αὐρήλιος Παμοῦρ, s. Παμοῦρ & Τακοσε	**42**.1, 31 (w/o metronymic), 40 (w/o Αὐρήλιος, metronymic)

Αὐρήλιος Παμοῦρ(ις), s. Ψάϊς	**19.b**.1; **20**.3; **21**.3, 25; **24**.15; **41**.3, 23 (w/o patronymic); **50**.1 (w/o Αὐρήλιος)
Αὐρήλιος Παμοῦρ, s. Ψάϊς, grs. Παμοῦρ	**33**.3-4
Αὐρήλιος Παυσανίας, s. Οὐαλέριος	**4**.1, 19; **38.a**.1, 9 (w/o Αὐρήλιος, Οὐαλέριος), 22; **38.b**.1, 9 (w/o Αὐρήλιος, Οὐαλέριος), 22
Αὐρήλιος Παχοῦμις, s. Ἀλιτοῦς, br. Αὐρ.Πεκῦσις and Πεβῶς	**13**.1, 5 (w/o Αὐρ., patronymic), 17
Αὐρήλιος Πεβῶς	**43**.38
Αὐρήλιος Πεβῶς, s. Ἀλιτοῦς, br. Αὐρ. Πεκῦσις and Παχοῦμις	**13**.1, 4 (w/o Αὐρ., patronymic), 6 (w/o Αὐρ., patronymic), 15 (w/o patronymic)
Αὐρήλιος Πεβῶς, s. Παμοῦρ	**39**.2
Αὐρήλιος Πεβῶς, s. Τιθοῆς	**24**.13; **42**.37; **44**.23-24
Αὐρήλιοι Πεκῦσις, s. Ἀλιτοῦς	**13**.1, 4 (w/o Αὐρ., patronymic), 5 (w/o Αὐρ., patronymic), 13 (w/o patronymic)
Αὐρήλιος Πεκῦσις, s. Ψάϊς and Ταπολλῶς, grs. Παμοῦρ	**44**.1, 21 (w/o metronymic, papponymic), 27 (w/o Αὐρήλιος, metronymic, papponymic)
Αὐρήλιος Πετεχῶν	**31**.29, 41
Αὐρήλιος Πι[ ]ιωνος	**41**.29-30
Αὐρήλιος Πιπέρισμι	**49**.1, 20
Αὐρήλιος Πλουτογένης	**58**.5
Αὐρήλιος Πολυκράτης, s. Ὧρος	**58**.7
Αὐρήλιος Σαραπάμμων	**13**.16
Αὐρήλιος Σαραπάμμων, s. Ψάϊς	**24**.12-13
Αὐρήλιος Στώνιος, s. Τεπνάχθης	**13**.14
Αὐρήλιος Σύρος, s. Βησᾶς	**24**.20
Αὐρήλιος Σύρος, s. Ψάϊς	**45**.4
Αὐρήλιος Τιβέριος	**3**.1
Αὐρήλιος Τιθέριος, s. Ὡρπατῶς	**50**.9
Αὐρήλιος Τιθοῆς, br. Αὐρ. --	**24**.14
Αὐρηλίος Τιθοῆς, s. Πετῆσις	**8**.2; **9**.2
Αὐρήλιος Τιμόθεος, s. Ἁρποκρατίων	**8**.16
Αὐρήλιος Τιμόθεος, s. Τιβέριος	**3**.11
Αὐρήλιος Τιμόθεος, s. Τιμόθεος	**24**.16
Αὐρήλιος Τις	**24**.22
Αὐρήλιος Τοῦ, s. Βησεπώνυχος	**34**.1, 21, 27 (w/o Αὐρήλιος)
Αὐρηλίος Φαυστιανός	**21**.1
Αὐρήλιος Φιβίων	**21**.26
Αὐρήλιος Φιλάμμων	**49**.3, 20-21
Αὐρήλιος Φιλοσαρᾶπις ὁ καὶ Μίκκαλος	**25**.2
Αὐρήλιος Φοιβάμμων ὁ καὶ Τριφιόδωρος	**13**.18, 22

Αὐρήλιος Ψάις	**37**.23
Αὐρήλιος Ψάις, s. Παμοῦρ & Τεκῦσις, f. Παμοῦρ, grf. Ὧρος	**30**.5, 10, 22; **32**.6 (w/o Τεκῦσις etc.); **38.a**.2; **38.b**.2 (both w/o Τεκῦσις etc.)
Αὐρήλιος Ψάις, s. Πεκῦσις, grs. Παλιτοῦς, husb. Τατοῦπ	**8**.1, 14
Αὐρήλιος Ψάις, s. Πετε[	**3**.8
Αὐρήλιος Ψάις, s. Πετεμῖνις	**15**.2-3
Αὐρήλιος Ψάις, s.(?) Τρυφάνης	**24**.11
Αὐρήλιος Ψάις, s. Ψύρος	**33**.1, 28 (w/o Ψύρος), 30 (w/o Αὐρήλιος, Ψύρος)
Αὐρήλιος Ψάις ..δ[. .]ιος	**34**.25
Αὐρήλιος Ψεκῆς	**48**.10 (w/o Αὐρ.), 20
Αὐρήλιος Ψεναμοῦνις, s. Πετοσῖρις	**52**.13
Αὐρήλιος Ψενπνοῦθης	**24**.11
Αὐρήλιος Ψενπνοῦθης, s. Παχουμῶν & Ἀγάπη	**30**.3, 11, 24
Αὐρήλιος Ὡρίων	**14**.4
Αὐρήλιος Ὡρίων, s. Τιμόθεος	**8**.19
Αὐρήλιος Ὧρος, s. Μέρσις	**34**.2, 21; **38.a**.10 (w/o Αὐρήλιος, patronymic); **38.b**.10 (w/o Αὐρήλιος, patronymic); **51**.3; **52**.2; **57**.5; cf. also s.n. Ὧρος, s. Μέρσις
Αὐρήλιος Ὧρος, s. Παμοῦρ & N.N., grs. Αὐρ. Ψάις s. Παμοῦρ & Τεκῦσις	**30**.4-5, 7 (only Ὧρος), 22
Αὐρήλιος Ὧρος, s. Σύρος	**13**.1, 6 (w/o Αὐρήλιος), 19 (w/o patronymic)
Αὐρήλιος --]δης, s. Σαρμάτης	**30**.23
Αὐρήλιος .....οπ	**52**.1, 11
Αὐρήλιος -ρίων, s. Τιθοῆς, br. Αὐρ. Πεβῶς	**24**.13
Αὐρήλιος -ων, s. Ἀπολλώνιος	**56**.8
Αὐρήλιος --, s. Βησᾶς s. Ψάις	**24**.14
Αὐρήλιος --, s. -]ης	**39**.1
Αὐρήλιος --, s. Θεόδωρος	**35**.1
Αὐρήλιος --, s. Κόραξ	**3**.6
Αὐρήλιος --, s. Πασαιτ.[.] & Τσενεντῆρις	**2**.4
Αὐρήλιος --, s. Τιθοῆς, br. Τιθοῆς	**14**.6-7; **24**.13
Αὐρήλιος --, s. Ὧρος s. Μέρσις	**9**.1
Αὐρήλιος --	**3**.1, 11; **18**.3; **34.App**.1, 2; **36**.13, 16; **37**.2, 9, 22; **39**.20; **40**.1, 15, 20; **47**.2; **56**.4
Ἀφροδι( ), f.(?) Ἀπολλῶς, grdf. (?) Ναρσ( )	**61**.9

Βημοφάνης	**75**.15
Βῆς, s. Δημήτριος	**60**.4
Βησᾶς, s. Σῦρος	**72**.46
Βησᾶς, s. Ψάις	**24**.14
Βησᾶς, f. Αὐρ. Σοφία, husb. Τα....ς	**42**.6
Βησᾶς, f. Αὐρ. Σῦρος	**24**.20
Βῆσας	cf. Αὐρήλιος Βησᾶς; Ψενοῦφις (ὁμοίως) ὁ καὶ Βῆσας
Βησεπώνυχος, f. Αὐρ. Τοῦ	**34**.1, 21, 27
Βῆσις, f. Αὐρ. Ἰακῶβ	**32**.20
Βήσις	**30**.13
Γάιος	**5**.22
Γελάσιος	**7**.22; **16**.2; **29**.3
Γενᾶ	**5**.3, 29; **6**.2, 54; **23**.10; **24**.8; cf. also Αὐρήλιος Γενᾶ
Γενᾶ, s. Πακῦσις, f. N.N. (d.)	**23**.25
Γενᾶ, s. Παταιᾶς	**7**.2, 26
Γενᾶ / Ἰενᾶ, s. Φιλυς	**62**.2, 16, 24
Γενᾶ, f. Πινοῦτα	**24**.18
Γενᾶ, f. Πινούθης	**3**.9
Γενειλος	cf. Αὐρήλιος Γενειλος
Γερμανός, f.-ς	**19**.**a**.**App**.6
Δημήτριος, f. Βῆς	**60**.4
Δημοσθένης	**11**.7; cf. also Αὐρήλιος Δημοσθένης
Δομίτιος	vide Φλάουιος Δομίτιος Ἀσκληπιάδης
Ἐ̣λα κη	**86**.16
Ἑρμογένης	**23**.26
Ἑρμοκλῆς	cf. Αὐρήλιος Ἑρμοκλῆς
Ἔρως, f. Σαραπόδωρος	**23**.25
Εὐμάθιος	**78**.1, 12
Ευτρόπιος	cf. Septimius Eutropius
Εὐτυχής, s. Φαριᾶς, f. Ψάις	**60**.3
Ἐχεύς (?)	**53**.4
Ἠλίας	**39**.7; **75**.4, 35; **78**.6
Ἠλίας, s. Σαβεῖνος	**81**.2
Ἠλίας, s. Φάις	**68**.1
Ἠλίας, f. Τιθοῆς	**60**.11
Ἡλιόδωρος, f. Ὧρος	**66**.27; cf. also Αὐρήλιος Ἡλιόδωρος
Ἡράκλειος	**69**.7
Ἡρακλῆς	cf. Αὐρήλιος Ἡρακλῆς
Ἡρκουλανός	cf. Οὐαλέριος Ἡρκουλανός
Ἡρώδης	cf. Αὐρήλιος Ἡρώδης
Ἡρωδιανός	**53**.2
Ἡρ̣ ̣νιος, s. Θεόδωρος	**30**.17

Θατμε[	**12**.31
Θεόγνωστος	**67**.2; **71**.9; **72**.9
Θεόδωρος, f. Αὐρ. N.N.	**35**.1
Θεόδωρος, f. Ἡρ..νιος	**30**.17
Θεότιμος	**23**.24
Θερμοῦθις, d. Παπνούθιος	**61**.6
Θέων	**28**.4
Ἰακῶβ	**61**.2; cf. also Αὐρήλιος Ἰακῶβ
Ἰενᾶ / Γενᾶ, s. Φιλυς	**62**.2, 16, 24
Ἱερακ[	**39**.18
Ἱερακίαινα	cf. Αὐρηλία Ἱερακίαινα
Ἱλαρι-	**12**.30
Ἱλαρία, slave of Αὐρ. Οὐαλέριος	**48**.3
Ἰούλιος Ἀθηνόδωρος	**19.a**.1 (?)
Ἰσιδ( ), ch. Παπνούθιος	**61**.13
Ἰσίδωρα, d. Ἰωάννης	**61**.12
Ἰσίων	**67**.19
Ἰωάννης f. Ἰσιδώρα	**61**.12
Καλλικλῆς, s. Σύρος	**60**.5; cf. also Αὐρήλιος Καλλικλῆς
Καλλικλῆς, f. Πεβῶς	**24**.19
Καμέ	**71**.48
Καπίτων	**47**.3; **71**.39; **76**.7; **80**.1-2; cf. also Αὐρήλιος Καπίτων
Καπίτων, f.(?) Αὐρ.Ἱερακίαινα Τασηχθισος	**41**.1
Καπίτων, f. Αὐρ.Καπίτων	**45**.1
Καταϊ( ), ch. Ἀπολλ( )	**61**.7
Κέλε, s. Πατσῖρε, f. Ψάις	**50**.3, 13
Κλεόβουλος	cf. Αὐρήλιος Κλεόβουλος
Κλωδιανός	**74**.15
Κλώδιος (ὁμοίως), i.e. br. Μάρων	**24**.17
Κοπρία	**61**.4
Κόραξ	**23**.24
Κόραξ, f. Αὐρ. --	**3**.6
Κόραξ, f. Αὐρ. Καπίτων	**24**.15
Λαβουατος, grf. Παχοῦμις	**23**.24
Λέων	**17**.2; **23**.24
Λιλοῦς	cf. Αὐρήλιος Λιλοῦς
Λο	**87**.3
Λούδων, f. Τιμόθεος	**24**.12
Λούδων, s. Λ[	**24**.12
Μακάριος	**10**.8; cf. also Φλάουιος Μακάριος
Μαξιλλάριος (?)	**53**.5
Μαρ[.]α, d. Ἀπόλλων	**61**.11

Μαρία	**71**.42, 48, 50, 52
Μάρσις	cf. Αὐρηηλία Μάρσις
Μάρων, br. Κλώδιος (?)	**24**.17
Μέρσις, f. (Αὐρ.) ῟Ωρος	**9**.1; **34**.2; **38**.**a**.10; **38**.**b**.10; **51**.3; **52**.2; **57**.5
Μίκκαλος	vide Αὐρήλιος Φιλοσαρᾶπις ὁ καὶ Μίκκαλος
Μουσαῖος, f. -ίδης	**51**.9
Μύρων, s. Πεβῶς, grds. Σαρᾶς	**60**.7
Ναρσ( ), s. Ἀπολλῶς, grds.(?) Ἀφροδι( )	**61**.9
Νεῖλος	**17**.11
Νεστόριος	**72**.46
Νικαντίνοος	cf. Αὐρήλιος Νικαντίνοος
Ὀνόμαστος	**19**.**a**.11
Οὐαλέριος	**64**.3, 29; cf. also Αὐρήλιος Οὐαλέριος
Οὐαλέριος, f. Αὐρ. Παυσανίας	**4**.1, 19; **38**.**a**.1, 22; **38**.**b**.1, 22
Οὐαλέριος Ἡρκουλανός	**27**.2
Οὐαλέριος Οὐικτωρινιανός	**21**.20
Οὐῶνσις	**24**.3
Οὐῶνσις, f. Αὐρ. Γενᾶ	**18**.1; **23**.2, 31
Παβῶς, s. ΤιΘοῆς Χηνου	**23**.22 (cf. Αὐρ. Πεβῶς)
Παγχάριον	**7**.23
Πακῦσις	**68**.9
Π[α]κῦσις, f. Γενᾶ	**23**.25 (Π[ε]κῦσις also possible)
Παλάμμων, s. Παλάμμων	**46**.3, 36
Παλάμμων, f. Παλάμμων	**46**.3, 37
Παλιτοῦς, f. Πεκῦσις, grf. Αὐρ. Ψάις	**8**.1
Παμῖνις	cf. Αὐρήλιος Παμῖνις
Παμοῦρ(ις)	**31**.36; **66**.1; **71**.3; **72**.1, 52; **73**.1, 32; **87**.3; cf. also Αὐρήλιος Παμοῦρ
Παμοῦρ(ις), f. Αὐρ. Παμοῦρ hb. Τακοσε	**42**.1, 31, 40
Παμοῦρ(ις), f. Αὐρ. Πεβῶς	**39**.2
Παμοῦρ(ις), f. Αὐρ. Ψάις	**30**.5, 22; **32**.6; **38**.**a**.2; **38**.**b**.2; **50**.1 (w/o Αὐρ.)
Παμοῦρ(ις), f. Ψάις, grf. Αὐρ. Παμοῦρ	**33**.3-4
Παμοῦρ, f. Ψάις, grf. Αὐρ. Πεκῦσις	**44**.1; **76**.36
Παμοῦρις, s. (mother) Λο	**87**.3
Παπνούθιος	**61**.8
Παπνούθιος, f. Ἰσιδ( )	**61**.13
Παπνούθιος, f. Θερμοῦθις	**61**.6

Πασαι-, f. Αὐρ. N.N., hb. Τσενεντῆρις	**2**.4
Πάταϊ	**61**.8
Παταιᾶς	**3**.10; **16**.4
Παταιᾶς (N.N. ὁ καὶ Παταιᾶς?), br. Ψάις	**24**.19
Παταιᾶς, f. Αὐρ. Γενᾶ	**7**.2, 26 (both w/o Αὐρ.); **76**.34
Παταμῖνις, f. Ψάις	**23**.18; cf. also Πετεμῖνις
Πατσῖρε, f. Κέλε, grf. Ψάις	**50**.4, 13
Πανσανίας	**5**.2 (husband [?] of Ταμοῦ), 28; **6**.2, 54; **63**.2; cf. also Αὐρήλιος Πανσανίας
Παχοῦμις, grds. Λαβουατος	**23**.24; **70**.7 (w/o Λαβουατος); cf. also Αὐρήλιος Παχοῦμις
Παχούμιος	**30**.12
Παχουμῶν, hb. Ἀγάπη, f. Αὐρ. Ψενπνούθης	**30**.3, 24
Πεβῶς, s. Καλλικλῆς	**24**.19; cf. also Αὐρήλιος Πεβῶς
Πεβῶς, s. Σαᾶς (?)	**66**.26
Πεβῶς, s. Σαρᾶς, f. Μύρων	**60**.7
Πεβῶς, s. Τιθοῆς Χηνου	**23**.22 (see also Αὐρ.Πεβῶς)
Πεκύσιος	**71**.18
Πεκῦσις, f. N.N.	**2**.11
Πεκῦσις, f. Ὧρος	**72**.2, 51 (cf. l. 13); cf. also Αὐρήλιος Πεκῦσις
Πεκῦσις, s. Ψάις, grds. Παμούρ	**76**.3 (w/o Ψάις, Παμούρ), 36
Πεκῦσις, s. Παλιτοῦς, f. Αὐρ. Ψάις	**8**.1, 14
Πετε[, f. Αὐρ. Ψάις	**3**.8
Πετεμῖνις, f. Αὐρ. Ψάις	**15**.2-3
Πετεμῖνις (?)	**74**.26; cf. also Παταμῖνις
Πετεχῶν, s. Ἀμμώνιος	**69**.17; cf. also Αὐρήλιος Πετεχῶν
Πετῆσις, f. Αὐρ. Τιθοῆς	**8**.2; **9**.2
Πετοσῖρις, f. Αὐρ. Ψεναμοῦνις	**52**.13
Πινοῦτα, s. Γενᾶ	**24**.18
Πινούθης, s. Γενᾶ	**3**.9
Πιπέρισμι	cf. Αὐρήλιος Πιπέρισμι
Πισίστρατος	**46**.2, 36; **63**.3, 41
Πκουρ[. .]ς	**24**.11
Πλουτογένης	**75**.22-23; cf. also Αὐρήλιος Πλουτογένης
Πολυκράτης, f. Αὐρ. Δημοσθένης	**8**.18; cf. also Αὐρήλιος Πολυκράτης
Πορφύριος	**23**.23
Πρεμενοῦρις f. Ψεκῆς	**3**.7
Πτολεμαῖος	**53**.3
Πτοῦ, f. Φλ. Μακάριος	**46**.34
Ῥαχῆλ	**61**.5

Ῥιραῦς	**29**.3
Ῥουπίλιος (?) Φῆλιξ	**1**.9-10
Σαᾶς (?), f. Πεβῶς	**66**.26
Σαβεῖνος, f. Ἠλίας	**81**.2
Σαβεῖνος, f. Τιθοῆς	**60**.10
Σαμοῦν, s. Τιθοῆς	**11**.2; **12**.2, 36
Σαπ..ς	**23**.24
Σαρα[π-	**3**.9
Σαραπάμμων	cf. Αὐρήλιος Σαραπάμμων
Σαραπίων, f. Αὐρ. Οὐαλέριος	**48**.2
Σαρᾶπις	**6**.53; **76**.2, 36
Σαραπόδωρος, s. Ἔρως	**23**.25
Σαρᾶς, f. Πεβῶς, grf. Μύρων	**60**.7
Σαρμάτης, f. Αὐρήλιος --]δης	**30**.24
Σεμνή, w. Σιβιτύλλος	**41**.26
Σεν-	**66**.23
Σενορ-	**19**.**a**.6
Septimius Eutropius v.c.	**26**, Fr. I.1, 3, 5, 7
Σερῆνος	**27**.3
Σιβιτύλλος, husb. Σεμνή	**41**.26
Σινεύς	**6**.17, 22, 50
Σῖρις	**78**.1, 11
Σόις, s. Ἀκοῦτις	**21**.6
Σοφία	cf. Αὐρηλία Σοφία
Σπου..μ( ), f. Αὐρ. Τιθοῆς	**24**.18
Στρατήγιος	**26**, Fr. II.6, 7; **75**.3, 34-35
Στώνιος	cf. Αὐρήλιος Στώνιος
Σύριος	**80**.6
Σύρος, f. Αὐρ. Ὧρος	**13**.1, 6; cf. also Αὐρήλιος Σύρος,
Σύρος, f. Βησᾶς	**72**.46
Σύρος, f. Καλλικλῆς	**60**.5
Τα....ς (gen.), m. Αὐρ. Σοφία, w. Βησᾶς	**42**.6
Ταα	**23**.6; **24**.18
Ταγάπη	**74**.25
Τακοσε, m. Αὐρ. Παμοῦρ, w. Παμοῦρ	**42**.2 (cf. also s.nn. Αὐρηλία Τακῦσις, Τεκοσε, Τεκῦσις)
Τακῦσις	cf. Αὐρηλία Τακῦσις
Ταμοῦ, w. (?) Παυσανίας	**5**.7
Ταοῦπ	cf. Αὐρηλία Ταοῦπ
Ταπολλῶς, m. Αὐρ. Πεκῦσις, w. Ψάις, d.-in-law Παμοῦρ	**44**.1
Τασηχθισος	cf. s.n. Αὐρηλία Ἱερακίαινα
Τατοῦπ	cf. Αὐρηλία Τατοῦπ

Ταύρις	**43**.25
Τάψαις	cf. Αὐρηλία Τάψαις
Τβῆκις	**2**.7
Τεκοσε	**65**.1, 51 (cf. also s.nn. Αὐρηλία Τακῦσις, Τακοσε, Τεκῦσις,)
Τεκῦσις, w. Παμοῦρ, m. Αὐρ. Ψάις	**30**.5 (cf. also s.nn. Αὐρηλία Τακῦσις, Τακοσε, Τεκοσε)
Τεπνάχθης, f. Αὐρ. Στώνιος	**13**.14
Τιβέριος, f. Αὐρ. Τιμόθεος	**3**.11
Τιβέριος, f. Ὧρος	**60**.2
Τιβέριος, f. N.N.	**3**.8; cf. also Αὐρήλιος Τιβέριος
Τιθέριος	cf. Αὐρήλιος Τιθέριος
Τιθοῆς	**10**.2; **24**.18; cf. also Αὐρήλιος Τιθοῆς
Τιθοῆς, s. Ἠλίας	**60**.11
Τιθοῆς, s. Σαβεῖνος	**60**.10
Τιθοῆς, s. Σπου..μ( )	**24**.18
Τιθοῆς, f. Αὐρ. Πεβῶς	**24**.13; **42**.37; **44**.24
Τιθοῆς, f. Αὐρ. [ ]ς	**14**.7
Τιθοῆς, f. Σαμοῦν	**11**.2; **12**.1, 35
Τιθοῆς Χη(υ)ου, f. Ὡρίων & Πεβῶς	**23**.22, 25
Τιθοῆς, f. --	**24**.14
Τιμόθεος	**5**.20; **6**.4, 27, 52; **70**.2, 15; cf. also Αὐρήλιος Τιμόθεος
Τιμόθεος, f. Αὐρ. Τιμόθεος	**24**.16
Τιμόθεος, f. Ψάις	**60**.8
Τιμόθεος, f. Αὐρ. Ὡρίων	**8**.19
Τιμόθεος, s. Ἁρποκρατίων	**23**.15
Τιμόθεος, s. Λούδων	**24**.12
Τις	cf. Αὐρήλιος Τις
Τοῦ	Cf. Αὐρήλιος Τοῦ
Τριφιόδωρος	cf. Αὐρ. Φοιβάμμων ὁ καὶ Τριφιόδωρος
Τρόδα	**23**.23
Τρυφάνης, s. Ψάις Τρυφάνης	**73**.10
Τρυφάνης, f.(?) (Αὐρ.) Ψάις	**24**.11 (with Αὐρ.); **50**.2, 11-12; **71**.40 (Τροφ.), 48 (Τρυφ.); **73**.2, 33
Τσεμπνούθης	**71**.43
Τσενεντῆρις, m. Αὐρ. N.N., w. Πασαι-	**2**.4
Τσενπαμοῦν	**12**.6
Φαριᾶς, f. Εὐτυχής, grf. Ψάις	**60**.3
Φαυστιανός	cf. Αὐρηλίος Φαυστιανός
Φαυστῖνος	cf. Φλ. Φαυστῖνος
Φῆλιξ, Ῥουπίλιος (?) Φῆλιξ	**1**.9-10
Φιβίων	cf. Αὐρήλιος Φιβίων

Φιλάμμων	**19**.b.2; **64**.2, 29; **65**.1, 51; **71**.36, 49; **72**.39; **79**.6; cf. also Αὐρήλιος Φιλάμμων
Φιλοσαρᾶπις	cf. Αὐρήλιος Φιλοσαρᾶπις ὁ καὶ Μίκκαλος
Φιλούμενος	**62**.5, 10, 14, 19, 23, 27, 33
Φιλυς, f. Γενᾶ / Ἴενᾶ	**62**.2, 16, 24
Φλ. Δομίτιος Ἀσκληπιάδης	**15**.1
Φλάυιος Κολλοῦθος	**30**.26
Φλ. Μακάριος, s. Πτοῦ	**46**.34-35
Φλ. Φαυστῖνος	**23**.1
Φοιβάμμων	Cf. Αὐρήλιος Φοιβάμμων ὁ καὶ Τριφιόδωρος
Χῶλος	**24**.11, 18; **65**.41
Χη(υ)ος (?)	**23**.22,25
Ψάις	**24**.19; **65**.39; **66**.4, 21; **67**.5; **71**.2, 49; **72**.9; **74**.1, 35; **75**.18 (ὁ μέγας), 21; **79**.3; cf. also Αὐρήλιος Ψάις
Ψάις, s. Ἀλέξανδρος	**60**.9
Ψάις, s. Εὐτυχής, grds. Φαριᾶς	**60**.3
Ψάις, s. Κέλε, grs. Πατσῖρε	**50**.3, 12
Ψάις, s. Παμοῦρ	**50**.1
Ψάις, s. Παμοῦρ, f. Αὐρ. Παμοῦρ	**33**.4
Ψάις, s. Παμοῦρ, f. Αὐρ. Πεκῦσις, husb. Ταπολλῶς	**44**.1, 21, 27; **76**.36 (w/o Αὐρ., Ταπολλῶς)
Ψάις, s. Παταμῖνις	**23**.18
Ψαις, s. Τιμόθεος	**60**.8
Ψάις, s.(?) Τρυφάνης	**50**.2, 11; **71**.39 (Τροφ.), 48 (Τρυφ.)
Ψάις, s.(?) Τρυφάνης, f. Τρυφάνης	**73**.2, 33
Ψάις, s. Ψεναπολλῶς	**60**.1
Ψάις, br. Παταιᾶς	**24**.19
Ψάις, f. Βησᾶς	**24**.14
Ψάις, f. Ἠλίας	**68**.2
Ψάις, f. Αὐρ. Ἡρακλῆς	**14**.8
Ψάις, f. Αὐρ. Παμοῦρ	**19**.b.1; **20**.3; **21**.3, 25; **24**.15; **41**.3; **50**.1
Ψάις, f. Αὐρ. Σαραπάμμων	**24**.13
Ψάις, f. Αὐρ. Σύρος	**45**.4
Ψαρᾶπις	**66**.1
Ψεκῆς, s. Πρεμενοῦρις	**3**.7; cf. also Αὐρήλιος Ψεκῆς
Ψεκῆς, s. Ψεννοῦφις	**23**.18
Ψεναμοῦνις	cf. Αὐρήλιος Ψεναμοῦνις
Ψεμπνούτης	**70**.1, 16 (cf. also s.n. Ψενπνούθης)
Ψεναμοῦνις	**21**.11-12, 17; **80**.2
Ψεναπολλῶς, f. Ψάις	**60**.1

Ψεννοῦφις, f. Ψεκῆς	**23**.18
Ψενοῦφις ὁ καὶ Βῆσας	**24**.17
Ψενπνούθης	**23**.23; **24**.11; **74**.18 (cf. also s.nn. Αὐρήλιος Ψενπνοῦθης, Ψεμπνούτης)
Ψύρος, f. Αὐρ. Ψάις	**33**.1
Ὧρ	**75**.24
Ὡρίων, s. Τιθοῆς Χηου	**23**.25; cf. also Αὐρήλιος Ὡρίων
Ὧρος	**24**.15; cf. also Αὐρήλιος Ὧρος
Ὧρος, b.(?) Παμοῦρ	**72**.8
Ὧρος, f. Αὐρ. Ἡλιόδωρος	**13**.20
Ὧρος, f. Αὐρ. Πολυκράτης	**58**.7
Ὧρος, s. Ἡλιόδωρος	**66**.27
Ὧρος, s. Μέρσις, f. Αὐρ. N.N.	**9**.1 (see also Αὐρ. Ὧρος, s. Μέρσις)
Ὧρος, s. Παμοῦρ	**30**.5, 7; **72**.6
Ὧρος, s. Πεκῦσις	**72**.13
Ὧρος, s. Τιβέριος	**60**.2
Ὡρπατῶς, f. Αὐρ. Τιθέριος	**50**.9

Incomplete names:

-θης	**3**.7
-νοῦφις	**2**.8
-ιανός	**3**.17
-ίδημος	**51**.9
-ουτβαντς	**3**.7
-ρυλλος	**63**.34
-σις	**3**.9
-σίδης	**37**.10
-των, f. Παταΐᾶς	**3**.10
-υει (?)	**35**.1

VI: GEOGRAPHICAL NAMES

(A) Countries, Provinces, Towns

Αἴγυπτος	**1**.10; **23**.20; **76**.16; **81**.5
Αἰγύπτιος	**33**.27; **34**.20; **41**.31; **46**.11-12; see also Index III
Ἀλεξάνδρεια	**29**.5
Ἀνταιοπολίτης (νομός)	**30**.4; **32**.5; **42**.5; **43**.3; **44**.5
Ἀντινόου (πόλις)	**71**.16; **77**.30

Ἕλλην	**8**.13; **41**.22; see also Index III
Ἑλληνιστής	**67**.20
Ἑρμοῦ πόλις (ἡ μεγάλη)	**21**.27; **51**.1-2 (ἡ μεγάλη); **52**.4, 14; **66**.21
Θηβαΐς	**2**.2; **19**.**a**.1; **20**.2
Ἰβίτης νομός	**2**.11
Ἰβιτικός	**45**.15
Ἰβιτῶν πόλις	**2**.4; **13**.18, 22; **35**.4
Μεσοβή (μερ.)	**28**.5; **68**.12
Μῶθις	**77**.11
Μωθίτης νομός	**3**.1; **8**.2; **9**.1; **15**.3-4; **18**.3, 4; **23**.2; **24**.2; **33**.2-3; **34**.**App**.1; **41**.4; **45**.3-4
Μωθιτῶν πόλις	**4**.2, 3; **13**.2; **19**.**a**.**App**.5, 7; **20**.4, 9; **21**.1, 3-4; **25**.3; **27**.4; **30**.6; **32**.2-3; **34**.1-2; **35**.2; **38**.**a**.1, 3; **38**.**b**.1, 3; **39**.2; **41**.2, 26-27, 30; **42**.2-3; **44**.2; **48**.3; **52**.1-2
Ὄασις Μεγάλη	**9**.6 (w/o Μεγάλη); **19**.**a**.**App**.5; **20**.5; **21**.1; **25**.1-2; **30**.6, 9 (w/o Μεγάλη); **42**.3; **44**.2-3; **51**.3 (w/o Μεγάλη); **77**.11 (w/o Μεγάλη)
Πανοπολίτης	**30**.4
Ῥωμαϊκός	**77**.30
Ῥωμαῖος	**19**.**a**.**App**.4
Τριμιθιτῶν πόλις	**49**.1-2 (cf. also 'b', Τριμῖθις)
Χώρα	**21**.2; **23**.29

(b) Villages

Ἀφροδίτης κώμη	**30**.4, 7, 10, 24 (w/o κώμη); **32**.4-5; **42**.4, 8; **43**.3, 39; **44**.4, 25
Ε...... ἐποίκιον	**8**.2
Θιον (?) ἐποίκιον	**45**.3
Κέλλεως κώμη	**3**.1, 10; **4**.3; **8**.1, 18, 19; **9**.1; **13**.1-2, 14, 16, 20; **14**.8; **15**.3; **18**.2; **19**.**a**.2; **19**.**a**.**App**.6 (w/o κώμη) **20**.3-4; **21**.3, 7; **23**.2; **24**.2, 20; **30**.6; **32**.2; **33**.2; **34**.2, 26; **34**.**App**.2; **38**.**a**.2, 6; **38**.**b**.2, 6; **39**.1; **41**.4; **42**.2, 7, 38, 40; **43**.38-39; **44**.2; **45**.2, 36; **47**.3 **49**.4; **50**.10; **52**.3; **56**.9; **74**.35 (w/o κώμη) **79**.5 (w/o κώμη)
Κεραμείων κώμη	**34**.1
Μαδιώφριος (?) κώμη	**2**.11
Πακέβκ- (?)	**35**.3

Πανεώους χωρίον **62**. 2-3, 17
Πμ(οῦν) Βερι βορινοῦ **5**.12
Πμοῦν Κε.( ) κώμη **49**.2-3
Πμοῦν Παμω **21**.12
Πμοῦν Τάμετρα ἐποίκιον **41**.2-3
Πμ(οῦν) Τεκαλε **6**.12
Συνορίας κώμη **30**.4
Τουπχα κώμη (?) **47**.2
Τπακε κώμη **52**.1
Τριμῖθις **27**.3; **29**.8
[ ]μηση κώμη **35**.2

(c) Other

Πόλεως Ἀπηλιώτου ἀμφόδου **51**.2-3

VII: RELIGION AND MAGIC

(a) Religion

ἀναγνώστης καθολικῆς ἐκκλησίας **32**.21
Γῆ **48**.5
δαίμων **85**.b.18; **87**.1
διάκονος **24**.11
διδάσκαλος (?) **69**.18 (cf. introd.)
ἐκκλησία καθολική **24**.3; **32**.21; **58**.8
Ζεύς **48**.5
Ἥλιος **48**.5
Θεός **19**.**a**.**App**.18; **24**.5; **63**.4; **65**.11, 14; **67**.3, 15; **68**.22; **71**.3, 8, 14; **72**.11; **85**.**b**.19a (?); **87**.4; **88**.3
ἱερεύς **13**.14
μοναστήριον **12**.18-19
παράκλητος **63**.29
παντοκράτωρ **24**.5
πρεσβύτερος **24**.11; **32**.21; **48**.20 (?)
πρεσβύτερος καθολ. ἐκκλησίας **24**.3; **58**.8
χριστιανότης **48**.4

(b) Magic

Ἀγαθ]ὸς Δαίμων	**85**.**b**.17-18 (?)
βαμ[εαζα (?)	**85**.**a**.13
Βηλ Βηλ	**85**.**a**.9
ΓΑΒΡΙΗΛ	**86**, right margin
ζωτρα	**85**.**b**.17 (?); **87**.1
Θαναλβλαναθ	**86**.8
Θερμουθις	**85**.**b**.17 (?); **87**.1
ια .[	**85**.**a**.9
ιαηγαρ	**85**.**b**.18 (?); **87**.2
ισαχ = Ἰσαχ ?	**85**.**b**.21
κ· κν	**85**.**a**.10
κοπφιη	**85**.**a**.8
λιθαβιοχ[	**85**.**b**.20
ΜΙΧΑΗΛ	**86**, left margin
ΟΥΡΙΗΛ	**86**, right margin
ΡΑΦΑΗΛ	**86**, left margin
σαλ[αμαξα (?)	**85**.**a**.12
σαρχαθον	**85**.**b**.17-18 (?); **87**.1
σεραμικκη[	**85**.**a**.7
σεσεμφθα	**85**.**b**.17; **87**.1
υιεδ( )	**85**.**b**.21
φθη[	**85**.**a**.10

— Vowels

α	**86**.7, 9
α ε η ι ο υ ω	**85**.**a**.14
εαε	**85**.**b**.3
εε	**86**.6, 10
ηηη	**85**.**b**.4; **86**.5, 11
ιιι	**85**.**b**.5; **86**.4, 12
οιηυε	**85**.**b**.11
ooooo	**85**.**b**.6; **86**.3, 13
υοιηεω	**85**.**b**.10
υυυυυυ	**85**.**b**.7; **86**.2 14
ω	**85**.**b**.15
ωοιη	**85**.**b**.12
ωυ	**85**.**b**.14
ωυο	**85**.**b**.13
ωυοιηε	**85**.**b**.9
ωωωωωωω	**85**.**b**.8; **86**.1, 15

VIII: OFFICIAL AND MILITARY TERMS AND TITLES

αἰδέσιμος	**48**.9-10
ἀνδρεία	**3**.2; **21**.19
ἀπαιτητής	**15**.4; **17**.2-3
ἀπὸ λογιστῶν	**29**.3
ἀποδέκτης	**29**.7
ἄρξας	**4**.1, 19; **8**.17; **19.a**.5; **19.a.App**.5; **21**.1, 27; **23**.7; **25**.3, 4; **37**.10; **38.a**.1, 22; **38.b**.1, 22; **48**.2, 18
βοηθός	**26**, Fr. II.11
διάδοχος ἐξάκτορος	**23**.3, 26
διασημότατος	**1**.10; **3**.2, 17; **19.a**.1; **20**.1; **21**.20; **23**.1; **24**.1
δοῦξ	**3**.2 (?), 17 (?); **24**.1
ἔκδικος χώρας	**21**.2
ἐκσκέπτωρ	**54**.13-14
ἐκσπούγκτωρ	**21**.9; **77**.13
ἐξάκτωρ	**23**.4, 26
ἔπαρχος Αἰγύπτου	**1**.10
ἐπιεικεία	**21**.18
ἐπικριτής	**15**.4
εὐγένεια	**5**.4-5, 9, 19
εὐλάβεια	**71**.4-5
ἡγεμών	**3**.2 (?), 17 (?); **15**.2; **19.a**.3; **20**.6; **21**.20; **23**.1
ἡγούμενος Θηβαίδος	**2**.2; **19.a**.1; **20**.1-2; **26**, Fr. I.1, 3, 5, 7 (praeses Thebaidos)
ἱππεύς	**46**.35
κώμαρχος	**21**.6, 16-17; **23**.2, 10, 31
κόμες	**3**.6; **15**.2
κωμογραμματεύς	**3**.15; **14**.7; **45**.35
λαμπρότατος	**3**.6;; **15**.1; **26**. Fr. I.1, 3, 5, 7 (vir clarissimus); cf. also Index II, Consuls)
λειτουργός	**23**.3, 4, 12
λογιστής	**25**.1; **29**.3 (*ἀπὸ λογ.*); **69**.17
ὀφφικιάλιος	**2**.3; **21**.9
πολιτευόμενος	**54**.17
πραιπόσιτος πάγου	**27**.3
praeses Thebaidos	**26**, Fr. I.1, 3, 5, 7
πρίγκιψ	**53**.7; **54**.4
πρόεδρος	**25**.3
στατιωνάριος χώρας	**23**.29
στρατηγικὴ τάξις	**23**.5

στρατηγός **19.b**.5; **54**.16-17
στρατιώτης **21**.8-9; **26**, Fr. I.4; **70**.12
σύμμαχος **23**.11, 23
σύνδικος **25**.4
ὑπομνηματογράφος **54**.13, 19-20, 22
τάξις **2**.2, 3, 8; **23**.5; **24**.1
φλαυιάλιος **15**.2

v(ir) c(larissimus) **26**. Fr. I.1, 3, 5, 7

IX: PROFESSIONS, TRADES AND OCCUPATIONS

ἁμαξηλάτης **54**.4-5
<ἀ>μαξιλλάριο<ς> ? **53**.5 (?; cf. note ad loc.)
ἀναγνώστης **67**.20
γεωργός **6**.40; **78**.3-4; **81**.12
διδάσκαλος **69**.18 (cf. index VII)
δρομεδάριος **79**.7
ἐπιστολεύς **54**.24
ἐπιστοληφόρος **54**.11
καθαρτής **6**.45
καθηγητής **53**.12?
καμηλάτης **77**.15
καμηλίτης **51**.3; **52**.2
κεραμεύς **61**.2; **66**.22; **74**.2, 35 (?)
ὀψωνιαστής **23**.6
παραχύτος **3**.9; **60**.9
πραίκων **53**.6 (?); **54**.6
ῥήτωρ **54**.2
τέκτων **5**.29; **6**.12; **8**.2; **11**.3; **21**.12; **33**.1; **60**.6; **70**.2, 15
χαλκεύς **3**.7; **61**.7

X: MEASURES AND MONEY

(a) Measures

ἀρτάβη **11**.4-5, 9-10; **16**.5; **32**.14; **47**.15; **79**.9, 10

δίσσακκον	**72**.32 (?)
κάγκελλος	**6**.14, 19, 30, 42, 50; **10**.6-7, 11
κεράμιον	**49**.6-7, 23
μ(ετρητής ?)	**61**.5
μάριον	**45**.14, 15, 31, 32, 38; **61**.5 (?); **80**.4
μάτιον	**54**, passim; **61**.5 (?)
μέτρον, δημόσιον μ.	**79**.8-9
μέτρον τῆς κώμης	**49**.7, 24
μνᾶ	**61**.6
μόδιος	**61**.11
ξέστης	**64**.22
οὐγκία	**89**.1, 2, 3, 4, 5
πενταχοεία	**49**.9-10
πῆχυς (τεκτονικός π.)	**4**.6, 7; **38**.**a**.7-8, 8 (w/o *τεκτονικός*); **38**.**b**.7, 8 (w/o *τεκτ.*)
τριχοῦς	**50**.5
χο(ῦς)	**61**.3, 4; **90**.7
χοῦς, Ἰβιτικὸς χοῦς	**45**.15

(b) Money

ἀργυρίου δραχμή	**62**.3, 7-8, 17-18, 26, 29
ἀργυρίου ... νόμισμα	**34**.23 (w/o *ἀργυρίου*); **35**.8
ἀργυρίου παλαίου Πτολεμαικοῦ νομίσματος τάλαντα	**19**.**a**.**App**.16-17
ἀργυρίου Σεβαστῶν νομίσμα	**34**.7; **34**.**App**.6; **41**.7; **42**.12
ἀργυρίου Σεβαστ- τάλαντον	**39**.9
ἀργυρίου καινοῦ τάλαντον	**19**.**a**.9
ἀργυρίου τάλαντον	**10**.4; **29**.5-6; **31**.37 (?), 39-40; **33**.12; **41**.24-25; **42**.13, 16, 33, 35, 40; **43**.6, 9; **44**.9; **46**.7-8; **78**.4-5; **90**.1
δίχαλκον	**66**.20
δραχμή (cf. sub *ἀργυρίου δρ.*)	**28**.2, 4, 5; **34**.8, 23; **41**.8, 25; **53**.14; **62**.4, 9, 12, 13, 18, 21, 22, 26, 30, 31, 32; **66**.5, 27-28
ἡμιωβέλιον	**28**.5
μυριάς	**76**.9, 10, 21
νόμισμα	cf. sub *ἀργυρίου νόμισμα*
νόμισμα τετραχρύσουν	**29**.5-6
νομισμάτιον	cf. sub *χρυσοῦ νομισμάτιον*
νοῦμμος	**31**.39-40; **34**.7, 23; **41**.8; **55**.10
ὁλονομισμάτιον	**12**.13
πεντώβολος	**28**.5

τάλαντον (cf. sub *ἀργυρίου - τάλ.*) **10**.12; **11**.8; **13**.9; **29**.6; **34**.7-8, 8, 22-23, 23; **34.App**.6-7; **35**.9; **37**.20; **41**.8; **42**.13; **43**.18, 36; **44**.10; **46**.9, 21, 27, 37; **47**.6, 7-8, 13-14, 17; **53**.14; **54**, passim; **61**.7, 8, 10, 12, 13; **66**.5; **70**.8; **78**.5; **90**.3
χαλκοῦς **28**.4
χρυσοῦ νομισμάτιον **8**.6 (w/o *χρυσοῦ*), 15; **18**.7-8, 8 (w/o *χρυσοῦ*); **44**.7, 8, 22, 27; **45**.9-10, 10, 28; **64**.14 (w/o *χρυσοῦ*)

XI: TAXATION

φόρετρον ἀνδριάντων **29**.4, 8
χρυσάργυρον **76**.11-12
χρυσάργυρον πραγματευτικόν **15**.5

XII: GENERAL INDEX OF WORDS

ἀβίωτος **21**.5
ἀγαπητός **67**.1, 16
ἅγιος **86**.17
ἀγνοέω **76**.12
ἀγοράζω **66**.10, 18; **72**.30, 34, 37
ἄγραφος **9**.10
ἀγρός **73**.28
ἄγω **21**.18; **39**.16; **65**.22
ἀδελφ[**4**.9
ἀδελφή **9**.3; **12**.6, 21, 32; **13**.6; **65**.2, 51-52; **71**.53; **72**.7; **74**.11; **76**.5
ἀδελφός **5**.19-20; **6**.1, 4, 10, 26-27, 48, 52, 53, 54; **7**.1, 5, 22, 25; **10**.1, 8, 15; **11**.1; **12**.20; **13**.1, 17, 19; **16**.3-4; **17**.8, 11; **23**.17, 19; **24**.13, 14, 17, 19; **63**.38; **64**.1, 10, 28; **65**.40; **67**.4-5, 13, 19; **68**.29; **70**.1; **71**.2, 9, 17-18, 22; **72**.1, 2, 8, 38-39, 51; **73**.1, 4, 32; **74**.5, 32, 34; **75**.1-2, 17-18, 32-33, 35; **76**.1, 36; **78**.1, 6, 8, 11; **79**.1, 6, 14; **80**.1
ἀδιάθετος **9**.5
ἀδιαίρετος **13**.8

ἀδικέω **3**.3
ἀεί **21**.7
ἄθλιος **3**.16; **23**.19
αἱρέω **8**.9; **34**.14; **36**.6; **38.a**.14; **38.b**.14; **39**.14
αἴρω **74**.14
αἰτέω **23**.28
αἰῶν **88**.25, 26
αἰώνιος **38.a**.1; **38.b**.1; **88**.3
ἀκόλουθος **2**.8
ἀκούω **24**.6; **65**.16; **72**.12; **76**.25
ἀκριβής **76**.25
ἄκων **27**.5
ἀληθής **71**.1
ἀλλά **5**.11; **10**.9; **11**.11; **16**.5; **17**.3; **23**.19; **64**.13, 17, 24; **65**.37; **71**.18, 19, 33; **72**.26; **78**.6; **79**.11
ἀλλήλων **8**.5; **13**.2; **30**.7, 8, 19; **34**.7; **34.App**.6; **35**.8;
ἄλλος **6**.29, 32; **9**.12; **10**.10; **13**.1; **23**.3, 10; **24**.11; **30**.17; **55**.4; **62**.12, 21, 25, 29, 31; **68**.10; **69**.2; **71**.49; **72**.21; **75**.20; **77**.23
ἀλλότριος **15**.10
ἄλογος **24**.7
ἅμα **21**.11; **66**.17
ἅμαξα **46**.7
ἀμέλεια **6**.43-44; **46**.17-18
ἀμελέω **7**.7; **11**.11; **16**.6; **66**.11, 26; **68**.20; **70**.12; **71**.24; **78**.7; **80**.3
ἀμέριμνος **72**.29
ἀμφημερινός **86**.18
ἄμφοδον cf. Index VI.c
ἀμφότερος **8**.1; **40**.2; **63**.24
ἄν (cf. also ἐάν) **21**.5; **30**.13, 17; **36**.6; **42**.25
ἀναγκαῖος **18**.7; **20**.16; **40**.2; **41**.6; **42**.11; **43**.5; **44**.6; **45**.8-9; **47**.5; **71**.16-17
ἀνάγνωσις **22**.3
ἀναγνώστης **67**.21 (cf. also Index VII s.v.)
ἀναγράφω **51**.2; **63**.10
ἀναδέχομαι **6**.28, 34
ἀναίτιος **15**.12
ἀνακομίζω **41**.14
ἀνάλωμα **30**.20; **53**.1; **54**.1
ἀναμφίβολος **76**.22
ἀναμφίλογος **42**.23
ἀναπόρριφος **34**.5
ἀναφαίρετος **38.a**.4; **38.b**.4

ἀναφέρω **23**.27
ἀνδρεία **3**.2; **21**.19
ἀνδριάς **29**.4, 8
ἀνεκδίκητος **23**.15
ἀνεπίλημπτος **34**.5; **48**.7-8
ἀνεπιτήδειος **82**.5
ἀνέρχομαι **6**.21
ἄνευ **33**.16; **44**.13; **46**.13
ἀνήκω **68**.8
ἀνθρώπινος **23**.14; **76**.24
ἄνθρωπος **12**.15; **19.a**.15; **20**.9, 13; **65**.9, 25; **76**.13
ἀνοίγω **30**.11-12
ἀνοικοδομέω **30**.18-19
ἀνοικοδομή **38.a**.7; **38.b**.7
ἀνταμείβομαι **63**.30
ἀντί + Gen. **5**.21; **41**.9, 11
ἀντίγραφον **23**.29; **48**.1, 21
ἀντίγράφω **12**.14
ἀντικαταλλάσσω **30**.8, 13, 22
ἀντικαταλλαγή **30**.2
ἀντικνήμη **30**.6
ἀντίλημψις **88**.22
ἀντιλογία **33**.17; **43**.14-15; **44**.13; **45**.17; **46**.12-13
ἀντιποιέομαι **8**.10; **38.a**.16; **38.b**.16
ἀντίτυπον **19.a.App**.20; **31**.21
ἀνυπέρθετος **33**.16; **41**.13; **42**.23
ἄξιος(?) **27**.7
ἀξιόω **2**.9; **6**.20-21; **7**.7; **8**.17; **20**.17-18; **21**.19; **23**.26; **30**.25; **43**.40; **44**.25; **45**.37; **46**.35; **49**.27; **71**.43-44, 48, 50; **72**.36; **73**.27; **74**.8, 31
-αξιόω **63**.37
ἀπάγω **3**.15
ἀπαιτέω **66**.27; **70**.11; **76**.8, 28; **78**.3
ἀπαίτησις **15**.7, 15, 16 (?); **76**.11
ἀπαλλάσσω **68**.10; **85.a**.15; **85.b**.19; **86**.16; **87**.3
ἅπας **8**.4; **13**.3; **23**.4; **30**.8; **34**.4; **34.App**.4; **35**.5; **37**.6; **38.a**.5; **38.b**.5; **39**.5 (see also πᾶς)
ἄπειμι **30**.9
ἄπειρος **63**.5
ἀπελευθερόω **48**.4-5
ἀπελευθέρωσις **48**.1, 9, 13, 18-19, 21
ἀπεντεῦθεν **30**.17
ἀπέρχομαι **26**, Fr. II, 9; **68**.12; **71**.15-16, 20-21
ἀπέχθεια **24**.2

ἀπέχω **8**.15; **34**.8, 22; **36**.1; **37**.19; **66**.9

ἀπηλιώτης **30**.12; **38.a**.6, 8, 9; **38.b**.6, 8, 9; **39**.7

ἀπηλιωτικός **4**.5

ἁπλοῦς **3**.5; **8**.6; **9**.9; **33**.18; **38.a**.16; **38.b**.16; **40**.10; **41**.15; **42**.26; **45**.18; **49**.10; **65**.5, 18

ἀπό **2**.4, 11; **3**.1, 10, 11; **4**.2, 12; **6**.12; **7**.24; **8**.1, 2, 3, 7, 10, 18, 19; **9**.1, 2; **13**.1, 3, 14, 16, 18, 20, 22; **14**.8; **15**.3, 6; **18**.2, 4; **19.a**.2; **19.a.App**.6; **20**.3, 8; **21**.3, 12; **24**.2, 13, 15, 16, 20; **27**.4; **29**.3; **30**.6, 8, 14, 19, 24; **32**.2, 7; **33**.2, 4; **34**.1, 2, 3, 6, 10, 15, 26; **34.App**.1, 2, 3; **35**.2, 4, 5, 14; **36**.3, 7, 16; **37**.1, 3, 5, 6, 7, 9, 22; **38.a**.2, 4, 5, 15; **38.b**.2, 4, 5, 15; **39**.1, 3, 4, 8, 11, 20; **40**.2, 20; **41**.2, 4, 26, 30; **42**.2, 7, 17, 37, 40; **43**.1, 11, 24, 38; **44**.2, 3, 10, 24; **45**.2, 5; **47**.1, 3, 9, 20; **48**.8; **49**.1, 4; **50**.5-6, 9; **51**.3; **52**.1, 2, 14; **58**.7; **72**.27-28; **74**.26; **78**.3; **81**.5; **83**.11; **88**.11

ἀπογίνομαι **43**.24-25

ἀποδίδωμι **2**.10; **8**.9; **18**.8-9; **33**.10; **34**.14-15; **36**.7; **42**.25, 34; **43**.13-14, 37; **44**.23; **47**.13, 14; **49**.8

ἀπόδοσις **41**.11; **42**.19; **43**.13; **44**.12; **46**.18-19, 25

ἀποκαθίστημι **13**.9; **33**.13; **41**.12-13; **42**.21

ἀπολαμβάνω **23**.23

ἀπολαύω **63**.21, 22

ἀπολύω **42**.20; **65**.11

ἀπόνοια **24**.6

ἀποσπάω **23**.13

ἀποστέλλω **6**.5, 18, 36-37, 42-43, 50-51; **7**.9; **29**.4-5; **72**.35; **73**.9, 27, 31; **80**.7

ἀπότακτος **42**.15, 22

ἀπουσία **21**.10

ἀποχή **6**.41; **29**.7, 8; **49**.10; **50**.7, 11; **51**.7; **52**.6-7; **62**.5, 10, 13, 19, 23, 27, 33

ἀργύριον **43**.10, 27; **46**.20-21; **55**.10; **61**.1; **70**.6 (cf. also Index X.b)

ἀριθμέω **42**.11

ἀριθμός (?) **35**.10

ἀριστερός **23**.13; **30**.4, 6

ἀρκέω **23**.18

ἁρπάζω **20**.11

ἄρτι **72**.14; **74**.18

ἀσθένεια **88**.14

ἄσμενος **63**.19-20

ἀσπάζομαι **7**.4; **12**.3, 4, 7-8, 20, 31; **64**.4; **65**.38, 40-41, 41; **66**.2, 3; **67**.12, 14; **68**.2; **70**.3; **72**.7-8; **73**.4, 6; **74**.3, 6, 7
ἀστεῖος **67**.18
ἀσφάλεια **13**.10; **31**.21; **42**.27; **43**.26, 28; **44**.16-17; **45**.18; **46**.17; **47**.18; **50**.7; **51**.7; **52**.7; **76**.18
ἀσφαλίζω **15**.13-14
ἀσφαλισμός **24**.7
ἀτελής **20**.12
αὖ **21**.12
αὐθαδία **21**.4
αὐθαιρέτως **23**.17
αὐτός **2**.3; **3**.8, 9, 11, 17; **4**.3; **6**.23, 28, 29, 34, 46; **8**.1, 2-3, 3, 9, 16; **9**.2, 3; **11**.8; **12**.19, 32; **13**.1, 14, 15, 16, 18, 20, 21; **14**.6, 7; **15**.6, 7; **18**.4; **20**.8-9; **21**.7, 14, 15, 19, 26; **23**.7, 8, 18, 19, 20, 23, 26; **24**.12, 13, 14, 15, 16, 20; **26**, Fr. I.4; **26**, Fr. II.10; **30**.5, 7, 12, 24, 26; **31**.39; **32**.7, 8, 22; **33**.4, 5, 14; **34**.3, 13, 25; **34**.**App**.3; **36**.5, 15; **37**.3, 22, 23; **38**.**a**.3, 12; **38**.**b**.2, 12; **39**.3, 13, 21; **40**.19; **41**.27, 29; **42**.7, 8, 37, 38; **43**.40; **44**.3, 4, 24, 25; **45**.5, 12, 30, 33; **46**.10, 20, 32; **47**.19; **49**.25; **50**.8, 9; **51**.10; **52**.3, 12; **54**.23, 26; **56**.7; **58**.6; **62**.6, 7, 11, 20, 25, 28; **64**.11, 12, 14, 15, 19-20; **65**.20-21, 23, 25-26, 29, 40, 45; **66**.3, 5, 18, 24, 25, 27, 29; **67**.22; **68**.5; **70**.8, 9, 10-11; **71**.21, 47, 51; **72**.7, 24, 26, 35; **73**.6, 12, 14, 17, 22, 28, 30; **74**.8, 28, 29, 30-31; **76**.8-9, 9, 12, 13, 17, 21, 26, 29, 30; **77**.17; **78**.2, 7; **80**.6; **88**.11, 18
ἀφοσίωσις (?) **64**.16
ἀφανίζω **5**.16; **68**.17-18
ἄφιξις **71**.11
ἀφίστημι **24**.6; **30**.19-20; **74**.26
ἄχυρον **55**.3
ἄχρι(ς) **13**., 7; **41**.11; **42**.19; **43**.13; **44**.12; **46**.25

βάλλω **12**.18; **71**.51; **72**.34
βαρυκέφαλος **72**.43
βασιλικός **77**.12
βαστάζω **71**.35
βατέλλιον **71**.26, 50
βέβαιος **4**.14; **8**.11; **19**.**a**.**App**.21; **13**.11; **30**.21; **31**.22; **33**.20; **34**.17; **37**.13; **38**.**a**.17; **38**.**b**.17; **40**.10; **41**.18; **42**.27; **43**.28-29; **45**.20; **48**.14; **49**.11

βεβαιόω **8**.15; **30**.19, 23, 25; **34**.9, 23-24; **35**.11; **36**.3; **37**.20-21
βεβαίωσις **4**.11; **8**.9, 15; **30**.19, 23, 25; **34**.10, 14; **35**.11, 13; **36**.3, 6; **37**.21; **38.a**.14; **38.b**.14-15
βία **19.a.App**.18; **20**.6
βίαιος **20**.6, 10
βιβλίδιον **20**.17
βιβλίον **21**.18
βίος **20**.15
βλέπω **65**.43
βοηθέω **3**.14
βοηθός **88**.21
βορρᾶς **30**.11; **38.a**.7, 11; **38.b**.7, 11; **39**.6
βούλομαι **3**.2; **7**.18; **13**.3; **42**.20; **43**.15; **63**.7; **69**.9-10; **76**.4, 7-8
βραχίων **88**.6-7

γάλα **8**.5
γαμέω **9**.3
γάρ **3**.4, 14; **6**.51; **21**.10; **23**.15; **63**.9, 17, 28; **64**.19; **65**.16; **67**.20; **70**.9; **72**.24, 30, 33, 43, 47; **73**.23
γείτων **4**.7, 11; **30**.11, 13, 17; **38.a**.9, 11; **38.b**.9, 11; **39**.6
-γεννάω **34**.6
γένημα **6**.35-36; **31**.38
γεοῦχος **52**.6; **68**.24; **81**.4
γερδιακός **19.a.App**.11
γίνομαι **8**.6; **15**.7, 11, 12, 15; **18**.8; **19.a**.8, 13; **21**.6; **23**.21-22; **24**.4; **28**.3; **29**.6; **30**.14-15; **34**.8, 23; **35**.9; **37**.20; **39**.9; **42**.13, 16; **43**.18; **44**.8, 10; **45**.10, 14, 32; **46**.9, 18; **47**.7; **54**.23, 26; **62**.4, 9, 13, 18, 22, 26, 30, 32; **65**.17; **66**.23; **67**.20; **76**.10; **78**.5; **79**.10
γλεῦκος **73**.23
γνώμη **38.a**.14; **38.b**.14
γόμος **51**.4; **52**.5, 12; **66**.4, 7, 8, 25
γράμμα **3**.8, 9, 11; **8**.16; **13**.14, 16, 18, 20, 21; **14**.6; **21**.26; **24**.12, 15, 16, 20; **30**.24, 26; **32**.22; **34**.25; **36**.15; **37**.22; **39**.21; **40**.19; **41**.15; **42**.38; **43**.40; **44**.16, 26; **45**.34; **46**.32-33; **47**.20; **49**.25-26; **50**.8; **51**.10; **52**.13; **58**.7; **63**.7, 11, 20; **68**.6, 23; **69**.6; **71**.31, 38; **78**.3
γραμμάτιον **56**.2
γράφω **3**.5, 8, 9, 10; **4**.13; **5**.21; **7**.18; **8**.10, 16; **9**.13; **13**.10, 14, 15, 17, 20, 21; **14**.6; **19.a.App**.19, 20;

	21.26; **24**.12, 14, 16, 19; **29**.6, 9; **30**.21, 24, 26; **31**.20; **32**.22; **33**.18; **34**.16, 24-25; **36**.15; **37**.12, 21-22; **38.a**.16; **38.b**.16; **39**.21; **40**.10, 19; **41**.15, 29, 30; **42**.38; **43**.28-29, 38; **44**.25, 26; **45**.18, 33, 36; **46**.32; **47**.19; **49**.11, 25; **50**.8; **51**.9; **52**.12; **56**.7; **58**.6; **65**.3-4, 5, 31; **66**.11; **68**.25, 27; **69**.9; **71**.13-14, 21-22, 34, 48; **85.a**.4
γυνή	**8**.1, 5, 14; **9**.7; **12**.8; **41**.26; **43**.25; **66**.24; **76**.6
δαίμων	cf. Index VII
δάμαλις	**35**.6
δανείζω	**18**.5-6; **41**.5, 24; **42**.9; **43**.4; **44**.6; **45**.7
δαπάνη	**10**.11-12
δέ	**2**.7, 10; **3**.12; **6**.32; **7**.12; **9**.6; **13**.5; **15**.8, 11; **19.a.App**.15; **23**.6, 8, 9, 17, 21, 24, 29; **26**, Fr.II.10; **30**.11, 13, 15, 20; **40**.8; **42**.25; **46**.17; **47**.12; **63**.22; **64**.7, 21; **65**.10, 14, 18, 30; **69**.9; **71**.29; **72**.19, 29, 36, 44, 46; **73**.29; **74**.14, 17, 21, 31; **76**.13, 24
δεῖνα, ὁ/ἡ	**85.a**.5 (bis)
δεινός	**20**.5
δέκα	**15**.6; **67**.18; **71**.48; **73**.16
δεκαπέντε	**38.a**.8; **38.b**.7
δελματίκιον	**7**.11
δέλτος	**3**.17
δέομαι	**20**.18
δέρμα	**66**.18
δεσπόζω	**8**.8
δεσποτεύω	**30**.18
δεσπότης	**5**.1, 25-26, 28; **19.a**.3; **20**.17; **46**.1, 29, 36; **52**.6; **63**.28; **69**.6-7, 16; **74**.33; **75**.30-31 (see also Index I, II); **88**.2
δεσποτικός	**8**.6
δεύτερος	**13**.4
δέχομαι	**8**.6; **64**.9; **68**.6; **71**.48, 49; **72**.45
δέω	**63**.30
δή	**71**.21
δηλονότι	**63**.24
δῆλος	**6**.33
δηλόω	**6**.38; **12**.10, 17; **64**.7-8, 19; **74**.19-20
δημοσίᾳ (adv.)	**15**.13; **23**.19, 21, 31
δημοσία ῥυμή	**30**.11, 16; **38.a**.11; **38.b**.11
δημοσία χρεία	**23**.7
δημόσιον μέτρον	**79**.8

δημόσιον (τὸ δημ.) **4**.15; **13**.11; **31**.23; **34**.17; **37**.13, 21; **38.a**.17; **38.b**.17; **41**.18; **45**.21; **49**.12; **58**.3
δημόσιος λειτουργός **23**.7, 12
διά + Acc. **3**.13 (?); **5**.14; **9**.10; **13**.9; **48**.4; **65**.36; **68**.7; **71**.14; **72**.14, 32 (?)
διά + Gen. **3**.14; **4**.12; **5**.8; **6**.44, 50; **7**.10; **8**.6, 9; **12**.4, 14; **15**.7; **20**.17; **21**.18; **29**.3; **30**.5, 22; **34**.9, 15; **35**.13; **36**.2; **37**.8; **38.a**.15; **38.b**.15; **40**.4; **41**.6; **42**.11; **48**.9; **61**.8; **63**.7; **65**.24; **66**.4; **68**.7; **71**.32; **72**.45; **77**.7; **83**.4
διά + ? **3**.4 (?); **66**.16
δια- (verbum?) **24**.3
διαγράφω **29**.3
διαδικέω **19.b**.5-6
διάδοχος cf. Index VIII
διάθεσις **63**.15
διαίρεσις **13**.8, 9, 10, 13, 15, 17, 19, 21; **30**.15
διαιρέω **13**.3
διακόσιοι **33**.12-13; **62**.8, 21
διαλαμβάνω **19.b**.6-7; **22**.5
διαμένω **63**.35
διάνοια **21**.17; **63**.5-6
διαστολή **13**.13, 15, 17, 19, 21; **14**.5; **31**.32; **56**.6; **58**.6
διατρίβω **42**.8
διδάσκω **12**.19
δίδωμι **10**.7; **16**.3; **19.a.App**.8, 15; **23**.5; **26**, Fr. I.6; **32**.12; **62**.1, 4, 6, 9, 11, 13, 16, 18, 20, 22, 24, 27, 28, 32-33; **63**.34; **64**.14-15; **65**.15, 27; **66**.5, 17; **67**.22; **69**.4-5, 8; **70**.6, 10; **71**.44, 48; **73**.30; **74**.16, 17; **78**.6, 7; **80**.3, 6; **88**.23
διευτυχέω **21**.22
δίκαιος **12**.28; **19.a.App**.3; **30**.14
δίκη **26**, Fr. I.6
διό **6**.18; **71**.24; **76**.16
διοικέω **8**.8; **34**.13; **36**.5; **38.a**.13; **38.b**.13; **39**.13
δισσός **8**.10; **19.a.App**.19; **31**.20; **37**.12
διστάζω **74**.24
δισχίλιοι **78**.5
διψάω **71**.37
δοκέω **5**.18; **15**.13
δόκιμος **44**.7
δούλη **8**.4, 8, 14; **19.a**.6, 10, 13; **19.a.App**.10, 23
δοῦλος **87**.3
δύναμαι **20**.10; **21**.17, 21; **71**.34-35; **72**.33; **73**.27; **88**.16-17

δύναμις **88**.10
δυναστεία **23**.8
δυναστεύω **30**.18
δυνατός **63**.27-28
δύο **2**.7; **6**.10, 37, 45, 50; **8**.6, 15; **11**.4; **19**.**a**.7; **19**.**a**.**App**.12; **32**.14; **34**.8, 23; **37**.20; **41**.8, 25; **47**.9; **62**.30; **64**.14; **66**.5, 25; **90**.4
δυσκληρία **3**.4
δώδεκα **6**.14, 20, 30, 42; **62**.8-9
δωδέκατος **18**.10

ἐάν/ἤν/ἄν **4**.11; **6**.38; **8**.9; **13**.9; **19**.**a**.**App**.15; **34**.14; **38**.**a**.11, 14; **38**.**b**.11, 14; **39**.14; **40**.8; **46**.17; **47**.12; **65**.10, 14, 22 (ἤν); **66**.28; **68**.25; **69**.8; **70**.6, 10; **73**.15, 27; **76**.23
ἑαυτοῦ **23**.5, 11, 21; **67**.6
ἕβδομος **39**.5
ἔγγραφος **9**.10; **19**.**a**.10; **23**.26
ἐγγράφω **8**.7; **22**.4; **30**.21, 23, 25; **39**.18-19; **42**.36
ἐγγυητής **2**.10
ἐγγύς **43**.22
ἐγκαλέω **15**.9-10
ἐγχειρίζω **15**.6-7
ἐγώ **2**.10; **4**.4, 12, 14; **5**.1, 6, 21, 22, 26, 28; **6**.1, 39, 47; **7**.1, 9, 11, 12, 19, 24, 25; **8**.4; **9**.7, 8, 10, 11; **10**.1; **11**.1; **12**.1, 5, 6, 7, 8, 9, 14, 24, 35; **13**.4, 5, 6; **15**.8; **16**.1, 8; **17**.8; **19**.**a**.**App**.10; **20**.12, 15; **21**.7, 8, 10, 13, 19; **23**.9, 10, 11, 12, 15, 17, 19, 20, 21; **24**.1; **30**.11, 13, 14, 19, 22; **31**.22; **33**.19; **34**.4, 6, 11, 14, 16; **35**.6, 13; **36**.6; **37**.6, 13; **38**.**a**.6, 9, 15, 17; **38**.**b**.6, 9, 15, 17; **41**.6, 9, 14, 16, 17, 26; **42**.10, 21, 24; **43**.5, 23, 24, 25, 30; **44**.6, 14, 17; **45**.8, 10, 19, 29; **46**.1, 5, 10, 15, 29, 36; **47**.5, 19; **48**.3, 6; **49**.6, 23; **50**.1; **52**.6; **64**.1, 18, 21, 23, 28; **65**.2, 4, 7, 12, 27, 32, 34, 35, 44, 52; **66**.10, 11, 12, 18, 19; **68**.1, 3, 24, 26, 27; **69**.7, 10, 16; **70**.1, 15; **71**.5, 19, 25, 27, 33, 39, 41, 43, 44, 47, 49, 50, 52, 54; **72**.1, 20, 22, 26, 36, 37, 38, 51; **73**.1, 10, 11, 18, 21, 27, 31, 32; **74**.1, 4, 9, 11, 27, 30, 33, 34; **75**.1, 14, 34; **76**.1, 5, 36; **78**.1, 2, 11; **79**.1, 13; **80**.1; **81**.1, 3, 7, 9, 15
ἔδαφος **38**.**a**.6, 9; **38**.**b**.6, 9
(ἐ)θέλω **5**.9; **6**.40; **19**.**a**.**App**.15; **41**.12; **64**.16; **66**.8, 12, 19; **68**.27; **70**.5-6, 10; **71**.51; **72**.15; **74**.20

ἔθος	**19.a.App**.4; **23**.5; **46**.24
εἰ	**5**.18; **6**.25; **21**.4; **26**, Fr. II.4; **31**.18; **66**.29; **67**.4; **68**.23; **72**.18, 25, 30, 39; **74**.20, 28; **76**.24
εἶδος	**73**.10, 18
εἰκάζω	**65**.9-10
εἴκοσι	**38.a**.8-9; **38.b**.8; **62**.21-22, 32; **73**.16
εἰκώς, τὰ εἰκότα	**6**.52
εἰλικρινής	**63**.9-10
εἰμί	**2**.9; **3**.3; **4**.11, 14; **5**.17; **8**.11; **13**.8, 10, 11; **20**.14; **21**.12, 16; **23**.6, 8, 14, 15; **24**.3, 6; **30**.10, 13, 17; **31**.19, 20; **33**.21; **34**.16; **38.a**.11, 17; **38.b**.11, 17; **41**.18, 22; **42**.17; **44**.11; **47**.9; **48**.14; **49**.11; **63**.5, 27; **65**.7, 8; **67**.4, 9, 11; **71**.33, 36; **72**.11, 40; **74**.12; **76**.14; **87**.3; **88**.20
εἰς	**3**.13, 15; **6**.6, 31, 39, 50; **9**.5, 6, 8; **12**.18; **18**.6; **23**.20; **26**, Fr. I.6; **29**.5; **30**.8, 14; **31**.21; **34**.6; **39**.7; **40**.2; **41**.6; **42**.10; **43**.5, 24; **44**.6; **45**.8; **47**.5; **48**.8; **49**.6, 22; **51**.7; **52**.7; **54**.9, 19; **63**.16; **66**.21; **68**.12; **71**.16, 46, 51; **72**.18, 25, 35; **74**.10; **76**.18; **79**.4; **88**.25
εἷς	**6**.13, 19, 50; **10**.10; **13**.3, 4; **18**.8; **31**.37; **32**.11; **44**.7, 22; **45**.10; **46**.8-9, 27; **47**.7, 16; **49**.7, 24; **50**.4; **51**.5, 6; **65**.4; **66**.4; **72**.21, 27; **76**.10, 21; **80**.4; **81**.8
εἰσέρχομαι	**72**.47-48
εἴτε	**6**.32
εἴωθα	**21**.5
ἐκ (ἐξ)	**2**.7; **3**.17; **4**.5; **20**.13; **23**.21; **30**.20; **34**.9; **35**.1; **38.a**.6; **38.b**.6; **71**.13; **77**.9
ἕκαστος	**6**.13; **13**.3; **21**.4, 8; **23**.5; **30**.15, 18; **33**.11; **42**.15; **43**.8; **44**.9; **71**.28, 45
ἑκάστοτε	**23**.15
ἑκάτερος	**19.a.App**.19
ἕκατον	**35**.9; **62**.4, 18, 26, 30
ἐκδίδωμι	**19.a.App**.18; **31**.21; **42**.26; **43**.28; **44**.16; **46**.14-15; **50**.6; **51**.7; **52**.6
ἐκδικία	**21**.22; **23**.14, 28
ἐκδύνω	**23**.19
ἐκεῖ	**71**.19; **73**.28
ἐκεῖνος	**76**.23
ἔκθεσις	**61**.1
ἐκλαμβάνω	**3**.17
ἑκούσιος	**13**.9; **38.a**.14; **38.b**.14
ἐκπέμπω	**63**.17

ἐκπλέκω	**74**.30
ἐκπλήττω	**72**.28
ἔκτος	**30**.10, 22
ἐκφαίνω	**63**.8; **72**.48
ἐκφέρω	**23**.21
ἐλᾴδιον	**65**.21-22
ἐλαίη	**52**.5; **65**.10; **74**.15, 17-18
ἔλαιον	**45**.14, 15, 31, 38; **49**.6, 23; **61**.3; **80**.4; **90**.7
ἐλαιοποιεία	**49**.9
ἔλεγχος	**23**.21
ἐλέγχω	**23**.17-18
ἔλεος	**88**.15
ἐλευθερία	**48**.7
ἐμαυτοῦ	**2**.10; **8**.5
ἐμβάλλω	**26**, Fr. II.3
ἐμμένω	**13**.15, 17, 19, 21; **30**.20-21
ἐμός	**9**.11; **23**.9, 28; **65**.19
ἐν	**4**.15; **5**.11; **6**.50; **8**.2, 15; **11**.8; **13**.4, 7, 11; **19.a.App**.7; **20**.7; **23**.4, 12; **24**.8; **26**, Fr. I.2; **26**, Fr. II.11; **29**.5; **30**.4, 9, 10, 11; **31**.23, 39; **32**.4, 8; **34**.7, 17, 23; **35**.2; **37**.4, 7, 13, 19; **38.a**.17; **38.b**.17; **41**.2, 7, 18; **42**.4; **43**.2, 39; **44**.4, 25; **45**.3, 21, 30; **46**.21; **49**.2, 9, 12; **52**.4; **55**.10; **58**.3; **61**.1; **63**.4, 5, 9; **64**.24; **67**.3, 15; **68**.20, 29; **71**.3; **72**.22, 47; **73**.8, 14; **74**.35; **75**.10; **76**.14, 15, 30; **77**.11, 30; **85.a**.4; **85.b**.2
ἐνδέκατος	**44**.12
ἔνδον	**63**.14
ἕνεκεν	**26**, Fr. II.9; **71**.17
ἐνθάδε	**65**.17-18, 26, 27, 46-47
ἐνθαδί	**71**.15
ἐνθυμέω	**23**.16
ἐνιαυτός	**32**.13; **33**.11; **71**.45
ἐνίστημι	**19.a.App**.9; **32**.10; **42**.17; **43**.12; **44**.11
ἐννέα	**29**.6; **31**.40; **64**.22
ἔννομος	**4**.14; **8**.11; **13**.11; **31**.23; **33**.21; **40**.10; **43**.29; **45**.20-21; **48**.14; **58**.3
ἐνοίκιον	**32**.12; **33**.10
ἐνοχλέω	**74**.27
ἐντάσσω	**19.a**.16
ἐνταῦθα	**19.a.App**.7; **52**.4; **71**.23-24
ἐντεῦθεν	**9**.9; **42**.10; **48**.7
ἐντέλλω	**6**.3
ἐντολή	**3**.5, 8, 9, 10; **50**.3

ἐντός **13**.6
ἐξακολουθέω **4**.12; **8**.9; **34**.14; **35**.13; **36**.6; **38.a**.15; **38.b**.15
ἑξακόσιοι **44**.9-10
ἑξάμηνος **19.a**.12
ἐξαυτῆς **5**.10
ἔξειμι **13**.8; **19.a**.11; **38.a**.12; **38.b**.12; **39**.13; **76**.27
ἑξήκοντα **62**.12
ἑξῆς **3**.5; **24**.2; **35**.5; **39**.4
ἐξορκίζω **23**.26
ἐξουσία **8**.8; **34**.13; **36**.5; **38.b**.13
ἐπαγγέλλω **24**.6-7
ἐπακολουθέω **2**.2; **13**.9; **21**.5
ἐπάν **44**.15
ἐπανέρχομαι **6**.7-8
ἐπάνω **66**.7, 8, 25
ἐπάξιος **63**.29
ἔπαυλις **30**.10, 11, 23
ἐπεί **6**.8; **24**.2; **65**.25; **74**.12, 32
ἐπείγω **5**.23; **63**.13
ἐπειδή **5**.11, 23; **9**.3; **71**.20; **76**.4
ἐπεισέρχομαι **21**.11
ἐπεκτείνω **63**.9
ἔπεργον **42**.14, 23, 34
ἐπέρχομαι **4**.12-13; **8**.10; **21**.13; **23**.11; **30**.19; **34**.15; **35**.14; **36**.7; **38.a**.15-16; **38.b**.15-16
ἐπερωτάω **3**.5; **4**.15, 21; **8**.11-12, 16; **9**.15; **13**.11, 14, 15, 17, 20, 21; **14**.5; **19.a.App**.21; **30**.21; **31**.24, 33-34; **32**.15-16; **33**.21-22; **34**.17, 24; **36**.14; **37**.14, 21; **38.a**.18, 23; **38.b**.18, 23; **40**.10-11, 19; **41**.19, 28; **42**.28; **43**.30; **44**.18; **45**.22, 32; **48**.15, 19; **49**.13; **51**.7; **52**.7; **56**.2, 6-7; **58**.3
ἐπί + Gen. **3**.5; **4**.14; **8**.10; **9**.13; **13**.10; **19.a.App**.20; **20**.10; **21**.15; **23**.8, 10, 14, 22; **24**.6; **30**.3, 5; **31**.22; **32**.11; **33**.8, 18; **34**.16; **37**.12; **38.a**.16; **38.b**.17; **41**.15; **43**.26, 29; **44**.17; **45**.18; **47**.18; **51**.2
ἐπί + Dat. (*ἐφ' ᾧ/ᾧτε*) **8**.7; **13**.9, 13, 15, 17, 19, 21; **14**.5; **18**.8; **31**.31; **41**.9, 28; **42**.8; **45**.10, 29; **46**.9; **56**.5; **58**.6; **65**.7
ἐπί + Acc. **6**.46; **8**.4; **13**.3; **19.a**.7; **19.a.App**.11 **23**.14, 27; **30**.8; **34**.4; **34.App**.4; **35**.5; **37**.5; **38.a**.5; **38.b**.5; **39**.4; **47**.8; **54**.23, 26; **63**.8; **72**.43
ἐπιβάλλω **43**.21
ἐπιβουλεύω **21**.7
ἐπιδημέω **30**.7
ἐπιδίδωμι **21**.18, 26; **23**.26, 29; **24**.21; **57**.6-7

εὔνοια **48**.6; **63**.19
εὐπορία **42**.24; **44**.14-15
εὑρησιλογία **41**.13-14; **46**.14
εὑρίσκω **6**.10, 26, 33; **15**.9
εὐσέβεια cf. Index I
εὐσεβής **63**.23, 32
εὐτυχέω **5**.26-27; **46**.30-31; **64**.27; **69**.15; **72**.42
εὐτυχής **24**.8
εὐφημία **63**.7
εὐφραίνω **63**.12
εὐχαριστέω **88**.19
εὔχομαι **5**.7, 25; **6**.47; **7**.6, 20; **10**.14; **11**.12; **12**.3-4, 33; **16**.7; **17**.7; **46**.28-29; **63**.36; **64**.4-5, 26; **65**.49; **66**.13; **67**.16; **68**.5, 28; **69**.13; **70**.13; **72**.4, 41; **73**.25; **74**.4, 33; **75**.9, 26-27; **76**.31; **78**.7-8; **79**.13; **80**.8; **81**.14
ἔφοδος **23**.24
ἔχθρα **24**.2
ἔχω **5**.24; **7**.19; **8**.8; **9**.9; **18**.5; **19.a.App**.19; **21**.14; **23**.22; **26**, Fr. I.2; **30**.3, 5; **31**.35; **34**.13; **36**.5; **40**.2, 17; **41**.5; **42**.9, 32; **43**.4, 35; **44**.5, 21; **45**.7, 28; **46**.5; **47**.4, 14; **49**.5, 22; **50**.2; **64**.11; **65**.26, 44; **66**.12; **68**.26, 29; **69**.11; **70**.9; **71**.7; **72**.18, 21-22, 27; **73**.18; **74**.19, 32; **76**.20, 29; **90**.5
-έχω **77**.5
ἕως **13**.4, 5; **42**.25; **47**.10; **55**.6, 9; **73**.17; **74**.13; **83**.2, 3

ζάω **65**.12
ζημία **65**.26
ζητέω **6**.8; **66**.17; **76**.27
ζίζυφον **11**.10; **54**.3, 12, 15, 18, 24, 26
ζμύρνη **89**.4
ζ[μυρνόμελαν **85.a**.4 (?)
ζωή **88**.10, 17-18

ἤ **4**.11; **7**.12; **8**.10; **9**.11; **11**.7, 9; **27**.6; **30**.13, 17; **38.a**.11, 16; **38.b**.11, 16; **41**.12; **68**.25; **71**.36; **73**.16; **74**.20; **76**.28; **80**.6
ἤδη **23**.28; **70**.8
ἥδομαι **63**.17
ἡδύς **7**.19; **66**.12; **69**.10
ἡθμός **50**.5

ἡλικία **20**.12
ἡμεῖς **3**.4, 5; **8**.4, 9, 11; **13**.3, 8, 9, 10; **18**.6, 8; **19.a.App**.19, 20; **21**.5; **23**.5, 6, 13, 16; **30**.18; **39**.6, 7; **40**.3; **63**.2, 6, 27, 28, 36; **65**.12, 17, 36, 46; **71**.8, 11, 30, 31; **72**.13, 15, 21, 29-30, 45; **74**.16, 20, 22, 32; **76**.28; **88**.20, 23
ἡμέρα **5**.13; **21**.10; **42**.17; **72**.47; **73**.16; **81**.8; **82**.1; **85.b**.2; **88**.17
ἡμέτερος **6**.17; **23**.3; **24**.6; **72**.10; **77**.4
ἡμίσεια **30**.11; **34**.4, 11, 22, 27; **35**.6; **77**.16, 18
ἥμισυς **34**.23; **76**.10, 22; **79**.10
ἡσυχία **21**.18
ἥττων **23**.9
ἤτοι **42**.22

θαλλίον **52**.5
θανάσιμος **23**.12
θάνατος **23**.13-14
θαρρέω **23**.8
θαυμάζω **64**.5-6; **65**.3, 30; **68**.10-11; **69**.1; **70**.4; **71**.28-29, 48; **72**.19
θαυμαστός **72**.33
θεῖος **63**.16
θέλω cf. s.v. ἐθέλω
θεοσεβής **63**.15
θυγάτηρ **19.a.App**.10; **23**.25; **61**.12; **68**.4; **74**.7-8
θύρα **21**.11; **30**.12

ἴασις **88**.8
ἴδιος **18**.6; **30**.20; **40**.2; **41**.6; **42**.10; **43**.5; **44**.6; **45**.8; **47**.5; **48**.3; **49**.6, 22
ἰδού **6**.51; **64**.19; **71**.18; **73**.8
ἱκανός **63**.29
ἱμάτιον **71**.46
ἵνα **5**.15, 20, 23; **12**.30; **52**.5; **65**.20; **73**.11, 21; **80**.5
ἰνδικτίων cf. Index IV
ἴσος **30**.11; **72**.12
ἵστημι **41**.10-11
ἱστός **71**.51
ἰσχάς **51**.5
ἰχθῦς **71**.49

καδμεία	**89**.5
καθαρός	**6**.19; **47**.16
καθαρτής	**6**.45
καθεξῆς	**23**.5
καθολικός	cf. Index VII
καθόλου	**15**.16
καθώς	**12**.16-17
καιρός	**5**.17; **6**.31; **18**.9; **20**.8; **24**.8; **45**.12; **49**.10; **63**.30; **73**.22-23
κακός	**23**.28-29; **26**, Fr. II.9; **82**.2, 3, 6, 8, 9, 14, 16, 19, 21, 24, 26, 32; **83**.5, 6
καλός	**64**.25; **65**.8; **82**.12, 13, 14, 15, 16, 17, 18, 19, 20, 22, 23, 25, 27, 28, 29, 30, 31, 33; **83**.1, 8, 9, 10, 11, 12, 13, 14, 15, 16
κα.ός	**83**.7
καλόχρωμος	**72**.36-37
κάμηλος	**27**.6; **51**.4
καμηλών	**38**.**a**.9-10; **38**.**b**.9-10
κἄν	**71**.31; **72**.20
καρπίζω	**2**.9-10
καρπός	**5**.14; **63**.22; **74**.17
κατά + Acc.	**7**.5; **8**.13; **11**.10; **19**.**a**.10, 11; **19**.**a**.**App**.3; **21**.10; **23**.4, 5, 27; **24**.2; **30**.5, 10, 14, 22; **33**.27; **34**.20; **41**.10, 22, 31; **42**.15, 35; **43**.8; **44**.9; **46**.23; **50**.3; **63**.27; **67**.13; **71**.6, 28, 45; **74**.5, 8; **80**.4; see also Index III
κατά + Gen.	**23**.21
καταβάλλω	**26**, Fr. II.11
κατάγαιον	**13**.4
καταγράφω	**8**.3
κατάκειμαι	**4**.15; **13**.11; **31**.23; **34**.17; **37**.13-14; **38**.**a**.17; **38**.**b**.17-18; **41**.18-19; **45**.21-22; **49**.12; **58**.3
καταλαμβάνω	**26**, Fr. I.4; **68**.23; **72**.43; **74**.32
καταλείπω	**9**.7
καταλλαγή	**30**.21
καταλλάσσω	**30**.18, 24-25
καταμένω	**8**.2; **19**.**a**.**App**.7; **30**.4; **32**.3-4, 7-8; **35**.2; **41**.2; **43**.2; **45**.2; **49**.2
καταντικρύ	**30**.12; **43**.23
καταξιόω	**71**.31-32
κατασπορά	**5**.18
καταστάσιος	**20**.7
κατασχίζω	**21**.11

κατασωτεύομαι	**23**.16
καταφεύγω	**20**.16; **23**.28
καταφυγή	**88**.21
κατέχω	**23**.9; **44**.15; **73**.20
κάτω	**41**.16
κεῖμαι	**74**.12
-κεῖμαι	**77**.6
κελεύω	**5**.8-9; **20**.18; **65**.11; **66**.12; **69**.10
κέλλα	**13**.4, 5, 6, 7; **32**.11; **33**.8, 14
κεφάλαιον	**41**.12; **42**.14, 19, 21, 33; **43**.7, 13; **44**.7, 13, 22
κηπίον	**39**.5
κλεπτ-	**23**.17
κληρονομία	**12**.28 (?); **30**.8-9; **39**.8 (?); **43**.24
κληρονόμος	**12**.26
κληρόω	**23**.3, 5, 6
κλιβανωτός	**71**.27
κοινός	**13**.7; **76**.29
κοινωνέω	**15**.15-16
κοινωνία	**30**.10-11
κοινωνός	**23**.9
κόλλημα	**22**.5
κολοβός	**42**.5
-κομιδή	**77**.20
κομίζω	**63**.18, 31
κόμμι	**61**.5
-κόπτω	**19.a.**15
κόρα	**71**.44
κοῦκι	**52**.5
κραταιός	**88**.6
κρατέω	**66**.28
κριθή	**10**.6; **11**.5; **55**.2; **61**.11; **78**.4; **79**.8
κρίκιον	**71**.50-51
κρίνω	**19.a.App**.9; **71**.33
κρύπτω	**66**.20
κτάομαι	**13**.3
κτῆνος	**5**.24; **27**.6; **77**.7
κύημα	63.15-16
κυθρίδιον	**71**.49
κυρία (Subst.)	**5**.6; **12**.5, 6, 8; **68**.3; **71**.52
κυριεύω	**8**.8; **30**.18; **34**.10; **36**.4; **38.a**.12; **38.b**.12
κύριος (Adj.)	**3**.5; **4**.13; **8**.10; **9**.13; **13**.10; **19.a.App**.20; **30**.21; **31**.20; **32**.15; **33**.17; **34**.15; **37**.12; **38.a**.16; **38.b**.16; **39**.17; **40**.9; **41**.18; **42**.27; **43**.28; **44**.16; **45**.17; **47**.18; **48**.14; **49**.10

κύριος (Subst.) **3**.2; **6**.1, 47; **7**.1, 25; **10**.1; **11**.1; **12**.1, 9, 35; **16**.1, 8; **17**.7; **19**.**a**.**App**.3 **20**.6; **21**.19; **23**.3, 28; **24**.1; **50**.1; **63**.1, 33; **64**.1, 28; **68**.1, 24; **70**.1, 15; **71**.1, 9, 47; **72**.1, 51; **73**.1, 32; **74**.1, 33, 34; **75**.1, 13-14, 34; **76**.1, 36; **78**.1, 11; **79**.1, 13; **80**.1; **81**.1, 3, 14; **88**.4; see also Index I
κώμη **3**.4, 11, 12; **4**.5; **8**.3; **9**.2; **14**.7; **15**.6; **19**.**a**.**App**.7 **23**.3; **24**.6, 13, 15, 17; **32**.8; **33**.5; **37**.1, 3-4, 8, 23; **40**.2; **43**.1, 2; **44**.4, 24; **49**.7, 24 (cf. also Index VI.b)
κωμήτης **28**.2, 5
-κωμήτης **21**.13

λαμβάνω **33**.15; **63**.35; **64**.14; **65**.9; **66**.3, 16, 17, 20, 22, 29; **67**.8; **68**.24; **74**.20; **78**.2; **85**.**a**.3
λαμπρότατος see Index II, VIII
λατρεύω **88**.18-19
λέγω **13**.7; **63**.20; **72**.46; **76**.6-7
λειτουργέω **72**.13-14
λειτουργία **23**.6; **72**.17, 25-26
λειτουργός, δημόσιος **21**.12; **23**.3, 4, 12 (δημόσιος)
λευκός **34**.4-5; **34**.**App**.4
λευκόχρωμος **35**.7
λήθαργος **65**.37-38
λίβελλος **3**.2; **23**.14
λινουφικός **12**.19-20
λίψ **30**. 12; 17; **38**.**a**.8, 9; **38**.**b**.8, 9; **39**.7
λογίζομαι **43**.11; **44**.10; **46**.22
λόγος **9**.8, 9; **13**.9; **26**, Fr. I.6; **43**.8; **44**.8; **46**.6; **53**.1; **54**.1; **55**.1; **64**.18, 24
λυπέω **72**.44
λύχνος (?) **50**.5
λύω **76**.26

μάθησις **19**.**a**.**App**.11
μαλακία **88**.13
μάλιστα **71**.35
μανθάνω **65**.46; **66**.8, 19; **67**.22; **70**.9; **74**.14, 21
μαρτυρέω **8**.18, 19; **14**.8; **30**.26; **37**.24; **48**.20; **58**.8; **63**.11; **76**.35
μάρτυς **23**.24, 25
μαῦρος **30**.12
μαφόρτιον **65**.32

μέγας **20**.9-10; **51**.2; **75**.19; **85.a**.16; **85.b**.19a (?); **87**.4
μελαγχαίτης **42**.5
μέλι **64**.22, 25
μέλλω cf. Index II
μέλω **65**.33-34
μέν **6**.25; **13**.4; **63**.31; **67**.4; **72**.12; **74**.28
μένω **64**.6
μέρος **4**.5; **12**.24; **19.a.App**.15; **19.b**.6; **30**.10, 22; **34**.12, 13; **37**.6, 7, 19; **39**.5, 12; **43**.21; **74**.16
μέσος **23**.12
μετά + Acc. **19.a**.12; **22**.3; **47**.7 (+ Acc.?), 11; **70**.5; **73**.10 (?); **77**.30
μετά + Gen. **5**.6, 13; **6**.21; **7**.4; **12**.7, 9, 31; **19.a.App**.4; **21**.14; **23**.3, 6, 7, 11; **39**.12; **42**.22, 34; **48**.5; **68**.4; **70**.4; **71**.17, 22, 25, 40, 53; **73**.10 (?), 12, 14, 16-17, 22
μεταξύ **19.b**.6
μεταπέμπω **71**.19
μεταφέρω **3**.4
μεταφορά **3**.13
μεταχειρίζω **23**.15
μετέρχομαι **9**.11; **23**.7; **76**.4-5
μέτριος **3**.3; **20**.14; **63**.12; **77**.2
μετριότης **23**.9
μέτρον **6**.35
μέχρι **69**.3; **76**.14
μή **3**.8, 9, 11; **5**.15; **7**.7; **8**.16; **11**.11; **13**.8, 9, 14, 16, 18, 20, 22; **14**.6; **15**.9; **16**.6; **21**.4, 15, 26; **23**.14; **24**.12, 15, 16, 20; **26**, Fr. II.4; **30**.24, 26; **32**.22; **34**.25; **36**.15; **37**.22; **39**.21; **40**.19; **42**.39; **43**.40; **44**.26; **45**.34; **46**.33; **47**.13, 20; **49**.26; **50**.8; **51**.10; **52**.13; **58**.7; **64**.16; **65**.14; **66**.11, 26, 29; **68**.6, 17, 20, 25, 26; **70**.10, 12; **71**.15, 24, 34; **72**.21, 44; **73**.20; **74**.20, 24; **78**.6; **80**.3; **81**.6
μηδέ **5**.16; **15**.12; **21**.12; **24**.6
μηδείς **3**.3; **24**.7; **76**.29
μηδε[**40**.5
μῆκος **13**.5
μήν **2**.9; **6**.52; **42**.15, 18, 35; **43**.8, 11; **44**.9, 11; **45**.30; **46**.11 (?); **47**.8-9, 9, 10-11; **68**.11; **90**.4
μηνύω **21**.19
μήτε **21**.12
μήτηρ **2**.4, 7; **9**.7; **12**.5; **30**.3, 5, 9; **35**.1; **42**.1, 6; **44**.1; **65**.43-44; **68**.4; **71**.42, 48, 50, 52; **73**.5; **74**.4, 6, 11, 25

μικκός **65**.21
μικρός **71**.42; **72**.7, 31, 37
μιμνῄσκομαι **64**.20-21
μισθός **53**.12; **54**.7, 13, 19, 22; **65**.7; **71**.47; **73**.19; **74**.19
μισθόω **31**.30; **32**.9, 19; **33**.6-7;
μίσθωσις **31**.20, 31, 36; **32**.15; **33**.17-18, 29
μισθωτός **31**.30, 42
μνημονεύω **65**.35-36, 36-37
μοναχός **13**.10
μόνος **23**.6; **32**.10; **47**.9; **63**.28; **72**.24, 31-32; **77**.28
μυριάς **43**.18, 36; **46**.8, 9, 26-27; **47**.6, 8, 13; **90**.1

ναῦλον **53**.13
νεομηνία **45**.13; **46**.11; see also Index III
νέος **30**.2
νεοχάρακτος **8**.6
νή **71**.14
νῆψις **67**.7
νομίζω **68**.21-22
νομός **8**.3; **9**.3; **19**.**a**.**App**.8; **30**.7; **33**.5; **44**.4; **45**.6 (cf. also Index VI.a)
νόμος **21**.5, 15
νόσος **88**.12
νότινος **30**.10; **68**.21
νότος **30**.11; **38**.**a**.7, 10; **38**.**b**.7, 10; **39**.6
νοῦς **63**.10
νυκτερινός **86**.18
νῦν **8**.4, 7; **13**.3; **23**.22; **30**.8; **34**.3, 10; **34**.**App**.4; **35**.5; **36**.3; **37**.4, 5; **38**.**a**.5; **38**.**b**.5; **39**.4, 11; **42**.7; **63**.21
νυνί **42**.4; **72**.45
νύξ **23**.20

ξύλον **68**.18

ὅδε **13**.8, 13, 15, 17, 19, 21; **20**.17; **21**.18; **23**.14; **43**.27; **49**.10
ὅθεν **19**.**a**.16; **23**.25
ὀθόνιον **51**.5-6

οἶδα **3**.8, 9, 11; **5**.17; **8**.16; **13**.14, 16, 18, 20, 22; **14**.6; **21**.26; **24**.12, 15, 16, 20; **30**.24, 26; **32**.23; **34**.25; **36**.15; **37**.22; **39**.21; **40**.19-20; **42**.39; **43**.40; **44**.26; **45**.34; **46**.33; **47**.20; **49**.26; **50**.8; **51**.10; **52**.13; **58**.7; **65**.34; **71**.36-37; **72**.21; **73**.23; **77**.21
οἰκ- **13**.5
οἰκέω **37**.4; **42**.4; **43**.39; **44**.4, 24
οἰκία **13**.4; **19.b**.8; **23**.20, 21, 22; **30**.12, 16, 17; **32**.11; **33**.8-9; **37**.7, 19; **38.a**.10; **38.b**.10; **43**.22; **73**.8; **74**.26
οἰκογενής **19.a.App**.10
οἰκοδομέω **68**.13-14
οἰκονομέω **8**.8; **30**.18; **38.a**.13; **38.b**.13
οἰνάριον **23**.17, 20
ὀκτακόσιοι **10**.13
ὀκτώ **6**.50; **62**.12
ὀλίγος **9**.4; **63**.22; **74**.9-10
ὁλοκληρέω **5**.7-8; **7**.6; **72**.4-5
ὁλοκληρία **88**.8-9
ὅλος **26**, Fr. II.10; **30**.16; **32**.13; **40**.6; **72**.47; **73**.8; **83**.4
ὁμιλέω **64**.12
ὄμνυμι **2**.5; **24**.4
ὁμοίως **24**.17; **62**.31; **63**.34
ὁμολογέω **2**.5; **3**.5; **4**.4, 16, 21; **8**.3, 12, 16; **9**.9, 15; **13**.3, 8, 11, 14, 15, 17, 19, 21; **14**.6; **18**.5; **19.a.App**.8, 21; **24**.4; **30**.8, 21; **31**.24, 34; **32**.16; **33**.6, 22; **34**.3, 18, 24; **34.App**.3; **35**.4-5; **36**.15; **37**.5, 14, 21; **38.a**.4, 18, 24; **38.b**.4, 18, 24; **39**.4; **40**.2, 11, 19; **41**.5, 19, 28-29; **42**.9, 28; **43**.4, 31; **44**.5, 18; **45**.6, 23, 33; **47**.4; **48**.4, 15, 19; **49**.5, 13, 21; **51**.4, 8; **52**.3, 7; **56**.3, 7; **58**.3; **76**.19
ὁμολογία **9**.13; **13**.8, 10; **14**.4; **19.a.App**.19; **31**.19; **40**.9-10; **41**.27; **56**.5, 10; **58**.5
ὁμότυπος **13**.10; **30**.21
ὅμως **63**.11; **71**.34
ὀνικός **5**.24; **52**.4-5
ὄνομα **7**.5-6; **23**.6, 23; **67**.13; **71**.6-7, 28; **74**.5; **83**.24-25
ὄνος **5**.22; **20**.11
ὀπίσω **30**.16
ὁπόταν **41**.12; **42**.20; **43**.15
ὅπου **12**.19
ὅπως **6**.20, 50; **64**.6, 15; **68**.11; **74**.19; **88**.15
ὁράω **12**.30; **67**.11-12; **70**.12
ὁρίζω **46**.19

ὁρμάω **27**.5
ὁρμή **9**.5
ὅρος **41**.28
ὅς **4**.11; **7**.8, 18; **8**.7, 9; **13**.5, 13, 15, 17, 19, 21; **14**.5; **19.a.App**.19; **21**.14; **23**.23, 28; **28**.3; **30**.11, 13, 17; **31**.20, 31; **34**.14; **36**.6; **38.a**.11, 14; **38.b**.11, 14; **39**.14; **43**.13; **56**.5; **58**.6; **63**.14; **64**.23; **65**.7, 17; **66**.9, 12; **68**.27; **69**.8, 9; **72**.40, 47; **77**.30; **85.a**.5; **87**.3; **90**.2
ὁσημέραι **21**.7; **71**.12
ὅσος **63**.27; **65**.44
ὅσπερ **8**.6; **23**.20; **34**.8; **41**.17
ὅστις **23**.11; **71**.13
ὅτι **3**.3; **6**.10, 39; **15**.14; **64**.9; **65**.6, 26, 31, 35, 45; **66**.8, 19; **68**.22; **70**.5, 10; **71**.22, 35, 37, 49, 51; **72**.13; **74**.14, 21, 26; **87**.3; **88**.19-20, 23
οὐ(κ) **5**.23; **6**.33; **21**.17; **23**.18; **24**.4; **27**.6; **65**.3, 33, 36; **70**.5; **71**.20, 34, 36, 48; **72**.15, 18, 19, 24, 27, 32; **76**.27
οὐδέ **19.a.App**.14; **20**.6; **64**.12; **66**.20; **71**.30
οὐδείς **9**.9, 11; **12**.11; **20**.5; **64**.10-11; **65**.5; **66**.17, 19, 22, 23; **76**.30
οὐκέτι **3**.4
οὐλή **30**.3, 5
οὖν **5**.18; **6**.16, 50; **63**.31; **64**.11; **65**.8, 43; **73**.9; **74**.28
οὔπω **65**.45; **69**.4; **74**.18
οὐράνιος **2**.5
οὔτε **72**.22, 23
οὗτος **3**.13, 16; **5**.14; **6**.21-22; **12**.27; **13**.8; **15**.6, 10, 11; **18**.8; **19.a.App**.15; **21**.19; **23**.15, 18, 25-26, 29; **24**.4, 8; **26**, Fr. II.2; **32**.13; **34**.5; **41**.14; **42**.15, 26; **43**.8; **44**.9, 16; **46**.15; **48**.9, 13; **50**.6-7; **56**.5; **63**.8, 10, 13; **64**.18, 20; **65**.6; **67**.8; **71**.21, 49; **72**.14-15, 18-19, 43; **86**.17
οὕτως **1**.12; **21**.16
ὀφειλή **43**.26
ὀφείλω **42**.32
ὀφθαλμός **23**.13
ὄφλημα **42**.25
ὄχλησις **24**.7
ὄψις **23**.28
ὀψωνιαστής **23**.6

παιδίον	**26**, Fr. II.2; **71**.23
παῖς	**23**.15
πάλαι	**71**.13
παλαιός	**30**.17
πάλιν	**6**.32; **39**.6; **63**.22-23; **69**.8; **88**.24
πανάγιος	**88**.24
πανταχοῦ	**8**.11; **48**.14
παντελής	**15**.10
πάντοθεν	**4**.11; **38.a**.11; **38.b**.11; **66**.17-18
παντοῖος	**44**.14
πάντως	**10**.9; **17**.3; **65**.16; **72**.14; **79**.11
πάνυ	**63**.17; **72**.44; **73**.4; **74**.32
πάππος	**30**.5, 9, 22
παρά + Acc.	**21**.8; **65**.22
παρά + Dat.	**3**.2; **7**.5; **11**.5; **46**.5; **64**.7; **67**.4, 10; **72**.39; **73**.21
παρά + Gen.	**2**.4; **6**.11; **8**.6; **15**.2; **18**.6; **19.a**.2; **19.b**.2; **19.a.App**.2; **20**.3; **21**.3; **23**.2, 13, 23; **24**.1; **31**.35; **32**.9; **33**.7; **34**.8; **40**.2; **41**.7, 24; **42**.10, 20; **43**.4; **44**.6; **45**.8; **47**.4; **49**.5, 22; **50**.2-3; **51**.4; **52**.4; **64**.9, 11, 14; **65**.51; **70**.9; **71**.48, 49
παραβαίνω	**13**.8; **19.a.App**.15
παραβάλλω	**23**.11
παραδίδωμι	**9**.8; **45**.11, 29
παρακρεμάσιον	**71**.49
παραλαμβάνω	**51**.4; **52**.4, 11
παραμένω	**41**.9; **71**.15
παρασκευάζω	**26**, Fr. II.10
παράστασις	**27**.6
παρατήρησις	**82**.2, 4, 7, 9
παραφέρω	**41**.16
παραχωρέω	**4**.4, 20
παραχώρησις	**4**.13
πάρειμι	**2**.10; **7**.8; **19.b**.5; **42**.18; **43**.11; **45**.12; **48**.20; **69**.4; **76**.15
παρεπιδημέω	**21**.8
παρέχω	**2**.10; **11**.6; **42**.14; **43**.7; **44**.8; **46**.10; **52**.5-6; **70**.7; **73**.19; **76**.16; **80**.5-6; **81**.10
παρουσία	**23**.3
πᾶς	**4**.12; **5**.8; **8**.7, 9, 10, 15; **12**.2, 4; **13**.13, 15, 17, 19, 21; **14**.5; **15**.11; **23**.4, 18; **30**.19, 21, 23, 25; **31**.32; **34**.10, 15; **35**.11, 12, 13, 14; **36**.3; **37**.7, 21, 24; **38.a**.15; **38.b**.15; **39**.18; **42**.24, 36; **43**.14; **44**.13, 14; **46**.13; **48**.8; **56**.6; **58**.6; **63**.25, 37; **65**.18; **66**.2;

	67.12; **70**.3, 4; **72**.3, 9-10, 11; **73**.7-8, 27; **74**.3; **81**.12; **88**.11-12, 12-13, 14
πάσχω	**23**.14, 29; **24**.7; **76**.24
-πάσχω	**77**.10
πάτηρ	**9**.8; **11**.6; **12**.1, 34, 36; **16**.1, 8; **26**, Fr. II.2; **30**.5, 9, 22; **50**.1; **69**.2; **74**.1, 15, 34; **75**.14
πείθω	**34**.9; **36**.2; **39**.10-11
πεκούλιον	**48**.6
πελύκιον	**21**.11; **71**.25-26
πέμπω	**5**.19; **6**.16, 50, 51; **65**.24, 29, 31, 34; **66**.7, 9, 19; **67**.18-19; **71**.43, 50; **72**.23, 32-33; **74**.9, 13; **79**.4
πένης	**3**.16
πεντ-	**12**.25
πέντε	**10**.7; **13**.1, 8; **38.a**.8; **38.b**.8; **45**.14, 31
πεντακισχίλιοι	**39**.9; **42**.13, 33
πεντακόσιοι	**42**.16, 35
πεντασσός	**13**.10
πενταχοεία	**49**.9-10
πεντεκαιδέκατος	**45**.16
περί + Gen.	**6**.8; **7**.18; **8**.9; **9**.9; **12**.10, 17; **15**.11; **19.a**.14; **19.b**.7; **34**.13; **36**.5; **38.a**.13; **38.b**.13; **39**.13; **64**.8, 13, 20; **65**.4, 17, 18, 46; **66**.11, 23; **68**.9, 27; **69**.1, 9; **71**.10; **72**.12, 29
περί + ?	**31**.37
περιέχω	**13**.13, 15, 17, 19, 21; **14**.5; **31**.32; **56**.5; **58**.6;
πίμπλημι	**63**.25
πίμπλησις	**72**.17
πινακίδιον	**67**.17
πίπερι	**89**.2
πιπράσκω	**8**.3, 8, 14; **34**.3, 11, 22; **34.App**.3; **35**.5; **36**.4, 14; **37**.5, 18; **39**.4, 11-12; **73**.17
πιστεύω	**7**.10; **65**.19
πίστις	**76**.18
πιστός	**12**.15; **65**.24
π[ιττάκιον	**85.a**.3 (?)
πλάγιος	**30**.5-6
πλεονεξία	**20**.7
πλευρά	**23**.13
πληγή	**21**.14, 14-15; **23**.12
πλήρης	**8**.7; **34**.9; **35**.10; **36**.2; **37**.20; **88**.8, 9
πληρόω	**9**.10; **44**.15; **65**.13; **76**.20
πλήσσω	**23**.13
πλοῖον	**53**.13
-πλοῦς	**9**.13; **30**.21

πνεῦμα **88**.14
πνευματικός **63**.21
ποθεινότατος **63**.1; **71**.2
ποιέω **3**.2; **5**.20; **6**.22-23, 27-28; **9**.5, 6; **12**.29; **23**.4, 16; **64**.17; **65**.8-9; **70**.11; **72**.40; **73**.11, 15, 27
ποκάριον **72**.20
πολλάκις **71**.18-19
πόλεμος **23**.12
πόλις **4**.3; **28**.1; **34**.3; **34**.**App**.3; **52**.3; see also Index VI.a
πολύς **1**.17; **3**.15; **5**.4, 26; **6**.48; **7**.4, 20, 23; **12**.3, 34; **17**.9; **20**.8; **23**.8, 10; **46**.30; **63**.5, 38; **64**.4, 26; **65**.2, 26, 49; **66**.2, 3; **68**.3, 28; **69**.13; **70**.3, 14; **71**.4, 41; **72**.3, 41; **73**.3, 25-26; **74**.3, 5, 7; **75**.6, 11, 27-28; **76**.31-32; **78**.9; **79**.14; **81**.15
πορίζω **20**.15-16
πορφύρα **61**.1; **72**.31; **73**.29; **74**.10, 14, 23
ποσάκις **12**.9-10
ποτε **15**.9; **24**.6; **74**.29
ποτίστρα (?) **55**.11
πούς **30**.6
πρᾶγμα **5**.16, 21; **9**.10; **15**.10-11; **68**.8, 21
πραγματευτικός **15**.5; cf. also Index XI
πρᾶσις **8**.10; **30**.14; **34**.15-16, 27; **37**.12
πράττω **15**.16 (?)
πρεσβύτερος cf. Index VII
πρό **12**.2; **23**.14; **65**.6; **66**.2; **67**.22; **70**.3; **72**.3; **74**.3; see also Index III
προαίρεσις **63**.33
προβολή **55**.5, 8
προγράφω **19**.**a**.**App**.23
προδηλόω **19**.**a**.**App**.14, 17
προηγουμένως **5**.3-4; **71**.4; **73**.2-3; **75**.5-6
προθεσμία **46**.20; **47**.12
προίξ **23**.16
πρόκειμαι **3**.8, 9, 10; **4**.20; **8**.5, 14, 15; **13**.13, 15, 17, 19, 21; **14**.4, 5; **21**.25; **23**.31; **30**.21, 22, 23, 24, 25; **31**.29, 31, 33, 40, 41-42; **32**.19, 20; **33**.28, 29; **34**.12, 21, 24; **36**.13-14, 14; **37**.18-19, 20, 24; **38**.**a**.23; **38**.**b**.22, 23; **39**.19; **41**.11-12, 23, 24, 28; **42**.32, 36-37; **43**.26-27, 35, 37; **44**.21, 23; **45**.27; **46**.26; **48**.18, 19, 20; **49**.8-9, 21; **51**.8; **52**.11, 12; **56**.4, 6; **57**.6; **58**.5
προλέγω **6**.50; **19**.**a**.14-15; **21**.16; **23**.10; **24**.7-8; **28**.3
πρόλοιπος **46**.6; **73**.29
πρόνοια **71**.7-8

προοράω — **72**.16
πρός + Acc. — **5**.10, 22; **6**.16; **8**.5, 7; **9**.4, 9; **13**.6, 10; **19.a.App**.9, 11; **20**.15, 16; **21**.21; **23**.21, 28; **24**.7; **26**, Fr. I.4; **30**. 8, 15, 17; **32**.10; **34**.10; **35**.8; **36**.3; **38.a**.7, 12; **38.b**.7, 12; **39**.11; **42**.27; **43**.11, 28; **44**.16; **46**.16; **48**.6; **50**.7; **63**.14, 26, 33; **69**.2; **70**.7; **71**.11, 30; **72**.15, 27, 45; **73**.22; **76**.30; **77**.22; **85.a**.2, 6; **85.b**.1, 16
πρός + Gen. — **23**.13
πρός + ? — **3**.14; **28**.4; **66**.23
προσ.[— **39**.15
προσαγορεύω — **5**.5; **7**.24; **63**.38; **71**.5, 8, 27, 38-39, 41, 52, 53; **72**.3-4, 5, 38; **73**.3; **75**.8, 12-13
προσδοκέω — **69**.5; **71**.12-13, 20, 23
προσέχω — **67**.6
προσήκω — **19.b**.9; **21**.21-22
προσθήκη — **81**.7
προσκαρτερέω — **23**.7
προσκυνέω — **75**.10
πρόσοδος — **28**.4
προσοκνέω — **23**.7 crit.app.
προσομολογέω — **63**.32
προσπο[— **3**.14
προστίθημι — **77**.30 (?)
πρόστιμον — **13**.9
προστυγχάνω — **26**, Fr. II.8
πρότερος — **3**.13; **26**, Fr. I.2
προτίθημι — **15**.13; **23**.31; **77**.30 (?)
πρόφασις — **26**, Fr. II.9; **74**.24
προχωρέω — **21**.4
πτύξ — **67**.18
πυλών — **13**.5-6, 6
πωλέω — **65**.22-23, 28; **66**.24
πῶλος — **34**.4, 11, 22, 27; **65**.28
πῶς — **65**.3; **71**.29, 48; **72**.19

ῥιγοπύρετον — **85.b**.1
ῥόπαλον — **21**.14; **23**.11, 22
ῥύμη, δημοσία ῥ. — **30**.11, 16; **38.a**.11; **38.b**.11
ῥώννυμι — **5**.24-25; **6**.46; **7**.20; **10**.13-14; **11**.12; **12**.33; **16**.7; **17**.6; **46**.28; **64**.25; **65**.48; **66**.13; **67**.15; **68**.27-28; **69**.12; **70**.13; **71**.47, 54; **72**.10, 40-41, 50; **73**.24-25; **74**.33; **75**.25; **76**.30-31; **78**.7; **79**.12; **80**.8; **81**.13

σαβάνιον **72**.34
σάκκος **72**.32
σαπρός **82**.2, 3, 6, 7, 8, 9, 9-10
σεαυτοῦ **48**.13
σείω **26**, Fr. I.2
σεληνοδρόμιον **82**.11
σημαίνω **3**.14
σημειόω **31**.42
σήμερον **9**.6; **32**.9; **34**.8; **35**.10; **47**.4-5
σιδηροῦς **71**.51
σιτοβολεῖον **13**.5
σῖτος **6**.14, 19, 30, 42, 50; **32**.14; **47**.16
σκέπασις **23**.21
σός **5**.9, 10; **21**.18; **43**.28; **44**.16; **70**.4; **71**.4, 11; **73**.24; **77**.21
σπέρμα **85**.**b**.18 (?); **87**.2
σπεύδω **6**.15; **63**.25-26
σπουδάζω **74**.32
σπουδή **73**.11-12, 24
σπυρίδιον **51**.6; **63**.31
στατήρ **71**.48
σταφίς **51**.5
στέγη **13**.4
στήμων **71**.48
στόμα **63**.6
στρατηγικός **23**.5; cf. also Index VIII
σύ **4**.4; **5**.5, 25; **6**.34, 43, 47; **7**.4, 5, 6, 8, 20; **8**.3, 6, 7, 8, 15; **9**.3, 8, 9; **10**.14; **11**.5, 12; **12**.3, 4, 10, 17, 33; **13**.1, 19; **16**.7; **17**.6; **18**.6, 9; **19**.**a**.**App**.8, 19; **20**.16; **26**, Fr. II.4; **30**.8, 9, 23, 25; **31**.21, 35; **32**.9, 11, 12; **33**.7, 8; **34**.3, 8, 10, 11, 12, 22, 24; **34**.**App**.3; **35**.5, 11; **36**.3, 4; **37**.5; **38**.**a**.4, 10, 11, 12, 13; **38**.**b**.4, 10, 12, 14; **39**.4, 11, 12, 13; **40**.2; **41**.6, 9, 10, 13, 24; **42**.10, 14, 21, 25, 26; **43**.5, 7, 27, 28; **44**.6, 8, 15, 16; **45**.8, 11, 29; **46**.10, 15, 28; **47**.4, 14; **48**.5, 6, 8; **49**.5, 8, 22; **50**.3, 6; **51**.4, 7; **52**.4, 6; **64**.4, 7, 13, 18, 24, 26; **65**.5, 11, 13, 14, 15, 16, 19, 20, 22, 31, 34, 35, 38, 39, 48; **66**.2, 3, 8, 9, 13, 19; **67**.4, 5, 19; **68**.3, 6, 8, 10, 28, 29; **69**.12; **70**.3, 7, 11, 13; **71**.15, 20, 25, 46; **72**.2, 3, 5, 6, 8, 18, 23, 29, 40, 41; **73**.3, 4, 5, 6, 7, 9, 19, 20, 21, 25; **74**.3, 5, 27, 32, 33; **75**.6, 9, 26; **76**.17, 19, 20, 27, 31; **78**.7; **79**.12; **80**.8; **81**.10, 13; **88**.5, 7, 15, 18, 19, 20, 25
συγκληρονόμος **13**.8

συγκόπτω	**20**.13-14; **21**.14; **23**.12, 13
συγχωρέω	**81**.6-7
συλλειτουργός	**23**.8
σύμβιος	**21**.9-10, 13; **71**.6, 40; **72**.5-6; **73**.6-7
συμπείθω	**13**.8
συμφωνέω	**8**.5; **34**.6-7; **34**.**App**.5-6; **35**.7-8; **39**.8
σύν	**13**.6, 19; **30**.10, 16; **44**.23; **46**.22; **68**.22
συναγορεύω	**26**, Fr. II.10
συνάγω	**42**.22, 34; **73**.12
συνακτικός	**67**.21
συνεπιπάρειμι	**19**.**a**.4; **19**.**a**.**App**.4; **41**.25-26
σύνεργον	**74**.13
συνεργός	**26**, Fr. I.2
συνευδοκέω	**2**.10-11; **19**.**a**.4-5; **19**.**a**.**App**.4, 25
συνεχῶς	**63**.13; **74**.27
συνηθεία	**3**.12
συνήθης	**23**.4
συννόμως	**22**.4
συνταγή	**11**.10-11; **74**.9; **80**.5
συντίθημι	**13**.9, 15, 17, 19, 21
σύστασις	**68**.29
σφόδρα	**77**.1
σχεδόν	**77**.16
σχιστός	**68**.18
σχολάζω	**68**.11-12; **72**.24
σχολή	**72**.26
σῶμα	**21**.15; **41**.30; **44**.26; **45**.36; **76**.14, 26-27
σωματίζω	**37**.23
σωτήρ	**88**.20
τάξις	**2**.2, 3, 8; **23**.5; **24**.1
τάσσω	**26**, Fr. I.2; **77**.30
τάχος	**75**.11
τάχυς	**7**.9; **65**.23; **66**.11; **72**.43; **74**.13
τε	**15**.4; **21**.16; **23**.13; **30**.9, 19; **63**.5, 19
τεκμήριον	**63**.19
τέκνον	**19**.**a**.**App**.3; **71**.40-41, 53, 54; **73**.5, 7
τεκτονικός	**4**.6, 7; **38**.**a**.7-8; **38**.**b**.7
τελετή	**86**.17
τελέως	**68**.9
τέλος	**23**.4
τέσσαρες	**3**.14; **16**.5; **62**.22, 32
τεταρταῖος	**86**.18

τέταρτος **37**.6, 19; cf. also Index II
τετρακισχίλιοι **10**.5; **11**.8-9
τετραχρύσους **29**.5-6 (cf. Index X.b)
τέχνη **19.a.App**.11
τέως **5**.14; **71**.7; **73**.20
τηρέω **65**.6, 20, 45
τίθημι **3**.8, 9, 10; **13**.13; **14**.4; **33**.28; **41**.27; **48**.18; **56**.4; **58**.5
-τίθημι **88**.5
τίκτω **85.a**.5; **87**.3
τιμή **6**.50; **8**.5, 15; **11**.7; **34**.6, 22; **34.App**.5; **35**.7; **36**.1; **37**.19; **39**.8; **45**.11, 30; **46**.6-7; **54**.21; **65**.24, 30; **66**.9, 25
τιμιώτατος **71**.1, 12; **75**.16-17
τις **3**.15; **6**.39; **7**.10; **12**, 31 (?); **13**.9; **23**.6, 14; **26**, Fr. II.6; **31**.18; **40**.8; **43**.14; **64**.9; **66**.17, 20 (?); **76**.6, 24
τίς **65**.36; **88**.20
τίς ποτε **74**.29
τοίνυν **21**.6, 16; **65**.8, 43; **70**.6
τοιοῦτος **34**.5; **63**.36; **72**.28
τόκος **41**.10, 11; **44**.23; **46**.22; **47**.15
τολμάω **21**.21
τόμος **22**.5
τόπος **3**.15; **4**.10; **20**.10; **23**.8-9, 11; **38.a**.6, 13, 23; **38.b**.6, 14, 23; **65**.7, 19-20
τοσοῦτος **63**.8; **68**.7; **70**.5; **71**.29, 32
τότε **20**.7, 12; **64**.24
τουτέστιν **47**.15
τραπέζα **37**.8
τρεῖς **79**.10
τρέφω **19.a.App**.13
τριάκοντα **26**.Fr. II.10; **62**.30; **73**.29
τρίς **66**.9
τρισχίλιοι **41**.8, 25; **66**.28; **70**.8
τριταῖος **86**.17
τρίτος **33**.27
τρίχους **50**.5 (cf. Index X.a)
τρόπος **8**.9; **34**.14; **36**.6; **38.a**.14; **38.b**.14; **39**.13
τροφεύω **8**.4
τρύγη **18**.9 (?)
τυγχάνω **21**.13, 21; **30**.9; **88**.16
τύπος **3**.15
τυραννία **23**.10, 15

τυραννικῶς **20**.11
τύχη **2**.5; **23**.5 (cf. also Index I)

ὕβρις **23**.22
ὑγιαίνω **12**.4; **64**.5; **68**.5; **74**.4; **76**.23
ὕδωρ **3**.4; **77**.8
ὕαλος **50**.6
υἱός **5**.7; **6**.23; **9**.11; **12**.7, 9, 16, 17, 32; **19**.**a**.11,12; **21**.11, 17; **30**.7; **60**.2; **63**.1; **64**.8, 15; **65**.39; **67**.1, 22; **68**.1; **71**.6, 10; **72**.6, 13, 23; **73**.9, 21; **74**.2, 35 (?); **81**.1
υἱωνός **30**.6
ὑμεῖς **6**.16; **19**.**b**.6; **63**.9, 20, 26-27, 29, 32-33, 38; **67**.10, 13-14, 14, 16; **68**.22; **71**.53; **72**.43
ὑμέτερος **63**.6, 14-15, 18-19; **71**.37-38
ὑπάγω **27**.5
ὑπάρχω **4**.4; **8**.4; **33**.7-8; **34**.4; **35**.6; **37**.6; **38**.**a**.5-6; **38**.**b**.5; **39**.5
ὑπέρ + Gen. **3**.8, 9, 11; **6**.13, 18, 31; **7**.8; **8**.11, 16; **10**.5, 10, 11; **13**.9, 10, 14, 15, 18, 20, 21; **14**.6; **19**.**a**.**App**.17, 20; **21**.26; **24**.12, 14, 16, 19; **29**.4; **30**.19, 24, 26; **31**.36, 38; **32**.12, 22; **33**.10, 19; **34**.12, 16, 25; **36**.15; **37**.13, 22; **39**.21; **40**.19; **41**.17, 29; **42**.14, 38; **43**.7, 30, 40; **44**.8, 17, 25; **45**.11, 19, 29, 33, 38; **46**.5, 32; **47**.17, 19; **49**.25; **50**.8, 12; **51**.10; **52**.12; **56**.7; **58**.6; **62**.2, 7, 16, 25, 28; **64**.23; **66**.6; **73**.30; **76**.9, 10, 28; **78**.4
ὑπερβολή **48**.4
ὑπέρθεσις **43**.14; **44**.13-14
ὑπερπηδάω **23**.20
ὑπερτίθημι **5**.14-15
ὑπερῷον **13**.5, 6
ὑπεύθυνος **15**.12-13
ὑπηρετέω **41**.10
ὑπηρεσία **72**.25; **77**.22
ὑπό + Acc. **41**.10; **48**.5
ὑπό + Dat. **23**.3
ὑπό + Gen. **8**.4; **20**.8; **23**.9, 18; **29**.9; **34**.11; **41**.16; **44**.15; **70**.11
ὑποβάλλω **15**.5; **23**.22
ὑπογραφεύς **13**.11; **41**.17
ὑπογραφή **3**.5; **4**.14; **8**.10; **9**.13; **13**.10; **19**.**a**.**App**.20; **31**.22; **33**.18-19; **34**.16; **37**.12; **38**.**a**.17; **38**.**b**.17; **41**.15; **43**.29; **44**.17; **45**.18-19; **47**.18-19

ὑπογράφω	**3**.5; **8**.11; **33**.20; **34**.16; **37**.12-13; **41**.16-17; **43**.30; **44**.17; **45**.19-20; **47**.19
ὑποδείκνυμι	**7**.12; **74**.25, 29-30
ὑποδειξ-	**7**.17
ὑποκάτω	**85.b**.17, 18 (?); **87**.1, 1-2
ὑπόκειμαι	**21**.15; **42**.24-25
ὑπόμνημα	**3**.17; **53**.10
ὑπομνηματίζω	**2**.8
ὑποτίθημι	**43**.20
ὑφαιρέω	**23**.17, 20
ὑψηλός	**88**.7
ὑψόω	**88**.24
φαίνω	**21**.15; **72**.43
φανερός	**15**.11
φέρω	**63**.15; **64**.21; **71**.25
φήμι	**6**.9
φιλαδελφία	**75**.7
φίλος	**41**.17
φοίνιξ	**16**.4; **78**.4
φόνος	**23**.15, 17
φόρετρον	**29**.4, 8; **64**.13; **66**.6; **71**.44-45 (cf. also Index XI)
φορέω	**86**.16
φόρος	**62**.2, 7, 16, 25, 29
φροντίζω	**23**.9
φυγαδεύω	**3**.12, 16; **23**.19
-φυλακία	**81**.9
φυλάττω	**15**.8
φωτεινός	**63**.26
χαίρω	**4**.3; **5**.3; **6**.3; **7**.3; **8**.3; **9**.3; **10**.3; **11**.4; **12**.2; **13**.2; **15**.4; **16**.3; **18**.5; **27**.3; **30**.7; **32**.8; **33**.6; **34**.3; **34.App**.3; **35**.4; **37**.4; **38.a**.3; **38.b**.3; **39**.3; **41**.5; **42**.8; **43**.3; **44**.5; **45**.6; **46**.4; **48**.3; **49**.4; **50**.2; **52**.3; **63**.4, 18; **64**.3; **65**.2; **66**.1; **67**.3; **68**.2; **70**.2; **71**.3; **73**.2; **74**.2; **75**.4; **76**.3; **78**.2; **79**.3; **80**.2; **81**.3
χαλκός	**50**.4
χαλκοῦς	**71**.26
χαμαίρετος	**8**.4
χαρίζω	**38.a**.4, 13, 22; **38.b**.4, 13, 22-23; **71**.46 (?)
χάρις	**38.a**.4, 16; **38.b**.4, 16; **65**.13, 15; **72**.11; **74**.23

χάρτης **53**.8; **54**.21
χείρ **8**.6-7; **34**.9; **36**.2; **41**.6; **42**.12; **72**.22; **88**.3
χειρόγραφον **42**.26; **43**.27; **44**.27
χθές **21**.10
-χίλιοι **13**.9; **66**.5-6
χιτώνιον **65**.33; **66**.4, 24, 25; **74**.10
χοι- **7**.12
χοιρίδιον **6**.5, 9, 25, 37
χοῖρος **23**.16, 17, 18
χορηγέω **71**.46 (?)
χράομαι **23**.10; **63**.13-14; **64**.17
χρεία **18**.7; **23**.7; **40**.3; **41**.7; **42**.11; **43**.5; **44**.7; **45**.9; **47**.6; **49**.6, 23; **65**.25; **68**.25; **71**.17; **72**.18; **74**.12, 32
-χρεία **77**.26
χρεωστέω **64**.23; **74**.28, 29
χρῆμα **3**.13
χρηματίζω **19.a.App**.3
χρηστότης **5**.11
χρονίζω **76**.15
χρόνος **5**.27; **6**.48-49; **7**.21; **8**.4; **9**.4; **12**.34; **13**.3; **17**.9-10; **19.a**.7; **19.a.App**.12, 14, 17; **21**.6; **30**.8; **34**.4; **34.App**.4; **35**.6; **37**.6; **38.a**.5; **38.b**.5; **39**.5; **43**.11, 20; **44**.10; **46**.31; **64**.27; **65**.50; **68**.7, 28; **69**.14; **70**.5, 14; **71**.32; **72**.42; **73**.26; **75**.29; **76**.32; **78**.9; **79**.14-15; **81**.16
χώρα **21**.2; **23**.29; **77**.14
χώρημα **30**.11, 16, 17
χωρίζω **88**.11
χωρίον cf. Index VI.b
χωρίς **6**.43; **19.a.App**.3, 18; **41**.13; **43**.14; **45**.17; **46**.12; **53**.13

ψιλός **4**.10; **38.a**.23; **38.b**.23; **39**.6, 7
ψυχή **63**.27
ψυχικός **63**.23

ὦ **74**.32
ὦμος **77**.9
ὠνέομαι **8**.7; **34**.11; **36**.4
ὥρα **69**.8; **72**.27; **78**.2
ὡς **3**.8, 9, 10; **4**.15; **5**.8, 17; **6**.50; **8**.15; **13**.11, 13, 15, 19, 21; **14**.5; **21**.14, 15; **23**.12, 17, 20; **30**.3, 5, 21,

23, 25; **31**.23, 33, 40; **32**.20; **33**.29; **34**.17, 24; **36**.14; **37**.13, 20, 24; **38.a**.17, 23; **38.b**.17, 23; **39**.19; **41**.18; **42**.36; **43**.37; **44**.23; **45**.21; **48**.12, 19; **49**.12; **52**.12; **56**.6; **58**.3; **64**.7, 8; **68**.19, 25; **71**.1; **72**.43; **74**.18, 27

ὥσπερ **33**.14-15

ὥστε **15**.6; **23**.7

1: FRAGMENTS OF AN OFFICIAL DOCUMENT (A PREFECTURAL DECREE?)

2: DOCUMENT ON OATH

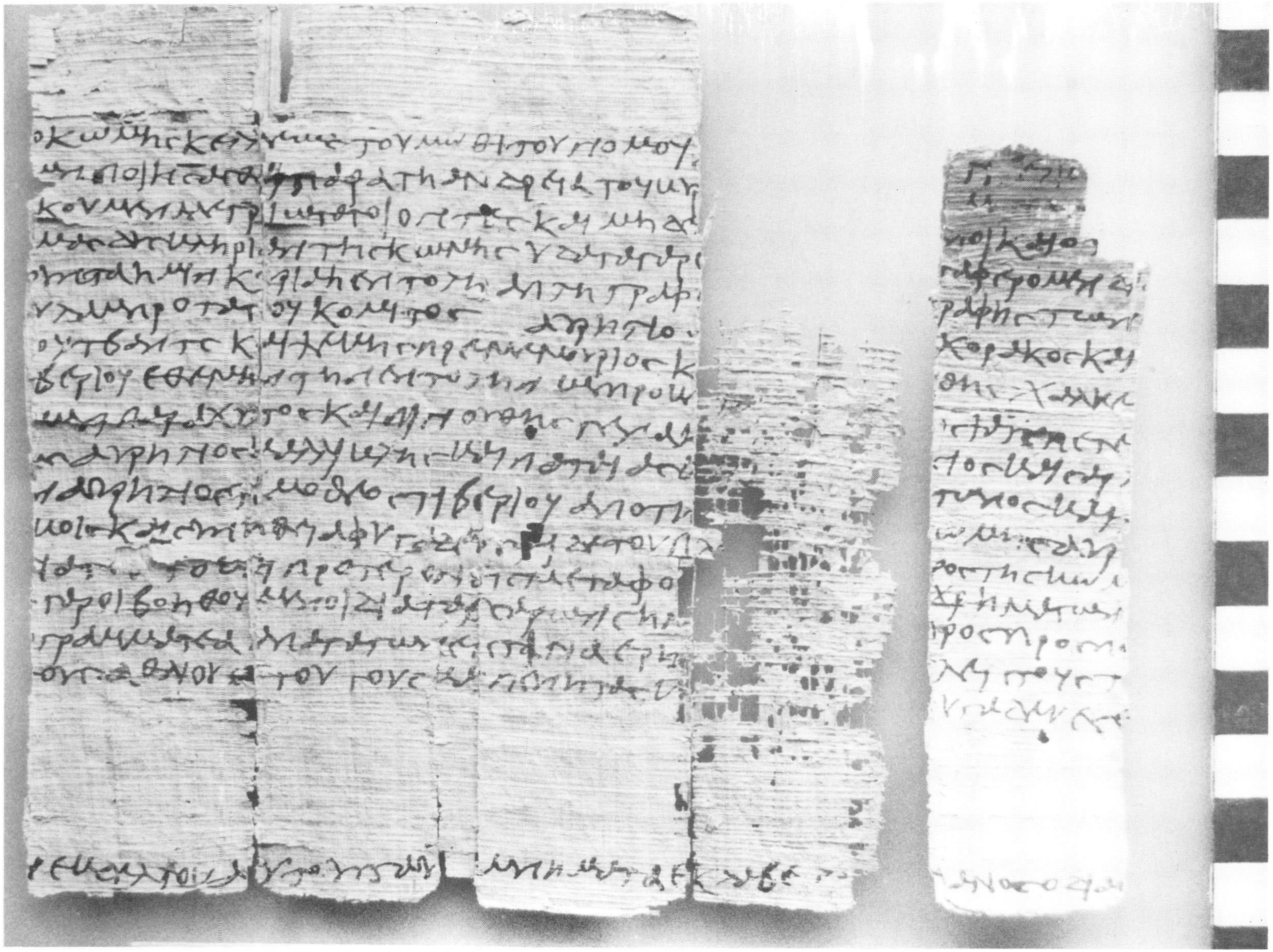

3: DOCUMENT CONCERNING IRRIGATION

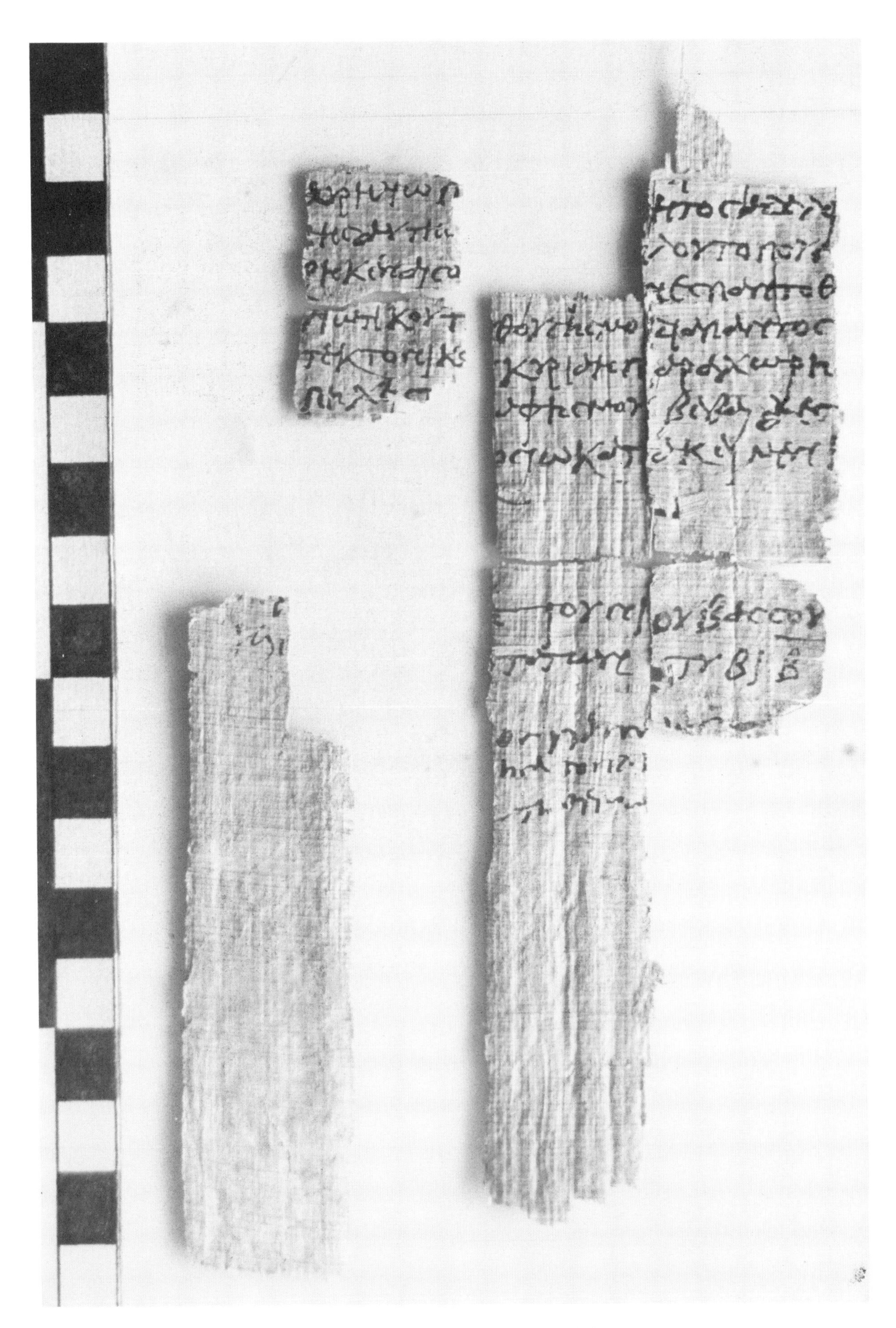

4: CONTRACT OF *PARACHORESIS*

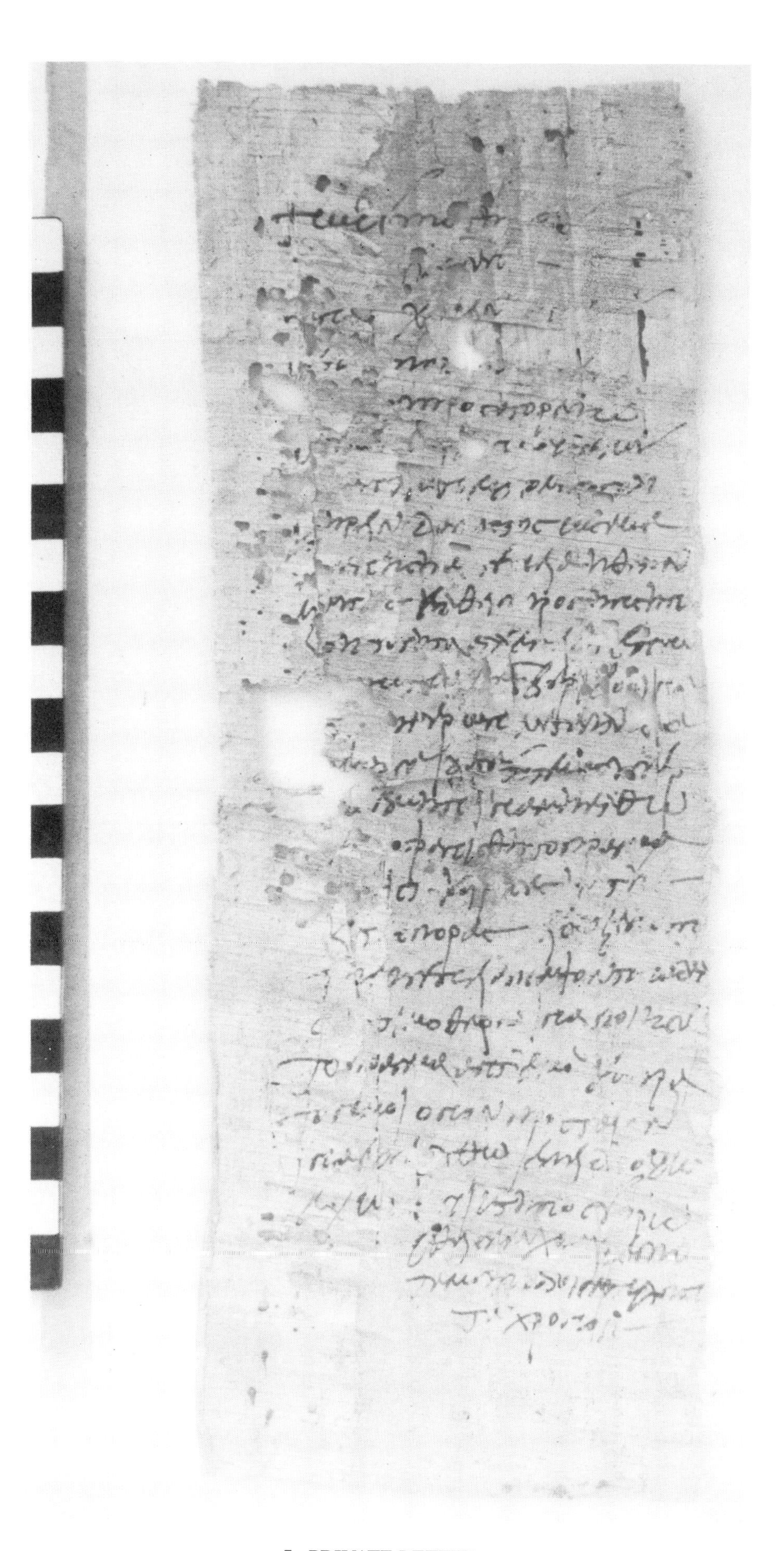

5: PRIVATE LETTER

6: PRIVATE LETTER

7: PRIVATE LETTER

8: SALE OF A SLAVE

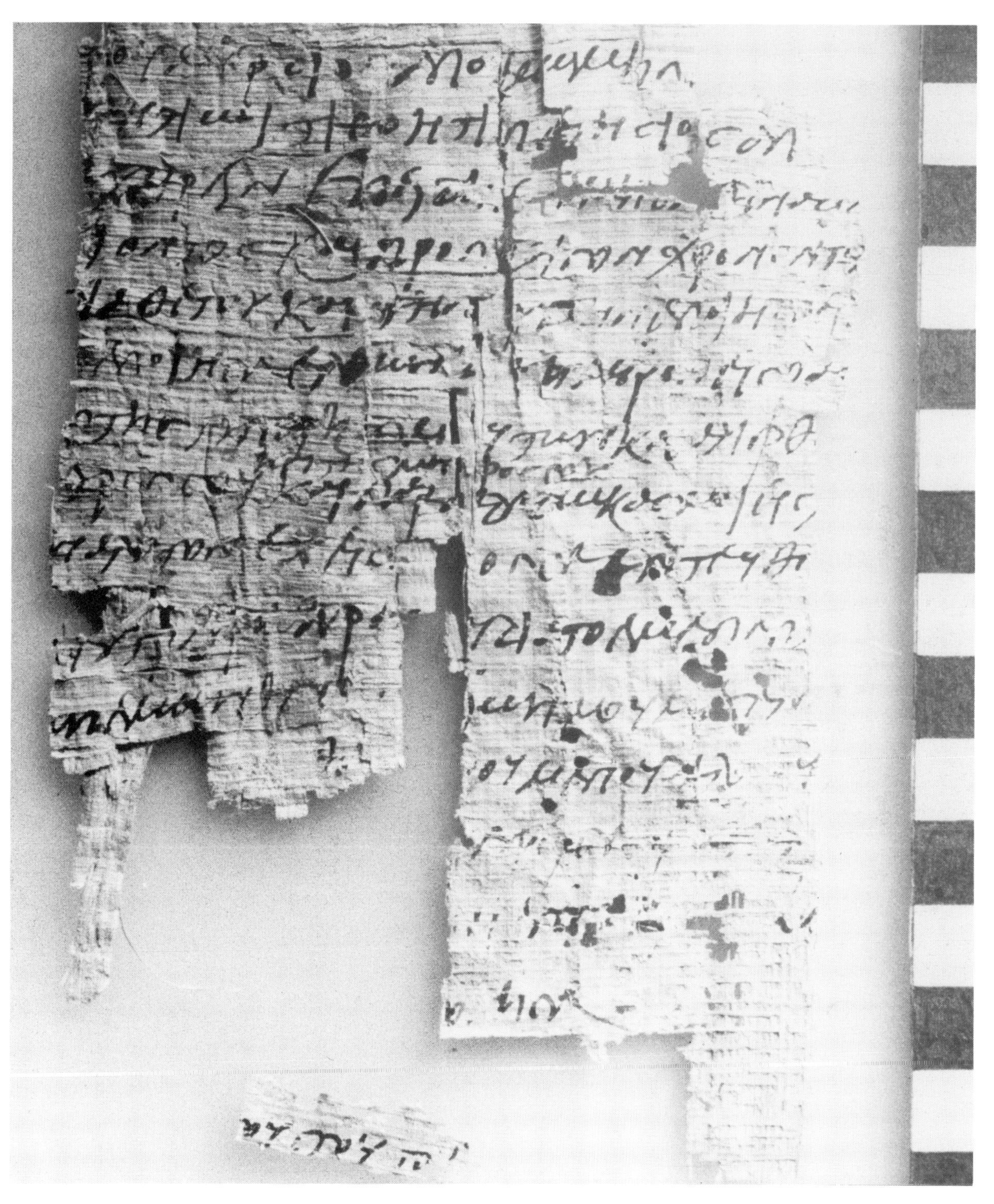

9: PRIVATE AGREEMENT

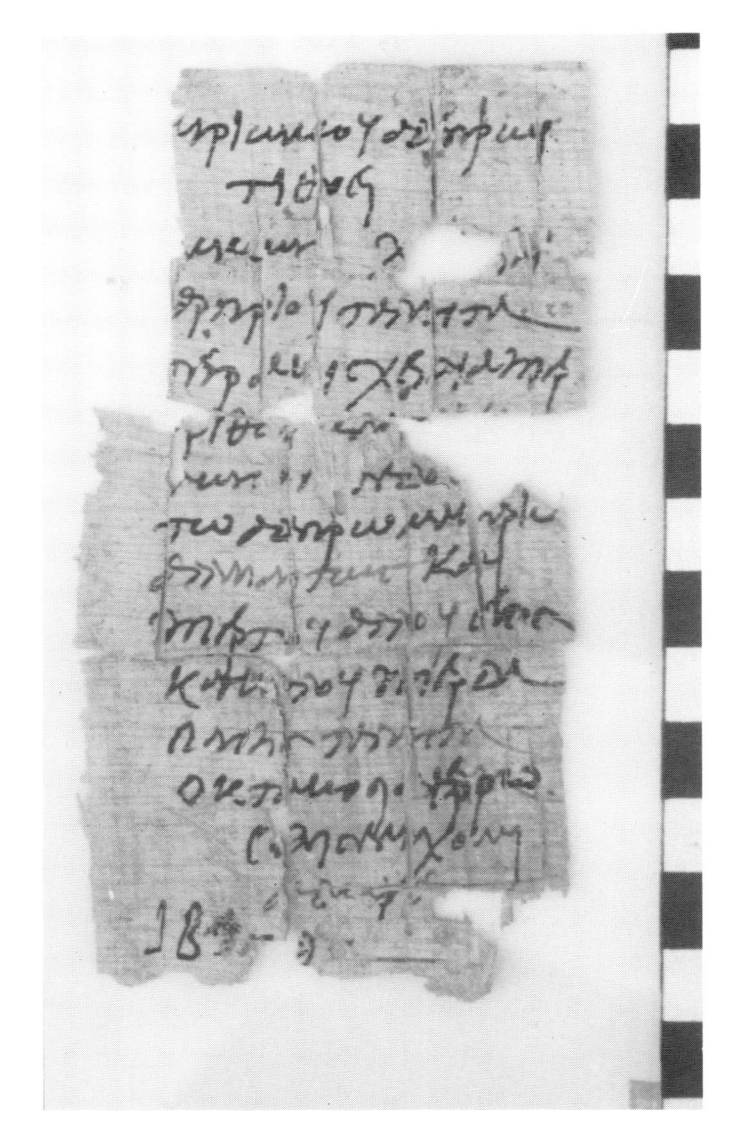

10: ORDER OF PAYMENT

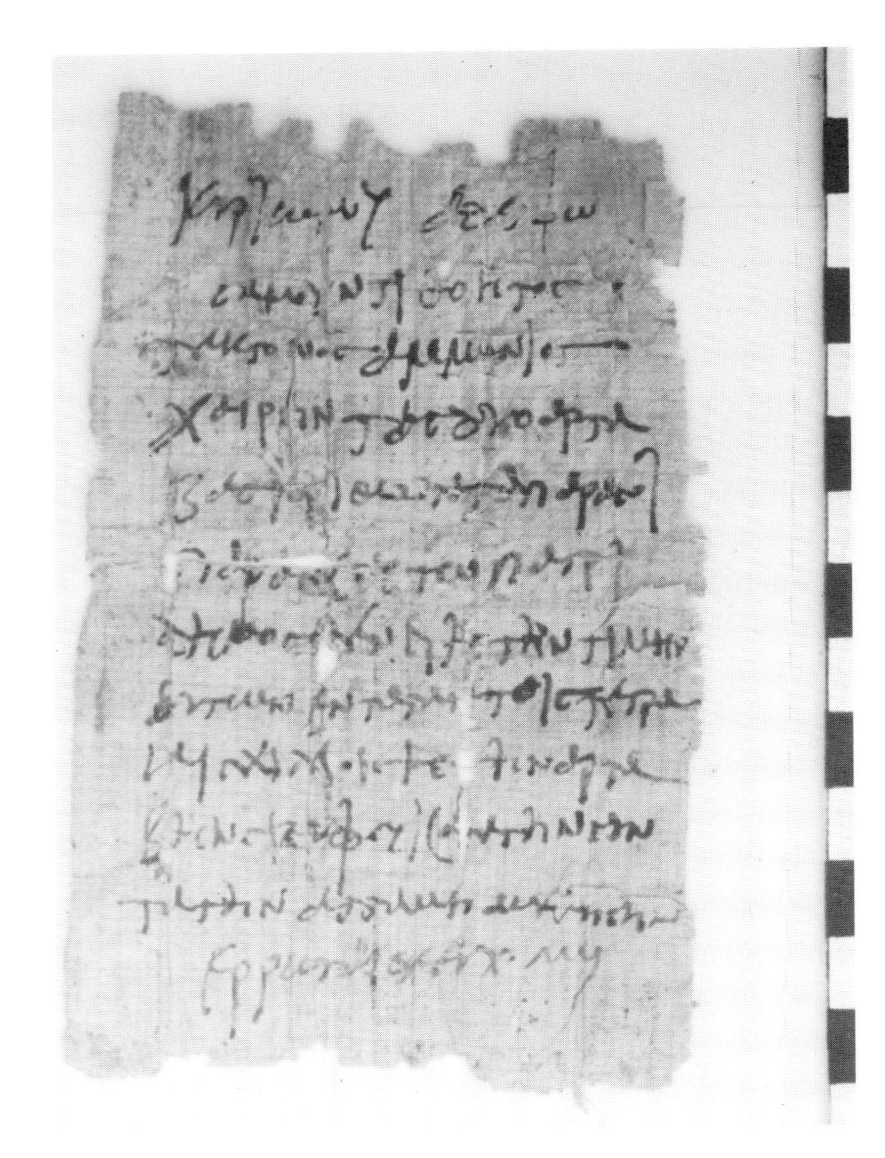

11: ORDER OF PAYMENT

12: FRAGMENTS OF A PRIVATE LETTER

13: DIVISION OF PROPERTY

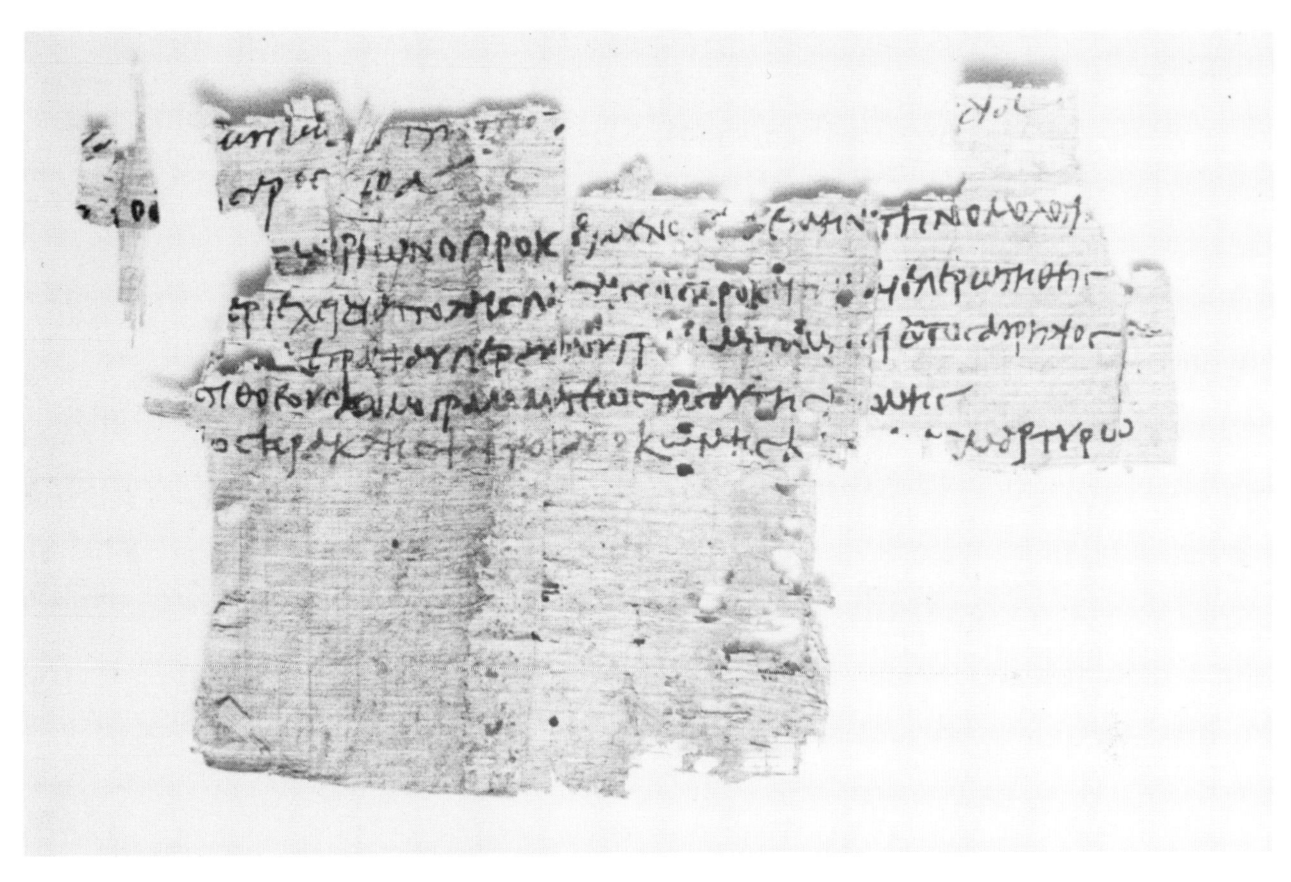

14: FRAGMENT OF AN AGREEMENT

15: PUBLIC DECLARATION TO THE PRAESES THEBAIDOS

16: BUSINESS NOTE

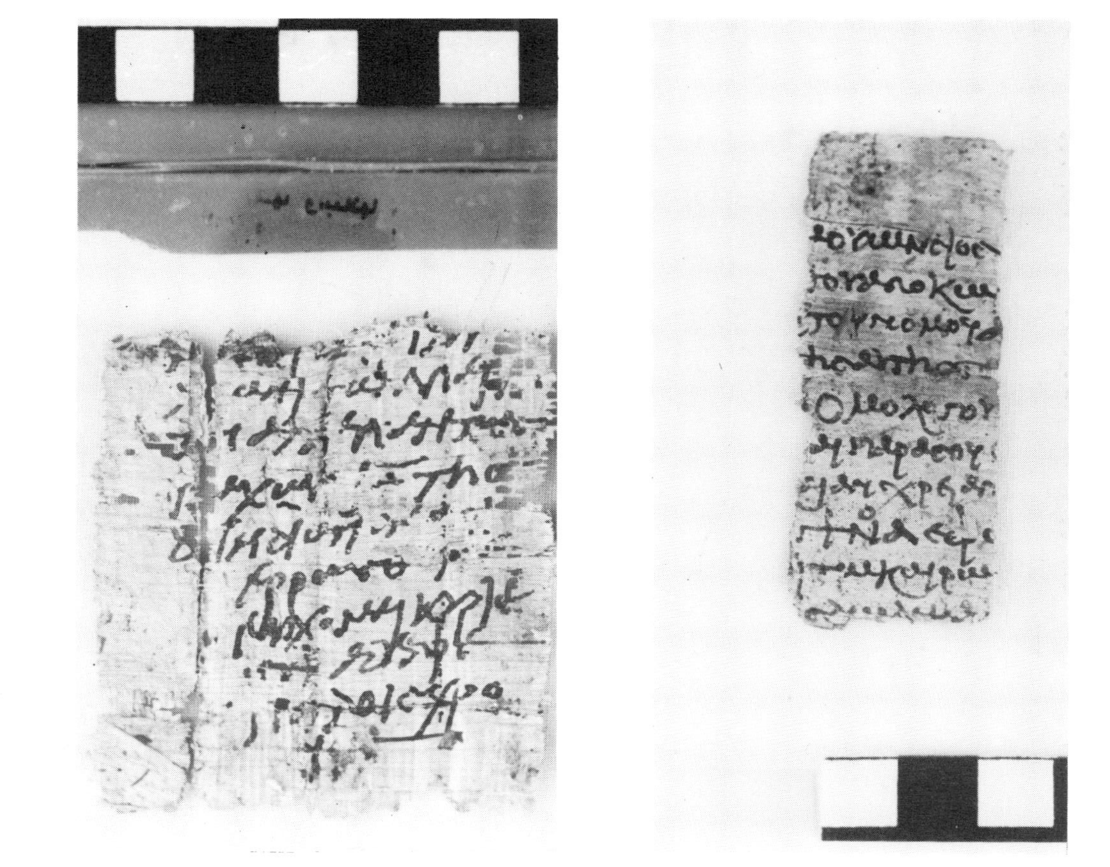

17: END OF A LETTER

18: FRAGMENT OF A LOAN OF MONEY

19.a: PETITION TO THE PRAESES THEBAIDOS

19.a.appendix: CONTINUATION OF **19.a**?

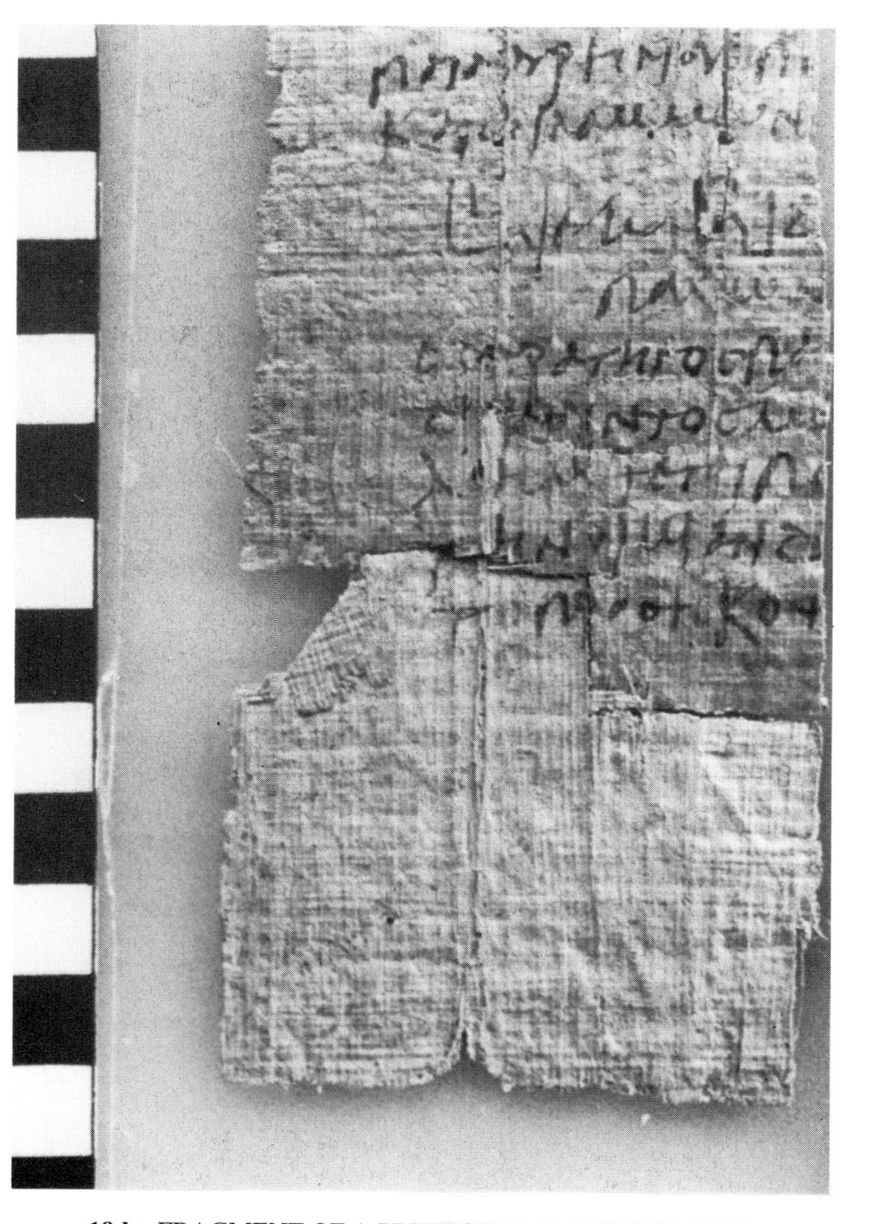

19.b: FRAGMENT OF A PREFECTURAL HYPOGRAPHE

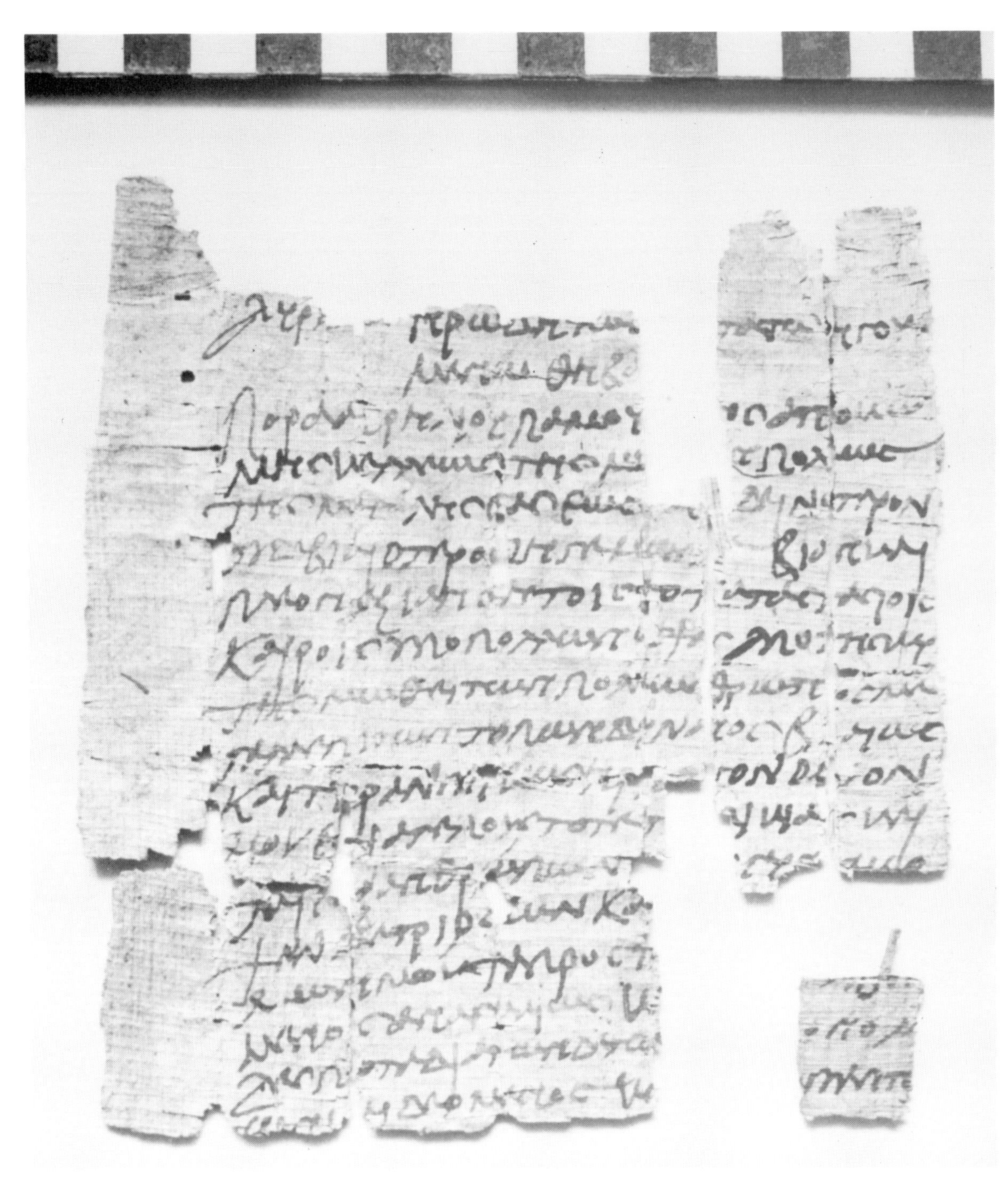

20: PETITION TO THE PRAESES THEBAIDOS

21: PETITION TO A FORMER MAGISTRATE

22: PART OF A DATED PREFECTURAL (?) HYPOGRAPHE

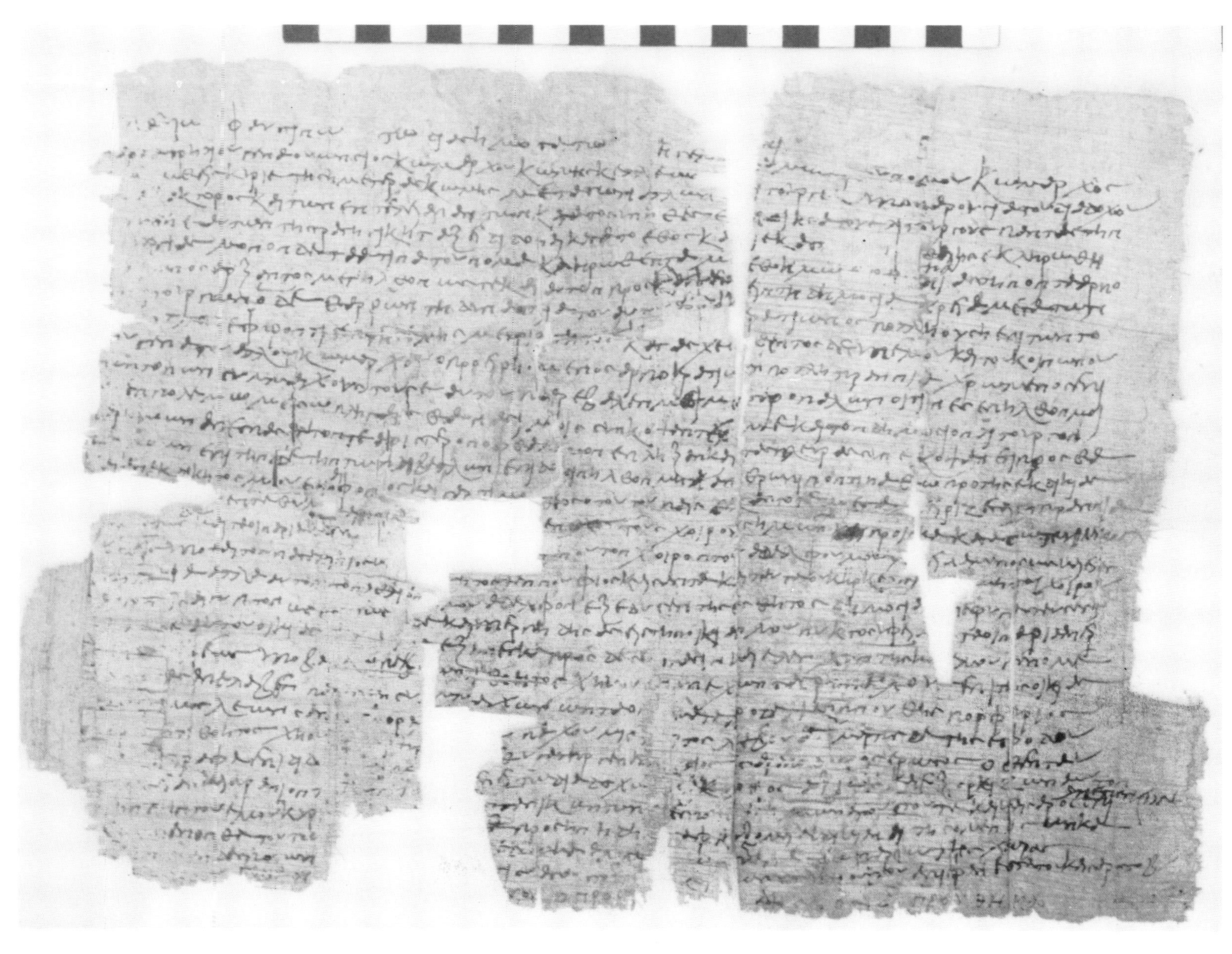

23: PETITION TO THE PRAESES THEBAIDOS

24: OFFICIAL DECLARATION TO THE OFFICE OF THE DUX

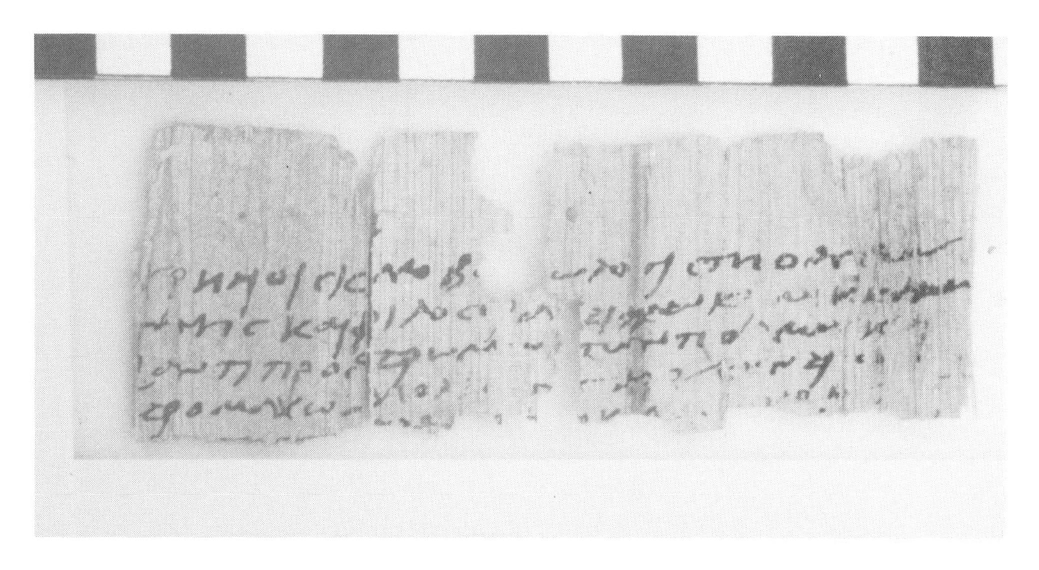

25: ADDRESS OF AN OFFICIAL DOCUMENT

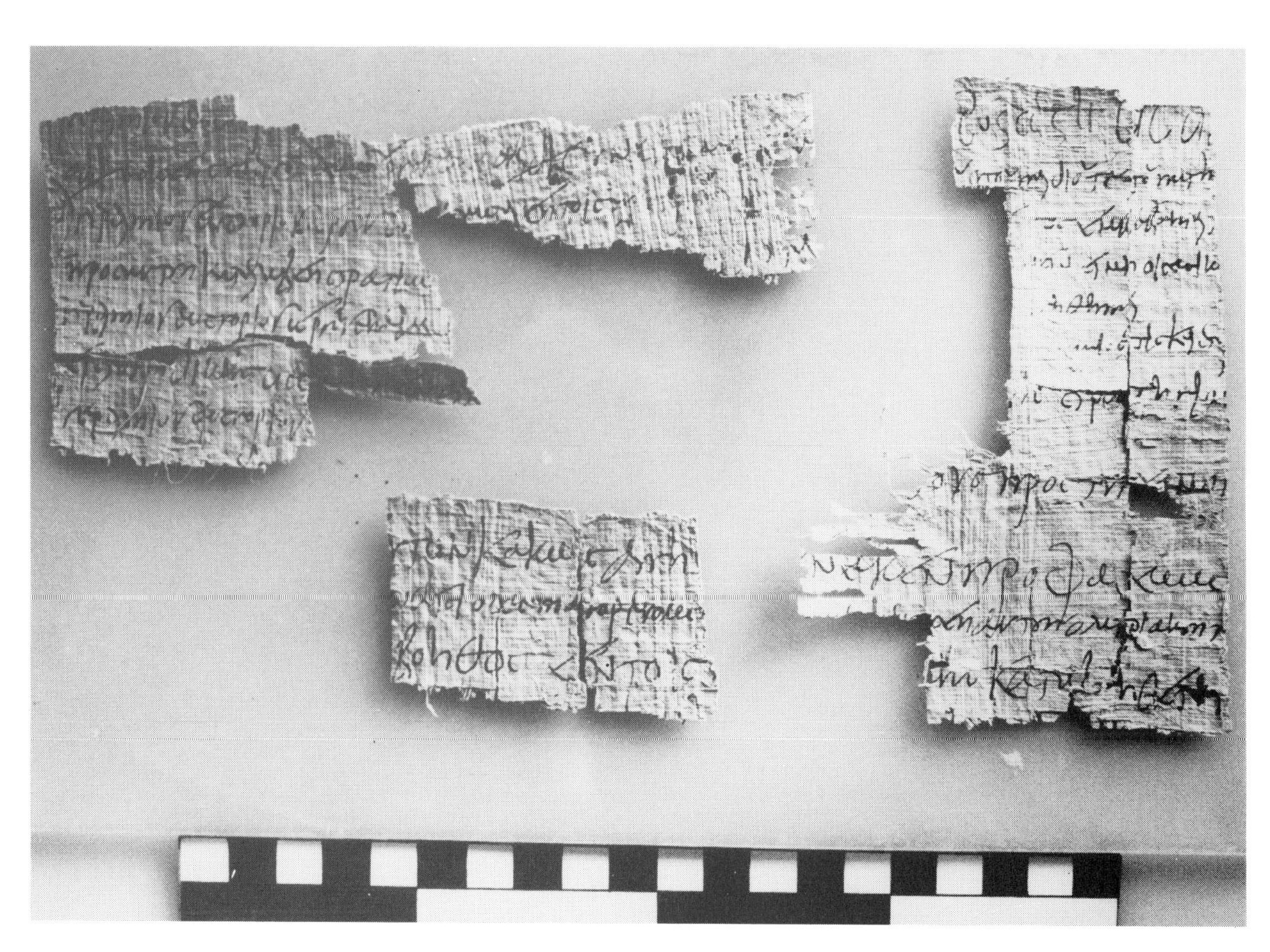

26: REPORT OF JUDICIAL PROCEEDINGS

27: OFFICIAL DOCUMENT

28: ADMINISTRATIVE ACCOUNT

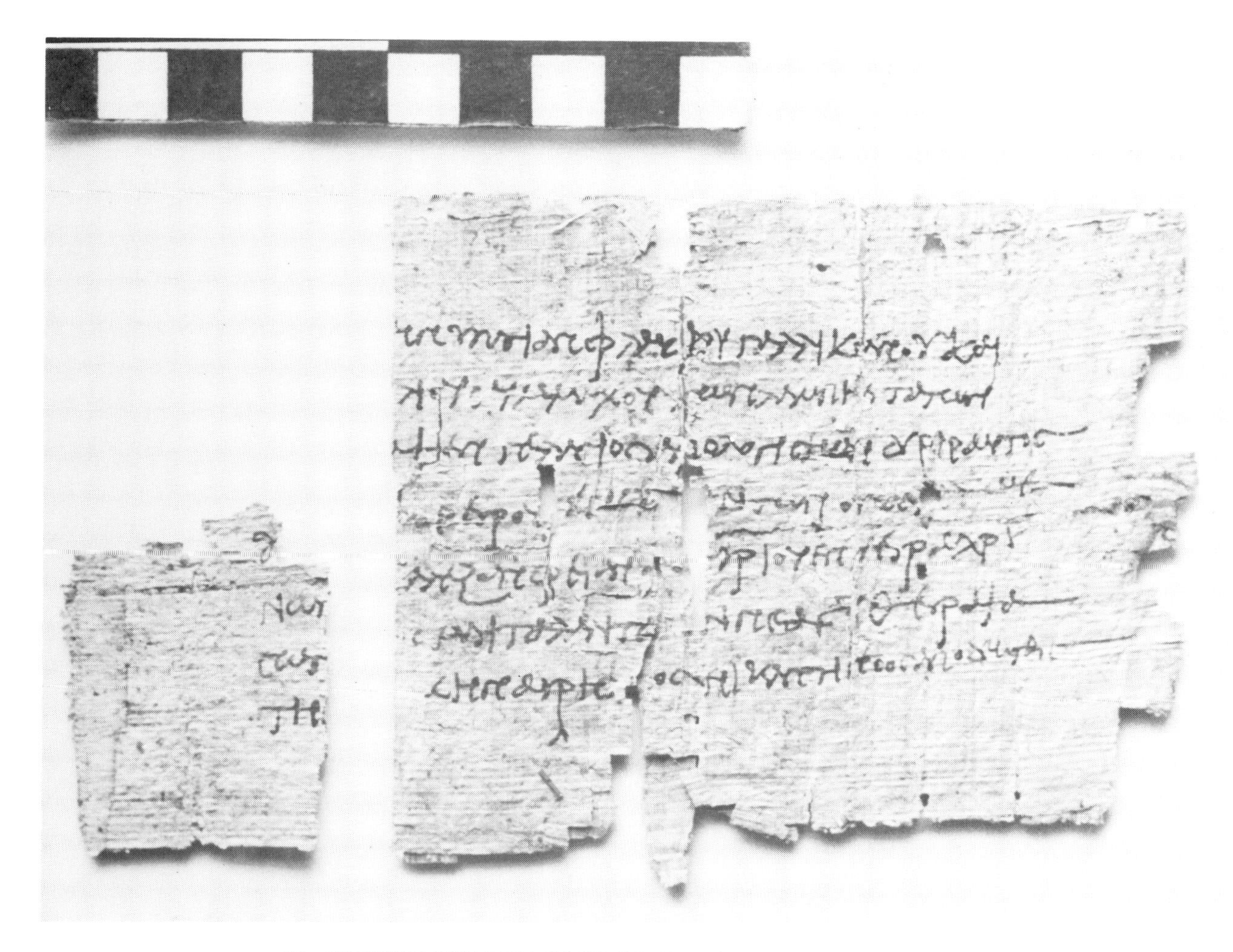

29: RECEIPT FOR THE COST OF TRANSPORTATION OF STATUES

30: EXCHANGE OF PROPERTY RIGHTS

31: LEASE OF A HOUSE (?)

32: LEASE OF A ROOM

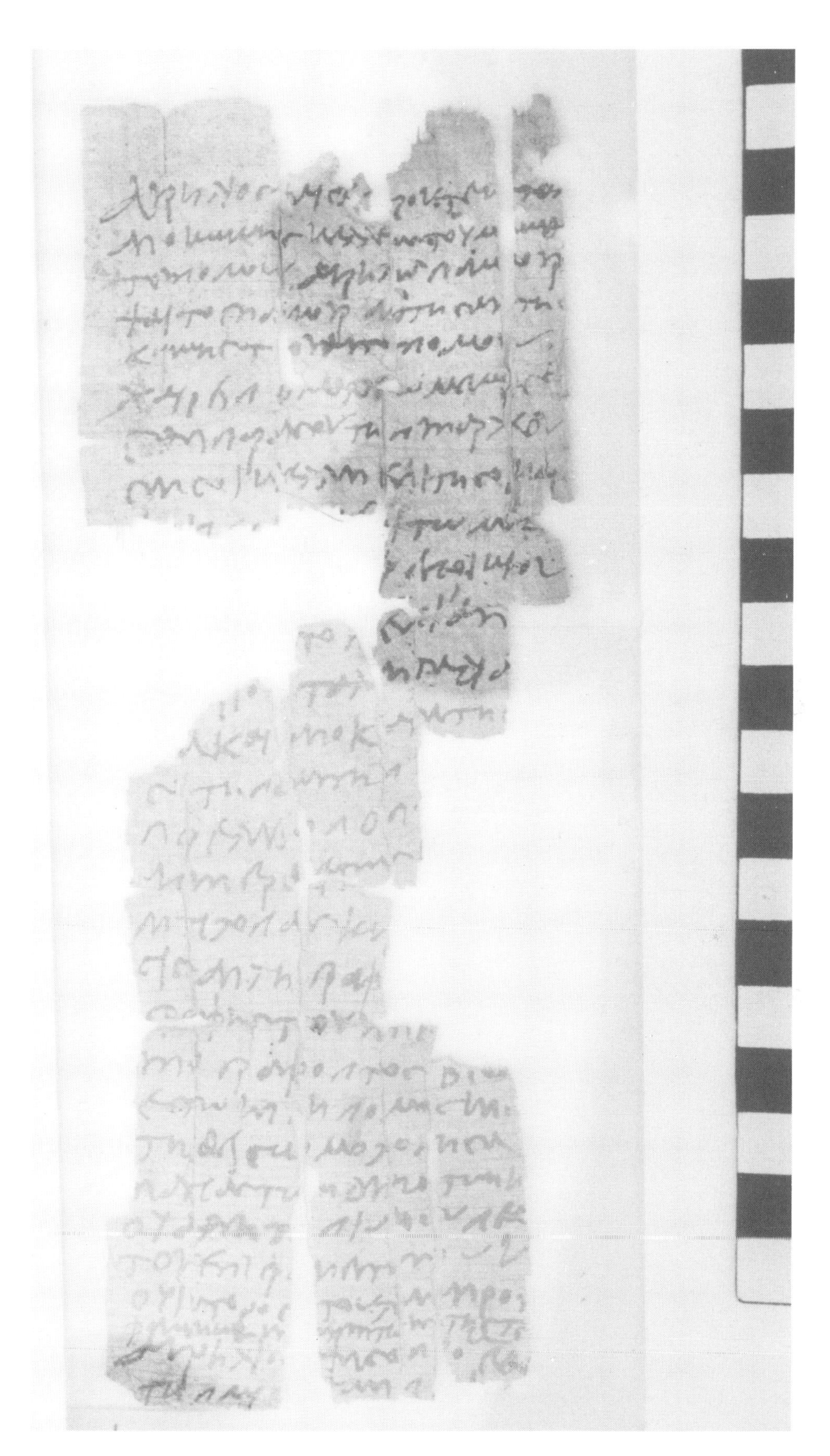

33: LEASE OF A ROOM

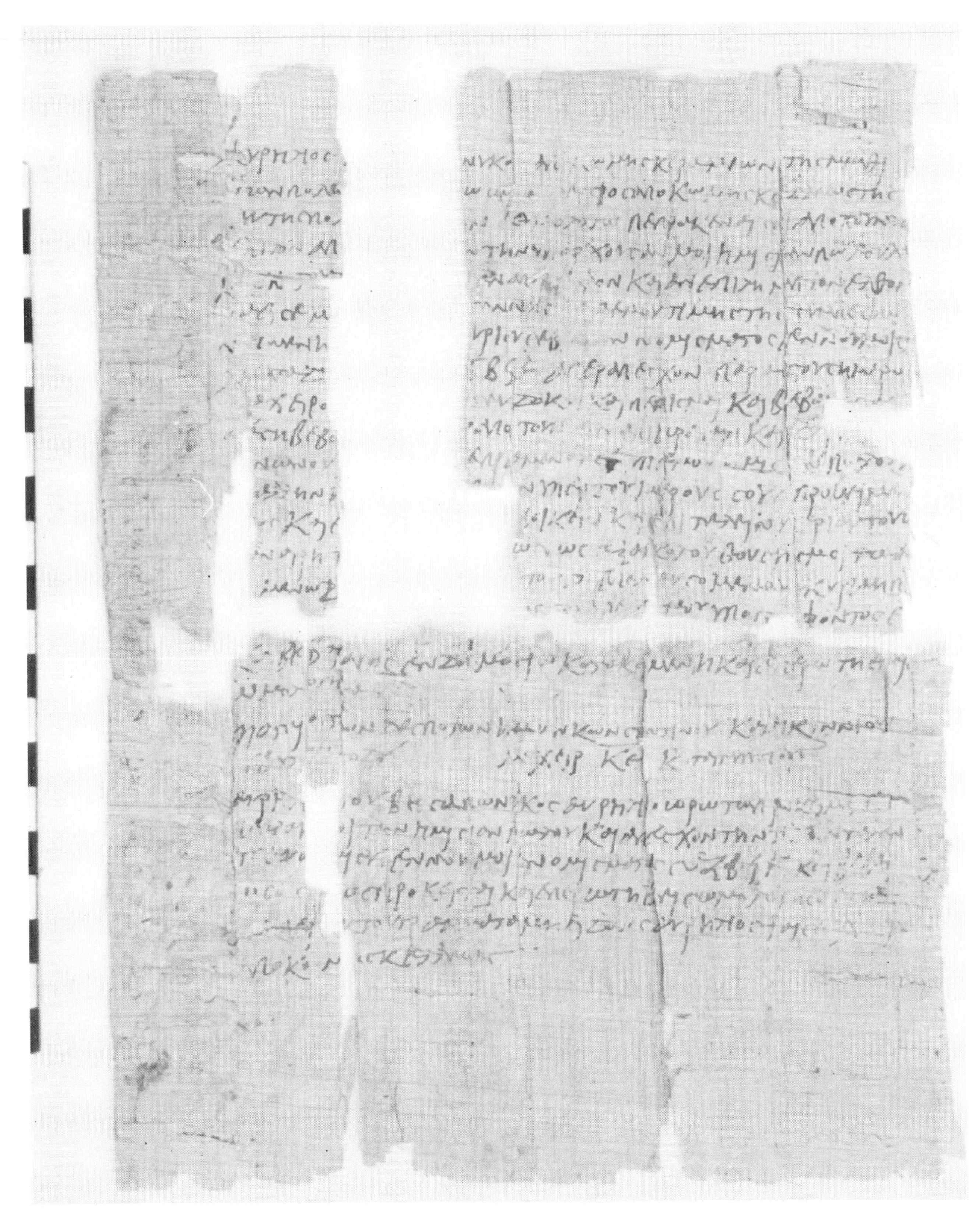

34: SALE OF HALF OF A FOAL

34, appendix: This fragment is not illustrated

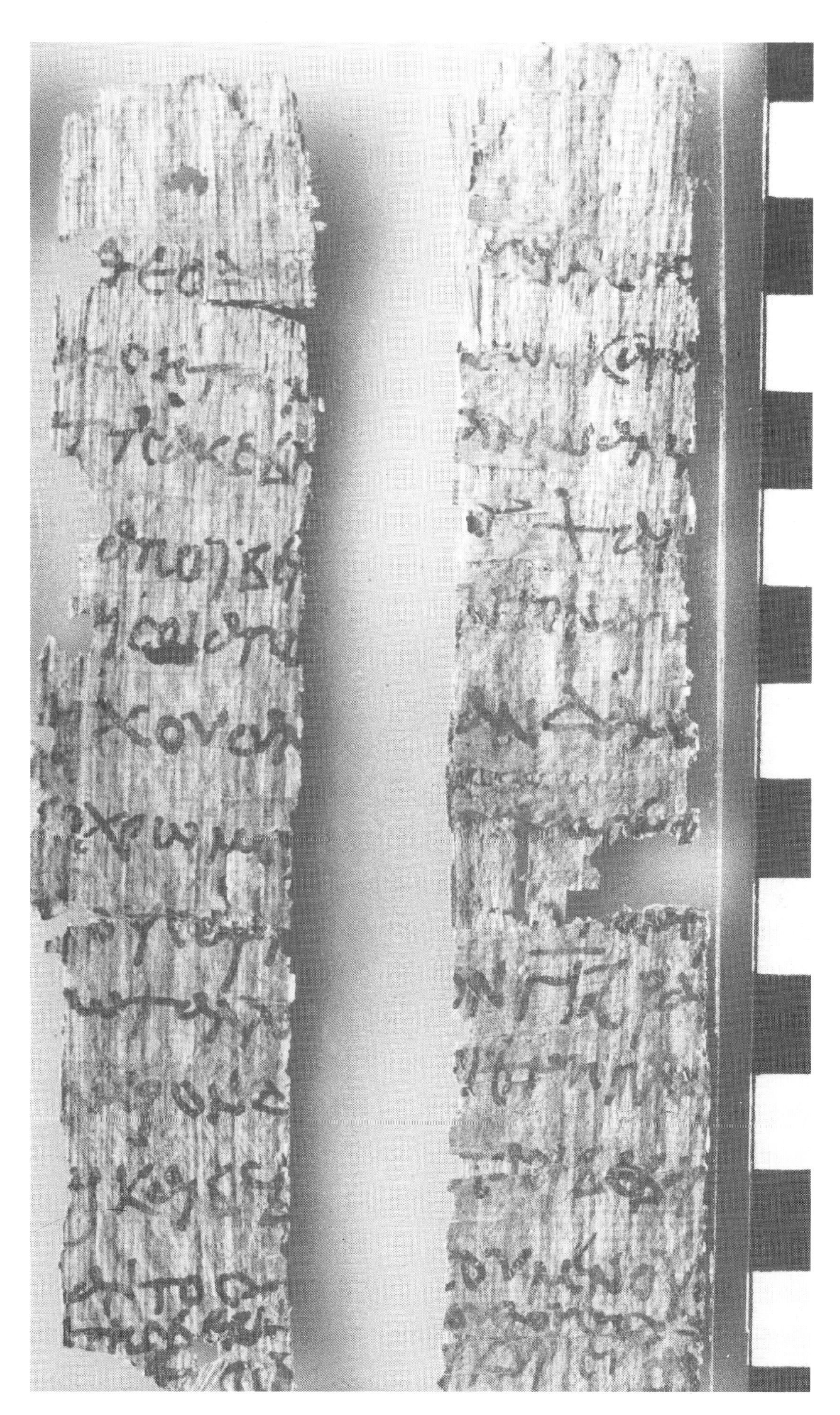

35: SALE OF A HEIFER

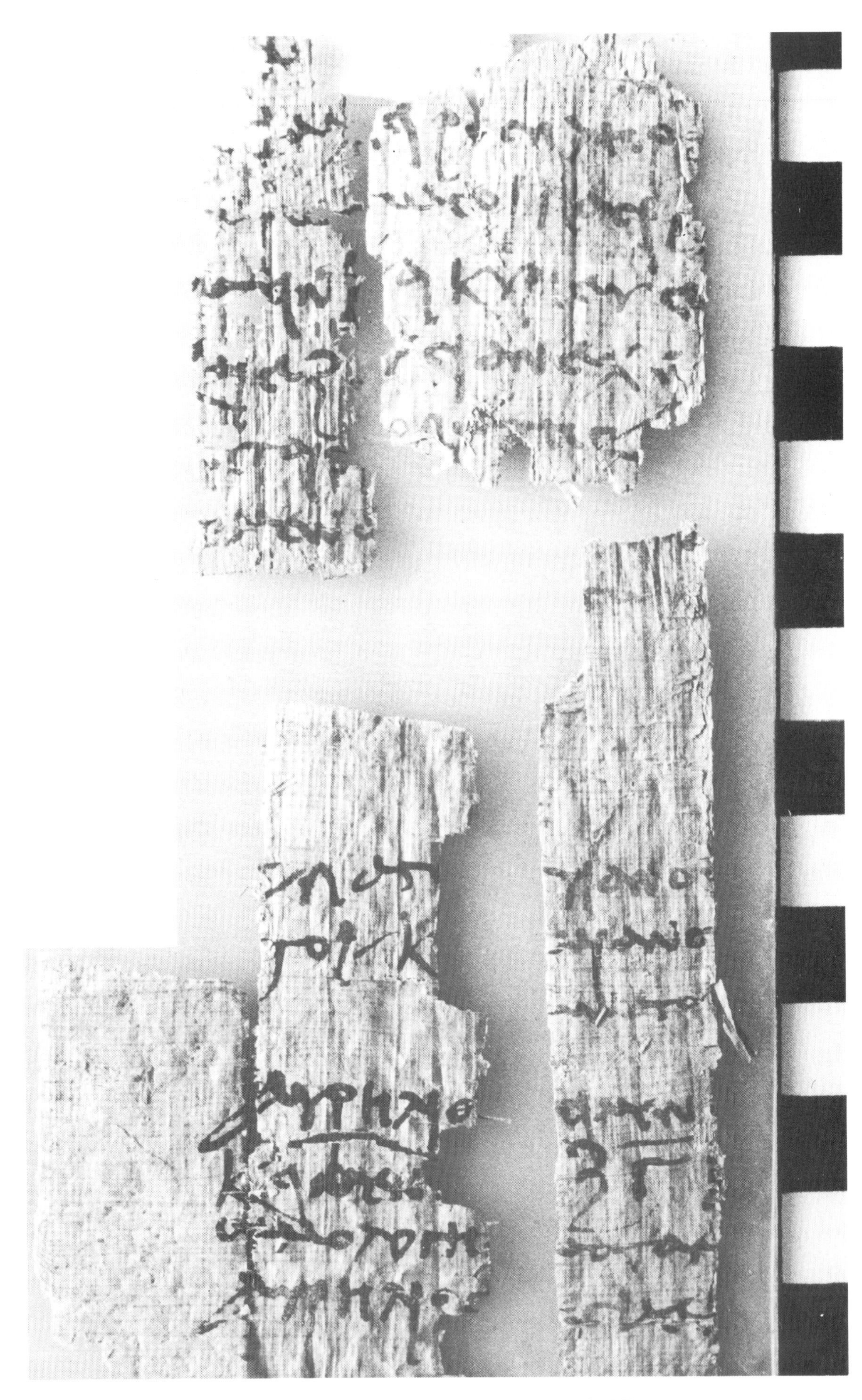

36: FRAGMENTS OF A CONTRACT OF SALE

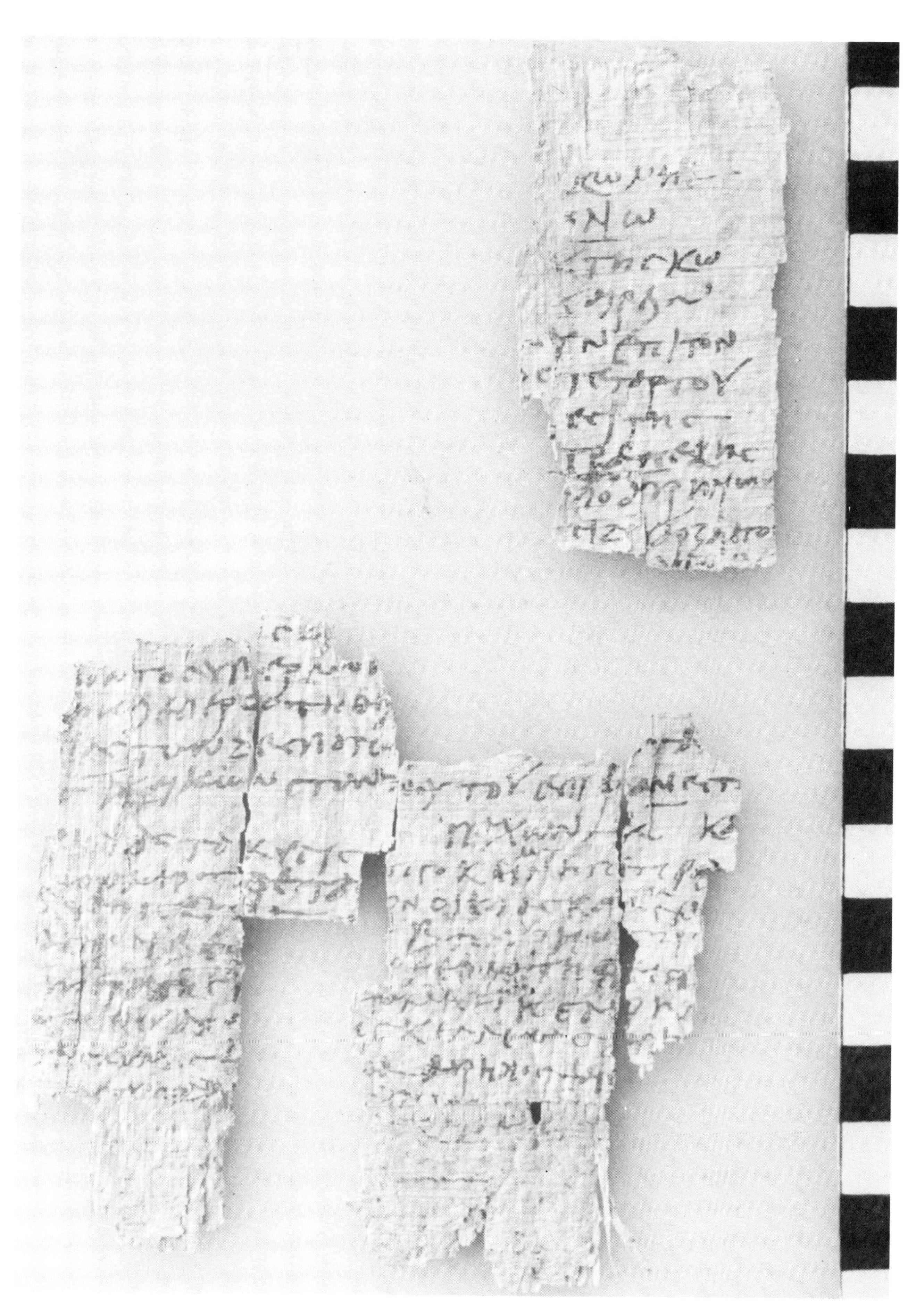

37: SALE OF PART OF A HOUSE

38.a: PROPERTY GIFT

38.b: PROPERTY GIFT

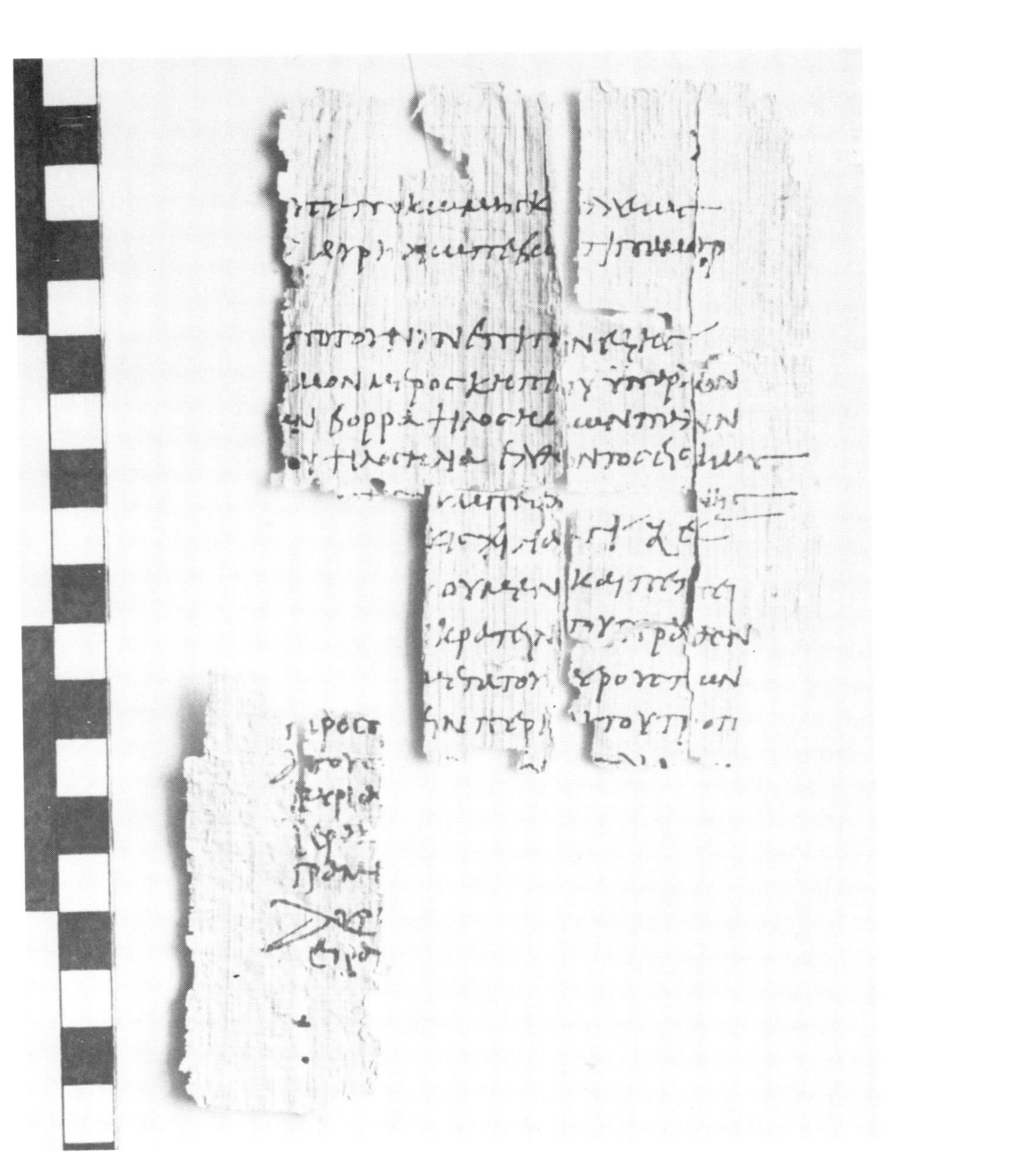

39: SALE OF PART OF AN ORCHARD

40: FRAGMENT OF A LOAN

41: LOAN OF MONEY

42: LOAN OF MONEY

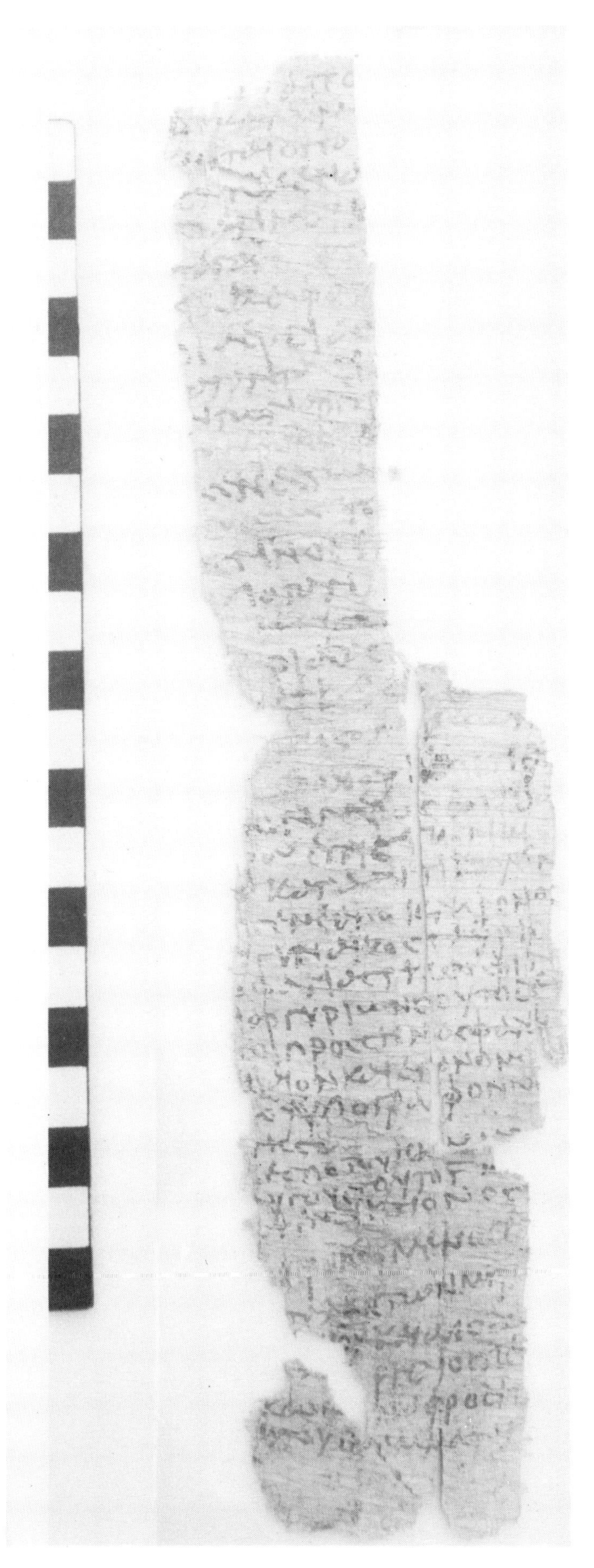

43: LOAN OF MONEY WITH MORTGAGE

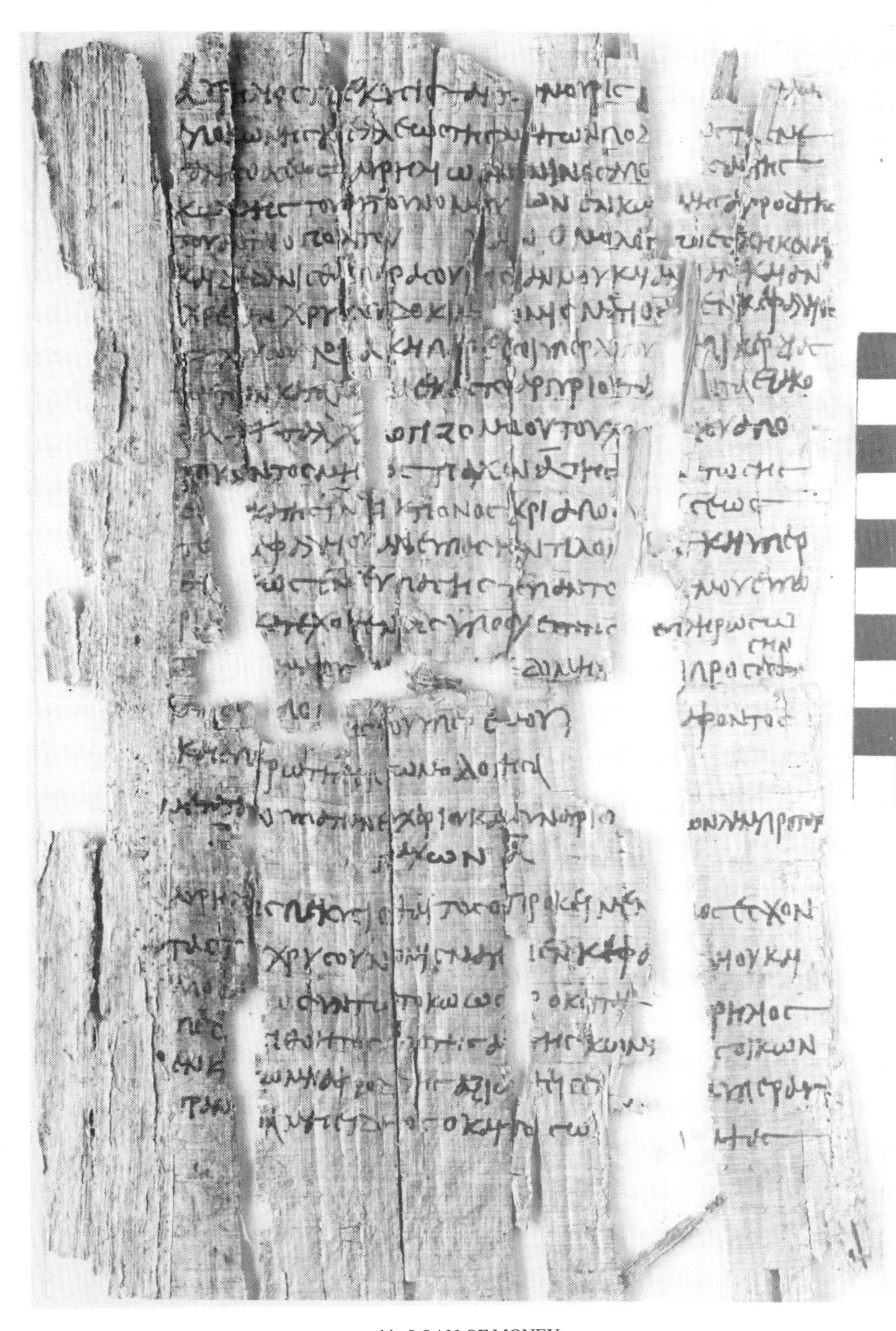

44: LOAN OF MONEY

45: LOAN OF MONEY

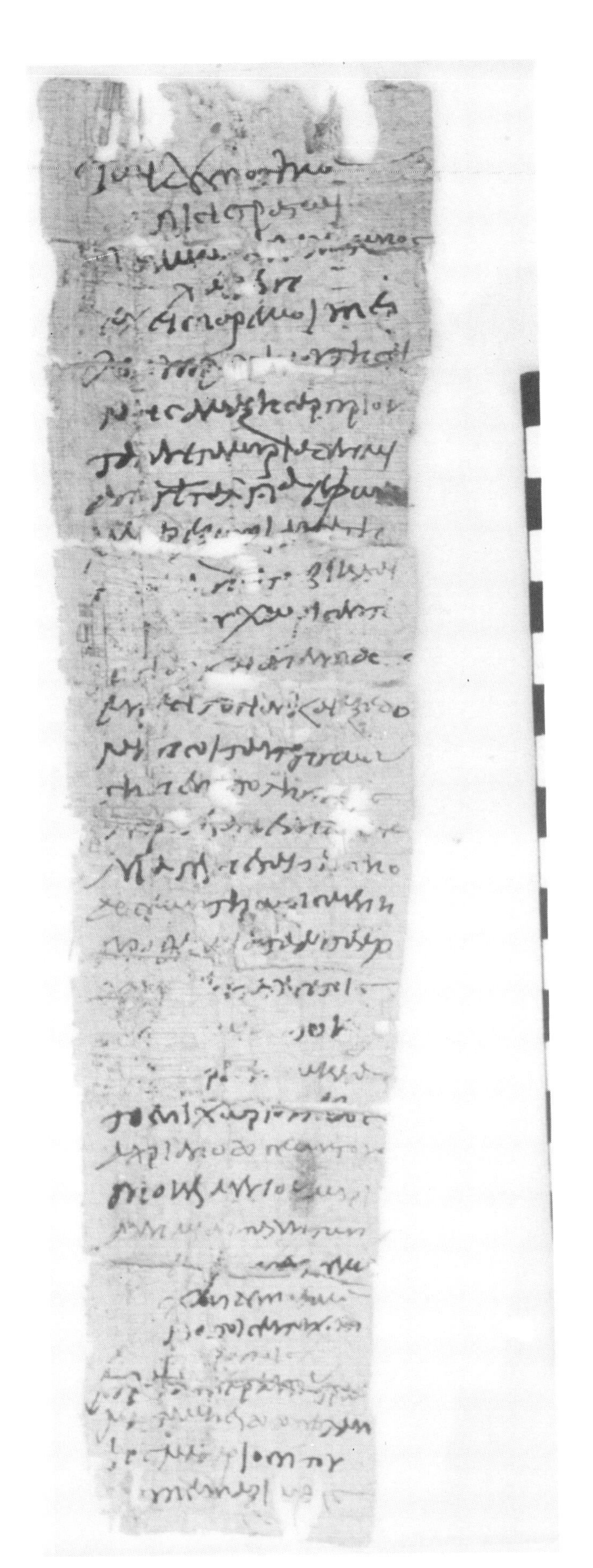

46: LOAN OF MONEY

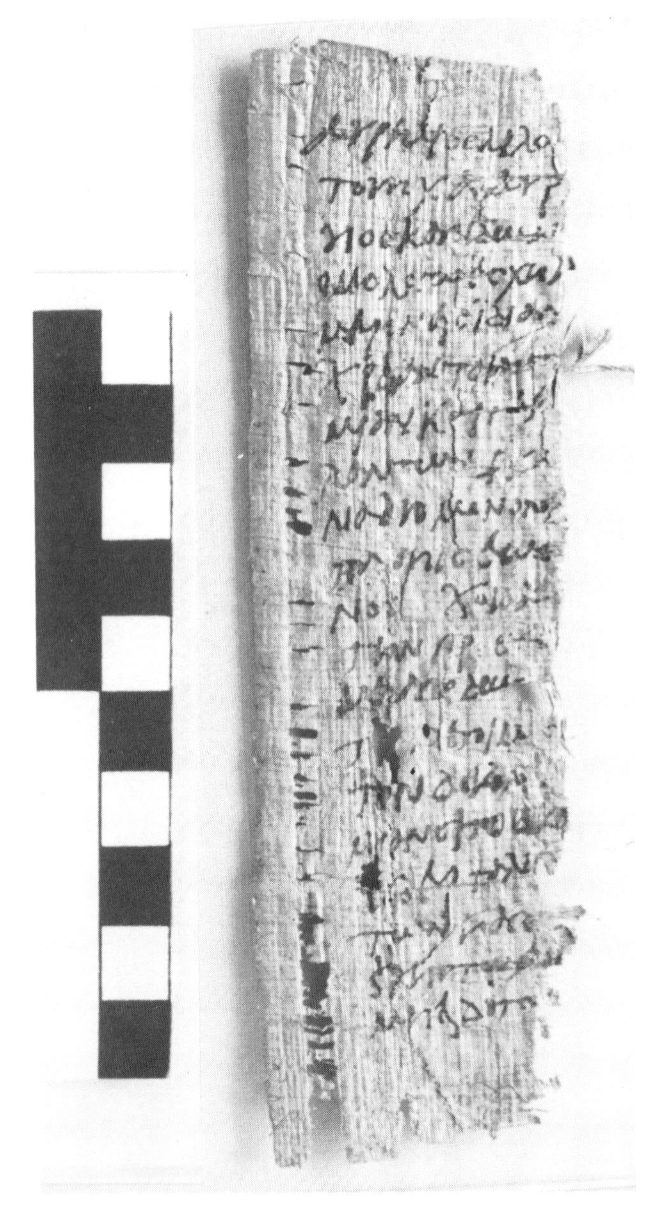

47: LOAN OF MONEY

48: MANUMISSION OF A FEMALE SLAVE

49: LOAN OF OIL

50: RECEIPT FOR VARIOUS OBJECTS

51: TRANSPORTATION RECEIPT

52: TRANSPORTATION RECEIPT

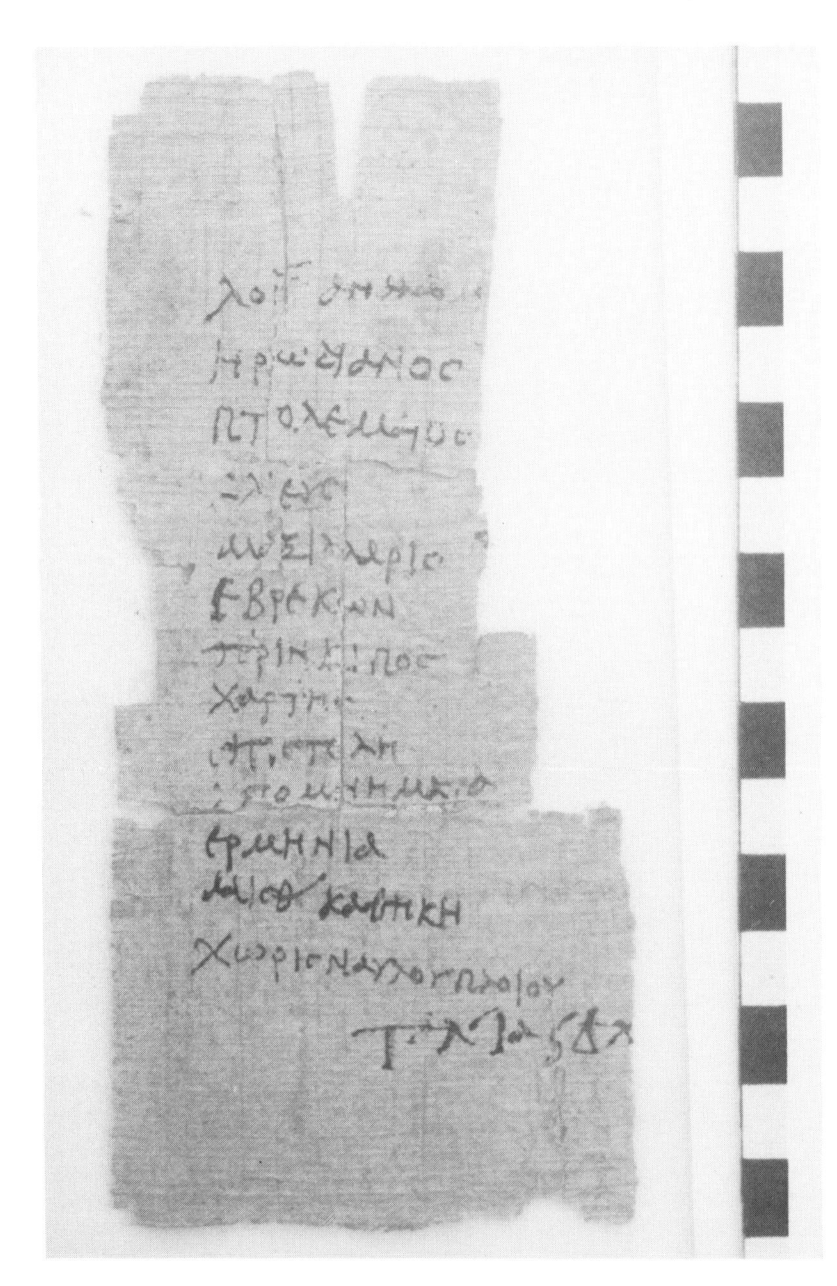

53: LIST OF EXPENSES

54: LIST OF EXPENSES

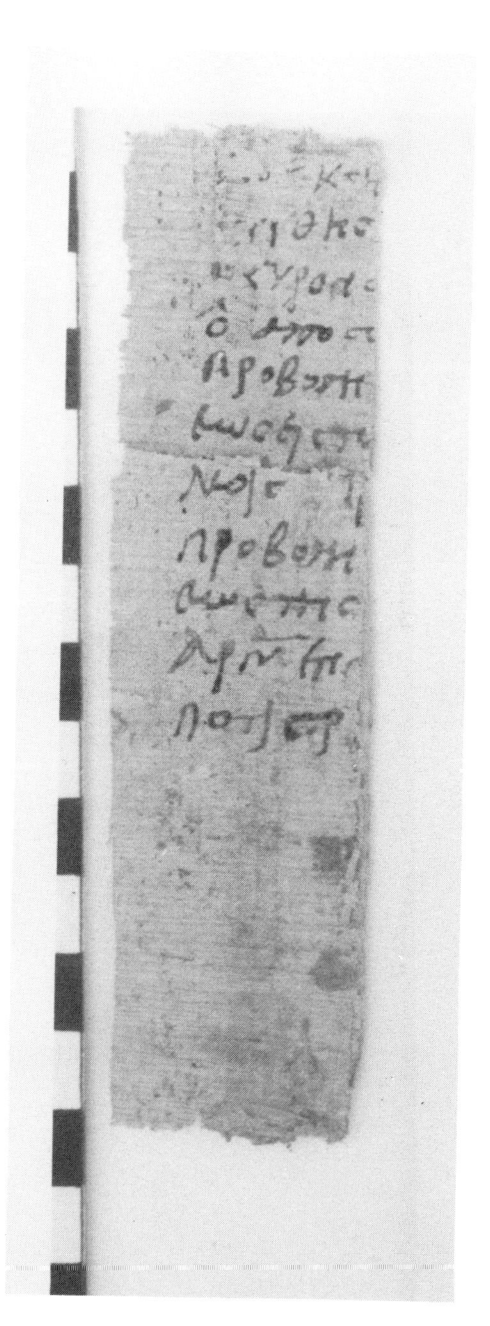

55: LIST

56: SUBSCRIPTION TO A DOCUMENT

57: This fragment is not illustrated

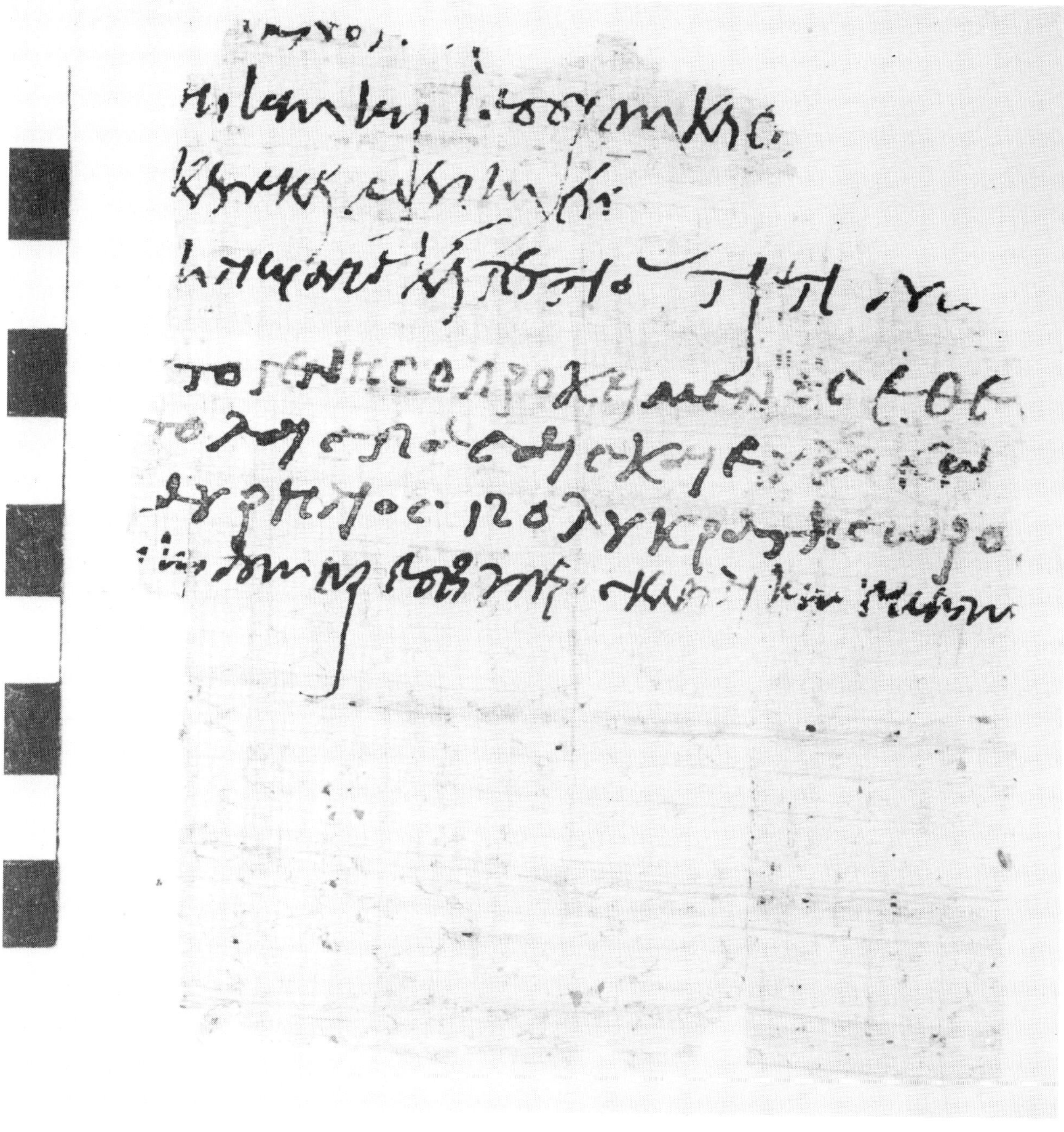

58: FRAGMENT OF AN AGREEMENT

59: CONSULAR DATE

60: LIST OF NAMES

61: LIST OF MONEY ARREARS

62: LIST OF RENT PAYMENTS

63: MANICHAEAN LETTER

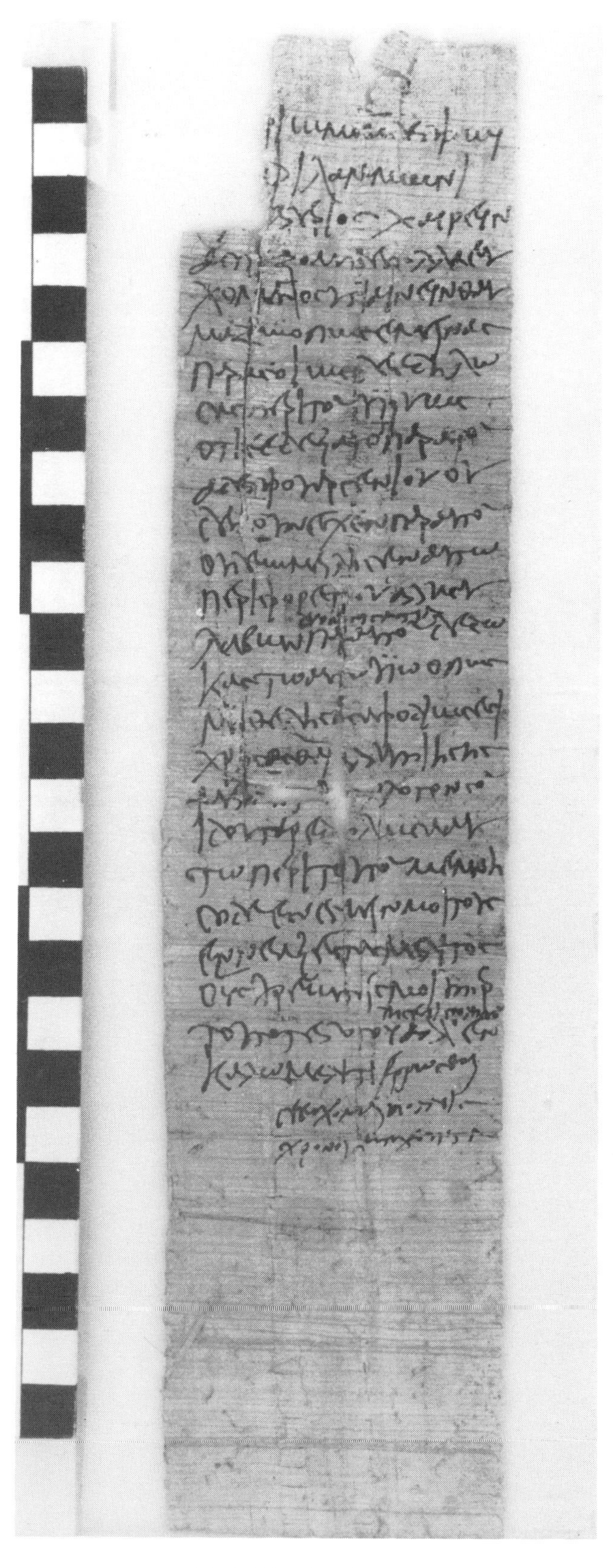

64: PRIVATE LETTER

65: PRIVATE LETTER

66: PRIVATE LETTER

67: PRIVATE LETTER

68: PRIVATE LETTER

69: PRIVATE LETTER

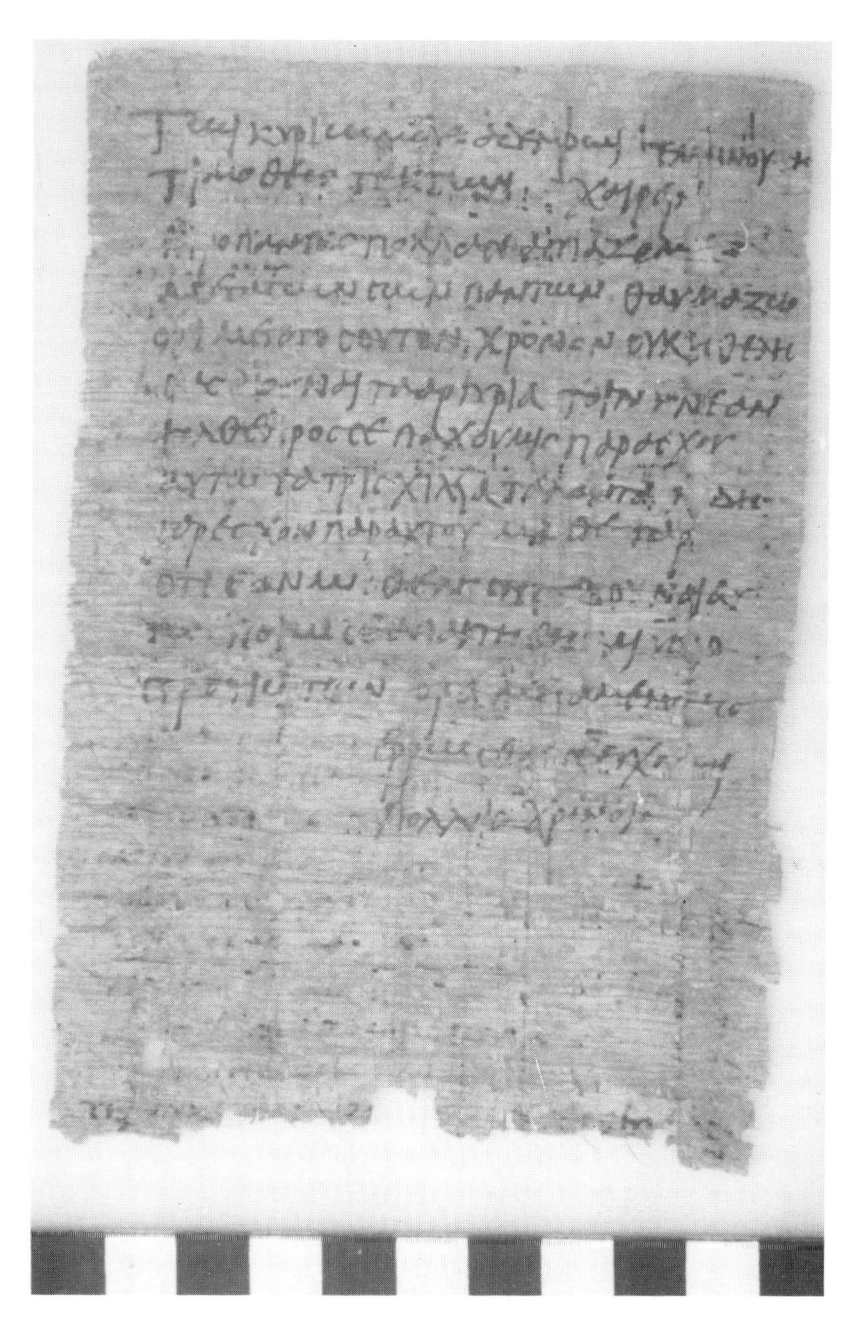

70: BUSINESS LETTER

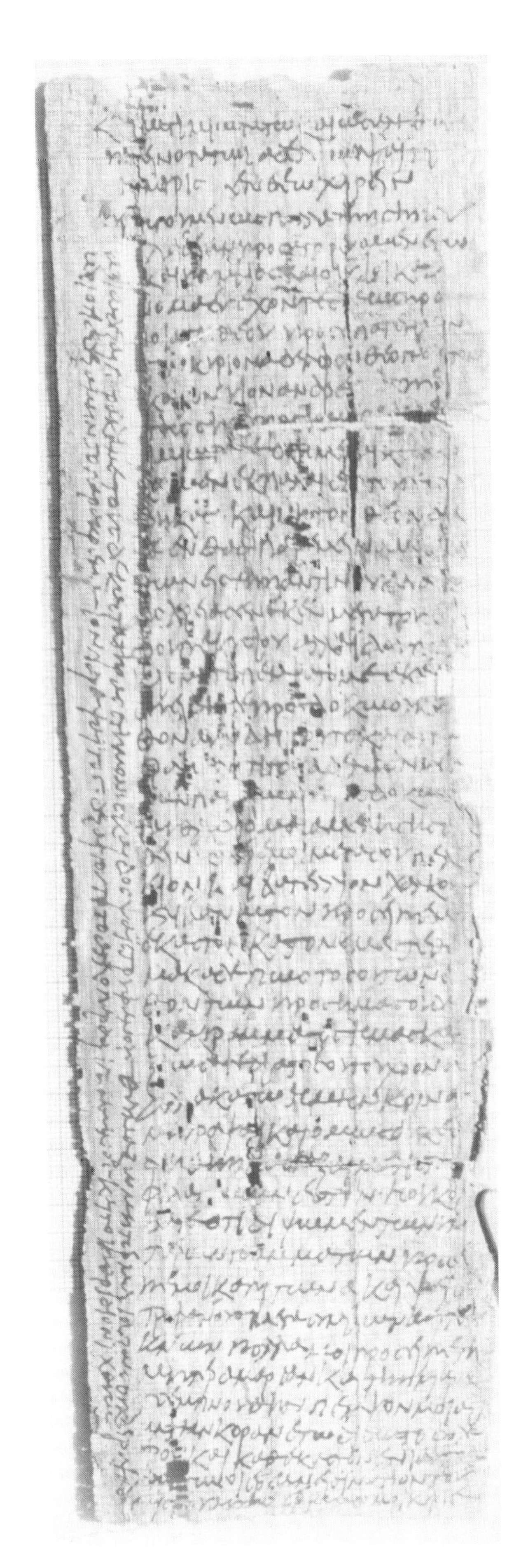

71: PRIVATE LETTER

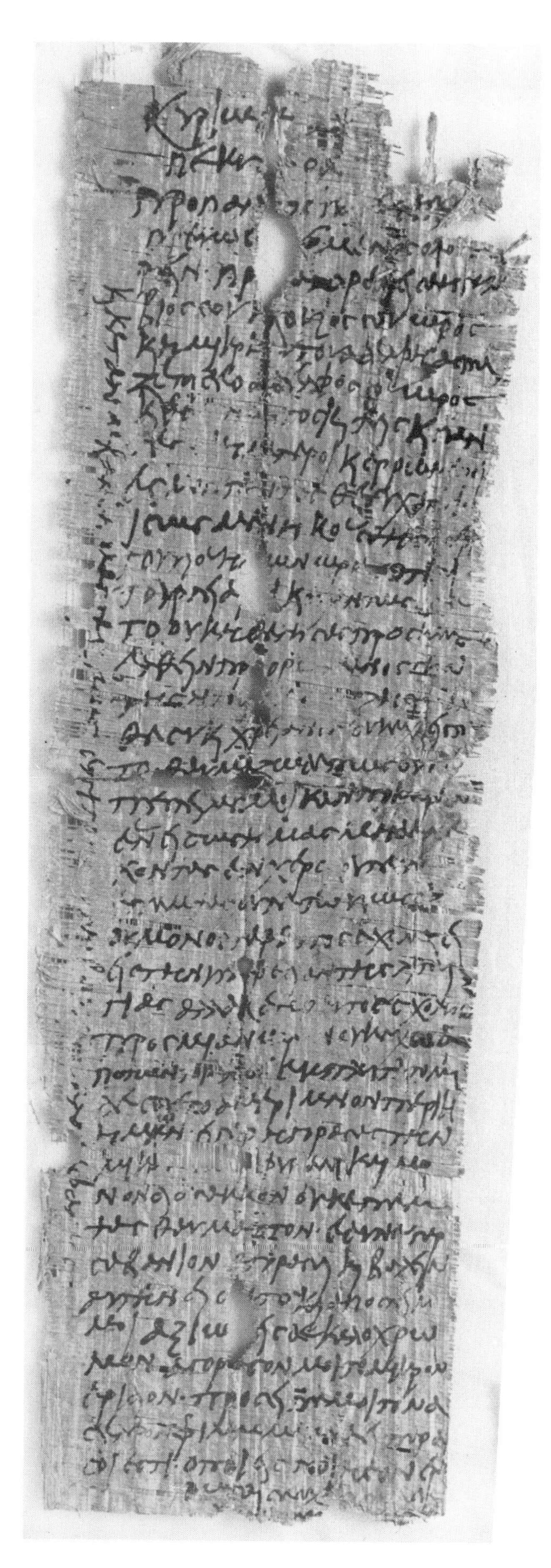

72: PRIVATE LETTER

73: PRIVATE LETTER

74: PRIVATE LETTER

75: PRIVATE LETTER

76: PRIVATE LETTER AND SURETY

77: This fragment is not illustrated

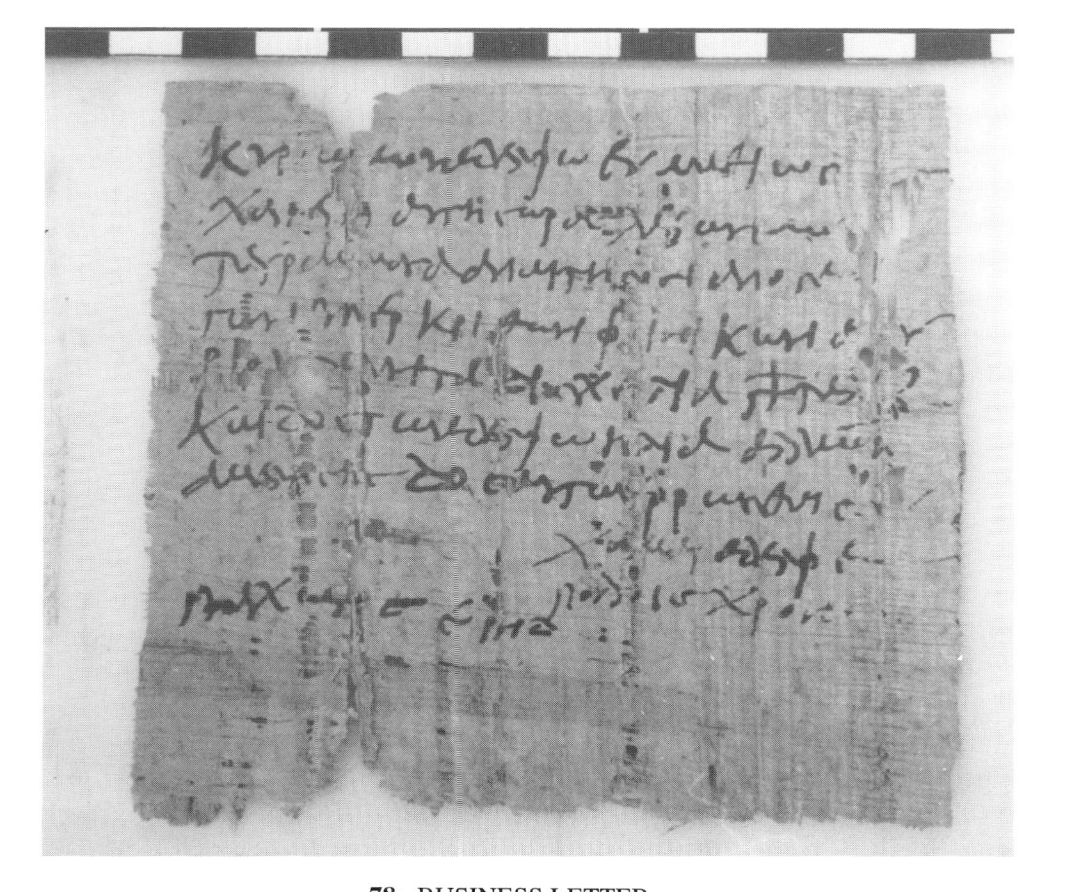

78: BUSINESS LETTER

79: BUSINESS LETTER

80: BUSINESS LETTER

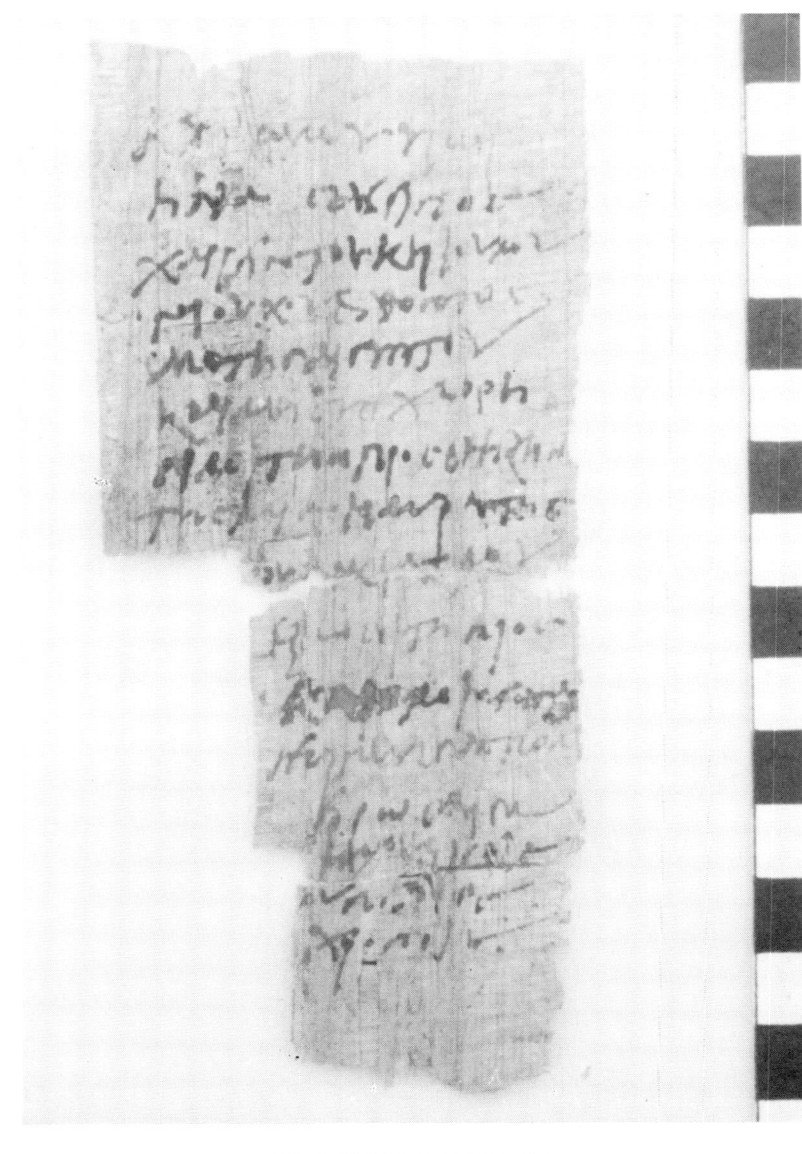
81: BUSINESS LETTER

82: CALENDAR OF GOOD AND BAD DAYS

83: CALENDAR OF GOOD AND BAD DAYS

84: GREEK HOROSCOPE

85.a,b: MAGICAL FORMULARIES

86: FEVER AMULET

87: FEVER AMULET

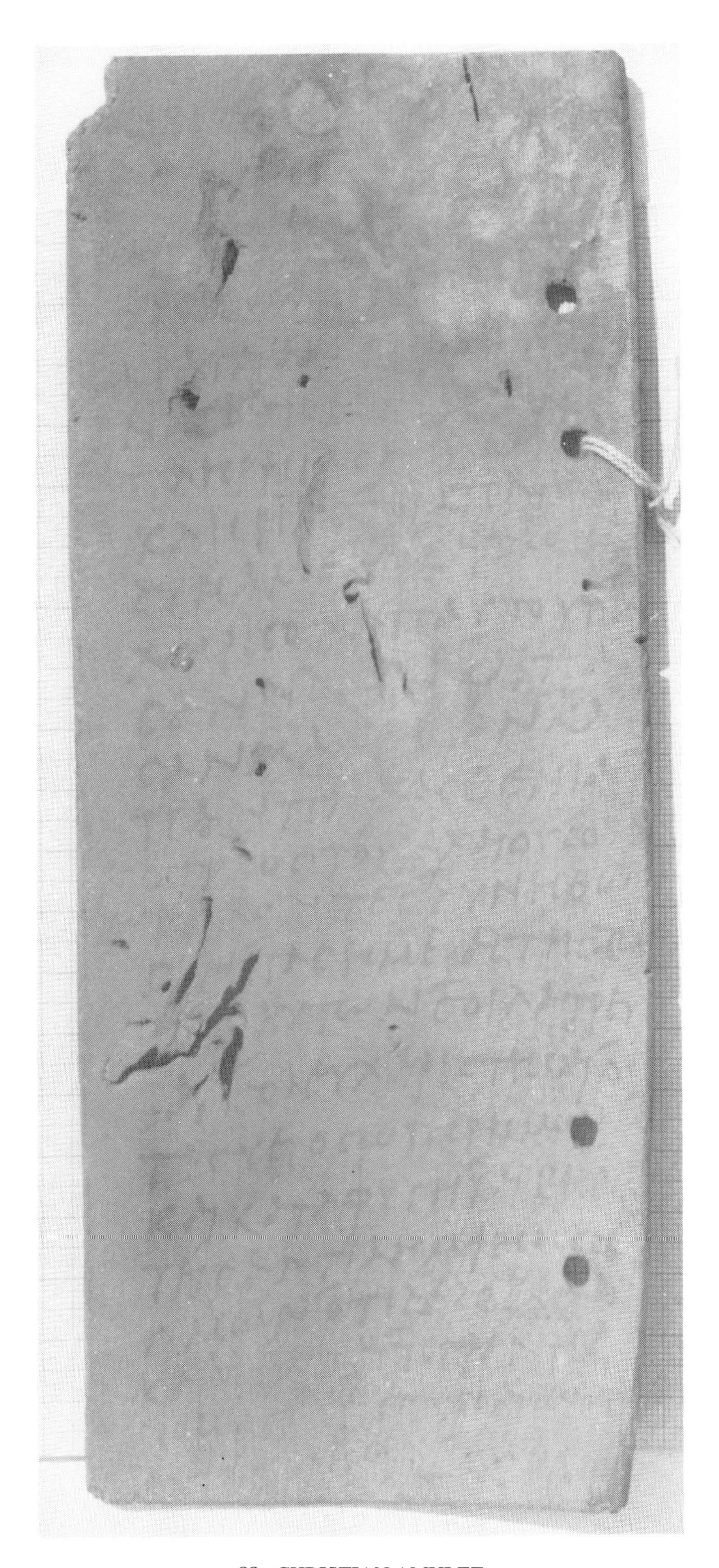

88: CHRISTIAN AMULET

89: MEDICAL PRESCRIPTION

90: SCHOOL EXERCISE: CALCULATION